The Emanuel Hirsch
and
Paul Tillich Debate

A Study in the Political Ramifications of Theology

The Emanuel Hirsch
and
Paul Tillich Debate

A Study in the Political Ramifications of Theology

A. James Reimer

BR
115
·P7
R4334
1989

Toronto Studies in Theology
Volume 42

The Edwin Mellen Press
Lewiston/Queenston
Lampeter

Library of Congress Cataloging-in-Publication Data

This volume has been registered with The Library of Congress.

This is volume 42 in the continuing series
Toronto Studies in Theology
Volume 42 ISBN 0-88946-991-1
TST Series ISBN 0-88946-975-X

A CIP catalog record for this book
is available from the British Library.

The Edwin Mellen Press
Box 450
Lewiston, NY
USA 14092

The Edwin Mellen Press
Box 67
Queenston, Ontario
CANADA L0S 1L0

The Edwin Mellen Press, Ltd.
Lampeter, Dyfed, Wales,
UNITED KINGDOM SA48 7DY

Printed in the United States of America

To

Margaret

The Emanuel Hirsch
and
Paul Tillich Debate

A Study in the Political Ramifications of Theology

Table of Contents

Preface

This study began in 1975 as a modest essay on the 1934-1935 controversy between Paul Tillich and Emanuel Hirsch, written for Professor Herbert W. Richardson in a doctoral course at the University of St. Michael's College, Toronto. I had had a long-standing interest in the theology of Paul Tillich, fascinated particularly with his earlier life in Germany, his conflict with the Nazi regime, and his 1933 emigration to New York City. He was one of the first Protestants academics, together with many Jewish friends, to experience the harsh fate of those who opposed the National Socialist revolution occurring in Germany at the time. He was suspended from his philosophy professorship at the University of Frankfurt in the spring of 1933. I had myself studied at Union Theological Seminary in 1971-1972, where Tillich had taught for his first 22 years in America, and envisioned doing a major study on Paul Tillich, especially on the relation of his theology to his politics. Richardson suggested I begin by examining the 1934-1935 debate between Tillich and Emanuel Hirsch, an early friend of Tillich's but someone who took a very different theological and political path in 1933. Convinced that Hitler and National Socialism were divinely inspired instruments for German national renewal, Hirsch had become a passionate spokesman for the so-called "German Christians," those who urged the German Evangelical Church to throw its full support behind National Socialism. It was inconceivable to me that a serious Christian theologian could have supported Hitler. I had never heard of Emanuel Hirsch, let alone read any of his works, and began what I expected to be a rather straightforward exposé of what I presumed must be Hirsch's flawed theology, and a simple apology for what I uncritically assumed to be Tillich's more intelligent and coherent position.

It did not take long, however, before I realized that the issues were considerably more complex than I had imagined. In the process of studying the writings of Emanuel Hirsch, meeting friends and colleagues of his, and talking to some of his post-war students, I found myself increasingly fascinated by this intellectual giant—one of the more impressive and enigmatic of German theological scholars of this century—and his particular way of grappling with the "crisis of modernity." Here was a man with an astounding historical knowledge of the western philosophical and theological tradition; someone engaged with modern critical thought at its deepest levels, fully aware of both the positive and the negative consequences of the Enlightenment for modern Christianity and society. Hirsch had few illusions about power and party-politics, and saw within National Socialism both the dangerous possibility of disastrous ruin for Germany and the potential for a new uniquely German post-monarchical, post-democratic synthesis of freedom and community. There was for him no turning back to the previous age of either German Pietism or Lutheran Orthodoxy, and yet he was deeply religious, shaped by the theology of Martin Luther, on the one hand, and Soren Kierkegaard, on the other. Here was someone for whom theological integrity and social-political engagement were taken with utmost seriousness. How was it possible for a thinker of this stature to make the political choices he did in 1933? This became my quest.

To complicate matters even further was my discovery that Tillich and Hirsch had been friends since their youth, individuals with similar family backgrounds and similar liberal theological training, evidently attracted to each other both personally and intellectually. I found there was extensive unpublished correspondence between them, that from the beginning they followed each other's intellectual careers, read and occasionally reviewed each others books, were privy to each other's intimate personal lives, Hirsch frequently playing the role of confidante to Tillich. I came to recognize that whether or not I agreed with Hirsch's final theological and political judgments, I would need to take him seriously. Most important for my study, I would need to consider carefully his criticisms of Tillich's theology, for here was someone who understood Tillich's personality and intellectual position better than most.

In the end, consequently, what began as a relatively innocent study and defence of Tillich's 1934-1935 charges against his old friend Emanuel Hirsch, a kind of case study of Tillich's struggle against the Nazis, turned into a rather lengthy study of the intellectual development and tragic personal fate of two individuals caught in the historical web of one of the most earth-shattering events of modern history. I realized that if we are ever to begin to understand what happened in Germany under Hitler and the Third Reich, what happened in other parts of the world at the same time that in some way contributed to the course of those events, and why it was that highly intelligent and religious thinkers supported the movement, we will need to enter empathetically into the thought-worlds of people like Paul Tillich and Emanuel Hirsch. This is what I have attempted to do as fairly as possible in the following study. I am convinced that the historical theologian studying this era is called to make critical historical judgments where necessary, but needs at the same time to demonstrate empathy for his subjects, and take seriously the theological integrity of individuals who appear to have made wrong political choices, and drawn wrong political conclusions from their theological presuppositions.

The core and focal point of this study is the 1934-1935 public debate between Tillich and Hirsch in German periodicals: an analysis of Tillich's two sharp open letters to his friend and political opponent Hirsch, charging him with plagiarism and the sanctification of a finite, earthly reality (National Socialism and the German nation); and Hirsch's response in which he persuasively defends himself against Tillich's charges and makes counter-charges of his own. Initially, this formed the first part of my work, with all the subsequent chapters being an attempt to understand the background to this debate and gain clarity on the accuracy of the charges made. In the present structure, however, the 1934-1935 exchange is the culmination of the study as Part Three: chapter eight concentrating on Tillich's two open letters against Hirsch; chapter nine devoted to Hirsch's response; and chapter ten summarizing the reverberation of the debate throughout German academic and church circles, critically evaluating the accuracy of the charges and counter-charges in the light of the whole study, and concluding with a few suggested implications of Tillich's and Hirsch's thought for the political task of theology in general.

Part One and Part Two ought to be read as moving toward Part Three, the hub of the study, as concentric circles, often dealing with similar materials but becoming smaller and increasingly more focussed on the issues separating Tillich and Hirsch in 1933, 1934 and 1935. Part One is the outer circle, in which the biographical-intellectual portrait of the two friends is painted with a rather large brush. Many of the later theological and political themes are first introduced here in the context of their family background, early education and first meeting (chapter one); their different experiences, writings, teaching and intellectual development during the war years and the Weimar Republic (chapter two); the radical rupture in their relationship in 1933 due to their different political responses to Hitler and National Socialism, and their subsequent divergent professional careers (chapter three); and finally a kind of epilogue to the study in chapter four—the final phase of their lives, where they have occasion to meet each other briefly and reflect on their lives and their friendship.

Part Two is the second circle. Having introduced most of the relevant issues and many of the writings in Part One, I here concentrate on a more detailed analysis of the major writings having to do specifically with their political ethics and theological presuppositions during three periods: World War One, 1914-1918 (chapter five); the Weimar years, 1918-1933 (chapter six); and the triumph of National Socialism, 1933 (chapter seven). Chapter seven is the bridge to Part Three (the goal of the study): an examination and critical evaluation of the theological and political convictions separating Tillich and Hirsch in 1933, as publicly debated in 1934 and 1935.

The confrontation between Tillich and Hirsch is not simply one more casuistic squabble between two pedantic theologians. It deals on the deepest level with one of the more critical questions facing theology in the modern era, or for that matter, in any age: What is the relation of the divine to the human? Assuming that God acts within human history, even within political movements, what are the criteria by which divine presence in finite events can be identified?

The charges that Tillich and Hirsch level against each other in regard to the above questions are of universal significance, and their fateful decisions in the early 1930s had far-reaching consequences and implications for their contemporaries and future generations.

The history and evaluation of this era in German history is highly sensitive and complex, full of pitfalls, and allows for no simplistic moral judgments and generalizations. My intention, therefore, is not simply to collect evidence with which to support one side over against another, but rather to trace as fairly as possible the theological and political development of these two thinkers in their own right, from their early adult years to their fateful choices of 1933. In the end, I do make judgments—this is too serious an era for its students to remain in the illusory neutral realm of armchair analysis. The atrocities of the period call for unequivocal denunciation, and their causes—including intellectual presuppositions—need to be traced and unmasked if they are to be avoided in the future. The historical causes of these atrocities, however, reach back further than we tend to think, and responsibility frequently rests on the shoulders of more sides than one likes to admit.

In this study of Tillich and Hirsch I attempt to understand why their lives and thought evolved the way they did and why they made the choices they did in 1933. There are here, we shall see, two radically different, nevertheless consistently argued, ways of reading history and historical events, of interpreting Christianity and of perceiving the theological task, each of which even today continue to have their strong advocates. My conclusion, therefore, consists not so much in choosing finally between Tillich and Hirsch, as in explicating their distinct theological "models," showing how these two different theological modes of thinking are consistent with two divergent apprehensions of social and political ethics, and pointing out, finally, some of the problems in each of their respective approaches. Only through an intensive struggle with the thought and lives of both Tillich and Hirsch in the years leading up to the triumph of National Socialism can we hope to understand their fateful choices in 1933, learn from them and avoid their pitfalls. Only by thoroughly understanding the nature of the theological and political battles that raged in the 1920s and early 1930s can we hope to better understand why it was that thinkers such as Tillich and Hirsch—with great intellectual powers and personal integrity, individuals with similar social and religious roots—made such radically different choices in the face of one of the most fateful revolutions of the twentieth century.

I am indebted to numerous individuals and institutions for the role they have played in the various stages of conceiving, researching, writing, typing, indexing and copy-editing of this study. I want first of all to thank Gregory Baum who saw me through the initial form of this study as my doctoral thesis. Herbert W. Richardson first suggested the topic to me and helped me particularly in the early stages. I gratefully acknowledge all those who through personal conversations or correspondence have contributed to my understanding of the personal lives and writings of Tillich and Hirsch. These include, in Germany, Hans-Joachim Birkner, Horst Bögeholz, the late Hayo Gerdes, Hans Hirsch (the son of Emanuel Hirsch), Hans Martin Müller, Trutz Rendtorff, Horst Renz, Joachim Ringleben, the late Klaus Scholder, Hans-Walter Schütte, Wolfgang Trillhass; and, in North America, James Luther Adams, Walter Bense, Wilhelm Pauck and Aarne Siirala. Frau Gertraut Stöber, Göttingen, Germany, graciously assisted in the early stages of research, particularly in transcribing most of the difficult handwritten Hirsch letters to Tillich into German typescript. I express my special appreciation to Walter Buff, personal friend of Emanuel Hirsch and long-time archivist of Hirsch materials in Hannover, Germany. Buff not only made available to me much valuable material, but has carefully and critically read large portions of this study, and given me invaluable assistance in understanding not only the life and thought of Emanuel Hirsch but the times in which he lived. I gratefully acknowledge the contribution of Pamela Fawcett in typing the initial manuscript, Carol Kieswetter for entering the final version on computer, Bruce Uttley for implementing the document layout, Margaret Loewen Reimer in her assistance with the bibliography and hours of proof-reading, Dave Kroeker for his careful work as copy-editor, and Tim Wiebe and Daryl Culp for helping to prepare the index. Finally, I thank Andover Library, Harvard Divinity School, for giving me access to the Tillich Archive, the province of Ontario for graduate scholarships, the Social Sciences and Humanities Research Council of Canada for doctoral fellowships, the University of Waterloo and Conrad Grebel College for grants at various stages of manuscript preparation.

July, 1989
A. James Reimer

PART ONE

A BIOGRAPHICAL-INTELLECTUAL PORTRAIT

1
Theological Beginnings
and the Start of a Friendship
1907-1914

An Intimate Friendship Begins

Emanuel Hirsch and Paul Tillich were life-long friends who from the beginning engaged each other in a rigorous personal, political and theological exchange of ideas. Their growing differences surfaced during World War I, intensified during the 1920s, and culminated in a public rupture of their friendship in a 1934-35 debate over National Socialism. It is the depth of their friendship, which never totally dissolved, that gives their split over Hitler a tragic poignancy. The falling apart of these two towering German intellects caught on opposite sides of momentous political events serves as a case study for the more general rupture that was occurring within German society and the German Evangelical Church at the time. Tillich and Hirsch evidently first met at a Wingolf student gathering sometime in the fall of 1907 in Berlin.[1] It appears they were quickly drawn to each other intellectually, and subsequently developed an extraordinarily close and lasting friendship.[2] What gave their

1. What appears to be the first extant note by Hirsch to Tillich, dated February 11, 1908, is found in the Andover-Harvard Theological Library, Harvard Divinity School. Most of Hirsch's original letters to Tillich have been preserved in the Tillich Archives of the Andover-Harvard Theological Library; references to them will hereafter simply take the form "Hirsch to Tillich, date." Hans-Walter Schütte says Tillich and Hirsch first met at a Wingolf meeting toward the end of their studies in 1908. "Subjektivität und System," *Emanuel Hirsch Paul Tillich Briefwechsel 1917-1918* (Berlin und Schleswig-Holstein: Verlag die Spur, 1973), p. 43 (hereafter cited as *Hirsch Tillich Briefwechsel*). In a letter to Tillich, dated February 17, 1963, however, Hirsch himself recalls an occasion in November 1907 when he visited Tillich's bedside, the latter being sick with a fever. It was on that occasion, says Hirsch, that he first called Tillich by his first name, which suggests that they had known each other for some time. Hirsch to Tillich, February 17, 1963. It was Horst Bögeholtz who first drew this discrepancy to my attention.

2. Marion Pauck suggests that the two "were drawn together by their classical education as well as by their common talent for definition and analysis." She mentions that "Friends who accompanied them on long walks in Berlin said it was almost impossible to tell their thinking apart, it was so nearly identical. This provides a clue to the bitterness of their later split. As long as the friendship lasted, it yielded untold richness and intellectual stimulation for both." *Paul Tillich: His Life and Thought,* Vol. I (New York: Harper & Row, 1976), p. 30 (hereafter cited as *Tillich: Life*). Contrary to what Pauck suggests here, the friendship of Tillich and Hirsch, and the love they had for each

intellectual affinity for each other a particularly personal touch, especially on the part of Hirsch, was the latter's unrequited love for Tillich's sister, Johanna. His desire to marry her, however, was thwarted by the sudden surprise announcement of her engagement to another close friend of Tillich's, Pastor Albert Fritz ("Frede").[3] The high value which Hirsch placed on friendship and fidelity within personal and intimate relationships is perhaps expressed most poignantly not only by his continuing relationship with Tillich to the end of the latter's life but also with Fritz, and more particularly his discreet friendship with Johanna till her death in January 1920. This is ironically demonstrated in the small play that Tillich and Hirsch co-authored and presented to a small group of friends at an engagement party for Johanna in September 1912.[4]

While the differences between Hirsch and Tillich becomes evident early on, what is truly remarkable, as we shall see, is the extent of their early similarities. They had similar backgrounds. Although Tillich was raised in a more cosmopolitan environment, both grew up in strict orthodox Lutheran pastors' homes. They had similar theological-academic beginnings. Both studied under liberal theology professors in Berlin. They had similar intellectual passions and interests. Both were well versed in modern critical philosophy and intent on applying critical thought to theological questions. Neither was satisfied with an uncritical acceptance of orthodox Lutheran formulations. These similarities all helped to shape the intense early friendship of the years leading up to World War I.

---

other, never did end but continued to the end of their lives. Schütte, a close acquaintance and student of Hirsch, also talks about the intimacy of their early friendship: "E. Hirsch, about two years Tillich's junior, found in Tillich not only an equal but a superior friend. He was indebted to this acquaintance for what was possibly his deepest source of stimulation." Schütte, "Subjektivität und System," *Hirsch Tillich Briefwechsel* p. 43. All translations from German works are mine, unless otherwise indicated.

3. The depth of Hirsch's own feelings for Johanna and the extent to which they remain part of Hirsch's consciousness, shaping his own views on how married men should relate to other women, surfaces in his private correspondence with Tillich. See particularly Hirsch to Tillich, June 21, 1921. I am greatly indebted to Gertraut Stöber, Göttingen, for her transcription of most of these letters from the hard-to-decipher handwritten German to a typewritten German version. Marion Pauck says of the surprise engagement: "For Emanuel Hirsch the surprise was a painful one. He too had fallen in love with Johanna, and had determined to ask for her hand, but waited too long and suffered despair at the knowledge. Johanna, for her part, had never considered him as more than a friend." *Tillich: Life*, pp. 35-36. Hirsch married in November 1918, and, despite his ongoing affection for Johanna, stressed the importance of faithfulness within the marriage bond.

4. The play, which was presented September 16, 1912, consists of 11 characters, with Tillich playing the part of county court president (*Landgerichtspräsident*) and Hirsch the part of a philosophical expert on marriage. *Der Prozess: eine individual-typologische Vorehekomödie verfasst von Paul Tillich, Gelegenheitsdichter und Zufallskomödiant, meistens Doktor der Philosophie unter respektive Gegenwirkung der "Prinzesskafécommission 'Gemischtes Bis'" sowie des philosophischen Ehesachverständiger "Mane Hirsch."* An unpublished manuscript in typewritten form, Tillich Archive, Marburg, Germany.

Hirsch: Early Religious-Intellectual Development

Emanuel Hirsch was born on June 14, 1888 in Bentwisch, Westpriegnitz, not far from Berlin, where he grew up. His father, Albert Hirsch, came from a family of farmers and artisans. It was only through much persistence that his father was able to overcome family resistance to his becoming a Lutheran pastor. His mother was a descendant of generations of sailors, some of Huguenot ancestry. Referring to Emanuel's home environment, Walter Buff says: "The spirit of his parents' house, a serious, reserved, orthodox piety, that despite all its firmness still preserved a great practical tolerance, exerted a strong and enduring influence on him."[5] This deep inward piety characterized Emanuel Hirsch till the end of his life and found expression in books like *The Meaning of Prayer*, first published in 1921.[6]

Displaying his father's singlemindedness, Emanuel demonstrated his own independence of spirit by beginning his theological studies at the Kaiser-Wilhelm University in Berlin in 1906 despite his father's objections to his studying under liberal theology professors. This spirit of independence and inclination to think for himself is evident in an unpublished autobiographical sketch, "über mich selbst."[7] In this sketch Hirsch describes how he was determined to find out for himself whether his liberal professors were in error. His father finally acquiesced to his son's ultimatum only to observe painfully how the liberal critique of dogma began to influence young Emanuel. But his father was surprised, adds Hirsch, to find "that my attitude to Jesus and his passion, to prayer and obedience, were not hurt in the least, and the religious influence of my parents continued in my life even after they surrendered their theological influence."[8] Hirsch says he experienced his theological studies not as an undermining but rather as a deepening of his Christian faith.

These early years of study gave Hirsch insights that were to become dominant themes in his thought to the end of his life. The most important source of information for these early years of study is a series of three autobiographical essays written by Hirsch in 1951.[9] In the first of these, "Meine theologische

5. Walter Buff, "Emanuel Hirsch," *Die Spur: Beiträge, Mitteilungen, Kommentare* (Berlin: Bund Evangelischer Lehrer, 1968), p. 76.

6. *Der Sinn des Gebets. Fragen und Antworten* (Göttingen: Vandenhoeck & Ruprecht, 1921). A second completely reworked edition was printed in 1928.

7. This unpublished autobiographical sketch was not accessible to me but is referred to at some length by Hans-Walter Schütte in his "Subjektivität und System," *Hirsch Tillich Briefwechsel*, pp. 39ff.

8. *Ibid.*, p. 39.

9. All three were published in 1951 in the German periodical known as *Freies Christentum:* "Meine theologischen Anfänge," 3,10(1951), pp. 2-4; "Mein Weg in die Wissenschaft (1911-16)" 3,11(1951), pp. 3-5; and "Meine Wendejahre (1916-21)" 3,12(1951), pp. 3-6. It is noteworthy that, as Jens Holger Schjørring rightly observes, "In these notes Hirsch says very little about his practical-political engagements during the First World War and their theological inferences." *Theologische*

6 Emanuel Hirsch and Paul Tillich

Anfänge," Hirsch says virtually nothing about his earliest childhood years, except that he was inclined toward observation and reflection and that he grew up in a simple, pious, church-committed pastor's home, little affected by the streams of modern thought. He makes three initial but highly significant observations about the first years of theological study: (1) Critical theology ironically saved him for the Christian faith by deepening his hidden personal piety, forcing him to grapple with the great ideas of Christian history and to struggle for the final meaning and content of traditional Christianity; (2) From the start it was clear to him that he would have to side with "critical" theology, distinguishing between the truth of the heart—"the pious self-reflection of the heart" before God, and "the critical alertness of the researcher and the thinker;" (3) From the beginning he was convinced that he would have to follow an independent theological course which was neither liberal nor orthodox: "I could become neither a liberal nor an orthodox theologian," he says. "From the beginning I had to stretch myself toward something that lay beyond both,..." On the one hand, he would need to be more critical than liberalism was; on the other, he would have to maintain some of the pious innocence of traditional faith. He was destined "to follow a road hard to travel and still harder to make comprehensible to others."[10]

It is important to understand, as the above comments clearly indicate, that Hirsch considered himself neither liberal nor orthodox-conservative, but tried from an early age to combine a certain traditional piety with a strongly critical perspective. He was an independent thinker who, influenced greatly by the modern critical method (theological liberalism), was intent on reinterpreting traditional concepts for the modern age without losing a traditional sense of religious piety. To call Hirsch's views reactionary in the sense of wanting to recover traditional orthodox categories in their pristine purity with the intent simply to defend the theological (or political) *status quo* is to misunderstand this highly critical theological element in Hirsch's thought.

The two basic issues which preoccupied Hirsch's thinking from early on were the *epistemological* problem—the possibilities and limits of human knowledge of that which lies beyond the senses, and the *historical* question—the historical

Gewissensethik und politische Wirklichkeit: Das Beispiel Eduard Geismars und Emanuel Hirschs
(Göttingen: Vandenhoeck & Ruprecht, 1979), p. 59/n. 16 (hereafter cited as *Theologische Gewissensethik*). Schjørring's study of Hirsch and Geismar in many ways parallels methodologically my own study of Hirsch and Tillich.

10. Hirsch, "Meine theologischen Anfänge," p. 3. In private correspondence Walter Bense has made the interesting suggestion that Karl Barth is too often considered the primary spokesman for neo-orthodoxy, and that in fact Barth, Tillich, *and Hirsch* could be seen as representing three distinctive neo-orthodox alternatives in the 1920s. (Bense to Reimer, July 1, 1976). Hirsch's self-proclaimed critique of liberalism, on the one side, and strong defense of the classical theology of Luther, on the other, would lend some support to Bense's suggestion. What Bense's thesis does not adequately take into account is Hirsch's emphatic critique of Lutheran orthodoxy and scholasticism, as we shall see.

nature of that which lies at the foundation of the Christian faith. The first question compelled him to undergo a thorough study of Kant's major writings, which by the end of the first year had destroyed for him the religious metaphysics upon which traditional church dogmatics and "vulgar" piety were built. The second question was addressed by the Berlin faculty through biblical criticism and a study of the history of dogma in a way that convinced Hirsch that the major doctrines of the church were products of human-historical thinking, which needed to be subjected to the same historical examination and criticism as any other aspect of the history of religion. In a remarkable admission, Hirsch says: "I could never again build up what collapsed for me at that time: honesty did not allow it."[11] Instead, in his later thought he tended to pursue even more rigorously the implications of these early critical insights.

What Hirsch lost in epistemological and historical certainty regarding the Christian faith he now gained in an *existential* understanding of Jesus, Paul, and Luther. Hirsch calls this experience an intellectual "earthquake" with its source in the hidden, nameless mystery of God. The person and teacher who now became one of the most influential mentors in Hirsch's development was Karl Holl.[12] It was Holl, the man largely responsible for the renaissance of Luther scholarships in Germany in the early part of the 20th century, who gave Hirsch his entry into Luther studies. Holl, who called himself a student of Ferdinand Christian Bauer, "was as a critic of history and dogma, as a relentlessly sagacious analyzer of dogmatic and theological history, at least in his younger years when I heard him, much more radical than Harnack, the person nearest to him."[13] According to Hirsch, it was Holl who now contributed to a further dismantling of his childhood faith; at the same time, however, Holl led him into an understanding of Luther's doctrine of justification, to a new comprehension of the mystery of guilt and forgiveness, and to a personal deepening of his Christian faith.[14]

11. Hirsch, "Meine theologischen Anfänge," p. 3.
12. In one of his letters to Tillich, Hirsch makes the statement that he knew Holl's soul as well as his own. Hirsch to Tillich, July 10, 1921. In the words of Schjørring, "Hirsch's Luther studies are unthinkable outside of the influence of Karl Holl. This is evident not only in their theological agreement, but also in the fact that through the impact of the war both felt themselves called to revive the Lutheran understanding of the relation between gospel and society. Both wanted to make Luther's thought relevant for the social problem; both however wanted also to hold fast to the historical analysis of the time-bound character of Luther's assertion." *Theologische Gewissensethik*, p. 59.
13. Hirsch, "Meine theologischen Anfänge," p. 3.
14. While Hirsch's theological relationship to Holl is crucial for understanding Hirsch's theological development and his theological stance in the 1920s and 1930s, it must remain the topic of a separate study. It should be noted, however, that Hirsch, despite his great admiration for Holl and Holl's Luther work, and despite the profound influence of Holl on his own thought, perceived his own dogmatics and ethics to have developed beyond that of Holl's and in independent directions. *Ibid.*

Reflecting on these theological beginnings years later, Hirsch identified three motifs which distinguished his own thinking from most other academics and practical theologians. First, he believed "that truth in relation to God exists alone in and for subjectivity," an insight corroborated by his study of Luther—particularly Luther's view of the hidden God—and the emerging influence of Kierkegaard. Hirsch found in these thinkers the willingness to subject truth to the discipline of human knowledge, to dispense with objective ecclesiastical and dogmatic props, and to surrender to the divine mystery.[15] Second, Hirsch experienced the freedom of religious and theological thinking which saw itself *en route,* not fixed, characterized by a kind of *Gelassenheit* in the midst of the shaking of the foundations of belief. Hirsch discovered that the hidden love of Jesus is present more as a "light on the dark and dangerous road of knowledge, than when it hangs as a chandelier in the temple of a purely confessionally-proper doctrine."[16] The third motif, closely related to the second, was the eroding of the distinction between being a non-Christian and being a Christian, and between being a Christian and becoming a deeper Christian, both forming a unity in the dialectic of the human movement toward God.

What is particularly significant in Hirsch's early theological development, as he describes it, is the extent to which he struggled with the Kantian epistemological revolution—that is, with the impossibility of traditional certainty concerning objective knowledge about God and divine matters. Hirsch's thinking was profoundly shaped by the insights of modern historicism, namely, the essentially historical nature of the foundations of the Christian faith. What was thus shattered by modern critical theory and historicism was replaced by the certainty of a subjective "knowledge" of the hidden God as emphasized by Luther and Kierkegaard. It is precisely this strong emphasis on subjectivity that becomes central for Hirsch's theological stance in the 1930s and in his debate with Tillich in 1934-35.

In the second autobiographical sketch, "Mein Weg in die Wissenschaft (1911-16)," Hirsch describes his decision to give his life to academia instead of to the institutional church, a choice strongly encouraged by his mentor, Karl Holl. He came to consider his academic life as a service to God.[17] After the successful completion of his church examination in 1911, he accepted a position in October 1912 as supervisor of a seminary (Stifsinspektorat) in Göttingen. Then in spring of 1914, after completing his doctoral studies, he accepted an offer by the Bonn faculty to a similar position at the seminary there, where he continued his studies toward his *Habilitation,* turning down an offer for a well-paying job as assistant pastor of a Berlin church.

15. Hirsch, "Meine theologischen Anfänge," p. 4.
16. *Ibid.*
17. Hirsch, "Mein Weg in die Wissenschaft," p. 3.

As lecturer (*Privatdozent*) in Bonn Hirsch says he learned to understand the notions of ethos and providence in three ways. These ensuing observations reveal the extent to which Hirsch became aware of the ambiguities of the human situation, of human history, of one's religious, ethical, and vocational choices. On reading these 1951 reflections upon earlier events, one gets the distinct impression that Hirsch is implicitly saying something highly significant about his choices in 1933.

First, except for that which pertains to outward discipline and order, he says, he realized that there is no ethical-religious law that is able to interpret clearly for one what is right in unclear situations. The encounter of the individual conscience with God in such situations has a riddle-like character. One cannot know beforehand whether one is making the right decision or not in ambiguous situations—whether one understands and is in fact doing God's will. One discovers God's will only through taking risks, only in retrospect, only when the dice have fallen. Even then one does not understand in any final sense but only gradually as one takes further risks, thinks through and suffers through one's choices.[18]

Second, in the context of such ambiguity, such incomplete understanding of life, Hirsch says he became convinced that one must have a sense of being pardoned which is stronger than any autonomous certainty about the direction one is pursuing (*zielbewussten Selbstführung*). "Already as a student," he remarks, "I had moved far beyond the usual belief in the providence of pietistic piety [*pietistischer Frommigkeit*]." "In its place," he says, "There grew within me the presentiment [*Erahnen*] of a power which...through the harsh fate of being, awakened and kept alive in me, or more accurately, forced out of me, stretched and tried, purified and limited a will for that which was determined for me, which bade me to take the next step without a thoroughly thought-through program or aim."[19] This view of providence, this sense of a power which is both the expression of one's own personality and will *and* is capable of placing an ultimatum before one, even against one's own will, this power which determines one's fate and destiny in life, is central to Hirsch's thought and experience. It lies at the heart of his view of law, bondage, and obligation, concepts which were so important for him in the 1930s.

Third, Hirsch realized during these early years at Bonn that Luther was right in his insight that all vocations are equal before God and that one's duty in life must take precedence over feelings of personal self-fulfillment. "All human activity, the special as well as the ordinary," he says, "has its ethical imprint in the fact that it can be truly fulfilled only through strict self-limitation, through placing the essential task over and above personal desire. It miscarries when its greater or lesser historical and intellectual significance becomes the basis and

18. *Ibid.*
19. *Ibid.*

justification for a final personal feeling of worth."[20] What is demanded of intellectuals and artists is commitment—a forgetting of the self.

Although these reflections upon the years 1911 to 1916, made by Hirsch in 1951, are surely filtered through his experiences of 1933 to 1945 and later, they are important in giving us his own perceptions of how the insights of those earlier years prepared him for the crucial events and decisions of the 1920s and 1930s. Hirsch became convinced that ethical decisions had an ambiguous character about them, that there is a providence which determines fate and destiny and compels one to take certain steps not necessarily part of a well thought-through program, and finally, that what is demanded of one is a strong sense of duty, obligation, and commitment in life which goes beyond personal self-fulfillment, a sense of vocational obedience to God, the hidden ground of one's life.

What gave Hirsch's theology its most distinctive character, however, was a unique combination of the philosophy of Fichte and the theology of Luther.[21] The thought of the German Idealist Johann Gottlieb Fichte (1762-1814) had a deep and abiding influence on Hirsch. It was Tillich, ironically, who first urged Hirsch to study Fichte as a means of solving the epistemological problem encountered in Kantian metaphysics, particularly as related to the concept of God.[22] Tillich, who had first seriously encountered the thought of Fichte at the University of Halle, gave his own inaugural lecture at the University of Breslau on Fichte's concept of freedom. However, he was soon drawn more to Friedrich J. Schelling (1773-1854), who he felt offered more adequate solutions to the

20. *Ibid.*

21. Hans-Walter Schütte rightly points out that Hirsch's affinity for Fichte lies at the heart of the debate between Hirsch and Tillich in 1917-18. Schütte observes that "The Christian content, that for E. Hirsch was connected with the name of Luther and the unfolding of which constituted and was to constitute an important part of his work as a writer, received in the Fichtian philosophy its formal conceptual clarification, as it were. This perhaps surprising combination of Luther and Fichte proved itself to be extremely consequential for the theology of Hirsch." "Subjektivität und System," *Hirsch Tillich Briefwechsel*, p. 40. The extent to which Fichtian thought actually shaped Hirsch's understanding of Luther is a highly complex subject and must remain the topic of an independent study. But that it played a highly significant role in Hirsch's thought is beyond dispute.

22. *Ibid.*, p. 43. See also Hirsch, "Brief an Herrn Dr. Stapel," in *Christliche Freiheit und Politische Bindung: Ein Brief an Dr. Stapel und Anderes* (Hamburg: Honseatische Verlagsanstalt, 1935, p. 46. According to Schjørring, Hirsch's interpretation of Fichte is of decisive importance for Hirsch's thought as a whole. Fichte became a model for Hirsch in that Fichte combined his philosophical definition of morality with a practical emphasis: "Hirsch considered the significance of Fichte to exist in the fact that he developed a philosophy of religion defined by logical stringency, inner decisiveness and value for all areas of life." Fichte overcame the last residue of dogmatism in his theory of knowledge. Particularly important for Hirsch was Fichte's understanding of God in relation to personal and social morality, "a morality which could not be described merely in formal categories, but could also be condensed into a material ethic." *Theologische Gewissensethik*, pp. 54-55, 55/n. 9. Despite this positive valuation of Fichte, Hirsch remained critical of Fichte's tendency to think of personality and of God in conceptually abstract terms, of not viewing life and existence in a sufficiently dialectical way, and of not placing thought itself under critical judgment.

questions raised by the idealist tradition.[23] Hirsch, however, following the advice of his friend Tillich, devoted himself to two years of intensive study of Fichte. In 1913 Hirsch completed his inaugural dissertation on Fichte, published in two parts in 1914. Also in 1914 he completed a second thesis, his *Habilitation* requirement, on Christianity and history in Fichte's philosophy. This was published in 1920.[24]

Hirsch continued to struggle with Fichtian thought, attempting to relate it to Christianity. This wrestling with Fichtian categories, combined with his later intensive study of Luther and Reformation theology, largely shaped the course along which Hirsch's thought was to move for the rest of his life.[25] Fichte, he says, helped him break through "the narrowness of the theological horizon and through the hollowness of theological conceptuality." Through Fichte he gained a fresh perspective on all questions relating to human-historical life and a clarity about the severity and compass of the contemporary crisis concerning the "relation of the ethical-religious to the human, that which is Christian to that which is human...."[26] He sees his early study of Fichte, which was done independently of

23. It was an oral examination/lecture on August 22, 1910, on the topic "Die Freiheit als philosophischen Prinzip bei Fichte," which qualified Tillich to lecture in philosophy. See *Register, Bibliographie und Textgeschichte zu den Gesammelten Werken von Paul Tillich, XIV* (Stuttgart: Evangelisches Verlagswerk), p. 223 (hereafter references to the *Gesammelte Werke* will take the form *GW* Vol., page)."

24. Hirsch's inaugural dissertation was first published as *Die Religionsphilosophie Fichtes zur Zeit des Atheismusstreites in ihrem Zusammenhange mit der Wissenschaftslehre und Ethik* (Göttingen: Vandenhoeck & Ruprecht, 1914). A second publication was *Fichtes Religionsphilosophie im Rahmen der philosophischen Gesamtentwicklung Fichtes* (Göttingen: Vandenhoeck & Ruprecht, 1914). His second thesis on Fichte was published as *Christentum und Geschichte in Fichtes Philosophie* (Tübingen: Mohr, 1920).

25. In 1926 Hirsch published a major book dealing with the relation of German Idealism to Christianity, *Die idealistische Philosophie und das Christentum. Gesammelte Aufsätze, Studien des apologetischen Seminars* (Gütersloh: Bertelsmann, 1926). A book on related issues appeared in 1930, *Fichtes, Schleiermachers und Hegels Verhältnis zur Reformation* (Göttingen: Vandenhoeck & Ruprecht, 1930). Hirsch came to be known as a Luther scholar through his many writings on Luther's theology, compilations and editions of Luther's works, too numerous to list here. For an exhaustive listing of Hirsch's works on Luther see *Bibliographie Emanuel Hirsch 1888-1972*, edited by Hans-Walter Schütte (Berlin und Schleswig-Holstein: Verlag die Spur, 1972). One early significant work dealing with Luther's concept of God is Hirsch's *Luthers Gottesanschauung* (Göttingen: Vandenhoeck & Reprecht, 1918). Many of Hirsch's later writings grow out of his study of Luther and are attempts by Hirsch to apply Luther's theology to the contemporary German and European situations: *Die Reich-Gottes-Begriffe des neueren europäischen Denkens. Ein Versuch zur Geschichte der Staats- und Gesellschaftsphilosophie* (Göttingen: Vandenhoeck & Ruprecht, 1921 [hereafter referred to as *Reich-Gottes-Begriffe*]); *Schöpfung und Sünde in der natülich-geschichtlichen Wirklichkeit des einzelnen Menschen. Versuch einer Grundlegung christlicher Lebensweisung. Beiträge zur systematischen Theologie* (Tübingen: Mohr, 1931). An important book for understanding Hirsch's struggle with early Lutheran and Reformation theology is his *Die Theologie des Andreas Osiander und ihre geschichtlichen Voraussetzungen* (Göttingen: Vandenhoeck & Reprecht, 1919).

26. Hirsch, "Mein Weg in die Wissenschaft," p. 4.

his teachers (including Karl Holl, who did not have a good opinion of German Idealism), as being part of the general pre-war disposition of Germany's youth—a mood of protest against Western positivism and a search for a more adequate foundation for a genuine German humanity and culture.[27] His attraction to Fichte was also rooted in his conviction that one could not develop a profound spirituality solely on the basis of Kant's philosophy and ethics. Fichte provided Hirsch with his particular understanding of subjectivity, which finds further elaboration in Hirsch's later extensive interpretation of Kierkegaard, and which also provides him with a particular way of reconciling that which is human with that which is Christian.[28] Hirsch's intensive engagement with Luther, coming after his struggle with Fichte, brought him to a new level of intellectual development and gave his understanding of God, human personality, ethics, and history a Lutheran stamp significantly different from that of Tillich.

Tillich's Early Intellectual Formation

Paul Tillich was the first child of Johannes Oskar and Wilhelmina Mathilda. He was born on August 20, 1886 in Starzeddel, a small industrial town in the province of Brandenburg, now in Poland. Like Hirsch, Tillich grew up in the religious environment of a Lutheran pastorate, although his parents, he says, represented the "privileged class."[29] In 1890 the family moved to Schönfliess-Neumark, where his father, a minister of the Prussian Territorial Church, became superintendent of a group of parishes. The town had 3000 inhabitants and had a medieval fortress and Gothic-like character, which Tillich suggests may have had something to do with his "romantic" inclinations. This

---

27. "Über mich selbst," as referred to and quoted by Schütte in "Subjektivität und System," *Hirsch Tillich Briefwechsel*, p. 41.

28. Hirsch came to be known as a specialist on Kierkegaard, interpreting, editing, and translating works of Kierkegaard too numerous to list here. See Schütte (ed), *Bibliographie Emanuel Hirsch*, pp. 11-12.

29. Tillich says of his "privileged class" home environment: "Belonging to the privileged class, therefore, aroused in me very early the consciousness of social guilt that later became very important in my life and work." *On the Boundary: An Autobiographical Sketch* (New York: Charles Scribner's Sons, 1936), pp. 19-20. In this autobiography, written just one year after his 1934-35 debate with Hirsch, Tillich describes how he was destined to stand on the boundary between "alternative possibilities of existence." He begins by describing himself as standing between two temperaments: that of western Germany, represented by his mother from the Rhineland, with an "inclination to meditation tinged with melancholy, a heightened consciousness of duty and personal sin" and a regard for authority, and eastern Germany, represented by his father from Brandenburg and "characterized by a zest for life, love of the concrete, nobility, rationality and democracy." It was his father, he says, whose influence was dominant and with whom he struggled to develop his own position (pp. 14-15). Here we find another similarity between early Hirsch and early Tillich—both struggled against strong authoritative fathers in their attempt to develop their own independent spiritual and intellectual personalities.

romanticism, he says, entailed a special relationship to history and to nature, a "predominantly aesthetic-meditative attitude toward nature as distinguished from a scientific-analytical or technical-controlling relation."[30] It is for this reason, he adds, that Schelling's philosophy later had such a profound impact on him, and why he found himself at odds with Ritschlian theology and its natural allies in American Calvinism and Puritanism. The latter had a more moral and technical stance toward nature as something to be controlled without a sense of the "mystical participation in nature," without a view of nature as "the finite expression of the infinite ground of things."[31]

One of the roots of his attitude toward history and nature, says Tillich, was the Lutheran emphasis on *Infra Lutheranum,* which, in contrast to the *Extra Calvinisticum,* asserted that "the finite *is* capable of the infinite, and consequently that in Christ there is a mutual indwelling of the two natures."[32] A related aspect of Tillich's early formation was the experience of the "holy" in nature and history, so that the mystical experience of divine presence became the starting point for his thinking about God, methodologically prior to the ethical, logical, and systematic aspect of theology, a factor which he says made Friedrich Schleiermacher and Rudolf Otto congenial to his own Christian mysticism.[33]

The concern with the relation of the "human" and the "divine," and the reconciliation of these two realms, was to preoccupy both Tillich and Hirsch and was to lie at the heart of their differences. Tillich, despite his commitment to the prophetic tradition as later expressed through religious socialism, was to move much more in a mystical direction in his attempt to reconcile the Christian concept of God with nature and human history. Hirsch, despite his emphasis on subjectivity and the inner human encounter with the mystery of God, was to emphasize much more concretely the personal-ethical way of bridging the abyss

30. Paul Tillich, "Autobiographical Reflections," in *The Theology of Paul Tillich,* edited by Charles W. Kegley and Robert W. Bretall (New York: The Macmillan Company, 1964), p. 4.

31. *Ibid.* Here we find an early difference between the temperaments of Tillich and Hirsch. Tillich's stance towards history and nature tended to be more mystical than Hirsch's, whose inclinations were more personalistic and ethical. This distinction later finds expression in their different concepts of God—Tillich developing a more mystical-dialectical notion and Hirsch a more "traditional" theistic and personal-ethical view.

32. *Ibid.,* p. 5. Tillich here is describing not so much the theology of Luther himself, but what he perceives to be a general difference between continental Reformed Calvinist theology and Lutheran theology as he came to understand it.

33. *Ibid.,* p. 6. In his 1912 thesis on Schelling Tillich wrote: "Mysticism is the religious expression for the immediate identity of God and man." The Christian church, says Tillich, has always struggled for a solution of the antinomy between "identity" and "opposition" between man and God: "Mysticism and guilt-consciousness, the feeling of unity with the absolute and consciousness of opposition to God, the principle of the identity of absolute and individual spirit and the experience of contradiction between Holy Lord and sinful creature:. . . " *Mysticism and Guilt-Consciousness in Schelling's Philosophical Development* (Lewisburg: Bucknell University Press and London: Associated University Presses, 1974), pp. 30, 27.

between the divine and the human.

If "romanticism" was one of the first factors in Tillich's early formation, the experience and rejection of "Prussian authoritarianism" was almost as important. Conservative Lutheran authoritarianism and militant bureaucratic centralism, says Tillich, characterized every facet of Prussian society in the late 19th century: the king and emperor at the top, the military beneath, the civil service in general, the public schools, and finally the family. Where this authoritarianism affected Tillich most immediately was in the home. Both his parents had strong personalities. His father was a "conscientious, very dignified, completely convinced and, in the presence of doubt, angry supporter of the conservative Lutheran point of view."[34] His mother, while from the more liberal and democratic Rhineland, had been influenced by the rigid morality of the Reformed tradition. "The consequence was a restrictive pressure in thought as well as in action, in spite (and partly because) of a warm atmosphere of loving care. Every attempt to break through was prevented by the unavoidable guilt consciousness produced by the identification of the parental with the divine authority."[35] Tillich's breakthrough to an autonomous position came mainly in the philosophical discussions with his father. "It is this difficult and painful breakthrough to autonomy which has made me immune against any system of thought or life which demands the surrender of this autonomy."[36]

This early struggle against authoritarianism lies at the basis of his later rejection of the principles of heteronomy on the one side and self-sufficient autonomy on the other, in favor of theonomy—a synthesis and superseding of both.[37] It also helps to explain his early feeling of repulsion toward National Socialist totalitarianism and his passionate rejection of what he rightly or wrongly perceives to be his friend Hirsch's captivity to theological and political heteronomy.[38] Important for our comparison of these two thinkers' personal and intellectual formation is this double motif in Tillich's early development: (1) his

34. Tillich, "Autobiographical Reflections," *The Theology of Paul Tillich,* p. 8.
35. *Ibid.*
36. *Ibid.*
37. In a 1923 essay Tillich defines "theonomy" in the following way: "Theonomie ist die Einheit von heiliger Form und heiligem Gehalt in einer konkreten Geschichtslage. Die Theonomie erhebt sich in gleicher Weise über die Formindifferenz der sakramentalen Geisteshaltung wie über die Gehaltsentleerung der formalen Autonomie. Sie erfüllt die autonomen Formen mit sakramentalem Gehalt. Sie schafft eine heilige und zugleich gerechte Wirklichkeit." Theonomy is the synthesis of prophetic form and sacramental content. Without the sacramental content, the prophetic becomes empty, formal, destructive autonomy; without the prophetic formal dimension, the sacramental content becomes idolatrous heteronomy. "Grundlinien des Religiösen Sozialismus," *GW* II, p. 94.
38. Tillich's charge that Hirsch had a heteronomous view of God and religious experience surfaces again and again, as we shall see below. Hirsch, for his part, refuted this charge, as is evident in the unpublished letter by Hirsch to Walter Buff (August 3, 1970), provided by Walter Buff, Hanover; and also Hirsch's letter to Tillich (May 22, 1918), *Hirsch Tillich Briefwechsel,* p. 32.

"romanticism," which expressed itself early in an intensely mystical understanding of God and religious experience, in contrast to Hirsch's more
"personal-pious" experience of God, and (2) his early passionate protest against
all forms of heteronomy, which began with a protest against his father and
continued to express itself in his philosophical, theological, and political rejection of all forms of heteronomous authority, in contrast to Hirsch's much greater
sense of the need for the individual to submit and bow before the discipline and
ethical claims of a higher power.

After his family moved to Berlin in 1900, where his father became superintendent and minister of the Bethlehem congregation and *Konsistorialrat*—a
member of the Brandenburg consistory responsible, among other things, for
examining ministerial candidates. Tillich entered the Friedrich Wilhelm
Gymnasium in Berlin, from which he graduated in 1904. He began his theological training in Berlin and in the years from 1904 to 1909 he studied at the
universities of Berlin, Tübingen, Halle, and again at Berlin. From January 1909
to the autumn of that year Tillich was an assistant to Pastor Ernst Klein in
Lichtenrade, near Berlin, where he spent much of his time studying Schelling.
Here Hirsch visited Tillich.[39]

Tillich's ministerial training continued alongside his academic education.
After passing his first church examination in the spring of 1909, and after
spending one year at a seminary in Berlin, he served a year as vicar in Nauen,
near Berlin. In July 1912 he passed his final church board examination and was
ordained minister of the Evangelical Church of the Prussian Union, Berlin.
From 1912 to 1914 he was assistant preacher in a workers' district of Berlin.[40]
During these years Tillich wrote and published two dissertations on Schelling,
one on Schelling's religious-historical construction, for the University of
Breslau in 1910, and the other on mysticism and the consciousness of guilt in
Schelling's thought, for the University of Halle in 1912.[41] By 1912 Tillich had
decided that he wanted to become a university professor; while serving as assistant pastor he began working in his spare time on his *Habilitationsschrift* (qualifying thesis) for the University of Halle. His Habilitation thesis dealt with the
concept of the supernatural prior to Schleiermacher.[42]

39. Pauck, *Tillich: Life*, p. 30.
40. *Ibid.*, pp. 29-39. For much of this biographical data on Tillich I am indebted to Marion
Pauck's biography.
41. Tillich, *Die Religionsgeschichtliche Konstruktion in Schellings Positiver Philosophie. Ihre
Voraussetzungen und Prinzipien* (Breslau: Fleischmann, 1910); translated into English with an
Introduction and Notes by Victor Nuovo as *The Construction of the History of Religion in
Schelling's Positive Philosophy* (Lewisburg: Bucknell University Press, 1974 [hereafter this work
will be cited as *Schelling's Positive Philosophy*]); Tillich, *Mystik und Schuldbewusstsein in
Schellings Philosophischer Entwicklung* (Gütersloh: Bertelsmann, 1912), translated with an
Introduction and Notes by Victor Nuovo, *Mysticism and Guilt-Consciousness in Schelling's
Philosophical Development* (Lewisburg: Bucknell University Press and London: Associated
University Presses, 1974).

Like Hirsch, Tillich was preoccupied with the need to bridge the human and the divine, the historical and the transcendent, the philosophical and the theological. His love of the Greek language and culture began in his *Gymnasium* years in Königsberg and Berlin, and was to turn into a life-long attempt at synthesizing the humanist and Christian traditions. His student years at Halle, 1905 to 1907, were particularly significant in his intellectual development. Here he listened to and debated with great theologians. Here he learned that Protestant theology was not outdated but could "without losing its Christian foundation, incorporate strictly scientific methods, a critical philosophy, a realistic understanding of men and society, and powerful ethical principles and motives."[43] Here also Kierkegaard's "dialectical psychology," as he calls it, made its first impact.

At the University of Halle Tillich met the teacher that was to have a profound influence on his interpretation of Luther and Reformation theology, comparable to the influence of Holl's understanding of Luther on Hirsch. The teacher was Martin Kähler. If, as we shall see later on in this study, the "two-kingdom doctrine" and the "law-gospel dichotomy" were to become Hirsch's key to Luther's theology, the insight into the "Protestant principle"—which he gained from Kähler—became Tillich's key to Reformation theology. The Protestant principle came to represent for Tillich the protest against all forms of heteronomy. Kähler helped to mediate this principle to Tillich: "The power of the Protestant principle first became apparent to me," says Tillich, "in the classes of my theological teacher, Martin Kaehler, a man who in his personality and theology combined the tradition of Renaissance humanism and German classicism with a profound understanding of the Reformation and with strong elements of the religious awakening of the middle of the nineteenth century."[44]

For Tillich the Protestant principle is rooted in the doctrine of justification through faith. Here, too, Tillich pays tribute to his mentor Martin Kähler who, he says, was responsible for his "insight that the principle of justification through faith refers not only to the religious-ethical but also to the religious-intellectual life. Not only he who is in sin but also he who is in doubt is justified through faith."[45] Justification, therefore, liberates one from both religious-ethical and intellectual heteronomy. The Protestant principle as derived from the

---

42. Tillich, *Der Begriff des Übernatürlichen, sein dialektischer Charakter und das Prinzip der Identität, dargestellt an der supranaturalistischen Theologie vor Schleiermacher.* First part: (Königsberg/Newmark: Madrash, 1915). Second part: Unpublished manuscript: Theol. Habilitationsschrift, Halle-Wittenberg. Cf. *Register und Bibliographie, GW* XIV, p. 139.

43. Tillich, "Autobiographical Reflections," *The Theology of Paul Tillich*, p. 10.

44. Tillich, "Author's Introduction," in *The Protestant Era,* trans. by James Luther Adams (Chicago: The University of Chicago Press, 1966), first published in 1948, p. ix.

45. *Ibid.,* p. x. See also "Foreword," in *The So-Called Historical Jesus and the Historic Biblical Christ* by Martin Kähler, as translated, edited, and with an Introduction by Carl E. Braaten (Philadelphia: Fortress Press, 1964), pp. xi-xii.

doctrine of justification through faith is, however, not only a rejection of heteronomy as represented by papal infallibility, but is also a rejection of "self-complacent autonomy," as in secular humanism. It calls for theonomy, a "self-transcending autonomy."[46] This early encounter with Reformation theology under the teaching of Martin Kähler, combined with Tillich's study of Schelling, was to shape Tillich's thought in a way parallel to the influence of Fichte and Luther studies on Hirsch's thought.[47]

Two Different Theological Temperaments

In this first chapter we have traced briefly the early childhood experiences, intellectual development, and theological education of Tillich and Hirsch. We have described the start of an unusually intimate friendship between two individuals who were rooted in remarkably similar soil. Both grew up in strict Lutheran parsonages and struggled for independence from strong Prussian parental authority figures who nevertheless tolerated diverse opinions. Each inherited from his parents an intense religious make-up and appetite for theology and philosophy—characteristics which eventually attracted the two men to each other. Both channelled their astute minds to the pursuit of theological answers to questions left unsolved by their Lutheran upbringing. Neither was satisfied with the dogmatic formulations offered by traditional evangelical piety and rigid orthodoxy. For both, Protestant scholastic orthodoxy was shattered by the historicism and scepticism of liberal professors in Berlin.

Although both Tillich and Hirsch became preoccupied with solving the problems raised by modern critical thought, particularly as posed by Immanuel Kant, concerning the relation of the "human-historical" to the "divine-suprahistorical," early differences in theological temperament began to appear during these years. The pivotal question in this study, looking at Tillich and Hirsch in retrospect, is why these two friends and theological giants, with such similar religious backgrounds, interests, and theological education, were to take such radically different political paths in 1933. This entire study is essentially a search for the elusive answer to that question. Naturally, there is no one key that unlocks the

---

46. Tillich, "Author's Introduction," *The Protestant Era*, p. xii.

47. Tillich himself says, "For what I learned from Schelling became determinative of my philosophical and theological development." *Perspectives on 19th and 20th Century Protestant Theology*, edited and with an Introduction by Carl E. Braaten (New York: Harper & Row, Publishers, 1967), p. 142. In the opinion of Victor Nuovo, Tillich's Schelling dissertations, both of which he translated into English, "reveal the first formulation of the method and system from which he never departed and the principal themes with which he was concerned throughout his career." Nuovo argues that "Tillich's dissertations reveal the 'deep structure' of his thought, which may be likened to a 'language' with which one 'speaks' about existence." Translator's Introduction," *Schelling's Positive Philosophy*, p. 12.

door to this mystery. There is rather, as we shall find, a constellation of factors that determines their divergent political-theological destinies. We shall find in the following chapters that it was their different response to World War I and its aftermath that lies at the basis of their 1933-35 split. But even this explanation leaves us with a prior question: What was it in their pre-war development that prepared the ground for their opposite reaction to the war and the events of 1918? A purely socio-political account, although important, will not suffice to explain these differences.

A psycho-historical analysis by itself, albeit significant, is also inadequate. Hirsch himself is not given much to psychological introspection. We know that he came from a long line of peasant and artisan stock but this does not seem to figure strongly—at least not in Hirsch's own mind—in the ultimate course which his life was to take. We are also told that he inherited from his home a deep inward piety and an independent spirit which remained with him to the end of his life. We know that he had to overcome the resistance of his strict father to study with liberal professors in Berlin. We will also find that his health problems, making him ineligible to fight in World War I, tended to intensify his patriotic sentiments. The significance of these socio-psychological factors in shaping his theological and political temperament cannot be denied. Tillich, much more of an autobiographical thinker than Hirsch, is much more inclined to dwell on the influence of his "privileged class" status, the "romantic" surroundings of his early childhood, and his struggle for autonomy from his authoritarian father in the shaping of his personal disposition, his future theology, and his political choices. In fact, with Tillich one gets the distinct impression that he occasionally over-indulges in this kind of psychological self-examination, and that he gives too much credence to psychological factors in the shaping of his theology and politics. While their ancestral roots, their different socio-economic class status, and their divergent early psychological environments clearly had a role to play, these in my opinion do not hold the final key to explaining the different paths Tillich and Hirsch were to follow.

What was decisive was the formation of different theological and philosophical temperaments. Tillich and Hirsch came under the influence of different teachers and made some crucial theological choices in the pre-war years which began to move them in different directions. Hirsch's studies in Berlin had the effect of undermining traditional objective supports for faith in favor of inward certainty and the importance of subjectivity. He became convinced that he would have to embark on an independent course beyond the liberalism of cultural Protestantism, on the one hand, and the rigidity of Lutheran orthodoxy, on the other. At this point the influence of Karl Holl was crucial in nudging him on to a new synthesis in which an existential interpretation of Jesus, Paul, and Luther was decisive. His study of German Idealism through the eyes of Fichte and Kierkegaard combined with his devouring of Luther was to stamp forever his distinctive amalgam of inward piety and his sense of moral obligation to his country. During his early years as lecturer in Berlin he became increasingly convinced of the ambiguities of the human situation and of all ethical-vocational choices. He developed a view of Providence which saw divine will in a person's life not in terms of clear absolute ethical norms but of risk. It was through taking risks in unclear situations that one expressed one's commitment to the hidden God of history.

From the beginning Tillich was attracted more to a mystical view of the divine in its relation to history and nature. For him the indwelling of the two natures in Christ came to be paradigmatic for the dialectical relationship of the finite and the infinite, the finite being within the infinite and the infinite within the finite. This mystical starting point was to determine his theology as well as his political ethics, in which the struggle against all forms of non-dialectical heteronomy and totalitarianism became an obsession. His intellectual development and dialectical theology were permanently stamped by his studies at the University of Halle, the traditional seat of German pietism, where he came under the spell of Martin Kähler. It was from Kähler that he inherited some of his basic theological concepts, especially his understanding of justification and the Protestant principle. His education at the University of Halle, the influence of Kähler, and his intensive work on the mystical theology of Schelling gave shape to a theological temperament and a concept of God and human history which was increasingly to distinguish him from the thought and temperament of his friend and future opponent Emanuel Hirsch.

No single set of factors is adequate to explain the different destinies of these two thinkers. One could presumably see these two figures as simply caught in a web of historical, socio-psychological circumstances which gave shape to two divergent temperaments, creating a religious socialist out of one and a religious nationalist out of the other. While there is undeniably some truth to this view, it does not do justice to their own self-perceptions, nor does it adequately reflect the freedom with which they made their choices in 1933 and the responsibility they personally took for these decisions. What is decisive—and this is the thesis of this study—is the early theological-philosophical education of Tillich and Hirsch that, tested and tried, confirmed and modified by their experiences in World War I, together with their own freely chosen paths, played a primary role in setting the course which their lives were to take.

2
A Theological, Political and Personal Parting of the Ways 1914-1933

Theological and personal differences between Paul Tillich and Emanuel Hirsch were already evident in the years preceding World War I. It was the war, however, and their different responses to the war that permanently changed both them and their relationship to each other. Each enthusiastically volunteered for military service at the outbreak of the war in 1914. Hirsch was rejected for health reasons and was left to observe the tragic consequences of the war as a pastor and teacher. Tillich became army chaplain on the western front and there experienced first hand the impotence of traditional theological categories in the face of meaningless suffering and death. How these war experiences gave shape to their theology and how this in turn had fateful consequences for their future lives—their intellectual development and political choices—provides us with a key to understanding their opposing positions in the debate of 1934-35.

Hirsch Develops a National-Political Consciousness

The period from 1914 to 1921 was a time of transition for both Tillich and Hirsch. Tillich's experience of the horrors of war as army chaplain made him into a class-conscious religious socialist.[1] Hirsch's experiences as teacher in Bonn, as pastor in southern Germany, as patient struggling against blindness, and as someone back in academic life in Bonn, all helped to increase his national consciousness and antipathy to socialism.[2] He became increasingly

1. According to Marion Pauck, Tillich was "utterly transformed" by the war. "These years," she says, "represent *the* turning point in Paul Tillich's life—the first, last and only one." *Tillich: Life*, p. 41. That this was the *only* turning point in Tillich's academic career is debatable. It has been argued that Tillich's North American concentration on psychological and ontological themes represents a major shift from his earlier concentration on social- and political-ethical themes in Germany. Stumme makes precisely this point in his "Introduction," *The Socialist Decision*, trans. by Franklin Sherman (New York: Harper & Row, 1977), p. ix. While such a shift is evident, it should be noted that Tillich's psychological and ontological interests appear even in his earliest writings and a strong case can be made for the consistency of his thought both on psychological-ontological and on political-ethical issues.

2. According to Walter Buff, Hirsch preferred not to use the term "nationalism" to describe his

more committed to the renewal of national dignity and to a "political theology" which would take seriously its task and responsibilities at the vortex of the nation. It is no accident, therefore, that Hirsch called his third autobiographical essay, "Meine Wendejahre (1916-21)."[3]

During his two years of study and teaching in Bonn, 1914 to 1916, the main outline of what were to be his life-long areas of academic interest took shape: German Idealism and the history of European and German theological and philosophical thought; Reformation theology; the philosophy of religion, history, and the state; and church history—particularly the history of early Christianity and historical Jesus studies.[4] Although his natural inclination, he says, lay in the direction of systematic theology, he chose church history because the Bonn faculty offered no *habilitation* degree in theology. For a number of semesters he was the only teacher in the area of church history, a burden which he saw as an alternate form of military service.[5]

own view because he perceived it as characterizing an unholy love of the fatherland and as an absolutization of one's own nation and state. He preferred to talk about love for the fatherland, national consciousness, or national feeling. Personal letter, Buff to Reimer, September 20, 1979.

3. Hirsch describes these years in retrospect with the words: "Mein Leben war in schmalen stillen Gleisen gelaufen, rein in der Richtung auf Geist und Innerlichkeit zu. Sollte ich ein rechter theologischer Lehrer werden, der in den heraufziehenden Zeiten der Not und Krise des Volkes seinen Mann stand, so war hier etwas nachzuholen. Die Lenkung griff ein und warf mein persönliches Leben in eine Reihe von Wenden und Krisen hinein, in denen mein wesentlicher Wille gleichsam kunstgerecht erprobt, klargestellt und zurechtgehämmert wurde." "Meine Wendejahre," pp. 3-4. In my reading I have not found any specific reference by Hirsch to his own work as "Political Theology." Nevertheless, there is considerable justification, as we shall see, for describing Hirsch's theology in this way.

4. In his study of church history Hirsch became especially interested in the powerful role played by great historical individualities in the movement of history. The most important of such historical figures was of course Jesus himself, and Hirsch became fascinated with the historical human Jesus, his temptations, his God-forsakenness, and the relation between faith and history that this entailed. He became convinced of the "essential opposition between Jesus and Old Testament Jewish religion and piety." His particular view of the human historical Jesus, he says, was to predetermine his travelling a lonely road during the coming age of dialectical theology. "Mein Weg in die Wissenschaft," p. 4. His numerous writings touching on these subjects include *Studien zum vierten Evangelium. Text, Literarkritik, Entstehungsgeschichte, Beiträge zur historischen Theologie* (Tübingen: Mohr, 1936); *Das vierte Evangelium in seiner ursprünglichen Gestalt verdeutscht und erklärt* (Tügingen: Mohr, 1936); *Das Alte Testament und die Predigt des Evangeliums* (Tübingen: Mohr, 1936); *Die Auferstehungsgeschichten und der christliche Glaube* (Tübingen: Mohr, 1940); *Frühgeschichte des Evangeliums. Erstes Buch: Das Werden des Markusevangeliums* (Tügingen: Mohr, 1941); *Zweites Buch: Die Vorlagen des Lukas und das Sondergut des Matthäus* (Tügingen: Mohr, 1941); *Betrachtungen zu Wort und Geschichte Jesu* (Berlin, 1969).

5. Hirsch describes his teaching in Bonn between 1914 and 1916 in the following way: "Diese Arbeit war bis etwa Spätherbst 1916 mein Kriegsdienst, und er gab mir den Freunden draussen und den bald nicht fehlenden kriegsversehrten Studenten gegenüber das Gefühl der Ehre und Verbundenheit zurück, dass mir meine Untauglichkeit zum Kriegsdienst (ich war ein überkurzsichtiger, schwächlicher Mensch, der nur ganz wenige Pfund über hundert wog, und Heben und Tragen war mir ärztlich verboten) zu nehmen drohte." "Mein Weg in die Wissenschaft," p. 4.

In 1916 Hirsch terminated his position on the Bonn faculty and became pastor of a church in Schopfheim, in the Black Forest area of Germany, where he immersed himself in a variety of pastoral and administrative duties from February to October, 1917, activities which were cut short by a serious eye disease.[6] His pastoral work had the effect of making him more reflective, leading to the development of an independent theological stance marked by ever greater simplification and inwardness.[7] The next few years were difficult ones: the eye disease left him partially blind, financial difficulties faced him and his new bride,[8] and he encountered a series of rejections by German theological faculties and by the church.[9] Hirsch did not seem to fit into the traditional ecclesiastical schools of thought. The apprehension that German theological faculties had toward Hirsch appears to have been due partly to the "rumor of my riskiness and also because of my oddness [*Querheit*], which did not fit any theological and ecclesiastical direction," says Hirsch.[10] His opportunity came in 1921 when he was finally offered the church history professorship in Göttingen despite strong resistance from a majority of the faculty. At about the same time he was given the demanding but also prestigious editorship of *Theologischen Literaturzeitung,* a scholarly periodical founded and initially edited by Adolf von Harnack.[11]

Hirsch's difficult personal and professional experiences during and immediately following the war nurtured in him an inner identity with and conformity to the national German destiny, to an inner understanding of what he calls the crucial question for him during the period of transition. He learned to experi-

6. In the winter of 1917 18 Hirsch had to give up his church work because of an eye disease which despite an operation resulted in the loss of sight in his left eye. In August of 1919 he developed the same disease in his right eye. Through advanced medical treatment the eye was saved, leaving him with another 25 years of partial eyesight. He became totally blind in 1946. This struggle with blindness contributed to his somewhat "tragic" perspective on life.

7. Hirsch says of this pastoral experience, "So wurde Theologie zu Meditation, und Reflexion zur Gebärerin der Worte, auf deren schwanker zerbrechlicher Brücke das Geheimnis des Göttlichen zum Nächsten ging. Orthodoxer ist meine Theologie bei dieser Umschichtung wahrlich nicht geworden. Es war eher eine Vereinfachung und Verinnerlichung, bei welcher die Ferne zur Begrifflichkeit der Amtsgenossen, die Fremdheit zu dem, was ich theologische Schnurrpfeifereien nannte, noch steig." "Meine Wendejahre," p. 4.

8. Hirsch married in November 1918.

9. For some reason his home church turned down his application for pastoral work. Further, within a period of a year and a half, five German theological faculties almost hired him and then turned to someone else.

10. "Meine Wendejahre," p. 4.

11. In the words of Hirsch himself: "Dann setzte sie mich zu Herbst 1921 (gegen den Willen der Fakultätsmehrheit und mit dem Separatvotum des greisen N. Bonwetsch, eines streng orthodoxen Lutheraners) in das Göttinger kirchengeschichtliche Ordinariat und warf mir zum Überfluss gleich noch die Schriftleitung der von Harnack und Schürer gegründeten 'Theologischen Literaturzeitung' zu, welche durch die Inflation in Seenot geraten war und eines das Segeln gegen den Wind nicht scheuenden jungen Steuermanns bedarfte." *Ibid.*

ence "non-being" and the "abyss of the *deus absconditus* [the absence of God]."
Philosophically, he had for some time perceived God as the "thought-consuming
boundary [*die das Denken verzehrende Grenze*] which had a grotesque-comical
quality in contrast to the gravity of the philosophical-dogmatic doctrine of
God."[12] Religiously, he came to realize the need for giving one's life and will
over to the "mysterious hidden one [*rätzelhaft Verborgenen*]." "In its depth," he
adds, "the relation to God is not simply one of thought, but lived antinomy."[13] It
is not in despair but in obedience to the call to service and work that one's
encounter with this mystery of the hidden God makes a man out of a theologian.

Hirsch's pre-war philosophical and theological evolution was given shape by
his study of German Idealism, especially in its Fichtian version, as we saw in the
previous chapter. This second period of his life (1914-1933) was determined
primarily by his experience of political events and his intensive study of Luther.
It would be unfair to regard his intellectual development—particularly his interpretation of Luther—as simply a product of his attempt to make sense out of the
social-political events which engulfed all of Germany during these years.
Nevertheless, it is clear that Hirsch turned to Luther's theology for his own theological and political orientation during this time of national crisis.
Socio-political experiences and intellectual-theological development influenced
each other in a dynamic, dialectical process.

Since a more thorough analysis of Hirsch's political views and his appropriation of Luther's categories will be the subject of a later chapter, we allude here
only briefly to some of the themes essential to Hirsch's intellectual and personal
development. Strongly influenced by his mentor Karl Holl, Hirsch came to feel
that Luther's theology—particularly Luther's view of the relationship of law and
gospel, his concept of God and the doctrine of justification, and his understanding of the two kingdoms—had special relevance for Germany's socio-
political problems during the war and the post-war period.

Hirsch was especially interested in the ethical import of these theological
doctrines. He was impressed by the paradoxical nature of Luther's concept of
God in which God's judgment and grace, anger and forgiveness, hiddenness and
revealedness always went hand in hand. This paradoxically determined both
human freedom and human bondage, forgiveness and judgment. As Jens Holger
Schjørring formulates it, "This meant further that the ethical attitude, the principle of morality which arises out of freedom in the Christian life, contradicts all
the versions of misunderstood Christian ethics which Hirsch (and with him
Holl!) saw everywhere present in the years 1917-18: the ascetic pacifism of Leo
Tolstoi, the religious-socialist ethic of the Swiss Leonhard Ragaz, the utopianism of social democracy (which in Hirsch's eyes was a disguised form of
egoism and blatant Godlessness) or also British utilitarian morality, which was

12. *Ibid.*
13. *Ibid.*

intended simply to cover up indigent world-imperialistic ambitions and served, for instance, as a legitimation of the hunger blockade against Germany."[14]

Hirsch adamantly maintained that in fidelity to Luther's doctrine of the two kingdoms, the kingdom of the world and the kingdom of God—the visible community of society and politics and the invisible community of love and universal brotherhood—must be clearly distinguished. And yet he came to reject the total separation and isolation of these two realms from each other. His study of Fichte and German Idealism had convinced him of the dialectical relationship between the realm of the spirit (*absoluter Idealität*) and the realm of human history in which human action actualizes itself.[15] How to distinguish and yet bridge these two realms emerged as one of the central dilemmas for Hirsch.

It was through his understanding of the human conscience—a concept which came to be pivotal for his view of human personality, of both human spirituality and human action—that Hirsch solved the problem of bridging the two realms. He became convinced that the individual conscience was the point at which the individual's relationship to God intersects with the individual's relationship with the world. As Schjørring puts it, "Faith in the Reformation sense could therefore for Hirsch not be reduced to a passive forensic act, but was much more to be understood as an act which made the personality dynamic, gave the will tenacity, and created a new disposition [*Gesinnung*]."[16] It would be inaccurate, however, to perceive Hirsch's solution to the problem of relating the divine and the human realms as a totally individualistic one. Hirsch saw God's sovereignty as existing not only over the individual conscience but as extending to the nation and to history as a whole. Central to Hirsch's view of history, as he developed it during these years, was his notion of the hidden sovereignty of God—God as the sovereign Lord of history, the "unfathomable dynamic will," the "invisible, mysterious driving-force of history," which he liked to call a "theistic view of history."[17]

As we shall more fully examine in a later chapter, Hirsch, on the basis of his unique combining of German Idealism and Luther's theology, developed a "conservative" political ethic dedicated to national renewal. He was highly critical of the November revolution of 1918, of all forms of social and parliamentary democracy, and of international pacifism. He saw pacifism as simply playing into the hands of British imperialism. He defended a uniquely German view of the authoritative state which stood in continuity with Bismarck's vision of the official state. It was a theory of the state quite distinct from that of the British Calvinist tradition (characterized, as he saw it, by a utilitarian morality in the service of world imperialism) and the French socialist tradition (stamped by

14. Schjørring, *Theologische Gewissensethik,* p. 60.
15. *Ibid.,* p. 71.
16. *Ibid.,* p. 60.
17. *Ibid.,* pp. 66, 72-73.

its utopian vision of universal brotherhood and a secular kingdom of God). For Hirsch such a German authoritative state was fully consistent with Luther's views regarding the two kingdoms and the legitimate God-ordained authority of government.[18]

During and immediately following the war years Hirsch wrote and published an impressive number of theological-political treatises devoted to these questions, works in which he attempted to address seriously the social and political realities in Europe and in Germany.[19] The most important of these politically-oriented writings was without a doubt his book *Deutschlands Schicksal*, first published in 1920, of which he says: "It was a small piece of daring, to give these lectures in the summer of 1920 and then immediately to send them to press."[20] Viewing the German nation and ethos as threatened by an alien Anglo-Saxon view of the state, a state emptied of all ethical-religious content, Hirsch felt called to defend a theory of the nation-state uniquely appropriate to Germany, one in which the "national" and the "human," the "human" and the "Christian" were held together in a distinctively German way.[21] This controversial book was greeted with enthusiasm by post-war nationalist groups such as the Young National Lutherans, who were passionately committed to national renewal.[22] The book helped Hirsch gain a permanent position at the University

18. *Ibid.*, pp. 63-79.

19. These writings include "Unsere Frage an Gott," *Evangelische Wahrheit* 5,22(1914), pp. 370-372; "Volksernährung und Biergenuss," *Wingolfs-Blätter* (1916); "Ein christliches Volk," *Der Geisteskampf der Gegenwart* 54,7(1918), pp. 163-166; "Rauschgeist und Glaubensgeist," *Der Geisteskampf der Gegenwart* 55,2(1919), pp. 40-42; "Was die Liebe tut," *Der Geisteskampf der Gegenwart* 55,10(1919), pp. 192-193; "Nation, Staat und Christentum, 30 Thesen," *Mitteilungen zur Förderung einer deutschen christlichen Studentenbewegung* 6(1923), pp. 82-84; "Zum Problem der Ethik," *Zwischen den Zeiten* 3(1923), pp. 52-57; "Zur Grundlegung der Ethik. Eine Auseinandersetzung mit Albert Schweitzer," *Die Tat* 16,4(1924), pp. 249-260.

20. "Meine Wendejahre," p. 5. Hirsch recognized that this venturing out of the traditional academic areas of concern into social and political matters as a theologian was not without risks. He was driven, however, by an inner courage: "Meine schon einige Jahre bestehende Vorstellung, dass ich als Nichtsoldat neben meiner eigenen Arbeit her die eines Gefallenen mittun müsse, hatte sich in den langen Monaten des Dunkels zu einem Entschluss verdichtet. Falls ich Licht zur Arbeit wieder empfange, solle es nicht bloss theologischem Forschen und Lehren im engeren Sinne dienen, sondern (ohne jede Verkürzung solchen Dienstes) auch noch dazu, meinem Volke in der es mit innerer Auflösung bedrohenden geistigen Krise durch helfendes Denken den Weg zu finden." *Ibid.* The book referred to is *Deutschlands Schicksal: Staat, Volk und Menschleit im Lichte einer ethischen Geschichtsansicht* (Göttingen: Vandenhoeck & Ruprecht, 1920). The third edition, which we will be using, was published in 1925. Hereafter referred to as *Deutschlands Schicksal*.

21. "Meine Wendejahre," p. 5.

22. *Deutschlands Schicksal* evoked immediate response from the German theological community. Hirsch describes the reaction as follows: "Die Staats- und Geschichtslehre des jungen nationalen Luthertums, die sich in den Jahren nach dem Zusammenbruch bildete, knüpft deutlich an es an. Ich habe von da an unter den jungen nationalen evangelischen Theologen und darüber hinaus unter den eine nationale Wiedergeburt ersehnenden geistigen Deutschen manche persönlichen Freunde gehabt und bin stolz darauf gewesen. Aber ich spürte von Anfang an die durch das eherne Schicksal

of Göttingen, a post he held from 1921 to his resignation in 1945. *Deutschlands Schicksal* was to be the forerunner of Hirsch's 1933-34 lectures and book under the title *Die gegenwärtige geistige Lage*, which he viewed as an elaboration of his earlier book and which in effect initiated the Hirsch-Tillich debate of 1934-35.[23]

During these years and right to the end of his life in 1972, Hirsch steered an independent course, not readily classifiable in terms of theological movement or ecclesiastical party. Throughout his life he was a controversial figure in theological, ecclesiastical, and political circles but remained a powerfully influential and creative thinker both in the political and the churchly arenas.

Nevertheless, while holding strong political views and being sharply critical of the Weimar Republic, Hirsch, like Tillich, was more of a theoretician than a partisan activist in theological-political matters. His party affiliations during the Weimar years are not entirely clear. From an unpublished letter to Karl Barth on August 9, 1921, it is evident that Hirsch at that time held no political party membership, although his sympathies lay with the conservative German National People's Party (DNVP). He stresses in this letter to Barth that he is opposed to every international-type of party that undermines a sense of nationhood and statehood. At the same time he criticizes the DNVP for its economic views and for its tactics, and as a Christian expresses reservations and some disillusionment with the sham and pretense that seem to characterize all political parties.[24] According to Walter Buff, Hirsch did not join the DNVP until the late 1920s.[25]

Despite his suspicion of political parties, Hirsch became an influential figure in a movement in Germany in the 1920s and early 1930s committed to providing a theological base for a growing nationalism. This movement, which was dedicated to national-political renewal, in the early 1930s played a significant role in making the German Evangelical Church open to the National Socialist "revolution." Included in this circle of "political theologians" were such well-known theological personalities as Paul Althaus, Friedrich Gogarten, Wilhelm Stapel,

schmerzhaft gezogenen Grenzen dieser Wirkung. Theologie und Kirche gingen unter dem Einfluss der dialektischen Theologie weithin andere, entgegengesetzte Wege und verschlossen sich, soweit sie das taten, auch um des Gegensatzes zu 'Deutschlands Schicksal' willen allen Einwirkungen meiner theologischen Arbeit. Da wurde es natürlich schwer, wenn nicht unmöglich, radikalen jungen Stürmern und Drängern zur richtigen Einsicht in das Verhältnis des Christlichen und des Humanen zu helfen. Für mich persönlich aber ist 'Deutschlands Schicksal' der Anfang zu einer unerschöpflichen Gedankenbewegung geworden, die mich immer tiefer in das Durchdenken der allgemeinen geistigen Lage unseres Zeitalters hineinführte." *Ibid.*

23. Hirsch, *Die gegenwärtige geistige Lage im Spiegel philosophischer und theologischer Besinnung: Akademische Vorlesungen zum Verständnis des deutschen Jahres 1933* (Göttingen: Vandenhoeck & Ruprecht, 1934). Hereafter cited as *Die gegenwärtige geistige Lage.*

24. Personal letter, Hirsch to Barth, August 9, 1921. Karl Barth Archiv, Basel, Switzerland. Supplied by Walter Buff, Hannover, Germany.

25. Personal letter, Buff to Reimer, June 19, 1980.

and Emanuel Hirsch, for whom the concept of *Volk* (variously translated as people, nation or folk, and having strong ethnic connotations) became a central category for all theological-political thinking.[26]

Tillich Becomes a Class-Conscious Socialist

While Hirsch was studying and lecturing in Bonn, 1914 to 1916, and engaged in pastoral work in Schopfheim in 1917, Tillich took temporary leave from his academic and professional career (in 1914) to serve as army chaplain in France for four years. The first hand experience of the horrors of war changed his political and theological views dramatically. He turned from an enthusiastic and patriotic supporter of the war effort into a critic and ardent class-conscious socialist. Immediately after the war he helped found the Berlin Religious Socialist or "Kairos Circle," intent on reconciling Christian theology and socialist thought. As army chaplain in the context of extreme suffering and constant, meaningless death, Tillich's theology became more and more radical and eschatological, his understanding of justification grounded on the paradox of "faith without God."[27] This growing eschatological and even "sceptical" religious orientation was to distinguish Tillich's theological perspective from that of Hirsch in the coming years.

Tillich's professional academic career began only after the war (in 1919), when he accepted a position as lecturer (*Privatdozent*) in theology at the University of Berlin, where he taught until 1924, preoccupied mainly with developing a "theology of culture." Like Hirsch, Tillich was interested in medi-

---

26. Klaus Scholder devotes substantial space to the rise of German conservative political theology in the 1920s and shows how Paul Althaus, Friedrich Gogarten, Wilhelm Stapel, and Emanuel Hirsch in particular all helped to give shape to this new type of modern theology, which saw "the responsibility for the national community as a decisive theological task, which theology and the church could not withdraw from under any circumstances." According to Scholder, "Gewiss ist jede Theologie politisch. In der modernen politischen Theologie aber wird die politische Ethik zur Schlüsselfrage theologischen Verstehens und kirchlichen Handelns. Das ist ihr allgemeines Merkmal und Kennzeichen." *Die Kirchen und das Dritte Reich: Band I: Vorgeschichte und Zeit der Illusionen 1918-1934* (Frankfurt/M: Verlag Ullstein Gmb H, 1977), p. 125ff, 130. One of the most valuable contributions of Scholder's study is that he takes seriously the theological-political thought of such German Christians and National Socialists as Emanuel Hirsch.

27. In a private letter to Maria Rhine, dated November 27, 1916 he says about his newly acquired eschatological emphasis: "Und dann das Leiden der Menschen—ich bin reinster Eschatologe; nicht dass ich kindliche Weltuntergangsphantasien hätte, sondern dass ich den tatsächlichen Weltuntergang dieser Zeit miterlebe. Fast ausschliesslich predige ich das Ende." *GW* XIII, p. 70. A year later, December 5, 1917, Tillich wrote the following to Rhine: "Und nun Weihnachten! Ich meine damit das theologische Problem, dass wir angeschnitten haben! Ich bin durch konsequentes Durchdenken des Rechtfertigungsgedankens schon lange zu der Paradoxie des 'Glaubens ohne Gott' gekommen, dessen nähere Bestimmung und Entfaltung schon lange den Inhalt meines gegenwärtigen religionsphilosophischen Denkens bildet...." *Ibid.*

ating the truths of traditional Christianity with those of modern culture, and was especially concerned with harmonizing the insights and methods of various disciplines such as theology, philosophy, sociology, art, and politics. Tillich's numerous writings during the years following the war reveal not only his interest in theology and culture in general, but also in theology and politics in particular.[28]

Unlike Hirsch, however, who perceived himself as much more of a socially constrained (*gespannte*) person, Tillich had a gregarious quality about him—a passion for personally experiencing the creative and chaotic aspects of modern culture.[29] Tillich says of this period in his life: "The situation during these years in Berlin was very favorable for such an enterprise. The political problems determined our whole existence; even after revolution and inflation they were matters of life and death. The social structure was in a state of dissolution, the human relations with respect to authority, education, family, sex, friendship, and pleasure were in a creative chaos. Revolutionary art came into the foreground, supported by the Republic, attacked by the majority of the people. Psychoanalytic ideas spread and produced a consciousness of realities which had been carefully repressed in previous generations."[30]

Tillich was not only a careful observer of these phenomena but participated actively in them, an involvement which, he says, "created manifold problems, conflicts, fears, expectations, ecstacies, and despairs, practically as well as theoretically."[31] His personal participation in the new modes of life and thought brought him into conflict with family, friends, and church. Correspondence between Tillich and Hirsch during these years shows how it brought him into conflict also with his friend Hirsch, who strongly disapproved of Tillich's style of life, particularly his relationship to women, and who consequently urged him to transfer from the theology faculty to philosophy.[32]

28. Among these early writings are *Der Sozialismus als Kirchenfrage* (Berlin: Gracht, 1919). Also in *GW* II, pp. 13-20; "Über die Idee einer Theologie der Kultur," *Religionsphilosophie der Kultur* (Berlin: Reuther & Reichard, 1919). Also in *GW* IX, pp. 13-31; "Christentum und Sozialismus (I), *Das neue Deutschland* 8(1919), pp. 106-110. Also in *GW* II, pp. 21-28. "Christentum und Sozialismus (II)," *Freideutsche Jugend* 6(1920), pp. 167-170. Also in *GW* II, pp. 29-33; "Masse und Persönlichkeit," *Die Verhandlungen des 27. und 28. Evangelisch-Sozialen Kongresses* (Göttingen: Vandenhoeck & Ruprecht, 1920). Also in *GW* II, pp. 36-56; "Masse und Religion," *Blätter für Religiösen Sozialismus* 2(1921), pp. 1-3, 5-7, 9-12. Also in *GW* II, pp. 70-90; *Masse und Geist. Studien zur Philosophie der Masse* (Berlin, Frankfurt/M.: Verlag der Arbeitsgemeinschaft, 1922). Also in *GW* II, pp. 35-90; "Kairos (I)," *Die Tat* 14(1922), pp. 330-350. Also in *GW* VI, pp. 9-28; "Grundlinien des Religiösen Sozialismus. Ein systematischer Entwurf," *Blätter für Religiösen Sozialismus* 4,8-10(1923), pp. 1-24. Also in *GW* II, pp. 91-119; *Kirche und Kultur* (Tübingen: Mohr, 1924). Also in *GW* IX, pp. 32-46; "Christentum, Sozialismus und Nationalismus," *Wingolfs-Blätter* 53(1924), pp. 78-80. Also in *GW* XIII, pp. 161-166.

29. Hirsch himself points to this difference in temperament between himself and Tillich in a private letter, dated June 21, 1921.

30. Tillich, "Autobiographical Reflections," p. 13.

31. *Ibid.*, p. 14.

In 1924-25, Tillich, strongly encouraged by his friend Karl Becker, minister of education, accepted the associate professorship in theology at the University of Marburg. He stayed for only three semesters but it was a period which left an indelible mark on him and on some of his life-long friends who were his students there.[33] It was at Marburg that he first experienced the "radical effects" of neo-orthodox theology on students, that he came into contact with existentialism through the person of Martin Heidegger, and that he first began working on his systematic theology. That year he also published his important book, *Die religiöse Lage der Gegenwart*. In it he attempted, through an examination of the various social, political, and artistic phenomena of modern cultural life, to understand and unmask the hollowness of the "spirit of capitalism," based on self-sufficient reason and autonomy.[34]

Despite his sharp critique of modern capitalism, Tillich's stance toward modernity, and especially modern technology, remained dialectical. From 1925 to 1929 Tillich was professor of philosophy and religion at the Dresden Institute of Technology, and for part of this period (1927 to 1929) also adjunct professor of systematic theology at the University of Leipzig. The technological and

32. As we shall see below, a group of five letters from Hirsch to Tillich, between June 11 and June 28, 1921 all deal with rumors about Tillich's relationship to various women and how Hirsch had a totally different view of what should constitute such relationships.

33. Marion Pauck describes these three semesters in Tillich's teaching career as a time which "though painful, helped him to establish himself." The students were mostly Barthians, and strongly under the influence of professors Rudolf Bultmann and Martin Heidegger, and tended to neglect other views, particularly those related to theological and cultural liberalism. Gradually Tillich gathered a group of students around himself, students enarmored by his unique way of speaking about faith and God, quite distinct from that of Karl Barth. Pauck, *Tillich: Life*, pp. 94ff.

34. For Tillich, in this book, "the *spirit of capitalist society* which occupies a central place in the following discussion does not mean the spirit of individual men or of a class or a party. It is rather a symbol for an ultimate, fundamental attitude toward the world." *The Religious Situation*, trans. by H. Richard Niebuhr (New York: The World Publishing Company, 1967), p. 27. This book was first translated in 1932 from the German *Die Religiöse Lage der Gegenwart* (Berlin: Ullstein, 1926). What is this capitalist attitude? It is an attitude in which "there is no trace of self-transcendence, of the hallowing of existence. The forms of the life-process have become completely independent of the source of life and its meaning. They are self-sufficient and produce a self-sufficient present. And all phases of life which are subject to the spirit of rationalistic science, technique, and economy bear witness to the time as one which is self-sufficient, which affirms itself and its finitude." *Ibid.*, p. 48. Tillich's book does not begin with "traditional" theological and Lutheran theological categories but rather with an analysis of the inadequacies of modern culture. He examines various protests against the religion of self-sufficiency inherent in modern culture—in science, art, politics, ethics, and religion—and then proposes his own more adequate view of culture, namely a "believing-realism," which combines a faith in transcendence with a realistic acceptance of the historical reality of the present situation. For a discussion of what Tillich means by "believing-realism," or "belief-ful realism," as H. Richard Niebuhr translates Tillich's concept, see "Translator's Preface," *Ibid.*, pp. 13ff. It is noteworthy that Hirsch's 1934 book, *Die gegenwärtige geistige Lage*, which roused the ire of Tillich and in effect occasioned the public dispute between the two friends in 1934-35 bears a remarkably similar title to Tillich's *Die religiöse Lage der Gegenwart*.

cosmopolitan nature of these major urban cultural centres, like Berlin earlier and Frankfurt later, and New York City after 1933, always held a fascination for Tillich. It saved him "from a romantic rejection of technical civilization" and taught him "to appreciate the importance of the city for the development of the critical side of intellectual and artistical life."[35] It was in the huge urban metropolis where he learned sympathetically to understand Bohemianism, as well as social and political movements that germinate in large cities. Many of Tillich's writings during the second half of the 1920s, most of which grew out of speeches and lectures, deal with his attempt to interpret Christian theology dialectically in its relation to the creative, open, and dynamic aspects of modern urban cosmopolitan culture.[36] Always Tillich applied a dialetical method: "Question and answer, Yes and No, in an actual disputation—the original form of all dialectics is the most adequate form of my own thinking," Tillich observes self-reflectively.[37] It was a method of theological thinking which Hirsch felt kept his friend Tillich from taking strong positions, from making clear commitments in actual historical situations, and in effect undermined Christian faith itself.[38]

In 1929 Tillich became professor of philosophy and sociology at the University of Frankfurt, where he remained until April 1933. His inaugural lecture at Frankfurt and his numerous writings and publications during the next four years indicate to what an extent Tillich was preoccupied with social and political ethics during these his "golden years" in Germany.[39] He came to know

35. *On the Boundary*, p. 17.

36. Some examples of these writings are "Logos und Mythos der Technik," *Logos* 16(1927), pp. 356-365. Also in *GW* IX, pp. 297-306. "Das Christentum und die Moderne," *Schule und Wissenschaft* 2(1928), pp. 121-131, 170-177. Also in *GW* XIII, pp. 113-130; "Die technische Stadt als Symbol," *Dresdner Neueste Nachrichten* 115(1928), p. 5. Also in *GW* IX, pp. 307-311; "Das Christentum und die moderne Gesellschaft," *The Student World* 21(Geneva, 1928), pp. 282-290. Also in *GW* X, pp. 100-107.

37. "Autobiographical Reflections," pp. 15-16.

38. In his review of Tillich's "Religionsphilosophie" (Berlin: Ullstein, 1925), Hirsch is critical of Tillich's dialectical method, which he considers an escape from the immediacy of life into the highest form of abstraction: "Auch T.s Abriss der Religionsphilosophie ist kein zugängliches Buch. So krystallklar und sauber T.s Gedankenentwicklung ist, sie liegt doch im Elemente allerhöchster Abstracktheit, in der die Unmittelbarkeit des Lebens so gut wie verloschen ist." *Theologische Literaturzeitung* 51,5(March, 1926), p. 98. Actually, Hirsch perceived Tillich's philosophy of religion as a fundamental attack on Christian faith itself. In the same review, Hirsch says: "Dennoch, wer ein schlichtes ja Gottes zu Christus und damit auch zum Christen kennt, wer es als Aufhebung der ihm von Gott aufgezwungenen Personheit versteht, bloss geisttragende Gestalt, d.h. bloss Ort von zugleich gerechtfertigtem und gerichtetem Sinnvollzuge zu sein, wer den Glauben an ein diese Welt zerbrechendes ewiges Gottesreich festhält, wem der lebendige Gott kein Symbol ist, sondern das Urgrund alles Lebens selbst,—der wird T.s Religionsphilosophie als zentralen wissenschaftlichen Angriff auf den christlichen Glauben empfinden müssen. So geht es mir." *Ibid.*, p. 102.

39. His inaugural lecture was entitled "Philosophie und Schicksal," appeared in *Kant-Studien* 34(1929), pp. 300-311. Also in *GW* IV, pp. 23-35. Other writings of the next few years which deal with social and political issues as they related to religion and theology include "Sozialismus," *Neue*

intimately a wide range of scholars from many different disciplines, including leading figures of the Institute of Social Research and representatives of the famous Frankfurt School of Critical Theory.[40] Here his political views took shape in the context of regular conversations with other leading intellectuals with whom he had heated discussions on economic, social, political, philosophical, and theological issues.

In the 1920s Tillich avoided direct partisan political involvement devoting himself to a theoretical elaboration of religious socialism, yearning and struggling for a just social order in the Jewish prophetic tradition—a new society which would transcend party lines.[41] Despite his reluctance to join a political

Blätter für den Sozialismus 1(1930), pp. 1-12. Also in *GW* II, pp. 139-150; "Religiöser Sozialismus," *Neue Blätter für den Sozialismus* 1(1930), pp. 396-403. Also in *GW* II, pp. 151-158; *Religiöse Verwirklichung* (Berlin: Furche, 1930); *Protestantisches Prinzip und proletarische Situation* (Bonn: Cohen, 1931); Also in *GW* VII, pp. 84-104; "Sozialismus: II. Religiöser Sozialismus," *Die Religion in Geschichte und Gegenwart*, Hrsg. Hermann Gunkel und Leopold Zscharnack (Tübingen: Mohr, 1931), pp. 637-648. Also in *GW* II, pp. 159-174; "Das Problem der Macht. Versuch einer philosophischen Grundlegung," *Neue Blätter für den Sozialismus* 2(1931), pp. 157-170. Also in *GW* II, pp. 193-208; "Kirche und humanistische Gesellschaft," *Neuwerk* 13(1931), pp. 4-18. Also in *GW* IX, pp. 47-61; "Zehn Thesen," *Die Kirche und das Dritte Reich. Fragen und Forderungen deutscher Theologen*. Hrsg. Leopold Klotz (Gotha: Klotz, 1932), pp. 126-128. Also in *GW* XIII, pp. 177-179; "Der Sozialismus und die geistige Lage der Gegenwart," *Neue Blätter für den Sozialismus* 3(1932), pp. 14-16; "Protestantismus und politische Romantik," *Neue Blätter für den Sozialismus* 3(1932), pp. 413-422. Also in *GW* II, pp. 209-218; *Die sozialistische Entscheidung* (Potsdam: Protte, 1933). Also in *GW* II, pp. 219-365; "Das Wohnen, der Raum und die Zeit," *Die Form* 8(1933), pp. 11-12. Also in *GW* IX, pp. 328-332. These representative writings indicate the extent to which Tillich was concerned with the social and political questions arising out of the modern Western, European, and German situation and impinging on religious, theological, and ecclesiastical thinking. Hirsch is right, however, when he says Tillich's interest in social-political questions developed later than his own.

40. Theodor W. Adorno wrote his dissertation on Kierkegaard's aesthetics under Tillich's supervision and with Tillich's assistance became a University lecturer (*Privatdozent*) in 1931. Tillich led seminars together with Max Horkheimer, sponsored him for an appointment to a philosophical-sociological chair in 1929, and helped him in 1930 to become director of the neo-Marxist Institute of Social Research. He also became well acquainted with other leading intellectual figures, including Adolf Löwe, Karl Mannheim, and Friedrich Polloch, with whom he entered into controversial and heated discussions on economic, social, political, philosophical, and theological issues, in the context of a discussion circle that met regularly for this purpose. For biographical information on Tillich's years in Frankfurt and his contacts with leading intellectuals, see Pauck, *Tillich: Life*, pp. 110ff; John R. Stumme, "Introduction," *The Socialist Decision*, pp. ix-xxvi, Stumme, *Socialism in Theological Perspective: A Study of Paul Tillich 1918-1933* (Missoula: Scholars Press, 1978), pp. 44ff, and Martin Jay, *The Dialectical Imagination: A History of the Frankfurt School and the Institute of Social Research, 1923-1950* (Boston and Toronto: Little, Brown and Company, 1973), pp. 24, 25, 29, 31, 66. This friendship with Jewish neo-Marxists during the Weimar years helps to explain why Tillich earlier than many recognized the dangers of National Socialist anti-semitic attitudes and why Tillich was one of the first to lose his academic chair together with some of his Jewish colleagues.

41. In 1936 Tillich described his aversion to being identified with any particular party in the following way: "Admitting that I stand on the boundary of Marxism adds nothing new politically to

party, however, he finally did join the Social Democratic Party in 1929 as did many of his friends in the wake of the growing strength of National Socialism.[42] A second overt political action at about the same time was his involvement in the founding and editing of the *Neue Blätter für den Sozialismus*.[43] While he explicitly denounced and eventually resigned from the Berlin Wingolf fraternity in protest of what he considered to be its right-wing views, and while he publicly derided National Socialist views, he did not participate in officially organized anti-National Socialist political action.[44] He concentrated rather on a theoretical analysis of the political situation in Germany and on explication of his own general political orientation, a socialism deepened by and grounded in a religious view of life.

what I have said about my relationship to religious socialism. It does not commit me to any political party. Were I to say that I have stood between two political parties, the 'between' would have to be interpreted differently than it has been elsewhere in these pages. It would mean that I do not inwardly belong to any party and never have, because what seems to me most important in the political realm is something that is never fully manifest in political parties. I desire and always have desired a fellowship that is bound to no party, although it may be nearer to one than to another. This group should be the vanguard for a more righteous social order, established in the prophetic spirit and in accord with the demand of the Kairos." *On the Boundary*, p. 90. It is interesting that Hirsch, too, despite his strong commitment to the National Socialist German Workers' Party (NSDAP) after 1933, had earlier (in 1921) expressed strong reservations and disillusionment with the sham and pretense that seem to be a part of every political party. Personal letter, Hirsch to Karl Barth (August 9, 1921), Karl Barth Archiv, Basel. Provided by Walter Buff.

42. Again in 1936, Tillich wrote of this decision to join the Social Democratic Party: "Hence it was with difficulty, and only because of the political situation of the time, that I was able to bring myself to join a party that had become as bourgeois as the Social Democrats in Germany." *On the Boundary*, p. 21. Tillich *may* have been a member of the Independent Social Democratic Party (USPD) as early as 1919. See Stumme, *Socialism in Theological Perspective*, pp. 24ff, 58, n. 62.

43. That Tillich saw this as in some sense a political act even though he himself was not engaged in practical party politics is evident from his own statement: "So too it was with my relations to the Social Democratic Party. I became a member in order to influence it by contributing to the elaboration of its theoretical base. For this purpose I joined with my friends of the religious-socialist group to found the magazine *Neue Blätter für den Sozialismus*. Through it we hoped to revitalize the rigid theology of German socialism and to remold it from a religious and philosophical standpoint. I myself did not engage in practical politics, but since many of my co-workers were very active politically, our magazine was drawn into the problems of the existing political situation. Of course, I did not refuse specific tasks. But I did not look for them, perhaps once more to the detriment of theoretical work that was intended to serve a political end and to supply the conceptual form of a political movement. On the other hand, even those comparatively rare contacts with practical politics interrupted the concentration that my professional work so urgently required." *On the Boundary*, p. 34.

44. See Pauck, *Tillich: Life*, pp. 125ff. According to Pauck, "Despite explosions and premonitions Tillich failed, as many German citizens also failed, to involve himself in consistent and continuous participation in anti-Nazi political activity. In several fiery exchanges his friend Adorno urged him to reject Nazi language and ideology more directly. He finally did so in his book *The Socialist Decision*." *Ibid.*, p. 126.

Increasing Confrontation Between Two Friends

Having outlined briefly the personal, intellectual, and political development of Tillich and Hirsch separately from the years 1914 to 1933, we turn now to their personal friendship during this period and their growing conceptual and professional divergence. To do this we rely heavily on published and unpublished correspondence between Tillich and Hirsch and on their reviews of each other's writings. Unfortunately we cannot get a complete picture of their relationship during this time from their correspondence; first, because there is a lengthy period between 1923 and 1933 when there seems to have been no correspondence between them—at least none that is extant—and, second, because the rather extensive correspondence between them during the years 1919 to 1922 is incomplete. From these years only Hirsch's letters to Tillich have been preserved.[45]

Our picture of the Tillich-Hirsch relationship in the years 1915 to 1935 is therefore constructed on the basis of the following documents: (1) a single letter to Hirsch, dated November 12, 1917, writen by Tillich upon first hearing from his sister Johanna of Hirsch's hospitalization in Bonn; (2) a set of six letters (one of them an undated draft), three by Hirsch and three by Tillich, bearing 1917 and 1918 dates and dealing largely with theological issues, edited and published by Hans-Walter Schütte in 1973;[46] (3) a series of four letters, all from Hirsch to Tillich, in the years 1919 to 1921, dealing primarily with theological-political questions; (4) a group of five letters, again all by Hirsch to Tillich, in June 1921, having to do with sexual and marital issues; (5) two letters by Hirsch in 1921 and 1922 concerning personal and political differences; and (6) a series of reviews, one by Hirsch of a Tillich book in 1926 and three by Tillich of Hirsch's books in the years 1921 to 1927. These letters and reviews give us an enticing glimpse into the intellectually stimulating interchange between these two seminal theological figures of post-war Germany.

Two Different Concepts of God and Religious Experience:
Correspondence of 1917-1918
The first letter, dated November 12, 1917, is occasioned by Tillich's hearing,

---

45. Most of Hirsch's letters to Tillich have been preserved in the Tillich Archive, Andover-Harvard Theological Library, Harvard Divinity School. It appears, however, that Hirsch did not preserve most of the letters written to him, including those of Tillich, with the exception of those published by Schütte in 1973. I want to thank Andover-Harvard Library for having given me access to the unpublished correspondence from Hirsch to Tillich. I have not been given permission by the Hirsch estate to quote verbatim from these letters, so I have restricted myself to rough paraphrasing in the English language.

46. Hans-Walter Schütte was a student and friend of Hirsch towards the end of the latter's life and received special permission by Hirsch to publish this particular set of letters.

through his sister Johanna, of Hirsch's hospitalization in the Lazareth hospital in Bonn. It is a brief one-page letter devoted mainly to Tillich's understanding of the concept of justification as it relates to the paradox of faith without God. An atheist, he proposes, can consider himself justified by a reality which stands beyond the God that he denies. This theological conviction, Tillich concludes, arises and of an observation of the catastrophic Nietzschian-like negativity that the destructiveness of war has effected, evident particularly in Berlin. He ends with the hope that Hirsch will write and sends greetings to his bride to be.[47]

We turn now to the set of six letters between Hirsch and Tillich in 1917 and 1918, published by Hans-Walter Schütte with Hirsch's permission in 1973. Hirsch is writing from the Bonn eye clinic where he is receiving treatment for his eye disease. Tillich is army chaplain in France. All five letters are heavily theological and deserve more thorough treatment than is possible in this context. The central concern for Tillich, as he expresses it in his initial letter dated December 1917, is his growing theological scepticism. He wonders how to reconcile theoretical-intellectual doubt with the certainty of faith. He considers three possible ways of overcoming such scepticism: (1) the mystical attempt to transcend the subject-object split; (2) intellectual certainty arrived at on the basis of a scientific concept of God; and (3) the overcoming of scepticism and doubt through an emphasis on the ethical-religious experience of reality. While Hirsch has opted for the third alternative, Tillich finds himself espousing the second possibility. The science of religion, through a phenomenological analysis of the subjective moment of religion, can help once again to build up what science (*Wissenschaft*) has dismantled and destroyed. Tillich maintains that only the subjective moment of religion is immune from scepticism. He perceives the decisive difference between himself and Hirsch as follows: while Hirsch in the final analysis considers doubt (*Zweifel*) to be unethical, he (Tillich) believes such doubt (or scepticism) to be a moral requisite for an honest intellect.[48]

In his response to Tillich's letter, Hirsch holds that there are two basic types of religious experience which are beyond demonstration and therefore beyond scepticism, the first one of which Tillich has adequately described—namely, the dialectic of the spirit, the subjective-objective identity which is the presupposition of all life and thought and which can be scientifically and phenomenologi-

47. Personal letter, Tillich to Hirsch, November 12, 1917. Published in *Briefwechsel und Streitschriften: Theologische, philosophische und politische Stellungnahmen und Gespräche.* Ergänzungs- und Nachlassbönde zu den Gasammelten Werke VI (Frankfurt/M: Evangelisches Verlagswerk, 1983), p. 97. This letter and all six letters edited and published by Hans-Walter Schütte in *Hirsch Tillich Briefwechsel 1917-1918* are reprinted in the supplemental volume to *GW* VI. There exist at least two earlier letters by Hirsch to Tillich, one undated one in which Hirsch asks Tillich where in Hegel or Schilling he can find a good critique of Kant's ethics, and another, dated May 16, 1912 which is handwritten and very difficult to read.
48. Personal letter, Tillich to Hirsch, December, 1917, Schütte, *Hirsch Tillich Briefwechsel 1917-1918*, pp. 9-13.

cally explained. On this first level Hirsch agrees with Tillich. Both of them are after all deeply indebted to German Idealism, especially the thought of Fichte and Hegel, in their understandings of the dialectical life of the spirit. But there is a second form of religious experience which stands beyond scepticism and which Tillich and others in the idealist tradition ignore. It is the unmediated spiritual experience of God as the "Other" and the "Strange One," that stands prior to all conceptual interpretation, is the true source of all religion, and cannot be intellectually or scientifically examined. God himself can never be identified with or reduced to this dialectical life of the spirit. While Hirsch admits that he became aware of God through his (God's) ethical demand, God himself always remains hidden and prior to all ethics and human works.[49]

Tillich's opening remarks in his February 20, 1917 reaction to Hirsch's letter illustrate the kind of academic admiration with which he regarded Hirsch: "Your letter is the most profound that a theologian has written since Schelling's 'positive philosophy.'"[50] Tillich goes so far as to call other systematic theologians, including Troeltsch, "dwarfish" beside Hirsch. Nevertheless, Tillich's entire letter is an argument against Hirsch's notion that God as the "Other" can be experienced in an unmediated form. There is, according to Tillich, no experience of the "Absolutely Strange One" which is prior to all conceptual interpretation. The ethical bowing of the spirit to something higher, to something "Other" or "Strange," is phenomenologically correct, but in so doing the spirit still remains within itself. His struggle with Hirsch, Tillich admits, reflects a struggle taking place within himself. Tillich wants to maintain the unity of the experiencing self. His own thinking is moving him ever more deeply into the three moments of what he refers to as autonomous life-immanence (*automen Lebens-immanenz*), as it is expressed in modern literature and poetry; autonomy instead of bowing submission, life instead of a giving-up-of-the-self, immanence instead of transcendence.

In a letter dated May 9, 1918, Tillich elaborates on this initial response. He has just finished reading Rudolf Otto's book, *Das Heilige*. He has been inspired by its anti-supernaturalistic spirit of mysticism, a spirit which he considers to be reminiscent of the later Schelling and which is congenial to his own sense for paradox, for "practical irrationalism, anti-logic, anti-moralism"—something reinforced by his experiences on the war front.[51] Tillich concludes this letter by saying: "I believe we have come closer together," an attitude characteristic of much of the Tillich-Hirsch correspondence and reflecting a deep respect by both

49. Undated draft of a personal letter by Hirsch to Tillich, *ibid.,* pp. 14-20. This letter by Hirsch to Tillich is a lengthy treatise in itself, with a complex and intricately argued defense of Hirsch's view of religious experience. My synopsis of this treatise does not do justice to Hirsch's argument but simply attempts to isolate his basic points in response to Tillich.

50. Personal letter, Tillich to Hirsch, February 20, 1917, *ibid.,* p. 21. This letter is mistakenly dated February 20, 1918 by Schütte.

51. Personal letter, Tillich to Hirsch, May 9, 1918, *ibid.,* p. 28.

for each other's intellectual positions as well as a sincere longing for points of agreement on basic issues.[52]

Hirsch begins his May 22, 1918 answer to Tillich's letter in a similarly accommodating tone: "Dear Paul! I thank you for both of your letters. I will try to answer you, although at times I have only a small residue of strength at my disposal, and against you I always need to employ my whole spirit. I have the feeling that you have come significantly closer to me. Yes, we are perhaps even closer together than you believe. For you have not completely understood me on the philosophical side."[53] While Hirsch largely agrees with Tillich's analysis of the dialectic of the spirit, he feels Tillich's viewpoint is too rationalistic and not paradoxical enough. It is precisely a paradoxical understanding of the relationship between God and man, he maintains, that prevents "heteronomy and other theological naiveties" of which Tillich is so critical.[54] Hirsch calls his own position "theistic idealism." He accepts the idealist analysis of the dialectic of the spirit but maintains that behind this dialectic there is the Christian God before whom all systems are relative; knowledge is imperfectible and every system—Tillich's as well as Hegel's—is subject to the judgment of history.

Hirsch perceives two differences between himself and Tillich, both having to do with their divergent notions of God. First, says Hirsch to Tillich, "You do not attempt to understand *theistically* the dialectical relationship....You, therefore, have to explain it away from the standpoint of your philosophy of spirit." Second, "I have perceived," says Hirsch, "that what you mean [when referring to God as "other" or "strange one"] is more aesthetic and more moderate in tone than what I mean."[55] Hirsch maintains that his own theism is grounded in Luther's theology and suggests that Tillich ought to read his soon-to-be-published work, *Luthers Gottesanschauung.* His own concept of God cannot be adequately described as supernaturalistic but as a kind of idealistic-theistic realism: "It is true that the idealistic system has acquired a realistic undertone with me," he says. "The idealistic theory of knowledge is right but it has religious realism for a hidden presupposition."[56]

52. *Ibid.,* p. 30. In his previous letter Tillich had concluded by saying: "Nun leb wohl! Ich habe den Eindruck, dass wir nicht so weit voneinander entfernt sind, als ich zuerst dachte! Die 'Quarte' in das System der Kultur will auch ich schlagen, nur nicht durch eine Supra-Kultur." *Ibid.,* p. 27. Tillich wants to critique culture from within culture. He rejects the nature-supranature duality which he feels Hirsch is continuing to perpetuate.

53. Personal letter, Hirsch to Tillich, May 22, 1918, *ibid.,* p. 31.

54. Hirsch says: "Dass diese Grundposition nicht zu Heteronomie und sonstigen theologischen Naivitäten führen muss, habe ich in meinem Briefe zu zeigen versucht, und Du könntest das gewiss noch sehr viel besser als ich; gerade wenn man sich den philosophischen Ausdruck der religiösen Paradoxie erarbeitet hat, ist man gefreit gegen alle unphilosophischen heteronomen Wendungen des Gedankens. Du degegen bist in Gefahr, dass eine ganz elementare religiöse Kritik an Dir nicht nur Deinen Rationalismus (um den wäre es nicht so schade), sondern auch alle Vernunft hinwegschwemmt." *Ibid.,* p. 32.

55. *Ibid.,* p. 35. Emphasis is mine.

In his last letter of this published series, dated July 7, 1918, Hirsch adds a few clarifying notes on his previous letter, particularly with regard to his concept of God. He agrees with Tillich that God must not be seen as an object, adds that Luther did not view God as object, and expresses amazement at how successfully Luther withstands philosophical scrutiny. He maintains against Tillich, nevertheless, that God cannot be drawn down into the "dialectical see-saw of the spirit."[57] The concept of God and the human relationship to God, he stresses, must be taken with ultimate seriousness and cannot be seen simply in terms of a person's suspension between two polar opposites. He (Hirsch) is intellectually not naive and has put his own position under thorough philosophical scrutiny: "I think that you will also perceive in my simple presentation [*Darstellung*] that I have subjected that which I say to thorough [*auf Herz und Nierens*] examination before my philosophical conscience. *I am not at all naive.*"[58] While Tillich protests against all objectifications of God, it is, ironically, Tillich himself, says Hirsch, who is in danger of objectifying God: "You make—in your letters at least—the consciousness of the infinite into something with which the spirit plays. Thereby, however, it becomes something finite, something objectified. For something to be an object does mean, does it not, that it exists as a moment in the [life of the] spirit."[59]

What is especially noteworthy in this early debate between Tillich and Hirsch, despite their frequent allusions to a mutual coming together philosophically, is the significant difference between their concepts of God and the nature of religious experience. Hirsch defends what appears to be a more traditional, *theistic* notion of God, God as "Strange" and "Other," one who reveals himself to human beings in an unmediated way, prior to all conceptualization, and one who demands a humble, obedient, ethical response and commitment

56. *Ibid.*, p. 36. The concluding sentences of the letter read as follows: "Ich hoffe, wir kommen zusammen. Du wirst Dich für Deine Kritik an mir am ehesten richtig einstellen, wenn Du mich nicht unter das Schema des Supranaturalismus bringst, das trifft mich nicht. Wohl aber hat bei mir das idealistische System einen realistischen Unterton bekommen. Die idealistische Erkenntnistheorie ist richtig, aber sie hat einen religiösen Realismus zur geheimen Voraussetzung."

57. Personal letter, Hirsch to Tillich, July 7, 1918. *Ibid.*, p. 37.

58. *Ibid.*

59. The German reads: "Vielleicht darf ich die Dinge auch auf den Kopf stellen und sagen: Du bist viel eher als ich in Gefahr, Dir Gott zu vergegenständlichen. Du machst—brieflich wenigstens—das Unendlichkeitsbewusstsein zu etwas, womit der Geist spielt. Damit wird es aber verendlicht, vergegenständlicht. Gegenstand sein heisst doch wohl, Moment im Geiste sein. Nur das ist nicht Gegenstand, bei dem es in der Art, wie wir davon reden und denken, zum Ausdruck kommt, dass es nur per paradoxian in uns ist." And then Hirsch concludes with what becomes a familiar motif in this series of letters: "Ich habe seit Deinem Besuch das bestimmte Gefühl, dass wir uns zusammenphilosophieren werden." *Ibid.*, p. 37. In fact, they did not come closer together philosophically, but moved increasingly further apart; nevertheless, this recurrently expressed desire on both sides to come to some kind of agreement on theological issues does demonstrate the strong feeling of friendship they continued to have throughout these years and right to the end of their lives.

(*Hingabe*)—a giving up of autonomous egocentricity. Tillich, who strongly protests all forms of heteronomy and supernaturalism, asserts in these early letters the importance of autonomy rather than a giving-up-of-the-self,[60] an immanent transcendence rather than an absolute transcendence. He understands the experience of God as part of the dialectical life of the spirit itself, as "relatively transcendent," as an "Other" but an other that is a polarity within the life of the spirit itself. Tillich is more concerned with preserving the unity of the experiencing personality or consciousness.

While both Tillich and Hirsch were deeply influenced by German Idealism and its view of the dialectical nature of the life of the spirit, Hirsch, unlike Tillich, wants to place the life of the spirit in the context of a theistic understanding of God as a creator who is separate from the spirit and who in fact created the spirit. Like Tillich, he also rejects any "objectification" of God but protests what he perceives to be Tillich's drawing of God into the dialectical life of the spirit itself. He argues that Tillich's dialectical view of the spirit is right as far as it goes but maintains that behind this stands the Christian Creator God. The relation of humanity to God, of spirit to God, must, he alleges, be seen paradoxically. It is this emphasis on paradox, says Hirsch, that saves him from the kind of heteronomy and supernaturalism which Tillich falsely accuses him of and is so concerned to overcome. We shall see later that these variant philosophical and theological presuppositions have a determinative role to play in their subsequent divergence in social and political questions as well.

These early letters, representing a kind of mini-debate and foreshadowing the much more dramatic controversy of 1934-35, provide us with some important clues to understanding why Tillich and Hirsch moved in such different political directions during the Weimar years and the early years of the Third Reich. Their divergent early concepts of God and perceptions of religious experience have a direct bearing on their later political ethics. For Hirsch God is in some sense absolutely transcendent, demanding unconditional ethical obedience and submission both in personal and social issues. Tillich perceives God more immanently as part of the autonomous historical life of the spirit. Hirsch's concept translates more easily into a "conservative-national" social-political ethic while Tillich's view lends itself more readily to a radical prophetic, eschatological, and socialist-political ethic. Nevertheless, there are also some significant similarities between the two thinkers and their theological-philosophical presuppositions, affinities that help explain the unjustified charge of "plagiarism," which Tillich will level against his friend and political opponent in 1934.

---

60. Actually, in his mature theology, Tillich rejects both heteronomy on the one side and autonomy on the other and espouses what he calls theonomy, a category which we will return to below. In these letters, however, Tillich is more concerned with protesting all forms of heteronomy (submission to an external law), and argues for a relative autonomy.

Early Personal and Political Differences:
Correspondence of 1919-1922

As noted above, while Tillich and Hirsch corresponded frequently and substantively on a variety of issues between 1919 and 1922, only Hirsch's letters to Tillich have survived. Consequently, we have a rich but one-sided view of the Tillich-Hirsch friendship during these years, a relationship which is remarkable for its intimacy and candidness. While one-sided, the numerous letters by Hirsch to Tillich during these four years do nevertheless give us a good idea of the issues discussed and the positions taken, as well as valuable insight into Hirsch's own thought and how he perceives their relationship.

The first set of four letters deal primarily with personal and political issues. On May 14, 1919 for instance, Hirsch talks about his view of war. He argues that although love ought to be seen as the highest principle, justice between egocentric nations must be taken seriously as well. He criticizes Tillich's socialist orientation—comparing his view of state and authority to the sixteenth Anabaptists—and defends the concept of national renewal, stressing the importance of the individual and the need for a powerful charismatic leader with a strong sense of responsibility for the nation.[61] A July 5, 1919 letter is more personal in tone and indicates that although they are moving politically further apart (this was about the time that Tillich helped to found the Religious Socialist "Kairos Circle" in Berlin), Hirsch is determined if at all possible to maintain their intimate friendship and love for each other. He promises to read Tillich's books even if their worldviews are moving them in different directions, and even if, as he suspects, Tillich is not equally interested in keeping up with his own writing and thinking. He hopes especially that Tillich will read his soon-to-be-published book on Andreas Osiander.[62]

The background for Hirsch's October 8, 1920 letter is not entirely clear but is obviously related to Tillich's strained relation with the Berlin church. His increasing theological and political radicalism, and possibly also his marital status, seem to have put in jeopardy his position in the church and his continuing receipt of a Martin Kähler stipendium in the theological faculty.[63] Hirsch has

---

61. Personal unpublished letter, Hirsch to Tillich, May 14, 1919. It is interesting to note Hirsch's call already in 1919 for a powerful charismatic leader who will govern the nation responsibly under God, a motif which recurs frequently in his writings and helps to explain his pro-Hitler orientation in 1933.

62. Personal letter, Hirsch to Tillich, July 5, 1919. The book Hirsch is referring to is his *Die Theologie des Andreas Osiander und ihre geschichtlichen Voraussetzungen,* a major book on Reformation theology. The next letter by Hirsch to Tillich is more than a year later and suggests that at this point their correspondence broke off for a period, Tillich apparently not wanting to continue the given discussion.

63. On May 16, 1919 the Evangelical Consistory of Brandenburg probed Tillich about his political activities, probably prompted by his lecture to a group of Independent Social Democrats in early 1919 in Berlin-Zehlendorf. Whether Tillich actually was a member of the USPD is a disputed ques-

just returned from a tiring trip to Berlin and a visit with Karl Holl with whom he discussed Tillich's case. The situation appears to have been complicated by the fact that Tillich's own father held a leading position in the consistory of the Province of Brandenburg with head offices in Berlin. Hirsch, obviously critical of Tillich's stance and sympathetic to the church's dilemma, nevertheless, appears to have come somewhat to the defence of his friend before Holl. In the letter Hirsch pays tribute to Tillich's intellectual power and informs him that he is sending his latest book (presumably *Deutschlands Schicksal*) to him, a book which he says will clearly show the differences in outlook between them. He mentions that he has read Tillich's work on theology and culture so often that he knows it thoroughly, including all its hidden discrepancies.[64] Hirsch suspects that his own book will probably antagonize Tillich, but expresses the conviction that they must try now to practise as much overcoming love as possible in understanding each other's opposing intellects.

In the years 1920 to 1922 Tillich published a number of small works on the relationship of the proletarian masses to personality, religion, and the spirit.[65] Hirsch's views on these issues clearly differed fundamentally from those of Tillich. His April 19, 1921 letter to Tillich is devoted largely to a critical analysis of Tillich's writings on the subject. In this letter, ironically (ironically because in 1934 Tillich charges Hirsch with having sanctified the National Socialist movement) Hirsch charges Tillich with "hallowing" the proletariat.[66]

The workers, Hirsch maintains, have the same right as the entrepreneurs and the farmers to fight for their legitimate interests in the name of justice but they must never consider themselves a religious or holy movement. Hirsch accuses Tillich of perceiving the masses as an appearance of the divine. This, he claims, is a form of paganism devoid of any attitude of repentance before the Eternal.

tion. Nevertheless, soon after this Tillich gave his reply to the Berlin church, entitled "Christentum und Sozialismus. Bericht an das Konsistorium der Mark Brandenburg," *GW* XIII, pp. 154-160. This reply is translated by James Luther Adams as "Answer to an Inquiry of the Protestant Consistory of Brandenburg," *Metanoia* 3, 3(September 1971), pp. 10-12. For a discussion of these events see Stumme, *Socialism in Theological Perspective,* pp. 25ff. Tillich's basic point in this "Answer" is that there must be room in the church for Religious Socialists. Tillich's theological and political radicalism, combined possibly with his marital problems—his estrangement from his first wife Grethi after the war, culminating finally in February 1921 in an official divorce—is the personal context within which this letter by Hirsch to Tillich (October 8, 1920) ought to be read.

64. Hirsch is referring here to Tillich's "Über die Idee einer Theologie der Kultur," *Religionsphilosophie der Kultur.*

65. "Masse und Persönlichkeit (1920)"; "Masse und Religion (1921)," and *Masse und Geist* (1922). Hirsch is referring to the first and possibly to the second of these three works of Tillich in his April 19, 1921 letter to Tillich.

66. Both Tillich and Hirsch use the term "holy" as applied to earthly historical events and movements. Because the charges of deifying an earthly reality, levelled by each against the other, hinge to a great extent on their perceptions of what constitutes the holiness of an event, a more precise understanding of what each means by the "holy" quality of earthly events will be developed in a subsequent chapter.

This ethical dimension of humility and penitence by the individual personality before God is precisely Christianity's step beyond paganism. Hirsch emphasizes that God's love enters human history and the structures of society only from beyond and within individual, obedient hearts. A socialist order, as espoused by Tillich, is a cultural matter, while the kingdom of God is a matter of the individual conscience in its relationship to the Eternal. Every earthly order which does not subject itself to this hidden kingdom of God within itself will collapse. In an appendix to this letter Hirsch adds that, while in the winter of 1918 his letter was one of political passion, the present letter is one of passion for the gospel; he urges Tillich to have a similar passion for his own understanding. He maintains that in their works two different spirits are struggling with each other.

The differences that evolved between Hirsch and Tillich during the post-war years were, however, more than only theological and political. They were also highly personal, including differences on sexual ethics and how as a Christian and a theologian one should relate to women. A group of five letters from Hirsch between June 11 and June 28, 1921 all deal with highly sensitive matters relating to sexual ethics. They contain gossip about the Bohemian style of life that Tillich and other Religious Socialists were allegedly engaged in in Berlin, gossip which, mixed with truths, half-truths, and falsehoods was spreading among students and faculties in other German universities.[67] Some understanding of Tillich's personal style of life during the years 1919 to 1924, when Tillich lived in his Taunusstrasse apartment in Berlin—a period which he himself describes as a time of "creative chaos"—is necessary background for this series of highly personal letters by Hirsch to Tillich in June of 1921.[68] Our

67. This set of five 1921 letters by Hirsch to Tillich are all written from Bonn, where Hirsch was a *Privatdozent,* and are dated June 11, June 14, June 21, June 26, and June 28. Hirsch has just been appointed to a professorship in Göttingen and announces to Tillich in the first of these letters that he will be leaving for Göttingen on October 1, 1921. He says that he has heard rumors in Bonn that the Berlin Religious Socialists are questioning the hallowedness of marriage both theoretically and practically and offers to act as a mediator in trying to clear Tillich's name and separate truth from falsehood. The succeeding letters develop into rather extensive discussions on the nature of marriage, sexual ethics, and acceptable relationships between men and women.

68. For Tillich's own description of this period of "creative chaos" in his life, see his "Autobiographical Reflections," pp. 13-14. For the personal and tragic events in Tillich's life, including his marriage to Grethi Wever in 1914, the loss of their child in infancy, her affair and consequent child (in June 1919) with Tillich's friend Richard Wegener, her desertion of Tillich in the spring of 1919, and Tillich's subsequent relations with various other women, see Pauck, *Tillich: Life,* pp. 79ff. According to Pauck: "Tillich rationalized his not unsullied reputation. He was keenly grateful to Hirsch for his honesty and love, and admired his personal strength, which he went so far as to call a heroic religious ethic. Yet he rejected his advice. He did not want to pay the high price of the loss of nature, the demonic, the world of art, intuitive truth, and mysticism. So far as his own reputation was concerned, he felt that to have one at all was a blessing. He sensed that the split between his life and his work must be overcome, but knew at the same time that he could never return to the old ways from which he had freed himself in such tortuous fashion." *Ibid.,* p. 84. This

intent here is not to delve deeply into Tillich's sexual life, nor to examine in detail these letters by Hirsch. After all, the intellectual integrity and consistency of a person's work must surely be judged on its own merit, apart from the private life of that person. And yet one has the feeling that behind these differences on sexual ethics—Hirsch's attitude to relationships with women was defined by much more rigorous self-discipline, self-control, and traditional views of Christian fidelity than Tillich's—there exists a different concept of God and the ethical claims God places on the individual.

The letters do shed light on the extent of their intimacy, their frankness with each other, and the extent to which their differences touched upon highly personal issues. Hirsch warns Tillich against using human relationships for the purpose of intellectual and creative stimulation. He emphasizes that a pure love must remain on a non-erotic level if one is to preserve a variety of serious human relationships. While Tillich may have a more open, attractive, and spontaneous personality, he may be lacking in genuine depth, suggests Hirsch.[69] He is concerned that Tillich abide by certain conventional moral standards for good conscience sake, and for the sake of his reputation and the cause of Religious Socialism—a cause which is vulnerable to attack at the slight hint of scandal. Tillich will need, urges Hirsch, to abide by accepted standards of morality if he wants to overcome the fundamental weaknesses of the bourgeois order.[70] Hirsch proposes that Tillich transfer from the faculty of theology to philosophy to avoid public scandal and that he consider withdrawing from the Wingolf organization, which is committed to an older morality.[71]

In subsequent letters Hirsch leaves behind the discussion of personal sexual and marital matters and addresses the issue of scholarly method and rigor. A July 10, 1921 letter is devoted largely to what must have been an inquiry of Tillich's concerning the work of Karl Holl and the latter's opinion of his own work. Hirsch says he knows Holl's soul well and adds that Holl is not an enemy of Tillich's but does view Tillich's work with some serious misgivings. Holl misses in Tillich's method that discipline and rigor necessary for solid intellectual work, an appraisal with which Hirsch agrees although he is convinced that Tillich has the capacity for rigorous scholarly work, that Tillich has in fact a greater intellect than he himself has, and that he needs simply to subject this intellect to the rigors of self-disciplined work.[72]

side of Tillich's life has also been described in sensational detail by Hannah Tillich in her *From Time to Time* (New York: Stein and Day Publishers, 1974).

69. Personal letter, Hirsch to Tillich, June 21, 1921.

70. Personal letter, Hirsch to Tillich, June 11, 1931.

71. Personal letters, Hirsch to Tillich, June 26 and June 28, 1921. In all of these letters it is remarkable how existentially Hirsch becomes involved in Tillich's personal problems and how much concern he expresses for Tillich's reputation and academic career, despite their growing theological and political divergence. Repeatedly, Hirsch expresses his profound sense of love and loyalty to Tillich.

Hirsch's critique of what he perceives to be Tillich's lack of scholarly and methodological rigor becomes much stronger half a year later in a letter dated January 27, 1922. Tillich has just sent Hirsch his book, *Masse und Geist*. In this letter Hirsch gives a lengthy analysis and critique of this work. He begins by observing how their intellectual development is moving them increasingly further apart and how common propositions are now difficult to find. Tillich has become for Hirsch an interpreter and representative of modern thought and of the modern crisis, the assumptions of which Hirsch strongly rejects. But it is particularly Tillich's method that Hirsch finds inadequate. Tillich's strength lies in schematizing concepts, but there is a lack of seriousness and inner commitment, a lack of passion for drawing final conclusions. Hirsch charges Tillich with failing to subject historical reality to a serious analysis, something which demands personal commitment. Tillich's reflections remain abstract and incomplete.

Having said this about Tillich's method in general, Hirsch goes on to discuss more specifically Tillich's *Masse und Geist*. It quickly becomes evident in this part of the letter how far apart the two actually are in their theology, their theological method, and their political-social ethics. Hirsch here offers what may be another key to understanding the differences between them in the later debate. It has to do with Hirsch's different view of the personality type and the mass type, to use Tillich's phraseology. For Hirsch, individual personality must be seen primarily in terms of the relationship of the individual conscience to God and only secondarily in terms of social function and relationships. Hirsch feels that Tillich's dialectical approach has robbed him of respect for the evangelical religion of conscience before God. In Tillich's attempt always to mediate between two antitheses and move on to a higher synthesis, he is unable to decide for or against any one particular side.[73]

The 1917-18 correspondence between Tillich and Hirsch represents an early "rupture" between the two as far as theological-philosophical presuppositions are concerned. Their exchange of letters in the years 1919-22, as we have considered in the preceding pages, appears to have centered more on political and personal issues. One might say that the earlier debate set the theoretical stage for the later more concrete and practical divergence. Their differing views of the nature of religious experience and concepts of God constitute the theoret-

72. Personal letter, Hirsch to Tillich, July 10, 1921. Hirsch suspects that Tillich's education in essential matters and scholarly rigor at the University of Halle has been inadequate. He suggests that Tillich retreat from Berlin to some quiet small town. Only in such inner loneliness and retreat, not through dramatically influencing many people, can an intellectual power be nurtured. In a letter to Eduard Geismar, dated January 26, 1926 Hirsch says about Tillich that he "is one of our most gifted young, but unfortunately totally pagan thinkers." Cited by Schjørring, *Theologischer Gewissensethik*, p. 131.

73. Personal letter, Hirsch to Tillich, January 27, 1922. Again, behind this letter one senses two different conceptions of God and the individual's relation to God.

ical presuppositions for their divergent lifestyles, academic work habits, and more importantly, their opposing political convictions of the 1920s.

Growing Intellectual Divergence:
Reviews of Each Other's Books, 1922-1927
Tillich's writing on mass and personality, religion and spirit in the years 1920 to 1922, culminating in his *Masse und Geist,* and Hirsch's 1920 book *Deutschlands Schicksal* mark a fundamental theological and political parting of the ways more than a decade before their major rift in the early 1930s. This earlier divergence is illustrated by the rather abrupt termination of correspondence between 1922 and 1933. While their letters of 1921 and 1922 were a sincere attempt, at least on the side of Hirsch, to understand the other's position and to maintain a friendship, they now enter a lean period remarkable for its absence of direct contact (if the lack of correspondence is any indication). However, interest in each other's writing appears to have continued. What we have are a number of rather substantive reviews of each other's books—at least three by Tillich and one by Hirsch.

In 1922 Tillich reviewed both Hirsch's *Die Reich-Gottes-Begriffe des neueren Europäischen Denkens. Ein Versuch zur Geschichte der Staats und gesellschafts-Philosophie* (1921) and *Der Sinn des Gebets* (1921).[74] In the first, Tillich briefly summarizes Hirsch's analysis of the English-liberal-utilitarian, French-utopian-socialist, and German-idealist-humanist theories of state and society. Tillich recognizes the power of Hirsch's critique both of English utilitarianism and French secular socialism but cannot understand why Hirsch subsumes religious socialism, with its attempt to go beyond the secularization of the kingdom of God within the socialist movement, under socialism in general. Tillich also criticizes Hirsch for not dealing with a fourth type of social teaching, namely that of the conservative Lutheran doctrine of society, with its feudalistic and militaristic elements. Despite these criticisms, Tillich hopes for a second edition of the book both for the sake of its inherent value and for the purpose of expanding its scope, placing the issue of the kingdom of God in a context wider than simply Reformation thought.[75] Hirsch's book and Tillich's critique touch on their important different understandings of the kingdom of God and will be considered in a later chapter.

In Tillich's second review, of Hirsch's *Der Sinn des Gebets,* he once again criticizes the latter's concept of God and what he perceives to be Hirsch's heteronomous view of an individual's relation to God. He criticizes Hirsch for objec-

74. "Emanuel Hirsch: Die Reich-Gottes-Begriffe des neuren europäischen Denkens. Ein Versuch zur Geschichte der Staats- und Gesellschafts-Philosophie," *Theologische Blätter* 1(1922), pp. 42-43; "Emanuel Hirsch: Der Sinn des Gebets," *Theologische Blätter* 1(1922), pp. 137-138.

75. "Emanuel Hirsch: Die Reich-Gottes-Begriffe," p. 43.

tively placing God and humanity over against each other, something which, according to Tillich, "conforms neither to the nature of the Unconditioned, which stands beyond the opposition of subject and object, nor...the conditioned, which is being irremediably crushed by the objectified Unconditioned."[76] For Tillich this is the deepest source of legalism in prayer, a form of heteronomy, and leads to a one-sided autonomous reaction. Tillich continues his criticism of Hirsch in a similar vein five years later in his 1927 review of Hirsch's *Die Idealistische Philosophie und das Christentum*, a book which Tillich praises as possibly the "most mature that the work of the last 20 years on Idealism has produced," and which he highly recommends especially to those interested in understanding Fichte.[77] Once more Tillich's criticism pertains to what he considers to be Hirsch's objectification of God. While he is pleased that Hirsch joins the idealist tradition in its struggle against objectifying God, he argues that Hirsch's particular understanding of the lordship of God, of the I-You relationship between the human being and God, and of God's ethical demand cannot help but lead to such an objectification, even against Hirsch's own intentions. "The isolated I-You relationship which is not founded in ontology leads to a new 'dogmatic objectification' of the divine 'You'—in so far as that level of being in which every objectification is superseded is not understood."[78] Once again this review reveals to what extent the differences between Tillich and Hirsch in these years are related to their different conceptions of God, the human relation to God, and the nature and basis for the ethical demand.

We have at least one review by Hirsch of a Tillich book during these years. In the winter of 1926 Hirsch reviewed Tillich's *Religionsphilosophie*.[79] He begins by explaining why Tillich's 1923 "System der Wissenschaften nach Gegenstanden und Methoden," which he calls "one of the most mature (*reifsten*) achievements of the new German systematic philosophy," was not reviewed in the *Theologische Literaturzeitung* (edited by Hirsch).[80] Two of his reviewers had given up on the task because of its difficulty. This new book is also not easily accessible, he adds. He has decided to review this book by the friend of his youth personally, even though he finds himself in almost total opposition to its contents. Hirsch goes into an extensive exposition of Tillich's theological

76. "Emanuel Hirsch: Der Sinn des Gebets," p. 138.
77. "Christentum und Idealismus. Zum Verständnis der Diskussionslage," *Theologische Blätter* 6(1927), pp. 29-40. Also in *GW* XII, pp. 219-238. Actually, in this review Tillich discusses the work of Friedrich Brunstäd, Emil Brunner, Wilhelm Lütgert, and Emanuel Hirsch. His review of Hirsch's *Die idealistische Philosophie und das Christentum*, appears in the last few pages. See *GW* XII, pp. 235-238.
78. *Ibid.*, p. 238.
79. "Paul Tillich: Religionsphilosophie," *Theologischen Literaturzeitung* 52,5(March 1926), pp. 97-103.
80. *Ibid.*, p. 97. Hirsch is referring here to Tillich's *Das System der Wissenschaften nach Gegenständen und Methoden. Ein Entwurf* (Göttingen: Vandenhoeck & Ruprecht, 1923). Also in *GW* IX, pp. 109-294.

method, his view of the relation of religion to culture, his notion of God as symbol in which theonomy and autonomy are reconciled, his belief that faith carries within itself both atheism and theism, and his view of the demonic will. Interestingly, Hirsch places Tillich within the tradition of Barthian dialectical theology and argues that Tillich has in fact consistently taken this theology to its final conclusion; namely, that all that can be said about God and God's yes to that which is human and historical must be couched in paradoxical terms. A theology that wants consistently to be dialectical, he says, must end up espousing Tillich's radical symbolism concerning God. Hirsch, who defends the notion of a living God who is no symbol but the primal ground of all of life, sees Tillich's philosophy of religion as an academic attack on the Christian faith itself.[81] Despite this he praises Tillich's book as not only clever, containing a wealth of ideas, but a serious piece of writing in which a "total person struggles with all his power to answer the greatest and deepest questions—a work, therefore, which enriches everyone who has the power to engage himself in a spiritual struggle with it."[82]

Other than these four reviews and occasional references by Hirsch to Tillich in larger works,[83] we have little direct evidence of the widening gap in their thinking up to their open debate and rupture in 1934-35—except for two short notes which we will allude to in the next chapter.

We have established in the foregoing survey and analysis of biographical materials, published works, private correspondence, and reviews that the differences between Tillich and Hirsch did not erupt suddenly in the years 1934-35 but were there theologically as early as 1917-18, politically and personally in the immediate post-war years and in their writings of the early 1920s, and that they became ever more pronounced on various levels in subsequent years. Substantial *theological* differences—different perceptions of God, the nature of religious experience and ethics—form the basis of their 1917-18 debate. Basic *political* differences—differences in their view and experience of the war, their convictions concerning political solutions for Germany, their understandings of the relation of "personality" to the "proletarian masses"—are evident in a series of letters by Hirsch to Tillich in the years 1919 to 1921 as well as in publications of the early 1920s. *Personal* and domestic differences are obvious in a series of letters on sexual ethics by Hirsch to Tillich in 1921. *Methodological* differences—differences in regard to what constitutes rigorous scholarly work

81. "Paul Tillich: Religionsphilosophie," p. 102. In a short January 1927 "clarification" Hirsch reiterates his high regard for Tillich's book *Religionsphilosophie,* and defends Tillich against the charge of atheism made by a certain D. Traub. "Erklärung," *Monatsschrift für Pastoraltheologie* 22, 3 (1927), pp. 62-63.

82. "Paul Tillich: Religionsphilosophie," pp. 102-103.

83. See, for instance, Hirsch's references to Tillich in his 1931 *Schöpfung und Sünde,* pp. 90-97, notes 2, 8, 42, 54. It is clear from references like these that Hirsch continues consciously to develop his own theology over against that of Tillich's.

and methodology—are expressed by Hirsch in letters to Tillich in 1921 and 1922. More substantial theological and methodological differences become blatant in a series of published reviews of each other's works in 1922, 1926, and 1927. These growing differences in theological, political, personal, and scholarly-methodological questions all provide important background for understanding the nature and accuracy of the charges they levelled against each other in the 1934-35 debate.

Nevertheless, these obvious growing differences dare not hide the existence of significant similarities on a number of important levels. It was their similarities that initially drew them intellectually and personally to each other. It was these which motivated them to correspond with each other, to read and review each other's books, to struggle seriously and persistently with each other's spirits, and created that deep yearning for agreement that each expresses over and over again. Finally, it was these similarities that made the 1934-35 rupture so vehement and painful.

3
Two Separate Roads:
The Rupture of a Friendship, 1933-1945

We have up to this point traced the intellectual development and friendship of Paul Tillich and Emanuel Hirsch through two time periods: the beginning of their friendship from 1907 to 1914, and their growing intellectual separation between 1914 and 1933. In this chapter we turn to the crucial year of Hitler's *Machtergreifung* (Hitler became chancellor of Germany in January, 1933) and the years of the Third Reich, up to 1945, including of course the years of Tillich's and Hirsch's public debate in 1934-1935, to be dealt with separately in Part Three. The years 1933, 1934 and 1935 are the culmination of both the differences and the similarities of their theological and political thought. On the one hand, these years represent the final rupture of their relationship due to their irreconcilable differences, a friendship which had been fraught with increasing points of tension in the preceding years. Quite simply put, their different diagnoses of World War I, the revolution of 1918/19 and the Weimar Republic, and their different prognoses of and recipes for Germany's future got the better of their personal friendship. This final rupture had its immediate cause in Hirsch's strong support of the "German Christians" and the National Socialist movement, and Tillich's harsh critique of the new turn of events, which resulted in his ouster by the National Socialists from his chair at the University of Frankfurt, and his fleeing into exile in New York, where he began a new career on foreign soil. Their public controversy of 1934-1935 was the outward expression of this fundamental split between them, open for all to see.

On the other hand, however, the passionate nature of this controversy suggests that there was something deeper going on then simply two friends splitting up because of different political choices in 1933. Their heated exchange, particularly the vehemence with which Tillich attacked his old friend's 1934 book, *Die gegenwärtige geistige Lage*, suggests that Hirsch represented a kind of alter-ego for Tillich. What surfaces in the 1934-1935 exchange are not simply the differences between these two theologians but some substantial similarities. The central thesis of this study, argued at length in a later section when we deal with the charges and countercharges of the controversy, is that, despite their obvious differences, there are some structural similarities between Tillich's Religious Socialist and Hirsch's Religious Nationalist categories which help to explain the intensity of the confrontation between them. It is in this light, I will argue, that the charge of "plagiarism" made by Tillich against Hirsch must be understood.

In a later chapter we will be analyzing substantively a few of the major theological-political works of Tillich and Hirsch in the years 1933 to 1935. Here we concentrate more on biography; that is, on a cursory overview of their lives, the positions they took, and their shorter writings during the years of the Third Reich, 1933 to 1945.

Hirsch and the German Church Struggle

The Crisis of Modernity

Robert P. Ericksen is right when he, in his excellent recent study of three Lutheran theologians who supported Hitler and National Socialism, argues that what helps to explain the positions of Gerhard Kittel, Paul Althaus and Emanuel Hirsch in 1933 and following was their profound sense of the "crisis of modernity."[1] The industrial and technological revolution had undermined shared traditional and family ties in favor of a pluralism of disparate cultures and ideals. The democratic revolution had sought to entrench individual rights and personal freedoms again at the expense of shared traditional values. The modern intellectual revolution had undermined rationalism and empiricism which had been the pillars of truth beginning with the Renaissance and solidified with the Enlightenment. Theology, particularly modern German theology felt the brunt of this intellectual crisis of modernity. The myths of religion, science and reason were broken by the turn of the century and shattered in August, 1914. World War I and the years of the Weimar Republic brought home to all serious theological thinkers in Germany that the noble tradition of nineteenth-century German liberal theology was at an end. Karl Barth's crisis theology (variously called crisis theology, Word of God theology, dialectical theology or neo-orthodox theology) was simply the extreme example of this disillusionment with and rejection of the previous age of liberal theology. The various theological fronts as they developed in the 1920s and 1930s in Germany (including Barth's crisis theology, on the one side, Hirsch's *nomos* theology, on the other, and Tillich's *kairos* theology in the middle) were distinguished from each other, not by whether or not they recognized this crisis of modernity (they all did this) but how they sought to deal with this crisis.

What separated those theologians who supported Hitler and the National Socialist revolution, like Kittel, Althaus and Hirsch, from those who were

---

1. Robert P. Ericksen, *Theologians Under Hitler: Gerhard Kittel, Paul Althaus and Emanuel Hirsch* (New Haven: Yale University Press, 1985), pp. 1-27. Hereafter cited as *Theologians Under Hitler*. Although I read Ericksen's work toward the end of my own research, in this chapter I am indebted to his excellent historical study for additional biographical information on Hirsch.

staunch opponents, was not the lack of a coherent intellectual position. Hirsch, for example, in the words of Ericksen, "was also intelligent and respectable, and he devoted himself more fully [than most] to seeking an understanding of the Western intellectual and spiritual heritage. He also peered more deeply into the crisis of the age. Instead of protecting him from error, this effort made him a more committed supporter of Hitler and Nazism."[2] What distinguished these pro-Hitler theologians from their critics was the fact that "They shared a commom attitude towards German nationalism and traditional conservative, German Christian values. Each of them opposed the development of pluralism in German life, which is to say that each opposed the advent of modernity....So each of them envisioned an ideal of Germany in which authority, obedience and nationalistic unity would produce community."[3] Each of them (Kittel, Althaus and Hirsch) had an underlying ambivalent attitude toward the Enlightenment which they saw as in some sense the cause of the modern crisis. Each of them rejected some, if not most, aspects of the Enlightenment.

Hirsch's attitude towards the Enlightenment and its fundamental assumptions is perhaps the most difficult to assess. He, more than either Kittel or Althaus, "enthusiastically welcomed the scientific, rational heritage of the Enlightenment as the self-evident intellectual position for modern man. That is, he endorsed intellectual modernism while opposing political, social and cultural modernism. The resulting tension provided the challenge of Hirsch's lifework."[4] Each of them, however, according to Ericksen, saw their own theological and political positions as ways of recovering a lost social, moral and religious cohesiveness in the context of a modern pluralistic world. Each of them viewed the Weimar Republic with disdain, as reflecting the negative consequences of the Enlightenment in microcosm, and welcomed the advent of National Socialism as a new start for Germany.

In a 1920 letter to a trusted friend, Hirsch, who had just been given a professorship at the University of Göttingen, made some prophetic comments about himself. His intent, he says, is to follow an independent course and he predicts that he will be severely criticized by both the right and the left. The right will consider him dangerous because he is so close to them while still not totally one of them. The left will see him, as they do already, inclining toward the right despite his education in critical thought and some of his radical-sounding statements. He hopes that he may accomplish some unique achievement and be a mediating theologian for the future generation.[5] As we examine and evaluate Hirsch's role in the German church struggle it is important to remember this basic intent (not to retreat back behind the Enlightenment, as

2. *Ibid.*, p. 121.
3. *Ibid.*, p. 189.
4. *Ibid.*
5. A letter dated August 29, 1921. Referred to in an unpublished manuscript "Abschied von Emanuel Hirsch" by Walter Buff, Hannover, Germany.

Ericksen at points suggests, but to move forward *both theologically and politically* to a new post-modern age as a mediating theologian) which Hirsch had early already set for himself. An independence of spirit, not easily classified in terms of left or right, always characterized Hirsch even at the points where he appears, on the surface at least, to accommodate his thinking about the theological task of the church too much to that of the so-called National Socialist "rebirth" of Germany.

A number of recent studies of Hirsch's role in the German Church Struggle confirm my own thesis in this study; that Hirsch's decision to give unqualified support to Hitler and National Socialism in 1933, as well as his ardent work on behalf of the German Christians and Ludwig Müller's candidacy for the newly established office of *Reichsbischof*, the authoritative head of a new *Reichskirche*, was not an opportunistic one, as some have maintained, but was generally consistent with his prior intellectual and political development.[6] This is not to deny that there were not opportunistic elements in his writings and actions during the Third Reich; that during the heated church-political events, particularly in the spring and summer of 1933, political considerations may not have at points outweighed his deeper theological convictions. On the whole, however, there is a remarkable continuity between everything he wrote and stood for before and after the 1933 watershed.

Hirsch's political views as expressed in the numerous treatises written during the 1920s, the most important being his 1920 *Deutschlands Schicksal*, in which he articulated a conservative political ethic critical of the revolution of 1918 and the Social Democratic government of the Weimar years, and calling for a return to a Bismarkian-type of authoritative and centralized German nationstate under the helm of a strong charismatic leader, were in fundamental continuity with what he now in 1933 saw Hitler and the NSDAP espousing for the new Germany. It has in fact been suggested that his 1934 *Die gegenwärtige geistige Lage*, consisting of a series of lectures given in 1933 sympathetically interpreting the events of that year, the book which angered Tillich and compelled him to write his first open letter to Hirsch, was a kind of fourth edition of *Deutschlands Schicksal*.[7] Hirsch's earlier theological views, particularly his interpretation of Luther's theology during the 1920s, especially the law-gospel distinction and the separation of the two kingdoms, could now be readily appropriated in support of Bishop Müller's vision of a national German people's church which called for the autonomy of the German Evangelical Church in its primary task of preaching the gospel and administering the sacraments, on the

---

6. See Ericksen, *Theologians Under Hitler*, p. 123; Jens Holger Schjørring, *Theologische Gewissensethik*, p. 152.

7. That *Die gegenwärtige geistige Lage* (1933) can be seen as a kind of fourth edition of *Deutschlands Schicksal* (1920) was suggested to me by Walter Buff, Hannover, in a conversation, June 16, 1978. The significance of this is that it underlines the continuity between Hirsch's earlier and later thought.

one hand, and the giving of unqualified allegiance to the new totalitarian state, on the other. Further, there was a direct connection between his scholarly work on Kierkegaard—he wrote the concluding section of his monograph on Kierkegaard in the fall of 1933—and his political support of National Socialism. The two-fold Kierkegaardian emphasis on God's radical breaking into history, on the one side, and a turn to inward subjectivity, in which the individual alone stands humbly and obediently before the Lord of history, on the other, became the theological and philosophical basis upon which Hirsch developed his notion of "risking" an unequivocal commitment to the national rebirth of Germany, fully aware of all the dangers involved in taking such a risk.[8]

In 1933 Hirsch brought his impressive historical, theological and philosophical learning to bear on the movement now under way, the "holy storm" sweeping across Germany, which he saw as God's direct encounter with the German people. His enthusiastic support of this mass movement was premised on his deep conviction that the underlying intention of Hitler and the NSDAP leadership could be trusted, and that they considered both the Catholic and the Protestant churches as indispensable for the German ethos. He was certainly convinced by Hitler's declarations that the Party wanted to cooperate with the two major Confessions in the fight against materialism and godlessness, and for the creation of a new God-fearing German state.[9] In his March 23, 1933 speech to the Reichstag, Hitler had said: "The Government, being resolved to under-take the political and moral purification of our public life, is creating and securing the conditions necessary for a really profound revival of religious life....The National Government regards the two Christian Confessions as the weightiest factor for the maintenance of our nationality....*The National Government will allow and secure to the Christian Confessions the influence which is their due both in the school and in education.*"[10] Hirsch took these public utterances at face value and saw them as indicating a genuine shift away from the previous Weimar vision of a secular state. This becomes clear in a number of his smaller writings of the period.

Ericksen's assertion that Hirsch "endorsed intellectual modernism while opposing political, social and cultural modernism" is accurate only if one interprets political, social and cultural modernism narrowly in terms of democratic pluralism. Hirsch saw his own intellectual and political stance not as a retreating behind the age of the Enlightenment or modernity but as a new mediating synthesis which went beyond, not behind, the modernity of the Enlightenment and the nineteenth century. This was clearly expressed in a number of his writings in the first few years of the Third Reich: "Vom

---

8. Schjørring, *Theologische Gewissensethik*, p. 159ff.

9. *Ibid.*, p. 178.

10. Cited by Ernst Helmreich, *The German Churches under Hitler: Background, Struggle, and Epilogue* (Detroit: Wayne State University Press, 1979), p. 131. The italics are Helmreich's. Hereafter referred to as *German Churches Under Hitler*.

verborenen Suverän (1933)," "Rede auf der Kundgebung deutscher Wissenschaft (November, 1933)," "Weltanschauung, Glaube und Heimat (January, 1936)," and "Die Lage der Theologie (February/March, 1936)."

The Hidden Sovereign

For a clarification of his political views "Vom verborgenen Suverän" is probably the most important of these writings.[11] In this seminal piece of political thinking Hirsch carefully shows how during the Weimar period he and a circle of like-minded thinkers began developing a new evangelical conception of the state. It went beyond, although was in some sense continuous with, the a) Reformation teaching of unconditional obedience to the divinely instituted ruling authority (*Obrigkeit*), and the b) nineteenth-century conservative view, which saw the state as based not on the sovereignty of the majority but on the divine right of the monarchy and princes to rule. What distinguished the nineteenth-century view from the Reformation teaching, was that it made obedience conditional on the type of authority in existence and thus, theoretically at least, was willing to condone counter-revolution. The November 1918 revolution against Kaiser and King was viewed by Lutheran conservatives as disobedience to legitimate authority and ought therefore to be resisted. Neither the sixteenth- nor the nineteenth-century conceptions were reconcilable with the Weimar theory of state in which the elected parliament, on the one hand, and the elected president, on the other, were subject not to a higher authority but to the sovereignty of the citizens themselves. Hirsch himself rejected the November revolution not because it was a revolution but because it was a particular kind of revolution. In this he was closer to the nineteenth-century understanding of the state than the Reformation view of unconditional obedience. Nevertheless, even though he made no bones of his opposition to the Weimar Republic he had never countenanced a counter revolution in the given situation.

The new concept of state which Hirsch and some fellow Lutherans now developed in this difficult situation (the Weimar period) was premised on a view of authority in which everyone is subject to the hidden sovereign: nationality. Not the given ruling authority (as in the Reformation sense) nor a particular state (as in the nineteenth-century sense) but nationality as a whole now became the criterion for all political thinking and activity. This is how Hirsch describes it:

> Every member of the nation is called upon, through his decisive self-incorporation (Sicheingliederung) into the nation, to interpret and discharge the will of this hidden sovereign in his particular place and with the power of authority given to him, and thus to cooperate in achieving and structuring the right form of state. Every actual or alleged power in the state must be tested and judged by an individual decision of conscience in the light of the

11. Hirsch, "Vom verborgenen Suverän," *Glaube und Volk* 2, 1(1933), pp. 4-13.

criterion which is in accordance with the will of the hidden sovereign, allowing itself to be limited by God according to the measure of its power of authority and must accordingly then be treated with a trusting yes or a resisting no.[12]

Nationality, this somewhat ill-defined basis for (what Hirsch refers to as the "boundary" of) all social and political activity, the norm to which the people as a whole (including their leaders) are subject, is not to be equated with a particular form of state but is the necessary source for every healthy state. Hirsch and his political confreres were fully cognizant of and wanted to distance themselves from the prevalent mythologizing and glorifying of the nation, which they considered a misunderstanding of a right relation to nationality, and which they were persuaded the young German freedom movement would eventually overcome. What was required was the stringent education of individual consciences concerning the true nature and mission of the nation and the self-limitations that must be accepted before God.

While Hirsch and those like-minded wanted to preserve a continuity with the Reformation teaching as well as the essence of the Old Prussian understanding of obedience and loyalty to the state, the new Evangelical concept of the state based on the sovereignty of nationality was different from the nineteenth-century view in at least two respects. First, it was ready to allow for any historically given form of state as long as it could be used to fulfill the true potential and mission of nationality. The Weimar state clearly did not live up to this standard. Nevertheless, as a provisional political form, struggling for German freedom and a new national self-understanding, even the Weimar state could be affirmed in a qualified way. It allowed for individuals like Hirsch himself to develop a new political consciousness. In some sense, second, the democratic form of state, while not appropriate for Germany, in its modern emphasis on the free participation of all its citizens could be seen as an intermediate stage toward a nationally-conscious state in which all members of the nation have rights and assume responsibility for structuring society.

The development and actualizing of this third way, as Hirsch calls it, is a slow, difficult process and requires patience, especially if it is to resist simply accommodating itself to the tactical politics of the day. Hirsch is particularly critical of the ideological misuse of Reformation theology to legitimate the prev-

12. *Ibid.*, p. 7. The German reads as follows: "Jedes Glied des Volks ist durch sein bestimmtes Sicheingliedern in das Volk gerufen an seiner Stelle und mit der ihm gegebnen Vollmacht, Deuter und Vollstrecker des Willens dieses verborgnen Suveräns zu sein und damit rechte Staatlichkeit mit zu erfüllen und zu gestalten. Jede wirkliche oder beanspruchte Gewalt im Staate muss nach dem Massstabe des, das nach dem Willen des verborgnen Suveräns recht ist, geprüft und geurteilt werden in eignem Gewissensentscheid, der sich selbst nach dem Masse seiner Vollmacht durch Gott begrenzen lässt, und danach muss dann im Ja des Vertrauens oder Nein der Abwehr gehandelt werden." The original is in italics.

alent call for a dictatorship by those who have no intent of accepting the Reformation teaching of unconditional obedience to existent authority whatever that may be. For many of these opportunists the call for a return to a Reformation understanding of authority is, according to Hirsch, simply a camouflage for their own immediate political desires. *He considers his own view to be more dialectical, one in which the Reformation teaching is genuinely superceded and appropriated for a modern form of political life which is neither conservative, democratic nor socialist.*

In the current situation, therefore, the Evangelical Church must, on the one hand, guard its independence from all people, movements and powers which are struggling with each other in Germany; and, on the other, recognize and accept its indissoluble bond with the nation as a whole in the hour of struggle for a new national being and state. This precarious position of the church is not without its dangers but it is a risk worth taking. Hirsch is highly critical of those theologians who are not willing to take this risk into the future and simply return to the safety of the Bible, catechism and confession. God's gospel is not a law established once and for all. The gospel does not free human beings from the risk of thinking and acting in new ways appropriate to new historical situations: "We are coworkers with God in helping to shape history, and in the struggle for a new space, a new possibility and a new form of state for our nation."[13]

Hitler as the Instrument of Providence
As the opposition to Hitler's Germany grew, both internally and externally, Hirsch's own resolve to give unconditional support to National Socialism seemed to solidify. This is evident in his November 11, 1933 "Rede auf der Kundgebung deutscher Wissenschaft," in which he attempts to justify his interpretation of the events of 1933 and his view that National Socialism and Germany ought to and would unify themselves behind the Führer despite all resistance.[14] Nothing, according to Hirsch, had helped to disintegrate morality and great ethical ideas as much as the Treaty of Versailles, which tried to construct national community on the basis of untruth and lies. For the younger generation everything seemed hopeless. There was no goal and no place of work. Hirsch remembers himself becoming bitter and thoroughly convinced that if the nation, the natural basis of human life, was sick so was evangelical faith and life. The two were simply inseparable. Added to this was the fact that Marxism had split the German nation down the middle. He became persuaded that as long as this fundamental division between Germans existed there could be no substantive corporate life; the privatization and neutralization of everything ethical and religious would simply continue to increase.

13. *Ibid.*, p. 13.
14. Hirsch, "Rede auf der Kundgebung deutscher Wissenschaft: veranstaltet vom sächsischen Gau des nationalsozialistischen Lehrerbundes zu Leipzig am 11. November 1933," pp. 55-58.

This feeling of hopelessness and despair changed dramatically in the year 1933. Suddenly Hirsch observed new hope and joy in the eyes of his students, the recognition that they now had a government that expected discipline and sacrifice from the present generation. The only appropriate response to this miraculous renewal of hope and confidence in the nation was: "Thank God, now we have been given a foundation, an opportunity, upon which to build, on which to build also the proclamation of the highest and ultimate things. Thank God, our work as teachers of truth and educators of spirit and faith has once more become meaningful."[15] The Marxist division of the nation had been overcome. Hirsch concludes this small article with an affirmation of trust in Hitler's religious integrity, as one who openly admits that he is nothing but the instrument of providence and the creator of all things. "We Germans," Hirsch says, "are on the way out of the land of unbelief, back to that which is holy, something we were in danger of forgetting, and without which we can not live as individuals or as a nation."[16] His final affirmation of loyalty to Hitler is unrestrained and enthusiastic: "Living within me there is an affirmation of this hour, a heart-felt gratitude to God, who after a long period of shame and night has arisen aflame within all of us. If tomorrow the *Führer* calls us, one and all, men and women, something within me responds affirmatively. I say yes as a German, as an Evangelical Christian and theologian, as a teacher in the university. I say this as one small voice within a great chorus, which responds to the call of the *Führer:* We say yes, we will follow him. Heil Hitler!"[17]

Faith and Modern Secularity
While Hirsch was one of the few well-known German Lutheran theologians who did not publicly change his official position toward National Socialism, some of his writings by 1936 did, indirectly at least, suggest serious disappointment, not with Hitler but with how the church had failed to come to his support. Thus, three years into the Third Reich, in January 1936, he wrote a small article, "Weltanschauung, Glaube und Heimat," in which he interprets the struggle of the church as a painful transition into a new form of Christian understanding and theology. National Socialism, he says, has provided a true service to the Christian churches, not only in saving them from the threat of Bolshevism, but

15. *Ibid.*, p. 57.
16. *Ibid.*, p. 58: "Wir Deutsche sind auf dem Wege fort aus dem Lande des Unglaubens, zurück zu dem Heiligen, das wir zu vergessen in Gefahr warren, und ohne das wir nicht leben können als einzelner und als Volk."
17. *Ibid:* "Das 'Ja' zu dieser Stunde ist in mir lebendig, ist von Herzens Grunde in mir lebendig als ein Dank gegen den Gott, der nach langer Schande und Nacht uns allen in Flammen aufgegangen ist. Wenn auf morgen der Führer uns ruft, uns zu dem neuen nationalsozialistischen Deutschland zu bekennen, Mann für Mann, Frau um Frau, so antwortet es aus mir: Ja. Ich sage es als deutscher Mann, als evangelischer Christ und Theologe, als Lehrer der Universität. Ich sage es mit als eine kleine Stimme in dem grossen Chor, der auf den Ruf des Führers antwortet: Wir sagen Ja, wir folgen ihm. Heil Hitler!"

in compelling them to think through what authentic faith in the gospel means in the modern world: "For it has brought us into the situation, in which we are lost if we do not completely learn anew the Lutheran distinction between law and gospel and the earthly and the eternal kingdoms."[18]

In this article Hirsch clearly places the National Socialist revolution in the context of modern western European history. Major changes have occurred in the political, industrial, intellectual and religious self-understanding of Europeans in general and Germans in particular which make it impossible to return to a previous pre-Enlightenment confessional age. *National Socialism is, according to Hirsch, an authentic attempt to find meaning in a modern, post-Enlightenment secular world.* Following the destruction of the Thirty Years War, it was still possible to build up the German nation on the basis of shared values, an inner religious cohesiveness, a unity grounded in a common biblical, Lutheran-confessional worldview. Germans had a sense of having an authentic religiously-grounded homeland (Heimat). But gradually, over a period of two centuries, this sense of homeland was destroyed. This happened, on the one side, through modern technology and economics, and, on the other side, through the dissolution of the biblically-defined worldview by the modern intellectual spirit. Hirsch is unambiguous in asserting the futility of attempting to recover the old sense of cohesiveness: "We dare not make the meaningless and hopeless attempt to return to the nursery of biblically- and confessionally-bound post-thirty-years-war German existence. We must accept the [present] situation and within it build up a new German homeland for ourselves and our descendents."[19]

The National Socialist revolution had, in Hirsch's view, made possible the building up of a new German homeland on the basis of a new fusion of morality and order, and a new life-preserving worldview. The demonic atomization of modern economic and intellectual life were being overcome. "All of this will take place, however, on the foundation and by means of the [present] technical and economic age. And it will occur on the foundation and by means of an insight into human life and its ultimate coherence which accepts with unreserved honesty the demise of the biblical and confessional picture of the world brought about by the intellectual labors of humanity of the last century."[20]

Hirsch does not perceive National Socialism as a narrowly-defined German phenomenon but as having significance for the fate of modern European culture. It can be properly understood only in the western context of *modern secularity.* At the very heart of the movement, nevertheless, there remains the *religious* question: What happens now in a post-confessional age to the Christian faith

---

18. Hirsch, "Weltanschauung, Glaube und Heimat," *Zweifel und Glaube*, (Frankfurt a.M: Verlag Moritz Diesterweg, 1937), pp. 52-64, p. 64; originally published in *Deutsches Volkstum* (January, 1936), pp. 17-25.

19. *Ibid.*, p. 54.

20. *Ibid.*

that has in the preceding centuries played such a decisive role in the building up of a German homeland? The only way the Christian faith can continue to play a significant role in western and in German social history is if the eternal kingdom and the earthly kingdom are clearly distinguished. The kingdom of Jesus Christ is not of this world; it can no longer be seen as overtly determining the external order of corporate national life. In this the contemporary Evangelical Christian view clearly differs from the Jewish religion of law, on the one hand, and pagan tribal religion (which has unfortunately seen a rebirth in Germany) on the other. The new German view of life and society under National Socialism no longer boasts of having biblical-confessional roots. Christians must, therefore, conceive the Christian faith as concerned primarily with eternity and as the hidden ground of human existence. As such, it is not devoid of significance for social life but is influential only as a *hidden* power which helps to structure corporate life and a common worldview.

Neither Jewish heavenly law (*jüdische Himmelsgesetz*) nor pagan holy tribal law (*heidnische heilige Volksgesetz*) properly separated the eternal and earthly realms. This is where the Christian proclamation truly supercedes both, for Christ is the end of the law, and brings the freedom to enter unreservedly into the building-up of corporate life in accordance with one's own national needs and demands, without thereby confusing the eternal and the earthly spheres. The German worldview and the Christian faith are, therefore, two different things which can coexist with integrity in one and the same person; even though one cannot assume that all members of the German nation have such a personal Christian faith.

The fourth article alluded to above, "Die Lage der Theologie," is coloured by a deep disappointment with how the Evangelical church has been torn apart by the German church struggle and has failed to grasp the opportunity of the hour truly to shape the movement of national renewal.[21] What has become clear to Hirsch is that where theology tries domineeringly to determine the shape of the church it tends to split the church apart. Despite his disappointment, however, he remains steadfast and clear about what he sees as demanded by the hour.

Hirsch begins by addressing the issue of the so-called "worldview-struggle [*Weltanschauungskampf*]," dismissing with some scorn those who think that the primary enemy in this regard is the German Faith Movement, which he considers to be an insignificant minority and passing phenomenon. The real issue is that without a united spiritual homeland, without the discipline that is possible in the context of a coherent worldview grounded in a common faith in God, the German nation is bound to go to ruin. The real task for the church and theology is not to struggle against the growing movement of national renewal but as believing Christians to serve and assist it. What is required is a proper

---

21. Hirsch, "Die Lage der Theologie," *Deutsche Theologie,* 3, 2/3(February/March, 1936), pp. 36-66.

understanding of the distinction between gospel and worldview. Some theologians had already in the years between 1918 and 1933 begun to separate these, seeing the gospel as freely granting entry into eternal life and worldview as providing the necessary stability and coherence of earthly life.[22] Where they went wrong was in leaving the average person concerned with natural-historical realities to his own secular worldview devoid of ethical and religious idealism. "Never will we learn correctly to distinguish worldview and gospel from each other if we do not dare ethically and religiously to give honour to the whole national and human sphere of our natural-historical existence, understanding it as the place where God calls and finds human beings, and where Christianity can be received in a dynamic way, and from this to draw the consequences for our theological thinking and ecclesiastical work."[23]

What in the mind of Hirsch makes the events of 1933 such a momentous watershed in German history is that they are the culmination of a new worldview which has been in the making over the past three hundred years, a process which is not yet completed. What this new perception of reality will finally look like is not yet entirely clear, for what is being lived through is a transition period. The Old Protestant form of theology and the church is less and less able to meet the needs of this newly developing worldview. This transition from a nineteenth-century worldview, and its accompanying theology, to the coming new one is incredibly difficult for theology and the church but must be faced with courage. "We have been both nakedly and destitutely suspended for some time between the form of Christian faith which has become a thing of the past for us, and the new, which has not yet arrived."[24]

What makes this transition to a new worldview so difficult for theology and the church is that the traditional Reformation understanding of the Bible and the dogmatic presuppositions of Lutheran orthodoxy and confessionalism no longer shape the thinking of the vast majority. Traditional theological assumptions have become outmoded, even though there are essential insights there that can be appropriated for the new situation. The Reformation rediscovery and transformation of the gospel by Martin Luther can be useful in the present only if through it we can somehow develop a new Christian understanding adequate to our situation. A simple recovery of outmoded theological dogmas will not do. Hirsch is particularly critical of those who still uncritically hold on to Old Protestant orthodoxy which encapsules the gospel in an inflexible set of dogmas which no longer have the power to enlighten the modern situation. Luther himself always recognized that doctrines were human and temporally conditioned and must be subordinated to the gospel itself. He had a dialectical understanding of the relation between the gospel and the historical situation which can

22. *Ibid.*, p. 40.
23. *Ibid.*, p. 41.
24. *Ibid.*, p. 42.

be a point of contact even for today's generation.

The task and mission of the Evangelical Church cannot be reduced to a political-party program either on the left or the right. This is so because the "Political community and the community of faith do not stand under the same law of life." "In the political community the primary intent is rational self-assertion in the face of all the powers of being; in the community of faith and worship the primary goal is to have the requisite openness to the mysterious divine truth which testifies to itself. A church which uses its teaching and its confession as a party program and a marching order has betrayed the primary purpose of the community of faith and worship and has become a pseudopolitical community."[25] This happened in the nineteenth century under the guise of a scientific worldview in which truth became partisan. "It is clear to any thinking person," says Hirsch, "that a church which bases itself rigidly on doctrine and confession, no matter how skilfully, could not be other than a worldview party, acting as a front against another worldview, and would thus remain a laceration in the community of those who ought to believe and worship together."[26] Here Hirsch is obviously thinking not only of the Barthians and members of the Confessing Church, who had drawn up a list of six confessional theses against the German Christians at the Barmen Synod of May 29-31, 1934, but also of other conservative Lutherans who, while not part of the Confessing Church, were calling for a retrenchment in old Lutheran orthodoxy against the less confessionally minded German Christians.

The Ecumenical Movement

During the years of World War I and the Weimar Republic Hirsch's political utterances were largely of a theoretical nature. In the early 1930s, and particularly in the Spring and Summer of 1933, however, he became much more deeply embroiled in active church politics. The controversial positions he took during these tumultous years can be properly understood only in the light of his theological and political presuppositions as they have been outlined in the preceding pages. One of the first church-political issues that drew him into battle was the ecumenical movement. As early as 1925, at the time of the world conference in Stockholm, he had questioned the wisdom of German participation in the international ecumenical network, charging that the call for church unity across national boundaries was politically motivated, and suggesting that the boundaries of the *Volk* and the church should ideally coincide. Hirsch's role in the debate intensified in 1931, on the occasion of an international ecumenical leadership meeting in Hamburg, when he and Paul Althaus published a joint protest against German participation in international ecumenism.

25. *Ibid.*, p. 62.
26. *Ibid.*, p. 63.

Like his protest against international pacifism, so Hirsch's critique of world-wide ecumenism was premised on his conviction that in all such international organizations Germany was always at a disadvantage. This was the consequence of the political situation after the unjust Treaty of Versailles with its false war-guilt clause, the destructive reparation demands by the allies, and the exclusion of Germany from having colonies. In this light any international church cooperation on the part of German Evangelical leaders simply tended to further cover up the international exploitation of Germany. Hirsch and Althaus were not alone in holding such views. While there was a substantial negative response to their 1931 statement, both domestically and abroad, they received growing support within Germany, and they seemed to have had a remarkable influence in turning parts of the official German Evangelical church leadership against the ecumenical movement.[27]

In his "Oxford 1937 und Herr Oldham" Hirsch again came out publicly criticizing the world ecumenical organization and its subsidiary committees for, despite their superficial commitment to dealing with world social problems, not openly denouncing the real political injustices perpetrated against Germany ever since the Treaty of Versailles.[28] Dr. J.H. Oldham, chairman of the research commission of the ecumenical council had, in anticipation of the July 12-26 world conference in Oxford, written a book on "Church, Nation and State," in which he identified the threat to the Christian Church posed by the new totalitarian regimes of Russia, Italy and Germany. Hirsch is highly critical, first of all, of Oldham's comparison of the National Socialist state with that of Russia. But, more importantly, he accuses Oldham, this international English Christian, of stirring up anti-Christian sentiments in Germany, precisely at a time when the new regime had finally, after years of national dishonour and humiliation, given back to the young generation honour, freedom and bread. Instead of spreading propaganda against Germany, and labelling Bolshevism and National Socialism as identical threats to European culture, the Christian churches of the world ought to be grateful to German National Socialism for creating a European bulwark against anti-Christian Bolshevism. Instead, Oldham, says Hirsch, was using his official position to propagate his own private views, to act as a political agent for a particular perception of the world situation and thereby damaging Christianity and the Church. What would happen, asks Hirsch, if German National Socialist Christians would use the forum of the World Conference to push through a joint statement against the threat to Christian and church discipline posed by the democratic freedoms in England, North America

27. See Ericksen, *Theologians Under Hitler*, pp. 142-144.

28. Hirsch, "Oxford 1937 und Herr Oldham," *Deutsches Volkstum: Monatsschrift für das deutsche Geistesleben* (March, 1937), pp. 196-203. This article was written by Hirsch in anticipation of the July 12-26, 1937 Oxford ecumenical world conference, the theme for which was *Church, Community and State,* a theme on which Oldham, chairman of the research commission of the ecumenical council, had just recently published a book.

and France?

Behind Hirsch's comments there is the firm conviction that there is an essential difference between Anglican and Reformed Christianity, on the one hand, and German Lutheran Christianity, on the other. According to the Lutheran view, there is only one possible common Christian and churchly word and that is the proclamation of Jesus Christ; that is, the proclamation of eternal life through the free gift of God's love in Jesus Christ. How this is rooted in and takes effect for individual Christians in their own national life and culture can not be clarified by an international church conference. It can be determined only by individual Christians and teachers, representing relatively small circles of individuals, who fully participate in the life of their own nation. Hirsch acknowledges that Anglican and Reformed Christianity have never fully accepted the Lutheran teaching concerning law and gospel, and have consequently had a different understanding of the relation of church and state; but what astounds him is how naively Oldham tries to shape a world conference according to the Anglican-Reformed perception of Christianity and the relation of church to public life.

In conclusion, Hirsch challenges Christians from all over the world, who will be gathering at the Oxford conference, to join together with German Christians in recognizing the freedom of the individual Christian conscience, and the unity that rests in personal faith in Jesus Christ, without becoming embroiled in national and church politics. As far as German National Socialist Christians are concerned, Hirsch confidently asserts: "We will, as disciples of Jesus Christ, as those who are dedicated in faith to the gospel, follow our own path on this earth in trust and commitment to our nation and our state, and will give our life and blood in the struggle to complete the German National Socialist reconstruction."[29] It is clear from this that Hirsch, while having been disappointed by the theological and ecclesiastical disunity within Germany due to the German Church Struggle, had not become disillusioned with National Socialism as such and its form of national renewal even by the late date of 1937.

The Dehn Affair

A second political issue Hirsch became embroiled in, one that was closer to Hirsch's academic-institutional concerns and that was an important indicator of his future stance on questions involving university appointments, was the "Dehn Affair". Guenther Dehn (1882-1970) had been appointed professor of practical

---

29. *Ibid.*, p. 203. In an article written later that year, "Nachruf auf Oxford," Hirsch reflects further on the ecumenical movement in light of the Oxford conference, criticizing not so much the respected leaders of the movement as the institution itself: "It is the fault of the institution," he says. "The ecumenical movement, as it has been developed [*aufgezogen*] up to this point, is a form of international church-parliamentarianism. The essence of parliamentarianism is such that the capacity and responsibility of qualified individuals—many qualified individuals—are lost in irresponsible and unsubstantial talk." *Deutsches Volkstum* (October, 1937), pp. 738-740, p. 740.

theology at the University of Halle in 1932, despite his outspoken pacifist leanings and harsh criticism of German militarism and conservative nationalism. Dehn's appointment at Halle met with growing unrest among and objections from conservative students there and soon gained national attention, drawing into the debate theologians of the stature of Hirsch, on the one side, and Karl Barth, on the other. On January 27, 1932 Hirsch and a theological colleague at Göttingen, Hermann Dörries, issued a joint statement in which they in effect sided with the students against Dehn. Initially, Hirsch had deliberately not become involved in the controversy, critical of the undisciplined actions of the students and fearing that his participation might simply create more unrest. But with the 1931 publication of Dehn's *Kirche und Völkerversöhnung* he found himself no longer able to remain silent.

In their joint statement Hirsch and Dörries affirm the importance of academic freedom and the one condition of all academic appointments: academic qualification for research and teaching. Further, they recognize the need, in the face of present confusion amongst Germans concerning the war-question, for allowing theological teachers freedom to think through in an impartial way their own position on this important issue of conscience. Nevertheless, having said this, they go on to demand the following conditions of all academics, even those with pacifist leanings such as Dehn: "...first, a recognition that the nation and its freedom, despite the ambiguity [*Fragwürdigkeit*] of creaturely existence, are divinely hallowed goods even for Christians, demanding a total commitment of heart and life; and [second], as a consequence of this recognition, support of the passionate desire for the freedom of our nation, which is being enslaved and defamed by power-hungry and greedy enemies."[30] This recognition was what German young people had rightly found lacking in Dehn, and for this reason Dehn in his public statements had undermined his own effectiveness as teacher of these young people. Hirsch and Dörries conclude by expressing their gratitude to and solidarity with the German youth in their commitment to freedom and the nation.

The German Christians
This brings us to the more specific political involvement of Hirsch with the German Christians and the National Socialist cause. Like many other conservative nationalists Hirsch had until 1932 supported the rightwing German National People's Party, somewhat sceptical of Hitler and the more radical National Socialist German Workers' Party (NSDAP). As the fateful victory of Hitler and the National Socialists became ever more certain, however, he switched his loyalty to the NSDAP. He explains his decision in a strategic letter to a local Party newspaper, *Göttinger Tageblatt*, on April 9, 1932, on the eve of the presi-

---

30. Hirsch and Hermann Dörries, "Zum halleschen Universitätskonflikt," *Die Wartburg* 31, 2(1932), pp. 46-47, p. 47. See also Ericksen, *Theologians Under Hitler*, p. 48.

dential election, headed "Ich werde Hitler wählen!"

> You know that I am not a National Socialist and that I have more than mild doubts about the NSDAP. You also know that I consider Hugenberg to be the right statesman for the present difficult times, although he is not recognized as such by the *Volk*....But I cannot get around the fact that a situation has developed without my assistance. And Hitler now is the only representative of a will to break with the mistakes of the twelve years from 1919 to 1931, the only candidate on 10 April to offer a new German beginning.[31]

The shift in Hirsch's political allegiance represents not an opportunistic move on his part but reflects rather his strong belief that something providential and fateful was taking place at the grass-roots level, and that Hitler had become the spokesman for the *Volk*. The people were speaking. At the same time it indicates his continuing ambivalence toward the Party and some of its policies, an ambivalence which quickly faded into the background. Hirsch, with his strong sense of tragic fate not only in his personal life but also in the life of the nation, once having made his choice, unflinchingly defended the new direction in which the National Socialists were now taking Germany. Actually, he did not officially join the Party until the remarkably late date of May 1, 1937, long after many of the Protestant theologians and pastors had become disillusioned with and forsaken the cause.[32] Why he joined at such a late date is not entirely clear, but it does once again indicate the non-opportunistic independence of Hirsch's disposition and political thinking.

What is much harder to assess is Hirsch's relation to the German Christians, that faction within the German Evangelical Church which gave credibility to and support to Hitler, including his racial policies, and the official church administration under the leadership of Ludwig Müller. According to Klaus Scholder, Hirsch "unquestionably belongs to those figures which are the most difficult to evaluate in the modern history of theology."[33] Following the first national convention of the German Christians in early April, 1933, in which the German Christians called for an accommodation of the Evangelical Church to the new state and the creation of a national German Protestant church (*Reichskirche*) under the leadership of a national bishop (*Reichsbischof*), Hirsch became a central figure at the very heart of German church-political events and the German church struggle.[34]

In order to evaluate fairly Hirsch's relation to the German Christians, it is important to distinguish between various factions within the movement. James

---

31. As cited and translated by Ericksen, *Theologians Under Hitler*, p. 146, 220/n. 112.
32. The Berlin Document Centre, Berlin, Germany.
33. Klaus Scholder, *Die Kirchen Und Das Dritte Reich*, p. 127.
34. *Ibid.*, pp. 178ff.

A. Zabel has conveniently divided these different German Christian groups into the conservative, opportunistic and radical wings.[35] All three had common roots in nineteenth-century German nationalist thought represented by thinkers such as J.G. Fichte and Ernst Moritz Arndt but each had a distinct ideology as reflected in their respective periodicals. The *conservative* wing was represented by the *Christlich-Deutsche Bewegung* (CDB), and existed as a distinct group from 1930 until its dissolution in the fall of 1933. It had in its ranks leading university professors such as Emanuel Hirsch, Heinrich Bornkamm and Paul Althaus. What was significant about this group, according to Zabel, was that it was made up largely of people from an "upper class" background who politically supported "a tradition of conservative Prussian-nationalism" and had affinities with the German National People's Party (DNVP) rather than the Social Democratic or Center Party. Because of their theological Lutheran Orthodoxy, however—they were the only group who put the term "Christian" before "German"—they could not accept the pre-Christian religious views of the more radical nationalist groups. Despite this, says Zabel, they "gave the Nazi efforts of 1933 the respectability and support of a large segment of German Protestantism."[36]

The second faction was the *Glaubensbewegung Deutsche Christen* (GDC), a group called into being by the Nazi Party itself, and which from its founding in June, 1932, by district Party leader Wilhelm Kube in Berlin, to its virtual collapse after the Sport Palace fiasco in November, 1933, became a kind of umbrella organization for all the various German Christian fronts.[37] In the mind of Zabel, what distinguished this group from the CDB was that it "saw the roots of modern evils in the Bismarkian empire and thus was looking for a new solution to German fate, which it specifically identified with the Nazi Party."[38] Zabel, somewhat unfairly in my opinion, simply labels this group "opportunistic" because of its desire to unite all the nationalist-minded groups behind National Socialist aims. Its writers, says Zabel, in effect put "Party principles first and Christian principles second" as reflected in its loose and opportunistic interpretation of the Party's espousal of a "Positive Christianity."[39] It rejected

35. James A. Zabel, *Nazism and the Pastors* (Missoula: Scholars Press, 1976). See also Helmreich, *The German Churches Under Hitler*, pp. 78ff.

36. Zabel, *Nazism and the Pastors*, p. 224.

37. For a short summary of the Sport Palace fiasco see Arthur C. Cochrane, *The Church's Confession Under Hitler* (Pittsburgh: The Pickwick Press, 1976), pp. 111ff; and Helmreich, *The German Churches Under Hitler*, pp. 149ff. On November 13 a mass rally of German Christians took place at the Berlin Sport Palace, in which radical speeches by representatives of the movement such as Joachim Hossenfelder and particularly Dr. Reinhold Krause discredited the German Christian movement.

38. Zabel, *Nazism and the Pastors*, p. 224.

39. The term "positive Christianity," as found in the NSDAP platform of 1920 was a rather ill-defined term that could mean a variety of things depending on who was using it. According to Zabel, "Just as the word 'Socialism' in the term 'National Socialism' was vague and open to various

the elitism of the CDB in favor of a radical egalitarianism from the perspective of the "lower class." It was more stridently anti-semitic in its sentiments and generally agreed with Nazi racial policy and authoritarian organizational structure as outlined in its ten guiding principles of June 6, 1932.[40] One of the central planks in its platform was the establishing of a national church under the leadership of a national bishop. Pastor Joachim Hossenfelder became the national leader of the GDC and Ludwig Müller, who later became the national bishop, was one of its early supporters, although he was forced to distance himself from Hossenfelder after November, 1933. Zabel states that, with the demise of the conservative CDB in 1933, some of its leading members, including Emanuel Hirsch and Paul Althaus, joined the opportunistic GDC. Although there may be some general justification for Zabel's characterizing of the GDC as "opportunistic" in its attempt to provide a common Protestant front in support of Nazis ideology, his analysis is not nuanced enough when applied to specific theologians like Hirsch, who on the whole cannot be labelled opportunistic.

The third faction, in Zabel's schema, was the Thuringian based *Kirchenbewegung Deutsche Christen* (KDC). This group with organizational beginnings as far back as 1927, led by two pietistic "revivalist" type pastors Siegfried Leffler and Julius Leutheuser, was the most radical and unorthodox of all the groups and survived under a variety of names until 1940. It attracted the lower strata of the populace, "people whose theology was emotional, fluid and enthusiastic,"[41] and was the most fanatic and revolutionary in its identification of "political faith in Hitler and belief in God,"[42] virtually giving divine and revelatory status to Adolf Hitler and German *Volk*-history. It was anti-intellectual and anti-doctrinal in orientation, emphasizing practical Christianity and religiosity above all else, and had no leading theologians in its ranks.

One of the intriguing questions, of course, is what Hitler and the Party elite thought of these various factions in the Evangelical Church who to a greater or lesser degree wanted to accommodate themselves so enthusiastically to the new state. In general it is clear that Hitler wanted to separate Party politics from

interpretations, so 'positive Christianity' was a useful term for the Nazis because it allowed the faithful to indulge in wishful thinking without having any concrete meaning." *Nazism and the Pastors*, pp. 112-113. For a detailed discussion of the various ways in which the term was used in Germany during the Hitler period see Zabel, pp. 111-129.

40. Principle no. 9 of "The Guiding Principles of the Faith Movement of the 'German Christians,'" stated that "In the mission to the Jews we perceive a grave danger to our nationality. It is an entrance gate for alien blood into our body politic. It has no justification for existence beside foreign missions. As long as the Jews possess the right to citizenship and there is thereby the danger of racial camouflage and bastardization, we repudiate a mission to the Jews in Germany. Holy Scripture is also able to speak about a holy wrath and a refusal of love. In particular, marriage between Germans and Jews is to be forbidden." Cochrane, *The Church's Confession Under Hitler*, p. 223.

41. Zabel, *Nazism and the Pastors*, p. 171.

42. *Ibid.*, p. 181.

church politics and repeatedly urged leading Nazis not to identify the Party with any particular church faction especially after obtaining power. But he did use the GDC as a means of consolidating power in 1932 and in the spring and summer of 1933. There is clear evidence that Hitler tried to distance himself from the GDC after the Sport Palace debacle, even abandoning his earlier friend and confidante Ludwig Müller, who increasingly became a lonely figure with little clout either within the Party or the Evangelical church. According to Helmreich, Hitler had never had much regard for the more fanatic nordic-religious wing of the German Faith Movement, although certain leading Party officials seemed to have participated in their annual rituals.[43]

Where did Hirsch stand with respect to the German Christians in general and the various factions within the diverse German Christian movement in particular? That is the question we want to address in the following pages. To get an accurate picture of this it is necessary to look at the chronology of events in the spring and summer of 1933 and a variety of Hirsch's published writings and personal correspondence during this time. It is fairly clear that ideologically, prior to early 1933, Hirsch must be placed in the ranks of the first group of German Christians identified by Zabel as the conservative *Christliche-Deutsche Bewegung*. He like other members of this faction had high regard for sound theological thinking although to label him Orthodox Lutheran, as Zabel characterizes those who belonged to this group, is somewhat misleading, especially in the light of Hirsch's persistent critique of Lutheran orthodoxy and confessionalism (Old Protestantism). Paul Althaus, for instance, considered Hirsch's demythologizing of the resurrection as unorthodox and thought that "Both Hirsch and Bultmann followed the logic of their research to uncomfortable, disconcerting conclusions."[44]

As we have seen above, Hirsch wanted to pursue a third way, beyond Old Protestantism and nineteenth-century theological liberalism, one which took Luther's theology seriously but adapted it to a new age both intellectually and politically. He was highly critical of scholastic Lutheran dogmaticians who wanted to hold rigidly to fourth-century views on Christology and the Trinity in an era when these doctrines had little or no significance for the majority of Germans.[45] In this he had more in common with the second group in Zabel's schema, the *Glaubensbewegung Deutsche Christen*, who were less dogmatically oriented and intent on adapting or reinterpreting traditional theology in light of present political and church needs and tasks.

Having said this, however, it is important to stress that Hirsch's identification with the German Christians in the winter and spring of 1933 was more nuanced than it is often made out to be. Schjørring is right when he says that Hirsch did

43. Helmreich, *The German Churches Under Hitler*, pp. 407ff.
44. Ericksen, *Theologians Under Hitler*, p. 83.
45. *Ibid.*, p. 183.

not simply take over uncritically the German Christian understanding of the church and its relation to the state. Schjørring cites an April 15, 1933 letter by Hirsch to the territorial bishop of Hannover, August Marahrens, in which Hirsch says of the German Christian concept of a national church that it is both impossible for various historical and theological reasons and unavoidable in the present situation. Hirsch in this situation became a political-church-realist and supported the need for an "evangelical nuncius" with full powers to represent the church before the National Socialist state, and urged that such a person be found in fourteen days. At this point in the process he suggested that the only possible three candidates for such a position would be Paul Althaus, Heinrich Rendtorff or possibly himself, the only three theologians who uncompromisingly recognized the aims of the young nationalist movement.[46]

Bishop Ludwig Müller and the New National Evangelical Church
On April 25, 1933, a few days after this letter to Marahrens, Hitler appointed the Königsburg army chaplain Ludwig Müller (1883-1945) as special laison officer between the state and the Protestant Churches. Müller quickly became one of the key figures in the church-political events of the next few months. It is at this point that Hirsch, recognizing the special confidence that Hitler had placed in Müller, swung his full support behind Müller, and became together with Karl Fezer, young and popular practical theologian at the University of Tübingen, a member of an inner advisory group around Müller.[47]

Müller's character and actions have been harshly judged by historians of the German Church Struggle. Klaus Scholder, for instance, has little praiseworthy to say about Müller: "Ludwig Müller, who by Hitler's decree of April 25 suddenly came out of anonymity and then in the Fall for a time was to become the first and only national bishop of the German Evangelical Church, was a weak character....He was, in his official position, a type of pious bureaucrat, one who knew how to adapt himself to all situations, the master of the language of the pietistic circle of Westphalia as well as the crude tone of the German military kasino."[48] According to Scholder's rather one-sided evaluation, Müller under the influence of questionable advisors found himself after the summer of 1933 in a growing web of lies and intrigue until he was totally unacceptable not only to the church but also to Hitler, who lost complete confidence in him. After 1935 he became a peripheral figure until his death in Berlin in 1945. Hirsch was one of these close advisors who supported Müller precisely because, initially at least, he had the support and confidence of Hitler, on the one side, and generally represented the German Christian view of a national people's

---

46. Schjørring, *Theologische Gewissensethik*, p. 179. See also Ericksen, *Theologians Under Hitler*, p. 147.

47. Scholder, *Die Kirchen Und Das Dritte Reich*, p. 403.

48. *Ibid.*, p. 391.

church (*Volkskirche*), on the other.

The fact is that Müller did represent a kind of middle position among German Christians and genuinely hoped to unify the church under the new church administration, a hope which to the disappointment of Hirsch, was shortly to be aborted. While Müller and this inner group of advisors identified with the German Christian cause they quickly realized that they would have to distance themselves from the more radical wing of the German Christians if they were to achieve this unity. The fundamental obstacle to church unity had always been the tensions between the three church confessional traditions: Lutheran, Reformed and United (a union of Lutheran and Reformed). The more radical German Christians wanted to de-emphasize these confessional lines in favor of one unified Evangelical church, conceived of largely in Lutheran terms. The conservative traditionalists, held to the inviolability of the various confessional streams, and were willing to more toward a loose form of church unity conceived of as a confessional association. Ludwig Müller and his inner circle tried to steer a middle course between these two positions, emphasizing the need for a substantive and constitutional union but one based on what the various confessions had in common. In effect, what Müller was calling for was a new confession which would gain the support of the German populace as a whole. To find this common element, he and his advisors now saw as the prayerful task of German Evangelical Christianity. What Müller had in mind became clear in a number of interviews in May, 1933, in which he called for a new confession that would be linked to the historical confessions and be the basis of a new *Reichskirche*. In fact Müller envisioned this new confession to be in line with the East Prussian German Christian guidelines which espoused that: "The eternal truth of God, as taught by Christ, must be proclaimed in a language and style understandable to the German soul."[49] As a result of his desire to steer a middle course Müller soon found himself in disagreement with Joachim Hossenfelder, by now the national leader of the German Christians, and had, together with Hirsch and Fezer, a hand in the drawing up of a new modified set of German Christian guidelines on May 16, 1933.[50]

The German church struggle in May of 1933 centred on a proposed constitution and the choice of a national bishop for the newly constituted Evangelical Church. It is particularly this latter issue which drew Hirsch into the heat of the battle. Müller was publicly nominated by the East Prussian wing of the German Christians on May 18, after the "Young Reformation Movement," representing the traditional confessionalists, nominated the well-known and respected Bethel-Bielefeld pastor Friedrich von Bodelschwingh. The national German

---

49. *Ibid.*, p. 396. It is somewhat ironical that in his call for confessional renewal Müller sounded somewhat like the confessional appeals of Hans Asmussen and the beginnings of the confessing church although clearly with different theological intent. See Scholder, pp. 395ff.

50. Schjørring, *Theologische Gewissensethik*, p. 180.

Christian movement, led by Hossenfelder, quickly backed the Müller nomination. We cannot here go into the details of the confusing events which followed, including late night meetings, charges and countercharges between the various church fronts, and so on, leading up to the election of Bodelschwingh on May 27. The German Christians, however, were unwilling to accept the choice and now questioned the legitimacy of the election procedures, undermining Bodelschwingh's leadership wherever possible. In the end Bodelschwingh was led to resign, which he did on June 24, and Müller won the newly-called church elections. He was officially elected *Reichsbischof* at the National Synod of the German Evangelical Church in Wittenberg on September 27. He was to be assisted by a Spiritual Ministry Council consisting of a lawyer and representatives of each of the three church traditions. In his inaugural address Müller announced: "The old has passed away. The new has emerged. The Church's political struggle is past. Now begins the struggle for the soul of the people."[51] Little did he know that the church struggle had in fact just begun and that the unity of the church would in a few months be in a state of ruins.

The important role that Hirsch played in the events surrounding the fight over a national bishop cannot be denied. He seems to have had a significant part in making Bodelschwingh's leadership untenable. On June 4, a statement which Hirsch had composed during the night of May 16-17 in which he unequivocally supported Müller for bishop, was published in the periodical *Evangelisches Deutschland*. On June 7 Hirsch published an appeal in the same journal calling for a plebiscite, in which the general church membership would be given the opportunity to voice their opinion on the proposed new constitution and national bishop.[52] According to Schjørring, who in general holds to the view that Hirsch's decisions and positions during 1933 were consistent with his thinking in the 1920s, Hirsch's actions during this stage of the struggle were politically determined and in every way accommodated Hitler's political interests.[53] Schjørring summarizes Hirsch's position at this point in the German Church Struggle: "There was in this phase not one essential point, in which he deviated politically from the party-line. Theologically and politically he came to the support of a moderate German-Christian course and was one of the few professors of theology who remained loyal to the *Reichsbischof* even when, after the proclamation of the German Christians in the Berlin Sport Palace on November 13, the collapse of the united front of the German Christians became apparent."[54] Thus, Hirsch could in August write to Eduard Geimsar that he was able to embrace without reservation the developments in Germany.[55] Schjørring cites the following letter by Hirsch to Müller in November, 1933: "I believe I

51. Cochrane, *The Church's Confession Under Hitler*, p. 111.
52. See Ericksen, *Theologians Under Hitler*, pp. 148-149.
53. Schjørring, *Theologische Gewissensethik*, p. 183.
54. *Ibid.*, p. 184.
55. *Ibid.*, p. 184, n. 79.

understand your, what is for me the authoritative, course and intent in a way that allows me to remain with the German Christians, and not follow the way of Fezer and Schumann. For that reason, I also gladly bear the risk of being called a heretic. My feeling is simple: *I do not forsake the banner at the moment when the firing intensifies.* I understand and respect the reasons of Fezer and his colleagues. They are sincere and pure. But I cannot join them when they *now* complete the *separation.* I do not feel their compunction of conscience."[56]

Hirsch's support of Müller and the newly established church administration was, however, not one of blind and naive loyalty as this quotation would suggest. He was genuinely concerned for a *united Church front.* In fact, he was soon to develop some deep reservations about the way things were going and the ruthless methods employed by Müller and the Church administrators in the spring, summer and early fall of 1934. In the spring of that year the polarization between the official Church administration and the opposition intensified as Müller and August Jäger, officer of church affairs in the Ministry of Science, Culture and Education as well as legal representative in the Church's Spiritual Ministry, began using coercive tactics to incorporate territorial churches into the national church. In the weeks just preceding Müller's installation as bishop the actions of Müller and Jäger became ever more strident as they tried unsuccessfully to bring recalcitrant territorial churches (the so-called "intact churches" of Hannover, Württemberg and Bavaria) into the fold.[57] Matters were made worse with comments by Müller like, "Adolf Hitler is so closely akin to the evangelical Church that he can almost be considered one of its members."[58] Despite this obvious lack of united Evangelical support, Müller's installation went forward with great pomp and ceremony in the Berlin cathedral on September 23, 1934, with only German Christian bishops and a few party officials present.

Hirsch felt uncomfortable enough with the course of events to write National Synod President Nikolaus Christiansen on September 16 asking for tolerance from him, Jäger and Christian Kinder, now national leader of the German Christians, for his own decision not to attend the installation ceremonies.[59] In this letter Hirsch is highly critical of the administration's actions in the preceding weeks, and says he cannot identify with installation services which are merely the celebration of the victors without general support, if he is to continue his work of responsibly helping to build up the new Evangelical

56. *Ibid.*, pp. 184-185, n. 79.
57. Helmreich, *The German Churches Under Hitler*, pp. 169ff. The "intact churches" were those territorial churches (primarily Bavaria, Württemberg and with some reservations Hannover) in which, in contrast to the so-called "disrupted or disturbed churches" where the German Christians had gained control, church leadership and administration remained in the control of the traditional authorities with sympathies for the Confessing Church. See Helmreich, pp. 163ff.

58. *Ibid.*, p. 170.

59. Personal letter, Hirsch to Nikolaus Christiansen, September 16, 1934. Provided by Walter Buff, Hannover.

Church. The letter reflects a growing disillusionment on the part of Hirsch with the way things were going. Nothing of the actions and proclamations of the previous weeks, says Hirsch, demonstrate the magnanimity of the victors in their responsibility to those who still need to be won to the movement. Every theological word and every gesture of comradeship has been lacking. His inner confidence in the *Reichsbischof* has been shattered with the growing recognition that Müller's position has become untenable. He reaffirms his commitment to the cause in general, including his work for the Church's constitutional committee, but he finds it impossible to identify with, let alone attend, the celebrations. He concludes with the hope that even now the celebrants will avoid fanning further the flames of resistance all over Germany.

Hirsch's evolving position during 1933 is fairly well documented in a series of eight short articles which he wrote that year and collected under the title *Das kirchlichen Wollen der Deutschen Christen,* a booklet dedicated to *Wehrkreispfarrer* Ludwig Müller.[60] The essays included in this small volume, when read chronologically, I believe show that Hirsch's decision to identify with the German Christians and Ludwig Müller is motivated not by sudden political opportunism but is the natural and consistent consequence of theological and political views held all along. The main principles of "Kurzer Unterricht in der christlichen Religion," May, 1933, for instance, had been written down as a personal confession by Hirsch well before he began his work for the German Christians. In the words of Hirsch, "I became a German Christian only because I knew that my collaboration could be affirmed in this spirit."[61] The twelves articles of the confessional statement revolve around the clear distinction between the eternal spiritual "community of brothers and sisters which extends through all of time and all lands" and the natural earthly community differentiated by families, nationalities and states.[62]

On May 5 Hirsch's "Die wirkliche Lage unserer Kirche" appeared, in which he outlines his reasons for urging the Evangelical Church to join the German Christians in unreservedly embracing and helping to shape what is happening in Germany under National Socialism.[63] For one thing, no amount of resistance to the efforts of the German Christians has any prospect of success in the face of the stormy will (*stürmischer Wille*) of the youthful movement. More important, however, is the tremendous opportunity that is being granted the Church to participate not only in the renewal of the state but also in the building up of a new national life. "The essential concern of the German Christians is to give us a nationally-rooted Church, so that the Church genuinely possesses a nation, and

---

60. Hirsch, *Das kirchliche Wollen der Deutschen Christen* (Berlin-Steglitz: Evangelischer Pressverband für Deutschland, 1933). Hereafter cited as *Das kirchliche Wollen.*
61. Hirsch, "Kurzer Unterricht in der christlichen Religion," *Das kirchliche Wollen,* p. 17.
62. *Ibid.,* articles 6 and 9, pp. 18-19.
63. Hirsch, "Die wirkliche Lage unserer Kirche," *Das kirchliche Wollen,* pp. 20ff. This article first appeared in *Monatschrift für Pastoraltheologie* 4, 5(May/June, 1933).

a nation possesses a Church."[64] Naturally, such an experiment, as envisioned by the German Christians, brings with it dangers, but faith always entails taking risks. This rootedness of the Church in the real life of the nation ought not to be seen as enslavement to earthly orders but, on the contrary, as genuine freedom to serve the Lord of Lords within the nation. Only in this way can the Church truly become the salt which can prevent the nation from going to ruin. What is demanded of theologians and pastors now is to set aside all criticisms and doubts and to risk, joyfully and without reservation, entering this new situation.

What follows are three articles specifically related to Hirsch's support of Ludwig Müller's candidacy for the office of national bishop. The first of these is the strategically important statement, "Volk, Staat, Kirche," composed by Hirsch during the night of May 16-17, in preparation for an important meeting at Loccum the next day, at which a recently appointed three-member committee met with Müller to discuss the creation of a new Church Constitution.[65] The very next day, on May 18, Ludwig Müller was publicly nominated for the *Reichsbischof* office by the East Prussian group of German Christians. After defending the National Socialist state's total transformation of German life and spirit, expressing the conviction that the new state recognizes that its work can not prosper without honouring the Christian faith, and after once more differentiating between the proper task of the church and the state, Hirsch emphasizes those areas where the Evangelical Church and National Socialism share a common responsibility: unselfish service to the nation. For the church this service ought to be seen as the preparation for the true task of the church which is to win people for the Kingdom of God. This preparatory service "Assists only in creating a form of national life and national spirit which is thoroughly imbued with Christian standards and Christian goals" conducive to the fulfillment of the greater mission of the Church.[66] It is in this light, concludes Hirsch, that the German Christian guidelines ought to be supported and Ludwig Müller nominated for the office of national bishop. "The person whom we are nominating for the office of *Reichsbischof*," says Hirsch, "has the confidence of all Evangelical Christians who, in their struggle for the renewal of our nation recognize their ultimate responsibility to God and the Gospel."[67]

In the second of these articles, "Nationalsozialismus und Kirche: Um die Berufung des evangelischen Reichsbischofs," May 28-29, 1933, Hirsch more specifically states his enthusiastic confidence in Hitler's personal deference to Christianity: "No single nation of the world has a comparable leading statesmen who takes Christianity with such seriousness; when Adolf Hitler concluded his

64. *Ibid.*, p. 22.
65. Hirsch, "Volk, Staat, Kirche," *Das kirchliche Wollen*, pp. 25-27. This article, written during the night of May 16-17, 1933, was first published in *Evangelisches Deutschland* 10, 23(June 4, 1933).
66. *Ibid.*, p. 26.
67. *Ibid.*, p. 27.

great speech of May 1 with a prayer, the whole world sensed in it a remarkable sincerity. The Church, therefore, has much to thank National Socialism for. Consequently, however, it [National Socialism] has something to expect from the Church, as well. She ought for God's sake not to engage in politics and for God's sake not to begin to appropriate for herself the state's mandate. Nevertheless, she ought joyfully to affirm a working-comradeship [*Arbeitsgemeinschaft*] with the evolving National Socialist state."[68] Hirsch does not want a Church which is being commandeered by National Socialism but one which sees itself as voluntarily and inwardly united with National Socialism in a common task.

With the prolegomena finished, Hirsch now comes to the matter at hand: a strongly worded and persuasive call for the church's support of Ludwig Müller for national bishop. Müller, says Hirsch, has for many years participated in the National Socialist struggle. He has known Hitler personally for some six years. He has strong leadership qualities. He has the strong support of numerous theologians who vouch that with him the majesty of the Gospel and the Church's confession will be safeguarded. Further, the German Christian guidelines that he has drawn up have been recognized by highly placed church officials.

Although Müller was eventually elected national bishop, after a rather sordid series of events leading first to the election and then the resignation of von Bodelschwingh, Hirsch's personal integrity and involvement in the proceedings from mid-May to early June was seriously attacked and left him embittered and disillusioned. In the third essay, "Zur Geschichte des Streits um den Reichsbischof," June 2 (published on June 7), 1933, Hirsch attempts to set the historical record straight, giving his own version of the Loccum meeting between Hermann Kapler, August Marahrens, Hermann Hesse and Müller and the subsequent events. He lays the blame for the disunity squarely at the feet of those who are not in tune with what is happening in the national renewal movement. Further, he accuses the Young Reformation Movement (*jungreformatorische Bewegung*) of pre-empting proper church procedures, by having announced the candidacy of von Bodelschwingh before more basic constitutional matters had been resolved. Consequently, the issue of the person rather than the office was brought into the foreground and the German Christians were put into the position of having quickly to nominate publicly their own counter-candidate, Ludwig Müller. What Hirsch now proposes is a national church plebiscite on both the new church Constitution and the person of a *Reichsbischof*.[69]

68. Hirsch, "Nationalsozialismus und Kirche: Um die Berufung des evangelische Reichsbishofs," *Das kirchliche Wollen*, p. 24. This article first appeared in *Völkischer Beobachter*, 26, 148/149(May 28/29, 1933).

69. Hirsch, "Zur Geschichte des Streits um den Reichsbischof," *Das kirchichen Wollen*, pp. 29-31. It first appeared in *Der Reichsbote*. Tageszeitung für das evangelische Deutschland, 130, 7(June, 1933).

Von Bodelschwingh did in fact resign on June 24, feeling that he could not carry out his duties under the newly appointed commissar of Prussian Churches, August Jäger. National church elections were held on July 23 in which the German Christians won two thirds of the seats. Ludwig Müller was elected national bishop at the first national synod of the newly constituted Evangelical Church in Wittenberg on September 27, 1933. On July 15 of that summer Hirsch published a short "Nachwort" on the struggle over the national bishop. He defends his June 2 statement, with further explanations and some new information observing that, since his personal integrity had been severely attacked, he had no option but to defend himself in order to preserve his reputation as a professor.[70]

The June 24 appointment of Provincial Legal Counsellor and die-hard National Socialist August Jäger as Commissioner of the Prussian Church signified an intensified political interference in church affairs. Jäger quickly dissolved various Prussian church bodies, replaced the superintendents of Provincial churches, and put German Christians into key administrative posts. Not only did this result in von Bodelschwingh's resignation but it brought in a flood of protests from dismissed officials, old governing bodies, pastors and laity.[71] It was in this context that Hirsch wrote his "Feiheit der Kirche, Reinheit des Evangelism," on June 30, 1933.[72] This short essay, together with the longer one, "Das kirchlichen Wollen den Deutschen Christen," July 15-16, 1933,[73] which Hirsch wrote in response to Karl Barth's famous tract *Theologische Existenz heute* (written in just two days, June 24-25, 1933) are especially important in outlining Hirsch's theological differences with the evolving theology of the Confessing Church, as later articulated in the six articles of the Barmen Confession, May 29-31, 1934.

The freedom of the church, Hirsch says in the first of these two essays, is not endangered by the National Socialist state but by those who do not recognize the opportunities and demands of the present hour; by those who drive the state to defend itself against the breaking up of the movement. The National Socialist revolution is more than a restructuring of the state and the economy; it wants to transform and mold people inwardly. It is in this inward shaping of the German people that the church must cooperate with the state. The church ought, therefore, not to speak of freedom *from* an affirmation of the present hour, but of freedom *to* serve God and the Gospel within the nation without state interfer-

70. Hirsch, "Nachwort," *Das kirchlichen Wollen*, p. 32. This article is dated July 15, 1933.

71. See Helmreich, *The German Churches Under Hitler*, pp. 137-141.

72. Hirsch, "Freiheit der Kirche, Reinheit des Evangeliums. Ein Wort zur kirchlichen Lage," *Das kirchliche Wollen*, pp. 27-28. First published in *Evangelisches Deutschland*, 10, 28(July 9, 1933), pp. 245ff.

73. Hirsch, "Das kirchliche Wollen der Deutschen Christen. Zur Beurteilung des Angriffs von Karl Barth (Theologische Existenz heute, München 1933)," *Das kirchliche Wollen*, pp. 5-17. Dated July 15-16, 1933.

ence. This freedom to call the National Socialist nation to obedience under the Gospel, Hirsch believes, is not endangered. Theologically, he grounds his position on a paradox. On the one hand, Christ is the decisive factor in the proclamation of the Gospel; nothing human and temporal can change this. On the other hand, the task of proclaiming Christ can be fulfilled only when human interconnectedness and human understanding provides the natural basis for speech. This second aspect, the natural side, is always conditioned by particular temporal and historical factors like nationality: "The natural pre-requisite for proclamation is most readily present when people are bound together through blood and destiny, in one common earthly circle."[74] The church's task, as a visible body, is conditioned by both of these aspects of proclamation. This has its dangers but, then, the church will always be a human church and bear the limitations and mistakes of the nation and the times. It is precisely God's grace which justifies in spite of, and allows the gospel to shine through, these shortcomings.

Barth and the Confessing Church

As has already been alluded to above, Hirsch's "Das kirchliche Wollen der Deutschen Christen," was a direct response to Barth's polemic against the German Christians in his famous essay *Theologische Existenz heute*. Hirsch begins his article with the statement that "For German Christians all conversation with Karl Barth is [now] impossible. He calls us 'wild public heretics.'"[75] The article is divided into four sections—the two tasks of the church in the present situation, Christian faith in God, Christianity and Germanness, and church leadership—each of which clarifies fundamental differences between Barthian confessional theology and German Christian theology.

First, Hirsch identifies the two tasks of the church: a) to proclaim the universal, voluntary church of Jesus Christ; and b) to engage in the task of nurturing ethical and religious discipline and education as a preparation for the primary task of proclamation. The fulfillment of both of these tasks is a form of obedience and service to Jesus Christ as Lord, who is Spirit, and as Spirit illumines our daily actions and decisions within our natural earthly life. The second of these tasks, the preparatory one, is conditioned by and changes according to the natural characteristics of nations and the particularities of the historical hour. This is what Hirsch thinks Karl Barth does not understand when he calls the German Christian response to God's imperative in the hour of the National Socialist revolution heretical, the fall of the church from obedience to the Word of God. One can only conclude, according to Hirsch, that Barth's understanding of the church as determined solely by the Word of God is totally ahistorical. Hirsch defends his orthodoxy and that of the German Christians by emphasizing

---

74. Hirsch, "Freiheit der Kirche," p. 27.
75. Hirsch, "Das kirchliche Wollen der Deutschen Christen," p. 5.

the second task as simply preparatory for the first and primary task; namely, proclamation of the one and only Gospel of Jesus Christ: eternal life and the mysterious presence of the Kingdom of God extending through all nations and times. Anyone, like Barth, who charges the German Christians of not recognizing this as the ultimate norm for all church activity bears false witness against the neighbor.

Second, Hirsch objects to Barth's Christology; particularly Barth's statement that God is present for us only in His Word, that the content of this Word is none other than Jesus Christ, and that Jesus Christ can be found nowhere but in the Holy Scriptures.[76] Hirsch accepts the centrality for the church of the living Word of God, which is Jesus Christ. He also holds to the Holy Scriptures as the primary bearer of this living Word, the norm for all proclamation in the Church. What he objects to is what he, rightly or wrongly, perceives to be Barth's too narrow a concept of Christ and the captivity of Christ and the Gospel to the biblical text.[77] Our knowledge of God in Christ is, for Hirsch, not the first nor the only witness of God to us. If God did not in some sense reveal Himself to us in the mundane events of daily life then the Word of the Gospel could never reach us, nor could we ever live according to the Gospel. Here Hirsch and Tillich share a common critique of Barth's theology. Tillich too argued contra Barth that unless God is already present to us in some prior sense His revelation in Christ could find no point of contact with us.[78] Hirsch's two critical statements against Barth's Word of God theology are the following:

Faith in Christ must become concrete in the form of a believing acceptance and structuring of the specific historical situation, and the believing acceptance and structuring of the specific historical situation must become genuine through faith in Christ....

Which is the word of God, through which Christ governs his church, in which he is present to us? Only that which is written down in the Bible? No, rather every living word of evangelical witness that spreads from mouth to ear, and from heart to heart by the miracle of the spirit.[79]

---

76. *Ibid.*, p. 8. Hirsch objects to the narrow Christology present in a statement like the following by Barth: "'In der Kirche ist man sich darüber einig, dass Got für uns nirgends da ist, in der Welt ist, in unserm Raum und in unsrer Zeit ist als in diesem seinen Wort, dass dieses sein Wort für uns keinen anderen Namen und Inhalt hat als Jesus Christus und das Jesus Christus für uns in der ganzen Welt nirgends zu finden ist als jeden Tag neu in der heiligen Schrift Alten und Neuen Testaments. Darüber ist man sich in der Kirche einig, oder man ist nicht in der Kirche.'"

77. Some of Barth's statements would seem to justify Hirsch's critique but Barth's Christology, the way it operates in his theology as a whole, is not as narrowly biblicistic as Hirsch here charges.

78. Tillich refers to this as the "mystical a priori," philosophically speaking, and the "theological circle," theologically speaking. See Tillich, *Systematic Theology*, Vol. I (Chicago: University of Chicago Press, 1951), pp. 8 ff.

79. Hirsch, "Das kirchliche Wollen," pp. 9-10.

The German Christians, Hirsch maintains, take both of these propositions with deadly earnestness. They demand that the Christian life become concrete in the actual situations in which people find themselves. The German Christians also believe that the evangelical witness can remain alive only if each new generation proclaims the truth of the Gospel with new language, new images and new experiential content.

Third, Hirsch challenges Barth's accusation that the German Christian interest in relating Christianity to Germanness, and church leadership to those of German blood is nothing but paganism. It is at this point in Hirsch's otherwise quite persuasive argument against Barth's theology that his thinking deserves unreserved critique. Even if one were in some sense to accept Hirsch's statement that "All human creating and structuring is bounded by and bound to the natural type [*natürlichen Art*] that we bring into life," one can in retrospect no longer accept the natural determinism implicit in this statement, let alone the identification of blood and congenital natural limitation. Clearly reflecting in his thinking the political and cultural ideology of the time, thereby also indirectly providing fertile soil for National Socialist racist ideology, Hirsch states: "When blood is corrupted, the spirit is also corrupted; for the spirit of the nations and peoples ascends from out of blood."[80] Despite his general independence of character, Hirsch here seems to have fallen prey to majority opinion in 1933 when he charges the church for not having guarded conscientiously this blood-heritage: "She has indifferently witnessed mixed marriages (as well as the being overrun by those who are inferior [*ebenso den überwuchern der Minderwertigen*]) without comprehending that these are justified only in exceptional cases, by virtue of particular divine leading."[81]

Hirsch clearly does not condone the ruthlessness with which the policy of racial purity is being put into effect by the state. He, nevertheless, admonishes the church not to evaluate what is happening solely in terms of the fate of individuals, but to recognize what is healthy and according to divine will in the transformation as a whole. Hirsch maintains that the tough questions have to be openly faced and not avoided. Here is where the German Christians need to be thanked. They have publicly asked the crucial polity questions. "None of them," says Hirsch of the German Christians, "has thought of dissolving the fellowship of communion [*Abendmahlsgemeinschaft*] with Jewish-Christians."[82] In other words, for Hirsch the Jewish question, as we will see below, pertains to the question of polity not soteriology. The deeper issue behind the tough questions relating to the blood-acceptability of non-Germans, the one which really divides the opposing factions in the German church struggle, is the need for Christianity and Germanness to find each other inwardly within the German

80. *Ibid.*, p. 11.
81. *Ibid.*
82. *Ibid.*, p. 12.

Evangelical Church. Barthian theology, Hirsch thinks, simply drives young people into the arms of the more radical German-religious groups.

Coming to the heart of his disagreement with Barthian theology, Hirsch identifies two theological reasons why he thinks there is such a resistance in the church to supporting a German-type of Evangelical Christianity. First, not enough theological work has been done on the concept of "the natural." The natural human being, natural law, natural knowledge of God have all remained illusory concepts applied indiscriminately to all people, and every historical type, state and economic order. What the legal profession has long since recognized—that that which is natural exists only as national-historical individuality [*nur als volkhafte geschichtliche Individualität*]—theology still has not learned. Every nation has its own distinctive national *nomos:* "The natural human being, natural law, natural knowledge of God, signifies concretely something else for Germans than for others."[83] Second, differentiation within that which is natural has not been seriously dealt with in theology. In Hirsch's opinion, when a person who is born anew in faith submits himself to the Lordship of God's spirit that which is natural is not annulled but used in the service of God. Christian thought, language and behaviour are nationally and historically modified (*abgewandelt*). The wonder of the biblical word is that under its lordship the national-historical character and the dynamic-creative, structuring power of a nation are not destroyed but enhanced.

Finally, fourth, Hirsch defends the German Christian concern for strong authoritative church leadership, including a national bishop, against Barth's charge that the German Christians are simply imitating and appropriating political ideas that do not suit the church. Reformed Christianity, says Hirsch, has never understood the Lutheran notion that the church is free to structure its polity in accordance with the demands of the hour, without making this church polity into dogma. The Evangelical church has always mirrored in its polity and constitution certain characteristics of prevailing political constitutional form. It is therefore natural that it would do so again under these new circumstances. This simply reflects the fact that the German Evanglical Church identifies itself inwardly with the German nation and state. The decisive aspect of this new authoritative leadership principle, which calls for an aggressive shaping of the church from top downwards, is the need to create space for individuals who have been given full power and responsibility to risk something new. This in no way compromises the church's ultimate allegiance to its one Lord Jesus Christ. Hirsch's defense of this strong leadership principle in the church is premised on a definition of the state which differs from Barth's view. According to Barth, "'The church believes in the divine institution of the state as the representative and carrier of public law and order [*öffentliche Rechtsordnung*] in the nation.'"[84]

83. *Ibid.*
84. *Ibid.*, p. 16. The original in its context reads: "Noch grössere Ferne zeigt aber Barth bei der

Hirsch calls this a liberal view in which the state is seen simply as executor of public order without any bearing on the private sphere of individuals. Hirsch gives his own alternate definition: "The state is that nation which, as an independent power, has through the Führer been legally and economically united and spiritually unified into a living community."[85]

Reading these various 1933 essays by Hirsch, collected under the general title of *Das kirchliche Wollen der Deutschen Christen*, one can begin to understand the reasoning behind Hirsch's (and the German Christian) unconditional support of a totalitarian regime, on the one hand, and their confession of ultimate allegiance to the one Lord Jesus Christ on the other. The two are seen to coexist as different realms of human experience. One has to do with earthly duty and responsibility, motivated by love; the other with the gospel of eternal life in Christ. Both realms, however, stand under the mysterious sovereignty of God as the Lord of history. "Totalitarianism" did not hold for Hirsch the same negative connotations that it does for us in retrospect. For Hirsch, it signified, as implicit in his definition of the state above, not a return to traditional authoritarianism but a freely chosen submission on the part of an entire people to specially gifted leaders. These leaders, including Hitler as political leader and Müller as church leader, were, ideally speaking, recognized by the people as embodying their own interests and destinies. They were given the power, responsibility and trust for harnessing every aspect of life in the struggle for national unity and independence.

According to Hirsch, the German Christians and those belonging to the Confessing Church have fundamentally different understandings of the church's relation to the political order, of church polity, and of God's relation to history (including revelation). Basic to the German Christian support of the National Socialist political order is the distinction between *worldview* and *gospel*. National Socialism is a comprehensive worldview, the gospel is not a worldview as those adhering to the Confessing Church mistakenly think. Consequently, Evangelical Christians can give unqualified support in helping National Socialists expand the traditionally restricted political sphere to a total, all-encompassing ordering of life. Not to do so would be to endanger the work of national renewal. In contrast to the purely *state-bound church* prior to 1918, and the complete separation of church and state between 1918 and 1933, the new vision is a church that is fully integrated with the life of the *nation and the state*. This does not endanger but rather enhances the church's freedom to pursue its primary task of proclaiming the Word of God and administering the sacraments.

dogmatischen Begriffsbestimmung des Staats: 'Die Kirche glaubt an die göttliche Einsetzung des Staats als des Vertreters und Trägers der "offentlichen Rechsordung im Volke".'"
85. *Ibid.*, p. 17. In the German context: "Ich stelle eine dem gegenwärtigen deutschen Staat gerecht werdende Begriffsbestimmung daneben, nicht als Dogma, sondern einfach als Erfassung der uns geschenkten Wirklichkeit: Staat ist das als unabhängige macht durch den Führer rechtlich und wirtschaftlich suzammengeschlossene und seelisch zur Lebensgemeinschaft geeinte Volk."

In other words, the National Socialist state and church share a common religious-ethical task: the nurturing of a common worldview among Germans. Consequently, nation, honour and race have the same significance for Christians as they do for non-Christians. What the Christians must object to is any absolutization of these in such a way that they become determinative for the individual's relation to God. The Confessing Church, in contrast, views the church's relation to the National Socialist state as a conflict between two different worldviews. For the Confessing Church only the Christian revelation in Christ (not nationality) can be the basis for developing a comprehensive worldview. The Party and the movement, it thinks, must be limited to the external political sphere, in the narrow non-worldview sense. Only then can the church submit obediently to it.

As far as church polity is concerned, German Christians believe that the external order and constitution of the church is a matter of Christian freedom. As long as the church is free to gather for worship, preach without interference Christ as saviour, and administer the sacraments, it is free to accommodate itself outwardly to the conditions of the historical and political situation. External order ought not to be made into a dogma or confession (as the Confessional front is doing). Under no circumstances can the church's confession, which has to do with the mystery of faith and eternal life, be made into a party program. The Confessing Church, on the contrary, sees the question of church order, while theoretically a matter of freedom, practically as having become a confessional question. It wrongly sees the German Christians as betraying the gospel for a political movement and dissolving the distinction between church and state. The Confessing Church wants to recover the confessional church which has been undermined by the modern spirit. In effect, Hirsch charges the Confessing Church with pitting a sixteenth and seventeenth-century scholastic orthodoxy (which it wrongly equates with the confession of Christ) against the German Christians and the *Reichsbischof*.

Finally, Hirsch rejects the Confessing Church's charge that the German Christians have other gods beside the one God as revealed in Jesus Christ. The first article of the Barmen Confession of May 29-31, 1934, had stated: "Jesus Christ, as he is attested for us in Holy Scripture, is the one Word of God which we have to hear and which we have to trust and obey in life and in death. We reject the false doctrine, as though the Church could and would have to acknowledge as a source of its proclamation, apart from and besides this one Word of God, still other events and powers, figures and truths, as God's revelation."[86] Hirsch firmly believes that God does reveal Himself in history to people and nations apart from Christ, but this form of revelation does not give us personal salvation. Personal salvation and the gift of eternal life are given to us in Jesus Christ alone. The Confessing Church, on the other hand, while

---

86. Cochrane, *The Church's Confession Under Hitler*, p. 239.

accepting that God works in nature and in history believes that God's presence in these is ambiguous and unrecognizable. The preaching of the church, it believes, has to continue as though 1933 and the National Socialist revolution is without divine significance and had never occurred.

We have spent considerable time examining Hirsch's role in the German Church Struggle in 1933, including his participation in the debate over the *Reichsbischof* and his theological differences with the Confessing Church, in order to gain some clarification of his relation to the German Christians. The simple categorization by the Barmen Synod (reflecting a particularly Barthian theological emphasis) of the German Christians (including implicitly also Hirsch's theology) as heretical does not do justice to the heterogeneity of the German Christian movement and the carefully articulated theological position of a man like Hirsch. Hirsch was quite realistic about what was happening and was clearly aware of the dangers inherent in the German Christian position. He had serious differences with some of the German Christians precisely over their fanatic confusion of the lines between Christianity and politics. He seems to vacillate between great optimism about the possibilities of the revolution sweeping Germany, and the great potential for religious renewal within the Evangelical Church and the German nation, and a foreboding about the possibility of the revolution miscarrying and the nation going to ruin. His relation to the German Christians was, consequently, quite stormy. While publicly, in his writings, he fully identified with the German Christians against the Confessing Church, he was, in his own words, an official member of the German Christians only briefly.

In his 1951 memoirs he makes the statement that, "It became naturally difficult, if not impossible, to help radical young *Stürmern* and *Drängern* towards a true understanding of the relation between that which is Christian and that which is human."[87] In a March 11, 1963 conversation with Walter Buff, Hirsch reflects on the years 1933-1934. He points out that in 1933 he refused to join the Berlin circle of the German Christians because of disagreements. In 1934 he became a member of the Hannover circle but left in August of that year because he could not prevent its members from fusing Christianity and the life of the nation. The German Christians, he says in this conversation, were unwilling to go along with his own rejection of the crusade idea and the fusion of the gospel and the nation, Christianity and the political community.[88] Hirsch comments further along the same line in a personal letter to Hans Grimm in 1958. In this letter he claims not to be able to comment accurately on the position of the German Christians because for the whole of 1933 and again after the Fall of 1934 he was a German Christian in general but did not belong to them officially. Hossenfelder, he

87. Hirsch, "Meine Wendejahre (1916-1921)," p. 5.
88. Personal letter, Walter Buff to A. James Reimer, January 11, 1980. The conversation was recorded by Buff himself.

adds, did not want him to be a member because he (Hirsch) was a free-thinker. After the Fall of 1934 he could not come to any agreement with the only group still left, the Thüringion faction of German Christians, because they demanded party-discipline and he (Hirsch) declared that he would not under any circumstances give up his freedom to have his personal, independent stance. The word of Emanuel Hirsch must always remain solely the word of Emanuel Hirsch.[89]

This internal squabble with the German Christians does not change the fact that Hirsch saw himself ideologically firmly in the German Christian camp in general. He identified specifically with that faction represented by Ludwig Müller and the official church administration, because of its potential for unifying the church in the spring, summer, and early fall of 1933 behind the new state and its vision for the new Germany. It was to this group that a growing number of Protestants who identified with the Confessing Church, which later crystallized around the Barmen Confession, stood firmly opposed.

The Non-Aryan Issue
Hirsch's attitude to the Evangelical Church's infamous Aryan paragraph illustrates how he went along with the discrimination against Jews in matters of church polity, on the one hand, while at the same time defending the non-discriminatory unity of all believers of whatever race in Christ, on the other. He was able to play both sides by once again neatly distinguishing between the two kingdoms: the realm of external structures, in this case matters of church polity which can be freely adapted to the exigencies of the situation, and the inward reality of God's undifferentiated grace. At the most important synodical meeting of the Evangelical Church of the Old Prussian Union, held in Berlin September 5-6, 1933, the following law was passed:

> He who is not of Aryan descent or who is married to a person not of Aryan descent may not be called as clergyman or official of the general church government. Clergymen or officials of Aryan descent who marry persons of non-Aryan descent are to be discharged. The determination as to who is to be regarded as a person of non-Aryan descent is made according to the provisions of the law of the Reich.[90]

It was this clause more than anything else which aroused opposition in the church and began the church struggle in earnest. According to Helmreich, "It was the attempt to introduce the Aryan paragraph into the church, to remove Jewish Christian pastors from their posts, that more than anything else ignited the so-called Church Struggle (*Kirchenkampf*) of the Hitler period, and

---

89. Personal letter, Hirsch to Hans Grimm, June 3, 1958. Hans Grimm Archive, Lippoldsberg/Weser. Made available to me by Walter Buff, Hannover.
90. As quoted by Helmreich, *The German Churches Under Hitler*, p. 144.

prevented the total regimentation of the Protestant church."[91] Various theological faculties were asked to give their opinion on whether this new legislation was consistent with the Word of God, the historic confessions of the church, and the new Church constitution.[92]

On October 7, 1933, Hirsch gave his own personal view on the matter in a written statement to the Church hierarchy, later expanded and published in *Deutsche Theologie*, May, 1934. The essay, entitled "Theologisches Gutachten in der Nichtarierfrage," is divided into four main sections: general presuppositions, the church (*Gemeinde*) of Jesus Christ and the concept of a people's church (*Volkskirchentum*), the church and ministry (*Amt*) in the German Evangelical peoples-church (*Volkskirche*), and concluding observations. Because of the importance of this essay for an understanding of Hirsch's basic orientation to the Jewish question we will devote considerable space in the following pages to outlining his underlying argument.

Hirsch's premise is that "Germans and Jews are two distinct peoples," who in their racial origins, history, and natural and sociological make-up have little in common with each other. "We are more strongly distinguished from the Jews than from any other of our national neighbors in Europe," Hirsch claims.[93] With only a few individual exceptions, assimilation as a whole has not been possible, Hirsch maintains. Assimilation, were it possible, would bring German racially-based nationality to ruin and mean the de-Christianizing of the German national order. The new National Socialist state has rightly recognized this danger and is trying to correct the domination of Weimar Germany by a foreign nationality, through a recognition of Jews as guests and foreigners in Germany. This policy unfortunately has bitter and painful consequences for individuals and families with Jewish backgrounds, but ought not to take away from the necessity of the process as a whole. Christians do not have the right to condemn the placing of a minority-group, which is not able to assimilate, into the category of "guest status." The task of Christians is to see to it that the differentiation between Jews and Germans is not extended into the metaphysical realm, a danger which is especially great among present-day Germans. "The category into which Jews ought to be placed is not that of those who are inferior, unworthy, depraved, but simply the category of those who are foreign, not suited to us, and with whom we cannot mix without suffering damage."[94]

91. *Ibid.*, p. 84.

92. *Ibid.*, pp. 145-146.

93. Hirsch, "Theologisches Gutachten in der Nichtarierfrage," *Deutsche Theologie: Monatschrift für die deutsche evangelische Kirche* 1(May, 1934), p. 182. This article was first presented to church officials on October 7, 1933 and appeared in an expanded form in May, 1934.

94. *Ibid.*, p. 184. The German reads as follows: "Die Kategorie, unter die der Jude zu stellen ist, ist nicht die die Minderwertigen, Unwerthaften, in die Substanz Verdorbenen, sondern einfach die Kategorie des Fremden, das für uns nicht passt, und mitdem wir uns nicht Vermischen können, ohne Schaden zu leiden."

Christians have a responsibility to those numerous individuals who find themselves caught on the boundary between two nationalities. They must help make their heavy burden bearable in this transition period from assimilation to sharper separation between Germans and Jews. Christians will also rejoice when later, after the process in general is no onger endangered, individual exceptions can be made for those who have become inwardly both Christian and German. Over and above this, Christians ought to keep their earlier made personal friendships with individuals of Jewish blood both on personal and human grounds. After this difficult 30-year transition period the relationship between Germans and those of Jewish blood will once again become easier.

Three important observations need to be made at this point concerning Hirsch's initial presuppositions. First, Hirsch's stance toward the non-Aryan clause followed consistently from his earlier writings about the blood-related nature of nationality and its centrality for the nation-state. Second, Hirsch clearly separated himself from the more radical anti-semitic polemic which labelled Jews as an inferior, corrupt and base race. He recognized the unfortunate tragic fate of individual Jewish Christians and urged Christians to maintain their personal friendship with those of Jewish background. In this he was in fact taking a stance which ran counter to much official propaganda and policy. It is true that Hirsch supports segregation but there is no inherent logic that leads from his espousal of racial differentiation to genocide. Nevertheless, third, and most incriminating, was Hirsch's underlying analysis in which he supported the general process of racial segregation both in society and the church. It is here where he in effect provided fertile soil for anti-Jewish policy both in the state and in the church. His sympathy for individual cases cannot exonerate him from this underlying structural discrimination against the Jewish converts, let alone the German Jewish community at large about which he, like most Evangelical Christians even in the Confessing Church, remained silent.

Hirsch's assertions regarding the relation of the church of Jesus Christ (*Gemeinde Jesu Christi*) to the church-of-the-people (*Volkskirchentum*) is premised on the clear distinction between the two. In line with Reformation teaching, Hirsch argues, the church is free to adapt its external polity (church laws, constitution, ministry as a civil vocation) to the historically-given character (Art) of the nation. In fact, he believes the church has an obligation to do so in order to shape the whole life of the nation and thus to nurture in the nation a receptivity to the Gospel. In its external structure, therefore, the church is not bound to New Testament church polity. This distinction is crucial for the Aryan question.

In the church of Jesus Christ all believers, irrespective of earthly and racial differentiation, are one. This unity is a three-fold one: all are sinners who stand under divine judgement; all are equally embraced by God's grace and mercy; and, finally, all have one and the same calling: to serve God and witness to this divine grace. This unity binds all Christians to each other as brothers and sisters symbolized most clearly in the Lord's supper. While this unity does not dissolve earthly and historical distinctions, it does mean that before God all believers stand as equal and united. Whoever is so captive to historical realities that earthly distinctions are extended into the spiritual realm of the Lord's supper is disobedient to the Gospel and gives up the right to belong to the church of Jesus Christ. In this spiritual context Hirsch is clearly espousing the unity of Jewish converts to Christianity, those members of the Evangelical Church which are of mixed blood, and those of unmixed German heritage. He does not address the question of the spiritual unity of all humankind of whatever race or religious affiliation before God.

Having spoken to the spiritual unity of all believers in Christ Hirsch proceeds, nevertheless, to make a strong case for taking seriously the vocational differences between Christians. Vocational differentiation is determined by external and historical factors such as station in life, nationality, gifts, education and personal character. To dissolve these differences would be to make the church of Jesus Christ ahistorical, a Greek distortion of biblical religion. The church of Jesus Christ is fulfilled not by removing it from historical movements but precisely in the recognition of God's mysterious and gracious presence in the struggles, sins and suffering of historical life. The flaw in Hirsch's argument is not in his taking seriously the historically-conditioned nature of the Christian calling but in linking historical differentiation to racial qualities. Here he reflects the racial ideology not only of National Socialism but of much of German thought in the nineteenth and early twentieth century.

Church polity, as an aspect of the national-church (*Volkskirche*) must, according to Hirsch, be seen as *casus instrumentalis*, a witness to the Christian proclamation within a particular historical and national context, and like all human community stands under sin and judgement. Nevertheless, it depends on *gratia praeveniens*; that is, it depends on God's graciously using the historically-conditioned church as a human means for the proclamation of the Gospel and the unity of all in Christ without thereby annulling the individual subject in his or her own particularity as member of a nation.

Hirsch applies his understanding of the Reformation distinction between the church of Jesus Christ and the national church as mandated within the context of a given historical situation (the two are dialectically related to each other) to the issue of whether Jews can hold the public office of pastor. Hirsch is unequivocal about his affirmation of the spiritual priesthood of all believers: namely, the spiritual right of all baptized Christians to proclaim the Gospel and administer the sacraments. The question is, however, whether the national church in its historical particularity has the freedom to demand certain national conditions to holding office. Here Hirsch is also clear. The Evangelical Church has always assumed as self-evident that, with certain exceptions (for example, missionaries in a foreign context), those who hold a public church office ought to belong to the given nationality of the church. This is so even within the different German groupings (Bavaria, Swabia, Schleswig-Halstein and so on).

According to Hirsch, the present opposition to the Aryan (or German) condition for holding office in Germany rests not on theological but on political grounds. The issue becomes one of whether Jewish-Christians are German or not. Here Hirsch reiterates his earlier contention; namely, that Jews (whether converted or not) belong to a foreign nationality which is alien to the German ethos. The German Evangelical Church, consequently, has the full freedom to deprive them of the right to hold office publicly. Where the issue takes on theological significance is where Jewish-Christians are deprived of being called brothers and sisters in the realm of the priesthood of all believers. If there are individual German Christians who have done this, although he is not aware of any, he would, together with the present leaders of the German Evangelical Church, judge such conduct as unChristian. To his Christian brothers of Jewish background Hirsch, as a German and as a Christian, admits that it is difficult to ask someone else to make a sacrifice that he himself is not required to make. Nevertheless, he urges Jewish-Christians voluntarily in love to make just such a sacrifice; namely, to give up the possibilities for their sons to become pastors within the new German Evangelical Church.

A fundamental presupposition of all that Hirsch has said up to this point is that no distinction can be made between Christians of German background and Christians of Jewish background as far as participation in Christian worship and the Lord's supper is concerned, without being disobedient to the Gospel. Should eventually some Jewish-Christians withdraw and form separate congregations, members of such congregations could still not be deprived of taking part with those of German background in public worship service or catechetical instruction. In short, should such separate Jewish-Christian congregations be established they would belong to the corporate body of the German Evangelical Church. Afterall, "Christ is the Lord of us all, and Christ knows of no distinction between Christian and Jews."[95] The only restriction would be that they could not hold public church offices or have voting privileges. Whether the creation of such separate Jewish-Christian congregations is feasible or not is an open question. There can be, however, no question of forcibly removing Jewish-Christians from the Church. This would be against the Christian principle of love.

Where Hirsch stands on the whole issue becomes quite clear in the concluding observations of the essay. He calls on both the opposition and the present church leadership not to make the non-Aryan issue into a dogmatic one but to keep it in the realm of church polity. It has to do with the relative demands of the historical situation and not the theological unity of all in Christ. Pastors who find themselves in disagreement with these polity decisions of the

95. *Ibid.*, p. 195.

church administration ought to continue to preach the gospel and bear patiently what they perceive to be a distorted church order. He admits that he himself has some disagreements with how the whole thing has been handled. Especially in light of the small minority of pastors affected directly (there are only 30 pastors of non-Aryan ancestry, of which 18 do not fall under the regulation) the leadership could have acted more effectively with a lighter hand. What is important for the future is that no pastoral candidates be accepted who are not willing to become full members of the student association [*Studentschaft*] and the SA. Despite his uneasiness about the indifferent and mechanical way in which things have been handled, Hirsch is fully behind the general intent of the new regulation. His basic areas of disagreement with the churchly opposition are the following: 1) its fundamental rejection of the distinction between Germans and Jews of non-German blood who speak the German language; 2) its belief that the German Evangelical Church ought to deal with Jewish-Christians as though they were fully German; and 3) its general opposition to the events of 1933.

The basic themes of this May, 1934 article had appeared in an earlier and much briefer statement by Hirsch, "Arier und Nichtarier in der deutschen evangelischen Kirche," published in 1933. This earlier essay also begins by affirming the spiritual unity of all Christians from whatever race or people—Jewish, black, mongolian and so on. Here Hirsch asserts that "This community in the hidden church of Jesus Christ, which runs through all peoples, times and lands, is also the final sustaining mystery within the visible church...."[96] While no differentiation is justified in the invisible church of Christ, the mysterious ground of the visible church, yet distinctions that are not spiritually grounded need to be made in the historical church. These distinctions—as those between black churches and white churches in America, German-speaking Lutherans and non-German-speaking Lutherans in Stockholm and Copenhagen, congregations of white immigrants and those of indigenous origins in colonial territories—are not spiritually based but have simply to do with functional and practical usefulness. Even in these cases, however, individual exceptions should be allowed: by allowing for such exceptions "we acknowledge that the standard [*Regel*] for our normally different way of behaving is a human-earthly standard derived from earthly necessities; we acknowledge that our [earthly] constituted church is not one and the same as the church of Jesus Christ."[97]

Hirsch now applies these nuanced distinctions directly to the German situation concerning the non-Aryian issue in church and state. He begins by saying that the church in its polity dare not remain indifferent to the developing ethos in the German state. A German order is being constructed on a thorough-going

96. Hirsch, "Arier und Nichtarier in der deutschen evangelischen Kirche," *Kirche und Volkstum in Niedersachsen*, 1, 2(1933), p. 1.

97. *Ibid.*, p. 2.

distinction between those of German blood and those of non-German blood. Hirsch, in effect, gives the strong impression in this article that the political restructuring of the German order is a difficult but necessary one, that the church as part of the German ethos ought not to resist this reordering of German society but energetically support it: "Further, the state has with its ruling concerning the non-Aryan question assumed the ethical task of deeply impressing [*einzubrennen*] upon the German people their responsibility to assure a distinctive German posterity. Its intent is to retain the natural blood-bond of the nation as the natural ground for German life and the German spirit. To all of this one must on grounds of Christian responsibility say yes, even though one is aware of the painful inner lot of individuals. A nation and a state in its dealings cannot be determined by deference to the lot of individuals."[98] The church also has a Christian responsibility to reflect these regulations within its own community. It ought, however, to do this in love. The church is, after all, a community based on good will while the state is a community ready to use coercion to enforce obedience.

In the light of these observations, Hirsch makes the following concrete suggestions for the church in the present situation. First, since the church has so few pastors with Jewish or half-Jewish blood, she need not request of pastors that they trace their racial origins. In general the church need not dismiss from their positions those who have served her loyally. In cases where the difficulties between a pastor with Jewish or half-Jewish blood and his congregation become unbearable a termination with a honorable pension would be in order. Good relations between pastor and congregations ought, however, not to be disturbed from without.[99] Second, future church leaders, however, will need to be selected on the basis of new criteria; standards which take seriously new views on comradeship and bondedness to the nation (*Volksverbundenheit*). One of the requisites will need to be that all candidates must have been members of the German student association (*Studentenschaft*) during their theological studies. "Thereby," says Hirsch, "the rigorous conditions of the German student association concerning the right blood type of pastors is fully met."[100] This way the church can fully support and gradually implement what the state is trying to do without taking extraordinary new church measures. On Christian grounds, however, the *Reichsbischof* should continue to be given the right by the state to

---

98. *Ibid.*, p. 3. Here is the original German: "Der Staat hat weiter mit seiner Regelung der Nichtarier-Frage die ethische Aufgabe übernommen, den deutschen Menschen die Verantwortung für eine Nachkommenschaft deutscher Art einzubrennen. Es ist sein Wille, dass deutsches Leben und deutscher Geist den tragenden Naturgrund in dem natürlichen Blutbunde des Volkstums behalten. Zu alledem muss man aus christlicher Verantwortung heraus ja sagen, auch wenn man um das schmerzliche innere Schicksal Einzelner weiss. Ein Volk und ein Staat kann in seinem Handeln nicht durch Rücksicht auf Einzelschicksale bestimmt sein."

99. *Ibid.*, p. 3.

100. *Ibid.*, p. 3.

make exceptions in individual, personal cases.

Third, concerning lay members in local congregations, Hirsch rejects a rigid either-or approach—either gathering all Jewish Christians in separate Jewish-Christian congregations, or incorporating them all into existing congregations. New Jewish converts and new mixed-marriage partners ought to join such Jewish-Christian congregations. Those, who have been long-standing members of our German-Christian congregations should not, however, be forced against their wishes to join such separate churches, particularly not those of mixed blood or mixed marriages. Finally, Hirsch considers it self-evident that there ought to be communion fellowship between such potential Jewish-Christian congregations and German-Christian congregations: "Someone who cannot without qualms (*grundsätzlich*) kneel before the altar together with a person of Jewish blood in order to receive the body and blood of the Lord, that person is still so immature in his Christianity, that at best he has renounced the right to participate in the discussion concerning basic church polity."[101]

Here, possibly more than anywhere else, we see the practical consequences for church life of Hirsch's political, philosophical and theological presuppositions concerning the nation, the state, Christianity and the church, as we examine them in this study. It can be said in defense of Hirsch that he does not use the derogatory anti-Jewish language that was prevalent among the more radical German Christians and National Socialist racist propagandists. He does affirm the spiritual unity of German-Christians and Jewish-Christians in Christ; a unity to be reflected in church fellowship around the altar. He also encourages compassionate behaviour on the part of individual German-Christians toward individual Jewish-Christians, and the making of exceptions concerning regulations affecting the non-Aryan issue. Here he seems to me to be at odds with much of the racial political rhetoric around him, and even take certain personal risks in expressing his views. *Where Hirsch is culpable, and where he reflects the prevalent ethos of his time, is in making race such a decisive category not only for German society in general but for the actual life of the church itself.*

There appears to be no evidence that Hirsch's theological or political views underwent any substantial change after 1933. In some of his later writings he reveals some disillusionment with Müller and some of the harsh measures and insensitive tactics of the church administrators, as well as disappointment over the church struggle and its splitting up of the church, admitting that he had been too optimistic in his earlier hope for theological and ecclesiastical unity. Despite this, however, his support for the revolution of 1933 and the general intent of National Socialism appears to remain firm. In fact his position seems to solidify.

---

101. *Ibid.*, p. 4.

Hirsch as Academic Dean

Records show that Hirsch belonged to numerous official Party organizations including the National Socialist German Students' League, the National Socialist *Volks* Welfare, the National Air Defense League, the Red Cross, the SS, and the National Socialist Teachers' League.[102] We have already mentioned that he joined the Party in February, 1937. In belonging to these various National Socialist associations he was no different from many others. Where he did make a unique contribution was in his role as academic dean of the faculty of theology at the University of Göttingen in the crucial years 1933 to 1938, a position which he held on the basis of good academic credentials.[103]

Robert Ericksen gives us a particular historical reading of what happened in the Göttingen theological faculty under Hirsch's tenure during these years.[104] Hirsch's role is somewhat difficult to evaluate. On the one hand, it could be argued that because Hirsch was well-connected with the officials in Berlin, he was able to and did protect his faculty from serious intervention by the Party. Apparently, no one from his faculty was removed for political opposition to the state or sent to the concentration camp, even though there was strong student sympathy for the Confessing Church and the theology of Karl Barth. On the other hand, Ericksen brings forth persuasive evidence in support of his claim that, "The aggressive, intimidating, unsettling role of Hirsch within the theological faculty" created tremendous conflict between Hirsch and the faculty and the students.[105] This despite the fact that in 1933 the vast majority of the faculty members supported the German Christians and the Hannover bishop, August Marahrens, in whose area of jurisdiction the important Göttingen theological faculty was located, was himself a supporter of Hitler and National Socialism. Even Hermann Dörries, one of the few supporters of the Confessing Church, was a conservative nationalist. Thus it would appear, from Ericksen's own account that a number of interpretations of Hirsch's role in the Faculty of Theology are possible.

Ericksen shows how already in the summer of 1933 the relationship between Bishop Marahrens and Hirsch began to deteriorate, the former distancing himself from the German Christians on the one side and the radical wing of the Confessing Church on the other on traditional confessional grounds. Marahrens was able to steer an independent course during the German Church Struggle, the Hannover territorial church being one of three "intact" churches during the period. Tensions also developed between Hirsch and the faculty, some of whom suspected Hirsch of denouncing them to the Berlin Ministry, an accusation

102. Ericksen, *Theologians Under Hitler*, p. 166.

103. *Ibid.*, p. 167.

104. In the following pages I am indebted to Ericksen's historical study, particularly his pages 166ff., for important biographical details.

105. *Ibid.*, p. 167.

which Hirsch denied.[106] According to Ericksen, "Hirsch maintained a flow of correspondence with Berlin, interspersed with personal visits, and he and the ministry put up a united and reasonably effective front against all Confessing Church-oriented activities touching upon the theological faculty."[107]

One of the most controversial issues Hirsch was involved in during his years as academic dean had to do with faculty appointments, especially the 1935 hiring of Walter Birnbaum to the position of practical theology. According to Ericksen's findings, Birnbaum's theology was decidedly nationalistic, his academic credentials were weak and he had been closely associated with Ludwig Müller and August Jäger in the battles of the church struggle. His appointment seemed to be little more that a political one. The controversy over Birnbaum was brought to a head by the boycott of his classes by Confessing Church-oriented seminary students, who also protested against Birnbaum sitting on their examining committees. Hirsch kept Bernard Rust, Minister of Church Affairs in Berlin, well informed estimating in one letter to Rust that about three-fourths of the theology students were under Confessing Church influence, but recommending non-interference, maintaining that the faculty could deal internally with the matter.[108] Further, Hirsch urged the supervisor of the seminary "to ban 'discussions on church-political questions in the public rooms of the seminary.'"[109] Despite Hirsch's self-perceived role as moderator and reconciler between the various sides, the year 1935 saw the lines drawn rather clearly between the "Confessing Church students, the church office in Hannover, and a very small group of faculty" on one side, and "Hirsch, a majority of the faculty, and the ministry in Berlin" on the other.[110] In the words of Ericksen, "Although he could not control students as fully as he would have liked, and although he eschewed violence, he employed intimidation and a hand-in-glove relationship with the government in his attempt to thwart the Confessing Church at every turn."[111]

Hirsch, says Ericksen, tried in the years 1935 to 1937 to curtail the activities of Confessing Church students such as retreats, *Ersatz* courses and separate theological examinations (without theological representation of the faculty) under the auspices of the Hannover office. At one point Hirsch sent copies of circular letters by Confessing students to the Ministry charging the students and the Hannover bishop of sympathies with the "'radical Berlin-Dahlem Confessing Church group' of Martin Niemöller."[112] As a consequence the Ministry published a decree on November 17, 1936 forbidding all substitute

106. Ericksen, *Theologians Under Hitler*, p. 167.
107. *Ibid.*, p. 168.
108. *Ibid.*, pp. 169-170.
109. *Ibid.*, p. 170.
110. *Ibid.*, p. 171.
111. *Ibid.*
112. *Ibid.*, p. 172.

courses. A group of fourty students protested to the *Reich* Minister in February, 1937, pleading for academic freedom. Hirsch in turn wrote to the Ministry suggesting that these protests be ignored and supporting the decree. The consequence of this was that in the spring of 1937 the Hannover office established theological examinations based on Confessional orthodoxy, independent of the Göttingen theological faculty. On May 16, 1938 the state officially cut off monies to students taking their examinations without faculty participation, an action which brought a further round of protests by Hannover students studying at various universities including Göttingen.

There seemed to be no resolution to the growing conflict between the Hannover Church office and the Confessing students, on the one side, and Hirsch, the faculty, and the Berlin Ministry, on the other, until Hirsch himself offered a compromise. He agreed to absent himself from the examinations. Birnbaum would participate, thus satisfying Ministry regulations, with the proviso that he would personally not examine students who were unalterably opposed to him. This uneasy solution seemed acceptable to the students and was approved by the Hannover church.

The tensions in the Göttingen theological faculty and in its relationship with the Hannover office decreased remarkably with the resignation of Hirsch from his deanship in 1938 and the outbreak of war. Birnbaum's role lessened during the war years especially after 1941 when he began travelling extensively lecturing to *Luftwaffe* personnel on the Russian front. Hirsch's influential role also diminished after he stepped down as dean even though he continued to teach and "enjoyed a reputation as perhaps the greatest theologian in Germany during those years."[113] He continued to research and write extensively after his "forced retirement" in 1945,[114] although by 1946 he was totally blind.

Between 1933 and 1945 there was no direct contact between Hirsch and Tillich (other than a rather enigmatic letter from Hirsch to Tillich in 1933 and the public debate in periodicals in 1934-1935). Their lives and thought—on the most obvious level at least—went in entirely different directions. Hirsch's more radical response to the crisis of modernity, his concept of nationality as the "hidden sovereign" to which all Germans owe unqualified allegiance in the earthly realm, his enthusiastic support of Hitler and the NSDAP as the instruments of providence, his boycott of the ecumenical movement, his influential role in the German Church Struggle on the side of Ludwig Müller and the German Christians, his double approach to the Non-Aryan issue, and his controversial tactics as Academic Dean at the University of Göttingen, all ran fundamentally counter to what Tillich believed in and stood up for. And yet, there was something which drew these two men together from an early age, something that fascinated each about the other even in the heat of the battle between

113. *Ibid.*, p. 176.
114. *Ibid.*

them. On a deeper level there was, I will argue, something in their thought which was similar. We turn now to a consideration of Tillich's career during the same period.

Tillich: "Between Native and Alien Land"

The details of Tillich's life and thought between 1933 and 1945 are much more widely known in the English-speaking world than are those of Hirsch, having been recounted in a number of autobiographies by Tillich himself, documented in great detail by Marion Pauck in her biography, and politically examined by numerous analysts most recently by Ronald Stone.[115] Consequently, we have deliberately gone into much greater detail analyzing the facts and positions of Hirsch in the Third Reich than we need to with Tillich during his years in America. We limit ourselves here, rather, to highlighting some of the major aspects of Tillich's career during 1933 and after his emigration which stand in relief vis-a-vis Hirsch during the same period.

Tillich titled the second-to-last chapter of his 1936 autobiographical sketch *On the Boundary*, written three years after his emigration from Germany to the United States, "Between Native and Alien Land." This phrase is a suitable metaphor for much of Tillich's life and written corpus but is particularly appropriate for describing his response to German nationalism in 1933, and his early years in North America. In contrast to Hirsch, for whom commitment to nationality (what he called the "hidden sovereign") became the criterion for all responsible historical thought and action, Tillich's attachment to his German homeland—its landscape, tradition, language, and destiny—was so instinctive, he says, that he "could never understand why it should have to be made an object of special attention."[116] Such a preoccupation with nationalism, according to Tillich, reflected insecurity and occurred in individuals who come from the periphery and feel driven to justify their patriotic feelings.

Despite his deep sense of rootedness in German culture, which he maintained to the end of his life. Tillich talks in this book about living on the boundary between alien country and native land, a life demanded by the God of the Jewish prophet and of Jesus. This Judeo-Christian God, says Tillich, "uttlery demolishes all religious nationalism—the nationalism of the Jews, which he opposes constantly, and that of the pagans, which is repudiated in the command to Abraham ['Go from your home...to the land that I will show you']."[117]

115. Ronald Stone, *Paul Tillich's Radical Social Thought* (New York: University of America Press, 1986).
116. Tillich, *On the Boundary*, p. 93.
117. *Ibid.*, pp. 91-92.

Tillich identifies two types of emigration that may be demanded of anyone and that characterize his own life: physical emigration from one country to another; and spiritual emigration: breaking with "ruling authorities and prevailing social and political patterns," or what he also calls personal-inward emigration: "parting from accepted lines of belief and thought; pushing beyond the limits of the obvious; radical questioning that opens up the new and uncharted."[118] Tillich was an emigrant in all of these senses: "In every sense of the word, I have always stood between native and alien land. I have never decided exclusively for the alien, and I have experienced both types of 'emigration.' I began to be an 'emigrant' personally and spiritually long before I actually left my homeland."[119]

The concept of emigration became an important category for Tillich's theology generally, reflected in various writings and speeches he made during his first few years in America, and separates his thinking and life sharply from the "rootedness" of Hirsch's orientation. He saw emigration, whether for reasons of Christian love, moral protest or political convictions, as an important spiritual category applicable to every Christian, indicating God's majesty and the unconditional moral imperative at certain times to leave all.[120] He defended the importance of "cultural cross fertilization" that resulted from emigres crossing national boundaries but added that such fruitful cross-cultural fertilization was "possible only because a common human nature binds individuals, groups and peoples to one another." "No one can understand that which is strange without rediscovering himself in it...." "The certainty of the existence of such an essential identity between human being and human being allows people to leave their homeland and emigrate to foreign countries."[121] In the following pages we look first at the events leading up to and following his "physical emigration" to New York City. Secondly, we take a cursory look at what might be described as his "intellectual" or "spiritual" emigration between 1933 and 1945, concentrating particularly on those aspects of his thought which link him or separate him from the views of his friend and now political opponent Emanuel Hirsch.

118. *Ibid.*, p. 92.

119. *Ibid.*, p. 93.

120. Tillich, "Christentum und Emigration," *GW* XIII, p. 190. First given as a speech to the "American Committee for German Christian Refugees," New York, June 6, 1936. Originally published in *The Presbyterian Tribune*, 52, 3(1936), pp. 13, 16, and then translated into German from which this quotation is taken.

121. Tillich, "Geist und Wanderung," *GW* XIII, p. 200. An address to the Graduate Faculty of the New School for Social Research in New York, April 13, 1937. Orginally published as "Mind and Migration," in *Social Research*, 4, 3(1937), pp. 295-305.

Physical Emigration

In the 1920s, as we have seen, Tillich like many other German intellectuals, including Emanuel Hirsch, shied away from direct political-party involvement even though much of his theoretical work was directly political in nature. In one of his autobiographical sketches, for instance, Tillich says his lectures in Frankfurt, and his public lectures across Germany "produced a conflict with the growing Nazi movement long before 1933."[122] With the growing popularity and strength of the National Socialist party, however, Tillich and many of his friends joined the Social Democratic Party. Tillich joined in 1929, taking a very different route than Hirsch who until 1932, when he threw his weight behind Hitler, supported the conservative German National People's Party.

A second politically-related act, which like the former was later to be held against Tillich by the Nazis, was his helping to found and sitting on the editorial board of a left-wing periodical, *Neue Blätter für den Sozialismus*. Interestingly, despite his penchant for theoretical political analysis and these politically-related activities he was considered by some of his friends during this time as being politically naive.[123] Any naive political optimism he may have had, however, quickly disappeared in the coming years, particularly in 1932 and 1933, as the political clouds hanging over his own future became ever more menacing, bringing out Tillich's true personal and political mettle.

In April 1932 he and a friend wrote a letter to the Berlin Wingolf student fraternity, of which he was a member, denouncing it for its discrimination against left-wing students and Christian students with Jewish background. They asserted their solidarity with Jews and socialists and threatened to resign, which they in fact did some time later. On a number of occasions Tillich publicly identified with Jews and vented his anger at the National Socialists.[124] On one occasion, in July 1932, fighting broke out between students at the University of Frankfurt, Nazi students and Storm troopers beating up Jews and left-wing students. Tillich, as dean of the faculty of philosophy, bravely defended the socialist and Jewish students calling for the expulsion of the National Socialist students.[125] Tillich's courageous criticism of the antisemitic ideology and acts of the Nazis, no doubt due in part to his long intimate association with Jewish friends and his own prophetic-theological orientation,[126] stands in marked

122. Tillich, "Autobiographical Reflections," p. 14.

123. Pauck, *Tillich: Life,* p. 125.

124. Hannah Tillich, in her autobiography, recounts how Tillich, after hearing Hitler speak close up, came "home shudderingly impressed by the demon in Hitler's eyes." She says, "Paulus felt the spell of the little man with the uncultured voice and the brutality of his wordy assault. He sensed great danger." *From Time To Time,* p. 149. She also recounts Tillich attacking Hitler directly in a speech in Kassel (*Ibid.*).

125. Pauck, *Tillich: Life,* p. 125. Hannah Tillich gives a moving account of this episode and says, "Paulus, who had been lecturing during the attack, had helped to carry battered students into a room behind his office." *From Time To Time,* p. 149.

126. For a good discussion of Tillich's views on the relation between Christianity and Judaism,

contrast to Hirsch's much more ambivalent attitude toward the Jewish question as we have seen above. Hirsch, while not openly antisemitic, nevertheless, saw a great gulf between what he calls the "Jewish spirit" and the German *nomos*, and, while emphasizing the unity of all Christians in Christ, including Jewish converts, and objecting to unduly harsh measures against the Jews, still on the whole defended the National Socialist attempt to separate Jews from Germans, and give them "guest status." The kind of double standard—one theological and the other socio-political—that Hirsch's stance to the Jewish question represented was anathema to Tillich.

Tillich's most important theoretical-political act, however, was the writing of *The Socialist Decision*, which appeared toward the end of 1932, and ought to be read side by side with Hirsch's *Die gegenwärtige geistige Lage* in order to gain a true picture of their similarities and differences. It was banned as soon as Hitler came to power, a few copies circulating secretly among friends.[127] On March 18 and 25 articles appeared in the *Frankfurter Zeitung* attacking the Johann Wolfgang Goethe University, especially its Jewish faculty, citing Tillich's favorable statements and writings about Jews and socialists as illustrating his "unreliability," and specifically quoting a sentence from *The Socialist Decision*. On April 13 long lists of *persona non grata* appeared in newspapers including left-wing intellectuals and members of Socialist and Communist Parties, and Jews. Tillich's name, together with many of his Jewish friends and others, appeared among those suspended from their university positions.

This was followed by an anxious period of uncertainty for Tillich, during which he consulted various friends throughout Germany concerning his future, as the political situation in Germany rapidly deteriorated. Tillich observed the public burning of books in Frankfurt, including his own *The Socialist Decision*, on May 10, 1933.[128] This period, the events leading up to and surrounding his dismissal from the university, his "murderous despair" over what was happening not only to him and his family but throughout Germany, is graphically described in highly personal terms by Hannah Tillich in her provocative autobiography, *From Time To Time*.[129]

and his outspoken criticism of all forms of antisemitism see Ronald Stone, *Tillich's Radical Social Thought*, pp. 77-78, 101-105, 146-149. Not only was Tillich unequivocal in his critique of Nazi antisemitism between 1933 and 1945, after World War II he urged Germans to face their guilt. Of Tillich's bold lectures at the Deutschen Hochschule für Politik in Berlin in 1953, on "The Jewish Question: Christian and German Problem," Stone says: they "are among the deepest of his writings." Stone adds: "Long acquaintance with the Jews and appreciation for Jewish philosophers conditioned him to become one of the best friends that Judaism had among the ranks of Christian theologians," p. 148.

127. For interesting background to Tillich's writing of *The Socialist Decision* see John R. Stumme, *Socialism in Theological Perspective*, pp. 47-50, and Stumme, "Introduction," *The Socialist Decision*.

128. Pauck, *Tillich: Life*, pp. 126-132.

129. Hannah Tillich, *From Time To Time*, pp. 147-156.

It was with great ambivalence and a sense of guilt, for leaving his homeland while others stayed behind,[130] that he finally accepted an offer by Columbia University and Union Theological Seminary, New York City, to come and teach there.[131] On September 9 the Prussian Ministry of Culture replied to a request by Tillich, granting him a one-year leave to teach abroad. During a meeting with officials at the Ministry, in an attempt to get his status clarified, he got the impression that his case was not very serious and that he might be reinstated at some future time.[132] In fact, his suspension was apparently at first seen only as a temporary measure. *Reichminister* Rust allegedly would gladly have reinstated Tillich but Tillich refused to accept the condition: to refrain from criticizing the National Socialist worldview.[133] After a series of farewell meetings and parties, including a final meeting with his father, whom he would never see again, Tillich, his wife Hannah and their daughter Erdmuthe left by ship for New York, where they arrived on November 3.[134]

His status with the German Ministry of Culture was not cleared up until December 20, when he received a letter in New York from the Ministry officially dismissing him from his job, and informing him that because of his belonging to the Social Democratic party and his socialist writings he was considered untrustworthy and could not be allowed to occupy a civil position in Germany.[135] Up to that point Tillich had still lived under the illusion that he might be able to return to Germany to teach after a year or two abroad. His disappointed expectations, and paradoxical attitude toward his homeland and even National Socialism are evident in an enigmatic January 20, 1934, letter to the Ministry for Science, Art and Education, Berlin. In this letter he expresses surprise at the earlier letter of dismissal from the civil service, recalling that ministry director Jäger had assured him of his "loyalty and that he thought that one year's stay in a foreign country would be of advantage to me both materially and personally." He goes on in the letter to defend his national reliability on the

130. According to Hannah Tillich, some of Tillich's Jewish friends wanted him to remain in Germany, and Tillich seriously considered staying and working in the underground movement, writing for them. Some of his political friends in the underground, however, advised him against it, considering him a danger, and urging him to work for them from abroad (p. 155).

131. Pauck, *Tillich: Life*, pp. 131ff. Pauck cites Harald Poelchaus as begging Tillich to stay because he was needed in Germany, and to join the underground resistance movement (p. 135). Somewhat ironically, Emanuel Hirsch, on the other side, urged Tillich to remain as well and work for the National Socialist cause.

132. Pauck, *Tillich: Life*, p. 136. Hannah Tillich recollects Tillich's account of his conversation with the secretary of education, in which the Ministry apparently wanted him to stay in Germany. After listening to Tillich's questions, particularly his query about the fate of the Jews and modern culture, the secretary recommended a leave of two years. *From Time To Time*, p. 155.

133. Introductory biographical remarks to "Die Amerikanische Zeit Nach Der Emigration 1933-1939," *GW* XIII, p. 185.

134. Pauck, *Tillich: Life*, pp. 135-138.

135. *Ibid.*, p. 148.

basis of his loyal participation in World War I, for which he was awarded the "Iron Cross First Class," and his years as a "theoretician of Religious Socialism," in which capacity he struggled "against the dogmatic Marxism of the German labour movement." In fact, he refers to having "supplied a number of concepts to the National Socialist theoreticians (probably having in mind his old friend Emanuel Hirsch)" and adds that his "last book [*The Socialist Decision*] was interpreted by the representatives of dogmatic Marxism as an attack upon them inasmuch as it points emphatically to the powers in man that bind him to nature." He adds: "The fact that as a theologian I adopt the biblical criticism of an unbroken sway of national powers could be regarded as evidence of my national unreliability only if National Socialism had not identified itself with the program of 'positive Christianity.' This, however, is the case. Hence I cannot, in this connection either, agree that national unreliability has in fact been demonstrated."[136] In effect he was in this letter asking the Nazi government to reconsider its decision of dismissal. In a further letter, dated June 15, 1934, Tillich was curtly informed that his protest could not be "sustained."[137]

This letter of Tillich's is highly significant for a number of reasons. First of all, it demonstrates the fluidity of the situation during the first year of National Socialist power, when officials in the various ministries themselves were not quite sure in which direction the new government would take them, reflected in the mixed messages Tillich received from civil servants. Secondly, it reveals Tillich's own uncertainty about the meaning of his exile. Was it in fact an exile, or was it simply a temporary leave of absence. It seems clear that initially, at least, he saw it as a leave of absence for which he had received official approval expecting to return shortly. Third, and more important, is the paradoxical way in which Tillich refers to his political contributions and loyalties. On the one hand, he makes clear his left-wing political perspective manifested in his theoretical work for Religious Socialism. In the same breath, however, he emphasizes his fight against dogmatic Marxism and his having indirectly supplied theoretical categories to National Socialist theoreticians. There is no doubt that Tillich for the most part held the National Socialists in great contempt, as both Marion Pauck and Tillich's wife Hannah in her autobiography take pains to point out. And yet there was something in his thought which led some, like Hirsch himself, to believe that Tillich could himself make a contribution to a National Socialist Germany. Marion Pauck captures the tone of the letter well when she says:

> The sometimes confused and imprecise tone of the protest seems to mar the image of a man of whom it was often said that he was the first non-Jew to be dismissed by the Nazi regime—a myth he never denied—and who was proud

136. This remarkable letter appears in full translated form in Pauck, *Tillich: Life*, pp. 148-150.
137. *Ibid.*, p. 150.

of his dismissal until the end of his life. Yet the letter reveals him, not as one proud of being singled out as an unreliable citizen and forced into emigration, but rather as the shrewd and practical man he was, caught in the ambiguities of history, reaching out to clear his name and trying to ensure that, failing all else, his pension would be available to him. The hero and the shrewd negotiator are one and the same.

The same man who wrote much later that life is ambiguous was himself ambiguous in a startling way in this letter, particularly in his statement that the Nazis had borrowed their terminology from him. Yet even this was altogether in keeping with his personality and his tendency to remain open to all possibilities, not taking an absolute stand when the future was inscrutable. The historic events of the next six months showed him the vanity of his attempt.[138]

In the winter of 1934 Tillich officially resigned from the Wingolf student organization, protesting the fact that Jews were excluded from its membership.[139] Gradually, his hope that the Nazi phenomenon would be short-lived, and that he might soon be allowed to return to his homeland to take up his teaching and writing there, gave way to a time of disillusionment; a "second death," the enduring loss of teaching position, homeland, and friendships, the first death being his experience of the First World War.[140] The public rupture of his friendship with Emanuel Hirsch was symbolic of the tragic consequences of the events in Germany not only for Tillich but for many in similar circumstances. Sometime in the summer or early fall of 1934 Tillich received a copy of Hirsch's book, *Die geganärtige geistige Lage,* in which the author comes out strongly in support of National Socialism, using categories which sound similar to Tillich's Religious Socialist ones. In the November, 1934 issue of *Theologische Blätter* Tillich irately attacks Hirsch's position, charging him with plagiarizing his own concepts. Hirsch responds to Tillich's charges in a letter to his friend Dr. Stapel, published as part of a book *Christliche Freiheit und politische Bindung* and Tillich gives a short rebuttle in a second open letter in the May, 1935, issue of *Theologische Blätter.* The documents of this debate and the issues concerning theology and politics as they arise out of this controversy are the central focus of this book and receive detailed treatment in later chapters.

What somewhat mitigated the trauma of this "second death" was Tillich's work with "Self-Help for Emigres from Central Europe," an organization founded on November 25, 1936, and devoted to helping refugees get in touch with each other and find jobs. Tillich was chosen first chairman and remained in this position for fifteen years.[141] Almost from the moment Tillich got off the

138. *Ibid.*, p. 151.
139. *Ibid.*
140. *Ibid.*, p. 153.

ship refugees of various kinds, many old friends, came streaming to his door. Tillich's office at Union Theological Seminary became a point of contact with the new world for many of these refugees, who, according to Pauck, became Tillich's first reading audience in North America.[142] He particularly identified with the fate of the Jews and, in the words of Pauck, "When the Jewish persecutions abroad grew increasingly flagrant, Tillich emphasized over and over again that not the Jews alone but Christianity and humanism were also being put to death."[143]

We need not here trace in any great detail Tillich's difficult first years in America, his gradual acceptance by the philosophical and theological establishment and his eventual rise to fame, a remarkable story told by Marion Pauck and others. What is significant for us here is that from 1933 to 1948 we have no record of any direct contact or correspondence between Tillich and Hirsch. They each pursued a very different course. While Hirsch took upon himself what he considered to be the fate of Germany, writing on behalf of the German Christians, siding with Ludwig Müller and the pro-Hitler administrators of the *Reichskirche* in the German church struggle with the Confessing Church, condemning the politics of the world ecumenical movement, and playing a leading role in theological academic affairs at the University of Göttingen, Tillich was engaged in his own form of pro-German but anti-Hitler propaganda from his offices at Union Theological Seminary in New York.

His many activities, addresses and writings from 1933 to 1939—on the meaning of emigration; on the work of "Self-help for Emigres from Central Europe;" on the European political and religious situation—are a rich resource not only for anyone trying to understand Tillich's thought but for an analysis of the period in general.[144] Of particular interest is his encounter with J.H. Oldham and the ecumenical movement. On the occasion of Tillich's first formal presentation to the Theological Discussion Group, founded in 1931 and of which he became a member in 1934, Oldham, chief organizer of the 1937 Oxford Ecumenical Conference and the brunt of Emanuel Hirsch's criticisms in a 1937 article, was present. According to Pauck's account, the two were immediately attracted to each other: "He (Oldham) and Tillich took to one another at once: Oldham was impressed by Tillich's analysis as well as by his concern for the future of Protestantism. Tillich quickly warmed to Oldham's enthusiasm for his point of view and expanded in his presence."[145]

Unlike Hirsch, Tillich wholeheartedly supported the ecumenical movement and when Oldham invited him to become part of the preparatory commission for

141. *Ibid.*, pp. 157ff.
142. *Ibid.*, p. 155.
143. *Ibid.*, p. 159.
144. A good selection of the writings of this period are collected in *GW* XIII, pp. 185-252.
145. Pauck, *Paul Tillich: Life*, p. 190.

the 1937 Oxford conference he willingly accepted. In this capacity he was given an opportunity during the spring and summer of 1936 to journey through England, Holland, France, Belgium, Switzerland and Italy, meeting many of his old friends although never crossing over into Germany itself. He lectured on the causes of National Socialism; discussed the creation of a religious league for the infusion of a dynamic religious socialist concern for social justice into Protestantism; met briefly with Karl Barth in Basel; had a poignant last farewell telephone conversation with his father; and even attended a seminar in Geneva in the presence of some pro-National Socialist German church leaders.[146] Although Tillich in 1937 returned to England to attend the Oxford Conference on Life and Work as a member of the "Commission on Socialism and Communism and their Relation to the Ecumenical Movement," he was not invited to attend later ecumenical conferences, a fact which, according to Pauck, he considered a personal affront. He attributed it to the fact that too many nonliberal theologians like Barth gave direction to the ecumenical movement. In Pauck's words: "It was in fact his own position between the church and the world, a position from which he spoke to those outside the church more than to those who stood within it, that prevented him from becoming a force in ecumenical circles, and not any personal ill toward his thought—although that, too, was sometimes expressed by conservative persons."[147] Thus while Hirsch deliberately remained aloof and highly critical of the ecumenical movement for church political reasons—he perceived it as an international forum for anti-German propaganda—Tillich unwillingly found himself left out of an ecumenical forum that he desired to be part of but for whatever reasons ignored him.

As an emigre Tillich decided not to become involved in any particular political party and he advised other emigres not to do so as well. Nevertheless, he did make a few forays into politics between 1938 and 1945.[148] On November 21, 1938 he broke his five year public silence concerning German politics, for

---

146. For a personal account of his travels, including among other things some reflections on the German church struggle, see "Die religiöse Lage im heutigen Deutschland" and "Eine geschichtliche Diagnose: Eindrücke von einer Europareise," *GW* XIII, pp. 226-248. The former was first published as "The Religious Situation in Germany Today," in *Religion in Life*, 3, 2(1934), pp. 163-173; the second appeared as "A Historical Diagnosis: Impressions of an European Trip," in *Radical Religion*, 2, 1(1936/1937), pp. 11-17.

147. Pauck, *Paul Tillich: Life*, p. 195.

148. Tillich describes his political activities and interests in America in his 1952 autobiographical sketch in the following words: "The political interests of my postwar years in Germany remained alive in America. They found expression in my participation in the religious-socialist movement in this country; in the active relation I maintained for years with the Graduate Faculty of Political Sciences at the New School for Social Research, New York; in my chairmanship of the Council for a Democratic Germany during the war; and in the many religio-political addresses I gave. In spite of some unavoidable disappointments, especially with the Council, politics remained, and always will remain, an important factor in my theological and philosophical thought." "Autobiographical Reflections," p. 19.

the first time attacking the Nazis at a public assembly. He addressed a Protestant group protesting Nazi persecution of the Jews on "The Meaning of Anti-Semitism."[149] He minced few words in this speech, emphasizing that "an attack on Christianity must necessarily follow an attack on the Jews, and the destruction of the German spirit and the German soul necessarily follow the destruction of Jews."[150] In short, the two were inextricably linked: the annihilation of the Jews meant an annihilation of Christianity. He clearly distinguishes the genuine Germany of the Middle Ages, of the Renaissance, of the Reformation, of Martin Luther, of the many great German thinkers, including Nietzsche, whom the Nazis now misuse, down to the uncompromising spirit of a man like Martin Niemöller from the demonic forces which now hold Germany captive in the service of the "irresistable weapons of a technological civilization."[151] He could, however, also become sharply critical of Luther and the Lutheran Church generally. In a 1936 article on "The Religious Situation in Germany Today," for instance, he attacks Luther's split between the religious and political sphere as contributing to the general political impotence of the church in the present struggle. Pressing social issues concerning the Jews, communism, even sterilization are perceived by most as purely political issues, the concern of the state for which the church as such as no responsibility.[152] He concludes with the hope that, despite all, this experience will in the end result in a "powerful community of human beings, races and confessions, the overcoming of their differences, the resistance against antisemitism, against the antichristian and antihumanistic spirit."[153]

These themes became ever more pronounced in Tillich's speeches and writings during the war years: in his more than a hundred religious-political addresses to the German people broadcast over the Voice of America between 1942 and 1945; his numerous political reflections in a short-lived New York journal *The Protestant* between 1941 and 1942 in which "He discussed war aims, stressed the allied Western nations' responsibility for Nazism because of the burden that the Versailles Treaty and war reparations had placed on Germany after 1919, and emphasized the need not only to conquer Nazism but to begin the construction of a new world order—indeed a world federation."[154]

149. Pauck, *Tillich: Life*, p. 196. Tillich himself states: "Nach fünf Jahren des Schweigens greife ich zum ersten Mal wieder in einer öffentlichen Versammlung diejenigen an, die ich für die wahren Feinde der deutschen Seele halte, die an einem Reich bauen, aber das Reich der Gerechtigkeit und Wahrheit zugrunde richten. Ich möchte mich dürch das, was ich sage, für das wahre Deutschland verbürgen." Tillich, "Die Bedeutung des Antisemitismus," *GW* XIII, p. 219. First appeared as "German Americans Take Stand For Democracy Against Nazis," in *German People's Echo*, 2, 48(1938), pp. 1-2.
150. Tillich, "Die Bedeutung des Antisemitismus," p. 216.
151. *Ibid.*, pp. 218-219.
152. Tillich, "Die Religiöse Lage im Heutigen Deutschland," *GW* XIII, pp. 228-229.
153. Tillich, "Die Bedeutung des Antisemitiomus," p. 220.
154. Pauck, *Tillich: Life*, pp. 200-201.

He helped to found and was the chairman of the ill-fated Council for a Democratic Germany, made up entirely of a diverse group of German fugitives from National Socialism intent on planning for post-war German reconstruction, but who could not agree with one another, an involvement for which Tillich was ironically blacklisted by the U.S. Army for a short period of time in 1945.[155] Tillich experienced some disillusionment with active politics after the war. The proposals of Tillich and the "Council for a Democratic Germany" for moderation and the post-war reconstruction of Germany along democratic lines were rebuffed by President Roosevelt.[156] He felt that a "sacred void" had replaced the time of kairos, concluding, as Pauck puts it, "that his program of religious socialism was too romantic for the times and that a more realistic way of living expectantly and hopefully in a vacuum had to be accepted."[157] According to Stone, Tillich's vision toward the end of World War II was basically the same as it had been during the Weimar Republic—against "totalitarian heteronomy" and for a "theonomous culture" that affirmed "autonomous humanity."[158] But he had become more pessimistic about the possibility of the *kairos* in the face of the demonic split between East and West, and his writings became less political focussing more on social and ethical questions, "Particularly, he displayed only a moderate interest in American politics. His religious-socialist vision was grounded in German interwar politics and was alien to the times of postwar American politics."[159]

Spiritual Emigration
As alluded to above, emigration became a metaphor not only for Tillich's physical existence between home and native land, but also a religious metaphor for Tillich's spiritual and intellectual life. In a 1936 address before the "American Committee for German Christian Refugees" he made the following appeal:

> I would like to close with an appeal to support emigration, be it for the sake of Christian love, moral indignation, or political conviction. But behind all these reasons there should be the recognition that emigration is a religious category, which applies to every Christian; for it points to the majesty of God and the exclusiveness of his demand that people at certain times ought to tear themselves away from home and family, homeland and nation, and all other

155. For a good overview of this period in Tillich's life, see Pauck, *Tillich: Life*, pp. 196-206; primary documents related to a variety of topics including "Council for a Democratic Germany," as collected in *GW* XIII, pp. 253-328; and his political speeches to his friends in Germany gathered together in a supplement to *GW* III.

156. Stone, *Paul Tillich's Radical Social Thought*, p. 112.

157. Pauck, *Tillich: Life*, p. 206. See also Tillich, "Autobiographical Reflections," p. 19.

158. Stone, *Tillich's Radical Social Thought*, p. 111.

159. *Ibid.*, p. 113. John Stumme makes a similar point in his *Socialism in Theological Perspective*, pp. 250-253.

things on this earth.[160]

In a similar vein, in a 1937 speech to the graduate faculty of the New School for Social Research, Tillich maintained that "between wandering and the spirit there exists not only an accidental but an essential relationship;" that "to wander belongs to the nature of the spirit," and that "it is a primal law of life simultaneously to remain steadfastly within oneself and to transcend oneself, at the same time to cultivate one's own and to estrange oneself from oneself."[161] Tillich also struck this theme in some of his war-time radio broadcasts to the German people in which he "encouraged them to emigrate spiritually, called them to a quiet and open resistance to National Socialism and contended instead for Germany's spiritual, religious and ethical 'rebirth' on behalf of and within a national community."[162]

This metaphor of emigration to describe the whole of life, the existence between one's own and that which is foreign to one, what Tillich frequently calls standing "on the boundary" or "on the frontier" between two equally alluring alternatives, is what perhaps most clearly separated him from Emanuel Hirsch and the later's unqualified allegiance to one's own—family, nationality, and country—the unavoidable God-given boundary ("boundary" now understood very differently from Tillich's usage of it) of all human existence. It is Tillich's concept of the "spiritual emigre," which characterized his life and attitudes long before his "physical emigration" from National Socialist Germany to North America, that lies at the basis of his very different perspective on politics, the Jewish question, the ecumenical movement, and the nation.

Why is it then that in 1933, in a letter to Tillich dated April 4, 1933 (some two months after Hitler had become chancellor of Germany), Hirsch expresses regret at Tillich's departure from the University of Frankfurt and at what he considers to be the curtailment of Tillich's intellectual evolution toward National Socialism evident in his last book (*The Socialist Decision*)? Hirsch suggests in this letter that Tillich really belongs to National Socialism even if he does not yet realize it, could have become a significant intellectual leader in the movement, and urges Tillich not to be led astray but to take his place where he truly belongs: the new Germany.[163] This appears to have been the last direct contact between Hirsch and Tillich until 1948 when Tillich visited Hirsch in Göttingen, except indirectly through a short congratulatory note from Mrs. Hirsch (Rose) dated July 10, 1935, on the occasion of the birth of Tillich's son.[164]

160. Tillich, "Christentum und Emigration," *GW* XIII, p. 190.
161. Tillich, "Geist und Wanderung," *GW* XIII, p. 191.
162. "Vorwort des Verlags," *An meine deutschen Freunde: Politische Reden*, supplement to *GW* III, p. 9.
163. Personal letter, Hirsch to Tillich, April 14, 1933.
164. Personal letter, Rose Hirsch to Tillich, July 10, 1935.

One approach to Hirsch's enigmatic letter of 1933 is simply to dismiss it as a gross misreading of Tillich's book. This does not take seriously the fact that Emanuel Hirsch probably knew Tillich's theology better than most having apparently read carefully virtually everything that Tillich had written and followed his career closely from the beginning as a personal friend and intellectual confidante. A more persuasive explanation is that there were in fact certain aspects of Tillich's thought that were similar to themes in Hirsch's own theology and usable by National Socialists themselves. This, as we have seen, is suggested by Tillich himself in his January 20, 1934 letter from New York to the Ministry for Science, Art and Education in Berlin. This would also help to explain the charges of plagiarism that Tillich levels against Hirsch in their 1934-1935 debate.

We will have opportunity in later chapters to look more comprehensively at these charges and counter-charges, and the differences and similarities, between Tillich's and Hirsch's theology. Here we want to touch on only one particular issue which may have led Hirsch to perceive Tillich as moving in his thinking toward National Socialist ideology: Tillich's view of nation and the myth of origin. A superficial reading of Tillich would suggest that Tillich's anti-National Socialism and 1933 exile to the United States, his dispute with his friend Hirsch, and his strong espousal of the socialist principle of universal human solidarity all entail an unambiguous rejection of all forms of nationalism. This is, however, to ignore some of the romantic elements in Tillich's thought which give him a great appreciation for those elements of rootedness in nature that are sometimes referred to as the "powers" or "myths" of origin, and an ambivalent "Yes" and "No" stance to modernity.[165] This provocative thesis and what this implies for a certain openness "not to the National Socialism of the terrorizing bands of brownshirts...but to National Socialism as an expression of

---

165. I have discussed this theses at some length in two essays of mine: "Nation and the Myth of Origin in Paul Tillich's Radical Social Thought," *Consensus: A Canadian Lutheran Journal of Theology*, 14, 2(1988), pp. 35-48; and "Paul Tillich's Theology of Culture—An Ambivalence Toward Nineteenth-Century 'Culture Protestantism'," *Religion et Culture*, ed. Michael Despland, Jean-Claude Petit, and Jean Richard (Quebec: Les Presses de L'Universite Laval Les Editions Du Cerf, 1987). Ronald Stone in his excellent analysis of Tillich's social and political thought in my view does not adequately account for this romantic element in Tillich's thought which make his relation to National Socialism more ambiguous than would at first appear. Stone accurately acknowledges that Tillich in his *The Socialist Decision* and other writings recognized that "the importance of loyalties to soil, blood, tradition, and social group had to be taken seriously" and that "socialism must affirm the nation more deeply than any nationalist ideology (*Tillich's Radical Social Thought*, p. 80)." He does not, however, show how there is in fact a deeper ambiguity within Tillich's thought which attracts him both to a romantic rejection of modernity, on the one hand, and a full affirmation of modern autonomous rational culture on the other, an ambiguity that is present in National Socialism itself. Consequently, Stone in his brief discussion of the Tillich-Hirsch debate of 1934-1935, does not account for why it was that Hirsch's categories sounded so much like Tillich's. He simply takes Tillich's word for it: the by now familiar accusation by Tillich that Hirsch had plagiarized his Religious Socialist categories and distorted them (pp. 87-89).

protest by mythical powers against a world which has lost its supporting ground" has been persuasively argued by East German scholar Detlef Döring.[166] We have seen earlier how Hirsch and his comrades Kittel and Althaus had an underlying ambivalence toward the Enlightenment, seeing it as responsible for the crisis and disintegration of value cohesiveness in the modern world. Theirs was not a simple rejection of the Enlightenment, however, as is especially evident in the thought of Emanuel Hirsch. Hirsch welcomed enthusiastically the scientific and rational enlightenment but opposed political and cultural modernism, a tension which characterized his life-work. His theology was a fusion of theological liberalism and political conservatism, and he saw himself as moving not back to a golden age of the past but forward to a new age, to a new synthesis in which the old political categories of left, right, centre—socialist, conservative, and liberal—were superceded. Tillich had some of the same ambivalence toward the Enlightenment and the modern world, as Döring points out. Tillich in his view of religion and culture, and particularly his view of theonomy, affirms the Enlightenment rational autonomy from the bondage of traditional authoritarianism and myths of origin, while at the same time recognizing the emptiness of pure formal autonomy and calling for a recovery of the myth of origin or what he sometimes calls religion as the priestly-sacramental substance of culture.

When one looks at his writings in the 1920s and early 1930s one is struck precisely by this combination of romantic and rational elements in his thought. What we find in these essays is a strong commitment to socialism but within this socialist decision a desire to retain romantic elements. Take his 1924 essay "Christentum, Sozialismus und Nationalismus," a highly critical warning to the conservative Wingolf student organization not to fall back into an unmediated pre-Christian identification of German bourgeois morality and nationality and Protestant Christianity.[167] What is interesting about this early essay is that although he unambiguously espouses political socialism, he, nevertheless, leaves positive room for family, *Volk* (the nation) and *Stand* (station in life). He argues

166. Detlef Döring, *Christentum und Faschismus: Die Faschismusdeutung der religiösen Sozialisten* (Berlin: Verlag W. Kohlhammer, 1982), pp. 36-37. In the words of Döring, "In dieser Gebrochenheit liegt Tillichs zwischen Bejahung und Verneinung schwankende Haltung gegenüber der Moderne begründet....Das führt Tillich nicht nur, wie schon erwähnt, in die Nähe der durch solche Begriffe wie Irrationalismus, Lebensphilosophie, Konservative Revolution zu kennzeichnenden, alle Lebensgebiete umfassenden Gegenbewegung zur modernen Welt, sondern schuf auch eine gewisse zeitweise Aufgeschlossenheit dem Nationalsozialismus gegenüber. Nur ist dabei nicht der Nationalsozialismus der terrorisierenden braunen Haufen gemeint, sondern der Nationalsozialismus als Ausdruck des Protestes mythischer Mächte gegen eine unerträglich gewordene Welt. Im weiteren wird es unsere Aufgabe sein, das Gegeneinander und Ineinander der beiden Prägungen, der mythischen und der rationalen, in groben Zügen innerhalb der Arbeiten Tillichs aus der Zei vor 1933 zu verfolgen, immer schon mit dem Blick auf seine spätere Faschismusdtheorie."

167. Tillich, "Christentum, Sozialismus und Nationalismus: Eine Auseinandersetzung mit der 'Marburger Erklärung' des Wingolf," *GW* XIII, pp. 161-166.

that the bourgeois spirit is also evident in vulgar Marxism, emptying corporate reality of all spiritual substance, reifying and rationalizing human relationships and destroying all immediate communal relationships embodied in family, nationality and station. Tillich makes the provocative point that Religious Socialism is committed to the struggle against these destructive forces of capitalism in relation to the nation, and thus is bound not only to political socialism but also to what he calls "religiously-grounded national movements;" even though in the end Religious Socialism cannot join these national renewal movements because they do not go to the root of the evil. They continue, without wanting to, to support the basic capitalistic attitude.[168] What becomes clear in this essay is that Tillich, while clearly opting for political socialism, still retains some ambivalence toward national renewal movements, because these movements correctly perceive the loss in capitalist society of something valuable— the irrational and mythical substance of individual and corporate existence—in a way that doctrinaire Marxists in Germany do not.

These same themes are taken up again in two articles which appeared in 1932 and 1933, in the context of the triumph of National Socialism and the Third Reich: "Protestantismus und Politische Romantik [1932]" and "Das Wohnen, der Raum und die Zeit [1933]." In the first of these he identifies two poles which characterize creatureliness and humanness: the "wherefrom (Woher)" or origin of human existence whereby human beings know themselves to be carried by a ground (tragenden Grund); and the "whereto (Wozu)" of human existence in which human beings perceive themselves as subject to a demand, an ought, as being directed toward a future goal. The first of these makes *space* primary and the second *time*.

What is interesting is Tillich's insistence that both of these primals are absolutely necessary moments of human existence: "We always stand within the origin, and we always have to tear ourselves away from it."[169] The problem with what Tillich calls *political romanticism* is its "attempt to return to the myth of origin on the basis of a broken myth of origin;"[170] that is, it uses the tools of the Enlightenment to recover that which has been broken by the Enlightenment. This is particularly the case with the second of two kinds of political romanticism. The first, *Conservative political romanticism*, is against anything new and wants simply to sanctify the old. It is represented by groups such as the farmers and farm-related craftsmen, the nobility, the military, the priests and certain segments of the civil service. The second, *revolutionary political romanticism* (with which Tillich identifies National Socialism and presumably also Hirsch's views) is represented by those groups which have been completely assimilated into the rational system but still yearn longingly for the powers of the origin, a

168. *Ibid.*, p. 164.
169. Tillich, "Prostestantismus und Politische Romantik," *GW* II, p. 209.
170. *Ibid.*, p. 210.

remythologization of consciousness. For the petit bourgeoisie and large sections of the myth-of-origin groups which have been disenfranchized by the economic crisis, political romanticism takes on this revolutionary character.

What is significant in this latter group is that for them the rational system has won the day and broken tradition. Technological reason is affirmed, however, only as long as it is useful. As soon as the dark side of capitalism manifests itself in the creation of a proletariat, this form of political romanticism rejects the rational system in favor of the myth of origin. The strength of political romanticism is its true recognition that being human depends upon being carried by a ground, a realization that becomes especially powerful at a time when the rational system and unfettered autonomy are in a state of crisis. The contradiction within political romanticism is that it ultimately depends on the destruction of the rational system and ends in chaos. This is what Tillich sees as the danger of National Socialism.

The romantic elements in Tillich's radical social thought are most remarkably present in the second of the above articles: "Das Wohnen, der Raum und die Zeit [Habitation, Space and Time]." All three concepts—*Wohnen* (to live in a house, to have a home), space and time—are given positive value, although in the end time is given priority. Space takes on meaning only as understood in its concrete diversity, as it relates to inanimate objects, plants, animals and human beings. To have and create space is the way everything that lives comes into existence and space takes on a primal and holy quality, particularly that space which has the character of preservation (*der Tragenden*), the ground (*Boden*). One's own house, the neighbor's house, village, city, country, and *Volk* (nation or nationality) all participate in the sanctity of space which gives us our existence.[171]

There are themes here which have a similar ring to some of Hirsch's views as we have seen them expressed in essays such as "Vom verborgenen Suverän," also published in 1933. There is, however, a difference; and that difference has to do with the priority of time over space. While time can never annual space—in fact, time becomes present for us only within space—we have again and again to forsake space for the sake of the future. Abraham was called to leave his living space (*Lebensraum*) for an unknown future and in this becomes the symbol for all of humankind. This is an especially important symbol during the present socio-political struggle, Tillich reminds his readers in 1933, when the gods and the power of limited space resist the breaking out into all-comprehensive space, the space of all of humankind. In other words, as we saw at he beginning of this discussion on Tillich, physical and spiritual emigration have greater theological and political significance for Tillich than allegiance to one's own. What is remarkable, nevertheless, particularly in the context of the times in which he is writing, and especially noteworthy in the light of his

---

171. Tillich, "Das Wohnen, der Raum und die Zeit," *GW* IX, p. 331.

struggle with Hirsch, is the weight he does give to the powers of origin, expressed in this second essay in terms of *Wohnen* and *Lebensraum*.

We will have occasion to discuss in greater detail some of these themes and the importance Tillich places on the myth of origin as the true origin, conceived by him more in terms of future goal (Telos) than a golden age of the past, when we consider his most comprehensive political work of the period *The Socialist Decision* in a later chapter. Our brief excursion into some of the shorter writings of Tillich, considered in the context of the political events that pushed Tillich out of his beloved country into a foreign land, help to explain why it was that the conflict between him and his friend Hirsch was so bitter. The line between them was clear on one level. We have listed their differences on matters concerning National Socialism, the Jews, the ecumenical movement, just to name a few. There is no doubt that Tillich's prophetic-eschatological theology, which put a premium on time and emigration over space and rootedness, distinguished his thinking in a fundamental way from Hirsch's two-kingdom theology, which made room for an unqualified allegiance to national ethos. Underneath these more obvious lines of demarcation, however, there were subterranean levels which bound these two men together personally, theologically and politically.

4

An Epilogue:
Years of Separation
and Intimations of Reconciliation

Contrasting Post-War Reputations

After the war years Tillich travelled, wrote, lectured, and taught at the major theological schools and universities in America.[1] In the process his own theology underwent a subtle shift. His earlier attention to theology and politics, particularly his attempt to bring together the insights of Marxism and Christianity, turned more and more into a preoccupation with theology and therapeutic psychology. While he retained an interest in social and political issues, there seems to have been some disillusionment with politics, reflected in his American writings which tend to focus more and more on psychology and systematic theology.[2]

Hirsch's career took an entirely different course. His 1945 resignation from the University of Göttingen, where he had taught for 24 years, brought his official university teaching career to an end. He wrote profusely, even after blindness struck in 1946, almost to the end of his life in 1972, including numerous short stories and novels.[3] While Tillich was acclaimed throughout America and

1. He taught at Union Theological Seminary, 1933-55, Harvard University and Divinity School, 1955-62, and University of Chicago, 1962-65.

2. According to Pauck, Tillich's one significant political involvement in the United States was his provisional chairmanship of the Council for a Democratic Germany, founded in 1944 and existing up to September 1945, an organization which was for a period falsely labelled as pro-Communist, and because of which Tillich was for a short while blacklisted by the U.S. army. Pauck says this experience frightened Tillich from further active political involvement in America and adds: "After the war he felt the tragic more than the elevating elements of historical existence and lost the inspiration and interest for active politics. By then, also, he had come to feel that he was far from an effective understanding of American political problems.... He announced that the productive time, the *kairos*, was over, that a 'sacred void' existed, and that mankind must content itself with a period of expectant waiting. From then on Tillich's thinking emphasized an old interest of his, namely, depth psychology, which unlike his dabbling in politics bore rich fruit; and he devoted himself almost entirely to the writing of his *Systematic Theology." Tillich: Life*, pp. 205-206.

3. Hirsch's *magnum opus, Geschichte der neuern evangelischen Theologie im Zusammenhang mit den allgemeinen Bewegungen des europäischen Denkens* (Gütersloh: Bertelsmann. Band 1, 1949; Band 2, 1951; Band 3, 1951; Band 4, 1952; Band 5, 1954), was written by Hirsch essentially

Europe, after the war Hirsch became more and more isolated from theological circles and from interaction with scholarly peers. His close identification with National Socialism, the "German Christians," and the *Reichskirche* in the 1930s brought him defamation of character and intellect. As a result at age 58, the age when other theologians—like Tillich—began reaping the reward of long hard academic labor, Hirsch was fated to spend his declining years alone and relatively isolated at his 66 Hainholzweg dwelling in Göttingen with a small group of private students and friends. It was only after repeated and persistent requests by students like Hayo Gerdes, eager to study privately with Hirsch, that he began in the 1950s to conduct weekly Thursday evening seminars in his private residence.[4]

The Renewal of a Relationship

Not until June 12, 1948, when Tillich made his first post-war visit to Germany, did he re-establish contact with Hirsch, of which we have a verbal report recorded by Pauck and at least two first-hand retrospective accounts by Hirsch himself.[5] While the 1948 visit appears to have been the only lengthy and substantive face-to-face encounter between them, we know of at least one rather

during the war years—begun in autumn of 1941 and completed in late summer of 1946 but published in five volumes between 1949 and 1954. See personal letter, Buff to Reimer, September 20, 1979. For a comprehensive list of Hirsch's major theological writings, editions of works, translations, and novels during the war years and after his 1946 blindness, see *Bibliographie Emanuel Hirsch 1888-1972*, pp. 10-13.

4. Being now totally blind, he selected certain students to help him prepare for these evening seminars by reading Schleiermacher, Hegel, and other theological classics. At the evening seminar he would lecture from memory up to three hours at a time. For information on the nature of these evening classes I am indebted to conversations with post-war students of Hirsch: the late Hayo Gerdes (June 6, 1978), Joachim Ringleben (June 6, 1978), Horst Renz (May 23, 1978), and Hans-Walter Schütte (May 18, 1978), among others.

5. Marion Pauck, relying largely on reflections by Gertraut Stöber and Paul Tillich, describes the visit in the following terms: "It was in many ways the most moving meeting of the summer. Hirsch stood waiting for Tillich in his Göttingen garden. He was almost entirely blind, very old, his hair uncombed. The two men talked of their work, Hirsch's family, his blindness, the loss of a son in Yugoslavia. Hirsch still clung to his belief that Hitler had been sent to create a unified German nation. His forced retirement and reduced pension caused by his Nazi sympathies embittered him. Despite all, he had continued to be enormously productive, a feat Tillich admired. Their farewell was particularly moving for Hirsch, who wrote Tillich later in the year how often he thought of their meeting, and thanked him for the gifts he had brought: a bottle of wine, two bars of chocolate, and a piece of soap." *Tillich: Life,* p. 214. It is not clear from Pauck's account how much of it is first-hand by Tillich himself and how much of it is second-hand, dependent upon Frau Stöber's report. It is also not clear when these reflections by Tillich and Stöber were made. It should be added here that there is at least one inaccuracy in the above account. Hirsch had two sons. The oldest, Peter, fell in Russia, and the youngest, Hans, now professor in Aachen, was taken a prisoner of war in Yugoslavia. Cf. Personal letter, Buff to Reimer, November 7, 1981.

lengthy telephone conversation initiated by Tillich at the time of his receipt of the Goethe prize in Hamburg in 1958 and another short personal courtesy visit.

What Hirsch says about these three direct contacts is highly interesting and informative about how he perceived his relationship with Tillich. In a June 19, 1948 letter to Hans Grimm, Hirsch describes the first visit, which had taken place six days earlier.[6] He calls Tillich a friend of his youth who has always been an internationalist and now has become completely American, having emigrated to the United States in 1935 (actually it was 1933), where he now teaches at one of the foremost American theological schools. Tillich, he says, offended him greatly in 1934 because of his hatred for the political events in Germany, but he now—in this visit—rectified these old matters. Both he and Tillich felt the strong bond of common memories and youthful ambitions. But, says Hirsch, the visit remained a conversation between a member of a conquered nation and one from a victorious one. During this meeting Tillich, according to Hirsch, spoke as if East Germany were lost to Russia and suggested that Hirsch too write off East Germany. Tillich advocated that West Germany accept a colonial-like dependence on America, particularly industrially. The only chance for West Germany was to accept this kind of dependent relationship in which Germans would be able to acquire the basic necessities of life. The conversation, remembers Hirsch, was conducted with civility; Tillich's attitude represented merely a sober acceptance of world realities rather than great moral passion. Tillich seemed to feel that humanity could, after all, learn something positive from it all once the horrors of the events could be forgotten.

In a reflective 1970 letter to his friend and long-time acquaintance Walter Buff, Hirsch writes a lengthy account of his three post-1945 encounters with Tillich and makes some rather telling observations about his relationship to Tillich and their personal and theological differences through the years.[7] The first and only substantive face-to-face visit after 1945, Hirsch recounts, occurred in mid-June 1948 and was arranged by a mutual friend. Tillich wanted to make amends for his 1934 article against Hirsch. Hirsch says he himself had always cast a certain spell over Tillich whenever the two of them were alone for a number of hours. This now happened again. Tillich's continual need to be recognized as a significant person and theologian faded. He talked about the

---

6. Personal letter, Emanuel Hirsch to Hans Grimm, June 19, 1948. Hans Grimm Archiv, Lippoldsberg-Weser, provided by Walter Buff. The fact that this letter was written by Hirsch himself so soon after the visit adds particular weight to its credibility, even though it is obviously a one-sided perspective.

7. Personal letter, Hirsch to Buff, August 3, 1970. This letter written by Hirsch two years before his own death, is a response to a letter by Buff to Hirsch, August 2, 1970. Because of its importance not only in giving us information about the contacts between Tillich and Hirsch after 1945 but also because of the insights it gives us into Hirsch's own thinking toward the end of his life about the nature of his relationship to Tillich over the years, we have paraphrased its contents here at some length.

world political situation, admitted that the whole propaganda campaign against Hitler's Germany was nothing other than a necessary guise with which to persuade the public, and admitted that the allies had much to answer for. The allies had desired and prepared for the war; to claim simply that Germany, intent on conquering the world, had begun the war was nonsense.

Tillich maintained, however, that Germany bore major responsibility and guilt for the war and also claimed that Hirsch himself shared in this guilt. He expressed the belief that it was God's will that in the present historical moment America and its allies ought to rule the world under the umbrella of American democracy. Germany had struggled against this American imposition of its form of democracy on the world and had thereby resisted the will of God and forced the allies into a war. The consequence was a legitimate punishing of Germany through the destruction of her political independence. When Hirsch asked Tillich how he reconciled his present defense of an American form of democracy with his earlier religious Marxism, Tillich replied that in America he had learned the meaning of middle principles. These middle principles allowed capitalism and socialism to coexist and adjust to each other until a democratic form of socialist society could evolve. Tillich maintained that he had remained true to his 1919 ideal but that he now recognized that capitalist democracy was a means to that ideal.

In the same letter to Buff, Hirsch refers to one more brief encounter, when Tillich paid him a courtesy visit as part of a tour. The visit lasted for only ten minutes. On this occasion Tillich spent much more time with other political friends in Göttingen than he did with Hirsch. The third more extensive conversation took place on the telephone in 1958 when Tillich received his Goethe prize in Hamburg and called Hirsch from his Hamburg hotel. The talk lasted for one-and-a-half hours and was, according to Hirsch, personally very tender. Hirsch gathered that it was a farewell call and that Tillich would never again visit him. Apparently, highly personal matters were discussed which Hirsch refused to divulge in his letter to Buff. Nevertheless, Hirsch does allude to an interesting theological aspect of the telephone conversation. Tillich had asked Hirsch what he thought about his theology and philosophy. Hirsch replied candidly, saying that he considered Tillich's thought to be a cultural philosophy vaccinated with selected elements of Evangelical theology, intended to save modern culture by secretly infusing it with religious and Christian ideas before its imminent and inevitable demise. For Tillich, Hirsch had told him, Christianity was good for little more than to fertilize a modernity in crisis. Tillich is to have responded by laughing heartily, adding that Hirsch was still as vulgarly mean to him as in the old youthful days, but that Hirsch's appraisal of him was essentially right.

Hirsch concludes his letter to Buff by making some general reflections about Tillich's theological and philosophical writings. First of all Hirsch admits feeling that sometimes in Tillich's later writings some of his own (Hirsch's) earlier ideas seem to reappear, and that generally there were many similarities in their thought due to their common early history. But, secondly, Hirsch holds that there was always a deep religious difference between them, something he had not sufficiently emphasized in his earlier debate with Tillich. He recalls that in one of their conversations after 1945 Tillich told Hirsch that his (Hirsch's) whole intellectual freedom was merely an illusion. Tillich had charged Hirsch with being heteronomous in his thinking because he considered the historical Jesus as Lord and Savior. Tillich, in contrast, rather than emphasizing the decisive importance of Jesus himself for personal life, stressed the spiritual, intellectual, and inspirational nature of the Bible as a whole, including the Old Testament. Tillich saw the Bible as a compendium of the whole human history of religion, the bearer of all of the important religious moments on the way toward the rational human culture of the future. Tillich put more weight than he himself on the importance of the prophetic message that God is always a political will, moving the world toward a future kingdom. According to Tillich, anyone who stresses this universal, many-sided nature of the Bible as the principle of intellectual-spiritual life is truly autonomous. Tillich felt that he (Hirsch) was a hoodwinked pietist wearing an autonomous mask. Hirsch concludes his letter to Buff by suggesting to the latter that he read the annotation in his (Hirsch's) edition of Schleiermacher's dogmatic sermons, where Schleiermacher maintains against Fichte and Hegel that he is a free servant of Christ. On this point, Hirsch adds, he considers himself on the side of Schleiermacher rather than Tillich.[8]

8. The rather important annotation that Hirsch is referring to here is from "Friedrich Schleiermacher, Dogmatische Predigten der Reifezeit, ausgewählt und erläutert," in *Friedrich Schleiermacher, Kleine Schriften und Predigten,* edited by Hayo Gerdes and Emanuel Hirsch, Vol. 3 (Berlin, 1969). Here Hirsch says: "The fine, profound analysis of a relationship to Jesus, in which we see ourselves as his 'free servants,' distinguishes the Christianity of Schleiermacher—which for him makes the freely affirmed inward dependence on the life and person of the historical redeemer into the genuine shape of religious autonomy—from radical autonomy, e.g., from Fichte's understanding of Christianity.... Fichte would have despised the inner personal binding of Schleiermacher to the redeemer as a servitude not worthy of man. The 'free servant' of Christ, that Schleiermacher wanted to be, would have been for him [Fichte] a heteronomous form-of-the-spirit deformed through superstition. The separation from Fichte, which is completed here by Schleiermacher, signifies obviously also a separation from Hegel and from vulgar liberal Protestantism. Schleiermacher would have certainly said no to Bultmann as well as Tillich and calmly borne the charge of hidden heteronomy which these would have had to make against him" p. 349, n. 4.

Final Contacts, 1948-1963

We have only a few extant letters from Hirsch to Tillich, and one from Tillich to Hirsch, from the latter years of their lives. Pauck cites an October 1948 letter by Hirsch, in which he thanks Tillich for the gifts of wine, chocolate, and soap and for his mid-June visit.[9] Ten years later we have a letter, written by Hirsch in July 1958, which is largely concerned with exchanging some of their books.[10] Later that same month, Hirsch writes Tillich a letter referring to books sent and received, adding a few remarks about their theological and philosophical-historical differences.[11] The one letter by Tillich, written from a Hamburg motel and dated July 12, 1958, is also a largely inconsequential note about books received and the difficulty of arranging a visit.[12] The last letter we have of Hirsch to Tillich is dated February 17, 1963. It is written in a highly conciliatory spirit and poignantly refers to some of their differences in style, to his own deep life-long love and affection for Tillich, although often entailing candid criticism, and to one of his earliest recollections of visiting Tillich—a visit to the latter's bedside in Berlin in November 1907.[13]

This completes our biographical portrait of Tillich and Hirsch from the time of their first meeting sometime early in 1907, until 1970—the last written reflection by Hirsch on Tillich that we have in our hands, some five years after Tillich's death and two years before Hirsch's death. In the process we have introduced all the main issues and assumptions—similarities as well as differences—that find more concentrated expression in their public debate of 1934-35, the political and theological nature of which remain to be more critically examined in subsequent chapters. One overwhelming conclusion that one arrives at after looking at these remarkable thinkers over the span of a lifetime is that despite their deep personal, political, and theological differences, their friendship and admiration for each other remained intact, enduring all the

9. Personal letter, Hirsch to Tillich, October 16, 1948. See Pauck, *Tillich: Life*, p. 318, n. 44. Pauck adds: "Hirsch was the only one of nearly fifty German friends and relatives of Paul Tillich who refused to be interviewed for this volume, for he was incapable of compromise. He knew he would have to tell the whole truth or nothing, and was hesitant to divulge what he knew of Tillich's private life to anyone."

10. Personal letter, Hirsch to Tillich, July 3, 1958.

11. Personal letter, Hirsch to Tillich, July 9, 1958. He says in the letter that after much thought he has decided to send Tillich a small work of his on the Old Testament, *Das Alte Testament und die Predigt des Evangeliums*. Hirsch adds that he considers this book to be central in isolating the fundamental theological, Christological, and philosophical-historical differences between them. He considers himself more of a Lutheran than Tillich, influenced by Schleiermacher, Kierkegaard, and Wilhelm Herrmann, and sees the Old Testament and the New Testament as separated by a large gulf. Tillich he perceives to have Anglo-Saxon Calvinist leanings, influenced by Martin Kähler, and someone who sees biblical religion as more of a unity.

12. Personal letter, Tillich to Hirsch, July 12, 1958. This must have been about the same time that Tillich and Hirsch had the lengthy hour-and-a-half telephone conversation.

13. Personal letter, Hirsch to Tillich, February 17, 1963.

vicissitudes of life, poignantly expressed in visits, conversations, and reflections after 1945, particularly toward the end of their lives. There is reflected in the fate of this particular friendship, torn apart by political events in the homeland, the fateful rupture within the German nation itself during the years of social crisis.

PART TWO

POLITICAL ETHICS AND THEOLOGICAL PRESUPPOSITIONS

5
World War I
and the Early Political Formation
of Hirsch and Tillich

In Part One we dealt broadly with the biographical and personal-intellectual aspects of Tillich's and Hirsch's development and friendship with each other. In Part Two we turn to a more specific examination of their political thought, best understood in its genesis and evolution within the social and political context of three main periods of German history: the war years, the "revolution" and the Weimar Republic, and finally the triumph of National Socialism. In previous chapters we alluded generally to the importance of Tillich's and Hirsch's different experiences during and interpretations of the First World War in the shaping of their political-theological thought—to a large extent foreshadowing their divergent political paths in the 1930s. In the present chapter we look more particularly at how World War I formed their subsequent outlook.

Tillich had little time for academic work during his four years as army chaplain on the western front. His substantive social-political writing began only after the war. It is possible, however, to construct his changing political attitudes during these years on the basis of his sermons, reports to superiors, and later autobiographical reflections on this time in his life. Hirsch, on the other hand, having been rejected for military service for health reasons, and despite his heavy pastoral and teaching duties, found time to reflect systematically on the war and on social and political questions facing the nation because of the war. These articles give us valuable insight into Hirsch's early political formation.

Hirsch's Early Reflections on War, Nation and State

War as a Holy Encounter with God
Hirsch's struggle with the question of "Germany's destiny" began in a short 1914 article, right at the start of the war, entitled "Unsere Frage an Gott," in which Hirsch sees war essentially as Germany's encounter with God and argues that to the extent that it is such it must be seen as a holy venture. A number of important themes in this early article are highly significant for and dominate Hirsch's political thought to the end of his life. It is clear that Hirsch has no

naive illusions about the romantic greatness of war as such. He is fully aware of the horror and suffering of war and its basic undesirability not only for one's own family and country but for peoples and families of other countries. "The war exists without our willing [it]," he says. "Now that it is here, however, we support it. We do everything we can to help our fatherland to victory, and demand of everyone that he employ all of his power on behalf of the threatened whole."[1] He is fully aware of the ambiguities of war for the Christian who believes that God is a God of peace for all humankind. Christians know that God is a God of peace who wants a kingdom of peace and love on this earth. They know that God is a God of the whole world, of the French, the Slavs, as well as of the Germans. They recognize the seeming contradiction in asking God's help for their own nation and not for the other side.

War occurs, however, when nations claim for themselves a place in the world. There exists no higher court of appeal than war in such circumstances, writes Hirsch. Only an appeal to weapons and force remains, which, if carried out with the proper intention (namely, as an appeal to God for his ultimate judgment), can with some legitimacy be called a "holy" venture: "A nation which grasps the sword, asks God whether God's eternal plan for humanity supports its espoused claim to power."[2] A sinful war is a war which arises out of a conscienceless, destructive intent, out of envy against other nations. While in smaller matters a nation may be willing to subordinate itself to others, in larger matters, where the very existence of a state is at stake, where its role in future world history is in question, it would be highly unethical and faithless for it to acquiesce and submit to others. It is through war that God decides the role of nations in history. In this sense there is nothing holier than a war carried on in the right spirit as an appeal to God, for it is in such a conflict that God decides a nation's destiny.[3]

1. Hirsch, "Unsere Frage an Gott," p. 370.
2. *Ibid.*, p. 371.
3. *Ibid.*, p. 372. A comparison with Tillich's views on the same subject is illuminating. While recognizing the importance of a pacifist witness within the universal church, Tillich rejects pacifism. See *Love, Power and Justice* (New York: Oxford University Press, 1954, 1960), pp. 122ff. Tillich describes the historic encounter and struggle between social groups and nations in the following way: "For every power group experiences growth and disintegration. It tries to transcend itself and to preserve itself at the same time. Nothing is determined *a priori*. It is a matter of trial, risk, and decision. And this trial has elements of intrinsic power united with compulsion whether the group or their representatives want it or not. These encounters are the basic material of history. In them man's political destiny is decided. What is their character? The basis of all power of a social group is the space it must provide for itself. Being means having space or, more exactly, providing space for oneself. This is the reason for the tremendous importance of geographic space and the fight for its possession by all power groups." *Ibid.*, p. 100. While Tillich here does not extol war as a means by which God decides the worthiness of nations, the way Hirsch does, still his analysis of the power struggle between nations for being and space, written of course many years later, is not that dissimilar from Hirsch's view.

In his defense of war that is fought in the right spirit, Hirsch tries to view with objectivity the fate of other nations. He says, in effect, that we cannot judge whether other nations, which are intent on destroying Germany, are carrying on the war in this right spirit or not. Speaking about these other nations Hirsch admits "...possibly our eyes have been blindfolded. Maybe it is the case that the role which God has, in their view, allotted them, can be actualized only when Germany no longer exists.... We, however, want to make sure that we Germans are able to conduct this war in the spirit of a holy war."[4] Germany, Hirsch feels, must struggle with God to the end. He is fully aware that in the end the Christian must hope for God's kingdom of peace at the end of history. This peace, however, will be fulfilled only when human understanding is complete, when all nations have come to an agreement among themselves concerning their true place in the whole of history. Till then each nation, including Germany, has the right to justify and defend its own understanding by appealing to God through the use of weapons, and through this to determine its God-given place in history.

A more comprehensive understanding of a Christian Lutheran view of nation, state, and war was developed by Hirsch during these years in three important articles: "Luthers Gedanken über Staat und Krieg [1916-17]," "Ein Christliches Volk [1918]," and "Der Pazifismus [1918]." The basic social and political theories developed in these three articles remained more or less constant for Hirsch for the rest of his life.

In the first of these, "Luthers Gedanken über Staat und Krieg," Hirsch outlines what he perceives to be Luther's understanding of state and war, one which he feels is with some elaboration applicable to the current situation.[5] The article is divided into four main sections: Luther's view of the Word of the gospel, Luther's understanding of the state and its use of the sword, Luther's concept of war as it grows out of his view of the state, and, finally, some general observations.

Luther's notion of the gospel applies to the individual conscience. Those who have been grasped by the Word of the gospel within their individual consciences have faith and stand within the *invisible* eternal kingdom of God. Out of this grows a new disposition, a voluntary doing of that which is good. Inwardly Christians are freed from the earth and its orders and are participants in a new community of voluntary love that requires no more law. The Christian as a child of God stands above but not against the state, doing on his own accord what the true state demands—maintaining peace, doing no one an injustice. In fact he does more: he loves and bears injustice. But it is precisely on this account that there is need for the state and the legitimate use of force.

---

4. "Unsere Frage an Gott," p. 372.
5. "Luthers Gedanken über Staat und Krieg," Sonderabdruck aus den *Wingolfs-Blättern* 46,7(January 1917), pp. 175-179.

The state and the office of the sword is an ordinance of God, since without the office of the sword the ill-nature of unregenerate humanity would transform the world into a hell. God has delegated to human beings a share of his own power. Christian morality is twofold: first, the Christian values freedom and rejects coercion, bearing injustice patiently; second, he values love, without which freedom would be impossible, a love which not only bears but also helps and serves. It is in this helping and serving function that love and the office of the sword in the hand of the state unite. God has called a few to carry out the office of the sword—the task to care for the life, honor, and good of many people. This is the calling of governmental authority. The state has the God-given duty to coerce, injure, even kill if necessary, when "peace" calls for it. The task of the state is to maintain peace amongst its subjects. The prince is not a person for himself but for others. The inner disposition of the prince as individual Christian is the same as that of any other Christian. He practises his special office out of love for those who are entrusted to him. Just as God requires clear proclamation from the preacher, he demands righteous and harsh judgment from the prince and his subordinates in magisterial offices. So for Luther the office of the bailiff, the executioner, and the preacher are equally honorable Christian callings.

Luther's concept of war, according to Hirsch, cannot be understood apart from his notion of the state and its legitimate function. The legitimacy of war is rooted in the legitimate office of the state. There are two conditions for a just war. First, it cannot be directed against governmental authority. Revolt is wrong. Unjust authority must be borne patiently and in love by Christians. A legitimate war can be fought only between two opposing independent states. The second condition is that war must arise out of the basic duty of the state to protect its subjects. In other words, it must be defensive. Luther rejects any war carried out on the basis of the personal motives of the prince for the sake of ambition or possessiveness. The enemy must already have drawn the sword before slaughtering can begin. Legitimate war is performed out of a service of love toward the neighbor, as is all true state-service, and is therefore the fulfillment of a holy duty.

In the final section of this important early essay, Hirsch makes some related observations illustrating Luther's conceptual achievements pertaining to nation, state, and war. Unlike the humanitarian or nineteenth-century ideal of culture, which saw in force the essential means for the advancement of the ethical-social ideal, Christian morality, says Hirsch, will always have to perceive state coercion as a problem and will find no other satisfying answer than that supplied by Luther. Ultimately, Christians whose view of force is shaped by Luther's theology will reject both the arguments of those Christians who reject war on Christian grounds, on the one hand, and those who enthusiastically support an international court of peace and justice equipped with coercive power, on the other.

Although Hirsch remains on the whole within the classic Just War tradition, at one point he appears to move beyond it—the right of a modern state to wage an offensive war under certain circumstances. In the above essay he admits to expanding Luther's theory of state and the use of force to fit the modern situation. Luther allowed only for a defensive war. What must be remembered, argues Hirsch, is that for Luther the concept of the state and the concept of war belong together, the state's essential function being the duty to preserve peace. In the contemporary world, however, the aim of the state has been expanded, demanding a rethinking of the concept of the just war. The new dimension that has been added to our understanding of the state since the time of Luther, according to Hirsch, is the concept of nationality (*Volksgedanken*). The state must be seen in the modern context as having the task of preserving the vitality of the nation, which includes the right to engage in more than a defensive war against other nations, narrowly defined.[6]

What is important in Luther's thought for us in the contemporary situation is that the legitimate aim of the state must also be the legitimate aim of war. Hirsch is aware that this elaboration of Luther's thought, which he believes remains true to Luther's intent, could be used by a conscienceless ruler to justify illegitimate wars. Ultimately there is only one way of preventing such a misuse of power, and that is that the prince brings a sensitive conscience to his task of ruling. The prince, according to Luther's theology, must place his view of state and war under the concept of duty and obedience. The question is not when war is *allowable*, but when war is a *duty*. Luther understood the work of war, as he did that of the state generally, in terms of obedience before a divine law; that is why he could see war as a divine work. The praising of war as a blessed and constructive power *per se* would have been foreign to Luther. Even war for the sake of duty was for him, speaking humanly, a great plague.

Finally, however, it must be remembered, says Hirsch, that for Luther the state was not the highest value. Inwardly, the Christian stands above the state and the nation. The Christian's only true home is the kingdom of God, in which everything is done voluntarily and out of love. This kingdom is already in some sense present as something hidden. Wherever there are genuine Christians, there the kingdom of God lives and grows. Eternity, with which the Christian is firmly bound up in his conscience, gives the Christian an inner disposition such that he does not lose himself and his soul to the state and to the world. This does not make the Christian into a weak citizen of the state, or worse, a secret enemy of the state. Luther was free of any such enthusiasm (*Schwärmerei*), which thinks of this world as possible without state order: "The kingdom of God is no cultural aim, achievable through human work, in some way able finally to replace the state. In this world the kingdom of God always remains

6. *Ibid.*, p. 177.

hidden, that which never becomes evident. The state is an indispensable order of creation and forces the hands of those whose hearts cannot be guided by the Word."[7] Even more important is the fact that precisely because the Christian is a child of God he will commit himself to the state: "To be Christian means loving and lovingly giving oneself to a resisting world. Where such a world-enduring and thereby world-overcoming love does not exist, there the hidden kingdom of God is still not alive."[8]

A Christian Nation-State

What is noteworthy about "Luthers Gedanken über Staat und Krieg" is the extent to which Hirsch formulates his view of the state, nation, and war on the basis of his understanding of Luther's theology and his willingness to expand and elaborate Luther's theology to meet the exigencies of the modern situation in which Germany finds itself. What this illustrates is the extent to which Hirsch's theology evolved contextually. His perception of the Christian nation finds further development in a second article, "Ein christliches Volk." He begins by addressing those who protest against the use of the term "Christian nation" on the grounds that only a minority of people within any nation have been grasped by the gospel within their conscience, and that the important distinction between even the best state and the kingdom of God must never be erased. Throughout his writings Hirsch himself is most concerned with keeping this distinction clear. He is quite ready to admit that a nation as such is not Christian but a pre-Christian reality: "National-community [*Volksgemeinschaft*] and a political system [*Staatsordnung*] will certainly never deny that in their roots they are pre-Christian. They belong to the works of God the creator and ruler, they are already granted to us through nature and history. Where people related to each other through blood and language are bound together through the common experience of fateful events [*Geschicke*] and the inspiration of common deeds, they become one nation and state. It is thus that we Germans became a people and a state. Thereby we fulfilled an earthly task given us by God. But we still have not made ourselves into Christians through this alone."[9]

Having said this, however, Hirsch goes on to defend the concept of a Christian nation, which he defines as a nation that has a "Christian-cultivated conscience [*christliche gebildetes Gewissen*]." The character of a nation is defined by that which it considers to be right. This general moral conscience is the great driving power in the life of the whole. Every nation has its own particular moral conscience, which can be either a right one or a distorted one. The life of the German nation, as that of other European nations, has been shaped largely by Christian values. One example of such a Christian value, deeply

---

7. *Ibid.*, p. 178.
8. *Ibid.*
9. "Ein christliches Volk," p. 164.

embedded in the German conscience, is the worth of every individual human being: "To mention at least one: we have a feeling for the infinite worth of the individual person. The personality of every individual stands before our conscience as something holy and inviolable, which also the state and its law cannot violate. This, however, we have learned from Christianity, that every person without distinction stands in free self-accountability before God [*Gott gegenüberstellt*] and thereby is granted a personal worth, that ultimately deprives [him] of the right to coerce the other."[10]

This is an example, says Hirsch, of how the German mind—its whole philosophy and worldview, its conscience—has been influenced by Christianity. In this sense Germany is a Christian nation and he calls Germans to exert every effort to keep Germany Christian and to make it ever more Christian in its ethos, for the conscience can change and the ethical demands of the gospel can easily disappear from the heart. Only through discipline and prayer can Germans remain what they are. Nevertheless, it is important to remember that the demands of the gospel can never be completely taken up into a nation's conscience. The gospel must remain the judge of a nation: "We have to make clear to ourselves and others that we have the right and the duty to judge legislation and public life in the name of the Christian conscience."[11] *The gospel can thus never be divorced from the political and social life of a people. The Christian must not limit himself to the winning of individuals to the Christian conscience, thinking that the morality of the mass will never be completely won over.* "If we stop being a Christian nation then the Christianity of even those who are serious about it [i.e. Christianity] will also remain unhealthy. And, contrariwise, the more we become a Christian nation the richer and deeper will true personal Christianity be able to develop."[12]

Pacifism: A Confusion of the Kingdom of Love and the Kingdom of Justice
In the third article, "Der Pazifismus," Hirsch much more systematically and substantially develops the themes touched upon in the first two.[13] The article is divided into three main sections: a systematic presentation of the basic assumptions of the pacifist ideal, a critique of those assumptions, and a defense of the right to wage a legitimate war. Pacifists, like their opponents, says Hirsch,

---

10. *Ibid.*, p. 165. This defense of the ultimate value of individual personality is important to remember, especially in the light of Hirsch's later defense of the totalitarian claims of National Socialism, which saw the worth of the nation as a whole as superceding the worth of the individual.

11. *Ibid.*, p. 166. It is not accurate to accuse Hirsch of being without criteria by which to judge the state and political movements within the state. The question is: What are these critical norms and are they adequate?

12. *Ibid.*

13. "Der Pazifismus," Sonderabdruck aus den *Wingolf-Blätter* (Mühlhausen: Paul Fischer, 1918), pp. 1-16. This essay was written during the period of the near-successful Ludendorff offensive.

recognize that any absolutizing of existing power relations would constitute an injustice. World peace presupposes that the boundaries between states are considered by each to be just and fair. Although, pacifism thus stands for the right of self-determination for all nations, disputes between nations are to be arbitrated by a world court. This presumes a world peace alliance in which all participating nations are to govern themselves through similar democratic forms. According to the pacifist vision, says Hirsch, only nations with a similar inner political structure can remain in peaceful fellowship with one another. This means, however, that such an international alliance for peace will presuppose common political, economic, legal, scientific, and cultural orders, erasing ever more the distinctions between peoples and nations.

According to Hirsch there are only two possibilities for humanity: either there is an emphasis on the diversity of nations and states leading to a diversity of life—something he himself espouses, or there is an evolving community (*Lebensgemeinschaft*) leading to a community of states (*Staatsgemeinschaft*). The pacifist ideal clearly leads to the latter—an international culture through a world peace alliance (*Weltfriedensbund*). What pacifists seem less ready to admit is the obvious conclusion to which their position must lead them: that groups and nations which do not share the same vision can be made members of this alliance only as subordinated colonial nations destined to remain dependent until they have been properly educated. While primitive nations with a relatively underdeveloped history and culture of their own might allow themselves to be thus dominated, more developed nations with a strong independent and unique spiritual and political identity will surely refuse to allow themselves to be thus subordinated and fused into a peace alliance. This is where the true limitation of the pacifist ideal becomes evident.

The pacifists want to climb to a new rung in the life of humanity, a level above the rung of power struggle and force. Force is to be used only against subhuman nature and the violators of peace. Human life is to be moralized. A new and richer working community will, they think, blossom on the basis of a new trust between nations. This *abstract* dream of world peace which lives in the minds of some pacifists will certainly never be realized, says Hirsch, though the *concrete* ideal has a certain realizability. But even this earthly kingdom of world peace will certainly never be eternal, for everything historical passes away.[14] Hirsch is quite willing to admit that not every nation is destined to live

14. Again it is instructive to note what Tillich many years later said in a similar vein about the relation of earthly achievements for peace and the union of humankind and the eternal kingdom of God: "Let us assume for a moment that this were possible. Under an unchangeable central authority all encounters of power with power are regulated. Nothing is risked, everything decided. Life has ceased to transcend itself. Creativity has come to an end. The history of man would be finished, post-history would have started. Mankind would be a flock of blessed animals without dissatisfaction, without drive into the future. The horrors and sufferings of the historical period would be remembered as the dark ages of mankind. And then it might happen that one or the other of these

out its own unique character (*Eigenart*) within its own particular state. Even great nations can be judged and subsumed into a higher whole. Since world kingdoms may be willed by God, nations which feel the call to be such a world kingdom have the right to strive for it. No one knows with certainty at a given moment where God's will may lead. The Germans now fight for their independence against the evolving world kingdom of the British. The Germans desire to have their own life and powerful state; their own conscience calls them to the hard duty of struggling to the end for their freedom and honor. Nevertheless, God's final word has not yet been spoken; the decisive answer to the German risk has not yet been given by God. It may be that God desires English sovereignty over the world.[15]

One thing the pacifist must realize about his envisioned kingdom of world peace is that the new world order he envisions would not be any better, any more just or moral than the present one. "Basically the world would still remain the old one. No political transformation is capable of changing common human life into a kingdom of righteousness or even of love."[16] In other words, the very foundation upon which the pacifist vision rests is misleading and deceptive. The powerful will never tolerate the shrinking of their own land space by other nations. The great capitalist powers would be able in a kingdom of world peace to exploit at will all nations of the earth. This would be the case particularly with democratic governments. Democratic states, as experience shows, are the most defenseless against the great capitalistic economic powers within their own nations.[17]

More important, says Hirsch, is the error of those pacifists who ground their vision—their ethic of justice—in Christianity. They confuse the kingdom of justice with the kingdom of God. The kingdom of justice belongs to the natural order. While the heart of morality is selfless love, that of justice is egoism. Justice is maintained by the use of ruthless force and is distinct from morality. The latter begins when a person on the basis of conscience acts voluntarily. In the following statement Hirsch expresses explicitly his perception of the nature of and distinction between the kingdom of justice and the kingdom of love:

blessed men would feel a longing for these past ages, their misery and their greatness, and would force a new beginning of history upon the rest.

"This image will show that a world without the dynamics of power and the tragedy of life and history is not the Kingdom of God, is not the fulfilment of man and his world. Fulfilment is bound to eternity and no imagination can reach the eternal. But fragmentary anticipations are possible. The Church itself is such a fragmentary anticipation. And there are groups and movements, which although they do not belong to the manifest Church, represent something we may call a 'latent Church'. But neither the manifest nor the latent Church is the Kingdom of God." *Love, Power and Justice*, pp. 123-124.

15. "Der Pazifismus," p. 6.
16. *Ibid.*
17. *Ibid.*, p. 7.

That is why the kingdom of justice [*Reich des Rechts*] is sharply distinguished from the kingdom of love. Even if we succeed in uniting all humans into one single community of justice [*Rechtsgemeinschaft*] and then in ushering in and establishing the most complete justice within it—we still always remain in the kingdom of the world. Nothing of that which Christianity actually desires would be actualized through this alone. The kingdom of God would still not be there. After all, in the kingdom of God, human beings, because they worship God and love each other, are to be of "one heart and one soul." Even in the most complete community of justice they are anything but that. They have merely reached certain common agreements over the way in which the pursuit of the particular intentions of each individual are to be allowed in the future.

On the other hand, it is possible for something of the kingdom of God to be present even while the community of justice is still incomplete. Where in general people are moved in their conscience by God and then freely commit themselves to the duty of love [*Liebespflicht*] which is demanded of them, there it begins to set in motion its concealed nature. It is something invisible, lives in the heart, binds souls one to another. It is therefore not an empty dream. For the best we have we are indebted to people who are at home in it [kingdom of God], who are firmly rooted in eternity.[18]

All those pacifists, says Hirsch, who think that the unification of humanity is a fulfilled community of justice leading to the kingdom of God have forgotten the words of the gospel and of Jesus when he says that the kingdom of God comes not with external signs but is within us.

The unrestrained development of justice into a pacifist world kingdom would devaluate life itself. What would be destroyed in particular is the life of the nation. Ancient history shows, says Hirsch, that natural, national communities are sublated (*aufgehoben*) into the common life of world kingdoms. Anyone with eyes to see can see that the international culture of our time is no less destructive of particular nations. In the following statement Hirsch expresses his own reasons for the importance of preserving particular nationalities:

Through our participation in the life of our nation we so-to-speak rid ourselves to some extent of the curse of egoism, which knows and values nothing but the small personal will. What the best law [*Recht*] cannot create is established through nature in the national community: the uncoerced agreement of many people in that which they think and desire, a natural inward binding-together [*Verbundenheit*], which exercises a power over persons [*Gemüter*], and from which only that which is corrupt considers itself free. That is why the national-community [*Volksgemeinschaft*], of all the

18. *Ibid.*, pp. 8-9.

phenomena of natural life, is the one in which man as Christian will find the most joy. Certainly it also reveals the raw and hateful signs that cannot be avoided by anything earthly. It lacks freedom and broadheartedness. It misleads to an inner locking-up-of-itself against the person who is not a fellow countryman [*Volksgenosse*]. It hardens the people included within it against spiritual values as well. At the same time it remains true that a person who has learned to love his fatherland possesses an inner preparation for the concepts of Christianity, as it springs from that which is nationally rooted.[19]

In this statement Hirsch reveals his awareness of the two-sidedness of the concept of nation and fatherland. He clearly sees its dangers (the exclusion of the stranger), dangers which were to actualize themselves so clearly in the National Socialist era much later, but dangers which Hirsch here finds are outweighed by the positive aspects of commitment to the nation.

Hirsch's recognition of the dangers of absolutizing a particular nation leads him to stress the transitoriness of a nation's lifespan: "Because the national ethos [*Volksart*] signifies the hardening of a natural particularity, which continues to have only a limited right, God cannot let nations live eternally. He must thoroughly plough over [*umpflügen*] the ground of the human world from time to time, in order to keep it receptive to the universal ideas which are in eternal flux."[20] If this were not the case, the history of humanity would degenerate totally. "Just because nations in God's time have need of judgment through world kingdoms we dare not conclude that world kingdoms are something for which we have to be joyful, that we have to see in them an ideal value worth striving for the way pacifism does."[21] In themselves world kingdoms only work destructively, leading to the loss of the natural well being of life. A genuine sense of community cannot be achieved through such international kingdoms. And when one is alienated from the ground of nature, one's spiritual and moral life is also damaged. It is for this reason that the creative powers of the human spirit are always revealed most profoundly in young aspiring nation-states and not in world kingdoms.

In the final part of "Der Pazifismus," Hirsch once more defends the right of the nation-state to wage a legitimate war. He repeats the arguments for war in

19. *Ibid.*, p. 10.
20. *Ibid.* In this context, when Hirsch refers to universal ideas, he is talking about justice, scientific truth, and so on, ideas espoused so passionately by many, particularly the pacifists. While he considers them important in making life richer and broader in some sense, still he argues that the roots of greatness and power do not lie with these universal ideas but with the "unfathomable dynamic" of life itself; namely, that "particularity and mystery, which constitute the beauty, the power and the health of life." This is why he feels that the unrestricted development of these universal ideas, including the purest of them all—the search for truth in science—must be limited. A dimension of the mystery in the dynamics of life must remain unresolved. *Ibid.*, pp. 9-10.
21. *Ibid.*, pp. 10-11.

somewhat greater detail than those we have already considered in an earlier essay of his. While war cannot be seen as a blessing in its own right, if fought in the right spirit it can be the servant of justice. War determines which nations have a right to maintain their own independent existence. Further, war can draw a nation closer to God. In lengthy periods of peace a nation's conscience, its relationship to God, can weaken, and humans can easily begin to rely on their own rational achievements. Nevertheless, in war God impinges on humanity and shows it that he is Lord of history, shattering its trust in human arrangements and laws.

We need not linger here on Hirsch's arguments in defense of war except to refer to his rather important discussion of the most difficult of all questions pertaining to war: "Does the commandment of love, as it is placed before us by the Sermon on the Mount, not contradict the destructive will which is expressed in war? Indeed, does it not contradict the simplest ethical concept of all, according to which we otherwise regulate community life?"[22] As before, Hirsch answers this crucial objection to war by making a distinction between the character and function of the state, which relies on coercion, and the commandment of love as demanded by the Sermont on the Mount: "Love entails the renunciation of right. Whoever is not ready to suffer injustice in personal matters does not yet love. Further, to love belongs the renunciation of force. Love does not demand what is not given to it voluntarily. The state would relinquish itself if in its concerns it would deal in this way. It must coerce. It cannot renounce its rights. In everything it does, including all its works of peace, this its nature, which is alien to love, emerges."[23]

Whoever thinks this is blatant disobedience to the demands of Jesus does not understand that the Sermon on the Mount applies to the conscience of the individual and not to the function of the state. In the Sermon Jesus wants to show us how we can become like our father in heaven, how we can become members of the *invisible* kingdom of God. These concepts are not applicable to the state and the national community. The latter are earthly realities which will cease to exist in eternity. The demand of love includes within itself the notion of self-sacrifice, for example. The Christian way of love teaches us that the highest fulfillment of personality is the apparent giving up of personality. But such self-sacrifice obviously does not apply to earthly existence and to the state; that would mean simple self-destruction. Nevertheless, this radical distinction between the two realms does not leave a nation without ethical and moral norms by which it must judge its actions:

22. *Ibid.*, p. 14.
23. *Ibid.*

We must therefore definitely reject the applicability of the Sermon on the Mount to the state as state. Nevertheless, national community and state are not phenomena free from every ethical law. They stand under the ethical idea of righteousness [*Gerechtigkeit*]. A nation ought not to concern itself with the inward only, but evermore with actualizing righteousness in its institutions [*Einrichtungen*]. Neither must it deal with unlimited arbitrariness internationally [*nach aussen*]. There exist respected historical laws that no nation dare ignore. Today, when there are so many small nations which suffer from megalomania, one must indeed remember that a nation sins not only when it allows itself to be pushed into a corner and does not utilize its God-given gifts toward the structuring of the world—that is the German error—but also when it creates tasks for itself, for the discharging of which it lacks a calling and capacities. Thus a nation can indeed begin a war when an aim, which appears to it as indispensable for the unfolding of its nature and life, cannot be attained in other ways. But woe to the nation that takes such a step lightly, that in boundless darkness or base rapacity transgresses against the rigorous spirit of historical righteousness. Nations must answer for their deeds, and the grandchildren atone for the crimes of the fathers.[24]

Here we see Hirsch clearly moving beyond the traditional conditions of a just war and defending even an offensive war. Nevertheless, he does not want to give the nation-state unlimited right for arbitrary action. He maintains that a nation must adhere to certain historical norms of justice. It must be held accountable for its actions even in foreign affairs and international relations.

Is there not then a split between state- or national-morality and the ethics of the individual? Hirsch answers that he has never yet found there to be an intolerable contradiction between the two. Ultimately the individual Christian's highest loyalty is to the commandment of love. The Christian statesman who takes upon himself the welfare of the nation, and on this ground unleashes a war, voluntarily takes upon his soul a difficult responsibility before God, risking that he has incorrectly interpreted the historical situation. He does it because he faithfully desires to fulfill his God-given office. He does it out of love for neighbor, just as the Christian soldier fights and destroys the life of other people out of service to his nation. It is such a loving commitment, a kind of self-sacrifice to his more sensitive nature, that is at work when he fulfills the hard duties of his office rightly.

Hirsch did not remain with general principles but became quite specific during these years in his concerns regarding domestic social issues—land reform, adequate housing for people, criticism of monopoly capitalism which exploits the poor through high rents and unreasonable profits from real estate.[25]

24. *Ibid.*, p. 15.
25. His 1917-18 article, "Deutsche Zukunft," for example, is devoted to a discussion of internal

His major preoccupation during the war years, between 1914 and 1918, however, relate explicitly to the pressing issue of war and its implications for Germany as a nation and a state. His thinking on these questions, particularly the important distinction between love and justice, between the *invisible eternal kingdom of God* and the function of the *visible, historical, earthly nation-state* is rooted in his interpretation and appropriation of Luther's theology. The kingdom of God is defined in terms of the individual's relationship to God, faith within the individual conscience expressed outwardly through self-sacrificial love to other individuals *as* individuals as well as to the nation in its struggle for survival. This is what is demanded by the Sermon on the Mount itself.

The nation-state as such, however, is a pre-Christian reality which binds people together in solidarity in an earthly, historical way, and is a reality divinely embedded in creation itself. Its primary function is the use of the sword to maintain peace and restrain chaotic evil. While Luther's theology is used by Hirsch to illumine the given historical situation in which Germany finds itself, he also expands and elaborates on it to fit the exigencies of the modern situation. The notion of state, for example, is expanded to include nationality, a concept with which Luther was largely unfamiliar. Hirsch maintains, however, that this extension of Luther's understanding of the function of the state to wage an offensive war on behalf of the nation-state remains true to the basic intent of Luther's thought.

Tillich's War Years: A Time of Disillusionment

In contrast to Hirsch who, as we have seen above, wrote extensively on social-political questions during the war years, Tillich's serious analysis of cultural-political questions began only after the war, although he did some academic work during his time as an army chaplain. Prior to 1914 he, like so many other German intellectuals, including Hirsch, was indifferent to politics, and wrote virtually nothing pertaining to social questions. It was the war, particularly the revolution of 1918, that awakened him to politics. While he was not in a position to write extensive theoretical treatises between 1914 and 1918, still from his

domestic problems. He urges the German government to solve its urgent social problems, such as land reform and inadequate housing, particularly for the families of fighting men. He is highly critical of profiteering through land sales and high rents, and supports the land reform program of the "Bund Deutscher Bodenreformer," a program which tried to solve social questions without falling into the error of communism, giving up private property altogether, on the one side, and the extremes of arbitrary capitalism on the other. Anticipating what would later become a key phrase in the platform of the NSDAP, he argues that the "Common good goes beyond individual will" (*Gemeinwohl geht über Einzelwille*). The government must have control over land and German soil and be able to limit arbitrary individual freedom to dispose of land at will. "Deutsche Zukunft," *Wingolfs-Blätter* 47(1917-18), pp. 1-8.

private letters, reports to superiors, sermons, and later autobiographical reflections we know that Tillich underwent a profound change during the war years, a change that determined his future political and theological life and thought.

For Tillich, the nineteenth century and with it his own idyllic and personal intellectual pre-war existence, came to an end on August 1, 1914—the beginning of World War I. In his "Autobiographical Reflections" he describes his war years and how they changed him:

> The First World War was the end of my period of preparation. Together with my whole generation, I was grasped by the overwhelming experience of a nation-wide community—of the end of a merely individualistic and predominantly theoretical existence. I volunteered, and was asked to serve as a war chaplain, which I did from September, 1914, to September, 1918. The first weeks had not passed before one's original enthusiasm disappeared; after a few months I became convinced that the war would last indefinitely and ruin all Europe. Above all, I saw that the unity of the first weeks was an illusion, that the nation was split into classes, and that the industrial masses considered the Church as an unquestioned ally of the ruling groups. The situation became more and more manifest toward the end of the war. It produced the revolution, in which imperial Germany collapsed.[26]

Tillich describes this change similarly in his 1936 autobiography, *On the Boundary*: "It was during the collapse of imperial Germany and the revolution of the last year of World War I that I began to understand such issues as the political background of the war, the interrelation of capitalism and imperialism, the crisis of bourgeois society, and the schisms between classes."[27]

The patriotism with which he and others had entered the war is described well by Tillich in one of his many sermons preached to soldiers at the front.[28] In a New Year's sermon, 1914-15, Tillich meditates on the events of the year just ending and how the love of the fatherland had grasped all of them at the beginning of the war: "We had to separate ourselves from our loved ones; only one love had a claim over us—that of the fatherland. Life and death had value only to the extent that we could benefit the fatherland."[29] The sermon is pervaded by a dark foreboding about the new year and the further horrors it would bring. Tillich nevertheless urges his listeners not to resign themselves to blind fate but to place their trust in God for strength to face the unknown future. While the sermon is remarkably free from nationalistic and patriotic language, it seems

26. "Autobiographical Reflections," p. 12.

27. *On the Boundary*, pp. 32-33.

28. Out of the time of World War I, around 100 fully worked-out sermons and approximately 30 sermon outlines of Tillich's have been preserved, most of which remain unpublished. Cf. *GW* XIII, pp. 70-71.

29. *GW* XIII, p. 81.

from reports written by Tillich during that first year that he had not yet as fully come to grips with the political dimensions of the war as he would shortly.[30] In a report to his superior, written in the second year of the war, this new consciousness is already subtly evident. He talks about the disappointments, the growing uncertainty about peace in the near future, and the presence of social bitterness.[31] This growing disillusionment with the realities and aims of the war and the effect it had on his preaching and theology, is alluded to in a series of private letters to Maria Rhine in 1916 and 1917. In them Tillich talks about the increasingly eschatological nature of his preaching.[32]

Both Tillich and Hirsch began with enthusiastic support for the war effort, patriotically volunteering to fight for the cause of their nation, but the war years had radically different effects on their political and theological views. Hirsch, as we have seen, developed an increasingly strong conviction that war at its deepest level was the legitimate struggle of nation-states for independent existence, victory depending to a large degree on the strength and solidarity of a people's spiritual will to preserve and realize their own unique God-given destinies. Tillich, on the other hand, became increasingly disenchanted with nationalism, with an explanation of the war in terms simply of a struggle between nations. He became convinced toward the end of the war that war was the expression of an international class struggle. Both Tillich and Hirsch were consistently to develop in very different ways these early political convictions into coherent political theories in the following decade—the years of the Weimar Republic.

30. Tillich is to have said that his superiors during the war urged him to influence the soliders more along patriotic lines than he was doing. Cf. *GW* XIII, p. 71.

31. "Bericht über die Monate November und Dezember 1915," handwritten manuscript of 1915 first published in *GW* XIII, pp. 77-79.

32. Personal letters, Tillich to Maria Rhine (also Maria Klein), October 15, 1916; November 27, 1916; December 5, 1917. In *GW* XIII, p. 70. Tillich's letters to Maria Klein have been published in *GW* V (supplement volume), pp. 111-123. Other correspondence and documents of this period also appear in this volume, pp. 77-110.

6
Religious Nationalism
and Religious Socialism:
Two Options During the Weimar Years

The Unstable Political Situation of the Weimar Republic

On November 11, 1918, after an unsuccessful attempt to have the harsh terms set by the victorious Allies modified, Germany—under compulsion—signed the armistice. While military operations ended, starvation continued. In fact, the Allies continued the blockade of food shipments for Germans while thousands died daily of malnutrition. "The memory of this horrible experience," says S. William Halperin in his 1946 classic, "lived on in the minds of Germans of every class. It bred a bitterness which the years assuaged but which could all too easily be resuscitated upon the first recurrence of adversity."[1] On June 28, 1919 a German delegation from Weimar signed the Versailles Treaty in the same hall where 48 years earlier Germany had experienced the great moment of the proclamation of the German Empire and the crowning of Wilhelm I as the German emperor. The "dictated settlement" consisted of severe terms which fueled the hostility of all parties, including right-wing nationalists and left-wing social democrats and communists, for decades: extensive territorial losses, unprecedented demilitarization and disarmament, an unrealistic demand for reparations, and the infamous "war criminals" articles and "war guilt" clause.[2]

Many Germans came to believe that Germany's defeat was due not so much to the defeat of the armies on the battlefields as to "subversive" elements within Germany, elements already growing in strength during the war years: pacifists, liberals, socialists, communists, and Jews.[3] Those who signed the armistice were

1. S. William Halperin, *Germany Tried Democracy: A Political History of the Reich from 1918 to 1933* (New York: W.W. Norton & Company, 1965), p. 103. This book was first published in 1946 by Thomas Y. Crowell Company.

2. E.H. Carr, *International Relations Between the Two World Wars 1919-1939* (London: Macmillan & Co. Ltd., 1965), p. 52. This book was first published under the title *International Relations Since the Peace Treaties,* in 1937. The "war criminals" articles called for the extradition and trial of ex-Kaiser Wilhelm II and other persons accused by the allies of having "committed acts in violation of the laws and customs of war," and the "war guilt" clause forced Germany to "accept the responsibility of Germany and her allies for causing all the loss and damage to which the Allied and Associated Governments and their nationals have been subjected as a consequence of the war imposed upon them by the aggression of Germany and her allies." *Ibid.,* pp. 46-47.

depicted by right-wing politicians as traitors and those who had successfully carried through the November revolution as "November criminals." The leaders of the Weimar regime were seen by many as traitors and cowards who had betrayed Germany. In the months following the signing of the treaty a change came over the German *Reichstag*. These elections showed a marked movement away from great initial enthusiasm and support by a large majority of ordinary Germans for moderate pro-democratic coalition parties of the Republic to an increasing disillusionment with democracy and its ability to run the country. The tide turned in favor of communism on the left and nationalist movements on the right.[4]

The early Weimar years bred a multiplicity of political parties each with a slightly different political vision for Germany. On November 9, 1919, after days of revolutionary chaos and strikes throughout Germany culminating in a general strike and demonstration in Berlin, Philipp Scheidemann, leader of the Social Democratic Party, appeared on the *Reichstag* balcony to proclaim the German Republic. Kaiser Wilhelm II fled to Holland where he formally abdicated his throne on November 28, 1919; the German government was left clearly in the hands of left-wing political forces. On July 31, 1919 the Weimar Constitution was officially adopted by a vote of 262 to 75, with opposition consisting almost completely of the Nationalist, Independent, and People's parties.

The revolution and the creation of the Republic seemed to have had the popular support of a large majority of the German people, although Halperin suggests that, had they had the option, most Germans might have preferred a more traditional parliamentary monarchy.[5] The overwhelming support for the Republic during the initial months is demonstrated by the fact that in the very first election of representatives to the national constituent assembly on January 19, 1918, the three strongly pro-democratic and pro-republican parties—the Social Democratic Party, the Center Party, and the Democratic Party—together received more than 75 percent of the total votes cast. These three now formed the "Weimar Coalition"—the first coalition government of the new Weimar Republic.[6]

3. Halperin, *Germany Tried Democracy*, p. 105.

4. *Ibid.*, pp. 153, 193ff. Halperin shows how the National Socialists and the Communists frequently competed for the same constituency vote, and on occasion supported the same cause, as for example the strike of the Berlin transport workers in November 1932. It would also appear that large sections of the populace vacillated in their support between left and right. *Ibid.*, pp. 509, 521. This is not to say that the left and right were intrinsically similar, although some have argued that there were some formal similarities between them (both were totalitarian worldviews), but to point to the instability of the situation.

5. *Ibid.*, p. 93.

6. *Ibid.*, pp. 126-136. These three parties together with the German National Party (Deutsche Volkspartei, DVP) are known as the "Great Coalition." Halperin gives us a helpful description of

The Republic, however, seemed to be crisis ridden from the start. Part of the problem was the proliferation of political parties, the result of a complex system of proportional representation, none of them ever obtaining an absolute majority on the basis of which they could act decisively. As it was, the indecisiveness and largely paralytic nature of the Weimar Republic became legendary, characterized by endless discussion, debate, political haggling, nonconfidence votes and frequent cabinet shuffles and calls for new elections. Tillich himself, while a strong defender of the pro-democratic and even revolutionary forces, alludes to this inherent weakness within a democratic system, evident particularly during the Weimar years.[7] Both left-wing and right-wing political groups in Germany, especially in the later years of the Republic, used this weakness to their own advantage.

The political thought of Tillich and Hirsch, the early formulations of which had already taken place during the war years, now matured and took on a clear and distinct shape in the context of post-war events in Germany through the decade of the 1920s. Hirsch's lament for the unified patriotic German spirit of 1914; his rejection of the forces within Germany, particularly liberal and left-wing pacifism, which he saw as aiding in the shattering of that spirit; his repeated and passionate denunciation of the Versailles settlement; his suspicion of democracy and the Weimar Republic; and his longing and struggle for national renewal and the restoration of lost national honor was shared by many German intellectuals, politicians, and ordinary Germans and cannot be understood apart from these larger national and international events.

each of the major parties in the newly-formed Republic and where they stood on the political spectrum. These included the middle class liberal Democratic Party, the moderately liberal People's Party organized by Gustav Stresemann; the conservative right-wing National People's Party; the Catholic Centre Party, which supported a "middle position" and was made up of both right wing and left wing elements; the Social Democratic Party, which was committed to a democratic, evolutionary, and gradualist approach to socialism; the more radical left-wing Independent Social Democratic Party (later known simply as the Independent Party); and the Communist Party. The nature and number of these and other parties changed throughout the Weimar period, especially in the dying days of the Weimar government, when the strength of the moderate middle class parties began to wane and lose their popular support. Tillich joined the Socialist Democratic Party in 1929. It is known that as early as 1919 Tillich had connections with the more radical Independent Social Democratic Party (USPD) but it is not clear whether he was a member or not. See Stumme, *Socialism in Theological Perspective*, pp. 24-25. Hirsch's party affiliations during the Weimar years are also not entirely clear. From an unpublished letter to Karl Barth on August 9, 1921, it is obvious that Hirsch at that time belonged officially to no political party although his sympathies lay with the conservative German National People's Party (DNVP). Hirsch stresses in this letter to Barth that he is opposed to every international type of party that undermines a sense of nationhood and statehood. At the same time he criticizes the DNVP for its economic views and tactics and as a Christian expresses reservations and some disillusionment with the sham and pretense that seem to be a part of every political party. Personal letter, Hirsch to Barth, August 9, 1921, Karl Barth-Archiv, Basel. Provided by Walter Buff, Hannover. According to Buff, Hirsch did join the DNVP in the second half of the 1920s. Personal letter, Buff to Reimer, June 19, 1980.

7. Tillich, *On the Boundary*, p. 44.

The "political theology" of the 1920s and early 1930s, of which Hirsch was a leading representative, grew out of the conviction that Germany was being unjustly treated and oppressed by foreign and domestic elements, that it was being exploited by the international community, and that the Weimar government lacked the will to rectify this national injustice. This new theological-political movement had as one of its central tenets the rediscovery of the centrality of nationality (*das Volk*) and the restoration and liberation of the German people from gross international injustice.[8]

Tillich's enthusiastic support of the revolution, his hopes for the democratic experiment of the Weimar Republic, and his development of a political theory which attempted to bring together the insights of Marxist socialism and Christianity can also not be understood apart from these larger social-political events. Hirsch's political thought, rooted in Luther's concept of the two kingdoms and a rediscovery of the importance of nationality, which binds together people of all walks of life and classes into a single organic unity, and Tillich's political thought, which sought to accommodate itself to and come to terms with the socialist forces within Germany through Religious Socialism, were not the only political options open to Germans. They were, however, two of the more important and distinct political visions during this decade of political crisis. In this section of our study we examine some of the important political writings of Tillich and Hirsch immediately after the war and during the 1920s and attempt to understand their political positions leading up to the National Socialist revolution in the 1930s.

Hirsch's View of National Destiny, The Church's Task and the Individual Conscience

In the years of 1918-19 Hirsch wrote a number of smaller articles which clearly

---

8. Scholder, *Die Kirchen und das Dritte Reich*, pp. 124-150. Scholder goes to great lengths to show how the category of nationality (*Volk*), rooted in the 19th-century romanticism of Herder, Arndt, and Fichte, was rediscovered in the 1920s and became a new ethical starting point for theology in the thought of Paul Althaus, Friedrich Gogarten, Emanuel Hirsch, and Wilhelm Stapel. A new kind of modern theology—political theology—was born, which had a completely different starting point than the previous liberal theology. "For Althaus and Hirsch and their friends the responsibility for the community of the nation became a decisive theological task, from which theology and the church could not withdraw under any circumstances. Here arose a new and modern type of theology: political theology. Certainly every theology is political. In the modern political theology, however, political ethics becomes the key question of theological understanding and church behavior. That is its general mark and point of recognition." *Ibid.*, p. 130. In my reading of the primary sources I have not found any reference by Hirsch himself to his own theology as "Political theology." Although I too use the term to talk about Hirsch's theology, the designation does not adequately account for the a) difference between "right wing" and "left-wing" political theologies, nor b) Hirsch's insistence that theology and politics can be related to each other only on the basis of a doctrine of the two kingdoms.

rose out of the revolutionary situation in Germany. In them he criticizes the revolutionary spirit, the democratic restructuring of Germany, the prevalent "spirit of intoxication [*Rauschgeist*]" that naively lauds the dissolution of German militarism and imperialism, and blames the monarchy for the collapse of Germany. He calls German evangelical Christians to become sober in their political judgments, to reject democracy in favor of the king and officialdom (*Beamtentum*), and to consider what true love—according to Luther's understanding of the New Testament—requires in the current situation.[9] During succeeding years Hirsch wrote numerous political articles and books outlining in great detail his basic understanding of the nature of society, the nation, the state, the two kingdoms, the individual conscience as the locus of morality and ethics, and what he considered to be "Germany's fate" and evangelical Christianity's task. The most systematic and important of these is without doubt his *Deutschlands Schicksal: Staat, Volk und Menschheit im Lichte einer ethischen Geschichtsansicht*, published in 1920. In the following pages we examine Hirsch's major political concepts in the light of these writings in the 1920s.

Society

In the 1934-35 debate Tillich suggests that Hirsch's support of the National Socialist movement revealed an inadequate and even naive social analysis. However, Hirsch's writings of the 1920s, particularly *Deutschlands Schicksal*, reveal a rather thorough knowledge of the Marxist analysis of society and a serious grappling with the class nature of society. It is clear that Hirsch reached very different conclusions than Tillich. For Hirsch, it is precisely the Marxist interpretation of society—which sees the nation as torn apart into an irreconcilable opposition between classes, the state as a tyrannical tool in the hands of capitalists, and the working class as having no fatherland—that has shattered the spirit of 1914.[10] It is the German fate that with the triumph of socialist forces in 1918 these Marxist ideas have triumphed over any concept of national identity and unity.

Hirsch is quite willing to recognize the social and economic class differences that have resulted from capitalism. While critical of them, he unequivocally rejects the Marxist solution. Hirsch maintains that socialism does not have an adequate scientific analysis and doctrine of society, that it lacks a clear concept of social justice, of a just worker's wage. The product of labor is seen as belonging to the total conglomerate of workers who are to have complete sover-

9. These include "Demokratie und Christentum," *Der Geisteskampf der Gegenwart* 54,3(1918), pp. 57-60; "Rauschgeist und Glaubensgeist," *Der Geisteskampf der Gegenwart* 55,2(1919), pp. 40-42; "Was die Liebe tut," *Der Geisteskampf der Gegenwart* 55,10(1919), pp. 192-193.

10. *Deutschlands Schicksal*, pp. 109-125. This influential book was first published in 1920, re-issued in 1922 with a new preface and a ten-page "*Nachwort*," and re-issued a second time without major changes in 1925. It is the 1925 edition that is being used in this study.

eignty in deciding how they will divide up this product amongst themselves. There is, however, no clear indication as to the positive principles by which such division is to take place.[11] There is no clear concept of how a common economy and common administration of diverse functions and goals is to be constructed and organized. What is not answered by the socialists is how the "right of individuals" and the "right of the whole" are to be adjudicated and under what conditions a community of creative life unfolds. Socialism avoids telling the workers to what end they are to be liberated and to what end they are to rule. All that is given is a negative answer; namely, that the masses, the proletariat, are themselves to determine what happens to their work and produce. Thus, by default, these adjudicative decisions are left to the rulers—the representatives of the proletariat. "The dictatorship of the proletariat demands therefore the dictator, the tyrant. Bolshevism is no abberation of the socialist ideal, but is its singular logical actualization."[12]

The greatest illusion of socialism, according to Hirsch, is that the rule of the proletariat will liberate and ennoble humanity. In actual fact, socialism, which transforms the whole of society into an office and a factory, leads to a tyranny without equal. There is one basic error in socialism: it does not recognize the moving power of human history, the inventive, creative, ordering, and structuring spirit within history.

All of this means for Hirsch that the socialist option must be outrightly rejected and countered with a clear and definite social ideal, the basic insight of which is "the nation-state, which stands together with all of its citizens in one community of purpose, creates room for each one of them for a free and healthy life, and from each one receives in turn life and love for a richer enfolding of its powers; it is within such a structure of common human life alone that the freedom and worth of the individual arrives at an inner accommodation with the right of the whole."[13]

Hirsch recognizes the problems that go along with this view of nation-state. One such problem is the inherent inequalities that exist between individuals and groups within a given nation. Nevertheless, each individual experiences his social situation as his fate (*Schicksal*), a fate which characterizes life itself and defies rationalization. Each individual must deal with his own fate, with the honor that every work of God demands. Every nation develops a diversity of inner life through the inequalities of its social relations, and each unique social relationship presents rich spiritual and moral opportunities.[14]

While Hirsch defends the importance of private property against socialism, he strongly rejects noninterventionist free-market monopoly capitalism, where

11. *Ibid.*, p. 116.
12. *Ibid.*, p. 118.
13. *Ibid.*, p. 120.
14. *Ibid.*, p. 122.

individual property owners exploit weaker individuals and ruin the national whole through unlimited arbitrary economic egoism. For this reason it is the right and the duty of nation-states to limit the power of economic ownership and to place it under strict regulations. The nation-state has the responsibility of protecting the weak; it must legislate to the benefit of the weak members of its society.[15]

Hirsch becomes quite explicit in his critique of the capitalistic spirit, arguing that soil must be subjected to strict legislation, that unequal possession of the earth is a cause of social injustice and exploitation and ultimately kills the state. The overcoming of capitalism—the unlimited exploitative freedom of private ownership—depends not on the abolition of private ownership but on a creative and flexible synthesis of the "freedom of ownership" and the "right of the state." Such a synthesis depends on the creative acts of individual leaders. Not every nation will arrive at the same solution. In every case, however, great wisdom will need to be combined with rigorous justice. Ultimately, a social ideal can only be approximated; it depends on individual leaders and citizens who have compassionate and loving spirits and who carry within themselves powers derived from the community of conscience in God (the Kingdom of God). State and society, in the final analysis, always remain expressions of external life and belong to the kingdom of this world.[16]

Nation

The most important political category for Hirsch is that of nation, the understanding of which radically separates him from socialist political theories and consequently also from the political thought of his friend Tillich. Technically, Hirsch distinguishes between *"Nation"* (nation) and *"Volk"* (a people), although the two are closely connected. The term *"Volk,"* a prior concept to "Nation," refers to a group of people with a common biological-racial, cultural, ethnic, linguistic, and religious heritage. It is more than a biological-racial entity but blood-relatedness is an important aspect of its group identity. It is family or tribe *(Stamm)* writ large. The word "Nation" refers to this people *(Volk)* having become conscious of its group identity in social, political, and historical terms. While Hirsch wants to maintain this technical distinction between nation and *"Volk,"* he tends in his writings to use them interchangeably.

In a 1924 article, "Die Liebe zum Vaterlande," Hirsch clarifies what he means by nationality and how one's love for it must be perceived. Human individuals, he says, do not grow in an isolated fashion—wild and mixed-up like flowers—but are born into and grow up within a national community *(Volksgemeinschaft)*. This is an historical fact which powerfully shapes individuals and which they experience as a law that defines and binds them in a vital

15. *Ibid.,* p. 123.
16. *Ibid.,* pp. 124-125.

association. The individual receives his external fate and inner being from this inescapable fact. This is why any conversion from one nationality to another is a slow and painful process that can be completed only in succeeding generations. Many would rather die than change nationalities. The character of one's nationality shapes one's soul or personality (*Seele*), which means that to estrange oneself from one's own nation is to experience estrangement from oneself.[17] To exchange one's own "fatherland" for another is in effect to dismantle one's soul and rebuild it for another. This is not to say that one soul, that of the German soul for instance, is better than another, only that it is different.

Love of the fatherland is nothing else than a feeling for the nation (*Nationalgefühl*). One feels the life of the nation to be one's own life. The life of one's fathers and their history becomes powerful within one and over one. "Thus the feeling for the nation is the root of all historical consciousness in humanity."[18] This respect for the past motivates people to great deeds in the present. This national consciousness binds us inwardly also to the state and creates in us a state-consciousness, for "If a nation is to develop its life completely in accordance with its own particular law, it must be bound together in an independent state."[19] The cause of the state is thus inevitably linked with the cause of the nation and becomes one's own cause. The great danger of recent economic development, says Hirsch, is the split of humanity into two classes or castes—masters and slaves, international capitalists and international proletariat. Within the nation, these antinomies must be superseded. In a limited sense, by analogy, nation-states create in the earthly realm what Christianity completes in the eternal realm—a classless community. "Thus the separation of humanity into nation-states in a certain sense advances toward Christianity, which also does not distinguish between those who are slaves and those who are free."[20]

In effect the nation-state is like a living and dynamic organism of which we are a part and which we experience as a law to which we are subject, as the part is to the whole.[21] We do not see it as an organic unity until we consider it in its

17. "Die Liebe zum Vaterlande," *Pädagogisches Magazin*, Heft 975 (Langensalza, 1924), p. 12.

18. *Ibid.*, p. 9.

19. *Ibid.*, p. 10.

20. *Ibid.*, pp. 11-12.

21. *Deutschlands Schicksal*, pp. 79-93. It is worth noting here that Tillich also uses the analogy of "organism" to describe both the individual and the social group. Tillich, however, more than Hirsch, points out the dangers of describing the social group as a biological organism: "But the individuals who constitute this organism are each independent centres for themselves, and so they can resist the unity of the social organism to which they belong. And here the limits of the analogy between biological and social organisms becomes visible. In a biological organism the parts are nothing without the whole to which they belong. This is not the case in social organisms. The destiny of an individual who is separated from the group to which he belongs may be miserable but the separation is not necessarily fatal. The fate of a limb which is cut off from the living organism to

connection with other nation-states. Then suddenly it takes on the shape of a living being, as a great individuality beside other individualities: "To every state belongs a land, a piece of this earth, which precisely it and no other has in its possession, and which is distinguished from every other piece of earth. And to every state belongs a population [*Bevölkerung*], a group of people, which lives exactly in it and in no other and has its particularity over against every other group."[22] This land, this people, is bonded together in a unity of life and will into an independent whole that is distinguished in its unique character (*Eigenart*) from foreign (*fremde*) unities of equal rank. This spirit and this will, which is the expression of a particular being and life, is always the "spirit and will of a definite people [*bestimmten Volkes*]. The unity of the State is inconceivable without national unity."[23] Even in a situation where many peoples (*Völker*) and tribes (*Stämme*) are bonded together into a common life, one dominant group which carries the state concept is still required. This group of people perceives the state as its particular purview and right. Only to the degree to which this ruling group, this nationality, is capable of assimilating (*einzuordnen*) the other groups into itself—into one all-encompassing national whole—will the state have an enduring stability (*Bestand*). This interpretation of state and national unity is necessary if life in a community, life within the nation-state, is to be experienced as a voluntarily-affirmed life and not as pure coercive power.

Law, State and Morality

This brings us to Hirsch's concept of law and the state.[24] The state for Hirsch is the unification of the diversities of the nation into one resolute will-of-life in the form of law both internally and externally: "To the extent that a state conforms to this definition of being [*Wesensbestimmung*], it is bound together with every one of its citizens in an inner community of goals carried by the national spirit which is proper to itself. In the general cause my own, the individual purpose, is

which it belongs is decay. In this sense no human group is an organism in the biological sense. Neither is the family the cell of a quasi-biological organism, nor is the nation something like a biological organism. This statement is politically significant. Those who like to speak of social organisms usually do it with a reactionary tendency. They want to keep dissenting groups in conformity and they use for this purpose biological metaphors in a literal sense.... A State has often been described as a person who has emotions, thoughts, intentions, decisions like an individual person. But there is a difference which makes all this impossible: the social organism does not have an organic center, in which the whole being is united so that central deliberations and decisions are possible." *Love, Power and Justice*, pp. 92-93.

22. *Deutschlands Schicksal*, pp. 79-80.

23. *Ibid.*, p. 80.

24. *Ibid.*, pp. 64-79. The term "*Recht*" is another one of those German terms which are hard to translate accurately into English. Depending on the context, it can be translated as "Right," "Law," or even "Justice." I have decided to translate it as consistently as possible with the word "Law," understood in its broadest sense, in contradistinction to "*Gesetz*," which refers to law or laws in the more concrete and specific sense.

included."[25] The state knows itself as a debtor to each one of its citizens "insofar as it guards the possibility of a free and healthy life, filled with individual moral content."[26] In turn the citizen knows the life of the state to be his own, to which he commits himself, gladly taking upon himself stately duties.

The state is the arm and will by which the concept of law becomes actual and concrete. Law (*Recht*) has three basic traits: (1) it has an inner majesty, a power that stands over and above all individual human wills, a power which binds people and binds them together; (2) it has a personal-majestic (*Selbstherrlichkeit*) quality which makes every individual subject to it; whoever does not want to submit to the law must be ready to withdraw from human community, for it is upon the principle of law that all freedom in society rests (in this way the law both frees and limits the individual); (3) the source of the majesty and authority of law is the supra-individual goal to which it is directed—namely, it binds together all relations between people through the concept of justice; it creates a unity and cohesion of life (*Lebenszusammenhang*) in which societal existence first gains its character of genuine community.[27]

The state is the means, the power structure, by which this abstract concept of law becomes actual. Simply put, the state has two primary aims: (1) it has real power and the means by which to carry through the nation's will by the use of force; and (2) it is a personality in a concrete sense which could not have arisen other than through powerful personalities. It is a well-ordered, firm, and enduring union (*Verband*), a bonding (*Zusammenfassung*) of a dispersed diversity (*zerstreuten Mannigfaltigkeit*) into a permanent unity of life and will.[28] There is therefore an inner connection between state and law, binding together individual members in a higher connection of rights and duties. Law and state exist only in mutual interaction with one another and do not exist separately. The state is the condition for all genuine human life, all peace and freedom, rooted in the state's power to protect law.

Justice is a critical norm by which to evaluate given relationships, not a codex of political definitions. Justice is a moral concept by which to critique the given situation, but it does not give us a positive and concrete picture of a perfect order.[29] Freedom, another closely related critical norm, is also a moral concept. In itself freedom appears to contradict the use of the force that is necessary for the state to enforce the law. A distinction, however, needs to be made between moral freedom and external freedom. The freedom which is guarded by the law is external freedom (*libertas in externis*).[30] Is it legitimate to

25. *Ibid.*, p. 109.
26. *Ibid.*, p. 110.
27. *Ibid.*, pp. 65-66.
28. *Ibid.*, p. 67.
29. *Ibid.*, pp. 68-69.
30. *Ibid.*, p. 69. Since every individual finds his individuality and independence only in the context of the will of the whole community, the submission of the individual to society and the state

endanger moral freedom in order to protect external freedom? Hirsch gives a positive answer to this question by showing how the seeming opposition between state and law on the one hand, and morality and freedom on the other, can be maintained without contradiction. He resolves the dilemma by applying them to two different spheres of human experience: State and law have to do with external justice, freedom, and duty; morality has to do with a higher realm of moral justice and freedom, a realm which lies beyond external order and structures. These two spheres are not totally distinct from each other, the sphere of the state and law being sustained by something higher but incapable of ever actualizing this higher realm in external structures. We are driven, therefore, to make a sharp distinction between the order of law within the realm of the state, based on the use of force, and the order of love within the realm of the kingdom of God, based on moral persuasion.

In a short but significant essay entitled "Demokratie und Christentum," Hirsch stresses that the gospel gives no direct guidance on the best form of state or its constitution.[31] While the New Testament indicates that we are to be subject to government authority (*Obrigkeit*), it does not tell us how this authority is to be structured. Thus, the claim that the monarchical state is the most appropriate form of government for Germany (something which Hirsch himself espoused) cannot rest its case on the gospel directly. It is rooted in an understanding of the particular situation in which Germany finds itself.

The gospel does not, however, leave us completely without at least some indirect guidelines. Two things can be said about the nature of the state which are consistent with the sense of the New Testament. For one, *the state stands above us* in the sense that it is an ordinance of God without which an ordered human community would be impossible, and through which God intends to actualize his intentions for human history. The state is much more than the sum of its present citizens. It belongs not only to the present but also to the past and to the future. Present citizens must in their political institutions respect the visions of their ancestors and the freedom of their children and grandchildren. The error of democracy lies in its assumption that the political institutions represent the majority of the present citizens.

The second thing that can be said on the basis of the commandment of love is that *the state is debtor to every one of its citizens,* and especially to the least and poorest among them. Above all, the state must see to it that people can lead healthy family lives and rear their children in modest but healthy homes. Many thousands lack this possibility for healthy human existence and no amount of self-sacrificial love by individuals as individuals can rectify this situation. Only the state through its law can prevent exploitative economic powers from depriving the weak of human worth and the means of existence.

is necessary for freedom to be preserved for all.
   31. "Demokratie und Christentum," pp. 57-60.

Christian love therefore demands strong resistance against a democratic form of government. The more democratic a state the more it tends to be dependent upon the great economic powers and the less one can expect social justice from it. True freedom goes beyond the freedom to vote. Christian freedom is an invisible spiritual good—the power of a free heart to interact with the living God and to serve worldly orders out of a loving conscience. Evangelical Christians ought to commit themselves willingly to the state, honoring it as a divine ordinance and not simply as a human creation. Therefore Hirsch believes "that a serious Christian should enter the present dispute on the side of the king and officialdom (*Beamtentum*) and against a democratic government."[32] A Christian will be able to do this in good conscience only if he works toward a state concerned with the spirit of social justice in economic life, and by guarding against the external enslavement of its citizens to an oppressive and miserable existence.

Two Kingdoms
Hirsch's distinction between the two spheres of human experience—the spiritual and the earthly—is grounded in Luther's distinction between the eternal kingdom and the temporal kingdom. The distinction is not simply one between the individual and the social realms, for the eternal moral sphere is also a communal or social one. It is a "community of conscience"; an actual, not an abstract community. It is a community in God and for God in which every individual retains his freedom. It is international and trans-temporal, one single church of God for the whole of humanity.[33] Earthly communities, however, cannot be universal in this sense but are characterized by external differentiations between nations, states, and laws—the necessary requirements for human-historical existence. In a remarkable statement Hirsch describes the distinction between these two realms as first understood by Luther and then later by Fichte:

> State and law belong to earthly, natural life; the kingdom of God in contrast is a spiritual power [*Grösse*], the community of conscience in God, experienced as a life-giving power. This separation is the great conception of Luther. He shattered the medieval view that the state is, according to its being, a member in the body of Christianity, and understood the state purely as a power in the order of creation. And this perception of Luther's was then once more newly discovered by Fichte in his own way. Before him one had, to be sure, distinguished technically between the doctrine of law and the doctrine of morality [*Sittenlehre*], but had not taken seriously the difference between law and morality in principle. Fichte however constructed his doctrine of law precisely on the concept that law [*Recht*] and morality

32. *Ibid.*, p. 5.
33. *Deutschlands Schicksal*, pp. 49-63. See especially pp. 59ff.

[*Sittlichkeit*] were two completely separate intellectual-spiritual worlds, each following its own inner laws; neither could be measured by the standard of the other. Both men were justifiably proud of this particular discovery of theirs. Whoever would understand human life must follow them here. It is entirely wrong to attempt to justify the state and its law by means of showing how it can ultimately be restructured toward the kingdom of God. Either one can comprehend it, particularly in its features that contradict morality, as a necessary ordering of human earthly existence, or one must set it aside as a lower rung of human community which has to be overcome.[34]

Hirsch's critique of anarchism, democratic pacifism, and communistic socialism (including variations of each), rests ultimately on his belief that they confuse these two realms. Each one of these worldviews in its own way presumes to actualize historically what must always remain an invisible reality. For Hirsch, the community of conscience in God, which is the deepest of all human communal relationships—the true place of all genuine freedom and love, can never become visibly institutionalized in an external order.[35] This is also why Hirsch rejects Tolstoi's interpretation of Jesus' Sermon on the Mount. In seeing Jesus' teachings as a critique of state, law, and nation, Tolstoi does not understand Jesus' distinction between the two kingdoms. Unlike Jesus, Tolstoi believes that the kingdom of God can be realized within the historical process.[36] Whoever wants to take Jesus' teachings seriously must recognize that the Sermon on the Mount pertains to the heart and to the conscience, and then fulfill his life and duty within the context of stately and societal orders.

What is probably the most important point to remember in Hirsch's view of the two kingdoms—the invisible community of conscience in God and the visible community of law, nation, and state—is that while the two must never be confused, there is a point of contact. This is one of the most difficult and most important aspects of Hirsch's political thought. In order to understand how these two distinct realms meet each other in the individual act of decision making, it is necessary to understand Hirsch's concept of history—a concept which he calls his "theistic view of history."[37] For Hirsch, human history has a double character: its metaphysical kernel (expressed in terms of the human concept of God) and the concrete historical expression of that metaphysical kernel. All historical reality has substance and life only through the fact that into it is mysteriously woven a supra-historical reality. No earthly reality, however, can ever be a pure expression of this supra-historical and metaphysical kernel.[38]

34. *Ibid.*, p. 72.
35. *Ibid.*, p. 126.
36. *Ibid.*, p. 138.
37. *Ibid.*, pp. 9-25.
38. *Ibid.*, p. 16.

The root of all human actions, which is the ethical decision, is circumscribed by historical conditions. The norms by which we make decisions have evolved and are conditioned by culture, nationality, education, and personal fate; therefore, no two persons will ever be completely in agreement. But inherent in this historically conditioned and accidental aspect there is a supra-historical ground, an eternal will, the Unconditioned, the Lord of history. Behind our ethical norms there stands a holy will to which we must be obedient: "Out of the certainty of its relation to an Eternal an individual soul unifies itself with the Eternal through an affirmation of particular duty."[39] Thus, our knowledge is always of a human and historically-changeable kind, so that our perceptions can never be a pure expression of a supra-human necessity but are simply allegories of that hidden depth which impresses itself upon our spirit. The human spirit can, however, have a basic certainty of its essential relation to eternal truth within itself.[40] Only through the fact that the human spirit has an inner relation to the final, unconditioned, holy will beyond itself, does it have a sure footing, life, and creative power.

The impact of the "community of conscience" upon the "earthly organized community" thus comes through the ethical decision making of individuals who have been awakened to a higher morality. Such individuals will devote their powers to improving the institutions and laws of the state, to approximating in the earthly realm the great ideas of justice, personal freedom, health, and naturalness of all relations without reducing the one realm to the other. The community of conscience will have an impact on external society indirectly through individuals who are members of that community of conscience. All ethical critiques of particular forms of law must honor the "once-established universal conditions of existence of right and morality upon this earth, and...not undertake in some way to improve on God's creation itself."[41] The invisible community of conscience and the visible community of state and society therefore stand in dynamic relationship to each other. *"One does not understand the historical, if one does not see it as a concrete inter-meshing of earthly-natural life with the ethical-religious. Both sides belong to history in the proper, genuine sense."*[42] The ethical-religious sphere, in which there is an immediate relationship to the eternal beyond history, is itself a concrete appearance within history.

It is because of this "theistic view of history" that Hirsch's separation of the two kingdoms does not lead to an irreconcilable split within the human personality. Humans participate in the all-powerful activity of God through the administration of law in the state, in which each person acts not as an individual for himself but for the sake of the whole. An individual demonstrates his belonging

39. *Ibid.*, p. 21.
40. *Ibid.*, p. 25.
41. *Ibid.*, p. 62.
42. *Ibid.*

to the community of conscience by how he exercises his God-given task of administering the law of the state, whether he administers for his own sake or for the sake of the whole. The kingdom of God is another name for the community of conscience, that spiritual power which shapes the disposition and from which there flows a creative and effective power into the world and organized earthly life. "The existence of the state and society in each of their forms depend on the fact that in them people selflessly, committedly, and genuinely ... oppose the power of particular egoism which destroys also the natural conditions of being and thus, according to the word of the Sermon on the Mount, become the salt of the earth. The kingdom of God is the life-bestowing mystery over all visible changes of history."[43]

In a most remarkable essay, *Die Reich-Gottes-Begriffe des neueren-europäischen Denkens,* Hirsch argues that there are two basic concepts behind the modern view of the state, both rooted in Reformation thought—particularly that of Luther and Calvin. The first fundamental assumption of modern social thought is the value of the "autonomous ethical personality" through which all humans have an equal right to unconditional, independent being. This is the fundamental critical norm of any doctrine of law. While the negative aspect of this value has been demonstrated in modern history, still the personality idea is a valid final norm of our perception of law. We will and should continue to measure every given law with reference to it.[44] While it has roots in the Renaissance, the most important expression of this concept of personality takes place in the Reformation, and particularly in Luther. Freedom from an earthly community on the one hand, and an ethical binding to this community on the other was uniquely worked out by Luther. His solution, which has not yet been surpassed, is based on his ethical pessimism in regard to historical reality. Because most people are brutal and selfish, an external order with coercive powers is required to restrain this selfishness. Only through it is the condition for the development of a higher personal life of freedom given.

The second basic concept of every modern doctrine of state is the perfected ethical-religious community—the kingdom of God or Christ. This concept of the kingdom of God is the "restless element" in the history of the modern doctrine of the state. Again, for Hirsch, it was Luther who most adequately understood the nature of this ideal ethical community. On the one hand, the kingdom of God was for him a heavenly reality, a union of souls in eternal love and life. On the other hand, this kingdom which is to be fulfilled only in the beyond is already present in earthly life in a hidden way. It is a spiritual reality in the human conscience which binds people together in a living community, as expressed in the Sermon on the Mount. This community of love which is international stands over against all earthly natural orders, above all earthly states

---

43. *Ibid.,* p. 126.
44. *Die Reich-Gottes-Begriffe des neueren-europäischen Denkens,* p. 6.

which constitute the kingdom of the world.[45]

Hirsch proceeds to discuss the three modern approaches to the kingdom of God and the state: the British liberal-utilitarian, the French utopian-socialist, and the German idealistic-humanist. What differentiates the German approach as formulated by Luther-Fichte from the others is that in it the two kingdoms are distinguished but not totally separated as in British liberalism, or collapsed into one another as in French socialism. The kingdom of God and the kingdom of the world are recognized as clearly distinct but as having a bearing upon each other. Both the freedom of the individual personality before God and the legitimacy of the state and society as authoritative, binding, earthly communities, can be valued simultaneously. The dualism between the two is a dualism in appearance only, not in essence. Participation in the natural orders must be understood as the way in which the moral will realizes itself, as the presupposition without which the ethical community cannot exist.[46]

Germany's Destiny and the Task of Christianity
Hirsch applies his theory of law, state, the two kingdoms, and ethical decision making directly to the German situation in the Weimar years. His theology and political theory become the basis upon which he now challenges Germans to commit themselves unreservedly to national renewal without deifying the nation. In his 1924 essay, "Die Liebe zum Vaterlande," Hirsch explains how this is possible for the Christian. The love of the fatherland becomes truly ethical only when it is grasped by the whole person as obedience and submission to God on the one hand, and unconditional and unreserved commitment to an earthly reality on the other: "Exactly this is the unconditionality that characterizes love for the fatherland, that it does not tolerate anything earthly as having equal right beside it. It wants the person and his power completely, without

---

45. *Ibid.*, pp. 6-7.
46. *Ibid.*, p. 28. In Tillich's review of this book he recognizes Hirsch's successful critique of the British utilitarian dissolution of the critical impact of the kingdom-of-God concept, and the secularization of the concept in socialism, but says he cannot understand how this critique applies to Religious Socialism, especially as it is influenced by Karl Barth. Tillich objects to Hirsch's throwing Religious Socialism into one pot with other socialist theories. Tillich also criticizes Hirsch for not analyzing a fourth type: namely, the conservative theory of society in which the typical Lutheran stance has most clearly expressed itself historically. He adds that "it would have been extraordinarily interesting to see how Hirsch, from his Lutheran perspective, would have extricated himself from the partly medieval-feudalistic, partly militaristic-power-political consequences of this position." According to Tillich, the kingdom-of-God idea, which he describes as the realization of the Unconditional in societal life, is the exciting element not only in occidental but in every theory of state. Hirsch, he says, has restricted himself too exclusively to the Reformation influence upon social thought. The impact of the Catholics, the sects, the Renaissance view of personality and its influence on economic life, and the socialist reaction to this, are all themes which could shed further light on the topic. Tillich encourages Hirsch to expand his treatment in future editions of the work. "Emanuel Hirsch: Die Reich-Gottes-Begriffe des neueren europäischen Denkens," pp. 42-43.

reservation."[47] If the eternal stood next to the earthly, as another earthly reality, then a hallowed love of fatherland would be impossible. But this is not the case. This would be to materialize the eternal and would then require a broken stance toward the fatherland. In fact, however, the eternal must be understood completely differently. We cannot divide up our time and powers between God and the world in this way. We must belong completely to God and his kingdom in our decision making; through this we discover God's will for us within the world. The God to whom we have decided to give ourselves is also the God who encompasses us in the world and who preserves the world. We cannot be true to him without being true to our earthly duty. "Every earthly relation is from and to God—if we make the right decision."[48] In our unreserved earthly love for our fatherland we are in effect being unreservedly faithful to God, who fulfills his historical intentions through nations and states.

It is important to remember, however, says Hirsch, that God has not only given one's own nation and state its right over the hearts of its members. One's own nation is only one powerful point of life in which world history takes place. Therefore no nation has the right to dispose of humanity and history in unrestrained and arbitrary ways. Each nation must contribute to its God-given work in world history, remembering that in world history a justice which stands above any particular nation rules. It must also remember that every nation is transient on this earth and will pass away. Death finally rules over nations.[49]

Hirsch has described the state as the highest earthly good of a nation, as the form in which alone a nation's life, freedom, and development is preserved. He has described the unreserved earthly love that a fatherland can legitimately require of its citizens. But now, in the Weimar years, Hirsch feels Germany no longer is a state in this sense. It has stopped being an historically effective and independent power in possession of its own particular life. Only an imitation of a state and a nation remains. Versailles has taken away Germany's freedom and threatens its very existence. Furthermore, German citizens do not have the kind of love for their fatherland that God requires of them. Nevertheless, the German spirit has not completely died and still lives on in some people who maintain the spirit that was dominant prior to 1914, a spirit which was largely replaced by the revolutionary German spirit of 1918.

What must be the aim in post-war Germany following the revolution and the Versailles enslavement is the regaining of that spirit which was lost through the war—"an independent state which protects us from foreign caprice (*Willkur*) and exploitation and assists our nation to establish a life of its own and an assured influence in the whole of human history."[50] "The state must once again

47. "Die Liebe zum Vaterlande," p. 20.
48. *Ibid.*, p. 23.
49. *Ibid.*, p. 29.
50. *Deutschlands Schicksal*, p. 146.

become a resolute will, a resolute personality."[51] Unfortunately, however, this will likely not come about through a return to the type of state that is most appropriate for Germany—the monarchy, which suffered a fatal stroke in the autumn of 1918.

In a most illuminating statement, Hirsch indicates sketchily his own vision for Germany's future in the prevailing circumstances: "The increase in the power of the president [*Reichspresident*] and the economic council at the expense of the *Reichstag,* the re-instatement of the department of civil service [*Fachbeamtentum*] in its old place would probably be the first measure required. Even more important is something spiritual: we must learn once again to consider our state and our law sacred."[52] The rulers, he says, could foster such an attitude if they would overcome class consciousness and become servants of the whole nation, of everyone equally. The way forward toward freedom and life will demand a great price and depend on German pride in its God-given character. Two things are required: (1) a clear view of humanity and history, of nation and state, which would sharpen one's sense of right and duty to do everything for one's own nation and state without regard for one's own person—together with the right concept of God and the gospel these truths could yet triumph over the many modern illusions; (2) something more personal: a faith in God which would awaken the qualities of the character and the soul that Germans now so badly need, and produce human beings with strong wills and warm, loving hearts.

Towards the end of the Weimar years Hirsch published his *Staat und Kirche im 19. und 20. Jahrhundert,* which he said belonged together with his *Deutschlands Schicksal* and *Die Reich-Gottes-Begriffe,* but which is distinguished from these earlier works by its sharper grasp of the current situation and its aims.[53] He begins by again emphasizing that the dynamic movement of history consists of the reciprocal relation between natural and religious life. Our awareness of eternity constantly limits everything that has its source in the natural character and power of the national and human spirit. The natural life is continually placed under the judgment and grace of supra-historical reality. This is what makes possible our relationship both to God and to healthy natural communities. This alone keeps the people who lead and shape those natural communities conscientious in their responsibility for the future of the whole.[54]

The burning issue of history is the relation of church and state, the state being the place where natural life has its content and form-giving coherence, and the church being the domain of religious life. Between 1789 and 1914, Hirsch says, a major change took place in the relationship between church and state. Before

51. *Ibid.,* p. 150.
52. *Ibid.*
53. *Staat und Kirche im 19. und 20. Jahrhundert* (Göttingen: Vandenhoeck & Ruprecht, 1929).
54. *Ibid.,* p. 5.

that the state and the church were closely bound to each other in a common enterprise; after that the state became a great power separate from the church and separate from Christianity and religion. The state became secular and religionless. The period after the war, the Weimar years, has simply brought out more sharply this separation which already occurred in the 19th century.[55] The basic reason for this is the existence of a new concept of the state, a concept which had its origin in the French Revolution and the 1791 declaration of rights. The state emerges as a sovereign common will constructed on the sovereign will of its individual citizens. Both the state and its citizens are now considered to be free, free from history, with the only enduring aspect being that of the constitution. All bonds have been dissolved, and all mediating powers between the state and the individual have been destroyed. In effect the state as defined by the majority of its citizens is now given an absolute power unknown previously.[56] The individual is now related directly and in an unmediated way to the state. What was earlier perceived as freedom has now become a form of tyranny, without any mediating institutions left to mitigate the central powers of the state. Capitalism and socialism are not genuinely opposed to each other but essentially desire the same thing—the linking of state power and economic forces over against the freedom of the individual. Hirsch believes that Europe is only now coming to the end of this post-1789 view of the state.

For Hirsch there is, however, an inherent truth in the new concept of freedom, a truth which Christianity must not reject. There is something eternally right about the belief that the individual conscience must live out its own understanding and not acknowledge anything that has not been internalized. For this reason the Evangelical Church has not been willing to give a simple yes or no to this new view of freedom. It has sought rather to develop a deeper concept of freedom, to go beyond a simple either-or and to develop a view of the state and its relationship to the church that corresponds to this deeper freedom. The great German idealist thinkers, particularly Hegel and Fichte, were especially concerned with understanding freedom in the context of the actualization of the universal spirit within the state. The individual is seen by them as having his freedom within the state. The state is viewed as the actuality of the living spirit which gives its citizens their ethical and religious depth. For both Hegel and Fichte "the invisible church was the inwardliness and depth of the life of the state itself."[57] Hirsch laments the fact that the state has been emptied of spirit,

55. *Ibid.*, pp. 8-18.
56. *Ibid.*, p. 23.
57. *Ibid.*, pp. 34-41, 37. Hirsch describes the Idealist view of freedom in the following way: "The individual has his freedom in the fact not that he determines the will of the state but that he recognizes himself once again in it and so possesses in his unification (Einigung) with it, through an understanding of the universal, the content of his own personal life. According to this the state is the body for the whole life of reason; also according to its ethical and religious depth it is the all-encompassing and all-restricting final powerful actuality of the living spirit." *Ibid.*, p. 35. While

that it no longer has concrete ethical-religious content, that we can no longer recognize ourselves—with our own affirmation of truth, goodness, and God—within it. The demonic aspect of the new concept of freedom is its self-assertion against all sense of duty and obligation.

Nevertheless, the Idealist solution, while it has much to say for it, cannot point the way into the future because it does not recognize the gulf between the two kingdoms. It collapses the spiritual and the natural into the one life of the spirit. Christianity must recognize the state as it has evolved, must accept its destiny as interwoven with humanity in the context of the modern spirit and its view of freedom. But the state must restrict itself to its earthly task and not infringe on the holy territory of the conscience and the spirit.[58] The state's earthly task is a threefold one: it must place our entire common life under the rule of law—through legislation and the administration of the law; it must take responsibility for the economic welfare of its citizens—through overseeing the economy with justice without itself controlling the economy absolutely and taking away individual initiative in economic matters; it must affirm its own independent power which seeks to preserve the freedom and independence of its citizens against other powers.[59] *What Hirsch is proposing is that the state limit itself to this threefold commitment to justice—law, economic order, power—and allow individuals room to develop their ethical-religious values in a separate sphere, so that it can in turn be renewed by this realm of the spirit. In this way it recognizes a higher order, it acknowledges that it cannot shape and control everything and that it is carried by the higher religious-ethical spirit of its citizens, and not the other way around.*

The development of this religious-ethical sphere is the special domain of Christianity and the church. Hirsch is convinced that the dominant spirit of the times stands in opposition to the spirit of Christianity. The state is presently being carried by this dominant spirit and it is Christianity's task to struggle against this spirit, to struggle for a new spirit without the assistance of the state. The state cannot be expected to hold to ethical-religious obligations which have disappeared from general consciousness. The religious-ethical values which Hirsch has in mind include monogamy, the place of the man as head of the family, the obedience of children to parents, the personal submission of the subservient to those who command, the linking of marriage and virginity, the sanctity of marital life, the sanctity of embryonic life, the sanctity of the freedom of conscience, and above all the duty to be obedient to the commands of God. "It has long become clear to us," says Hirsch, "that here, and not in the realm of

---

Hirsch criticizes German Idealism for collapsing the two realms—that of the moral-spiritual-ethical and the earthly-natural-historical—into the one life of the spirit, his particular understanding of individual freedom and political bondage is deeply indebted to the Idealist tradition. His interpretation of Luther's two kingdoms and how they relate to each other is greatly colored by German Idealism.

58. *Ibid.*, pp. 44-61.

59. *Ibid.*, pp. 46-47.

dogmas, is the crucial point of contention between the Christian religion and the spirit of the times."[60] *If Christianity were to bring about an inner transformation within itself then the state would once again also be filled with deeper spiritual-ethical content.*

The state no longer has the inner power necessary to nurture people in a way that is congenial to Christianity—the way it did in the 19th century. Neither does the state possess a national spirit. The responsibility for the vitality of the national spirit has fallen away from the state into the hands of individual families, groups, poets, and thinkers. More and more people will realize the illusory quality of freedom upon which the modern state is built; a freedom serving only the arbitrary will of the masses and public opinion. More and more people will realize that the Christian church alone, with its attempt to educate and cultivate its children according to its own conscience, is the bulwark against the growing omnipotence of the common will; that the church alone can rescue genuine individual freedom.[61]

The struggle for the conscience and the spirit, the fight against the power of sin begins in the heart of every individual Christian. Christianity must be committed to the re-formation (*Neubildung*) and sanctification (*Durchheiligung*) of earthly life, the guarding and deepening of nationality, understood from the perspective of the spirit of Christianity. This is the responsibility of Christianity.[62] Such a Christianity will be both a suffering and a fighting Christianity. Nevertheless, such a Christianity is not possible without the external church with its institutional orders, worship services, and activity. It is in the church that Christianity receives the shape of a definite working community.[63] It must become much more independent, proud, and conscious of its responsibility than heretofore. But the goals of the church, like those of the state, can be fulfilled only when individuals in their thinking, speaking, and living recognize themselves as immediately and independently responsible. The priesthood of all believers must be understood as an obligation for all Christians.

It is with these political and theological views that Hirsch entered the decade of the 1930s, the years that saw the Weimar Republic come to an end and Hitler's rise to power. As we shall see below, the views Hirsch expressed in 1933 and in his debate with Tillich in 1934-35 were quite consistent with what he had begun to say in the war years and throughout the 1920s. Before we examine Hirsch's stance toward National Socialism, however, we return now to the views of the other great protagonist in the debate, to see how Tillich's contrasting social analysis and political-theological thought evolved during the Weimar years.

60. *Ibid.*, p. 52.
61. *Ibid.*, p. 59.
62. *Ibid.*, p. 68.
63. *Ibid.*, p. 70.

Tillich's View of Religious Socialism
and its Commitment to the International Proletariat

Christianity and Socialism

Unlike Hirsch, Tillich, as we have seen, did not begin developing his political thought in any consistent systematic fashion until after the war. Beginning in 1919, however, he began to write prolifically on political and social questions. Since we cannot give an exhaustive treatment of Tillich's political, social, and theological thought,[64] we will examine here only a few of his major writings during the years of the Weimar Republic. This will help us gain valuable insight into Tillich's political and religious categories as they contrast with those of Hirsch. These writings also speak to some of the major political and theological charges later raised by Hirsch against Tillich.

In 1919-20 Tillich first wrote a number of articles on the question of how Christianity and the Christian church ought to view themselves in regard to the socialist movement in Germany; among his writings were "Der Sozialismus als Kirchenfrage," "Christentum und Sozialismus: Bericht an das Konsistorium der Mark Brandenburg," "Christentum und Sozialismus (I)," and "Christentum und Sozialismus (II)."[65]

In the first of these articles, Tillich argues that Christianity and socialism belong together. While it is true that the unconditionality of the religious principle is not dependent on specific cultural, social, or economic forms, the religious principle nevertheless becomes concrete only as it is expressed within definite forms of cultural life. Because Christianity considers the love ethic of Jesus the basic norm for communal life, Christianity has a greater affinity for some social and economic forms than for others. It must, for instance, oppose capitalistic and militaristic orders of society: it must oppose any social order which is based on the egoism of private and profit economics. But neither does Christianity uncritically join socialism. It has the task of bringing to socialism ethical and religious depth and thus to prepare for a new synthesis of religious

---

64. For such a comprehensive analysis of Tillich's political and theological thought in the Weimar years see Stumme, *Socialism in Theological Perspective: A Study of Paul Tillich 1918-1933*. Stumme's excellent book has been a most valuable resource in understanding Tillich's social and religious thought and frequent references will be made to this study in the following pages.

65. *Der Sozialismus als Kirchenfrage*, Leitsätze von Paul Tillich und Carl Richard Wegener (Berlin: Gracht, 1919). Also in *GW* II, pp. 13-20. Another version of this work in 1919 is "Christentum und Sozialismus. Bericht an das Konsistorium der Mark Brandenburg," *GW* III, pp. 154-160. Translated into English by James Luther Adams as "Answer to an Inquiry of the Protestant Consistory of Brandenburg," *Metanoia* 3,3(September 1971), pp. 10-12, 9, 16. The first of these two essays by Tillich appears to be a published and slightly revised form of the second, the original of which is in manuscript form: "Christentum und Sozialismus (I)," *Das neue Deutschland* 8(December 1919), pp. 106-110. Also in *GW* II, pp. 21-28; "Christentum und Sozialismus (II)," *Freideutsche Jugend* 6(1920), pp. 167-170. Also in *GW* II, pp. 29-33.

and social culture.[66]

Tillich stresses that distinctions must be drawn between socialism and Marxism, between the attitude of socialist parties toward the church and their attitude toward Christianity, between the socialist ideal (which is based on an ethic of love) and the empirical representations of the socialist ideal. There is no inherent opposition between the socialist ideal and Christianity. The negative disposition of social democracy toward the church is directed primarily toward the bourgeois capitalistic and nationalistic substructure of the church, which has itself little affinity with true Christianity and the ethic of love. In turn, materialism and "metaphysical atheism" are not essential to the socialist ideal but a residue of bourgeois culture within socialism. The revolutionary attitude of socialism can be seen as un-Christian only by those who equate Christianity with typical Lutheranism.

Tillich urges the church, therefore, to take a positive stand toward socialism and social democracy. It ought to commit itself to Christian social reform and tolerate within its ranks those involved in the socialist movement without expecting to win the worker movement as such for the church. This movement rightly views the church as too closely linked to the capitalistic state. Tillich does not expect the church to identify itself with the socialist movement but asks that it not exclude from its ranks those who enter the movement and struggle for a future linking of Christianity and a socialist order. He pleads with the church not to discriminate against socialists within the church. A church that refuses to be tolerant in this way, says Tillich, has given up the right to call itself a national church (*Volkskirche*) in a nation where nearly half of the people have decided for socialism.

In the third of these articles Tillich makes an even stronger case for the inherent unity of Christianity and socialism and the need they have for each other.[67] First, they must unite in their struggle against an unbroken heteronomy and for a genuine autonomy, deepened into theonomy. By theonomy Tillich means a free, unrestricted openness to being grasped by the Unconditioned within and through all things.[68] Here Christianity is being true to Protestantism,

---

66. *Der Sozialismus als Kirchenfrage*, p. 16. What Tillich says about the theological and ecclesiastical task with respect to socialism sounds similar to what Hirsch says about the Christian-theological duty toward national movements; namely, to give them ethical and religious substance and depth. The difference, as we shall see, is that Tillich's Religious Socialism claims to have a much more critical and self-critical stance towards socialism—the political movement with which it allies itself—than does the political theology of Young National Lutheranism, as represented by Hirsch, towards movements of national liberation.

67. "Christentum und Sozialismus (I)," pp. 21-28.

68. According to Tillich, "The unconditional is a quality, not a being. It characterizes that which is our ultimate and, consequently, unconditional concern, whether we call it 'God' or 'Being as such' or the 'Good as such' or the 'True as such,' or whether we give it any other name. It would be a complete mistake to understand the unconditional as a being the existence of which can be discussed. He who speaks of the 'existence of the unconditional' has thoroughly misunderstood the

which is on the side of autonomy and against any form of heteronomous church or sectarian legalism. There is some similarity between Tillich's view of the Unconditional ground of the historical-social order and Hirsch's "Theistic view of history" in which all historical reality has substance and life only through its being related to its supra-historical and metaphysical kernel. The difference is that Tillich views the relationship between the Unconditional and the earthly-historical in dialectical terms and Hirsch views it more in paradoxical terms. The second point at which Christianity and socialism need to unite is in their approach to world-shaping will. This world-shaping will must be saved from the emptiness and destructiveness of a pure technocratization of the world through an emphasis on faith as the experience of the Unconditioned. Christianity can affirm the immanent world-shaping will, seen in the context of the history of the spirit and of the kingdom of God coming into this world—but at the same time must put limits on this world-shaping will. According to Tillich, "that which can be shaped lies in the sphere of the technical—not the ethical, the categories of means and end—not of meaning and value. All shaping is technical, but the technical is not an end in itself, not the final end."[69]

Third, Christianity and socialism must unite in the sanctification (*Heiligung*) of cultural life in general and the socialist movement in particular. In order for this to be possible any strict separation between the beyond (*Jenseits*) and this world (*Diesseits*) must be rejected. What must be avoided is the opposition between Christianity viewed as a religion of the beyond (*Jenseitsreligion*) and socialism viewed as concerned with this world only (*Diesseitsstimmung*). When religion is seen as the experience of the Unconditioned with its yes and no to all earthly things and values, then the opposition between an absolute, fulfilled beyond and a relative, pluralistic world is overcome.

Here we see both a difference and a similarity between Tillich and Hirsch. Hirsch too calls for a "sanctification" of an earthly-historical movement, as we shall see again in the next chapter when we discuss Hirsch's stance toward National Socialism.[70] There is, however, a fundamental difference. *Hirsch wants to make a much sharper distinction between the religious-moral sphere (the beyond) and the earthly-historical sphere (this world) than does Tillich.*

meaning of the term. Unconditional is a quality which we experience in encountering reality, for instance, in the unconditional character of the voice of the conscience, the logical as well as the moral." "Kairos," *The Protestant Era,* translated by James Luther Adams (Chicago: The University of Chicago Press, 1966), abridged edition, p. 32, n. 1, first published in 1948. As we shall see later, Tillich's main concern with the socialist movement in Germany was that it was not sufficiently open to this unconditional element in itself. He saw the task of Religious Socialism to be that of making socialism aware of this religious dimension which is its true substance.

69. "Christentum und Sozialismus (I)," p. 26.

70. In 1934 Tillich accuses Hirsch of an unbroken sanctification or deification of National Socialism. It is interesting that in the early 1920s Tillich himself speaks of sanctifying the socialist movement and considers, as we shall see below, the mass movement of the proletariat as in some sense a holy movement, although never an unbroken holy movement.

Throughout his life Tillich was concerned with overcoming the distinction between the natural and the supernatural in a way that Hirsch was not. Even Hirsch, however, wants to maintain a bridge between the two realms. The difference is that for Hirsch the bridge occurs within the individual conscience. Tillich rejects this internalization of morality and ethics and sees the moral-religious realm, the kingdom of God, more in historical-immanent terms, as itself supplying norms not only to judge the external social-political order but to shape it positively. This is why for Tillich the Christian ideal of the kingdom of God and the socialist ideal of a universal, just and classless society have an intrinsic affinity. This is not the case for Hirsch. Hirsch rejects unequivocally any kind of intrinsic correlation between the invisible inner moral kingdom of God and the outer, visible, earthly order.

The fourth point at which Christianity and socialism need to become one is in their experience of universal human solidarity. Christianity in particular can provide the basis for such an experience of universal humanity. The cross of Christ can be viewed not only as the overcoming of Judaism (*Aufhebung des Judentums*) but also as the overcoming of Christianity to the extent that it absolutizes itself confessionally. It is here that Christianity can provide socialism with its particular substance—profound human solidarity. Socialism at the present lacks that feeling of community which creates unity from within the depth of the human—where the Unconditioned moves the soul.

It is in the fourth of these articles, "Christentum und Sozialismus (II)," that the differences between Hirsch and Tillich become truly pronounced. Tillich's main point here is that "Christianity and socialism must evolve into the future [*sich fortentwickeln*] and become one in a world and social order whose basis is an economic order shaped by justice, whose ethos is an affirmation of every human being because he is human, and whose religious substance is an experience of the divine in everything human, the Eternal in everything temporal."[71] Tillich admits that early Christianity was not genuinely socialist in its concerns. Early Christianity, he says, was concerned primarily with salvation from this world, not with its transformation, with the immanent breaking-in of the other-worldly kingdom of God, not with the improvement of the kingdom of the world.[72]

71. "Christentum und Sozialismus (I)," p. 33.
72. Tillich himself here espouses a certain kind of reading of the New Testament which not all scholars accept. Some recent theologians, such as the Mennonite John Howard Yoder, for instance, who calls himself a biblical realist, question the interpretation that Jesus' proclamation of the kingdom of God had to do primarily with an inward spiritual kingdom. According to Yoder, "Jesus was not just a moralist whose teachings had some political implications; he was not primarily a teacher of spirituality whose public ministry unfortunately was seen in a political light; he was not just a sacrificial lamb preparing for his immolation, or a God-Man whose divine status calls us to disregard his humanity. Jesus was, in his divinely mandated (i.e., promised, anointed, messianic) prophethood, priesthood, and kingship, the bearer of a new possibility of human, social, and there-fore political relationships. His baptism is the inauguration and his cross is the culmination of that

The unification of Christianity and socialism, therefore, must be based on a new idea—the idea of immanence, the idea that there is *one* reality. "It is," says Tillich, "the renunciation of the breaking-in of a transcendent kingdom of God and the replacing of this with the will to shape the kingdom of the world into the kingdom of God. One can question whether this idea is Christian or not. According to my conviction it follows from the basic principle of the Reformation—justification through faith alone."[73] In the doctrine of justification the opposition between the two worlds is overcome. Tillich maintains that his view can legitimately be called Christian even though Jesus and early Christianity did not perceive the kingdom of God in this way. It is a concept which is in harmony with the spirit of Christ.[74]

Here is a fundamental difference between Hirsch and Tillich. Hirsch has a much more traditionally theistic understanding of God; that is, a concept of God as absolutely transcendent, someone who can never be defined merely as a "quality of the relative" the way Tillich does here. Tillich's and Hirsch's political and theological differences, as illustrated in their 1917-18 debate, can be traced back to a different concept of God. Unlike Tillich, Hirsch is adamant in his refusal to define the transcendent kingdom of God as an historical-immanent goal for the world-shaping will. For Hirsch, the kingdom of God is, however, transcendent only in a very particular sense as well; namely, as the inward moral "community of conscience." Tillich ultimately rejects the kind of dualism that

new regime in which his disciples are called to share." *The Politics of Jesus* (Grand Rapids: William B. Eerdmans Publishing Company, 1972), pp. 62-63. See also Yoder, *The Original Revolution* (Scottdale: Herald Press, 1972), pp. 27-31.

73. "Christentum und Sozialismus (II)," p. 30. Tillich maintains that when freed from the medieval view of penance, justification means that the divine judgment stands in a paradoxical way over that which is relative, incomplete and unholy. As such the divine loses the character of that which is beyond, distant and supernatural, something that can be reached only through a negation of the world. The opposition between the two worlds is overcome in the doctrine of justification. In Tillich's words, "the Absolute is a quality of the relative and the relative is a quality of the Absolute. Both are one in the one reality, and the inner cleavage [*Spannung*], the paradox of the unity of the opposition creates the depth and the meaning of life." *Ibid.*, p. 31.

74. Tillich argues that if one wants to call this non-Christian, if one wants to deny the inner relation between the Renaissance and the Reformation, then one is driven to proclaim Christian only that which is Catholic—that is, that which is built on the distinction between nature and super-nature. Then, in fact, continues Tillich, we have not been Christian for a long time; then we cannot nor should we be Christian. Then we would need to find another name for the piety which fills us. "But whoever is of the belief that the spirit, which proceeds from Christ, has exhausted itself neither in Oriental nor Western Catholicism nor in Old Protestantism, but is capable of and possesses the conceptuality by which to create a new period of Christianity, for such a person there is no reason to look for a new name." "Christentum and Sozialismus (II)," p. 31. Hirsch, we might add, would agree with Tillich's description of early Christianity—at least his statement that Jesus and early Christianity did not perceive the kingdom of God as an earthly social order or political program— but would argue that Tillich's proposal for a new concept of the kingdom of God as an immanent reality which can act as a positive norm by which to shape external social reality is neither legitimately Christian nor true to the Reformation (Luther's) interpretation of Christianity.

Hirsch espouses in favor of a fundamental, ontological, dialectical monism.

Both Christianity and socialism, in Tillich's view, are concerned with establishing a just social order. Socialism wants to create a just social-economic order and a universal humanity beyond the contradictions of class, race, nationality, and confessions.[75] Whoever claims that the differences between rich and poor will always exist, that suffering, war, and race hatred are permanent realities of human existence; whoever wants to make economics a sphere of struggle by all against all, and the state as an independent organization of power; whoever struggles against individual egoism on the one hand and praises group egoism (the nation) on the other does not know anything about socialism. Although Tillich does not mention Hirsch by name here, he seems to have had people like him in mind, since economic, ethnic, and national distinctions, individual self-sacrifice for the ultimate earthly good of the nation, and the state as an independent center of power were recurring themes in Hirsch's thought.

Tillich believes that, like socialism, the spirit of Christ is intent on shaping the world according to the idea of justice for the sake of love. Like socialism it, too, is committed to the creation of universal human solidarity and community. Here again we see an important difference between Hirsch and Tillich. Although Hirsch readily admits the universality of the Christian community of conscience in Christ, this universality must and will always remain an inward, invisible reality of the kingdom of God. Historically, externally, and visibly humankind will continue to be divided along national, ethnic, and cultural lines as long as history remains history, as long as the sun shines. He categorically rejects the notion of a universal human culture and community in the external social and political sense. There is such a universal human solidarity in the Christian church as far as it represents the "community of conscience," but this cannot be actualized in visible, external, institutional, or political reality. Externally, socially, economically, and politically, the world is divided into conflicting human collectivities—nations and states.

Mass, Personality and the Holy

As we shall see in our next chapter, Hirsch perceived the National Socialist movement in the early 1930s as in some sense a "holy" movement, a "holy storm" sweeping Germany. It is this sacerdotal quality attributed to an earthly movement that Tillich is so critical of in the 1934-35 debate with Hirsch. Ten years earlier, however, Tillich himself had spoken of the proletarian movement and the nature of the masses as in some sense "holy" and representing a "Kairos" moment in Germany. In the following pages we examine Tillich's understanding of what he calls "the mass" (*die Masse*) as he expresses it in a series of articles between 1920 and 1922. These essays were published together under the title of *Masse und Geist* in 1922 and show one of Tillich's primary

75. "Christentum und Sozialismus (II)," p. 31.

socio-political categories to be that of "the mass" in contradistinction to Hirsch's parallel category of "nationality" (*das Volk*).[76] Tillich's writings on the nature, religion, and spirit of the masses grow out of and are a response to the events surrounding and following the revolution of 1918. He says as much when he notes that his basic ideas originated not out of partisan political prejudice nor out of sociological or philosophical reflection but out of the unavoidable power of recent world events which call for interpretation, and out of a serious considera- tion of the "dark depths of the life of the mass with its suffering, its formlessness and creative power."[77] Just as Tillich here sees his primary task as that of giving theological meaning to the phenomenon of the movement of the mass in the revolutionary epoch following 1918, so Hirsch in 1933, as we shall see, considers his primary task to be a theological interpretation of the phenomenon of the National Socialist movement.

In his *Masse und Geist*, which may be viewed as Tillich's counterpart to Hirsch's *Deutschlands Schicksal* since it was written during the same period,

---

76. *Masse und Geist. Studien zur Philosophie der Masse* (Berlin, Frankfurt/M: Verlag des Arbeitsgemeinschaft, 1922). Hereafter cited as *Masse und Geist*. Also in *GW* II, pp. 35-90. Earlier essays incorporated into this more major book were "Masse und Persönlichkeit," *Die Verhandlungen des 27. und 28. Evangelisch-Sozialen Kongresses,* ed. by W. Schneemelcher (Göttingen: Vandenhoeck & Ruprecht, 1920), *GW* II, pp. 36-56; and "Masse und Religion," *Blätter für Religiösen Sozialismus* 2(1921), pp. 1-3, 5-7, 9-12, *GW* II, pp. 70-90. Our references here are to *Masse und Geist* as it appears in *GW* II, pp. 35-90. Tillich uses the term "Masse" here in its singular form. We will use it in its singular (the mass) or plural (masses) form depending on the context.

77. *Masse und Geist*, p. 35. For Tillich to say as he does here that his reflections on the mass do not grow out of a partisan-political attitude is somewhat misleading. While Tillich may not have belonged to the Socialist Party as such, he clearly identified with the proletarian, socialist, and revo- lutionary cause in Germany during this period. John Stumme, in chapter 2 of his *Socialism in Theological Perspective* gives ample evidence of Tillich's political radicalism during the Weimar years: His early 1919 links with the radical Independent Social Democratic Party (USDP), his inten- sive involvement with the theoretical left-wing Kairos Circle in Berlin, 1920-1924, and his activity within socialism, 1925-1931, including his joining of the Social Democratic Party (SPD) in 1929, and his leading role in the left-wing *Blätter für religiösen Sozialismus* and later *Neue Blätter für den Sozialismus,* a paper devoted to the spiritual and political reshaping of socialism. In one sense it is true that Tillich transcended partisan politics during the Weimar years. While he saw his commit- ment to socialism as entailing a commitment to socialist parties, and while he supported the SPD, "he stayed on its periphery" and "had no discernible influence on party policies" (Stumme, p. 44). According to Stumme, this was due to his critical re-examination of Marxist theory at its basis. Stumme stresses that Tillich remained in the world of theoretical socialism and was in fact isolated from the proletariat and active political involvement. In Stumme's words, "Tillich was not a party ideologue, nor a politician, nor a 'prophet to politicians,' but a creative and critical theologian of politics" (p. 46). He was critical of the Communist Party and considered Bolshevism the "'roman- tic' version of religious socialism" which ignored the critical dimension within religion (pp. 46-47). All this, however, does not take away the partisan and ideological quality of Tillich's thinking which became, according to Stumme, increasingly more radical and Marxist towards the end of the Weimar Republic. He was committed to the transformation both of socialism and Protestantism in the hope of influencing the creation of a new social order in Germany. See Stumme, *Socialism in Theological Perspective,* pp. 15-51.

Tillich discusses three main aspects of the mass: mass and personality, mass and education (*Bildung*), and mass and religion. In the first Tillich examines five different mass types as they have evolved historically and have been depicted in various artistic periods, and various personality types as they have developed alongside of these mass types: the medieval *mystical* mass type, the Gothic and Renaissance *realistic* mass type, the baroque *dynamic* mass type, the impressionistic *technical* mass type, and the modern expressionistic *immanent* mass type.[78] These five mass types, he says, fall into three broad categories: the mystical, the technical, and the dynamic: "Those masses which are governed by an unmediated spiritual, mystical principle; those in which this principle is missing and instead external powers such as natural instinct or technique create mass-character; and those in whom an inner principle with moving power struggles for formation."[79] This latter mass type, which is a transitional one, comes to expression in modern expressionistic art and is "the mass of immanent mysticism." There is here "a new mystical mass in the making; only that the mysticism is not supernatural, escorted from above, but immanent, breaking out of the depth of the soul, remaining within earthly reality [*diesseitiger Wirklichkeit*]."[80] This dynamic mass is yearning for new organic mystical substance; a fourth kind of organic mass which is in the making and which Tillich tries to articulate and encourage.

Each of the above mass types has a personality type that corresponds to it. Tillich defines the personality as "the elevation of individuality to an independent bearer of authentic worth."[81] According to Tillich there are three personality types: the *substance* type (*Gehaltstypus*), the *form* type (*Formtypus*), and the *ethical* type.[82] The substance type of personality is characteristic of the early middle ages, in which mass is seen as the bearer of the spiritual substance of

78. In the *medieval mystical mass type* those who are led and those who lead are not independent autonomous realities but representations of ideal spiritual and supernatural forces. In the *realistic mass type* the individual personality is freed from the mystical mass and becomes real as individual. In the *dynamic mass type* these isolated individuals are drawn together within a dynamic, organic lifestream, having a new non-supernatural metaphysical base; supernatural religion has become an inner personal matter as people struggle for personal belief and renewal of society. The 19th century *technical mass type* represents the individualistic middle class in which mass is seen as an object of technique, social welfare, and disdain. In the 1920s the *immanent mass type* is born in which the mass itself becomes wholly subject, and leaders of the mass are seen as born from below, from the depth of the yearning of the masses. *Masse und Geist*, pp. 36-40. Interestingly, Hirsch also viewed Hitler not as a leader imposing his will on the masses from above, but as someone arising out of the German populace, from below and embodying within himself the ethos and will of the German people, who in turn voluntarily submitted themselves to him.

79. *Masse und Geist*, p. 40.

80. *Ibid.*

81. *Ibid.*, p. 41.

82. Tillich makes a distinction between substance (*Gehalt*) and content (*Inhalt*). Content is objective and accidental while substance is qualitative and essential. Substance gives form its meaning and significance. See Stumme, *Socialism in Theological Perspective*, p. 79.

personality. The leader does not stand above the mass but lives from and receives his spiritual substance from the mass. The form personality type is that represented in Renaissance art, in which every individual acquires significance in his own right without reference to the mass. Romanticism is based on the form type of personality but yearns for a recovery of the lost mystical substance. A new substance, however, is not a matter of will or desire; it is a matter of destiny, which comes upon the mass from within and from below, finding within the individual its consciousness.

The third type of personality is the ethical duty type, which corresponds in some ways to the dynamic mass, bearing a dialectical relationship to the form type and the substance type. It gained its historical significance during the Reformation in Protestantism and expressed itself in two directions: in the conservative Lutheran direction of dutiful subordination to officialdom (*Beamtentum*) and in the more liberal and democratic direction of Reformed piety. In the Lutheran ethical duty type (*ethischer Pflichttypus*) all members of state and society are evaluated in terms of their ethical subservience to fixed laws of duty, and the mass as such is seen as standing outside of this fixed formation of morality. The Lutheran ethical type is fundamentally conservative in its social ethics and is therefore hostile to the mass. But the hostility and opposition to the mass is even greater in Reformed (Calvinist) piety. Predestination is considered an absolute act of God isolating individuals from each other and the mass before the Absolute. This has profound implications for the world of economics and business where strong isolated individuals make their own way in their search for success.[83]

Consistent with his call for an organic mass type, a kind of immanent mysticism, Tillich here calls for the overcoming of the opposition between mass and personality, prevalent in Protestantism, through the birth of a new substance of humanity out of the depths of humanity itself. Such a new substance, however, is finally a matter of grace and destiny and cannot be manufactured through socialist or democratic techniques. No popular formation, no political or economic transformation that remains purely economic and political, can create such a new substance. Nevertheless, such a new substance can be longed for and prepared for by placing the relationship of personality to mass on a new basis. The foundation upon which a new understanding of mass and personality must be based cannot be the technical mass which destroys personality, nor the dynamic mass which tends only to be revolutionary and therefore transitional, but must be the mystical-mass which carries within it a unifying principle in which the opposition between subject and mass are overcome: "Everyone is subject insofar as he is a unique representation of the ground principle, and everyone is object in that through him the meaning of the whole comes to actualization."[84]

83. *Masse und Geist*, pp. 46-49.

In the second part of *Masse und Geist* Tillich discusses the education (*Bildung*) of the masses. He distinguishes between a purely *formal* mass—a biological conglomerate of individuals as separate entities without qualitativeness, and a *material* mass—a mass constituted of classes, races, and other collectivities which express the shaping power of the spirit within history. In this second concept of mass, tradition, custom, religion, and worldviews empower and limit the primal tendencies of life and give meaningful substance to the spiritual dimension of life. The formal mass, without material, spiritual, or social unity, results in pure negativeness—a mechanical mass in which the driving power is biological instinct—the immediate will to exist, the will to power. There is here a loss of spiritual form represented by religion, custom, family, home, and vocation. But in the depths of the mass there exists a principle out of which a dynamic mass can potentially arise which is not mechanistic, not unmediated biological instinct, but one which has spiritual substance. It can produce leaders whose subjectivity is not foreign to the mass but draws spiritual substance from it.

Tillich interprets the early Weimar years in Germany as vacillating between a mechanical and a dynamic mass movement. What is desperately needed now are educators and charismatic leaders who have an immediate relationship to the spiritual substance of the mass. But such leaders with immediacy to the masses are hard to find, least of all within individualistic-bourgeois culture. They can be found in confessional circles and socialist parties, but here also only in a broken way. The national idea, which occasionally has gripped the mass with a powerful dynamic and immediacy, has revealed its insufficient spiritual substance in the capitalist power struggle and in militarism. It has in fact mechanized the masses. "Since the national principle can never be the final spiritual foundation," says Tillich, "the protest of the masses against the predominance of this principle is spiritually justified."[85] The realization of a dynamic mass is, therefore, doubtlessly not possible outside of leaders being grasped by a propheticism derived from the mass itself. Tillich calls for educators of the mass who are concerned not to impose something foreign onto the mass but to draw out and express that inner dynamic of the mass itself, so that it can see its movement into the future as its own act, part of a cosmic drama moving toward the spiritually filled organic mass. It is interesting that Hirsch perceived Hitler's relation to the German populace in this way.

The third part of *Masse und Geist*, entitled "Masse und Religion," is the most important for our study. In it Tillich discusses the relation of mass to the holy and to religion and in the process reveals some of the similarities and differences between himself and Hirsch. *In the 1934 debate Tillich accuses Hirsch of sanctifying an earthly-historical movement (National Socialism) and considering it a*

84. *Ibid.*, pp. 52-53.
85. *Ibid.*, p. 66.

second source of revelation beside that of the kerygma. Here we see how as early as 1922 Tillich himself attributes a holy quality to the mass and sees it as a mediator of the holy to humanity. God, says Tillich in this essay, is not a reality beside other realities, not an object beside other objects, but is the a priori and presupposition of all questioning—the unconditionality of life. When one speaks, therefore, of "God and the mass" one speaks of "the revelation of that which is holy, the unconditionally-real which reveals itself through the mass."[86] The mass, although conditioned in itself, can in some sense legitimately be called holy when the unconditioned is revealed through it: *"The mass is holy: for it is the revelation of the creative infinity of the unconditionally-real* and to that degree the unconditionality of the unconditioned, seen through the category of quantity. There exists therefore a necessary relation between the holy and the mass; the holy could not be revealed as holy, nor the unconditional as unconditioned without it."[87] This applies, for Tillich, not only to the mass in abstraction but also to the mass in its concrete sociological sense: the proletariat.

Having asserted the holy aspect of the mass, Tillich is quick to qualify this assertion by saying that this relation to the holy must always be seen *paradoxically*. No individual form is ever capable of embodying the substance of the unconditionally-real other than through a paradoxical negation *and* affirmation of relative historical reality. No individual idea or form of the holy can ever be absolutized. This is most powerfully expressed by Tillich in the following statement:

> Neither a personality nor a community, neither a nation nor a church has a claim to absoluteness.... The unconditionality of the holy, which on the one side makes the unconditional demand, does not on the other side permit any being whatsoever to create a gulf between itself and another by which it itself is included in the sphere of the holy and the other is excluded. And that applies to all men and all circles, to all times and all Confessions; and it applies not only to the ethical-religious but also to the intellectual-aesthetic and to the legal-political spheres. That is the deepest reason why every profanation [*Entheiligung*] of the mass is unholy and necessarily leads to a pharisaical distortion of consciousness. Thereby the religious root of the common perverted attitude toward the mass is disclosed; the absolute divine judgment is pressed down into a relative human judgment; the absolute yes and no that befalls everyone at the same time becomes a yes to the individual and a no to the mass. Thereby, however, it is misconstrued and degraded in its essence. The holiness of the mass in the sociological sense is therefore grounded in the fact that the majesty of the holy reveals itself in it as grace, which, despite the unconditional valuation of the ethical form, does not allow

86. *Ibid.*, p. 71.
87. *Ibid.*, p. 72.

any being whatsoever to elevate itself above another before the unconditional.[88]

It is evident from the above statement that Tillich does not want to absolutize the mass nor the proletariat. *Nevertheless, for him the mass represents universal humanity through which the holy reveals itself. For Tillich the mass is a much more universal and all-inclusive category than is the nation and therefore intended to be less restrictive. What Hirsch's category of nation does for a particular group of people (Volk)—namely, provide an organic unity which overcomes class and caste differences—Tillich's category of mass is to do on a universal human scale.* However, there is built into Tillich's notion of mass an implicit restriction and partisan quality. While Tillich does not want to equate "the mass" with "the proletariat," the privileged status that the proletariat has within his schema becomes clear in his late writings. The proletariat is in fact the special representative of the dynamic mass and acts as a kind of deputy for universal humanity. So, despite his disclaimers, there is in Tillich's thought and in his discussion of mass a partisan commitment to a particular segment of humanity in a concrete sociological sense.

What distinguishes Tillich from Hirsch is not so much related to whether or not a holy quality is attributed to a finite reality, but to how this relation to the holy is described. Tillich is more dialectical and paradoxical in his terminology. What does Tillich mean when he uses the term "paradox?" The nature of paradox, emphasizes Tillich, is that it does not subjugate anything or any person to an abstract schema.[89] Paradox is not an antithesis that enslaves; rather it allows for the creative particularity and independence of every individual being. Thus the individual is paradoxically related to the mass and through the mass to the holy, both as the negation and the affirmation of particularity. The unholy arrogance of the pure self, as end in itself (*Selbstzwecklichkeit*), is superseded by the more universal end—that is, the actualization of unconditionality and holiness of pure substance (*Gehalt*). While Hirsch does not deny the paradoxical and dialectical nature of human existence, he feels that Tillich, in describing everything and all commitments paradoxically, in the end, despite his claim to the contrary, dissolves the solid commitment required in actual human situations into a free-floating individualism.

For Hirsch the individual plays a much more unique and important role in relation to the mass than for Tillich. In Tillich's schema, the mass mediates the universal, unconditional, holy substance to the individual; the mass is the "mediator of the great universal destiny."[90] Tillich argues that *"The individual is the*

88. *Ibid.*, p. 73.
89. It is noteworthy that Hirsch feels this is precisely what Tillich's dialectical method does—namely, through his systematic dialectical schema Tillich loses himself in theoretical and philosophical abstractions which are not rigorously rooted in the historical situation.
90. *Masse und Geist*, p. 75.

medium of revelation, the mass is the mediator of destiny; the invisible and visible community of ethically conscious personalities however is the bearer of all forms in the world of the spirit."[91] For Hirsch the nation has a God-given task on earth. It is the community in which the individual ego is both fulfilled and overcome. However, the relationship of the individual to the nation is for Hirsch different from the relationship of the individual to the mass in Tillich's thought. For Tillich the movement is from the mass as mediator of destiny and the world of the spirit to the individual as medium of that destiny. For Hirsch, in contrast, the movement is the other way. While it is true that for Hirsch the individual's destiny is determined to a great degree by the place where he finds himself in the historical situation, the individual stands more directly before the Absolute (God) and he expresses his ethical disobedience to God through his obligation and duty to the nation (*das Volk*). The nation represents the arena in which the individual acts out his obedience to God.

This difference between Hirsch and Tillich becomes even more pronounced in Tillich's critique of the Catholic ecclesiastical approach to the mass on the one hand, and the pietistic-individualistic approach on the other. In the former, the mass outside the church is seen as *mass perditionis*. The kingdom of God, however, says Tillich, can never be circumscribed by an empirical reality such as the church. The mass is always and everywhere *massa sancta* through the paradox of the unconditional.[92]

Pietistic individuals (and here Tillich seems to have had Hirsch in mind, even though Hirsch himself had a rather ambivalent relation to the pietist tradition), according to Tillich, make the opposite error. They reject the mass as such in favor of individuals joined together into a religious-ethical community, and regard anyone who does not participate in their particular ethical form as excluded from a relation to the Absolute. They should realize, declares Tillich, that they themselves are carried by the irrational substance which lives in the hidden depths of the mass and "brings every individual into destiny-like dependence on the eternal substance itself, the unconditionally real, the holy. That is the meaning and that is the necessity of the deeply paradoxical presupposition about the holiness of the mass."[93]

91. *Ibid.,* p. 76. In referring to "the invisible and visible community of the ethically conscious personalities" Tillich would seem to have precisely the views of Hirsch in mind. For Hirsch the "invisible community of conscience" made up of ethically conscious individuals is not merely the bearer of all forms in the world of the spirit but the bearer of spiritual substance itself, to use Tillich's terminology.

92. *Ibid.,* p. 77. In this connection Tillich makes an interesting observation concerning the kingdom of God: "The kingdom of God is however independent from every form, even of the churchly and confessional. It breaks into the world of relativity in every period and every place, wherever the unconditional is experienced through any relative form. Because it is independent from every form, however, it is mediated through the destiny-bearing mass which is never and nowhere a *massa perditionis*, but always and everywhere a *massa sancta* through the paradox of the unconditional." *Ibid.*

Having discussed the relation of the mass to the holy, Tillich devotes the latter part of *Masse und Geist* to the relation of the mass to religion. He distinguishes between two types of religion—the substance type (*Gehaltstypus*) and the form type (*Formtypus*), corresponding to the two types of mass (the organic and the dynamic). Consciousness of the divine, he argues, can take the shape of a "mystical comprehension of the unconditionally real [*Unbedingt-Wirklichen*]" or the "ethical and logical comprehension of the unconditionally valid [*Unbedingt-Gültigen*]."[94] The first, which is always the carrying principle (*tragende Prinzip*) of the second, is the cultic-pedagogical type and the second is the eschatological type. Tillich envisions and hopes for the synthesis of these two types of religion just as he envisions the synthesis of the dynamic and the organic mass. In this distinction and in his desire to combine them into a new synthesis Tillich is anticipating the distinction between priestly-sacramental and prophetic-eschatological approaches to religion, something that was to figure so strongly in the 1934-35 debate.

In the cultic-pedagogical type of religion, represented by the Catholic church, the presence of eternity is symbolized through myth and cult. Time becomes meaningless, "consciousness stretches not forward toward the creating of new actualities but rather upward toward the unchangeable truth and downward into the given sphere of life which is to be penetrated by that truth."[95] The eschatological type of religion, on the other hand, is directed exclusively toward the future. God is seen not as he-who-is (*der Seiende*) but as he-who-is-to-come (*der Kommende*). He is viewed not as static substance but as world-transforming will. *But this kind of eschatological piety, says Tillich, can only be a transitional form because any purely eschatological movement ends either in disappointment or in a return to cultic-pedagogical religion because the eschatological form always depends upon mystical-sacramental content.*

Protestantism represents a combination of the two in what Tillich calls the "ethical-cultic" type of religion. It has a paradoxical and contradictory relation to the mass. Insofar as it is cultic it has a proximity to the mass, but insofar as it stresses the ethical-personal side it can have no living relation to the mass. Such a relationship would be possible only through a new eschatological movement, but its quietistic ecclesiastical conservatism must reject this. As a consequence, eschatological sects and the extra-churchly eschatological movement of socialism find themselves outside this type and reveal the inadequacy of Protestantism.[96] The development of the ethical-cultic type of religion in Protestantism during the Reformation contributed to the development of the autonomy of the individual. The hierarchical authority of orthodoxy was

93. *Ibid.*, p. 78.
94. *Ibid.*, p. 79.
95. *Ibid.*
96. *Ibid.*, p. 81.

broken. Unfortunately, the mass lost the cultic-pedagogical form of its religious life. As a consequence it turned exclusively to the eschatological form, which corresponds to the dynamic mass type—a revolutionary movement into the future.

The Enlightenment aggravated the plight of the mass through its criticism of cultic consciousness but it did provide the mass with the notion of immanence. The revolutionary eschatological spirit of the Reformation united with the earlier tradition of divine law, natural law, and rational law and applied it to the transformation of the world into a kingdom of reason and justice. The kingdom of heaven was now seen as coming from above, not as a world-transforming act of God but as an act of humanity brought about by the spirit and the sword. This post-Enlightenment, revolutionary, eschatological spirit has filled and impelled the mass from the time of the French Revolution to present-day Communism toward sacrificial commitment and heroic struggle. This post-Enlightenment mass religion of the eschatological type is distinguished from the sectarian eschatological type of the Reformation period in that it is based on immanence. The consciousness of autonomy has replaced authoritarian obligation of whatever kind. Its hope for a world-shaping revolution is based not on the power of the supernatural but on reason which has a dialectical quality—namely, there is a moment when reason is taken out of human hands and becomes subject to a superior power of destiny that works through the historical process. Events receive the dimension and consecration of the holy. There is a community of spirit, a belief, a longing by the mass for a common experience of the holy.

The basis for community in this new immanent, eschatological, mass religion type is the *class,* the bearer of revolutionary faith. What is the class? "The consciousness of class is the historically-conditioned expression of the consciousness of humanity."[97] The class carries the movement but humanity is its aim—not humanity as a biological appearance but humanity as the bearer of all value. The class struggle is a struggle against nationalism, confessionalism, race-hatred, against those who exclude themselves from the universal human community. But there is in this class struggle an inner contradiction, an inner dialectic which tends to destroy the religious dimension of this modern eschatological mass movement. It is the contradiction between empirical necessity—which leads to class interest and class patriotism, and the ideal human community—which transcends everything material and empirical. The solution is not a return to a new form of transcendence and authority but the incorporation of the cultic-pedagogical experience of religion into the immanent eschatological type. This does not mean the rejection of a world-shaping will directed toward the future but the becoming conscious of the unconditional experience of the holy beyond pure technique and strategy.

97. *Ibid.,* p. 85.

The coming religion of the mass will need to combine both cultic and mystical substance with eschatological form, with the unconditional moral and ethical demand. "Wherever, however, the holy is livingly contemplated and experienced in the present, there the 'kingdom of heaven' is never only in the future but always already in the midst of and within us, and all shaping of the world is a working out of something already at hand, something contemplated and venerated, not a manufacturing of something which is [merely] thought or calculated, hoped for, or discovered."[98]

This new religion of the mass will therefore combine both mystical and activist elements. It will contemplate the holy and shape the world. It will evolve into a cultic-pedagogical type of religion without losing its eschatological impetus. Its view of transcendence will not be that of a "transcendent actuality...but of an inner 'transcending'...."[99] Tillich believes—and here he reveals his historical optimism about the mass in contrast to the historical pessimism of Hirsch—that to the extent that obstacles and reaction do not hinder it the religion of the mass is in fact already evolving in this new direction. The future religion of the mass is neither churchly nor worldly: "It sees the realization of the holy not in the soul and not in the church but in the world—that is its immanence."[100] It realizes that this immanentizing (*Verweltlichung*) cannot come through technique and strategy but only through souls (*Seelen*) and their community, out of which the power of the unconditional breaks forth. This is the transcending element. "Thus the religion which is coming to be unifies the eschatological and the cultic-pedagogical, the form- and substance-type of religion, on the foundation of immanence and builds a unity of both forms of the religion of the mass."[101]

While class consciousness and class patriotism are necessary as transitional forms between the present reality and the future universal ideal human consciousness, the distinction between the ideal religious human community and the empirical class-conscious community must always be kept in mind:

Not the empirical but the ideal class is the basis of the religious community. The critique from the perspective of the ideal, however, which is identical with the ideal human community, directs itself with equal energy against one's own class as against that of the opponent. In the technique [*Technik*] of the political struggle this is not possible. In the sphere of the religious feeling of community it is self-evident. One thinks of the "crypto-capitalism" of dictatorial leadership and party mechanism in the working class. All these are consequences of politically necessary things; and what is necessary also

98. *Ibid.*, p. 89.
99. *Ibid.*, p. 90.
100. *Ibid.*
101. *Ibid.*

has its legitimacy from the perspective of the holy. But it has as much illegitimacy as legitimacy in it. *Unconditionally holy is the ideal class alone, the ideal human community, the "kingdom of God."* [102]

This is an important statement because it reveals the difficulty in Tillich's thought with respect to the relationship of the empirical human community to the ideal human community. In his controversy with Hirsch in 1934-35 Tillich maintains that because Hirsch separates the two kingdoms so radically, relegating the kingdom of God to the inward private sphere and the kingdom of humanity to the outer public sphere, he cannot be sufficiently critical of external political movements, particularly the (Hirsch) movement that he himself identifies with. Tillich maintains that unlike Hirsch and others who support National Socialism, the Religious Socialists never uncritically supported the socialist proletarian cause.

On one level this self-evaluation on the part of Tillich is entirely true, as the above quotation indicates. Tillich never equates the "ideal human community" and the "ideal class" with the existing empirical human community, the socialist party, or the working class. This self-critical stance is abundantly clear in his writings during the Weimar years. But Tillich does have a problem defining the exact relationship of the ideal human community (the kingdom of God) to the empirical political movement with which he identifies. While not equating the two he does, it would seem, link them in an intrinsic sense. The empirical necessities of the political class struggle and the cause of the proletariat are in a real sense transitional stages in the movement toward the ideal human community, the kingdom of God. For Tillich the ideal human community is in fact the kingdom of God. It is this intrinsic connection between historical communities and the Kingdom of God that Hirsch so passionately rejects.

Excursus: Hirsch's Critique of Tillich's View of the Proletariat
We have devoted considerable time and space to a discussion of Tillich's *Masse und Geist* partly because it provides us with a convenient point of comparison with Hirsch's *Deutschlands Schicksal* of 1920. It is in fact this book that Hirsch gives an extensive and critical analysis of in his private correspondence with Tillich. It is evident from this unpublished correspondence that Hirsch carefully read Tillich's *Masse und Geist* and was highly critical of it. In an April 19, 1921 letter, Hirsch comments on fragments of the still unpublished book. In this letter Hirsch is especially critical of Tillich's notion that the individual personality is primarily the exponent of the mass—the symbols by which the mass understands and expresses itself. There may be such cases, admits Hirsch, but by and large this is not borne out by the facts. Great historical figures such as Jesus, Augustine, Luther, Rousseau, Kant, and Fichte were surely more than merely

102. *Ibid.*, p. 89.

exponents of the self-understanding of the mass.

Throughout his work Hirsch places great emphasis on the value of the individual personality for its own sake. In this letter Hirsch ironically accuses Tillich of deifying the mass, of cultivating and contributing to the self-deification and self-flattery of the proletarian masses. This is ironical because some 12 years later it is Tillich who similarly accuses Hirsch of hallowing the National Socialist revolution. In 1921 Hirsch—with foreshadowings of the theological critique that Tillich calls for from Hirsch in 1934—challenges Tillich to be more critical of the proletarian movement that he supports. In this letter Hirsch says that if Tillich's spirit becomes dominant within the proletarian movement, then all serious Christians will need to rise up unanimously against socialism. This would be unfortunate, says Hirsch, for it would lessen Christianity's critique of the current capitalistic reaction, a reaction which he himself also rejects.

What is needed, Hirsch says, is the drawing of a clear vertical line between the religious and the social spheres. The workers truly have the same right as the big entrepreneurs and the farmers to fight for their legitimate rights and interests in the name of justice. But if they consider themselves as in any way holy and rise up against the eternal will of God and conscience then they will rightly come to naught. Hirsch strongly criticizes Tillich for making the mass into an appearance of the divine in its natural concrete present. Tillich's analysis of the mass, he believes, lacks the call to repentance which is required also of the proletariat. The holiness of the mass in Tillich's thought, he believes, is not conditioned by the ethical. It is simply assumed to be holy. Tillich's view of the mass, claims Hirsch, comes close to paganism in positing a communal relationship with God without ethical conditions. The point at which Christianity moves beyond paganism is, in Hirsch's view, precisely in its emphasis on the ethical and the personal in relation to the transcendent and the eternal.

It may be, Hirsch allows, that Germany will in the future become a proletarian state, but in whatever way man transforms his earthly house it will still always remain a house of mud and clay. God's kingdom will remain something which abides within anticipating and obedient hearts. God's love penetrates every earthly order as something from beyond. The social order, in contrast to this kingdom of God, pertains to culture. God's kingdom will always remain a question of the conscience's personal relation to eternity. Without such a hidden kingdom of God which is both beyond and within culture, every earthly order collapses into the dust out of which it is built. According to Hirsch, the issue of restructuring the social order requires a serious consideration of the substantive issues—apart from mass pride and mass illusions—if a practical way between capitalism and the obligations of Christianity is to be found.[103]

---

103. Personal letter, Hirsch to Tillich, April 19, 1921.

In a January 27, 1922 letter to Tillich, Hirsch thanks him for sending a completed copy of *Masse und Geist* and then proceeds to criticize Tillich's analysis of the mass even more extensively. Their conceptual worlds, remarks Hirsch, have by now moved far apart and become so strange to one another that common presuppositions are hard to find. He recognizes Tillich's unusual capacity for schematization but criticizes him for lacking rigor and clarity, for failing to develop his thought to its ultimate conclusions. Hirsch thinks Tillich's thought lacks full ripeness and the weight of conviction. He considers Tillich's reflections on historical matters abstract and incomplete and remarks that it is unheard of that dialecticians like Tillich in constructing a mediation or synthesis between two antitheses ever decide for one of the antitheses.

More specifically, Hirsch dislikes Tillich's treatment of the *ethical* personality, in which he feels that Tillich is in fact engaged in a personal struggle with his own (Hirsch's) views. Tillich uses the concept of ethical personality only as a kind of sport for the purpose of building a logically consistent typology, he says. Further, Hirsch blames Tillich for not fully developing the relation of the personality types to the mass types. He is sceptical about Tillich's typology in general and his understanding of the individual in particular. Personality, says Hirsch, can and must be understood outside of its sociological relatedness. The notion of personality is a religious one expressing a relation to the eternal. It is defined by an individual's communion with God, by the relationship of the conscience to God. Tillich does not do justice to the ethical type because he does not recognize this. He perceives ethical norms and the ethical personality only in terms of social relationships. For Hirsch, however, the good is something eternal in relation to which social function is secondary. The ethical goal is to find one's way to God, to become God-like in one's communion with God even as a child relates to a father. Only because God wills to establish and promote community do social relations become an ethical concern.

What concerns Hirsch even more, however, is Tillich's renunciation of an unconditional ethical demand. Where one person can no longer confront another with an unconditional demand, there one loses the ability to show another the way to the eternal. Hirsch believes this rejection of an unconditional ethical demand is born, in Tillich's case, out of the unfounded belief that at the present a new life for all is emerging out of the mass. Christian belief in God, by contrast, stands or falls with the belief that new life comes not from below but from above. The person who believes that such new life comes from below deifies humanity. From this vantage point socialism, at its deepest level, is opposed to Christianity.[104]

---

104. Personal letter, Hirsch to Tillich, January 27, 1922.

Principles of Religious Socialism

Beginning in 1920 Tillich was deeply involved in the "Kairos Circle," a small intellectual group, not bound by confessional commitments, meeting on a regular basis for theoretical, social, political, and theological discussions. It is in the context of this circle of friends that Tillich forged his Religious Socialist views, the details of which are perhaps best expounded in his 1923 essay "Grundlinien des Religiösen Sozialismus."[105] In this work Tillich systematically discusses the stance, the goal, the struggle, and the way of Religious Socialism.

Religious Socialism adopts a prophetic stance in which (1) a sacramental-unhistorical attitude is united with (2) a rational-historical attitude and the historical moment is recognized as one of *kairos*. This prophetic stance does not fall either into a sacramental indifference to history or into a rational emptying out of spiritual substance, but unites the sacramental and the critical within a higher unity. According to Tillich, *kairos* "signifies the moment of time which is filled with unconditional substance [*Gehalt*] and unconditional demand [*Forderung*]."[106] The reason why he is so perturbed by Hirsch's political stance in 1934 is that he feels the latter has plagiarized his *kairos* doctrine but stressed only one side of it—namely, the sacramental side.

The goal of Religious Socialism, according to Tillich, is a theonomous culture in which "religious symbols are the final and most all-encompassing expression of autonomous cultural consciousness and the autonomous cultural forms are emanations of the fullness of the substance of the unconditional."[107] *Kairos* is the unique moment which has the possibility of becoming

---

105. "Grundlinien des Religiösen Sozialismus," *Blätter für Religiösen Sozialismus* 4,8-10(1923), pp. 1-24. Also in *GW* II, pp. 91-119. Again it must be said at the outset of this section that it is not our intent to give an exhaustive treatment of Tillich's political thought as it relates to socialism in general or Religious Socialism in particular. For such a comprehensive treatment see Stumme, *Socialism in Theological Perspective*. In chapter 3 of his excellent study, Stumme gives an extensive analysis of "The Meaning of Socialism" for Tillich. Stumme's main point in this chapter is that Tillich's particular understanding of socialism, developed from a theological-Protestant perspective, differs sharply from that of Marxist orthodoxy which dominated the German SPD at the time. For Tillich, socialism was, first, the expression of a particular socio-political group (the proletariat)—in this he agreed with socialist orthodoxy; second, however, Tillich perceived genuine socialism as a religious phenomenon which makes the ultimate, the eternal, the unconditional accessible to the proletariat; and, third, socialism is a prophetic movement in the tradition of the Jewish prophets, except that it goes beyond them in respecting the modern demands of autonomy. *Ibid.,* pp. 71-108, esp. 104ff.

106. "Grundlinien des Sozialismus," p. 94. The *kairos* concept was meant to express both a forward (horizontal) impulse and an upward-downward (vertical) direction, or historical-dialectical and paradoxical thinking. According to Stumme, "The notion of kairos thus combines the 'forward' thrust of the historical dialectic with the 'upward' relationship of the divine-human paradox." *Socialism in Theological Perspective*, p. 192. This category was Tillich's attempt to recover the utopian spirit inherent in socialism but at the same time to prevent it from becoming utopian—that is, from anticipating the full realization of the eternal within time without recognizing the eternal's shattering of time. *Ibid.,* pp. 189ff.

107. "Grundlinien des Sozialismus," pp. 97-98.

theonomous, a situation in which spiritual and social forms are filled with holy and unconditional substance.[108] Such a theonomous culture is distinguished both from a utopia of the beyond (*jenseitigen Utopie*), in which the emphasis on the ideal world devalues the conditional historical world, and this-worldly utopia (*diesseitigen Utopie*), which "leaves nature uncontested and desires to erect a rational social and spiritual structure on an irrational natural basis."[109]

Religious Socialism desires theonomy, not rational utopia. Religious Socialism is distinguished from utopianism in its emphasis on the individual, the concrete, and the historical. The difficulty with Tillich's language—his concepts of the unconditional, of the *kairos,* of theonomy—is that while he develops these categories precisely for the sake of becoming historically concrete, the categories themselves remain highly theoretical, abstract, and formal. The criteria by which an actual *kairos* or theonomous situation can be determined remain unclear and unspecific. Hirsch recognized this difficulty in Tillich's thought and with some justification accuses Tillich of failing to commit himself unambiguously within the historical situation.

This "dialectical ambiguity" (at least as perceived by Hirsch) is also evident in Tillich's discussion of concepts of "religious reservation" and "religious obligation" to culture. Culture and religion, says Tillich in this essay, can never

---

108. In 1922 Tillich first published an essay entitled "Kairos," in *Die Tat* 14(1922), pp. 330-350. Also in *GW* VI, pp. 9-28. It has appeared in English in Paul Tillich, *The Protestant Era,* translated by James Luther Adams (Chicago: The University of Chicago Press, 1948), pp. 32-51. In this essay Tillich develops the concept of the *kairos* as a summons to both a consciousness of the unconditioned and eternal, and a consciousness of history and the need for historical action. *Kairos,* he says, in contrast to a "mystical unawareness of history" (a pure contemplation of the timeless), on the one hand, or a "naturalistic unawareness of history" (capitivity of all time to this world and to recurrent cycles and eternally identical process), on the other, stresses the experience of the timeless within time. The *kairos* fights against any absolutizing of a special historical reality, whether in the form of a "revolutionary-abstract type" of historical consciousness which pronounces an absolute no to the past in favor of the future, or in the form of a conservative type of historical consciousness which absolutizes a moment or reality of the past as embodied in the church, a pure doctrine or a hierarchy. "The unconditional cannot be identified with any given reality, whether past or future; there is no absolute church, there is no absolute kingdom of reason and justice in history. A conditional reality set up as something unconditional, a finite reality to which divine predicates are attributed, is anti-divine; it is an 'idol.' This prophetic criticism launched in the name of the unconditional, breaks the absolute church and the absolute society; conservative ecclesiasticism and revolutionary utopianism are both idolatry." *Ibid.,* pp. 37-38. This means, likewise, that *kairos*-thinking must reject the "indifferent-type" of historical consciousness (here Tillich is quite certainly referring to Barthian crisis theology) which "remains abstract, beyond every special criticism and judgment." *Ibid.,* p. 39. Tillich's understanding of the historical and social nature of the kingdom of God, his understanding of what the actual future goal of Religious Socialism is, remains somewhat vague. Nevertheless, as is abundantly clear from Tillich's "Kairos" essay, Hirsch's accusation that Tillich is deifying an earthly reality like the mass or the proletariat—that Tillich is in some sense simply historicizing the kingdom of God—does not adequately take into account Tillich's emphasis on the Eternal's shattering of history, time, and all earthly utopias.

109. "Grundlinien des Sozialismus," p. 95.

simply be placed over against each other because culture is the form in which religion expresses itself. Religion is the substance which gives culture meaning. He maintains that "...all culture is actualized religion and all religion actualizes itself as culture."[110] The demonic is that which opposes unconditional form by identifying conditional forms with the unconditioned, thereby becoming destructive and self-destructive.[111] Because divine and demonic forms are always mixed together in every culture, religion and culture can never be easily identified or separated. Religion always has a double relation to culture, entailing both a no—which Tillich calls *"reservatum religiosum,"* and a yes—which he calls *"obligatum religiosam."* For this reason culture rightly rejects a culture-Protestantism, which robs culture of its transcendent religious substance, and why religion legitimately rejects the identification of religion and socialism, which robs religion of its very essence.

Religious Socialism, therefore, has a double stance toward culture and socialism, marked both by reservation and obligation. In his 1934 debate with Hirsch, Tillich accuses Hirsch of not having this double stance but of stressing only an unreserved commitment to the historical situation. Hirsch is fully aware of the dangers of such a commitment but considers Tillich's dialectical stance as much more irresponsible in that ultimately Tillich never finds himself on one side or the other. Even his commitment to socialism is not clear.

In the third part of this essay—in his discussion of the struggle of Religious Socialism—Tillich attempts to become more specific about the actual theoretical and practical commitments of the movement. In the theoretical sphere, Religious Socialism is committed to the fight against the rule of the demonic in the present, both in its sacramental and its natural forms. In its fight against these demons, Religious Socialism appropriates rational, liberal, and democratic elements, remaining fully aware of the demonic dangers inherent in liberalism and rationalism which tend to empty cultural forms of all spiritual substance. In sacramentalism, personality is dominated by a sacred relationship to soil, prop-

110. *Ibid.,* p. 95.

111. For Tillich, "The demonic is the elevation of the irrational ground of all individual, creative actualization of form [*Formverwirklichung*] in opposition [*im Widerspuch mit*] to the unconditional form.... The demonic is never formless. In that it is like the divine.... The demonic is observable as is the divine within the ecstatic, overwhelming, dreadful. While, however, the ecstatic of the divine affirms unconditional form and thus creates forms, the ecstatic of the demonic destroys form." *Ibid.,* p. 98. James Luther Adams explains Tillich's difficult concept of the demonic as follows: "The demonic cannot be understood, however, unless one realizes that it has positive significance. *Demonry* appears when the urge for form-creation, by stepping too high, drives on toward self-inflation and form-destruction. Hence it combines meaningful and meaningless elements, with the latter becoming predominant through the violation of universal norms. Neither element normally obtains complete sway in this world of ambiguity. If the meaningless element predominates to the point of complete disintegration, the demonic becomes *satanic.* The concept of the demonic, properly understood, combines destructive and creative elements." *Paul Tillich's Philosophy of Culture, Science & Religion* (New York: Harper & Row, Publishers, 1970), p. 51.

erty, family, clan, class, nation, and state hierarchy. The personality legitimately receives its substance and meaning from this sacramental structure but loses its autonomous aspect. The autonomous worth of personality suffers. This is the reason for the theocratic fight against all sacramentalism for the sake of justice, equality, recognition of personality, and liberation from enslavement to nature, most effectively represented by the Jewish prophetic tradition. It is within this tradition that Religious Socialism places itself. It sides with liberalism and democracy while recognizing the natural and demonic dangers inherent in the abstract and empty forms of freedom and equality.

Tillich attempts to apply this two-pronged fight of Religious Socialism to the fields of economics, law, state, and community. Religious Socialism is committed to the restructuring of economics, in which human eros in relation to property and things is transformed. There can be no talk of destroying technology and the machine; this would represent a return to the sacramental-demonic. What must be affirmed is a living personality which is adequate to the machine. Religious Socialism opposes any romantic reaction to the machine as well as the natural-demonic character of economic autonomy. The eros- and power-relationships between persons and property must be grounded anew on a mythic and cultic consecration of universal technical and economic processes.[112]

In the field of law, Religious Socialism joins theocratic liberalism in its fight against a sacramental understanding of law that defines the relationship between people in terms of a culticly-consecrated community in which individual personality is suppressed. But it is also critical of a formal and autonomous understanding of law that sides with freedom and equality but in which the living substance of the community disappears and is replaced by an abstract system of rational relationships. Such an understanding of law leads to a new distortion of free personality and the endless struggle by all against all, including the class conflicts of the capitalistic period. Religious Socialism supports the class struggle as an historically-conditioned reality, as a form of resistance to injustice brought about by the domination of capital. But in itself the class struggle is the expression of the demonic character of capitalistic economy. Religious Socialism must provide the class struggle with a theonomous economic perspective, one that sees the economy as rooted in the unconditioned.[113]

The state is the community which establishes and enforces law. It is the bearer (*Träger*) of all justice. Religious Socialism rejects both the sacramental-

---

112. "Grundlinien des Sozialismus," pp. 106ff. Stumme points out that while Tillich agreed that socialism involved a different economic structure than did capitalism, this was not his primary concern and he took a flexible approach to economics in a future socialist society. Tillich, according to Stumme, did not identify socialism with a particular economic system, or a particular political party, but rather with a meaningful society, a theonomous society in which economic and political forms were carried by their unconditional substance. See Stumme, *Socialism in Theological Perspective*, p. 106.

113. "Grundlinien des Sozialismus," pp. 108ff.

demonic understanding of the state, in which all authority represented by the ruling stratum of society is sacramentally grounded, and the natural-demonic view of the state which aims at the dissolution of the state in a universal organism of law as pure self-sufficient form. German political parties— conservative, aristocratic, center, liberal, socialist-communist, and nationalist— all represent either one or the other of these views of the state, or modifications of them. Religious Socialism, however, cannot attach itself in a fixed way to any of these political parties. It struggles against all sacramental, hierarchical, and autocratic forms of power, on the one side, and any elevation of the natural form of power—as in nationalism, which uses the rational form of the state for its own purposes—on the other. Religious Socialism supports a thoroughly rationalized democratic constitutional state (*der durchrationalizierte demokratische Rechtsstaat*) filled with the holy substance of a creative theonomy. "The state must be borne by the eros and inner power of those in whom the theonomous substance comes to expression most powerfully[114]

In external politics, similarly, the demonic character of a naturalistic nationalism which consecrates itself sacramentally must be opposed by an affirmation of the theocratic idea of law (*Rechtsidee*), not as empty power and eros-destroying form but as "the building-up of national and racial [*rassenhafter*] power."[115] The leading nations (*Führervölker*) must be the strongest carriers of the theonomous idea of humanity. For this reason Religious Socialists oppose a radical pacifism (like that of Tolstoi's) which does not acknowledge the aggressive affirmation of legal form (*Rechtsform*). Such pacifism overlooks the fact that only through force against arbitrariness (*Willkür*) can law assert itself. Religious Socialism rejects both mystical and naturalistic anarchism. It affirms

114. *Ibid.*, p. 113. When Tillich talks about Religious Socialism it is clear that he is not talking about a political party or a concrete political program. Religious Socialism, which represents the genuine socialist idea or principle, is a kind of "ideal type" in the Weberian sense but cannot be concretely identified with any actual historical party or movement. The Religious Socialist circle obviously included some of his friends in the "Kairos Circle" although it is not clear to what extent these colleagues would have agreed with Tillich's perception of Religious Socialism. It is precisely this rather vague ideal understanding of Religious Socialism (or genuine socialism) which makes Tillich particularly vulnerable to Hirsch's charge that he and his views represent a kind of intellectualism that ultimately cannot find itself concretely and unequivocally committed to an actual movement or community.

115. *Ibid.*, p. 113. Here again we are faced with the difficulty of translating terms such as *Recht*, *Rechtsidee*, and *Rechtsform*. We have translated *Recht* as law, but in fact it means more than the simple English term "law." It includes within it the idea of "right" and "justice" in a more general moral sense. Even in Tillich's Religious Socialism we occasionally find a strange romantic view of the role of nations and races as theonomous carriers and representatives of the universal ideals of humanity. In fact, Detlef Döring, in his recent book *Christentum und Faschismus*, argues that there exists in the Religious Socialism of Tillich an ambivalence in the face of National Socialism. This ambivalence, he says, rests in the fact that Tillich and his Religious Socialist circle shared with National Socialism a certain revolutionary-romantic protest against the decline of the west and a critique of modernity (pp. 43-60).

the need to use force to establish law both internally and externally. Only the holy community can renounce law in a symbolic way but no one can deny the state the right to use force in administering the law.

Finally, where does Religious Socialism as a movement concretely belong? It is a community of those who have an awareness of the *kairos* and who struggle for the destiny and grace of theonomy. It is a community which has a sense of solidarity with but can never identify itself wholly with any confession, church, cultural movement, or political party.[116] It espouses a theocratic and autonomous critique against all given symbols and stands closest to that confession which most clearly contains within itself the critical-theocratic element. This means that it has a certain affinity for and solidarity with the radical left wing of the Reformation. It is, however, not a religious sect; a sect is based not on autonomy and critique but on a new perception and transformation of old symbols. Religious Socialism, in contrast, is borne out of critical autonomy and in itself has no symbolic power. It is therefore not in itself a religious community.

Neither is Religious Socialism identical with a cultural movement or a political party. This means that it cannot be identified with political socialism nor can it be a new party alongside of political socialism. It calls itself socialist because it has appropriated the historical and material anti-demonic critique of socialism and supports the political struggle of socialism against the rule of political and social demons. Religious Socialism is, however, well aware of the extent to which political socialism is itself grasped by the demonic and knows that the socialist idea cannot be equated with political strategy.

Religious Socialism therefore rejects giving religious sanction to any socialist political party or any socialist economic program as such. It is open to the theonomous elements in other parties and movements. It cannot make community dependent upon party membership. But it demands acknowledgement of the socialist critique of culture and the socialist struggle against sacramental and natural demons. "They [Religious Socialists] can work in every party, confession, or movement insofar as these are given room to do their work and allowed to struggle against the demonic element."[117] Solidarity with socialist parties is possible of course but only in a provisional sense in order to guard against itself [Religious Socialism] becoming heteronomous and rationalistic.

---

116. Like Hirsch, Tillich was concerned with notions of the common good and community (*Gemeinschaft*). A meaningful society or socialist community would be one in which the class conflicts of the capitalist era would be overcome. According to Stumme, however, Tillich was somewhat hesitant to use the word "community" because of its romantic connotations. Cf. Stumme, *Socialism in Theological Perspective*, p. 195.

117. "Grundlinien des Sozialismus," p. 119.

The Proletariat and the Protestant Principle

It is evident when reading Tillich on Religious Socialism that he is faced with a fundamental problem in his political thought. On the one hand he develops his central categories of *kairos* and theonomy precisely for the purpose of making Religious Socialism socially responsible and genuinely conscious of history; another concept he uses for this purpose is "believing realism."[118] On the other hand Tillich is keenly aware of the danger inherent in socialism of equating God, the holy, the eternal, the ultimate, the unconditioned (all these concepts are more or less interchangeable for Tillich) with any particular historical cause, movement, party, or empirical reality for fear of absolutizing or deifying a conditional or finite reality. This means that Religious Socialism always remains strong in its critical and negative functions but weak in espousing any kind of specific, positive, concrete economic, political, or social programs. Tillich makes some general positive statements about what a meaningful or "substance-ful" socialist society might look like economically, legally, politically, and nationally (*staatlich*) but these remain rather vague. This difficulty, or perhaps more accurately this dilemma, becomes even more evident in Tillich's whole discussion of the situation of the proletariat in light of the Protestant principle.

One of Hirsch's theological charges against Tillich is that the latter has an inadequate grasp of and appreciation for Luther's doctrine of creation, and in particular Luther's doctrine of the two kingdoms as grounded in the law/gospel distinction. While a thorough study of how and to what extent Tillich's political ethics is rooted in Luther's theology would be helpful in trying to understand the Tillich-Hirsch debate, we cannot in this work go into any extensive examination of Tillich's indebtedness to and reinterpretation of Luther's theology.[119] All we

118. Tillich discusses what he means by "belief-ful realism" or "believing realism" in two essays: "Gläubiger Realismus," *Theologenrundbrief für den Bund deutscher Jugendvereine* 2(November 1927), pp. 3-13; also as "Gläubiger Realismus I," *GW* IV, pp. 77-87; and "Über Gläubigen Realismus," *Theologische Blätter* 7(1928), pp. 109-118; also as "Gläubiger Realismus II," *GW* IV, pp. 88-106. Tillich develops his concept of "believing realism" over against idealism on the one side and positivistic and empiricist realism on the other side. Believing realism stresses both the importance of concrete historical actuality and the unconditional ground and meaning of all historical reality. "Believing realism," says Tillich, "is a general stance towards actuality [*Wirklichkeit*]. It is not a theoretical worldview, but also not a life-praxis [*Lebenspraxis*]; it lies within a level of life beneath the split [*Spaltung*] between theory and praxis. It is not a particular religion or a particular philosophy. It is much more a basic attitude in every area of life which expresses itself in the structuring of every area. Believing realism unifies within itself in all decisiveness two elements, that which is actual [*das Wirkliche*] and the transcending power of belief." *GW* IV, p. 89.

119. While John Stumme, in chapter 6 of his study, attempts to give "The Theological Perspective" to Tillich's socialist thought, he does not deal with Tillich's interpretation of Luther and Lutheran theology in general in the context of the renaissance in Luther scholarship at the time, particularly that of the Karl Holl school in Berlin, of which Hirsch's understanding of Luther was a product. To what an extent Tillich's interpretation of Luther and Lutheran theology, in particular his

can do here is point to a few central themes.

Tillich was highly critical of Hirsch's interpretation and appropriation of Luther's two-kingdom doctrine. The main point of Tillich's critique is that Hirsch separated the two kingdoms too radically, relegating the kingdom of God to the private inward ethical and moral realm, and the kingdom of God to the external social and political sphere. Such a strict separation of the two spheres, grounded ultimately in an overly-strict law/gospel dichotomy, leaves the external sphere—that pertaining to economic, social, and political justice—without substantive critique and guidance from the prophetic perspective of the kingdom of God.[120] Tillich stressed that his *kairos* doctrine was an attempt to

view of the centrality of the Protestant principle, can stand the test of rigorous historical Luther scholarship is an extremely important question (also for the Tillich-Hirsch debate of 1934-35) which deserves the kind of concentrated study which is impossible in this particular work.

In his excellent essay "Paul Tillich on Luther," North American Tillich scholar James Luther Adams deals more explicitly with this complex question of Tillich's interpretation of Luther and Lutheranism in light of the Holl renaissance of Luther scholarship. He rightly points out that Tillich approached Luther not from the perspective of an historian (as Holl and to some extent Hirsch tried to do) but rather from the stance of a systematic theologian. Adams points out that Tillich was not strictly speaking as a Luther scholar and freely interpreted and reinterpreted Luther to accommodate his own existential concerns. Tillich was in fact highly critical not only of Lutheranism but also of Luther himself and at points preferred Calvinist theology. Tillich had a great admiration for Karl Holl's Luther interpretation which combined an "intimate inward understanding" with a "dispassionate method of research" (p. 307). Where Holl fell short, however, according to Tillich, is in giving "contemporary relevance" to Luther's thought and piety. Luther's revolutionary impulse got lost through various Luther transformations, particularly within Lutheran orthodoxy. Here Luther's initial breakthrough became interiorized and linked with conservative social ethics. Adams proceeds to show how Tillich himself transformed Luther's central insights (like the Protestant principle for example) for the contemporary social situation. In Adams' view, Tillich's whole theological method of correlation can in fact be seen as a particular way of relating law and gospel without separating them from each other, both of them having a positive place in the "creativity of love." "Here Tillich takes a view more akin to Karl Barth's than to Luther's. Accordingly, Tillich rejects the conventional Lutheran doctrine of the Two Kingdoms. In his view, Luther replaced the element of radical criticism by a strong historical positivism, thus over-emphasizing the role of force and the obligation of obedience to political authority. Tillich felt that one must go beyond Luther and deal with the question of how love and power—and love and justice—are to be united" (p. 330). *Interpreters of Luther: Essays in Honor of Wilhelm Pauck,* edited by Jaroslav Pelikan (Philadelphia: Fortress Press, 1968), pp. 304-334.

120. According to Stumme, Tillich always considered himself an evangelical-Lutheran Christian even in the context of the nonconfessional Kairos Circle (p. 33). He was deeply indebted to the Lutheran tradition for many of his fundamental ideas such as paradox, the perversion of human nature, and the dimension of the irrational (pp. 217-218). But it was in the area of social ethics that he parted company with traditional Lutheran theology. In its social ethics, in its understanding of the inward kingdom of God, it lacked that critical prophetic spirit which was needed for the inclusion of the revolutionary anticipation of the proletariat toward social transformation and the overcoming of injustice. "He preserved the freedom to decide freely among various political options and yet insisted that all judgments are to be seen in the light of the criteria of the kingdom" (p. 222). This is where Luther as well as Lutheranism, which neglected the horizontal in favor of the vertical, was inadequate to meet the social imperative. See Stumme, *Socialism in Theological Perspective,* esp.

avoid precisely this kind of sharp dualism, and it was for this reason that he replaced the doctrine of the two kingdoms with that of the "Protestant principle." For him the central insight of Luther was the protest against all heteronomy, against all idolatrous absolutizing of earthly realities. Although Tillich recognized the difficulty of moving from Lutheran theology to socialist thought, this critique of ideology implicit in Luther's thought provided Tillich with a way of linking Protestant theology with socialism.[121]

How Tillich understood this Protestant principle in the context of his political thought is most succinctly expressed in his 1931 essay entitled "The Protestant Principle and the Proletarian Situation."[122] This essay is one of the clearest expressions of how Tillich applies his theological method to a concrete historical situation. What he previously said more abstractly about the mass type in *Masse und Geist* is here much more explicitly and concretely discussed in terms of the proletariat in Europe. Tillich shows how Protestantism in Europe and North America and the proletariat have historically stood over against each other. Protestant churches have been linked with feudalism, the petit-bourgeoisie, big business, and successful entrepreneurs. "The proletarian situation, insofar as it represents the fate of the masses, is impervious to a Protestantism which in its message confronts the individual personality with the necessity of making a religious decision and which leaves him to his own resources in the social and political sphere, viewing the dominating forces of society as being ordered by God."[123] The implication for Protestantism is that there is one human situation which is excluded from it—namely, the proletarian situation. Protestanitism has consequently lost the universal character of its message and has limited itself to certain sociological groups. Socialism, which

pp. 217-225.

121. In his 1926 autobiography *On the Boundary*, Tillich says of the relation of Lutheranism to socialism: "The course of German theology after the war shows very clearly that it is practically impossible for a people educated as Lutherans to move from religion to socialism. Two theological movements, both Lutheran, were opposed to religious socialism. The first was religious nationalism which called itself 'young Lutheran' theology; its chief proponent was Emanuel Hirsch, a one-time fellow student friend who was to become my theological and political opponent. The second was Barthian theology, which is wrongly called 'dialectical theology.' Although Barth's theology has many Calvinistic elements, his strong transcendent idea of the Kingdom of God is definitely Lutheran. Both Barthian theology's indifference to social questions and Hirsch's sanctification of nationalism are so consistent with religious, social, and political traditions in Germany that it was futile for religious socialism to oppose them" (pp. 75-76). The question of whether Tillich was accurate in his depiction of Barth's or Hirsch's theology aside, the above statement does indicate clearly where Tillich thought the weakness of Lutheran theology lay.

122. *Protestantisches Prinzip und proletarische Situation* (Bonn: Cohen, 1931). Also in *GW* VII, pp. 84-104. Translated into English by James Luther Adams, as "The Protestant Principle and the Proletarian Situation," *The Protestant Era* (Chicago: The University of Chicago Press, 1957), pp. 161-181. Hereafter cited as "The Protestant Principle." The following references to and quotations from this article will be based on Adams' translation.

123. "The Protestant Principle," *The Protestant Era*, p. 161.

cannot be separated from the proletariat that it represents (although it is also not identical with it), therefore "poses for Protestantism the question concerning the meaning and the validity of its own unconditional and universal claim."[124] According to Tillich, the only way Protestantism can maintain this unconditional and universal nature of its message is by extricating itself from its present status without giving up its intrinsic character.

What is Protestantism's inherent character? It is the Protestant principle—a principle that transcends all its historical realizations. "What makes Protestantism Protestant is the fact that it transcends its own religious and confessional character, that it cannot be identified wholly with any of its particular historical forms."[125] More precisely, says Tillich, "The Protestant principle, in name derived from the protest of the 'protestants' against decisions of the Catholic majority, contains the divine and human protest against any absolute claim made for a relative reality, even if this claim is made by a Protestant church. The Protestant principle is the judge of every religious and cultural reality, including the religion and culture which calls itself 'Protestant.'"[126] The Protestant principle must not itself be seen as the highest ontological, metaphysical, or theological concept (such as God, the Absolute or Being) but "is the theological expression of the true relation between the unconditional and the conditioned or, religiously speaking, between God and man."[127] It guards against any usurping of the infinite and the unconditioned by a finite or conditioned reality. "It is the prophetic judgment against religious pride, ecclesiastical arrogance, and secular self-sufficiency and their destructive consequences."[128]

Historically, however, argues Tillich, Protestantism has failed to live up to its intrinsic critical and prophetic spirit. This becomes only too evident in its hostile stance to the proletarian situation. Tillich points to three major anti-proletarian tendencies present in historical Protestantism. The first is illustrated within Protestant orthodoxy, which has hardened and petrified dogma "into a system of doctrine that raises an unconditioned claim to truth."[129] In this it forgot the critical Protestant principle by giving a "quasi-sacramental dignity" to the biblical text and to pristine doctrine as expressed in the Protestant creeds. This makes the Protestant message unsuited to the proletariat which has no access in its dire situation to the achievements of the past. The proletariat is limited to the concepts derived from modern industrial society and looks toward a liberating future.

124. *Ibid.*, p. 162.
125. *Ibid.*
126. *Ibid.*, p. 163.
127. *Ibid.*
128. *Ibid.*
129. *Ibid.*, p. 176.

The second anti-proletarian tendency arises in Pietism, which considers religion "as an affair of the purely inner life" that "isolates the individual and limits the relation between God and the world to the relation between God and the soul."[130] Here the place of interaction between God and man is limited to the inner private realm totally separate from the social sphere; "The kingdom of God is the heavenly realm which the individual soul hopes to reach. Thus the forward-looking eschatological fervor of primitive Christianity is paralyzed and the world-transforming aspect of the idea of the kingdom of God disappears."[131] Although Tillich does not mention Hirsch by name in this essay, it appears from the 1934-35 debate that Tillich (not altogether fairly I might add) occasionally locates Hirsch's view of the two kingdoms in this pietistic tradition. According to Tillich, this individual piety has little significance for the social situation of the proletariat, which is more interested in the forward than in the upward direction. "Every attempt of this kind is felt by [the proletariat] as an attempt to divert attention from the political fight and as such is resisted."[132]

The third anti-proletarian tendency is Protestant liberalism, which has an ambiguous connection with the proletarian situation. On the one hand its view "is in accord with the proletarian outlook insofar as it is based on the autonomous attitude which is natural for proletarian thinking."[133] On the other hand, its link with the proletariat and the masses has been ineffective because it is captive to the "humanistic ideal of personality." It has produced a "theology of consciousness"—emphasizing the intellectual understanding and morality of the conscious religious personality, leaving untouched and suppressed the subconscious dimension. A consequence of this, like that of Pietism, is that the religious individual is left isolated from the social dimension of personality. Lutheranism and Calvinism contributed in different ways to this isolation of the individual. Luther's alliance with the princes against the peasants in the Peasants' Revolt (1525) "made it a permanent necessity for Lutheranism to depend upon absolutism and to repudiate democratic revolutionary tendencies."[134] In Lutheranism Protestantism allies itself with conservative patriarchal forms of society. In Calvinism, on the other hand, Protestantism allied itself with the middle classes and their struggle for economic independence, thus linking it with capitalist-liberal bourgeois social forms. Both Lutheranism and Calvinism in their own

130. *Ibid.*, p. 177.
131. *Ibid.*, pp. 177-178.
132. *Ibid.*, p. 178. Although Tillich's intuitions about the dangers of nationalism and about what was on the horizon for Germany if nationalism were to be triumphant were remarkably astute and accurate, here Tillich does not adequately recognize the power inherent in nationalism for gaining the support of the proletariat as later harnessed by the NSDAP in 1933. Tillich himself later acknowledged that Religious Socialism had not adequately recognized this power within nationalism.
133. *Ibid.*, p. 178.
134. *Ibid.*, p. 179.

distinctive ways have therefore historically been hostile to the proletariat.

While after World War I (in the Weimar years) Lutheranism had the opportunity to free itself from its old alliances, it maintained its traditional links with the pre-war monarchical groups. The church in fact supported conservative nationalistic circles hostile to the proletariat. Only misgivingly and not without antagonism has it tolerated the Religious Socialists who "have set for themselves the goal of freeing Protestantism from the sociological attachments resulting from its anti-proletariat past."[135] In the post-war years Protestants have surrendered almost totally to a nationalist ideology. "Only when the pagan basis of nationalism was openly expressed by various groups in recent years did a slight reaction against 'the myth of the nation' appear. Yet the old bonds between church and national state are still so strong that Protestantism mostly sides with those groups that have made the name 'nationalist' into a party slogan."[136]

Tillich does not mention Hirsch by name but is obviously including Hirsch and the young National Lutherans among these groups. This "nationalist ideology," says Tillich, is a further obstruction to any coming together of the Protestant church and the proletariat. Tillich urges Protestantism to separate itself from its historical manifestations and decide for the Protestant principle. He does not demand that the church become socialist in its thinking but rather that it use the Protestant principle as a critique of all its decisions and actions in light of "the disturbing and transforming reality of the proletarian situation."[137] This means that socialism should at least be taken seriously "as an expression of the proletarian situation." The Protestant "serves the 'man-made God' of his social group, class, or nation when he does not take seriously the reality of the proletarian situation as decisive for the future development of Protestantism."[138]

What exactly, in Tillich's eyes, is the proletarian situation? How is it related to socialism? How can the Protestant principle be legitimately vindicated in light of the proletarian situation? The "proletarian situation" functions as an ideal sociological type in Tillich's thought and cannot be equated absolutely with the empirical proletariat although it is intrinsically linked to it. Not *all* and not *only* the proletariat make up the type. The proletarian situation is "the situation of that class within the capitalist system whose members are dependent exclusively upon the 'free' sale of their physical ability to work and whose social destiny is wholly dependent upon the turn of the market."[139]

The Protestant principle has to do with a critique of the basic distortion within the human situation. It is this "self-contradiction within human existence" to which the theological notion of "original sin" also alludes. Not human finitude as such but the human "power of self-determination carries with it the

135. *Ibid.,* p. 180.
136. *Ibid.,* p. 137.
137. *Ibid.,* p. 180.
138. *Ibid.*
139. *Ibid.,* p. 164.

possibility of a perverted, destructive self-determination."[140] In the proletarian situation this Protestant principle is vindicated because here the distortion of human nature becomes uniquely visible in the social sphere. "This assertion can be theologically denied only by those who conceive of the relation between God and the world as exclusively a relation between God and the soul. But this is not consistent with either the prophetic message or the Protestant principle." For Tillich "The perversion of human existence is real in social, just as strongly as in individual, distortions and with even more primitive force; and collective guilt is just as real and perceptible as individual guilt; neither can be separated from the other."[141] The proletarian situation, in revealing the breaking up of society into antagonistic classes, "represents a distortion of essential human nature and a demonic splitting-up of humanity in general."[142] In their judgment of social perversion and guilt the socialist evaluation and the Protestant perception of the universal human condition agree. "The Protestant judgment becomes concrete, actual, and urgent in its application to the class situation of today; and the socialist judgment becomes universal, profound, and religiously significant if put in the frame of man's general situation."[143]

The distorted plight of the millions upon millions of rural and urban proletarians is obvious. This situation "is an escapable consequence of the demonic structure of capitalism."[144] The most obvious and basic contradiction of the capitalistic system is the class struggle, from which no one can extricate himself. "This does not mean that anyone should or could accept the class struggle as desirable. It is the symptom of a disease, or, symbolically speaking, it is the symptom of a demonic possession in the grip of which modern society lives."[145] What gives the proletarian fight its universal significance is that it is committed to overcoming the system which has produced the class struggle, the splitting-up and fundamental contradiction within human nature.

While the proletariat has the perpetual human tendency to build an ideological superstructure, and always does so, objectively speaking it is in a unique situation to unmask this basic perversion of humanity and the ideological distortion of it. "Anything that cannot rescue the proletariat from the perversion of existence in the capitalistic order is rejected. This refers to romantic-conservative as well as to progressive-idealistic ideas."[146] Here again the proletariat vindicates the Protestant principle which in the Reformation took shape in Luther's doctrine of justification by grace through faith. "'Justification' in this

140. *Ibid.*, p. 165.
141. *Ibid.*, p. 166.
142. *Ibid.*
143. *Ibid.*
144. *Ibid.*, p. 168.
145. *Ibid.*
146. *Ibid.*, p. 170. Tillich does not anticipate the power which the "romantic-conservative" view of existence as expressed by the NSDAP just a few years later would have over the workers.

sense is the paradox that man, the sinner, is justified; that man the unrighteous is righteous; that man the unholy is holy, namely, in the judgment of God, which is not based on any human achievements but only on the divine, self-surrendering grace. Where this paradox of the divine-human relationship is understood and accepted, all ideologies are destroyed. Man does not have to deceive himself about himself, because he is accepted as he is, in the total perversion of his existence."[147]

However, to be accepted by God, Tillich is quick to add, also implies a transformation in terms of anticipation. The object of this anticipation is the kingdom of God which is at hand, but never as an empirical object to be possessed. It can be possessed only through anticipation: "The paradox inherent in these concepts indicates the character of the relation of the infinite and the finite in the light of the Protestant principle and the idea of justification: possessing and not possessing at the same time."[148] The kingdom of God is both the ultimate which is anticipated and the present reality into which those who anticipate it are already drawn. No one, remarks Tillich, "can localize the divine that transcends space and time."[149]

The proletariat, especially after it became conscious of itself in the post-Marxist era, is also characterized by the passionate sense of this anticipation. "The Protestant principle provides the possibility for understanding the paradoxical character of anticipation as it is found in the proletariat, and, besides this, it has the power to guard against a distortion that threatens all anticipation, i.e., utopianism."[150] What is utopianism? "The attitude of anticipation develops into utopianism if it is allowed to lose its essential dialectical character and is held as a precise and literal intellectual anticipation—an anticipation that at some time in the future is to be replaced by a tangible, objective possession."

For Tillich, however, "The thing ultimately referred to in all genuine anticipation remains transcendent; it transcends any concrete fulfillment of human destiny; it transcends the other-worldly utopias of religious fantasy as well as this-worldly utopias of secular speculation."[151] This transcendence at the same

---

147. *Ibid.*, pp. 170-171. Stumme summarizes Tillich's concept of justification as follows: "Tillich perceived the Unconditional under two aspects, *Sein* and *Sollen*, grace and judgment, gift and demand, yes and no, ground and abyss, support and threat, promise and demand, import and form, the sacramental and the rational, etc. All of these polar terms are related to his interpretation of justification. The structure of his theology is found in the contrasts of Gospel and Law, and the problem of his theology is how to distinguish and relate these contrasts." *Socialism in Theological Perspective*, p. 88. According to Adams, Tillich's understanding of justification has essentially to do with the nature of prophetic criticism. "For Tillich this doctrine is the characteristically Protestant way of bringing everything finite, including rational criticism, under judgment. Prophetic criticism by means of the experience of justification drives rational criticism 'to its depth and its limit.'" "Paul Tillich on Luther," p. 310.

148. "The Protestant Principle and the Proletarian Situation," p. 171.

149. *Ibid.*

150. *Ibid.*, p. 172.

time, however, provides criteria and norms by which earthly reality is perpetually judged and changed; "it looks forward to continuous revolutionary shattering and transforming of the existing situation."[152]

Here it must be noted that when Hirsch charges Tillich with deifying an earthly historical reality by seeing the mass or the proletariat as holy, as in some sense paving the way for the kingdom of God, he is not sufficiently taking into account Tillich's dialectical and paradoxical understanding of the kingdom of God. It is, however, precisely the ambiguity of Tillich's combination of paradoxical and dialectical thinking about the unconditional and the conditioned, about the proletarian struggle for a classless society and the nature of the kingdom of God, his not-totally-successful attempt to combine a vertical upward looking ontological approach with a horizontal future-oriented historical understanding of the kingdom of God that makes Tillich vulnerable to Hirsch's charges.[153]

Divine action in human history, Tillich explains, can be theologically described in terms of providence and predestination, in which the "uncertainties of human freedom and self-determination" are placed in the context of "transcendent necessity." This transcendent necessity however never destroys empir-

---

151. *Ibid.* It is important to remember here, however, that transcendence for Tillich does not mean the transcendence of traditional supernaturalism, where transcendence is viewed as a kind of objective reality beside or beyond other objects. Transcendence for Tillich is a quality of being, an "immanent" transcendence which gives historical forms their ultimate meaning and substance. For Hirsch, in contrast, transcendence is viewed more in traditional theistic terms.

152. *Ibid.*

153. In an intriguing section on Tillich's "The Coming of the Kingdom," Stumme is critical of Tillich's confusion of paradoxical and dialectical, ontological and historical-eschatological thinking. He feels that precisely because of Tillich's understanding that the Unconditional "is independent of the modes of time," Tillich "defuturizes" the eschaton. He is driven, because he sees all historical events as equidistant from the Unconditional, the Eternal, to decide for the "priority of time over space," for the subordination of eschatology to ontology. Despite his intentions, therefore, Tillich is led to a *de facto* dehistoricizing of the kingdom of God, "he is forced to find the goal of history within history itself in the paradoxical reality of theonomy" (p. 239). Stumme suggests that transcendence might more adequately be understood as "the future that is coming [as Tillich did in *The Socialist Decision*] than as the eternal emerging from the depths of the present" (p. 240). *Socialism in Theological Perspective*, pp. 234-241. It is interesting that Stumme's criticism of Tillich is precisely the opposite of Hirsch's. Hirsch accuses Tillich of not preserving the absolute distinction and transcendence of God from historical reality. For Stumme, Tillich does not go far enough in historicizing the notion of the kingdom of God. For Hirsch Tillich's thinking goes too far, is not paradoxical enough; for Stumme it is too paradoxical—that is, too vertical and ontological. It seems that this so-called confusion between paradoxical and dialectical thinking in Tillich, if it is in fact a confusion as Stumme suggests, is a difficulty that is rooted in Tillich's theological method as such. While dialectical thinking has its strengths, one of its weaknesses, as Hirsch rightly charges and as Tillich himself vaguely admits in his *On the Boundary* (p. 13), is that in the midst of a social crisis— and surely the Weimar years leading up to the National Socialist revolution could be regarded as a social and political crisis in Germany—such a dialectical method is not an adequate basis upon which to make wholehearted social and political commitments.

ical human freedom; transcendent necessity and empirical freedom are symbols pointing to the relation of the unconditional to the conditioned. This same dialectic between freedom and necessity exists, he says, in the attitude of the proletariat to human history.

In the Marxian dialectic there is a residue of faith in providence, a combining of "universal necessity" and "historical responsibility."[154] "The course of the historical process leads with dialectical (not mechanical) necessity to the emergence of the *bourgeoisie* and the proletariat, to the victory of the proletariat over the *bourgeoisie*, and thence to the abolition of the class society."[155] This does not leave the proletariat passive but rather motivates it to revolutionary action. If the proletariat fails in its "calling" it will be replaced by some other instrument of destiny but the basic dialectic of human history will continue.

Protestantism too could conceivably miss its calling, be rejected and judged by its own principle. This would however not mean the denial of the Protestant principle or the anti-capitalistic principle. If Protestantism had remained more faithful to its fundamental principle, Tillich reflects provocatively, it would have developed a more positive stance toward the proletarian situation and given "a better interpretation of the proletarian struggle than the socialists, with their hopeless mixture of mechanistic calculation of historical necessities and petty tactics...."[156] Here again we see how Tillich's understanding of socialism is much less doctrinaire and partisan than Hirsch's later charges suggest. Tillich's critique of socialism itself, particularly its mechanistic and materialistic aspects, and his constant critique of blatant 19th century autonomous liberalism are not adequately accounted for by Hirsch.

Finally, it is ironic that precisely in its secularism, says Tillich, the proletariat vindicates the Protestant principle. In Protestantism's radical laicism, in its view that "everything is secular and every secular thing is potentially religious," in its conviction that "the relation to the unconditional permeates every moment of daily life and makes it holy," in Luther's concept of the "universal priesthood of all Christians," one finds, according to Tillich, this vindication of the secular character of the proletarian situation. Most Christian churches charge socialism with being "anti-Christian, anti-religious, and atheistic" but do not recognize the prophetic element within socialism.[157]

Protestantism ought to ask itself "whether, under the disguise of a secular theory and practice, socialism does not represent a special religious type,

154. In chapter 5 of his study of Tillich's political and theological thought, Stumme shows how Tillich managed in his thinking to transform the historical dialectic of Marxist thought. Stumme concludes that "Tillich went behind Marx and Hegel to the prophetic attitude of the Biblical tradition and placed the socialist dialectic within the context of transcendence, transcendence paradoxically present in history." *Socialism in Theological Perspective*, p. 198.

155. "The Protestant Principle and the Proletarian Situation," p. 173.

156. *Ibid.*, p. 174.

157. *Ibid.*, pp. 175-176.

namely, the type that originates in Jewish prophetism and transcends the given world in the expectation of a 'new earth'—symbolized as classless society, or a stage of justice and peace, or an era of perfect rationality, etc." "It must also be asked," continues Tillich, "in light of the Protestant principle, whether the proletarian movement does not represent a kind of lay movement, which, although remote from every theological self-expression, bears witness to the human situation, its distortion and its promise."[158]

This concludes our discussion of Tillich's political and theological views as they developed during the years of the Weimar Republic. There are some obvious formal similarities between Hirsch's and Tillich's thought during these years. They both sought to mediate between Christianity and political reality: Tillich attempted to unify Christianity and socialism; Hirsch tried to reconcile Christianity and German nationality. Methodologically, the category of "nation" plays a similar role in Hirsch's thought as does "the mass" or "the proletariat" in Tillich's.

However, this similarity is a formal one and must not hide the substantive political and theological differences between the two. Hirsch grounds his political views squarely on Luther's two-kingdom doctrine which divides the external political sphere from the individual sphere of conscience. Tillich rejects the two-kingdom doctrine and defends the Protestant principle—a protest against all forms of religious and political heteronomy—as more central to Luther's theology. These substantive theological differences overshadow the formal similarities and largely determine their choices in 1933. While both Tillich and Hirsch espouse a kind of political theology—a theology shaped by and determinative of political reality—one was a conservative political theology and the other a political theology of the left. Interestingly, in the 1920s Tillich's political theology allies itself self-critically with the socialist coalition and general ethos of the Weimar Republic while Hirsch finds himself in the minority opposition camp. In 1933 this is reversed: Tillich finds himself in the critical minority and Hirsch, while maintaining his independence, nevertheless finds himself on the side of the general ethos of the times.

158. *Ibid.*

7
Two Contrary Responses
to the Triumph
of National Socialism

National Socialism as the Culmination of the *Volk* Movement

The triumph of Hitler and National Socialism cannot be explained merely as a successful conspiracy and *coup d'état* by a few political-religious fanatics. It was rather the culmination and victory of a popularly-supported *Volk* movement espousing the importance of nation, race, and ethnicity, which Klaus Scholder calls the second great all-encompassing totalitarian ideology of the 19th century, Marxism being the first.[1] Characteristic of this *Volk* movement, which had its theoretical roots in the 19th century romantic tradition represented by such thinkers as Ernst Moritz Arndt, Johann Gottfried von Herder, and Johann Gottlieb Fichte, was a radical dualism: the fight of good against evil, light against darkness, idealism against materialism, purity against corruption.[2] World War I and the defeat of Germany played a decisive role in the evolution of *Volk* ideas, including strong antisemitic elements. During the crisis years of German politics (after 1918 and throughout the 1920s and early 1930s) such ideas moved from the peripheral concern of a few to the center of German politics, identifying a radical ethical dualist principle with the so-called Jewish materialistic spirit on the one side and the Arian idealistic spirit on the other.[3]

From his earliest speeches it is evident that Hitler moved within the sphere of ideas—religious, political, and cultural—that characterized this growing *Volk* movement, particularly in its ethical-dualistic form: the fight of Arianism for morality, common sense, and common good above personal good, against what he called Jewish-Marxist materialism.[4] What distinguished Hitler from the preceding *Volk* movement was his particular political vision, program, organization, and effectiveness.[5]

---

1. Scholder, *Die Kirchen und das dritte Reich,* p. 93. I am translating *völkische Bewegung* as "folk movement" in this particular context to retain its broader-than-simply-political meaning, including cultural, religious, ethnic, racial as well as political elements. For the historical material in the following pages I am deeply indebted to Scholder's massive study and allude to him repeatedly.

2. *Ibid.,* pp. 125ff.

3. *Ibid.,* p. 96.

4. *Ibid.,* p. 101.

The German Workers' Party (*Deutschen Arbeitspartei*) was founded on January 5, 1919. From the beginning it was one of a large number of politically-oriented nationalist groups linked to the popular nationalist movement and having strong religious overtones. It was this political group that Hitler identified with, although he did not found it. At a crucial February 24, 1920 meeting, Hitler's own personal leadership in this party became dominant. The party changed its name to the National Socialist German Workers' Party (*Nationalsozialistische Deutsche Arbeitspartei, NSDAP*). It adopted the famous 25 theses as its platform. Thesis 24 includes the well-known reference to the party's espousal of "positive Christianity": "We demand the freedom of all religious confessions in the state, insofar as they do not endanger its existence or strike against the ethical and moral feeling of the Germanic peoples. The party as such represents the standpoint of a positive Christianity without binding itself to any particular confession. It fights the Jewish materialistic spirit *within* and *without* us and is convinced that a lasting recovery of our nation can succeed only from *within* outward on the basis of: Common good before personal good [*Gemeinnutz vor Eigennutz*]."[6]

While Hitler, according to Scholder, identified himself to a large extent with the religious aspects of the *Volk* movement, he had a strong personal religious consciousness of his own destiny and God-appointed mission. He saw his own struggle as in some sense in continuity with that of Jesus himself, feeling that the victory of his ideas could be achieved only through the successful creation of a political party.[7] For this reason he sought to separate the religious and political aspects of the movement. It was not that Hitler was against religious ideas and religious reformation, says Scholder, but he saw the primary task of the NSDAP as being a political one. Some of the major early internal battles within the NSDAP were a result of Hitler's determination to bring the party out of a political, territorial, and religious ghetto that characterized the movement. He achieved this with remarkable success and political acumen.[8]

---

5. *Ibid.*, p. 102.

6. *Ibid.*, p. 107. This is my own translation of the German version as found in Scholder and varies only slightly from Arthur C. Cochrane's translation in his *The Church's Confession under Hitler* (Pittsburgh: The Pickwick Press, 1976), p. 221. The term "positive Christianity" was and has been given a variety of different interpretations following its initial use here. According to Scholder, at the time it was a summing up of the religious convictions of the folk-movement and signified a general German folk religion that transcended traditional Christian confessional boundaries and was aimed against the so-called Jewish materialistic spirit. For an extensive discussion of the diversity of meanings given to the term "positive Christianity" by German Christians during the 1930s see James A. Zabel, *Nazism and the Pastors*, pp. 111-129. According to Zabel, it was precisely the ambiguity of the meaning of the phrase which made it useful for the opportunistic *Glaubensbewegung Deutsche Christen (GDC)*.

7. Scholder, *Die Kirchen und das dritte Reich*, p. 109.

8. *Ibid.*, p. 123.

On January 30, 1933 Hitler became chancellor of Germany, second in power only to President Field Marshal Paul von Hindenburg, beginning the decisive phase of the National Socialist revolution. The next phase was devoted by Hitler and his party to *Gleichschaltung*—the elimination of political opposition, the consolidation of political power, to convincing opponents and the nation as a whole, including the church, of their credibility and the worthiness of their cause. In a remarkably short period of time Hitler and the NSDAP triumphed to become the sole political masters in Germany, a position they held for the next 12 years.

In the eight-week period from January 30, 1933 to the passing of the Emergency Laws in the Reichstag, Hitler proved himself, according to Scholder, to be a master politician, able to gain the trust and allegiance of a majority of Germans and of Christian churches through the use of well-designed political and religious tactics. Among those tactics were religiously-oriented speeches and the use of church buildings for political ceremonies. The Lutheran church, further observes Scholder, moved from restraint in early February to whole-hearted support by April.[9]

We need not recount here the complex series of events and elections between the years 1930 and 1933. Suffice it to say that German liberal middle-class politics was brought to virtual extinction.[10] The majority of the German electorate placed its trust in Hitler and National Socialism as the only hope for national rebirth, the only rescue from what, according to Scholder, appeared to many to be the genuine threat of an immanent Communist revolution similar to the one that swept Russia beginning in 1917.[11] In an earlier chapter we examined some

9. See Scholder, *Ibid.*, pp. 277-299. Scholder makes the important point that it is too simple and inadequate an explanation to see the religious element inherent in these speeches and ceremonies as solely National Socialist propagandistic strategy. According to Scholder, there clearly existed in Hitler "a religious element, a religious-folkish consciousness of being sent, which considered itself called by 'Providence' or by the 'Almighty'—concepts which Hitler characteristically much preferred to the concept 'God'—to a great work." "Something of this religious element," adds Scholder, "broke out more strongly during these weeks in which he moved so rapidly from one victory to another than it had ever done before or would hereafter" (p. 287).

10. For a good historical account of the political events in Germany during the Weimar years, the demise of the various traditional conservative, liberal, and socialist parties during the later years of the Republic and leading up to the electoral triumphs of the National Socialists in the early 1930s, culminating finally in the rather unusual circumstances surrounding the appointment of Hitler as Chancellor, see S. William Halperin, *Germany Tried Democracy*.

11. According to Scholder there were three reasons why Germans in March and April of 1933 were willing to submit themselves to the beginning rule of terror and force: fear of communism, the propaganda ability of the NSDAP, and a more positive reason—the belief that it was worthwhile to submit oneself and sacrifice one's self-interest on behalf of the nation in order to overcome the economic misery and political hopelessness of the Weimar period. Scholder, *Die Kirchen und das dritte Reich,* p. 328. Scholder stresses that a majority of Germans in these early months of National Socialist power perceived, rightly or wrongly, the communist evolutionary threat as a *genuine* threat and possibility, having before their eyes the communist reign of force in Russia. In these months

of the complex series of theological and ecclesiastical events which shook the German Evangelical Church in the years 1933 and 1934. One of these was the birth and short but powerfully influential life of the pro-National Socialist and pro-national church political faction known as the faith-movement of the German Christians (*Glaubensbewegung Deutsche Christen*) under the leadership of its 32-year-old leader Joachim Hossenfelder.[12] Another was the bitter struggle in the spring of 1933 over the nature of the national church (*Reichskirche*) and its bishop Ludwig Müller, a debate which ultimately split the church apart and led in 1934 to the creation of a separate ecclesiastical body known as the Confessing Church.[13] All of these events are relatively well-known aspects of

ecclesiastical decisions were made which drove the church into silence in the face of growing National Socialist terror against communists, Jews, and other actual or imagined opponents of the regime—symbolized by the erection of the first concentration camps in the latter part of March. It is bcause of this *perceived* threat of communistic terror, says Scholder, that many viewed the system-atic persecutions not as persecution but as justified measures by a government which had rescued Germany at the last moment from a communist takeover, believing that as soon as possible a normal state of law and order would return. Without justifying or de-emphasizing the silence of the church in face of growing terror and persecution, particularly of the Jews, Scholder argues that "Only under the impression of an immanent-threatening communistic terror was it possible to view the National Socialist terror not as terror but as a necessary and legitimate counter-measure" (p. 327). Emanuel Hirsch certainly viewed Hitler and the National Socialist regime as having saved Germany from a communist revolution.

12. For a good treatment of the rise, power, and collapse of *Die Deutschen Christen* in the German Evangelical Church in the years 1931-1933, see Scholder, *Die Kirchen und das dritte Reich*, especially pp. 239-274, 388-452, 701-742. Too often the German Christians are referred to in general terms as if to signify a homogeneous and theologically-unified faction with the German church. This is not to understand the diversity within the movement and the number of different groups that the term German Christians covered—some more moderate and others much more fanat-ical in their espousal of a racially pure *Volk* Christianity. In his book *Nazism and the Pastors*, James A. Zabel gives valuable insight into the diversity within the German Christian movement. Zabel examines in some detail three diverse German Christian groups: the more traditional, conservative *Christlich-Deutsche Bewegung (CDB)*, which was founded in 1930 and dissolved in the fall of 1933; the *Glaubensbewegung Deutsche Christen (GDC)*, which Zabel somewhat too summarily labels as opportunistic and concerned with Party principles first above any Christian principles, especially since for about one year (late 1932 to November 1933) it included under its umbrella the whole spectrum of Christian groups for the purpose of providing a common pro-National Socialist front; and the radical *Kirchenbewegung Deutsche Christen (KDC)*, which was centered in Thüringia and was the most enthusiastic supporter of Hitler and the National Socialists, combining a strong German Protestant pietistic ethos with a rejection of modern industrial society and a romantic yearning for the values of rural life—of all the German Christian factions it was the most durable and lasted into the war years. In Zabel's words: "The German Christian phenomenon progressed from diversity to unity and back again to diversity. The fact that German Christians only found unity in the feverish few months just preceding and following Hitler's takeover, points up the many different types of people involved in German Christian activities." *Nazism and the Pastors*, p. 21. Hirsch's own stance *vis-à-vis* the German Christians is much more equivocal and nuanced than Zabel credits him with as we have observed in a previous chapter.

13. Scholder deals extensively in his *Die Kirchen und das dritte Reich* with the background to, the nature of, and the outcome of the German church struggle concerning the *Reichskirche* and the

the struggle of the German church and are significant in understanding Hirsch's stance with respect to *Die Deutschen Christen, Reichskirche* and *Reichsbischof*. They shed important light on the practical consequences of his theology and his political ethics.[14]

The Rise of Political Theology

Of special interest for our study is the background and role of "political

Reichsbischof in the spring of 1933, including the longstanding (since the 19th century) call for church reform and the uniting of the various evangelical confessions and the 28 *Landeskirchen* (pp. 355-387); the struggle and church-political intrigues over the candidacy of Ludwig Müller versus Friedrich von Bodelschwingh, with the final election of the former (pp. 388-452); the founding of the *Reichskirche* in July and September 1933 (pp. 560-626); the collapse of the movement of German Christians in October and November 1933, not because of the resistance of the Confessing church but because of what Scholder calls the "illusory nature of its conception" concerning Hitler's alleged confession of Christianity, concern for the unification of the church, Party support of the German Christians, and the Party's fight against *"Schmutz"* and *"Schund"* (pp. 663-700); and the beginnings of the Confessing church at the meeting of the first "Free Synod" on January 3 and 4, 1934 in Barmen under the strong influence of Karl Barth (pp. 740ff.). The best overall English treatment of this whole period of German Protestant church and theological history, despite its somewhat one-sided and dated interpretation, still remains Arthur C. Cochrane's *The Church's Confession Under Hitler*, the first edition of which appeared in 1962. For a more recent survey of the events leading up to the Barmen Confession see Robert P. Ericksen, "The Barmen Synod and its Declaration: A Historical Synopsis," in *The Church Confronts the Nazis: Barmen Then and Now*, Herbert G. Locke, ed. (New York and Toronto: The Edwin Mellen Press, 1984), pp. 27-91.

14. Scholder makes frequent and extensive references to Hirsch in his massive work and finds him perplexing: Hirsch, Scholder claims, "belongs without a doubt to the figures most difficult to assess in the modern history of theology [*der neueren Theologiegeschichte*]. Universally educated, tremendously proficient, and with stupendous learning, he published a long row of significant works into the 1950s, parts of which remain unsurpassed even today" (pp. 127-128). Scholder calls him a "passionate political theologian," with an "unperturbed and hardnecked narrowness" (*von einer unbeirrbaren und hartnäckigen Beschränktheit*) in matters of Germany's destiny, a "glowing admirer of Hitler's" and somewhat misleadingly claims that Hirsch was a Party member of the folk-movement from the beginning (p. 128). Hirsch's relation to the folk-movement and particularly to *Die Deutschen Christen* was more ambivalent than Scholder makes out. Scholder erroneously claims that Hirsch was never a Party member of the NSDAP. In fact, Hirsch joined the Party in 1937. Scholder is certainly right, however, when he claims that Hirsch was never an opportunist either in 1933 or in 1945. Scholder discusses at length Hirsch's support of the cause of Ludwig Müller in the *Reichskirche* and *Reichsbischof* controversy (against the candidacy of Bodelschwingh) (pp. 403, 424, 428). In fact Hirsch was one of two or three of the closest church advisers to Müller and the German Christians supporting Müller after the other members of the close advisory circle had withdrawn their support (p. 179). In Scholder's words: "From the beginning of May until the end of the year Hirsch next to Fezer was the most important theological adviser to Ludwig Müller. With him and for him he fought for a *Reichskirche* which in its order [*Ordnung*] and in its proclamation would conform to the National Socialist revolution. This conformity [*Entsprechung*] was for Hirsch no *Gleichschaltung* in the sense that the church was to be brought politically into correspondence [*Übereinstimmung*] with the nation and the state, but it was the presupposition for the understanding and the credibility of its proclamation in the Third Reich" (p. 533).

theology" in the course of the events just mentioned. Broadly speaking there were four general theological options during the Weimar period in Germany: liberal Culture Protestantism, represented by thinkers such as Adolf von Harnack; Religious Socialism as represented by Paul Tillich; National Lutheranism as represented by Emanuel Hirsch; and Dialectical Theology as represented by Karl Barth.[15] The latter three were in various measures reactions against the first. Particularly significant, however, was the theological phenomenon which Scholder calls "Political Theology," a movement which drew its thinkers from a number of sources but was closely linked to National Lutheranism. A young group of theologians in the war and post-war years rediscovered the concept of *Volk*—a concept which became central for their theology and served to counter the individualism of Culture-Protestantism in defense of the virtues of community, solidarity, commitment (*Hingabe*), and self-sacrifice.

Among these theologians, for whom the concept of *Volk* became what Scholder refers to as a new ethical starting point for theology, were Paul Althaus, Friedrich Gogarten, Emanuel Hirsch, and the influential writer and publicist Wilhelm Stapel.[16] Whereas for liberal Protestant theology the starting

15. Cf. Scholder, *Die Kirchen und das Dritte Reich*, p. 64. Although Scholder clearly recognizes the shortcomings of Barthian dialectical theology, especially in the 1920s when through its preference for critique (the No) over affirmation (the Yes) it helped to take away crucial support for a vulnerable Republic, his preference for the Barthian theological position is evident throughout his book. "In the twentieth century," says Scholder, "no more radical critique of ideology has been developed than that of Dialectial Theology. It was aimed at and struck everything which raised an unconditional ideological claim, bourgeois capitalism as well as proletarian socialism, militarism as well as pacifism, nationalism as well as internationalism, the first definitely more and clearer but in principle the latter just as well. And it struck in particular measure and with particular sharpness there where the ideologies served Christian-churchly associations and props, as in liberal Culture-Protestantism, authoritarian national-Protestantism or religious socialism" (p. 64). It should be noted here that the term "Culture-Protestantism" has received a pejorative meaning for 20th-century theology largely (although not exclusively) through the anti-liberal polemics of the dialectical and neo-orthodox theologians of the 1920s. This purely negative connotation of the term, and with it the whole phenomenon of liberal theology at the turn of the century (including thinkers like Harnack and Troeltsch) has in recent years been substantially revised by historians like George Rupp and Friedrich Wilhelm Graf. See George Rupp, *Culture-Protestantism: German Liberal Theology at the Turn of the Twentieth Century* (Missoula: Scholars Press, 1977). Friedrich W. Graf, "Bürgerliche Seelenreligion? Zum politischen Engagement des Kulturprotestantismus," *Mittwoch* 2,76(April, 1986), p. 35.

16. Cf. *Die Kirchen und das Dritte Reich*, pp. 125ff. As dialectical theology was probably the most discussed theological topic at the end of the 1920s, according to Scholder (p. 61), Stapel's teaching of the *Volksnomos* belonged to one of the most discussed theological topics in 1933 (p. 536). Scholder points out that Hirsch and Stapel became the most important representatives of the new political-theological direction which in 1933 tried to interpret the National Socialist revolution theologically (pp. 530-531). He emphasizes the influence of Stapel's ideas on political theologians like Hirsch, particularly through the notion of *Volksnomos*—the law of life that conforms to the particular nature of a given nation, that defines the nation's inner and outer life, cult, ethos, government, and law (p. 534). Scholder stresses the similarities between the ideas of Stapel and

point had been the *individual*—ethically active within family, culture, society, and state to be sure—this new Political Theology stressed ethical responsibility not from the perspective of the individual but from that of the nation. Here, in the words of Scholder, "political ethics became the key question of theological understanding and church behavior; that is, its benchmark and point of recognition."[17]

Scholder's perceptive analysis of Political Theology in the 1920s and its political consequences in the summer of 1933 is most helpful for our own understanding of Hirsch's political ethics, his church/political decisions in 1933, and his response to the triumph of National Socialism. However, Scholder too quickly charges political theologians like Hirsch with making political ethics the starting point and the hermeneutic for theological understanding, especially in the summer of 1933. In so doing, Scholder does not adequately take into account Hirsch's repeated claim that his starting point is theological—particularly Luther's theology of the two kingdoms.[18]

It is difficult to assess the actual influence of Political Theology on the course of events within the Protestant church during the 1920s and early 30s. For Scholder, who is careful not to make a direct causal link between Political

Hirsch—for both the nation and nationality were aspects of God's creation itself revealed in a special way in the events of 1933—as well as the dissimilarities. According to Scholder, they differed, in their definition of the relation of church and state in the Third Reich. Stapel was more concerned with establishing a boundary (*Abgrenzung*) between the two while Hirsch was, in Scholder's opinion, more concerned with the coordination (*Zuordnung*) between church and state (p. 536). This is certainly an arguable point. Hirsch, through his understanding of the two kingdoms, was throughout concerned with the independence of the church in its proper sphere of activity—the spiritual realm. Scholder interestingly points out that the connection between the political theology of the 1920s and the church-political decisions that Hirsch and Stapel made in the summer of 1933 did not necessarily follow for all political theologians: Paul Althaus, who would have been expected to join the German Christians, found himself on the opposing side and Friedrich Gogarten, who had earlier been on the side of Karl Barth and dialectical theology, supported the German Christians in the summer of 1933, although he publicly announced his withdrawal before the end of the year (pp. 536-539).

17. Scholder, *Die Kirchen und das Dritte Reich*, p. 130.

18. Scholder's critique of political theologians like Hirsch is not only a criticism of the political theology of the right in the 1920s in Germany but of all political theology in the 20th century, including the more recent political theology of the left. In Scholder's opinion "Where political decision became the criterion for theology [as it did in the summer of 1933 according to Scholder]—and that happens in every political theology—politics and theology become blind, helpless and corrupt. That is an insight forcefully gained from the history of political theology in the twentieth century." *Die Kirchen und das Dritte Reich*, p. 133. This bias against all political theology runs like a thread through the whole of Scholder's book. A critique of Scholder's history of political theology in Germany in the 1920s and the 1930s, if one were to be made, might begin with a questioning of Scholder's basic understanding of the insights and intent of political theology in general. The political theologians of the right, in the 1920s and 1930s, and the more recent political theologians of the left, reject the notion that politics is the starting point of theology. Nevertheless, they maintain that all theology is intrinsically political. Whether this contention can be sustained is another matter.

Theology and the triumph of National Socialism as a political movement or the German Christians as an ecclesiastical movement, this new theology must at least be held co-responsible for helping to prepare the ground and making the church fertile for the reception of racial ideas. It helped to dismantle the barrier between Protestantism and the ideas of the NSDAP. It was, in the eyes of Scholder, the first and for a time the most important answer of German Protestantism to the popular nationalist movement.[19]

The discovery of the concept of *Volk* as the ethical point of departure for theology, together with the conviction that the church had an immediate responsibility for the religious and ethical education of the nation, was crucial in the years 1930 to 1933. It prepared the church to take a positive stance toward the *Volk* movement and to see it as good and worthy of support. According to Scholder, the readiness of the church to support National Socialism, to tolerate the anti-semitism that went along with the triumph of National Socialism, cannot be explained outside of the success of Political Theology in establishing the right of the nation as essential to the divine will in creation.[20]

While the Political Theology of Hirsch and his circle cannot as such be accused of espousing a consistent and systematic anti-semitism, nor of being simply a Hitler party within the church, it nevertheless represented a critical solidarity with the nationalist movement. In this way it helped to create fertile ground within the church for the affirmation of the *Volk* concept. This Political Theology legitimized popular racial attitudes over against liberal and socialist critics while distancing itself from fanatical exponents of a race-oriented German church. In this way, claims Scholder, it accommodated Hitler's own desire to separate the political from the narrow, fanatically religious stance within NSDAP ranks. In evaluating the Political Theology of the 1920s and 1930s one must remember that one is judging with the advantage of hindsight not available to the political theologians. Nevertheless, according to Scholder, Political Theology must be held at least partially accountable for the almost total accommodation of German Protestantism to the Third Reich in 1933.[21]

Hirsch's Interpretation of the Events of 1933 and His Support of National Socialism

Emanuel Hirsch was one of those "political theologians" who in 1933 sought to bring their impressive philosophical and theological powers and influence to bear on an interpretation of the National Socialist upheaval.[22] He urged the

19. *Ibid.*, pp. 132-133.
20. *Ibid.*, p. 135.
21. *Ibid.*, p. 150.
22. I have not so far found any specific reference by Hirsch to his own theology as "Political Theology," and am relying here on Klaus Scholder's designation of Hirsch as a Political Theologian.

German evangelical church to join hands with and give its unswerving support to the National Socialist revolution which was sweeping Germany.[23] In the following pages we want to present as clearly and fairly as we can Hirsch's interpretation of the events of 1933 and the grounds upon which he called evangelical Christianity to support the creation of a new Germany. It is our intent to show how Hirsch's stance in 1933 was not politically opportunistic and plagiaristic, as Tillich maintains in his open letter of 1934, but rather that it follows consistently—with certain additions, developments, and new terminology to be sure—from his earlier wartime and post-war writings. Unfortunately, as in previous chapters, we cannot examine Hirsch's many relevant writings of this period but must limit ourselves to a careful look at a series of lectures Hirsch gave in 1933 and published under the title *Die gegenwärtige geistige Lage im Spiegel philosophischer und theologischer Besinnung: academische Vorlesungen zum Verständigung des deutschen Jahre 1933*.[24] It was this book that initially angered Tillich and compelled him to write his first accusatory open letter to Hirsch—the letter which initiated the 1934-35 debate.

Hirsch divides his lectures in this book into two main parts: the first part deals with the events of 1933 from a philosophical perspective and the second interprets these events from a theological standpoint. In his preface, dated January 30, 1934 (the first anniversary of Hitler's becoming Chancellor), Hirsch points to the fluidity and uncertainty of the situation. There can be no objectively certain knowledge of the nature of present events, he says, the meaning of which is disclosed only as the events unfold and as people *dare* to make decisions in the face of them. Hirsch is fully aware of the dangers inherent in trying to interpret the situation. Through risking such an interpretation and commitment he sees himself as crossing beyond the boundary of traditional academia, moving from reflection into action. Only by risking such action, however, can one do justice to one's vocation as spiritual educator of German young people and co-shaper of a responsible theology that tries to help the church find its difficult way in the present situation. Hirsch is also aware of the need for the theologian to guard against losing himself totally within the movement. From 1918 to 1932, he says, he stood outside the mainstream, never dreaming in 1920,

23. While I have been urged not to use the term "revolution" for the National Socialist movement (since it was not a class revolution in the Marxist sense), many National Socialists did perceive themselves as a revolutionary movement. Paul Tillich in his *The Social Decision* alludes to National Socialism as a revolutionary form of romanticism (pp. 27ff.). I am using the term here not in the technical sense of a proletarian revolution but in a broader sense—namely, that National Socialism was a people's movement (with the support of elements from all levels of society) bent on a comprehensive transformation of German society.

24. It is intersting that some eight years earlier Tillich had written a book with a very similar title, *Die Religiöse Lage der Gegenwart*. Other of Hirsch's writings during this time include *Das kirchliche Wollen der Deutschen Christen* (1933); *Deutsches Volkstum und evangelischer Glaube* (Hamburg: Hanseatische Verlagsanstalt, 1934); "Theologisches Gutachten in der Nichtarierfrage," *Deutsche Theologie* 1(May 1934); "Vom verborgenen Souverän," *Glaube und Volk* 2,1(1933).

when he published his *Deutschlands Schicksal,* that he would experience such an awakening of Germany. He hopes that the "inward compass" which he developed during those years will stand the test of the present demands, a time which beckons all Germans to assist the church and the nation in finding the right direction. What the present demands above all is "clear and supportive thought." It is in this spirit, says Hirsch, that his book is published, directed to students first but also to pastors.

A Philosophical-Political Perspective on the German Awakening
Part One of *Die gegenwärtige geistige Lage* deals with the general intellectual crisis within German thought prior to and leading up to 1933, with the significance of the German awakening (*Umbruch*) of 1933 and with the new task of philosophy and theology. Hirsch begins by tracing the 19th-century notion of freedom and reason (*Vernunft*) as an intellectual attitude characterized by religious-ethical autonomy from all external restraints and obligations. This autonomous reason of the 19th century—the root of liberalism and individualism—manifests itself as a "world-structuring will" intent on the domination of nature.[25] While he recognizes the positive achievements of the 19th century, he is critical of its preoccupation with critique, diversity, opposition, debate, revolution, and struggle. Crisis and revolution, debate and emancipation are genuine and indispensable moments in human history, he admits, but no unity-creating historical actuality can have these as its sustaining ground. What is needed is the "dynamic power of truth which is inwardly binding in an ultimate way [*letzterinnerlich bindender lebendiger Wahrheitsmacht*]."[26] Tillich had said something similar in arguing that the technical and dynamic mass needed a mystical ground. According to Hirsch, Marxism and Bolshevism are the final result of the 19th-century worldview, representing the supreme rationalization and objectification of life—the triumph of technical will.[27]

The German awakening—the National Socialist revolution of 1933—must, according to Hirsch, be seen as a protest against the false individualism, the one-sided view of freedom and reason that characterized the 19th century. In its immediate sense it is of course an upheaval from below, an upheaval that has broken forth out of the indignity, death, hunger, defeat, betrayal, and unfaithfulness that Germany suffered in its years of post-war crisis. It is a rejection of the notion of unlimited reason and freedom and of self-sufficient scientific reflection, which are devoid of any sense of obligation to nation, state, tradition, discipline, or spirit. Instead, what is affirmed in National Socialism is a theoretical reflection that is rooted in and carried by the power of actuality (*Wirklichkeitsmacht*) and corporate life (*gemeinsamen Leben*). Analysis, oppo-

25. *Die gegenwärtige geistige Lage,* pp. 7-12.
26. *Ibid.,* pp. 12-17.
27. *Ibid.,* p. 18ff.

sition, and critique are seen to be helpful only within the context of an ethically- and religiously-defined, national corporate order and spirit which itself is beyond discussion and dispute.[28] A new view of law is in the making, a view in which the individual's relation to the whole is seen in a new way. Seen in its best light, National Socialism as viewed by its more intelligent supporters, is the attempt not to evade modernity as if it never happened but to combine the insights of the Enlightenment (socialism and reason) with a mythic and primal attachment to the origin (the national, primal, and irrational). This is the way Hirsch perceives it.

There is, according to Hirsch, a paradoxical aspect to the National Socialist revolution: it attempts to be both primal (*ursprünglich*) and reflective (*reflectiert*); it wants to overcome the life-destructive aspects of late occidental culture (*Spätkultur*) and build something new through the rational and technical means of recent culture. However, "The new will itself, regardless of how deliberately it applies itself, has not been artificially created by us: it has engulfed us as a *holy storm*. Furthermore, regardless of how resolutely it governs, it does not have creating, or the desire to create, as its core; it actualizes itself through nurture [*Erziehung*] and finds its ground and measure in that which is nation-oriented [*Volkhaft*]. That is why it will triumph over any destructive aspects of the late European culture out of which we have come that still cling to its officials [*Diener*] and representatives [*Träger*]."[29] This, says Hirsch, can be fully understood only by Germans who experienced the birth of this will in August 1914. Throughout *Die gegenwärtige geistige Lage* Hirsch idealizes the spirit of August 1914 as a time of great national spiritual and political solidarity which unfortunately was lost by the end of the war and trampled on during the Weimar years.

What truly separates this new experience of German existence as a nation and a state from the previous age, according to Hirsch, is the awareness of the "mystery of the boundary." Hirsch's concept of the boundary—a category which figures centrally in the Tillich-Hirsch debate—is difficult to understand and easy to caricature. Hirsch uses the Greek term "*horos*" to describe the concept of a boundary which cannot be crossed (*unüberschreitbare Grenze*).[30] The boundary cannot be equated with blood and race but is, nevertheless, illustrated by man's racial and biological origins. The boundary represents those historical and temporal givens and actualities which shape, determine, and limit all human reflection, will, and shaping power. The National Socialist upheaval, says Hirsch, represents a new and powerful consciousness of "the boundary of the origin itself on behalf of which reason and freedom are mere servants."[31] The

28. *Ibid.*, p. 28.
29. *Ibid.*, pp. 29-30.
30. *Ibid.*, p. 5n.
31. *Ibid.*, p. 33.

new consciousness of blood and race is the particular way in which the consciousness of the boundary is recognized in the present situation.[32] There is no doubt that Hirsch defends the importance of biological factors of blood and race in binding a nation together and in creating the solidarity of a common national *"nomos,"* but he adds that historically powerful nationalities are made up of blood ties between numerous and various clans and tribes, ties created and established through a common history.[33] These blood ties have only limited permanence and undergo constant change. Nevertheless, Hirsch maintains that it is to the credit of National Socialism that it has seen as its task the guarding of the German bond-of-blood which is being threatened from the outside. It is exactly at the point where Adolf Hitler speaks about the mystery of the bond-of-blood and the need to guard it, claims Hirsch, that there breaks through in him most forcefully that primal religious feeling which he (Hitler) senses so powerfully. "Here," thinks Hirsch, "one can feel the work of the almighty Lord for whom we are simply instruments."[34] Hirsch stresses that this experience of the boundary must be powerful in all areas of human-historical life and cannot be limited to the biological side.

In an important passage Hirsch distinguishes between two aspects of boundary—that of the "historical *horos*" and the "holy *horos*":

The boundary has always signified two things simultaneously. First, there exists before us and over us in our thinking and our action the Horos of historical actuality in its national particularity. In its ruling power it preserves for us our potentiality, our service and our direction. This Horos has now broken out amongst us with primal majesty so as to become through us and for us our Nomos. Secondly, however, in all of this the boundary also signifies for us the will and power of the Lord of history, who has indeed grasped and beckoned us within our historical actuality, but still remains the

---

32. Hirsch's view of blood and race and the extent to which these define nationality (*Volk*) is difficult to assess. He claimed Tillich had not fully understood his position on this. He rejects a simple biological materialism in defining nationality but says that biological factors are important. In Hirsch's words: "Vor allem, wenn man die Flachköpfe hört, die mitgetragen werden von der Oberfläche des unergründlich tiefen Stroms, könnte man meinen: hinter dem heutigen deutsche Reden von *Blut und Rasse* stecke nichts als biologischer Materialismus, und die dazu gehörenden politischen und volkshygienischen Massnahmen seien der widerspruchsvolle Versuch, ursprüngliche Unterlagen eines geschichtlichen Volkstums künstlich zu schaffen. Niemand wird leugnen, dass allerdings bestimmte—noch nicht allzu lange ins Licht des wissenschaftlichen Bewusstseins getretne—biologischen Tatsachen, die dem mit ihrer Gesetzmässigkeit Vertrauten auch zweckbestimmten Eingriff gestatten, uns als Ausgangspunkt gedient haben. Jedes geschichtsmächtige Volkstum ist ein Blutbund mehrerer Stämme mit zahlreichen Sippen, der durch gemeinsame Geschichte wird und besteht und an einem gemeinsamen nationalen Nomos Rückhalt und Festigkeit hat." *Die gegenwärtige geistige Lage*, p. 34.
33. *Ibid.*
34. *Ibid.*, p. 36.

Horos over against our as well as all of human-historical life in an incomprehensible majesty. The *historical horos* is at the same time also the *holy horos* (the emphasis is mine). And yet, on the other hand, the holy Horos is also that which, through the power of the Eternal, consumes [*der verzehrende*] the historical and makes it temporal. This appears to us as a paradox.[35]

If one dissolves this paradox and simply equates the "historical *horos*" and the "holy *horos*," or collapses one into the other, one slips into a pre-Christian national religion (*vorchristlicher Volksreligion*). If, on the other hand, one sees the "holy *horos*" only in terms of its consuming power, then one once more slips back into the preceding culture where God is known only as an ahistorical being and the providential power of the concrete historical boundary is violated. This is what Hirsch accuses Barthian Neo-orthodoxy of doing. In short, what Hirsch is saying here is that God is present within all of human-historical life (particularly in the German turning point of 1933) but must never be simply equated with it. On the one hand, abstract religious reflection (the implied reference here is, of course, to Barthian and some extent to Tillichian theology) demonically opposes the spirit of National Socialism. On the other hand, however, the German turning point in turn is itself always in danger of demonically deifying the concrete National-historical boundary as represented by the National Socialist "revolution."

Hirsch is obviously fully aware of and warns against the danger of self-deification in National Socialism. He wants paradoxically to walk the fine line between the two perils into a new period of German history. Only if the German turning point is understood in terms of the religious spirit moving and erupting within it can this tension be properly realized. Every human encounter with God, argues Hirsch, is characterized by the following tension: the hallowing of a particular historical moment and its content, and the distancing of oneself from the particular moment toward the hiddenness of God as the mystery which transcends and grounds all of history. Every encounter with God stands in danger of collapsing into one or the other. Only if this is recognized can our being grasped by the mystery of the boundary be a genuine encounter with God. Only then can it become the basis and goal of a new historical period and the restructuring of German life.[36]

35. *Ibid.*, p. 42.
36. In his two-fold understanding of the *"horos,"* in his view of both the holiness of a particular historical moment and its content and the need to distinguish between every earthly historical reality and the God who transcends all of history, Hirsch comes close to Tillich's view of the *"kairotic"* moment in which the unconditioned is experienced within the conditioned. But when Tillich accuses Hirsch of plagiarism at this point he does not adequately account for Hirsch's more traditional theistic presuppositions which—at least in the view of Hirsch—distinguish his use of these terms from Tillich's more philosophical language and assumptions. Hirsch, one might say, thinks paradoxically and Tillich dialectically.

Hirsch genuinely believes that this new historical period which Germany is entering is and will be qualitatively different from preceding periods. The new perception of nation and state—represented by the National Socialist revolution—is based on the willingness to lead and voluntarily allow oneself to be led. This principle must, however, be distinguished from previous forms of authoritarianism as well as from democracy. The unique character of the *authoritarian* state is that those who rule demand only the obedience and loyalty of their political subjects; all responsibility and decision making is centralized and members of the government carry out only what is commanded. In the *democratic* state those who are politically responsible for the state are merely delegates and employees of the bourgeoisie (*Bürger*); the middle classes are the actual rulers of the state. Those responsible are all subordinate to and under the constant supervision and critique of their true employers.

Hirsch maintains that one cannot equate the new German perception of leadership with the old authoritarian one. What is being realized in Germany is a new political reality which cannot be understood within the old schema. Something novel is occurring which entails a new view of the German nation, a new view of leadership and authority. There are two characteristics of this understanding of leadership which differentiate it from the old authoritarian concept. First, those led perceive and voluntarily accept their leader as one who has risen out of their own midst, out of a primal will (*ursprünglichen Wollen*). "That leader and nation discover each other and understand each other is a free gift of God, who brings about the historical hour. As such our political form has a historical quality which we are not free to dispose of."[37] One cannot predict with certainty what enduring shape this new political form will take. Hirsch thinks it improbable that this new perception of nation and state will evolve into pure authoritarian rule in the old style. He sees the leadership-state as a characteristically German political form and the authoritarian form as characteristically French. Second, each of the persons grasped by the historical hour and called to action views himself within his own circle as a leader with independent responsibility. Where previously Germans were subjected to government by administrators, they are now for the most part being led by free and daring men.

Hirsch maintains that evangelical theology has been and continues to be a vital and inalienable piece of the German *logos*.[38] The German nation and evangelical Christianity, he continues, have belonged together historically for more than a thousand years and whoever tries to separate the two endangers Germanness itself. For this reason it is legitimate for theology to weave itself into the German *logos* and act as the handmaid and preserver of the German

37. *Ibid.*, p. 64. We recall here that Tillich said something very similar about the leader of the coming age in his *Masse und Geist*.

38. Hirsch interprets *Logos* as "self-expressing living spirit [*sich aussprechender lebendiger Geist*]." *Ibid.*, p. 5n.

heritage.[39] What must be remembered is that Christianity consists of two things simultaneously: it is both a historical power and a matter of conscience, a national order (*Volksordnung*) and a personal relationship to God.[40]

While many great Germans may not have belonged to Christianity in the second sense, one cannot deny that all of them as members of the German *nomos*, shaped by the common Germanic-Christian nature, belonged to Christianity in the first, historical sense. In fact, Christianity in the first sense—as historical power, national order, and general spirituality (*Geistigkeit*)—draws its life from the hidden ember of Christianity in the second sense. A Christian people (*Volkstum*) for whom Christianity has become its inner fate—through its *nomos* and *logos*—can preserve and develop its own nature only through the openness of its individual members to the experience of the gospel; that is, being open to Christianity in the second sense. This fact constantly reshapes the nation's natural-historical life. Consequently, there will be recurrent crises, convulsions, historical revolutions and change in the nation's historical life. This is different from pagan nationalistic religions which encounter God only in a linear relationship to their nationality—as simply structuring their own natural-historical *nomos*.[41] One might say that Hirsch perceives the German revolution as an ongoing or perpetual restructuring.

The fate of the German church—of all evangelical Christians in Germany and of German evangelical theologians—is deeply intertwined with the German nation. A genuine theology is so much a part of the common historical life that in its spiritual expression and spiritual struggle it participates in the ultimate responsibility of Christianity for the gospel *and* for the perpetual penetration of the gospel into human-historical life. Precisely because its relation to the powers and decisions of the nation and the state is one of living tension, it is itself the expression of the historical hour; it is a mirror to and of the moving powers of corporate life and it must make the decisions that God expects of it in this historical hour.[42] It is precisely through its participation in the history of nation and state that theology must be a source of life both for evangelical Christianity and for the German nation.

The Events of 1933 Interpreted Theologically
Part Two of the lectures interpret the events of 1933 from a theological point of view. Hirsch begins with an extensive historical analysis of pre-war evangelical theology, arguing that the basic assumptions of the previous age—self-sufficient

39. *Ibid.*, pp. 69-70.
40. *Ibid.*, p. 70.
41. As we have noted earlier, in his view of *nomos* Hirsch was greatly influenced by Wilhelm Stapel's notion of *Volksnomos*. For Stapel, the nation had its own God-ordained order, "'a law of life which, in conformity to its nature, defined its inner and outer form, its cult, its ethos, its system of government, its law': the *Nomos*." Cf. Scholder, *Die Kirchen und das Dritte Reich*, p. 534.
42. *Die gegenwärtige geistige Lage*, p. 76.

reason, autonomous freedom, and historicism—defined and fragmented theology.[43] He and others became convinced that somehow faith and history must be bridged, that thorough historical-critical research must be combined with an existential experience of Christ in faith, and that the fragmentation and partisanship of pre-war theology could not provide an adequate foundation for the bonding of academic theology and the church. They believed strongly that the very essence of the church was at stake and that it could be rescued only through a genuine struggle for a new ground and structure for the whole of life.

It is in this context that evangelical theology in Germany became deeply involved in what Hirsch calls the "social question." There was a consensus among many theologians that academic theology bore some responsibility for the spiritual life of the nation and that it needed to participate in the shaping of German national life. Theology and the church had two options in attempting to answer the social question. One option was that of forming an alliance with the working classes under the banner of Marxism. While the majority of teachers, students, and the church as a whole rejected this option, some theologians (Hirsch is obviously thinking here of his friend Tillich) chose this path—a path, which, according to Hirsch, led away from the nation and the fatherland to an internationalism, away from a dynamic German spirituality into a doctrinaire world, away from the church into a world at enmity with Christianity. Thinkers who chose this option became convinced that the proletarian movement was the true protest against the demons of the period and the true bearer of a world-historical turning point. These theologians wanted to implant the seed of Christianity—Christian love and hope—into the proletarian movement and thereby maintain the integrity of Christianity.[44]

The second option was to attempt a gradual transformation of the common life from within, to improve the situation of the working masses through incorporating them into the nation, the state, and Christianity. "It was the way of actualizing social justice through the work of reform within the given situation and thus restoring the health of the nation and the state, and the good conscience of a church bound to nation and to state."[45] But this attempt also failed to stem the tide of Marxism which increasingly alienated the church from half of the German nation. What he and others learned from this period, says Hirsch, was that Christianity and the church is bound not only to spiritual conditions but to earthly conditions as well. They were saved from a "false spirituality" which prepared them for the crisis situation of later years.

43. *Ibid.*, pp. 78-101.

44. Hirsch's critique of this option is clear: "If one understands the will for the future [*Zukunftswillen*] and hope for the future [*Zukunftshoffnung*] of the Marxist route from the perspective of Christian eschatology, the Christian hope for the kingdom of God, then one certainly overlooked the small matter that here one faced a secularized religion, intensely hostile to religion, the foundation for which was not a Christian but a Jewish hope for the kingdom...." *Ibid.*, p. 98.

45. *Ibid.*, p. 99.

In the years 1914 to 1932—years defined by the shattering effects of war, defeat, and revolution—Germans were forced to ask the question concerning God (*Frage nach Gott*) in a new way.[46] It forced evangelical theology to look for a new third way, to reinterpret its view of the gospel and the relation of the gospel to the general spiritual life of the nation. What distinguished the theology of these crisis years from pre-war theology was that earth-shattering historical events which occurred outside of the theological sphere became decisive for theology.[47] Theology was forced to rethink the relation of that which is Christian to that which is human and historical. There was a deep realization that divine revelation could not occur outside of its reception within human experience, knowledge, and appropriation. A theological revolution took place first through a new interpretation and exegesis of Paul and the New Testament and, second, through a renaissance of Luther and Reformation studies. The young evangelical theologians were agreed in their opposition to Culture-Protestantism, which represented the fusion of God's kingdom with the kingdom of bourgeois culture. They saw Culture-Protestantism as denying the New Testament distinction between the present and the coming eon, and the Reformation teaching of the two kingdoms. Hirsch's emphasis on the *two kingdoms* is in effect a theological protest against Culture-Protestantism and its espousal of only *one kingdom*—liberal bourgeois culture sanctified by liberal Christianity. In their protest against Culture-Protestantism Hirsch and Tillich agree, although the latter's attitude to the previous age of liberal theology is much more ambivalent than the former's.

Out of theological ferment a new option was born—that of Young National Lutheranism, a movement with which Hirsch identifies himself. It stressed that the New Testament eschatological emphasis be combined with a sense of ethical obligation and obedience to the Lord of history within the given, actual, concrete historical situation and hour. It struggled against the ideas of the 1918 revolution and against the dream of an international world culture of Marxist or liberal-democratic orientation. It was committed to the preserving of German national freedom, calling, and renewal. It based its theological position on Luther's doctrine of the two kingdoms:

46. In such times of crisis—as in the war and post-war years when the very existence of the German nation was at stake—the Lord of history reveals himself as question: *"He is there as question.* And that means on the *one* side: he is felt much more dynamically and immediately than before when everything went on from one thing to another in its well-ordered path.... God exists as a question on the *other* side as well: he desires to be found through risk. He has become the question within the earthly question in a way that no one can avoid." *Ibid.,* pp. 102-103.

47. While Hirsch would certainly object to Scholder's characterization of his political theology as having political ethics as its starting point—for Hirsch the starting point remained theological (that is, Luther's theology)—he is quite willing to admit here the great extent to which external social and political events framed the question of God and helped to shape his theological perspective.

God has placed the Christian life in this state of tension [*Spannung*], that we serve the Eternal within the temporal. Now this view of Luther's was, however, a recasting of the New Testament Word: in place of the missionary message which anticipates an immanent miracle in a dying world culture, in which no one can feel at home any longer, the preaching of the divine kingdom of grace is internalized within man himself, who finds himself at home in an all-embracing earthly nation and state; the split between the two kingdoms situates itself in the paradox of inwardness.[48]

Young National Lutheranism saw as its main task the proper delineation of New Testament eschatology, of the nature of the eternal gospel, and of the nature of one's ethical commitment to the present historically-conditioned temporal reality. The whole Holl school of Lutheranism, including Hirsch, with its strong emphasis on ethical obedience, is in effect a kind of reform movement within Lutheranism, a movement which adds a strong ethical-moral component to the forensic notion of "justification by faith."

In the process of this theological rethinking, traditional Lutheran ethics underwent a significant evolution. First, the doctrine of justification was applied to the Christian's risking of an ethical commitment to a historical community; a community which on the one hand represents the arena of human sinfulness requiring justification by grace and on the other hand is precisely the forum in which human beings can and must express their unswerving obedience to the Lord of history and to the divine will within creation. Second, whereas the older Lutheran ethic had interpreted the concrete historical community as the state, the new view defined the historical community and the state in terms of nationality. These new Lutheran theologians had awakened to "nationality with its majesty, as the source of life and destiny, as the primal power of history, as the genuine bearer of the spirit, discipline, and life, yes, as the preparation for an encounter with God. In the nation one finds the boundary, with which the creator's will and life binds and unbinds human-historical life."[49] This kind of thinking freed these Lutheran theologians, including Hirsch himself, from a Christological narrowness in their concepts of revelation and grace. They recognized the reality of prevenient revelation and grace within history. In this rejection of a

---

48. *Ibid.*, p. 115. It is, as we have seen, precisely this internalization of the kingdom of God which Tillich rejects. For Tillich, relegating the kingdom of God to an inner reality robs it of its critical function with respect to social and political questions. Tillich sees this as problematic from an ethical point of view present not only in Hirsch's interpretation of Luther's theology but in Luther's own doctrine of the two kingdoms. These remarks by Hirsch reveal the extent to which Hirsch was willing to enter into a revisionist hermeneutics of the New Testament—in this case to de-eschatologize the New Testament view of the kingdom of God—in order to make the Christian gospel more readily adaptable to his understanding of the present historical circumstances. In doing this it seems he is in fact following the tradition of liberal biblical interpretation.

49. *Ibid.*, p. 117.

Christological narrowness Hirsch and the Young National Lutherans clearly parted company with the dialectical theology of Karl Barth, particularly as later expressed in the first and second articles of the Barmen Confession.[50]

Hirsch devotes a few masterfully argued pages to a discussion of the three existing theological options of the Weimar years, options which were opposed to Young National Lutheranism: the Theology of Crisis, Religious Socialism, and the Christian-conservative view.[51] His comments about Religious Socialism are particularly interesting and relevant. Despite its bitter opposition to Young National Lutheranism, Religious Socialism, observes Hirsch, had one thing formally in common with this its opponent: "that faith dared to make a historical decision."[52] Religious Socialism too was deeply concerned with the dialectic between that which is Christian and that which is human-historical and tried to relate the two through the concept of the *kairos*. In this section Hirsch is obviously thinking of his friend and opponent Tillich. He calls Religious Socialism "theological Marxism"—a label to which Tillich objected—and openly admits that it made an important contribution to Young National Lutheranism:

> In all of this, this philosophy of history of theological Marxism had a mission specially to Young National Lutheranism: it helped to liberate it from its original bourgeois narrowness; it helped it place the different historical decision that fell to it in a larger context. Without the inward struggle with this significant opponent (in the theological Marxist philosophy of history there was something that was lacking in Marxism, namely, spirit) the Young National Lutheran theologians would hardly have become dynamic enough to give themselves honorably to National Socialism, as the historical decision demanded of them and as the beginning of a new German historical period.[53]

In the light of Tillich's later charge of Hirsch's consciously-disguised plagiarism of Religious Socialism categories, it is important to point out that Hirsch himself here openly admits the extent to which the Religious Socialists influenced Young National Lutheran theology. Tillich himself in a 1933 letter to the National Socialist Ministry of Culture alludes to the fact that he apparently contributed conceptual categories to National Socialist philosophy.[54] This tends to lend support to the thesis not only that the 1933 political and intellectual situation was more fluid than is sometimes assumed but also that there were some rather remarkable formal similarities between the "political theology" of

50. See Arthur C. Cochrane, "The Theology of Barmen," in *The Church's Confession Under Hitler*, pp. 286-288.
51. *Die gegenwärtige geistige Lage*, pp. 118-123.
52. *Ibid.*, p. 120.
53. *Ibid.*, p. 121.
54. See Pauck, *Paul Tillich: Life*, pp. 148-150.

Religious Socialism and Religious Nationalism in the 1920s and 1930s.

We come now perhaps to the most important part of Hirsch's 1933 lectures—his discussion of the role of evangelical theology and the church in the present time. In this chapter Hirsch outlines his own view of Hitler and the National Socialist revolution more specifically and outlines what he perceives to be the relation between evangelical theology and National Socialism. Somewhat reminiscent of Tillich's 1921-22 claim, that Christianity and socialism needed to become one, Hirsch now, 12 years later, argues that "The young German evangelical theology and the present hour in nation and state belong together."[55] Only if theology opens itself up inwardly to the newness and greatness which has erupted and which is dedicated to the building of a new historical reality amongst Germans, can young Evangelical theology become what it is meant to be but could not become in the previous years of crisis. There is for Hirsch no middle way—only an either/or.

According to Hirsch, German evangelical theology and the present hour within the German nation and state belong together not in the sense of a confessional unity but rather in their common aim of educating Germans in their responsibility for the German *nomos* and *logos*. The primary question for evangelical Christianity, in Hirsch's opinion, is whether or not National Socialism and its worldview represents the sustaining natural-historical basis of life (*tragende natürlich-geschichtliche Lebensgrund*) for Germans of evangelical faith and spirit. If the answer is in the affirmative, then clearly the evangelical church has adequate space within the German nation and state, as shaped by the National Socialist movement and worldview, to nurture Germans in the evangelical faith through its proclamation, its catechetical instruction, and its pastoral care. It does not need additional space.[56] Because the German evangelical church ultimately has no historical possibility of life independent from the destiny of the German nation, the liberation of the German nation and its awakening to a new historical period also signifies a liberation and awakening of German evangelical Christianity.[57] Hirsch does not want to collapse evangelical Christianity into a particular political view of nation and state, as was the case in cultural Protestantism, but is arguing that German evangelical Christianity cannot be separated from its social and national ethos. Theology and the church

55. *Die gegenwärtige geistige Lage*, p. 132.

56. *Ibid.*, p. 133. Here Hirsch expresses a traditional Lutheran view of the church's appropriate sphere of responsibility—administering the sacraments and pastoral care—a realm separate from that of the state which deals with external socio-political and economic issues.

57. It is easy to understand why some Germans were so quick to link the political "revolution" with the awakening of the church when one sees the increases in church membership increased from an increase of 6300 in the first half of 1933 to an increase of 11,700 in the second half. That was an increase of 18,000 in the evangelical church in Thüringia in 1933—almost nine times as large as in the previous year. Similar stories could be told of other parts of Germany. This does not mean there were also some opposite trends in other parts. Cf. Scholder, *Die Kirchen und das dritte Reich*, p. 664.

hear a co-responsibility for the people together with the nation and the state in the present hour, before the Lord of history who has given each nation a special historical destiny.

Both Evangelical Christianity and National Socialism, Hirsch claims, are committed to the shaping of the same individuals within the German nation. It is this fact which defines the nature of their co-responsibility. Somehow Christianity, the nurturing of which is the special responsibility of Evangelical Christians, and the Germanness of the new German order, need to be related to each other.[58] What is required is a thorough rethinking of the relation of that which is Christian to that which is human-historical. The paradox of the evangelical faith is that it affirms a mystery; namely, that the ultimate decision concerning humanness takes place within the hiddenness of the individual human heart before God. This is something which is not immediately accessible to any national order (*Volksordnung*) or national-will-to-educate (*Erziehungswillen*). Here evangelical Christianity can make an invaluable contribution to the present National Socialist spirit—an act of gratitude for the possibilities of Christian proclamation and Christian rethinking that the new hour in Germany makes possible and preserves.[59]

Hirsch believes that the true task of the evangelical church is proclamation; it is in this that the church becomes what it was meant to be. But all proclamation becomes counterfeit when it tries to exist for itself, apart from human-historical and national life. The true proclaiming church does not insist on a place for itself. It has a unique task, but this task is within the living and historical space of the German nation. The people with which the church fulfills its task, and the people who hear its proclamation, whose faith and love are kindled by the divine word, are the same people who must take their responsible place within the social order, within national political life as unselfish coworkers in rebuilding the German national order and the German community. Only if this happens will the new life and order be a place where God is present in Jesus Christ, a place where the Eternal prepares the temporal and the national (*Volkhafte*) to be

58. *Die gegenwärtige geistige Lage*, p. 143.

59. In Hirsch's own words: "Ihre grösste Schwierigkeit und zugleich Verheissung aber hat sie daran, dass unser evangelischer Glaube mit dem Geheimnis steht und fällt, dass wir als Einzelne, in der Verborgenheit des Herzens, vor Gott treten, und dass die letzte Entscheidung über das Menschsein in diesem vor Gott ein Einzelner Sein liegt, welches für keine Volksordnung und keinen Erziehungswillen unmittelbar verfügbar ist. Damit trägt unser Glaube eine fruchtbare Parodoxie in die gegenwärtige sich bildende deutsche Geistigkeit hinein. Mit dieser Paradoxie aber vermag er der nationalsozialistischen Geistigkeit einen Dienst zu tun, der ein Dank mit der Tat werden könnte für alles, was die neue Stunde uns an Möglichkeiten christlicher Verkündigung und christlichen Neudenkens gewährt. Mit dieser Paradoxie wird evangelischer Glaube auf seinem Felde Hüter und Wahrer der früher von uns besprochnen unverlierbaren Grundparadoxie der politischen Bewegung selbst: dass sie ein unerhört bewusster und alles wagender menschlicher Gestaltungswille ist, der doch aus dem Geheimnis einer unverfügbaren heiligen Grenze alles menschlichen Schaffens und Gestaltens lebt." Hirsch, *Die gegenwärtige geistige Lage*, pp. 143-144.

its bearer (*Träger*) and instrument (*Werkzeuge*). Only if this happens—that is, only on the foundation of Christianity—can the insights and work of the people who embody the historical turning point in Germany be legitimately realized.[60]

Hirsch compares the 14 years of the evangelical church's existence within the culture of the Weimar Republic to that of the New Testament church's alien existence within a hostile pagan cultural environment.[61] In the context of this new historical turning point, as represented by the National Socialist awakening, the evangelical church once more finds itself in a more compatible social and political situation. It is a milieu which is normal for Germanic Christianity. One in which "the national reality is built up as a regimen of life which is open to and is shaped in its basic ethical and religious assumptions by Christianity."[62] For this reason—in contrast to the situation in which the New Testament church found itself—Hirsch believes that it is not God's intention in the present situ-

---

60. Because this is such an important and difficult passage, we need to quote Hirsch at some length in the original German: "Alles Verkündigen wird unecht und unverständlich, wenn es ein volks- und geschichtsüberlegnes Eigenwesen der Kirche und der in ihr Verkündigenden begründen soll. Gerade die Kirche, die wieder wesentlich verkündigende Kirche wird, darf nicht in einem Raume für sich stehen. Sie hat ihren besonderen Dienst, den niemand statt ihrer tun kann, aber sie hat ihn im Lebens- und Geschichtsraum des deutschen Volks. Die Menschen, mit denen sie ihren Dienst tut, und die Menschen, die auf sie hören, die vom die Kirchenrede brauchenden göttlichen Wort zu Glaube und Liebe entzündet sind, sie müssen von Herzen in allen neu sich bildenden Ordnungen, Kameradschaften, Zusammenschlüssen des volklich-politischen Lebens drin stehen als treue Helfer und Kameraden im Neuaufbau deutscher Volksordnung und Volksgemeinschaft. Und müssen es selbstlos tun, ohne dabei irgend etwas herausschlagen zu wollen. So, und nur so, wird alles neu sich bildende Leben eine Stätte der Gegenwart Gottes in Jesus Christus, eine Stätte, da das Ewige sich das Zeitliche, das Göttliche sich das Volkhafte bereitet zu seinem Träger und Werkzeuge. So, und nur so, kann die Einsicht der die Geschichtswende tragenden Männer, nur auf dem Boden des Christentums könne ihr Werk recht stehn und vollbracht werden, von uns aufgenommen und mit uns zusammen verwirklicht werden." Hirsch, *Ibid.*, pp. 149-150.

61. The German reads: "Wir sind in den letzten vierzehn Jahren daran gewesen, eine der neutestamentlichen Lage sehr ähnliche als unser Schicksal bereitet zu bekommen. So hat auch die neutestamentliche Gestaltung des Verhältnisses von Kirche und Welt unsern Willen und unser Gemüt vor eine Frage stellen müssen. Die Geschichtswende aber hat uns wieder in die Lage zurückgebracht, die für das germanische Christentum bisher die Regel gewesen ist: die volklich-staatliche Wirklichkeit baut sich grundsätzlich als eine dem Christentum geöffnete, von ihm in ihren letzten ethischen und religiösen Voraussetzungen mitgeformte Lebensordnung auf. Es ist nicht Gottes Wille, dass wir in dieser Lage, weil wir sie als noch nicht durchgeklärt empfinden, künstlich die neutestamentliche Kirchengestalt mit der ihr eigentümlichen Fremdheit und Abscheidung dem allgemeinen Leben gegenüber herzustellen suchen. Es ist nicht Gottes Wille, dass wir mit den ersten Christen den Bruch zwischen Gottesreich und Weltreich schauen als Bruch zwischen Gemeinde und Volksordnung. Das ist Gottes Wille, dass wir uns besinnen auf die Unterscheidung, die das reformatorische Christentum gemacht hat zwischen der verborgnen Kirche Gottes und der Kirche, die menschlich—geschichtliche Ordnung und menschlich—geschichtliches Werk ist." *Ibid.*, p. 151. Like Tillich, Hirsch is calling not for a restoration of primitive Christianity's view of the church and its relation to the world, but for a new church-state self-understanding, which for him (and here he differs from Tillich) is grounded in Luther's two-kingdom distinction.

62. *Ibid.*, p. 151.

ation that the distinction between the kingdom of God and the kingdom of the world should be seen in terms of the opposition between the church and the nation. Rather, it is God's will that a distinction be made, true to Reformation Christianity, between the hidden and invisible church of God and the church which is the product of human-historical order and work.

From the above comments it would seem that Hirsch suffered from simplistic illusions about the noble religious intentions and presuppositions that are at the basis of the National Socialist revolution. This is to misunderstand the realism with which he views the dangers inherent in the situation and the serious differences he had with some of the German Christians precisely over their uncritical and overly-enthusiastic views.[63] He seems, in fact, to vacillate between optimism about the tremendous possibilities of the revolution sweeping across Germany—including both the great potential for renewal within the evangelical church and the German nation—and a sense of foreboding about the dangers of the situation and the possibility of the revolution miscarrying. Some of this foreboding is evident in succeeding comments about the fluidity and uncertainty of the outcome of the current situation and the possibility of tragic suffering for the church. In the middle of a journey, he says, especially when the journey takes place within a stormy movement, one can only intuitively interpret the events and point the church in the right direction only by faith, with courage and an awareness of the dangers that are present to it. The evangelical church now needs people who are willing to take such risks, people who will give themselves wholeheartedly to the movement and help to shape it:

63. Hirsch's whole relation to the German Christians, as we have seen in a previous chapter, is complicated and at times confusing. On the one hand, in his writings during this period, he generally defends the German Christian stance and identifies himself with it. On the other hand, he officially belonged to German Christians only briefly and often criticized the more radical and overly-enthusiastic factions. In a March 11, 1963 conversation with Walter Buff (a conversation that Buff carefully took notes of), Hirsch reflected on the years 1933-34. He points out that in 1933 he refused to join the Berlin circle of the "German Christians." In 1934 he refused to join the Berlin circle of the "German Christians." In 1934 he became a member of the Hannover circle but left in August of that year because he could not prevent them from fusing Christianity and national life. The German Christians, he says in this conversation, were unwilling to go along with his rejection of the crusade idea and the fusion of gospel and nation, Christianity and political community. Cf. Personal Letter: Buff to Reimer, January 11, 1980. Hirsch comments on the same theme in a personal letter to Hans Grimm in 1958. In this letter he says he is not in the position to give any official or authentic presentation of the intentions of the German Christians because for the whole of 1933 and again after the Fall of 1934 he was a German Christian on the one hand but did not belong to them in any official way on the other. Hossenfelder, he says, did not want him to be a member because he considered Hirsch too much of a free thinker. After the Fall of 1934 he could not come to any agreement with the only group still left, the Thüringian German Christians, because they demanded party discipline and he (Hirsch) declared that he would not under any circumstances give up his freedom to maintain a personal stance—that a word of Emanuel Hirsch must always remain purely the responsible word of Emanuel Hirsch. Personal letter: Hirsch to Hans Grimm (June 3, 1958), Hans Grimm Archiv, Lippoldsberg/Weser, made available by Walter Buff.

We evangelical Christians can thankfully and honorably give ourselves to, and in the spirit of cooperation and support affirm the movement which is now transforming our national-stately [*volklich-staatlichen*] Nomos and Logos from the bottom up. We can do this, as no one can, out of an inner accountability before the Lord of history, and with the consciousness that in his Word and Gospel there exists a power with us and over us, that stands with majestic truth over all changes and movements of national-stately life, including the one that is now occurring, in a different way than we ourselves do.[64]

No one knows what will occur to the church in the immanent future. It may be faced with suffering and trial. But Hirsch believes and trusts that God can turn suffering into grace and blessing.

Hirsch's two-fold stance toward the nation is given more explicit theological expression in the short appendix to the book entitled "Das Ewige und das Zeitliche."[65] He rejects a false individualism which does not see itself as encompassed by and active within the national fatherland—the source of life and concrete earthly meaning. He rejects a false individualism that, instead of manifesting a self-sacrifical attitude on behalf of the nation, believes that the nation itself should be sacrificed for an international community. All historical internationalism, according to Hirsch, is rooted in a false individualism. But at the same time, Hirsch wants to recognize the limitation and finitude of the nation. While it is the highest earthly corporate reality, the nation must still be seen as temporal, as earthly, as something which will pass away. The myth of the "eternal" nation is not based on serious religious reflection and must be rejected. This paradoxical stance toward the nation, however, must not result in a half-hearted commitment and love for the nation but must inspire passionate involvement.

Hirsch bases his defense of the Christian's paradoxical relation to the eternal within the temporal on Luther's concept of freedom and bondage. The freedom and the bondage of the Christian constitutes a liberation from all earthly binding, on the one hand (through forgiveness and justification the Christian lives totally for and from God's love); but this very freedom, on the other hand, liberates the Christian to be bound to human-historical reality through an earthly calling. In love one becomes a dedicated servant within the temporal realm. In this dialectic, says Hirsch, we learn correctly to see our relation to the earthly embrace of the nation. It is precisely a *true* Christian individualism, which sees itself as free in God as individual, that can commit itself to the nation and

64. *Die gegenwärtige geistige Lage,* p. 153.
65. This slightly revised appendix, "Das ewige und das Zeitliche," was first published in *Glaube und Volk* 1,5(May 15, 1932), pp. 65-71. According to Hirsch, in it he develops the dialectical presuppositions which are at the basis of his lectures of 1933. It shows how and from where he arrives at his interpretation of the present hour in German history.

overcome a *false* individualism which is not bound to the nation. Precisely he who is free in God, who knows the contingency of the temporal, can be genuinely faithful in the earthly sphere. It is this basic understanding of the paradoxical nature of freedom and bondage, as grounded in Luther's theology, that Hirsch believes Tillich has not adequately acknowledged.

We have come to the end of our examination of Hirsch's political and theological stance toward the National Socialist revolution of 1933. In our study of Hirsch's thought as it evolved from 1914 to 1933 we have emphasized (in contrast to Gunda Schneider-Flume's thesis) the *continuity* of Hirsch's theological and political development as an argument against Tillich's charge of plagiarism and implicit opportunism which he levels against Hirsch in his open letter of 1934.[66] It is true that historical events of 1933 did profoundly influence and shape Hirsch's theological perceptions and formulations—as had the events of 1914 and 1918 earlier. It is true, as well, that the National Socialist revolution (representing the kind of leadership-oriented movement of national rebirth that Hirsch had longed and struggled for throughout the 1920s) and the theological ferment associated with it in the summer of 1933 provided Hirsch with and inspired him to use some new concepts and terminology, particularly that of *horos* and *nomos*. Further, it is true, also, that Hirsch's explication of the relation of the eternal to the human-historical (and the hallowedness of the historical moment) bore some resemblance to Tillich's notion of the *kairos*. Nevertheless, the charge that Hirsch plagiarized these categories from the Religious Socialists and disguised this plagiarism at that—simply does not bear up under a careful study of Hirsch's independent and consistent theological and political development from 1914 onward. Hirsch was much too independent and consistent a thinker—as Barth, his passionate opponent and colleague in the early 1920s, rightly acknowledged—deceptively to borrow from another man's thought.[67] Further, his political categories as he uses them in 1933 and earlier

66. One of Schneider-Flume's basic theses is that Hirsch's political and theological thought underwent a fundamental shift between the years of the Weimar Republic, which he opposed, and the triumph of National Socialism, which he wholeheartedly endorses. Schneider-Flume argues that this shift was a rather dramatic change from a decision-oriented ethics-of-conscience (*Gewissensethik*) in the 1920s to an ethics-of-actuality (*Wirklichkeitsethik*) in the 1930s conditioned partly by (1) the German turn of 1933 and partly by (2) the impossibility of inwardness to remain within itself and the inevitable necessity for it to be filled with some kind of content. Thus Hirsch's inward ethics-of-conscience and emphasis on pure "decision" (Schneider-Flume calls this "decisionism") turns in 1933 to an uncritical decision for and uncritical commitment and binding to a holy community. Gunda Schneider-Flume, *Die politische Theologie Emanuel Hirschs 1918-1933* (Frankfurt/M: Verlag Peter Lang GmbH, 1971). See especially pp. 128ff. In my argument for the continuity of Hirsch's thought throughout the years of the Weimar Republic and into the years of National Socialist rule I am supported by the analysis and views of Jens Schjørring in his *Theologische Gewissensethik*, see esp. p. 152.

67. Barth, *The German Church Conflict*, edited by A.M. Allchin, Martin E. Marty and T.H.L. Parker (London: Lutterworth Press, 1965). p. 30. In evaluating Hirsch's book, Barth states: "We can and must praise it [*Die gegenwärtige geistige Lage*] too for the fact that its author, in contrast to

are rooted in substantially different theological presuppositions than those of Tillich's: primarily Luther's two-kingdom doctrine, a dualism which Tillich finds alien to his own thought.

To determine the accuracy of Hirsch's interpretation of Luther's theology of the two kingdoms is beyond the scope of this study. Furthermore, to establish the extent to which Hirsch's interpretation of the two kingdoms underwent a substantial change to fit the situation toward the end of the Weimar years, as Schneider-Flume argues, would require a more detailed examination of Hirsch's early and later explication of Luther's two kingdoms than this study can undertake.[68] It is true that from 1918 to 1932 Hirsch found himself outside of and in opposition to the political mainstream as defined by the Weimar Republic. It is also true that his stance changed from one of "critical opposition" in the 1920s to wholehearted support when the National Socialists came into power in 1933. But this political shift did not, as Schneider-Flume suggests, represent a fundamental shift in Hirsch's theological-political views but was in continuity with his "conservative" understanding of the God-ordained nature and task of government and authority from the beginning. The basis upon which he distanced himself from the political assumptions of the Weimar Republic, to which he never swore an oath of allegiance, and his unequivocal support of Hitler and National Socialism in 1933 (he joined the Party only in 1937) was consistent throughout. It was based on what he perceived to be the legitimate task of temporal political authority. It was based on the strict separation of (1) the visible external political-legal sphere, governed by the norm of justice, the demand for obedience, and its particular God-given task of punishing evil and protecting the good through the appropriate use of force, from (2) the invisible internal spiritual sphere of conscience—the individual's hidden relation to God, governed by the norm of love and the reality of spiritual freedom. He believed that the political perceptions at the basis of the Weimar Republic together with theological-Marxist options of the period, such as Religious Socialism, were not consistent with the unique Reformation-Germanic-Christian understanding of the relation of the human-historical to the Christian as formulated most profoundly by Luther and Fichte. His support for National Socialism was not an

many of his fellow-believers, has, with what he declared today, remained in line with what he has always meant, intended and maintained. If anyone is genuine and has the right to speak in this affair, it is Emanuel Hirsch." In a very similar vein Barth writes in a personal letter to Hirsch in 1953, after many years of silence following their controversy in the 1930s, that, of all the German theologians known to him, Hirsch was the only one of those who supported Adolf Hitler and his cause who had the inner consistency and the moral right to take this step. Personal Letter, Barth to Hirsch, September 12, 1953. Karl Barth Archiv, Basel, made available to me by Walter Buff.

68. Schneider-Flume maintains that with Hirsch's growing disillusionment with German politics in the Weimar period his interpretation of the two-kingdom doctrine also underwent a change, the split between the two realms becoming ever more sharp and his intellectual secession from the existing state in favor of the duty of the spirit ever more pronounced. *Die politische Theologie Emanuel Hirschs 1918-1933*, p. 122.

opportunistic one but was conditioned by his firm conviction that the leaders of the historical turning point rightly understood their God-ordained, temporal, human-historical task and considered themselves accountable to the Lord of history. The success of the revolution, he thought, would depend to a great extent on how committed the evangelical church would be in its participation in the educational task of the new era in German culture.

Tillich's Critique of National Socialism and his Defense of a Genuine Socialist Decision in 1933

Having examined Hirsch's political thought in the early 1930s and his support of National Socialism in 1933, we turn now to Tillich's thought during this same period, giving special attention to his attitude toward National Socialism. We make reference to a number of Tillich's shorter essays, but focus primarily on *The Socialist Decision,* a book published by Tillich in 1933. This is one of Tillich's best and most systematic treatments of his political thought, parallel to Hirsch's *Die gegenwärtige geistige Lage* of about the same time. One of the important questions that we want to keep in mind in looking at Tillich's thought during these years is the following: What is Tillich's view of nation and nationality in view of his own commitment to Religious Socialism and the international proletariat in the 1920s, and in light of Hirsch's charge in 1934 that Tillich lacked a serious and binding commitment to a temporal historical community?

Yes and No to Nationality

As early as 1924 Tillich made some remarkably positive statements about nation and nationality while remaining critical of any identification of Germanness with Christianity. In a short article of that year entitled "Christentum, Sozialismus und Nationalismus," Tillich criticized the capitalist-bourgeois destruction of all immediate communal relationships, of the bourgeois attack against natural and spiritual realities such as family, nation, and station through the pure rationalization of existence and the unlimited will toward the capitalistic achievement of power.[69] Religious Socialism, he says in this essay, must be understood as fighting the destructive effects of the capitalistic reification and de-spiritualization (*Entseelung*) of corporate reality, as protesting the destructive effects of capitalism on the spirit and life of a nation and nationality. To this extent, Tillich goes on to say, the struggle of Religious Socialism makes common cause with the religiously-grounded national movement. This explains why it recognizes itself as having a considerable unity with religiously-based

69. Tillich, "Christentum, Sozialismus und Nationalismus," *Wingolfs-Blätter* 53(1924): 78-80. Also in *GW* XIII, pp. 161-166.

national movements while at the same time not being able to support them. In the end, they do not penetrate to the root of the evil, but, without wanting to, succumb to the general attitude of capitalism after all.[70]

Tillich is particularly critical of a Marburg Wingolf student declaration which too closely identified Christian and German morality. He unequivocally rejects such an identification, arguing that the creative impulses that erupt from the natural ground and history of individuals, communities, and nations can never be identified in an unmediated way with Christianity. In every moment there is a tension, a crisis, both a bonding and a repulsion between Christianity and these natural creative powers. Only through a perpetual "No" can the eternal realize itself within the temporal, the Christian within the nation. Any unmediated identification is a return to pre-Christian national religion and the worship of idols.

From the beginning, Tillich claims, his statements assumed that the task of the Christian vis-à-vis socialism was no different than the Christian's task vis-à-vis the national movement. Religious Socialism desired nothing else than to represent a critical force within the socialist worldview. It would not have occurred to Religious Socialism to say that it did not see any conflicts (*Gegensätze*) between Christian and socialist morality (*Sitte*). It recognized these conflicts profoundly and painfully, just as it recognized them between German and Christian morality. Would it not have been the task of the Wingolf, he asks, to represent this same kind of critical unrest, the cross and the judgment, within the national movement within which it legitimately finds itself and thus to understand others who consider their task in the same way within the socialist movement? Would precisely this not reveal the deep bond that exists between both movements?[71] This remarkable statement by Tillich reveals the rather sympathetic perspective from which he views the national renewal movement as represented by the Wingolf organization, even though he does not identify with it in any political sense. He concedes a certain legitimacy to the stance of those committed to national renewal upon Christian grounds and points out the common elements between Religious Socialism and religious nationalism. Most important, however, Tillich stresses the ultimate critical function that Christianity must always have to and within all political movements— something which he finds lacking in the Wingolf declaration.

In an important 1932 declaration, "Zehn Thesen," Tillich reveals his astute analysis of the political, religious, and ecclesiastical situation in a series of ten succinct propositional observations concerning National Socialism, Protestantism, and the relation between the two.[72] Because of their significance

---

70. *Ibid.*, *GW* XIII, p. 164.
71. *Ibid.*, pp. 165-166.
72. "Zehn Thesen," *Die Kirchen und das Dritte Reich* (Gotha: Klotz, 1932), pp. 126-128. Also in *GW* XIII, pp. 177-179.

and relevance for this chapter we briefly summarize them here.

According to Tillich, (1) A Protestantism which opens itself up to National Socialism and rejects socialism is once more about to betray its mandate in the world; (2) In its apparent obedience to the claim that the kingdom of God is not of this world, the Protestant church, like so often in its history, reveals its subservience to the victorious powers and their demons; (3) Insofar as it justifies nationalism and the ideology of blood and race through a doctrine of the divine order of creation, Protestantism gives up its prophetic foundation for the sake of an open or disguised paganism and betrays its task of witnessing to *one* God and *one* humanity; (4) Insofar as it gives the capitalistic-feudal form of rule (*Herrschaftsform*)—which National Socialism in fact serves to protect—the consecration of a divinely-willed authority, Protestantism helps to eternalize the class conflict and betrays its task of witnessing against the use of force (*Vergewaltigung*) and for justice as the standard for every social order; (5) Protestantism is in grave danger of being corrupted. From its beginnings it has lacked an independent group that represents it, a group outside of worldly powers and national divisions. It needs a prophetically-grounded socio-critical principle. It needs a Lutheran-based will to shape reality according to the picture of the kingdom of God. In Germany now, however, it is carried sociologically almost totally by groups who support National Socialism, and therefore it is bound to them ideologically and politically.

Tillich points out (6) that official declarations of neutrality do not change the stance of large numbers of theologians and laity within the Protestant church. In fact, these declarations become worthless, says Tillich, when at the same time the church takes measures against socialist pastors and congregations and when theologians who oppose "pagan nationalism" find no protection and support in the church; (7) Protestantism must preserve its prophetic Christian character by setting the Christianity of the cross over against the paganism of the swastika. It must testify to the fact that in the cross the hallowedness of nation, race, blood, and authority is broken and placed under judgment; (8) Protestantism, if it is to be true to its nature, must preserve its freedom from specific political directions and must allow Protestants to belong to any political party, even those parties which struggle against institutional Protestantism. At the same time it must place every party and all things human, even ecclesiastical action, under the judgment and hope of the essential, early Christian prophetic proclamation of the kingdom of God; (9) In this way it can point the political will of those groups who have now allied themselves together within National Socialism to a genuine and legitimate goal, a goal corresponding to its social necessity, and free the movement from the destructive demons to which it is now subject. Finally, Tillich predicts that (10) an open or disguised alliance of the Protestant churches with the National Socialist party in the suppression of socialism and the fight against Catholicism must, in view of the church's present expansion of power, lead to the future dissolution of German Protestantism.

These strong words by Tillich in 1932 reveal not only a remarkable grasp of the dangers inherent in the political and religious situation, and his disgust at the paganism of the swastika, but also indicate a rather ambivalent attitude to political movements dedicated to national renewal. Although Tillich clearly rejects the two kingdom doctrine which undergirds the nationalist movement and its capitalistic-feudal form of rule in favor of prophetic Christianity, he does not denigrate national movements as such—only their distortions and perversions. He even implies (Thesis 9) that the intentions of those groups supporting National Socialism, if freed from the demonic and destructive elements, could be directed to a legitimate goal within the movement. In short, Tillich suggests that there is a place within Protestantism for those who seriously struggle on the side of nationalism. What he unequivocally rejects is the one-sided identification of Protestantism with a particular national political vision to the exclusion of other options—in particular that of socialism. Protestantism, in other words, while allowing the representatives of various political options within its ranks, must itself never identify with one or the other but must in the name of justice maintain its critical social function vis-à-vis all political programs.

The Call for a Genuine Socialist Decision

Of all his early political writings, however, Tillich's *The Socialist Decision* is without doubt the most important, written in 1932 and published early in 1933, exactly at the time Hitler was consolidating his power. It culminates nearly 15 years of preoccupation with the relation of religion to socialist political thought. His astute analysis of political romanticism, bourgeois society, and the socialist principle must certainly rank this book among the best and most concretely political of all his writings. While the book is a call for opponents of socialism to make a socialist decision, it urges primarily those who use the name socialist—including National Socialists—to make a *genuine* socialist decision. Only through such a true socialist decision, says Tillich, can the fate of death which is threatening European peoples be averted. Tillich is engaged in a profound critique not only of political romanticism and bourgeois society but of distorted Marxism and socialism itself.

The book is a struggle *for* but even more *about* socialism; that is, it is an attempt to articulate a new understanding of socialism in opposition to "dogmatically bound socialism" and a socialism tied to a "limited number of slogans"—a narrow perverted socialism which is responsible for its present disrepute in National Socialist circles. As we look at this book in the next few pages we want to keep in mind one of our underlying questions in this section: What is Tillich's stance toward the "nation" and, more specifically, what is his view of National Socialism? This may help us evaluate Hirsch's public charge that Tillich was a free-floating critic in the tradition of 19th-century intellectual liberalism. A second question that we want to keep in mind is why Hirsch thought this book showed Tillich moving in the direction of National Socialism, as Hirsch expresses it in his personal letter to Tillich in 1933.

Tillich is only too aware of the ambiguities of the contemporary socialist movement and the fluidity of the whole political situation: "...nothing has yet been decided concerning the rightness or wrongness of this struggle against socialism. This is precisely the assumption from which this book proceeds."[73] Tillich wants to show the true nature of socialism and Marxism, and demonstrate to its opponents that their picture of socialism is not the right one.

Although Tillich feels that at the present National Socialism is an alliance of anti-socialist forces, he allows for the possibility that in the future National Socialism may lose the support of the bourgeois-capitalistic forces which have opportunistically sided with it. If this should happen, then National Socialism might yet join the proletariat in a common front against capitalism and feudalism: "The bourgeoisie ditches the revolutionary movement in the very moment when with its help the power of socialism has been overthrown. This could now result in National Socialism's reflecting on the second half of its name and seriously undertaking anticapitalistic actions. Thereby a linkage of groups related to the origin and the proletariat would become impossible, at least in principle, in the coming period of socialism. But things are too much in flux to justify having any definite expectations."[74] The interesting suggestion here by Tillich that National Socialism might yet become a genuine bearer of socialism for Germany may help to explain Hirsch's enigmatic statement about the National Socialist tendencies of this book.

While it is clear throughout the work that Tillich considers the genuine socialist principle superior both to the bourgeois principle and to that of romanticism—only socialism has the power to forge a future for Western civilization—the future of political romanticism (including National Socialism) is not transparent. He says in the conclusion to his book that the National Socialist revolution could move in either of two directions:

> The revolutionary form of political romanticism has only two options; either to revert to the conservative form (and the more decisive its victory, the more likely this is), or to become socialist. The latter would involve a casting off of the specifically romantic elements and an integration of the powers related to the myth of origin within the prophetic movement of the present day, namely, socialism. The unqualified superiority of the socialist principle is, of course, no guarantee of victory for the socialist movement. There is also, as Marx saw, another possibility: chaos. If, in the encounter between the bour-

73. *The Socialist Decision*, p. xxxii. I am using here Franklin Sherman's English translation (New York: Harper & Row, Publishers, 1977).
74. *Ibid.*, p. 170, 25n.

geoisie and political romanticism, the bourgeois principle should once again gain a complete victory, the increasingly severe crises would make chaos virtually inevitable. If on the other hand political romanticism, and, with it, militant nationalism proves victorious, a self-annihilating struggle of the European peoples is inevitable. *The salvation of European society from a return to barbarism lies in the hands of socialism.*[75]

It is socialism alone, according to Tillich, that will be able to assure that the "unlimited possibilities for technical domination of the world that have been created in the bourgeois period will remain under human control and will be employed for the service of humanity."[76] But while the key to the present social situation lies in the hands of the proletariat, it needs the support of origin-related powers without which it cannot be victorious. The future of the West could be one of socialism or of barbarism.

The meaning and future of the National Socialist revolution sweeping Germany is, thus, not at all plain to Tillich. On the one hand there are some positive things to be said for it. The revolutionary opposition of many origin-related groups to capitalism is "the strongest positive indication for a socialist victory."[77] The fact that this is happening under the banner of "blatant nationalism" and with the support of bourgeois groups engaged in a class struggle is a negative sign:

> Socialism is being forced by external pressure into a posture of defensiveness, surrendering its revolutionary energies to political romanticism.... Socialism can be victorious only in reliance on its own principle, in which powers of origin and prophetic expectation are combined. But expectation must play the major role. Only through expectation is human existence raised to the level of true humanity.... The hegemony of the myth of origin means the domination of violence and death. *Only expectation can triumph over the death now threatening Western civilization through the resurgence of the myth of origin. And expectation is the symbol of socialism.*[78]

It is evident from the above that, although Tillich is profoundly aware of the fluidity of the situation and of the ambiguity of the nature and destiny of the National Socialist upheaval—it could yet become the true bearer of socialism and take the "socialist" side of its name seriously—he fears the possible barbarization of the movement and with it of the Western world. He is unequivocal in his denunciation of the militant nationalism, the political romanticism, and the

75. *Ibid.*, pp. 160-161.
76. *Ibid.*, p. 161.
77. *Ibid.*, p. 162.
78. *Ibid.*

alliance with reactionary capitalist forces, that increasingly dominate the movement.

In our remarks so far we have introduced the central categories—political romanticism, the bourgeois principle, and the socialist principle—around which *The Socialist Decision* is organized. These now need further clarification in order for us better to understand Tillich's critique of National Socialism and his own socialist alternative.

Tillich's whole argument is based on the claim that there are two roots of political thought: (1) "The consciousness oriented to the myth of origin is the root of all conservative and romantic thought in politics";[79] and (2) "The breaking of the myth of origin by the unconditional demand is the root of liberal, democratic, and socialist thought in politics."[80] These two roots of all political thinking are grounded in the inner duality of human nature itself: being and consciousness, existence in itself and existence over against itself. These two—being and consciousness—form a unity. "A true consciousness...is one that arises out of being and at the same time determines it."[81] Conservative and romantic political thought stress the one side: myth of origin as grounded in being, the "whence" of existence, human captivity to birth, development, and death. Liberal, democratic and socialist political thought stress the other side: the breaking out of the cycle of birth and death, the "whither" of human existence, the "oughtness" and unconditional demand for something new.

Although Tillich stresses the unity of being and consciousness—the fact that the "whither" is not alien to but rooted in the "whence"—he clearly puts greater weight on the latter, on the unconditional demand to shape history in accordance with justice. In other words, the *ought* is more important than the *is*, even though the ought is rooted in the is. The origin itself is ambiguous and a distinction must be made between the "actual origin" and the "true origin." The intention of humanity is not fulfilled in the actual origin but in the true origin: justice. "Justice is the true power of being" and the intention of the origin.[82] True political thinking can occur only once the myth of the actual origin has been broken and its ambiguity revealed. The relationship between the "ought" and the "is" of human existence is therefore not simply one of balance or a typological dialectic. One must choose the demand of the true origin over the is of the actual origin. "One cannot be a spectator of the spirit; it makes demands, it calls for decisions."[83] Tillich is calling for a genuine socialist decision and

79. *Ibid.*, p. 4.
80. *Ibid.*, p. 5.
81. *Ibid.*, p. 3.
82. *Ibid.*, p. 3.
83. *Ibid.*, p. 7. On the theoretical level Hirsch's accusation that Tillich is a freely-floating intellectual critic who cannot commit himself to an earthly community is wrong. As this statement indicates, Tillich did in theory recognize the importance of not simply being a spectator, of the necessity of taking sides, of making a socialist decision. On a practical level, however, Hirsch correctly

commitment.

The Inner Contradiction of Political Romanticism

Part One of the book deals with political romanticism as rooted in the myth of the actual origin and its accompanying powers: the soil, blood, and social group. These powers of the origin are given priestly sanctity and viewed in terms of the law of cyclical motion so that nothing new can happen in history. Time is dominated by space. Being is seen as holy.

Political romanticism, observes Tillich, arises out of the legitimate recognition of powers of origin such as eros, fate, and death and an understandable resistance to the rationalization of all of human existence.[84] According to Tillich, "A weariness with autonomy can be discerned in all groups and levels of society. This is one of the most significant mood-determining elements in the background of contemporary political events."[85] But the problem with political romanticism is that it is built on an *inner contradiction:* it fights propheticism and the Enlightenment on the basis of a social and spiritual situation which has been shaped by propheticism and the Enlightenment. It is forced to use the very ethical and rational categories given to it by propheticism and the Enlightenment in its struggle for the recovery of the myth of origin.

Tillich argues that there are two forms of political romanticism: conservative and revolutionary. *Conservative political romanticism* tries to restore past forms in its struggle for the bond of origin against autonomy. Its central concept is that of the organic. *Revolutionary political romanticism* attacks autonomy and rationalism with the use of new forms and new ties to the origin. It stresses dynamic, innovative action and movement. It is clear that Tillich perceives both conservative and revolutionary romantic elements to be allied behind National Socialism at the present, but that revolutionary political romanticism is more characteristic of the essential nature of National Socialism.

The problem with revolutionary romanticism is that it is concerned primarily with the innovative and not the original. While in its emphasis on the dynamic principle it has a certain structural similarity to revolutionary socialism, its goals are unclear, impractical, and contradictory because (1) it cannot draw from tradition the way conservatism does, nor (2) can it rely on a rational and scientific

---

perceives that Tillich finds it difficult to make a concrete decision, to commit himself to a particular party or cause. The concrete nature of the socialist principle and the socialist decision is not clear.

84. Tillich's ambivalence to the Enlightenment tradition of rational autonomy is evident throughout the book. On the positive side, Tillich sides with the Enlightenment in its breaking free from the myth of origin. On the negative side, he rejects its total rejection of origin-related powers which remain intrinsic to all human existence; namely, the power of eros (the "union with the primal power of existence prior to analysis"), fate ("the primordial power resisting all efforts to shape or calculate existence"), and death (the "limit of the finite" which "poses the question of the meaning of finitude"). *Ibid.*, p. 25.

85. *Ibid.*, p. 169, 21n.

analysis of the present situation the way socialism does. Both forms of political romanticism, however, are preoccupied with the powers of origin: the soil (as represented by landowners and peasantry), the animal sphere (as represented by blood and race), and the social group (illustrated by its emphasis on community).[86]

The contradictory nature of political romanticism is particularly evident in its approach to tradition—tradition being that which stands between the origin and the present. A good example of this, says Tillich, is its attitude to national tradition. In its preoccupation with the myth of a national tradition political romanticism ignores the numerous particular religious, political, and regional traditions within the nation. Tillich unequivocally rejects its attempt to create a hegemonous Germanic national tradition:

> The attempt to create a unity bound to the origin by means of the old-Germanic heritage is completely hopeless, since as soon as the Germanic people appeared on the scene of history, they were grasped by the major streams of tradition already in existence and deprived of their original structure. To be sure, the Germanic substance was at work in the adoption and reformulation of these traditions; but there is no such thing as an original Germanic, and hence national, tradition, and such cannot be created.[87]

Even though Tillich refers to the reality of a "Germanic substance" in this passage, he nevertheless clearly perceives as hopeless any attempt to recover a lost Germanic heritage.

The essential contradition of political romanticism is that it desires "to base the irrational on reason, or intuition on analytic concepts."[88] It fights the notion of progress in the name of progress, it tries to achieve the victory of the myth of origin by means of a prophetic factor. It creates a modern form of apocalyptic thinking even though it rejects genuine prophecy. Revolutionary romanticism, for instance, maintains the fiction of a party while fighting the very notion of political parties. Ultimately the inner contradiction of political romanticism is inherent in its attempt to "return to the origin under the presuppositions of and by means of a society that has loosened itself from the origin."[89] Political romanticism attempts to do what is impossible and in this sense it is contradictory in the profoundest sense. "Human beings cannot renounce being human. They must think; they must elevate being into consciousness; they must transcend the given. But when this has happened, there is no way back. *One cannot by thinking abolish thought; one cannot consciously reject consciousness.* But

86. *Ibid.*, pp. 30-31.
87. *Ibid.*, p. 34.
88. *Ibid.*, p. 39.
89. *Ibid.*, p. 44.

the attempt to do just this, if we understand it from its roots, is the meaning of political romanticism."[90]

It is interesting at this point to recall Hirsch's own clear recognition of what he calls the inner paradox of the "German turning point." He calls the new stance toward reason and critical reflection "paradoxical" rather than "contradictory" and does not suggest that critical thought must be abolished but that it thus becomes subservient to the boundary of the origin as represented by nation and state. One of the problems of Tillich's astute analysis is that his "ideal types," while elucidating the social and spiritual situation in general, tend to do an injustice to any particular position such as Hirsch's, which Tillich would quite clearly have to classify under revolutionary romanticism.[91]

The Inner Conflict of Socialism

Part Two of *The Socialist Decision* is devoted to the principle of bourgeois society and the inner conflict of socialism. Tillich sees liberalism and socialism as having a common root—the break with the bond of origin in all of its aspects. Western bourgeois society, says Tillich, is the product of the *prophetic* break with the myth and bond of origin which occurred in Protestantism and the *humanistic* break with the origin which took place in the Enlightenment. Western bourgeois society proclaims and realizes a radical autonomous this-worldliness: *"Its principle is the radical dissolution of all conditions, bonds, and forms related to the origin into elements that are to be rationally mastered, and the rational assemblage of these elements into structures serving the aims of thought and action."*[92] Through objectification and rational analysis it subjects the world to its own aims and masters both human and nonhuman natures through technical and economic means. The two assumptions at the heart of the bourgeois principle are (1) the liberal idea of an objective natural harmony, and (2) the belief that the individual subject is the bearer of universal reason to which society and nature must be subjected.

Bourgeois society, however, is based on an inner conflict (in contrast to political romanticism which is based on an inner contradiction): there is implicit in bourgeois society a tendency to ally itself with pre-bourgeois (feudalistic) forms

90. *Ibid.*

91. Tillich explicitly uses the term "ideal type" when referring to the proletariat. By "ideal type" Tillich means "a concept that describes a social structure according to its decisive characteristics without regard to whether this structure is immediately and purely evident in experience." *Ibid.,* p. 62. Most of the categories that Tillich uses, including political romanticism (both conservative and revolutionary), the bourgeois principle, and the socialist principle function as "ideal types" for Tillich. While they are useful in describing general trends and movements in society, they tend to be unfair to particular movements and positions. This is partly the point of Hirsch's resistance in the debate with Tillich in 1934-35 to being evaluated by Tillich in terms of the latter's priestly-sacramental versus prophetic-eschatological framework—categories which Hirsch rightly perceived to be defined in terms of Tillich's Religious Socialist views.

92. *Ibid.,* p. 48.

because bourgeois autonomy is only a formal and dynamic principle without any substance of its own. It therefore depends for its substance on those groups which stand for the myth of origin. Bourgeois society cannot by itself provide the basis for its own existence and therefore constantly slips back into an alliance with pre-bourgeois forces. In this fact is revealed not a false consciousness, as is the case in political romanticism, but the genuine power and limit of the bourgeois principle.[93]

The birth of socialism goes hand in hand with a bourgeois radicalism which is committed to carrying through more consistently the democratic goals of the bourgeois principle, rejecting both reactionary romanticism and the alliance of the bourgeoisie with pre-bourgeois groups. Nevertheless, there is a fundamental difference between socialism and bourgeois radicalism: socialism rejects the bourgeois faith in harmony and progress because they contradict the proletarian situation. "The bourgeois principle as applied by liberalism does not lead to a harmonious society characterized by steady progress and contentment, but to crisis, class rule, and class struggle. The proletariat does not experience harmony, but *disharmony*. And on the basis of this experience, in which it becomes directly aware of its proletarian existence, it separates itself from bourgeois radicalism and becomes as much opposed to the radical as to the conservative bourgeoisie."[94]

Socialism has both a universal and a particular element. In its particularity it expresses the proletarian situation. Socialism and the proletariat are reciprocally related: "...the proletariat is just as much a creation of socialism as socialism is a creation of the proletariat."[95] In its universality socialism, through the will of the proletariat, attempts to transcend itself and move forward to a "classless society"—the symbolic name for a new form of society and human being. In its universality it reveals its indebtedness to the Christian-humanist tradition of the West. The socialist principle carries within it elements of Christianity, Greek humanism, and Jewish propheticism. Its universality consists of the "primordial human element: the demand, the transcendent, the expectation of the new."[96] The fight against utopian socialism—the danger of socialist intellectuals— depends on this inseparable link between the particular and the universal. According to Tillich, his book can be viewed "as an effort *to work out the universal element of socialism without giving up the particular element.*"[97]

Unlike political romanticism which is doomed ultimately to failure because of its contradictory nature, socialism is characterized by inner conflict related to

93. The false consciousness of political romanticism rests in the fact, according to Tillich, that "it does not recognize what meanwhile has transpired: the victory of the bourgeois principle, which can be reversed only through a collapse, not through nostalgic longing." *Ibid.*, p. 56.

94. *Ibid.*, p. 58.

95. *Ibid.*, p. 62.

96. *Ibid.*, p. 64.

97. *Ibid.*, p. 65.

its ambiguous link to bourgeois society. This inner conflict (or "antinomy" as Tillich also calls it) can be overcome by socialism acquiring a new form for itself. The inner conflict of socialism lies in the fact that the proletariat is a class within bourgeois society, lives off bourgeois resources, and at the same time struggles against bourgeois society. *"The proletariat must deny that power by which it struggles against the bourgeois principle, namely, the power of origin. And it must affirm that which it seeks to destroy, namely, the bourgeois principle. This is the inner conflict in which it stands."* [98] This is why, in Tillich's view, German socialism has been so impotent. The relation of the proletariat to the powers of origin are ambiguous but it is upon this relationship that it must fight against the alliance of bourgeois with pre-bourgeois forces. The only solution for the proletariat is to make a *genuine* socialist decision, which entails making "a clear decision for the powers of origin, while rejecting the forces of origin that have become bourgeois, together with the bourgeois principle itself."[99]

Tillich proceeds to discuss the inner conflict of socialism, as it is historically evident, in six concrete areas: belief, human nature, society, culture, community and economics. His radical critique of historical and political socialism in these six areas helps to explain his own aloofness from and lack of any enthusiastic engagement in socialist party politics. While he clearly sides with the socialist movement in general, the genuine socialist principle which he articulates remains highly theoretical. There seems to be in Tillich an element of profound disillusionment with historical-political socialism in Germany. It is precisely this critical distance of Tillich's socialist theory from historical-political socialism which appears to have kept Tillich aloof from actual political engagement. Gunda Schneider-Flume correctly perceives both the strength and the problems inherent in Tillich's social-political theory in this regard. The strength, according to Schneider-Flume, is that Tillich, in contrast to Hirsch, refuses to give any absolute earthly value to a political reality; he rejects all utopianism. The problem is that precisely because of this distance his social-political theory is incapable of achieving actual, practical, and concrete historical form.[100] It is exactly this problem also which gives some validity to Hirsch's

98. *Ibid.*, p. 68.

99. *Ibid.*

100. In an illuminating 1973 essay, Gunda Schneider-Flume compares and contrasts the political theology of Tillich, Hirsch, and Shaull. She argues that all three arrive at very different political judgments and valuations on the basis of similar theological presuppositions. The structural similarity between the three rests on the fact that each believes the divine penetrates history in a structuring and demanding way: Tillich describes it in terms of theonomy, Hirsch in terms of the boundary, and Shaull by means of the dynamic activity of God. The precise occasion at which this occurs is referred to by Tillich as *kairos,* by Hirsch as "the hour," and by Shaull as "the revolution." Schneider-Flume makes the point that "The belief in the possibility of mediating socialism and Christianity in Tillich, National Socialism and Christianity in Hirsch, and revolutionary change and Christianity in Shaull, rests on the conviction that Christian salvation and Christian truth can acquire

charge that Tillich fails to descend from his lofty stance of theoretical critique to make an actual commitment to an earthly community.

We cannot enter here into a lengthy treatment of Tillich's analysis of the inner conflicts of socialism in the various areas mentioned above. We allude only to his important comments about socialism's antinomous attitude to community and the nation. On the one hand says Tillich, socialism espouses the international community over against national imperialism and domination. On the other hand, it is forced to espouse the nation over against the "ideology of international citizenship." The bourgeois spirit is completely dedicated to the breaking down of all bonds of origin for the humanist ideal of individual emancipation, on the one side, but allies itself finally with the pre-bourgeois strata (particularly those espousing nationalism) to support the rule of capital.[101] The proletariat is forced to join hands with the revolutionary bourgeoisie in radicalizing the bourgeois principle and throwing off any alliance with the pre-bourgeois elements. The result is that the communal bonds of origin have been most completely dissolved in the proletarian situation, especially in the industrial proletariat. *"Every form of tradition or bond is seen, on the soil of capitalism, as a means of class rule."*[102]

But here the inner conflict within the socialist proletariat is particularly evident. On the one hand it "serves as the executor of all the dissolving powers of the bourgeois principle."[103] On the other hand it must attack the bourgeois principle of atomization, individualism, and harmony and propose a new form of community. To do this it must itself return to the powers of origin:

structure in historical-political reality." See "Kritische Theologie contra theologisch-politischen Offenbarungsglauben: Eine vergleichende Strukturanalyse der politschen Theologie Paul Tillichs, Emanuel Hirschs und Richard Shaulls," *Evangelische Theologie* 2,33(March-April 1973), p. 124. Unlike Hirsch and Shaull, however, whose "existential theology," according to Schneider-Flume, leads them to an unmediated and uncritical valuation of their particular historical-political commitments, Tillich's view of intellectual truth (*Sinnwahrheit*) as well as his understanding of paradox, disallow any consecration of historical-political reality. Tillich's critical stance, his view of a dynamic truth which perpetually transcends given reality, according to Schneider-Flume, makes his theological-political theory and social-political analysis qualitatively more profound than that of Hirsch and Shaull. While Schneider-Flume's thesis has much to say for it, she does not adequately deal particularly with Hirsch's theological presuppositions as derived from Luther's two-kingdom doctrine in clarifying the limited framework in which he sees his existential commitment to an earthly political reality. Another problem with Schneider-Flume's otherwise insightful essay is that in using only Shaull as a recent example of political theology she does an injustice to the diversity within contemporary political theologians, some of whom are concerned precisely with adequate theological criteria by which to make responsible political choices.

101. *The Socialist Decision*, p. 86.
102. *Ibid.*, p. 87.
103. *Ibid.*

Socialism must therefore fall back upon powers of origin in order to make community possible. But as soon as it does this, it finds itself aligned with the feudal ideology whose intent is to buttress its own class rule by pretending to offer a form of community based on the powers of origin.

This is especially true for the *attitude of socialism toward the idea of the nation.* In accordance with the bourgeois principle, socialism breaks through the national limitations and advocates an international ideal of humanity. In the last analysis, it must place humankind above the nation, and draw from this its conclusions regarding international law. At the same time, however, socialism is dependent for its own realization on national powers of origin. It has learned that the concrete community of place, race, and culture, is, in spite of the opposition of classes, stronger than the abstract identity of its destiny to that of the proletariat in other countries. It understands that it must actualize itself nationally if it is to actualize itself at all.... Socialism is thus thrown back upon the nation as a power of origin which it too cannot avoid. *The idea of the nation, however, had proven to be the most important instrument of domination in the hands of capital.* Socialism thus falls into the conflict of having to be internationalistic over against national imperialism, and on the other hand, nationalistic over against the ideology of international citizenship.[104]

In these highly revealing statements about the inner conflicts in the bourgeois stance toward the nation and about the antinomy of the socialist view of national and international community, we find the key to Tillich's own ambivalence toward the importance of nation and the nationalist revolution which was sweeping across Germany in the form of National Socialism—the movement which in its name tried to combine both nationalism and socialism.

The Need for a New Type of Socialism
In Part Three of his book Tillich outlines what he considers to be a way of overcoming the inner conflicts in socialism through a genuine socialist decision for the socialist principle. The inner conflict of socialism cannot be abstracted from the inner conflict of the proletarian situation—from the situation in which actual human beings find themselves. It is the real proletarian human being as related to the origin which reacts against the bourgeois principle that leads to depersonalization, objectification, and separation from the origin. In this, socialism has something in common with political romanticism: "They differ only in that, presupposing this relation to the origin, political romanticism seeks to reject the bourgeois principle, while socialism seeks to incorporate it."[105] Incidentally, Tillich observes that the proletariat understands what socialist theoreticians have

104. *Ibid.*, pp. 87-88.
105. *Ibid.*, p. 98.

never understood—"that a rational, analytical principle can never become the basis for individual or social life. It can never be more than a corrective and a critical norm."[106] The bond of origin and the proletariat do not contradict each other. In fact the proletarian being and movement are founded on the powers of origin but as filtered through the bourgeois principle.

Three principles—the power of the origin, the rejection of a belief in harmony, and the stress on the demand—interact and are combined in the socialist symbol of expectation: *"Socialism lifts up the symbol of expectation against the myth of origin and against the belief in harmony. It has elements of both, but it transcends both."*[107] Through this concept and symbol of expectation socialism is related to the prophetic tradition. Socialist propheticism, however, grows *"on the soil of an autonomous, self-sufficient world."*[108] Expectation has a historical "forward" impulse toward that which does not now exist—toward something novel within history itself. Here it parts company with political romanticism, which, according to Tillich, sees eschatology only in terms of the *"destiny of the individual soul"* and not in terms of history as a whole.[109] In political romanticism irrational powers hold individual and social life in their power. In genuine socialism "demand" and "promise"—the expectation that the new *"will* come" and the conviction that it *"should* come"—expectant waiting and responsible action, are held in tension.

Socialist expectation has both a prophetic and a rational character which separates it from political romanticism and constitutes both its profundity and its peril. Tillich caricatures political romanticism as frivolously self-abnegating autonomy and rationality.[110] In its prophetic character, socialist expectation

106. *Ibid.*, pp. 98-99. This statement is "ironical" because as we have seen and as Hirsch rightly perceived, Tillich himself, while realizing the need for an existential commitment and the inadequacy of merely an intellectual, rational, and analytical stance of critique, was one of those very intellectual theoreticians who remained aloof and at a distance from actual historical-political commitment and engagement. According to Detlef Döring, the Tillich circle of Religious Socialists was never engaged in church politics and never particularly concerned about influencing the wider population but remained a relatively small intellectual circle concerned with the theoretical dynamic relationship of Christianity and socialism. Only towards the end of the Weimar Republic did they lose some of their esoteric quality and begin to work together with related groups in the SPD in order to effect a reorientation of social democracy. Detlef Döring, *Christentum und Faschismus*, p. 19. It could be legitimately argued in favor of Tillich, on the other hand, that his very stance of critique, especially during the early 1930s and the triumph of National Socialism which led to his suspension and dismissal, was a form of political activism more important than any direct involvement in party politics.

107. *The Socialist Decision*, p. 101.

108. *Ibid.*

109. *Ibid.*, p. 103.

110. This is a caricature of a position like Hirsch's, for instance, who does not reject autonomy and rationality as such but rejects the 19th century concept of autonomy and rationality which is cut loose from any tie to historical national community. Freedom and reason are important but must remain subservient to one's social-ethical commitment to one's people (*Volk*).

remains transcendent and incalculable; in its rational aspect it is knowable and immanent. In an important passage Tillich describes the socialist view of the transcendent and immanent character of expectation, a view of transcendence that Hirsch would certainly reject:

> *Human expectation is always transcendent and immanent at the same time.* *More precisely, this opposition does not exist for expectation.* Any study of prophetic eschatological expectation shows this clearly. The coming order of things is seen in historical continuity with the present; it is immanent. And yet, the concepts used to describe the coming order presuppose a total transformation of the present, a suspension of the laws of nature. The immanent is in fact transcendent. Or, the coming order is sundered from the present by an intervening world catastrophe; it is transcendent. But the pictures by which all this is described are derived from the materials of everyday experience. The transcendent is in fact immanent. The same fluctuation can be found in the content of socialist expectation. It appears to be totally immanent: equality, freedom, the satisfying of human needs, etc. But when one examines the content of socialism's final expectation more closely, one finds that it presupposes a radical transformation of human nature, and in the last instance—since human nature constantly grows out of nature as such—a transformation of nature and its laws.[111]

Both prophetic and social expectation see life, therefore, as fundamentally open, and protest against both "false concepts of transcendence" and "false concepts of immanence."[112] One of the crucial differences between Hirsch and Tillich, as we have noted earlier in this study, is precisely their diverse views of transcendence. Tillich wants it both ways as the above statement clearly indicates: he sees transcendence as immanent and immanence as transcendent. He has in fact a dialectical view of transcendence. Transcendence is not a vertical transcendence in a paradoxical theistic sense, as Hirsch views it, but rather a dialectical transcendence: a radical future which stands both in continuity and in discontinuity with the present.

One of the problems, of course, is how to actualize socialism in Germany in the light of the contemporary situation. Tillich once again suggests that socialism *"must strive...for an alliance of the revolutionary proletariat with the revolutionary groups within political romanticism."*[113] The particular achievement of National Socialism in the present, he says, has been to accomplish a revolution through origin-related groups against bourgeois society. The revolutionary movement of political romanticism has a real element of expectation in it

111. *The Socialist Decision*, pp. 110-111.
112. *Ibid.*, p. 111.
113. *Ibid.*, p. 129.

as symbolized by the term "Third Reich," which alludes not only to the German Empire but conjures up the ancient image of the third age. Because this expectation is simply the recovery of unbroken origin, however, it is in danger of slipping back into conservative political romanticism and class domination, which appears to be the aim of its leader (Hitler). "If this should happen," remarks Tillich, "the realization of socialism in Germany would be impossible, unless new movements should arise out of economic or political catastrophe."[114]

The society which genuine socialism envisages would include factors of soil, blood, and social groups, tradition, commonly-held symbols, faith, and devotion. "It is these very forces, both in the proletariat and among the revolutionary origin-related groups, that are resisting class rule as we know it today. Through them alone can the classless society be realized."[115] Socialism, he maintains, depends on the support of outstanding, powerful individuals as well as on groups ready for ultimate sacrifice. Tillich makes the somewhat enigmatic statement that through the national and regional peculiarities of the proletariat this structure of the classless society is in the process of formation. "The place that the groups representing revolutionary political romanticism will occupy within this structure depends on whether they enter it as they are, without first having to go through a radical proletarianization. If they do enter as origin-related groups the tensions remaining between them and the proletariat can lead to fruitful political developments, as in Russia."[116]

Tillich proposes, finally, a genuine socialist view of the nation, freed from its ideological misuse by both political romanticism and the bourgeoisie:

But it is true here, too, that only what once had a genuine use can be misused. The idea of the nation cannot be destroyed by pointing to its perversion. The idea of the nation has energies deriving from the origin, and therefore has a claim to fulfillment—meaning not uncritical support, but also not destruction. Soil, blood, tradition, the social group—all the powers of origin are combined in the nation. The prophetic tradition thus relates to a people neither in such a way as to confirm it in its immediate self-awareness (as the "false prophets" do), nor to dissolve it for the sake of an immediate transition to a universal humanity (as bourgeois cosmopolitanism does). It seeks rather at once to judge and to support the nation. *The prophetic is always addressed to all humanity, but it always proceeds from amongst a people,* exhibiting thereby the unity of origin and goal that is typical of it.[117]

114. *Ibid.*, pp. 129-130.
115. *Ibid.*, p. 130.
116. *Ibid.*, p. 131.
117. *Ibid.*, p. 151.

Even though socialism has been forced into a negation of the concept of the nation partly against its own will, says Tillich, it must now *"enter into relationship with a people if it is to win acceptance among them."*[118] He adds that "For the sake of its own calling, socialism must affirm the nation, and with this, the tensions among the nations. But at the same time, it must destroy any claim that a particular people is directly identified with the absolute."[119] Its ultimate goal, however, must be humanity as a whole and the overarching reality of international justice, which stands beyond the tensions between nations. *"Socialism must affirm the nation more profoundly than nationalism can,"* says Tillich.[120] Socialism must liberate nations from the cyclical law of birth, development, and death, as espoused by political romanticism, and subject them to the prophetic demand.

In our extensive analysis of his *The Socialist Decision* we have tried to explicate Tillich's understanding of the nation as it relates to the socialist commitment. What Tillich espouses is both the *universality* and the *particularity* of genuine socialism. It is a rootless international proletariat that Tillich rejects. The proletariat must, he says, recover a lost sense of rootedness within a national peoplehood (*Volk*). But this national identity and loyalty is ultimately a means to an international end—the universal and just human community most adequately expressed in the prophetic vision of the kingdom of God. The way to this universal human good is *through* the national good, not *around* it. Ultimately, however, the universal community of love and justice must remain superior to the particular nation; it must stand as a judgment over and a critique of all particular national identities without dissolving them.

While blood, soil, nation, and ethnicity are important for Tillich he refuses to commit himself or bind himself uncritically and unreservedly to the German nation in Hirsch's sense because he is too aware of the ideological dangers inherent in such a stance. The "ought" and "whence" of human existence are finally on the side of a universal international order of justice. It is this dialectical understanding of the nation—affirming the myth of origin genuinely at work in one's ethnic rootedness in tribe and country while at the same time passionately denouncing the demonic oppression of "strangers" in the land in light of the prophetic vision of universal justice—that distinguishes Tillich's view of nation methodologically from that of Hirsch. In contrast to Hirsch, Tillich identifies himself with the Jewish prophetic critique of all religious nationalism, including Jewish nationalism, in favor of universal humanity, and claims as his model Abraham, whom God called to leave his own country.[121]

---

118. *Ibid.*
119. Ibid.
120. *Ibid.*
121. Tillich says in this regard: "The God who demands obedience of him is the God of an alien country, a God not bound to the local soil, as are pagan deities, but the God of history, who means to bless all the races of the earth. This God, the God of the prophet and of Jesus, utterly demolishes all

Tillich maintains that while he has always had an instinctive appreciation for the German landscape, language, tradition, and historical destiny, he has always lived on the boundary between alien and native land, never quite feeling at home in either.

While Tillich clearly defends the bonds of origin and nationality, he does not have nor espouse the kind of absolute commitment to a particular nation and ethnicity that Hirsch demands of him. It is at this point that we find one of the most profound differences between Tillich and Hirsch. Hirsch has a much more tragic sense of the givenness of life, of the fateful character and limitation that race, blood, ethnicity, and nationality place on human beings (it is this limiting factor of all human-historical life that Hirsch calls the "boundary") than does Tillich. Tillich refuses to accept this fateful captivity to birth, life, and death. It is his firm conviction that human beings can ultimately transcend the boundaries of ethnicity and work toward a universal humanity within history that most clearly separates him from Hirsch. Hirsch does not believe that the ethnic boundaries and national antagonisms can ever be overcome and be translated into an international community of love in the context of human history in any other than a spiritual sense. For Hirsch, the human relation to a *particular* national ethnicity can best be described in terms of the Lutheran concept of "bondage." Human beings find their *universality,* their union with all of humanity of whatever national culture, not in the arena of earthly justice and power but in the realm of "spiritual freedom." In marked contrast to Hirsch, Tillich believes and hopes that human beings will be able to shape earthly social structures in relative correspondence to the moral claims of the kingdom of God. To the chagrin of Hirsch, the universality of the prophetic promise for Tillich has some earthly, historical, and political possibility of realization; this envisioned just international order has a relative continuity with the kingdom of God.[122]

Ambivalence Toward Revolutionary Romanticism

Having said all of this, however, one must still account for the rather strange ambivalence that Tillich manifests in regard to National Socialism, not so much in its strictly political form but rather in its philosophical character. This somewhat equivocal attitude toward National Socialism is rooted in his ambiguous attitude toward modernity and Enlightenment reason on the one hand, and the stream of romantic, irrational, and nationalist thought that characterized 19th and 20th century critiques of modern scientific and technological reason on the

religious nationalism—the nationalism of the Jews, which he opposes constantly, and that of the pagans, which is repudiated in the command to Abraham." *On the Boundary,* pp. 91-92.

122. In Tillich's view, "The increased realization of a united mankind represents and anticipates, so to speak, the truth implicit in a belief in the Kingdom of God to which all nations and all races belong. Denying the unity of mankind as aim includes, therefore, denying the Christian doctrine that the Kingdom of God is 'at hand.' " *On the Boundary,* p. 96.

other. We earlier alluded to the enigmatic letter written by Hirsch to Tillich on April 13, 1933, in which Hirsch implies that Tillich really belongs with National Socialism and the new Germany. In fact, he suggests in this letter that Tillich's latest book, *The Socialist Decision*, shows the author moving in the direction of National Socialism.[123]

Tillich himself betrays a certain equivocation toward National Socialism and the new Germany in a January 20, 1934 letter to the National Socialist Ministry for Science, Art, and Education. In the letter he protests a December 20, 1933 letter from the Nazi Minister of Culture informing him that he has been officially dismissed from the civil service and will not be allowed to teach in German universities. Trying to persuade the new government of his reliability he says: "Later, I became co-founder of German Religious Socialism, on the basis of my experience with soldiers and officers in the trenches and on first-aid posts. As the theoretician of Religious Socialism I have fought throughout the years against the dogmatic Marxism of the German labor movement, and thereby I have supplied a number of concepts to the National Socialist theoreticians. Moreover, my last book was interpreted by the representatives of dogmatic Marxism as an attack upon them inasmuch as it points emphatically to the powers in man that bind him to nature."[124]

In her biography of his life Marion Pauck suggests there is a modest form of pragmatic opportunism in Tillich which refuses to reject outrightly any possibilities in fluid situations. She says about the 1934 letter: "Yet the letter reveals him, not as one proud of being singled out as an unreliable citizen and forced into emigration, but rather as the shrewd and practical man he was, caught in the ambiguities of history, reaching out to clear his name and trying to ensure that, failing all else, his pension would be available to him. The hero and the shrewd negotiator are one and the same. The same man who wrote much later that life is ambiguous was himself ambiguous in a startling way in this letter, particularly in his statement that the Nazis had borrowed their terminology from him. Yet even this was altogether in keeping with his personality and his tendency to remain open to all possibilities, not taking an absolute stand when the future was inscrutable."[125]

For Tillich this ambiguous stance toward the new regime in Germany was much more than simply a matter of personal pragmatism or opportunism, as

123. An unpublished letter by Hirsch to Tillich, April 14, 1933, the original of which exists in the Tillich Archive, Andover Library, Harvard Divinity School. The argument that Hirsch simply misunderstood Tillich's position as outlined in Tillich's book does not fit Hirsch's careful scholarly style nor his thorough knowledge of Tillich's intellectual development through the years.

124. The English translation of this letter is found in Pauck, *Tillich: Life*, p. 149.

125. *Ibid.*, p. 151. Referring to this same letter, Pauck says: "The sometimes confused and imprecise tone of the protest seems to mar the image of a man of whom it was said that he was the first non-Jew to be dismissed by the Nazi regime—a myth he never denied—and who was proud of his dismissal until the end of his life" (p. 151).

Pauck suggests. After our rather extensive treatment of Tillich's writings during the Weimar period and leading up to the triumph of National Socialism in 1933, we must conclude that there was in Tillich's thought a fundamental ambivalence towards romanticism, irrationalism, and nationalism and that it was this that was at the heart of his philosophical sympathy for some of the things the National Socialist theoreticians were saying. What must be stated much more strongly than Pauck does is that Tillich's positive view of the mythical ground of history made his so-called early resistance to National Socialism and Fascism less unequivocal than is generally assumed.

The nature of Tillich's ambivalence toward the philosophy of National Socialism is brilliantly examined by the East German scholar Detlef Döring in his recent study, *Christentum und Faschismus: Die Faschismusdeutung der religiösen Sozialisten*.[126] Because of the rather controversial but persuasive argument of Döring's book, and because it confirms the general position developed in our own study of Tillich and Hirsch, it is appropriate at this point to outline in some detail Döring's line of reasoning.

According to Döring, (1) Religious Socialism in Germany during the Weimar period can be divided roughly into two main types: (a) the more practical form which did not concern itself with theoretical speculation but was intent on bringing the church and the proletarian movement closer together. For this group the struggle against the disguised anti-Christian and anti-proletarian impulses within fascism was decisive from the beginning; (b) a more theoretically-oriented group around the periodicals *Zeitschrift für Religion und Sozialismus* (ZRS) and *Neue Blätter für den Sozialismus* (NSB), the latter concerned with Religious Socialism as a new worldview—a theoretical system of ideas. This faction shared some of the anti-modern sentiments espoused by supporters of National Socialism and consequently had a fundamental ambivalence toward fascism, something that was alien to the first more practically-minded group.[127]

(2) The Tillich Circle of Religious Socialists (or the *Kairos* Circle), Döring maintains, belonged to this second group, for whom the starting point was not

126. This book is the outgrowth of a dissertation at the University of Leipzig, East Germany, which Döring completed under the supervision of well-known church historian of the Weimar period and the German church struggle during the Third Reich, Kurt Meier. It should be pointed out that in my research I had reached my own conclusions concerning Tillich's ambivalent attitude toward National Socialism in its earlier phase independently of Döring's study. I came upon Döring's work in the later stages of my own work and his study simply helped me to strengthen and expand my own interpretation of the materials. What should also be noted is that Döring's study is written generally from a Marxist oriented approach toward fascism as the preface by Arnold Pfeiffer clearly indicates: "Die Arbeit steht im Bezugsfeld der marxistisch-leninistischen Geschichtsbetrachtung. Von daher erscheint der Einfluss von Konzeptionen, die den Nationalsozialismus als anti-modern und als totaliter begreifen und abwehren, wie eine Aberration von der 'wahren,' der soziologischen Erklärung" (pp. 5-6).

127. Döring, *Christentum und Faschismus*, pp. 12ff.

244 Emanuel Hirsch and Paul Tillich

first and foremost a commitment to traditional Christianity or the proletariat but the crisis within modern culture and civil society. They sought for a third way—a new form of socialism which would offer a new way of being in the modern world, a way beyond doctrinaire Marxism and beyond the formal emptiness of the bourgeois age. In this desire it shared some of the prevailing assumptions of the age—namely, a suspicion of the optimistic liberalism, progressivism, and rationalism of the previous age and a yearning for a medieval-type synthesis, a longing for restoration of authority and a rediscovery of the irrational-mythic dimensions of life and history.[128] Thus, in some strange sense, Religious Socialism and National Socialism germinated in the same fertile ground of the period.

(3) For Tillich and some of his fellow Religious Socialists, fascism was, as a result, not *ipso facto* a demonic opponent but rather a potential ally in the struggle against the liberalism of the previous age and for the coming of a new mode of being. Fascism, they thought, could be seen as a transitional phenomenon in Europe that, if it could undergo a course correction and extricate itself from its alliance with reactionary middle class and bourgeois capitalist forces, could still come to the support of a genuine socialist society.[129] (4) Döring depicts Tillich as being on the right wing of the Social Democratic Party (SPD), wanting to go beyond Marx in order to ground socialism anew and thus gain the support of the masses of petit bourgeoisie (who were increasingly being tempted by the nationalist movement) and the powerful youth movement in the fight against modern capitalistic development towards a socialist future.[130] One of the main elements of this "new socialism" as envisioned by Tillich *et al* was an emphasis on the totality of life including the primordial dimensions—what Tillich sometimes refers to as the sacramental aspects of reality. In his eyes the world ought to be desecularized and penetrated through and through with religious meaning, sanctified and carried by eternal truths. All human activities were to serve as fulfillment of God's demands. Herein, says Döring, lay the disguised yearning for the Middle Ages, the romantic component of this type of Religious Socialism.[131] In this way these Religious Socialists hoped human beings would be liberated from their enslavement to the machine and to economic materialism, and be able to overcome the alienation between subject and object, being and thinking, in a new dialectical view of life and history.

(5) Döring says Tillich perceives fascism as rising from the soil of the great kairotic events of the post-war period, a partly legitimate protest against the hubris of empty autonomous forms of the age.[132] Nationalism during the Weimar period was a protest against an overly-rationalistic perception of reality.

128. *Ibid.*, pp. 12-13.
129. *Ibid.*, p. 13.
130. *Ibid.*, p. 16.
131. *Ibid.*, pp. 17-18.
132. *Ibid.*, pp. 21-22.

The rediscovery of the irrational goal of life was closely bound up with the positive valuation of religion, state, and nation. The danger inherent in this movement was that it was readily susceptible to reactionary and anti-socialist forces. It was precisely this reactionary anti-socialist mentality which ultimately triumphed in the NSDAP and which Tillich unequivocally rejected, seeing it as a deterioration of the movement into barbarism.[133] (6) There existed in the later years of the Weimar Republic a large number of bourgeois youth who found themselves intellectually homeless. They were anti-capitalist, anti-Marxist, anti-individualist, and anti-rationalist. They found themselves between two fronts: alienated from the capitalistic status quo on the one side and the socialistic future on the other. The tentativeness and haziness of the National Socialist program appealed to them and captured their imagination.[134] What they found particularly attractive in the NSDAP was not only its anti-capitalist spirit and its struggle against the revolutionary proletariat but also the anti-intellectual element current in its philosophy. This mythic element found its supreme expression in Rosenberg's ideas, which for many became the substitute for the rationalistic-scientific worldview of the 19th century, and in the high value placed by the NSDAP on the nation and on unconditional surrender to an authoritative leader.[135]

(7) Thus National Socialism in its early years of power was a movement oscillating between two poles: it was simultaneously a reactionary anti-modern movement and a revolutionary anti-capitalist force with definite socialist leanings. The crisis within this movement in the early 1930s had to do with the struggle between these two poles: the reactionary forces under party leadership and the revolutionary forces represented by the left wing of the party.[136] It was

---

133. *Ibid.*, pp. 24ff.
134. *Ibid.*, pp. 26-27.
135. *Ibid.*, pp. 28-29.
136. *Ibid.*, p. 32. It has been argued in fact that National Socialism in its earliest stages had something of the socialist spirit and determination in its program but that with Hitler's need for money he formed a coalition with big capitalistic forces and as a result the socialist elements in the movement were increasingly forced out of the movement. See Döring, p. 127, 239n. S. William Halperin, in his *Germany Tried Democracy*, makes a similar point in his description of the early ideological leanings of Paul Josef Goebbels, Robert Ley, and the two Strasser brothers—Gregor and Otto. According to Halperin, speaking about Robert Ley and Paul Josef Goebbels in the mid-1920s, "The two men sought, with the aid of Otto Strasser, Gregor's brother, to push the movement farther and farther to the Left. They demanded the destruction of capitalism and the establishment of a 'corporate' socialist society. They declared themselves ready to co-operate with the revolutionary elements in other lands—Russia, India, and China—in order to bring about the fulfillment of this demand. On one occasion, Goebbels insisted that there were no essential differences between National Socialism and Communism. 'You and I are fighting one another,' he wrote in a letter to one of his Bolshevist adversaries, 'but we are not really enemies. Our forces are split up and we never reach our goal.' To this radical palaver Hitler took violent exception. He contended that the party must make itself the protector of private property and free enterprise. The issue was debated at a parley of district leaders in February 1926. Goebbels suddenly deserted Strasser and aligned

the former that ultimately triumphed under the leadership of Adolf Hitler, who eliminated the left wing of the party and joined forces with the industrial powers to gain total political-economic power. It was this early ambiguity inherent in the movement which helps to explain the ambivalent attitude of Tillich and his fellow Religious Socialists associated with the *Neue Blätter für den Sozialismus* toward the National Socialist phenomenon in the early 1930s. They saw it as a movement of the politically awakened middle classes and as a transitional phenomenon. Either it would separate itself from the revolutionary powers which were indisputably present within it and accommodate itself to the existing capitalistic system (which in fact it did very quickly) or it would follow a socialist course and come to see in socialism the answer to the demands and desires of the petit bourgeoisie.[137]

(8) Tillich's *The Socialist Decision* (the only place that Tillich devoted himself directly and substantially in a systematic way to National Socialism) must be understood in the light of the above ambiguity within the movement itself and in the context of his own declared propensity always to stand on the boundary, to find himself at home in two opposing camps simultaneously and always concerned with mediation and synthesis—particularly the synthesis between a formal world emptied of all substance and meaning and a theology which had become alienated from modern life. There is in Tillich's Religious Socialist thought, as manifested in this book, a distinctly irrational-mythic element, a strong critique of modernity and the attempt to overcome the modern through his notion of *theonomy*—not primarily a rational concept but one pointing to the irrational ground of all phenomena, the hidden divine power behind all events.[138] Tillich's position is a broken one between an affirmation and a negation of the modern: he affirms a *rational* modern culture in its autonomy and at the same time wants to give it a *mythical-irrational* stamp to sanctify that culture. He both is and is not a representative of the irrational stream of 20th-century thought. This creates in him an ambivalent attitude toward National Socialism—not the terrorizing National Socialism of the brown shirts but National Socialism as the expression of a mythical protest against an unacceptable modern world emptied of meaning and substance.[139]

(9) It was more specifically through his *kairos* doctrine that Tillich aimed to combine both the irrational-mythical and the rational elements in history. For Tillich a genuine socialist decision on the part of the proletariat is possible only as it decides in favor of the power of the origin against the bourgeois distortion of those powers of origin. Such a decision would bring socialism close to polit-

himself with Hitler" (p. 371). While Goebbels became one of Hitler's most trusted and loyal devo-tees, Gregor Strasser fell from the *Führer's* grace in December 1932.

137. Döring, *Christentum und Faschismus*, pp. 33-34.
138. *Ibid.*, p. 36.
139. *Ibid.*, pp. 36-37.

ical romanticism without joining it and without ultimately saying yes to it.[140] Tillich's fundamental ambivalence towards romanticism, nationalism, and irrationalism and consequently also toward National Socialism in the early 1930s (before it took a turn for the worst), is rooted in this longing for the romantic myth of origin—for an earlier period when blood, earth, and community encompassed all of life. He is also unable from the start, according to Döring, to give a rigorous and stringent critique of National Socialism because of his dialectical attitude toward the demonic; in every demonic manifestation there is for Tillich also a creative power and this holds true for National Socialism as well.[141] Political romanticism (NSDAP) shatters precisely at the point, however, where it affirms the power of the origin against the prophetic socialist thought in an unbroken and undialectical way.[142]

(10) In his *The Socialist Decision,* Tillich distinguishes between conservative romanticism and revolutionary romanticism. He sees revolutionary romanticism as the actualization of the dynamic mass of which he spoke so much in the early 1920s and whose intention he considers to be related to revolutionary socialism. Both seek a new land beyond present bourgeois civil society.[143] Where they differ is that while political revolutionary romanticism wants to revoke the bourgeois principle, socialism wants to appropriate it and move beyond it. The reason why the two fail to come to terms with each other is not primarily because of their essential differences, differences which cannot be denied, but more so because of the tragedy of the present situation. Both need each other, both need to fuse the rational and the mythical dimensions, as Tillich himself tries to do. Tillich still sees this coming together as a possibility in the early 1930s. The contribution of National Socialism is that it revolutionized the groups who adhered to the powers of the myth of origin against the capitalistic system. The "socialist" part of its name is not discarded as being merely demogogic but ought to be regarded as an expression of a genuine anticipation of a total transformation of society (its symbol being the "Third Reich"). Tillich sincerely hopes that at the moment when the middle class no longer sees an advantage in its alliance with revolutionary romanticism, National Socialism may still decide in favor of the second part of its name and enter into genuine anti-capitalistic actions. That would make possible an alliance between groups close to the myth of origin and the proletariat in the coming period of socialism.[144]

(11) According to Döring Tillich's ambivalence with regard to National Socialism (or political revolutionary romanticism) is illustrated in his two open letters to Hirsch in 1934 and 1935, in which he admits to a close connection

140. *Ibid.,* pp. 40-41.
141. *Ibid.,* pp. 50-51.
142. *Ibid.,* p. 52.
143. *Ibid.,* p. 54.
144. *Ibid.,* pp. 56-57.

between his own Religious Socialist categories and those of Emanuel Hirsch. Both expressed the desire for a new theonomy, a reintegration on the basis of a new mythos. The difference between them is that Tillich and the Religious Socialists put their confidence in the workers' movement to achieve this and Hirsch based his hopes on other sociological strata—the conservative middle-class revolutionary powers.[145] The attempt by Tillich and the Religious Socialists to win the masses over to a new myth-oriented socialism in support of the SPD failed to materialize. Tillich was to realize this soon after 1933.

Two Forms of Risk

As indicated earlier, our study of Tillich's religious and political thought in the 1930s—especially his strong critique of individualistic-bourgeois culture devoid of all immediate communal relationships through family, clan, tribe, nation, and state, his call for a genuine socialist decision in which the myth of origin would be taken seriously, and more generally his desire for a new synthesis of religion and culture in which the irrational-mythic dimension (the religious ground of all of culture) would once more be acknowledged—largely confirms Döring's thesis; namely, that Tillich did not reject fascism *ipso facto* as demonic, but that while he recognized the barbarous possibilities and direction of National Socialism, he saw in it—if it could correct its course—a potential ally in the struggle against the empty liberalism of the previous age and for the coming of a new mode of theonomous existence in European society.

Despite the areas of my agreement with Döring's thesis, there are in my opinion a number of deficiencies in his analysis. He does not, in my view, do justice to the critical theological elements in Tillich's political thought. I am thinking particularly of Tillich's use of the "Protestant principle" and the prophetic-eschatological concept of the "kingdom of God," as criteria by which all human-historical and political movements must be unambiguously judged.

Although it is true that Tillich makes some remarkably positive statements about the importance of the "myth of origin" (remarkable especially in the context in which they were made), and while the romantic elements in Tillich's thought cannot be denied (this is especially evident in his discussion of political romanticism and in his critique of doctrinaire Marxism), he remains unequivocal in his use of these theological criteria for the judging of all "isms." In his *The Socialist Decision,* Tillich is in fact quite unambiguous in his demand that the myth of origin (the "whence" of all human existence) must first be broken in the face of the "ought" of history (the "whither" of human existence). In fact it is at this point where Tillich parts company with those who support National Socialism, including his friend and political opponent Emanuel Hirsch. He sees

145. *Ibid.,* p. 57.

the invaluable contribution of the previous liberal age to be precisely that it broke through the myth of origin. One has first to accept the fundamental truth of the second root of all political thought—the liberal, democratic, and socialist rejection of the myth of origin—and to make a genuine decision for socialism before the myth of origin can once more be integrated into one's political thinking, now not as a return to the past but as the true origin, an origin which lies in the future society of justice, shaped by our understanding of the kingdom of God. The clarity with which Tillich applied his Protestant theological principle(s) to the political situation already in 1932 is especially evident, as we have seen, in his "Zehn Thesen" of that year. Here he unambiguously states that Protestantism can preserve its true prophetic Christian character only if it sets the Christianity of the cross over against the paganism of the swastika and the hallowing of nation, race, blood, and authority.

It is on the theological level that the differences between Tillich's and Hirsch's responses to National Socialism must finally be examined. What Döring's astute analysis does confirm for us as we look at their two contrary responses to the triumph of the National Socialist movement is the uncertainty and fluidity of the religious-political situation in 1933. Neither Hirsch nor Tillich were absolutely clear about where the movement was heading. For both the situation demanded the taking of risks. Their risks, however, took different forms growing out of their different theological perspectives. For Hirsch risk meant unconditional support of a movement which might go wrong, putting one's hand to the plough without turning back and thus accepting one's God-given responsibility in shaping the movement and helping to steer it in the right direction. Behind this risk was a particular understanding of what God demands of us in a given historical situation.

For Tillich, for whom there could be no such unreserved loyalty to an earthly movement while also remaining faithful to the "Protestant principle" of protest, risk in 1933 entailed being exiled from his homeland—living on the boundary between native and alien land. Behind Tillich's risk there was a different understanding of what God demands in an ambiguous situation. The dramatic public debate between Paul Tillich and Emanuel Hirsch in 1934-35, to which we now turn, helps to illumine the theological differences behind their divergent responses to National Socialism.

PART THREE

BASIC ISSUES OF THE 1934-1935 DEBATE

8
Religious Socialism
and the Kairos

The public confrontation between Paul Tillich and Emanuel Hirsch in their open exchange of 1934-35 was the culmination of their long struggle with each other's theological and political views from the time of their first meeting in 1907. Their early differences during the First World War, their increasing divergence during the Weimar period, and their contrary responses to Hitler and National Socialism in 1932-33 all led up to the dramatic rupture in their friendship in 1934-35. In Part Three (chapters 8, 9, and 10) we examine in detail the three primary documents in this public debate—the documents which constitute the climax of our whole study. We conclude with a look at the reaction to this debate in German theological circles, with an evaluation of the charges each levels against the other, and consider the political implications of this debate for the political task of theology. The first of the three documents is Tillich's initial open letter to Hirsch, written on October 1, 1934 and published in the November issue of *Theologische Blätter*, a journal edited by Tillich's friend and colleague Karl Ludwig Schmidt. Schmidt, like Tillich, had belonged to the small religious socialist movement in Germany in the 1920s and had been a member of the so-called Berlin "Kairos Circle."[1] This open letter, with which Tillich initiated the public debate between himself and Hirsch, was entitled "Die Theologie des Kairos und die geistige Lage: Offener Brief an Emanuel Hirsch."[2] The second document is Hirsch's response to Tillich's charges in a November 16, 1934 letter to his friend Wilhelm Stapel, a fellow participant in the Young National Lutheran movement, a movement dedicated to national renewal on the basis of

1. See John R. Stumme, *Socialism in Theological Perspective*, pp. 23ff. Schmidt, a New Testament scholar, was also a friend and faculty colleague of Karl Barth at the University of Bonn in the early 1930s. As a Social Democrat he too was under threat of suspension from his teaching position by the National Socialist government in 1933. See Klaus Scholder, *Die Kirchen und das dritte Reich*, p. 551. See also Eberhard Busch, *Karl Barth: His Life from Letters and Autobiographical Texts*, Tr. by John Bowden (Philadelphia: Fortress Press, 1976), pp. 201, 218, 268.

2. Paul Tillich, "Die Theologie des Kairos und die gegenwärtige geistige Lage: Offener Brief an Emanuel Hirsch," *Theologische Blätter* 11,13(November 1934), pp. 305-328. Also in *Briefwechsel und Streitschriften*, Ergänzung- und Nachlassbände zu *GW* VI, pp. 142-176. This letter has recently been translated into English by Victor Nuovo and Robert P. Scharlemann in *The Thought of Paul Tillich*, James Luther Adams, Wilhelm Pauck, and Roger Lincoln Shinn, eds. (San Francisco: Harper & Row Publishers, 1985), pp. 353-388. I am working here with the original German text and translations into English are my own.

Lutheran theology. Stapel, founder and editor of *Deutsches Volkstum*, had been influential in the development of some of Hirsch's key political concepts, particularly that of the *Volksnomos* (roughly translated, "the inner law of a national people").[3] Hirsch's letter was entitled simply "Brief an Herrn Dr. Stapel" and appeared, together with Hirsch's response to Danish theologian Eduard Geismar, in a book called *Christliche Freiheit und politische Bindung: Ein Brief an Dr. Stapel und anderes.*[4] The third and final document is Tillich's brief restatement of his earlier position in an open letter to Hirsch in May 1935. This final letter, in which Tillich leaves out some of the more passionate and personal elements of his first letter (in particular his charge of "plagiarism"), is entitled "Um was es geht: Antwort an Emanuel Hirsch." It too was published in *Theologische Blätter.*[5] Since we are not aware of any full-length analysis of this debate, and since Hirsch's side of the debate has not received the attention that it clearly deserves (Hirsch's response has never been translated into English) we devote chapters 8 and 9 to a rather detailed recapitulation of the arguments on both sides.[6]

3. Stapel founded the periodical *Deutsches Volkstum* in 1919 and was dedicated to a combining of a Christian-Lutheran (*"christliche-lutherische"*) orientation with a folkish-nationalistic (*"volkische-nationale"*) patriotism, having been strongly influenced by both Lutheran thought and by Fichte. Stapel, Paul Althaus, and Hirsch had strong affinities in this regard and could be considered "political theologians." In 1932 Stapel outlined his theological-political views in a book with the title *Der christliche Staatsmann. Eine Theologie des Nationalismus.* Of particular importance for Hirsch was Stapel's concept of the *Volksnomos* or *Volksgesetz*—the particular law and ethos of national peoplehood. While Hirsch differed from Stapel in some important ways, he himself on numerous occasions admits his indebtedness to Stapel for his *Nomos* concept. See Scholder, *Die Kirchen und das dritte Reich*, pp. 125, 131, 150, 533ff.

4. Emanuel Hirsch, "Brief an Herrn Dr. Stapel," *Christliche Freiheit und politische Bindung: Ein Brief an Dr. Stapel und anderes* (Hamburg: Hanseatische Verlagsanstalt, 1935), pp. 7-47. The second part of this book is directed to Eduard Geismar and is entitled "Kreuzesglaube und politische Bindung (Eine ökumenische Zwiesprache)," pp. 48-75. In the concluding section of this book, Hirsch lists in propositional form a series of theses outlining his basic theological and political tenets on the basis of Lutheran theology over against both Tillich and Geismar. An analysis of the Hirsch-Geismar debate by Jens Holger Schjørring has appeared under the title *Theologische Gewissensethik und politische Wirklichkeit: Das Beispiel Eduard Geismars und Emanuel Hirschs* (Göttingen: Vandenhoeck & Ruprecht, 1979). The first part of this book—namely, Hirsch's response to Tillich—also appears in *Briefwechsel und Streitschriften*, Ergänzungs- und Nachlassbände zu *GW* VI, pp. 177-213.

5. Tillich, "Um was es geht: Antwort an Emanuel Hirsch," *Theologische Blätter* 5,14(May 1935), pp. 117-120; also in Ergänzungs- und Nachlassbände zu *GW* VI, pp. 214-218.

6. Only a few studies of the Tillich-Hirsch debate of 1934-35 exist either in the German or English language, and these are short and sketchy. One such study is a short essay by Walter F. Bense, "Tillich's *Kairos* and Hitler's Seizure of Power: The Tillich-Hirsch Exchange of 1934/35," *Tillich's Studies: 1975*, John J. Carey, ed. (Tallahassee: North American Paul Tillich Society), pp. 39-50. Two of my own essays on the subject give overviews of the debate and examine the accuracy of the main charges on both sides in light of some of the biographical and theological presuppositions behind the controversy: A. James Reimer, "Theological Method and Political Ethics: The Paul Tillich-Emanuel Hirsch Debate," *Journal of the American Academy of Religion* XLVII/1

A Charge of Plagiarism in Tillich's First Open Letter to Hirsch

Tillich was suspended from his teaching position at the University of Frankfurt on April 13, 1933, although he was officially dismissed from his German professorship only on December 20, 1933, when he was already teaching in New York City. He had arrived in New York on November 3, 1933 to take up duties as a professor of religion and systematic theology at Union Theological Seminary. It was here, in 1934, that he received a copy of Hirsch's book, *Die gegenwärtige geistige Lage im Spiegel philosophischer und theologischer Besinnung,* the book which roused Tillich's ire. On October 1, 1934 he wrote his first stinging attack of Hirsch's book, entitled "Die Theologie des Kairos und die gegenwärtige geistige Lage: Offener Brief an Emanuel Hirsch." The letter consists of four parts: a short preface, in which Tillich makes some personal comments and briefly enumerates his basic charges against Hirsch; Part One, which consists of Tillich's attempt to show how Hirsch has appropriated the underlying categories of religious socialist thought—particularly the *kairos* doctrine—and emptied them of their intended meaning; Part Two, in which he provides what he considers to be a substantive critique of Hirsch's theological method itself; and a short final section in which he offers some concluding remarks.

In order to understand what is actually going on in this debate it is helpful to identify three basic levels: the personal, the political, and the theological. All three are important dimensions of the controversy. The most important level, I would argue, is the theological. Of second importance is the political level, which rests on certain theological assumptions; and third is the personal and biographical.[7] The personal undertone of the letter is evident throughout, no matter how much Tillich attempts to emphasize the more objective theological aspects of their disagreement. Tillich explains in the preface, for instance, that

Supplement (March 1979), pp. 177-192; and Reimer, "Theological stringency and political engagement: The Paul Tillich-Emanuel Hirsch controversy over National Socialism," *Studies in Religion/Sciences Religieuses,* 16,3(1987), pp. 331-345. Jens Holger Schjørring, in his *Theologische Gewissensethik,* devotes a few pages to the Tillich-Hirsch exchange in the context of his study of Hirsch and Geismar, "Die Auseinandersetzung zwischen Tillich und Hirsch," pp. 295-298. David Hopper, in chapter III of his book, *Tillich: A Theological Portrait* (Philadelphia: J.B. Lippincott Company, 1968), concentrates on Tillich's first open letter to Hirsch to shed light on Tillich's own theological evolution, "The Hirsch Affairs—And After," pp. 65-100. Gunda Schneider-Flume examines the debate in order to illuminate her study of Hirsch in her *Die politische Theologie Emanuel Hirschs 1918-1933* (Frankfurt/M: Verlag Peter Lang GmbH, 1971), pp. 145ff. Schneider-Flume has written an essay comparing the "political theology" of Paul Tillich, Emanuel Hirsch, and Richard Shaulls in which she again draws on the debate: "Kritische Theologie contra theologisch-politischen Offenbarungsglauben: Eine vergleichende Strukturanalyse der politischen Theologie Paul Tillichs, Emanuel Hirschs und Richard Shaulls," *Evangelische Theologie* 2,33(March/April 1973), pp. 114-137.

7. See Reimer, "Theological Method and Political Ethics," p. 173.

he had initially conceived the letter as a private one but that as his letter developed into a substantive attack on Hirsch's book, and realizing the possibility of a serious misinterpretation of the *kairos* doctrine, he decided to publish it as an open letter. There are times, says Tillich, when the "personal" and the "substantive" are inextricably bound together and this is one such occasion. Especially important in the situation, adds Tillich, is the need publicly to express more than one interpretation of the events of 1933.[8]

Tillich continues his personal comments in the first part of the introduction. He acknowledges the scholarly discussion that has gone on between them for many years, their growing opposition in substantive matters and the strain that this growing apart is having on their personal friendship. Their separation on important matters has become more evident to Tillich through his reading of Hirsch's latest book (*Die gegenwärtige geistige Lage im Spiegel philosophischer und theologischer Besinnung*). Tillich agrees with Barth that *Die gegenwärtige geistige Lage* is a highly significant book for understanding Hirsch.[9] He has chosen the "letter" form to indicate the conversational nature of their ongoing debate and the "public" forum to stress the fact that they are not simply engaged in a private conversation but are dealing with highly important public principles.[10]

The political and theological dimensions of the debate are closely intertwined with each other and can be identified only by carefully going through the text. Claiming that Hirsch's book has astonished him and others for a number of reasons, Tillich proceeds to make three opening charges. First, he accuses Hirsch of plagiarism, of appropriating all the decisive categories of his political and religious opponents of the last 14 years (the religious socialists) in order to give meaning to the new turn of events in German history. Second, he charges Hirsch with intentionally disguising his formal agreement with the religious socialist conceptual framework. Finally, what concerns Tillich most of all, is the implication that in his employment of these categories Hirsch may have

---

8. "Die Theologie des Kairos," p. 305.

9. In April 1934, in some reflections on the German situation, Barth makes the following comments about Hirsch's *Die gegenwärtige geistige Lage:* "I have just finished reading Emanuel Hirsch's new book....No-one should fail to study it. In contrast to almost everything that I have read of the productions of the German-Christian camp, it is a well-considered and also readably and interestingly written book, which has said, better than any previous book, the best that can be said for the German-Christian cause. We can and must praise it too for the fact that its author, in contrast to many of his fellow-believers, has, with what he declared today, remained in line with what he has always meant, intended and maintained. If anyone is genuine and has the right to speak in this affair, it is Emanuel Hirsch. This is what makes it so clear and certain that, and why, faced with this book, we must say No, No, and once again No, to this matter. Our denial is as unarguable as Hirsch's introduction and establishment of the subject in its basic theme." "On the Situation: 1933-34," Karl Barth, *The German Church Conflict*, ed. by A.M. Allchin, Martin E. Marty, T.H.L. Parker, tr. by T.H.L. Parker (London: Lutterworth Press, 1965), p. 30.

10. "Die Theologie des Kairos," p. 305.

brought them to their deepest meaning.[11] It is for these reasons that Tillich feels himself compelled to write this letter. While he would have preferred to remain silent, the use and misuse of the *kairos* doctrine in particular—a concept which had been associated with Tillich's own name for a long time—forces him to speak up publicly against his long-time friend.

Implicit in Tillich's three charges is the accusation against Hirsch of adopting alien categories for reasons of political opportunism, a motif that re-appears on numerous occasions throughout Tillich's letter. It seems, according to Tillich, that Hirsch is not at all clear in his own mind about the relation of intellectual integrity to the demands of the present political struggle.[12] In other words, Hirsch is conveniently adapting categories which he basically rejects just because they fit his present political ideology and the German climate. He is, in short, subordinating his theological beliefs and an honest historical analysis to partisan politics.

Hirsch's analysis of the situation would have appeared in a totally different light if he had admitted his dependence on religious socialist concepts. But nowhere, says Tillich, does Hirsch acknowledge the fact that Tillich's own work has provided him with the methodological basis for his own interpretation of 1933. Tillich finds especially offensive Hirsch's caricature of "Religious Socialism" as "Religious Marxism," the latter being a negatively-loaded term for the reading public. Tillich wonders whether it is an unconscious suppression on the part of Hirsch of his indebtedness to the religious socialists, a half-conscious fear of the consequences of such an acknowledgement, or whether it is simply political opportunism—the priority of politics over truthfulness.[13]

What Tillich finds most disconcerting is that Hirsch can use such similar-sounding language and concepts for such different political ends. These categories, says Tillich, should have led Hirsch to entirely different conclusions. Tillich says, for instance, that the sense of an historical turn and the crisis of the bourgeois era, the hope for a spiritual, social, and political renewal of Germany and of Europe were just as strong earlier for the religious socialists as they now

---

11. *Ibid.,* p. 306. The first more general accusation is expressed by Tillich as follows: "Das Erstaunen gründet sich auf die Tatsache, dass Du, um die neue Wendung der deutschen Geschichte theologisch zu deuten, alle entscheidenden Begriffe des vierzehn Jahre lang von Dir bekämpften und nun äusserlich überwundenen Gegners gebrauchst." He articulates his second and third charges with the words: "Aber diese Fruede ist durch ein Doppeltes getrübt: einmal durch die Tatsache, dass Du Deine Uebereinstimmung mit den religiös-sozialistischen Kategorien geflissentlich verhüllst, und zweitens durch die Tatsache, dass Deine Verwendung dieser Kategorien sie um ihren tiefsten Sinn bringst."

12. Here Tillich's implicit charge of political opportunism stands in contrast to Barth's evaluation of Hirsch, when he says of Hirsch's book: "We can and must praise it too for the fact that its author, in contrast to many of his fellow-believers, has, with what he declared today, remained in line with what he has always meant, intended, and maintained. If anyone is genuine and has the right to speak in this affair, it is Emanuel Hirsch." Barth, *The German Church Conflict,* p. 30.

13. "Die Theologie des Kairos," pp. 306-307.

are for the national socialists. Before National Socialism, Religious Socialism had already developed a strong critique of autonomy and anticipated a period of theonomy in which the demonic nature of class antagonism would be overcome, a time when the chasm between eternity and time would be bridged through the religiously-filled moment (the *kairos*).[14] Later on in the essay Tillich adds to this list of similarities. Hirsch's topics of analysis are the same as those of the religious socialists earlier: the attempt by autonomous reason, after the collapse of the religiously-based culture of the middle ages, to reconstruct society; the catastrophe of this rationally-based "worldshaping-will" during and following the First World War; the significance of the Reformation and the Counter-reformation for the rise of this autonomous reason; the importance of the three symbols of the modern age—science, technique, and economics—for the rational domination of nature; the struggle for human rights; the rejection of idealism; the overriding importance of Karl Marx and Friedrich Nietzsche for the 19th century.[15] The fundamental difference between himself and Hirsch, says Tillich, is that Hirsch begins his analysis with a belief in the revolutionary powers of the middle class rather than that of the proletariat.[16]

Part One of Tillich's letter is divided into four main sections: a) an identification of the specific categories that Hirsch has supposedly appropriated from the religious socialists; b) a demonstration of how Hirsch has emptied these categories of their meaning and distorted them; c) a discussion of their true intended meaning; and d) an exposé of Hirsch's alleged distortion of the new existentialist philosophy by adopting a sacramental stance.

Plagiarized Categories and Concepts
Tillich begins by listing briefly the main concepts that Hirsch has taken from the religious socialists. There is, first, the notion of the *demonic*—one of the central concepts of Religious Socialism. The religious socialists used it to signify the creative-destructive powers that exist within all periods of history. Hirsch, however, has used this concept to characterize a particular period of crisis, especially the Weimar period, and believes that the recent events in Germany have overcome this demonic period.[17] A second religious socialist category used by Hirsch is that of the *boundary*. Here Hirsch seems to feel the need to justify his own use of the concept with reference to older usages. But when Hirsch defines his concept as "holy middle," in contrast to earlier notions of the boundary as an infinitely deferrable limit (*unendlich hinausschiebbare Beschränkung*), he has in fact inverted the meaning of the boundary situation as explicated by Tillich and

14. *Ibid.*, p. 307.
15. *Ibid.*, p. 308.
16. *Ibid.*, p. 307. Tillich says to Hirsch: "You believe that the conservative and middle class revolutionary powers are a better starting point, yes have in principle brought fulfillment."
17. "Die Theologie des Kairos," p. 308. In Tillich's words, "You take over this central notion and interpret the German event as the overcoming of the agglomerated demons in the age of crisis."

Jaspers. Hirsch's use of the term "holy boundary," Tillich claims, is in fact a reformulation of the term "abyss" as he (Tillich) formulates it in his own work. Hirsch, like the religious socialists, says Tillich, portrays bourgeois society as the bearer of a religiosity without the experience of the abyss and the boundary situation.[18]

Third, and most important, is Hirsch's use of the notion of *kairos,* without ever using the term itself. Tillich expresses surprise at the fact that Hirsch avoids using the Greek *"kairos,"* after using the Greek word *"nomos"* as formulated by Stapel and translating the word "boundary" with the Greek word *"horos."* Instead, he uses phrases like "present hour," "historical moment," "historical hour," a "breaking through" (*Aufbruch*), "particular responsibility," and so on.[19] It is this disguised appropriation of the *kairos* teaching that now suddenly seems to create a basic methodological agreement between them.

Fourth, Hirsch defends an existentialist method of viewing history, an approach that Tillich in his last German lecture tried to develop as an "existentialist-historical method." Certain sentences of Hirsch's concerning an existentialist approach to history, says Tillich, are almost a verbatim repeat of Tillich's own writings.[20] Like Hirsch now, the religious socialists from the beginning tried to understand the German reality from within its existential depth and tried to take seriously the task of the hour.

Tillich argues that the logical consequences of Hirsch's demand for existentialist-historical thinking are, on the negative side, that he must break with Friedrich Gogarten's form of dialectical thinking, which sees the *kairos* philosophy as the "pest of history." Only by means of self-deception can he link himself closely with Gogarten. On the positive side, to follow through consistently he would need consequently to side with the religious socialists and, ironically, with Karl Marx, whom of all people he would least like to identify himself with. Unlike Kierkegaard, whom Hirsch relies upon, Heidegger, whom he rejects, and Jaspers, whom he fails to cite—all of whom stress the existence of the individual—it is in fact the young Marx who truly demands existentialist-historical thinking. Further, anyone who thinks existential-historically, including Marx himself, is dependent upon the old Jewish prophetic tradition. In this sense Hirsch, on the basis of his present claims, now clearly stands not only in the tradition of Marxism but of prophetic Judaism and religious Marxism, an identification he would surely find objectionable.[21]

18. *Ibid.*, pp. 308-309.
19. *Ibid.*, p. 309.
20. One such sentence, as cited by Tillich, is the following: "Die Existenz des Philosophierenden wird Mass der geschichtlichen Existentialität der Philosophie," *Ibid.*, p. 309. Tillich adds that this is almost a word for word repeat of one of the basic concepts of his own work, "Gläubiger Realismus," *Theologenrundbrief für den Bund deutscher Jugendvereine* 2(November 1927), pp. 3-13. Also in *GW* IV, pp. 77-87.
21. "Die Theologie des Kairos," pp. 309-310. Hirsch's strong anti-Marxist and anti-communist

Fifth, Hirsch espouses the idea of *dynamic truth,* a notion which is central to the *kairos* doctrine as developed by the religious socialists.[22] All the consequences of this dynamic view of truth are taken from the religious socialists, says Tillich. Similarly, in the sixth place, the category of risk (*Wagnis*), which is central to Hirsch's analysis, is akin to Tillich's own notion of the risk-character of knowledge as well as to his portrayal of knowledge in terms of destiny and risk in his article "Kairos und Logos."[23] Tillich adds a most interesting remark, which again reveals his own now strange affinity with Hirsch's thought, when he says that he and the religious socialists were aware that knowledge must occur within and for the community in order not to be freely-suspended will. The religious socialists tried to locate the "power of history" within the nation (*das Volk*).[24] However, Tillich later admits that they—the religious socialists—did not take seriously enough the power of the nation.

Seventh, Tillich notes Hirsch's reliance on the religious socialist polarity of autonomous and theonomous ages to explain the meaning of various historical epochs.[25] Hirsch characterizes late antiquity as a period of estrangement from God—in which God is viewed as ahistorically beyond being, the bourgeois age as the period of the self-sufficient power of reason and freedom, and pre-Christian paganism as an unbroken theonomy in which there exists a simple unity of historical being and the holy *horos.* Hirsch calls both pagan theonomy

critique is expressed repeatedly throughout his writings, as we have had occasion to examine in other parts of our study.

22. "Die Theologie des Kairos," p. 310. Hirsch's decisive sentence, according to Tillich, is this: "Vernunft ist der sich als Logos geistig verstehende und entfaltende Nomos bestimmten menschlich-geschichtlichen Lebens selbst, und Wissenschaft ist nichts als Zucht und Rechenschaft dieses wirklichkeitsbestimmten Logos vor sich selbst über die ihn bestimmende Wirklichkeit." Tillich adds: "Ohne hier schon auf Deine Formulierungen einzugehen, möchte ich Dich erinnern, dass das Problem, dass Du mit ihnen stellst, das Thema aller Arbeiten war, die sich um die philosophische Begründung der Kairos-Lehre bemühten, dass die Lösungen weit über unseren Kreis hinausgewirkt haben, dass wir seit jener Zeit von einer 'dynamischen Wahrheit' gesprochen und eine 'dynamische Methode' zu entwickeln versucht haben? Muss ich Dich daran erinnern?"

23. "Die Theologie des Kairos," p. 310. For Tillich's "Kairos und Logos" see *Kairos. Zur Geisteslage und Geisteswendung* (Darmstadt: Reichl, 1926). Also in *GW* IV, pp. 43-76.

24. "Die Theologie des Kairos," p. 310. In a sentence that sounds amazingly similar to something Hirsch might have said, Tillich says, "Für die Forderung, das Erkennen, um frei schwebender Willkur zu entgehen, aus der Gemeinschaft und für die Gemeinschaft geschehen müsse, zeugte der Religiöse Sozialismus durch seine Existenz. Er suchte innerhalb des Volkes den Ort der grössten 'Geschichtsmächtigkeit' zu finden, und aus der Gemeinschaft mit dieser Gruppe heraus die geschichtliche Existenz des Volkes und des Kulturkreises zu erhellen." Ironically, Hirsch will accuse Tillich precisely of representing the kind of "frei schwebender Willkur" that Tillich here disavows. See Hirsch, *Christliche Freiheit und Politische Bindung,* pp. 28-29.

25. "Die Theologie des Kairos," p. 310. In Tillich's words: "Deine Geschichtskonstruktion ist bestimmt durch den Gegensatz autonomer und theonomer Zeitalter, also die Grundvoraussetzung des Religiösen Sozialismus....Selbst die Heteronomie kennst Du, wenn Du von der 'Zerknickung der Gewissen durch widernatürlichen Zwang sprichst' und Dich zu zeigen bemüht bist, dass so etwas in der neuen Theonomie nicht beabsichtigt sei."

and modern autonomy demonic and defines a true theonomous time as one in which "The historical Horos is at the same time the holy Horos, and yet, on the other hand the holy Horos is also the one who with the power of the eternal consumes the historical as something which passes away."[26] The religious socialists, Tillich adds, spoke of theonomy as the "Breakthrough of the sustaining and destroying ground and abyss," within the historical forms of life.[27] Even heteronomy, a central concept for Tillich's own thought, is recognized by Hirsch when he speaks of the breaking up of the conscience through the forms that stand over against nature.

Finally, Hirsch's discussion of the development and task of Protestant theology, declares Tillich, contains most of the decisive concepts for which the religious socialists were earlier slandered by orthodox church theologians. These concepts included notions such as the "evangelical turn against itself," the "identify of theology with theonomous philosophy," the "recognition of the basic moving powers (*bewegenden Grundmächte*) of the common life," the overcoming of historicism through an emphasis on "Christ as the center of history," the critique of Barthian transcendence of history as implicit support for the demons of the time, and finally, the recognition that the concept of justification applies to thought as well as sin, something which, he says, Hirsch had rejected till now.[28] When Hirsch protests against the independent existence of the church in a transhistorical sense and against throwing traditional theology over people's heads like a sack—two protests that the religious socialists also strongly made—then it is difficult, according to Tillich, to understand why Hirsch sides with Gogarten rather than with Tillich himself.

The only explanation, for Tillich, is that in the present spiritual and intellectual struggle there exists tremendous confusion. Hirsch has not helped to clear up this confusion, although he could quite easily have done so. What deeply disturbs Tillich is the now sudden appearance of what seems to be a genuine methodological and substantive agreement between himself and Hirsch in so many particulars. Tillich finds especially jolting Hirsch's statement that "It is the power of the present hour in nation and state, that we now all together are forced into asking genuine and original questions," when these same questions were asked earlier by those whom Hirsch identified as his opponents.[29] Hirsch

26. *Ibid.*, p. 310.

27. *Ibid.*

28. Tillich here refers to some of his own writings on these subjects: On the identity of theology and theonomous philosophy see *Das System der Wissenschaften nach Gegenständen und Methoden* (Göttingen: Vandenhoeck & Ruprecht, 1923). Also in *GW* I, pp. 109-293. On the overcoming of historicism through an understanding of history from the perspective of Christ as the "center of history" see "Christologie und Geschichtsdeutung," *Religiöse Verwirklichung* (Berlin: Furche, 1930); also in *GW* VI, pp. 83-96.

29. "Die Theologie des Kairos," p. 311. Tillich adds: "Die Aelteren wissen noch von diesen Dingen und schütteln den Kopf. Wie kannst Du es aber vor den Jüngeren, die von allem dem nichts mehr wissen, verantworten, dass Du ihnen ein Bild von der Entwicklung gibst, dass ihnen jeden

now uses these same questions as a basis for his own method.

Distortion of Religious Socialist Categories
In the second section of the first part of the letter, Tillich attempts to show how Hirsch has emptied the religious socialist categories of their true meaning and distorted them. Hirsch has done this for political purposes, he says, and thereby has given Tillich and the religious socialists a bad name. The distortion is particularly evident in Hirsch's use of the *kairos* teaching. One of the most important distinctions made by the religious socialists was that between (1) a sacramental consecration (*Heiligsprechung*) of that which is given in time and space and (2) a prophetic understanding of the proclamation of the kingdom of God. For the religious socialists the kingdom of God was both *promised* and *demanded.* The eschatological nature of the *kairos* doctrine combined both human *responsibility* and human *anticipation,* but strongly resisted the idolatrous sacramentalizing of a historical hour. Tillich summarizes his critique of Hirsch's book with the statement, "You invert the prophetic-eschatologically intended kairos teaching into a priestly-sacramental consecration of a present *happening.*"[30]

The three theological-political alternatives that Tillich sees as being the most important in Germany in 1934 are (1) the Dialectical Theology of Barth, (2) the Young National Lutheran Theology of Hirsch, and (3) the *Kairos* Theology as espoused by Tillich himself and by the religious socialists. At one extreme, in Tillich's opinion, is the Barthian escape into the abstract supernatural realm with its "undialectical" understanding of history (Tillich, in short, does not recognize Barth's theology to be true "dialectical" theology). At the other extreme is Hirsch's "undialectical" collapsing of the supernatural realm into the here and now. In the middle stands Tillich's own theological position, which has a truly "dialectical" view of the relation between the divine and the human, the transcendent and the historical.[31] Tillich's conception of his own theology over against that of Barth and Hirsch is expressed most clearly in the following rather lengthy statement by Tillich:

Zugang zum Verständnis der wirklichen Entwicklung von vornherein verbaut?"
    30. *Ibid.*, p. 312.
    31. *Ibid.* While his treatment of Hirsch is extremely biased and includes some grave errors, David Hopper in his *Tillich: A Theological Portrait* does a relatively good job comparing and contrasting the thought of Barth and Tillich. Commenting on the divergent lines of thought between the two theologians after 1919, he says: "Barth pointed to God, the One who was other than man, the One who in Christ offered man forgiveness. Tillich, on the other hand, pointed to the possibilities of new creation that were to be found in the contemporary historical situation, possibilities existing alongside the destruction and decay of old structures of meaning" (p. 37). While the picture of Barth as having an inadequate view of creation and a totally negative appraisal of culture and history is clearly a caricature, it seems true nevertheless that Tillich was more ready than Barth to argue for a "positive" alliance between Christianity and culture. It was here that he had some affinity with Hirsch's position.

This eschatological moment belongs inseparably to the Kairos teaching, in original Christianity as in Religious Socialism. It binds us to Barth insofar as we dispute with him the graspable presence of the divine in a finite being or happening; it separates us from Barth because the eschatological is supernatural with him; with us it has a paradoxical character. We do not put the transcendent in an undialectical opposition to history, but believe that it can be understood as genuine transcendence only if it is understood as that which here and there breaks into history, shatters it and transforms it. In this conception you and I stand together. The theology of Kairos stands precisely in the middle between the theology of the young national Lutherans and dialectical theology. It observes the second as a deflection into the abstract-transcendent, the first as a deviation into the demonic-sacramental. Against both it advocates the prophetic-primitive Christian paradox, that the kingdom of God comes into history and yet remains *above* history. It is clear that such a dialectical position is neither adaptable nor was adapted to the undialectical requirements of the political church struggle. But I cannot give up the hope that in both camps theologians and non-theologians can be found who will find in the undistorted Kairos doctrine a way out of the blind alley into which you like Barth will in the long run necessarily lead theology and the church. Indeed, as long as the struggle rages we stand on the side that advocates the eschatological over against the assault of a demonized sacramentalism. Even if on account of that the high price of a supernatural narrowing and an orthodox hardening has to be paid, it is better that way than paying the price of the eschaton for an absolutization of a finite reality.[32]

On the one hand, what Tillich and Hirsch have in common is their more radical understanding of the human captivity to history. The transcendent can be grasped only from within the historical realm. On the other hand, however, Tillich and Barth agree in their overriding conviction that the transcendent must never be equated with the historical. Despite his rejection of Barthian theology on many grounds, in the present situation Tillich finds himself on the side of Barth against Hirsch. Tillich does, however, make a crucial admission; namely, that the dialectical approach of the *kairos* doctrine as envisioned by himself and the religious socialists "is neither adaptable nor was adapted to the undialectical requirements of the political church struggle."[33] This admission is an important

32. "Die Theologie des Kairos," p. 312. According to Hopper, "This quotation suggests that if there was some influence of Barth upon Tillich the most likely area of such influence was in the realm of eschatology....It should be observed, however, that there are independent roots for Tillich's eschatology in his definition of God as the Unconditional, the Ground of the subject-object cleavage, and in Schelling's strong condemnation of 'pharisaism.'" *Tillich: A Theological Portrait*, p. 79n.

33. Hopper makes the following significant observations: "It must be said in relation to the German church struggle that the theology of Paul Tillich did not figure large in the opposition to National Socialism. Much more important in this regard was the point of view of 'dialectical theol-

one, because it is precisely the inadequacy of this purely "dialectical" method of understanding history that Hirsch considers to be his fundamental critique of Tillich.

Tillich continues to elaborate on what a genuinely dialectical view of history meant for the religious socialists. They viewed the present struggle as a wrestling for that which was to come. Their commitment to a "believing realism" prevented them from ever romantically absolutizing a particular historical event.[34] Hirsch, on the contrary, says Tillich, attributes an "unbroken negativity" to the occurrences of 1918 and an "unbroken positivity" to the events of 1933. He gives absolute theological validity to these historical events and thereby turns theology into political propaganda. He describes the Weimar era (1918-1932) in totally negative terms—a time of "confusion and temptation," the "abyss of a nation and the end of history," a "deathly sick nation," and so on.[35] There is no such age, says Tillich. No age has the theological right to judge a previous age in such an unequivocal way. Nothing finite stands under an unconditional Yes or No. Judgments such as Hirsch here makes can be made only on the assumption that one lives in a time of fulfilled grace. That Hirsch perceives it as such can be seen, according to Tillich, in statements such as "The new will...has come over us and has grasped us like a holy storm."[36] Hirsch, says Tillich, has implicitly given the year 1933 "salvation history" meaning by comparing it to the year 33.

The religious socialists, in contrast, never used the *kairos* doctrine to give such absolute valuations to historical periods. They never saw the preceding Wilhelmian epoch as a time of complete sinfulness, although they had reason to do so since they blamed it for the defeat of Germany: "We never called ages sinful, but we called powers demonic."[37] The demonic is never unequivocally destructive, maintains Tillich, but it is always also creative and sustaining

---

ogy' represented by Karl Barth. To account for this one must observe that Barth's theology stood much closer to the traditional standards of the church's faith and thus provided a more objective and familiar rallying point than did Tillich's theological-philosophical formulations." *Tillich: A Theological Portrait*, p. 90.

34. In H. Richard Niebuhr's 1932 "Preface" to Tillich's *The Religious Situation*, he discusses at length Tillich's notion of "belief-ful realism," pp. 9-24. According to Tillich, as cited by Niebuhr, "By the connection of *belief-ful* and *realism* the most fundamental of all dualisms is called into question and if it is justly called into question it is also overcome. Faith is an attitude which transcends every conceivable and experiencable reality; realism is an attitude which rejects every transcending of reality, every transcendency and all transcendentalizing," p. 14. "Gläubiger Realismus" might be better translated as "believing realism" than Niebuhr's "belief-ful realism."

35. "Die Theologie des Kairos," p. 313. Hirsch's negative appraisal of the Weimar Republic is more nuanced than Tillich here suggests. What Hirsch rejects in the Weimar Republic is the loss of the religious element in its concept of the state and its espousal of self-sufficient reason and autonomy.

36. *Ibid.*

37. *Ibid.* Despite his disclaimers here, as we have seen earlier in this study, Tillich himself in the early 1920s came close to giving such salvific significance to the proletarian movement.

(*tragend*). The religious socialists understood the demonic dialectically.[38]

This view of the demonic as part of the creative urge (as distinct from the satanic which is the negative within the demonic)—the other side being a divine impulse—marks another significant difference between Tillich and Hirsch. According to Tillich, if one calls groups, persons, and trends demonic in an undialectical sense, the way Hirsch does, then one can triumphantly assume one's victory over the demonic when one's opponents are defeated. But this is a misunderstanding of the depth and power of the demonic. The religious socialists also recognized a demonic element within capitalism, for instance, but saw the demonic as disguised and believed that resistance to that demonic element lifted itself out of the world catastrophe in the form of a *kairos*. This *kairos* contained within it elements both of promise and demand in the form of "believing realism." Tillich maintains that instead of such a believing realism— virtually the only category of the religious socialists that Hirsch does not appropriate—Hirsch espouses an "unruptured enthusiasm that robs him of the critical overview and the critical word, that we as Protestant theologians and messengers of the present spiritual situation ought to expect from him."[39]

The Intended Meaning of Religious Socialist Categories
In section three of Part One, Tillich uses an example from theology and an example from philosophy to shed light on what the religious socialists actually intended with some of their categories. In the first place, theologically speaking, they were always concerned to guard against utopianism. Tillich defines utopianism as the absolutization of a finite possibility, a danger that is present in any prophetic-eschatological movement. Tillich and his friends in the socialist movement were keenly aware of this danger, and the *kairos* doctrine was in fact born out of the concern to prevent such an absolutization without giving up the need for human responsibility and passion. It was an attempt to give value to the historical movement and its power to shape the future without becoming utopian. While Hirsch, in Tillich's judgment, recognizes the possibility of

---

38. In his 1926 essay, "Das Dämonische," Tillich systematically explicates his dialectical view of the demonic. There he says: "Die Spannung zwischen Formschöpfung und Formzerstörung, auf der das Dämonische beruht, grenzt es ab gegen das Satanische, in dem die Zerstörung ohne Schöpfung gedacht ist. Gedacht ist—denn das Satanische hat keine Existenz wie das Dämonische. Um Existenz zu haben, müsste es zur Gestalt kommen können, also einen Rest von Schöpfung in sich tragen. Das Satanische ist das im Dämonischen wirksame negative, zerstörische, sinnfeindliche Prinzip, in Isolierung und Vergegenständlichung gedacht....Denn eine Versuchung, die nicht in den schöpferischen Kräften des Kreatürlichen wurzelt—etwa in dem mit dem Erkenntnistrieb verbundenen Machtwillen—, hat keinen Anknüpfungspunkt, ist keine Versuchung, weil sie keine Dialektik, kein Ja und Nein in sich hat. Mythologisch gesprochen ist der Satan der oberste der Dämonen, ontologisch gesprochen ist er das im Dämonischen enthaltene negative Princip." *Das Dämonsiche. Ein Beitrag zur Sinndeutung der Geschichte* (Tübingen: Mohr, 1926; also in *GW* VI, pp. 42-71), *GW* VI, p. 45.

39. "Die Theologie des Kairos," p. 314.

miscarriage within a historical event, he does not find a theological word to guard against such a miscarriage. It would have been Hirsch's task as a theologian to take the same critical stance toward the now victorious political movement in Germany as the religious socialists took against ideological enthusiasm in the socialist movement. Instead Hirsch has taken over the *kairos* teaching in a formal sense only, without its critical substance. The consequence is an unbroken sacramentalism.

Second, philosophically speaking, the religious socialists always struggled against the crass metaphysical materialism which engulfed the worker movement as an anti-religious front at the end of the 19th century. Out of this concern was born the concept of a "believing profanity" and a "latent church." Hirsch, on the other hand, has a one-sided view of materialism, when he talks about the "smut [*Schmutz*] of economic materialism."[40] He reduces the notion of materialism to "economic" materialism without struggling against a "metaphysical" materialism.

Hirsch's use of terms like the "smut of economic materialism" suggests a) that Hirsch is suppressing something that he has not come to terms with personally, and b) that he is unacquainted with economic materialism as a method of inquiry that arose in a struggle against the metaphysical materialism of Feuerbach and was in fact accompanied by a lofty ethical idealism which was ready for martyrdom.[41] Tillich adds: "The avowal of a positive Christianity belongs to your political program. But would you as a theologian not have had the task of unmasking the fate [*Verhängnis*] that accompanies every political espousal of religion and to bring it under as sharp a critique as we did materialism?"[42] Hirsch's theological duty, argues Tillich, would have been to use his conceptual tools "to unmask the ideological misuse that is perpetrated by reactionary forces and by the petit-bourgeois in their anti-proletarian class struggle with the help of religious confession."[43] Behind ideological theism often stands a much smuttier "practical materialism," says Tillich. In his opinion there is no more important task in the present hour than to unmask such an ideology. Instead, Hirsch takes every ideology, positive or negative, at face value—by

40. *Ibid.*, p. 315.

41. *Ibid.*

42. Tillich says: "Für Dich gab es keinen Kampf gegen metaphysischen Materialismus oder Religionsfeindlichkeit. Das Bekenntnis zum positiven Christentum gehört zu Deinem politischen Programm. Aber hättest Du nun nicht als Theologe die Aufgabe gehabt, dass mit jedem politischen Bekenntnis zur Religion verbundene Verhängnis zu enthüllen und unter eine gleich scharfe Kritik zu stellen, wie wir den Materialismus?" *Ibid.*, p. 315.

43. The German reads as follows: "Es wäre Deine theologische Pflicht gewesen, diese Denkmittel zu benutzen, und mit ihrer Hülfe den ideologischen Missbrauch aufzudecken, der von Reaktion und Kleinbürgertum in ihrem antiproletarischen Klassenkampf mit dem religiösen Bekenntnis getrieben worden ist. Es ist doch so, dass hinter dem ideologischen Theismus sich oft ein—nun wirklich schmutziger—praktischer Materialismus verhüllt, während hinter dem materialistischen Atheismus ein heroischer Idealismus stehen kann." *Ibid.*

what it says rather than by what it really is.

Sacramental Distortion of Existentialist and Socratic Philosophy
In the final section of Part One Tillich charges Hirsch with distorting the new existentialist philosophy—a philosophical movement which Hirsch himself defends. There is, first, Hirsch's false critique of Heidegger. Tillich agrees that Heidegger must be criticized from within existentialist philosophy. By his use of abstract historicity Heidegger masks the concrete historical givenness of his own ideas. The fundamental assumption of existentialism is its belief in the primacy of existence in opposition to idealism, which emphasizes existence only insofar as it corresponds to the idea as essence.[44] In his own work, Tillich declares, he tried to formulate his existentialist-historical categories through an analysis of oppression within historical existence. This existential oppression is not overcome through the victory of any one particular historical group. It is the task of every existentialist philosopher to unmask the existential oppression that is present in every historical reality. "In your critique of Heidegger," observes Tillich, "as in your own philosophical stance, you reveal yourself as an enthusiastic idealist, not an existentialist philosopher. Instead of unmasking, you consecrate."[45]

Second, Tillich criticizes Hirsch's demand for a renewal of the Socratic method. Historically everything militates against such a renewal. In contrast to the Socratic situation we live at the end of a rational-autonomous age and are moving into a new period of bondage. We live under the necessities of the late capitalistic organization of the masses that precludes a free discussion of fundamental principles. Tillich maintains that in his use of the Kierkegaardian symbol of Socrates, Hirsch is in fact hiding his real affinity with Nietzsche and his struggle against Socrates. Nietzsche protested against the Socratic method, and, according to Tillich, it is easy to show that many of Hirsch's ideas are already present in Nietzsche's thought. Unlike Socrates, Hirsch denies the critical study of philosophy; otherwise, he would have argued against the current vitalism, irrationalism, and voluntarism in the same way Tillich and the religious socialists spoke up against an emptied rationalism, intellectualism, and mechanism (for which, incidentally, they gained the reproach of fascism).[46]

44. *Ibid.*, p. 316. "Das, was die Existenz zur Existenz macht," says Tillich, "ist das, wodurch sie nicht in der Idee, im Wesen steht. So sah es der zweite Schelling, als er im Anschluss an seine Lehre vom Bösen den Gegensatz beiden Philosophien entdeckte...."
45. Ibid.
46. *Ibid.*, pp. 316-317. What Tillich is in effect blaming Hirsch for, is his lack of self-criticism within his own ideological framework. Tillich is not so much asking Hirsch to surrender his basic theological-political position as to become as self-critical in his stance as Tillich and his colleagues were within Religious Socialism. It is for this reason that Tillich says: "Wir hatten die Bedeutung des Vitalen, des Eros und des Willens mit solchem Nachdruck herausgearbeitet, dass wir uns immer wieder den Vorwurf des Fascismus zugezogen haben. Ich sehe nicht, dass Du die entsprechende umgekehrte Aufgabe von der Philosophie gefordert oder selbst in Angriff genommen hättest." *Ibid.*,

Finally, Tillich attacks Hirsch's teaching concerning *nomos* and the *logos*. Hirsch, Tillich says, robs the *logos* of its critical power on three levels. First, he binds the *logos* to the *nomos* of a historical actuality. Second, he acknowledges the *nomos* of only one particular nation, Germany. Third, Hirsch's *nomos* is subject to change and is dependent on the political power of a particular nation. The result is that the *logos* becomes contingent upon the group that happens to be in power at any given time. Practically this means that "You support those who in a great chorus with Nietzsche say that truth is the expression of the representative power group and its being. This stands in insoluble contradiction to everything Socratic; but also to the *kairos* teaching, which made an effort to base itself on the Socratic method."[47]

What Hirsch calls the *nomos* the religious socialists perceived in terms of the unity of oneness and inexhaustibility (*Einheit von Einheit und Unerschöpflichkeit*). Oneness makes logical perception possible. Inexhaustibility prevents knowledge from ever becoming static. This means that critical control is never lacking. Further, the religious socialists did not bind the *logos* to any one nation but linked it to the structure of an historical constellation in which a particular nation participates. "Fundamentally, it must be said above all that in this way the binding of truth to might is excluded to the extent that every power finds its limit in the collective constellation. No single structure can bind the *logos* to itself, just as no nation can bind God to itself. The first insight we attribute to Plato, the second to Amos."[48]

Finally, the religious socialists never understood the binding of truth to a historical actuality as excluding the notion that "truth" is the relative self-understanding and self-expression of a historical reality. Unlike the religious socialists, Tillich believes Hirsch has not adequately analyzed the distinction between "expression" (*Ausdruck*) and "valuation" or "Interpretation" (*Geltung*) and their relation to each other. Because Hirsch was always more preoccupied with the former (*Ausdruck*), he in fact missed what an event had to say at its deepest level.[49]

p. 317.

47. *Ibid.* In his *Die gegenwärtige geistige Lage,* Hirsch defined *nomos* as "Ordnung, Lebens- und Denkverfasstheit [order, the constitution of life and thought];" and *logos* as "Sich ausspre- chender lebendiger Geist [the self-expression of dynamic-living spirit]." *Horos* he defined as "unüberschreitbare Grenze [the boundary that cannot be crossed]" (p. 5).

48. "Die Theologie des Kairos," p. 317. One should say in defense of Hirsch here that, as we have seen, he also believed in a historical constellation of nations—a community of nations—each one fulfilling a particular God-given role in this constellation.

49. This is a difficult passage and bears citation in the German original: "Drittens haben wir unter Bindung der Wahrheit an eine geschichtliche Wirklichkeit niemals verstanden, dass die Wahrheit nichts als Ausdruck oder Selbstinterpretation dieser geschichtlichen Wirklichkeit sein soll. Wir haben das Verhältnis von 'Ausdruck' und 'Geltung' oft behandelt und sind zu der Auffassung gekommen, dass es für den Erkennenden nur *eine* Intention, nämlich die Geltung geben darf; dass aber gerade dann, wenn er am meisten und strengsten auf die Geltung, das An-sich, das Objektive

What is at stake in this first part of Tillich's letter to Hirsch is precisely the salvaging of his own theological method. Hirsch's book has revealed to Tillich the overwhelming fact that his own categories can, at least formally, be used to support a political program that is opposite to his own. It is for this reason that Tillich spends so much time, often somewhat repetitiously, showing how Hirsch has emptied particularly the *kairos* teaching of its intended meaning. This is especially clear in Tillich's concluding remarks to Part One: "I deny that the concepts themselves provide the possibility for such an application. You have had to remove a decisive element out of every one of them in order to force them into the service of your theological and philosophical intentions. Against that I must guard myself and want to guard myself further, by considering individual problems."[50]

One further observation needs to be made at this point. Tillich's charges against Hirsch in this first part of the letter rest on the assumption that Hirsch is in fact basically working with the same theological and philosophical categories that Tillich and the religious socialists presuppose, and that Hirsch's concept of the "hour" is, formally at least, the same as Tillich's concept of the *kairos*. Tillich's individual arguments rest on this basic charge: that Hirsch has taken over Tillich's concepts without understanding them and has thus distorted them. This is, of course, the basic question that needs to be answered: Is it in fact true that Hirsch has plagiarized these categories from his political opponents and is working within the same theological-philosophical framework? We have shown how Hirsch's stance in 1933 is in continuity with his earlier thought. The thesis of our study is that, while he owes a great deal to Tillich, the charge of plagiarism cannot be sustained. Hirsch is a highly independent thinker and his categories, although bearing some formal similarity with Tillich's own conceptions due to a common intellectual heritage, are substantially different in some crucial aspects. These differences are due in no small part to the different theological presuppositions Hirsch brings to his political convictions.

Revelation, Risk and the Kairos

Part Two of Tillich's open letter is divided into five sections: the nature of revelation, the need for a sociological analysis, the concepts of nation and state, the freedom and independence of the church, and the necessary dialectic of reservation and obligation. In the first of these Tillich asks whether Hirsch has not in

---

gerichtet ist, sich die Ausdruckskraft seines Denkens einstellt. Und zwar um so mehr, je weniger er sie beabsichtigt und je mehr er doch zugleich gefüllt ist mit der inneren Mächtigkeit seiner Gegenwart. Aber nicht diese inner Mächtigkeit ist das in jedem Erkennen Gemeinte, sondern die Wahrheit. Du hast diese Unterscheidung nicht herausgearbeitet, Du konntest es nicht, da Du selbst mehr um 'Ausdruck' als um 'Geltung' bemüht warst und darum—das ist die richtende Dialektik des Wahrheitsgedankens—auch den tiefsten Ausdruck dessen, was geschieht, verfehlt hast." *Ibid.,* pp. 317-318.

50. *Ibid.,* p. 318.

fact made contemporary German events into a source of revelation standing alongside the Bible. If this is the case, says Tillich, then those who perceive these same events differently would have to be excluded from a revelatory event. They would, like the Jewish Christians, find themselves with lesser rights in the German Evangelical church.

Tillich once more betrays a certain uneasiness and defensiveness about his own *kairos* category. "I ask myself," he ponders, "whether such a view can in any way be justified by the *kairos* concept. I do not see how, but I do admit that we did not in the last years adequately pursue the problems that arise here, and it is for that reason that such deviations of interpretation were not clearly enough excluded."[51] To the extent that Hirsch's book has forced a clarification of this problem, Tillich concedes, he is thankful for it.

Hirsch's book forced Tillich to understand and formulate more adequately the relation between "revelation" and *kairos,* the aspect of "being grasped" by a revelatory truth, and the element of "human risk." Revelation has two sides, Tillich claims. There is revelation *per se,* in which sense it is an objective, exclusive, and final criterion of one's thought and action. There can be no other revelation beside it. But revelation can become concrete for someone only by actualizing itself. In this more subjective sense it is part of a *"kairos-revelation"* correlation. The *kairos* is the situation from which humans enter into the revelatory experience. Every new situation changes the *kairos*-revelation correlation but not the revelation itself. "Revelation is that to which I know myself as being subjected, as the final criterion for my thought and action in an unconditional way. The *kairos,* the historical hour, can therefore never be revelation in itself; it can only point out the entrance to a new revelation-correlation. It marks the moment in which the meaning of revelation discloses itself anew for knowing and action, in which, for instance, the final criterion of truth becomes visible anew in the face of a temporal constellation, as for example the cross of Christ over against the capitalistic or nationalistic demonic."[52]

Take, for example, the category of risk (*Wagnis*), which is central to Hirsch's political theology. Tillich is willing to allow for the use of this term for a new

---

51. *Ibid.* Hopper argues that "Tillich's discovery, in the Hirsch affair, of the need to differentiate more sharply than he had between revelation and the kairos certainly revealed a major flaw in his earlier systematic efforts." He goes on to say that "Beyond this, however, one must note that the subtleties of Tillich's thought appear to have been too finely drawn to be determinative in the church's fight against National Socialism. It is ironic that in spite of his own firm stand against Nazism aspects of Tillich's philosophical and theological work lent themselves to the German Christian cause by fixing a source of revelation in general history and therefore in 'the natural orders of race, folk, and nation.'" Unlike the Roman Catholic Church, which also endorsed a natural revelation but was saved through its "own strong ecclesiastical structure" from "the 'enthusiasm of the moment,'" Tillich in his theoretical work was not rooted in such an ecclesiastical structure. "His theological appeal was experienced on a highly intellectual and individualistic level and never reached down into the life of the people at large." *Tillich: A Theological Portrait,* pp. 90-91.

52. "Die Theologie des Kairos," p. 318.

self-disclosure of revelation on the condition that a) Hirsch does not call the "standing-in-the-revelation itself" risk, and b) that Hirsch recognizes the relativity of that which is risked in all circumstances. "Revelation is prior to not the object of risk taking," explains Tillich.[53] Revelation is that which grasps me before my risk taking. While risk has its place in the *kairos*, it does not determine the revelation itself. In other words, the (1) revelatory community is not dependent upon the (2) risking community. There may be factions within the theological community but one group cannot exclude the other from revelation.

Tillich, Hirsch, and Barth are representatives of three such theological factions, each faction being a different form of risk taking. Tillich once again contrasts the three approaches:

> Risk carries within itself the consciousness of possible failure. It is neither unconditional nor exclusive. So, for example, in our case: For you and others kairos is that which you characterize as the "German hour"; for us it was that which one could characterize as the "hour of socialism" and of which according to our perception the German occurrence is a part that cannot in any way be understood in isolation from the whole. For Barth, who, without intending to do so, therein pays his tribute to the kairos, it is the hour of the liberation of the church from the secular elements which forced their way in during the bourgeois centuries, which is of course possible only because secularism as a historical phenomenon has become fragile in itself. All three interpretations of the kairos are forms of risk.[54]

It is evident from this statement that Tillich considers all three positions—his own as well as those of Hirsch and Barth—to be forms of risk; yet it seems here that Barth's stance is seen by both Tillich and Hirsch as a qualitatively different one from either of theirs. Unlike Barth's, Tillich's "hour of socialism" and Hirsch's nationalism or "hour of Germany" are both explicitly "political" options. They focus on the structure of the state.[55]

53. *Ibid.* "Offenbarung ist Prius, nicht Gegenstand des Wagnisses."
54. *Ibid.*, p. 319. It is interesting to read Barth's interpretation of Hirsch's concept of "risk": "In fact, in Hirsch there is lacking all and every 'assurance and security' whether from biblical exegesis, whether from connection with Church tradition. In fact, everything is not only basically, but also manifestly, 'risk'; that is, free speculation or brooding, a speculation into which 'the Gospel' and Luther are drawn at particular points, in which they have their very important and worthy place, yet speculation, arbitrary experiment, preaching on a theme and without a text (it might be that one would wish to take as a text the 'hour' experienced by Hirsch), a theologically valueless 'Kairos philosophy,' which indeed clears out all the theological elements like that of his religio-social antipode, Paul Tillich. And it is this which, as the basic thesis not only of Hirsch's book but also of the teaching and behavior of Müller's Church government and of the German-Christians in general, is their basic error." "On the Situation, 1933-34," *The German Church Conflict*, p. 31.
55. The "non-political" nature of Barth's theology, or its deflection into the "abstract-transcendent," as Hirsch and Tillich tend to caricature Barth's view over against their own, is a

Tillich's concern, as expressed above, is with whether Hirsch intends to exclude the other two factions—the Barthians and the religious socialists—from a valid place within the German Evangelical church. According to Tillich, the (1) "exclusiveness of the criterion [Revelation]" and the (2) "relativity of the concrete decision [Risk]" lie on different levels and must be kept distinct. His struggle with and opposition to Hirsch's book has clarified this distinction for him. "Attention to the first makes a theologian into a theologian, it gives him the final criterion; standing in the second gives him historical power and nearness to the present."[56] Hirsch, in Tillich's view, has unfortunately blurred the distinction by making the second primary and the first invisible.

The Need for a Sociological Analysis

In the second section of Part Two Tillich concentrates on a sociological-historical critique of Hirsch's book. What Tillich finds astonishing is that Hirsch could write a book about the present spiritual-intellectual (*geistige*) situation without giving a sociological analysis of the groups and classes which represent the various religious and intellectual trends in Germany and Europe. Many of Hirsch's judgments, says Tillich, are comprehensible only if one assumes that he has consciously or unconsciously repressed well-known socio-logical insights. Tillich adds that sociology is one of the best weapons against an unbridled enthusiasm.[57] Such a sociological analysis would have forced Hirsch to recognize the conflict between the bourgeoisie and the proletariat, the world economic crisis and the resulting crisis of the middle classes and the formation of a new social type—the unemployed. Instead of using images such as "spring" to describe the events of 1933, he would have had to employ the image of "late fall." He would have had to admit the worldwide nature of these phenomena rather than restricting himself to the crisis within Germany. His positive valuation of the present events might not have changed substantially but

---

highly debatable interpretation. This view has been severely questioned by the controversial rein-terpretation of Barth's theology by Friedrich-Wilhelm Marquardt, who argues that Barth's theology cannot in fact be separated from his radical social politics. Commenting on Tillich's and Barth's relation to the German Social Democratic Party, Friedrich-Wilhelm Marquardt says: "In contrast to Tillich, he [Barth] understood his socialism in terms of *praxis*, not in terms of religious and social theory." Marquardt asserts that "Barth's theology is in fact rooted (as Barth was aware on the theo-retical level) in his political involvement (*praxis*)." "Socialism in the Theology of Karl Barth," *Karl Barth and Radical Politics*, edited and translated by George Hunsinger (Philadelphia: The Westminster Press, 1976), pp. 48, 49. The late Third Reich church historian Klaus Scholder strongly disagrees with the Marquardt interpretation, maintaining that Barth's main point was that *theology* stands prior to *politics*. Scholder goes on to show, however, that precisely *because* of this priority of theology to politics, it had a powerful political potency in that it could critique ideologies of both left and right the way Hirsch's political theology and Tillich's Religious Socialism were unable to do in the 1920s and 1930s. See Scholder, *Die Kirchen und das dritte Reich*, pp. 546ff, 833/80n.

56. "Die Theologie des Kairos," p. 319.

57. *Ibid.*

at least he would have had some scientific (*wissenschaftliche*) basis for his position. "If you as theological historian had wanted to explicate the spiritual-intellectual situation of the present, you alone could have performed a great service if you would have paid attention to other sociological interconnections than those we see [on the surface], and if you would have pointed out the present sociological structure in central-Europe as background for the current spiritual-intellectual situation."[58] Hirsch would then have had to acknowledge the all-pervasive tension that exists beneath the present apparent political unity. This would have been a "genuine, concrete existential historical analysis."

This, says Tillich, would also have prevented Hirsch from making hostile innuendos and uncontrolled judgments about foreign lands, such as his comment that cultural imperialism is a "specifically French [Welsh]" idea, not to mention his negative remarks about Russia. "And when you are rightly roused to indignation over the 'lies of the world conscience' and the 'guilty silence of the churches concerning Versailles,' you could at least have called attention to the indignation evoked in the whole world—within the church and outside of it—for example, by the silence of the German church on the day of the Jewish boycotts."[59]

Tillich declares that it is Hirsch's unbroken sacramentalism that has prevented him from making a distinction between the passing of race laws, which he (Hirsch) supports on philosophical and theological grounds, and race hatred as clearly as the religious socialists distinguished between the necessity of the class struggle in capitalism and class hatred. With this interesting observation Tillich seems to suggest that there is in fact a certain structural parallel between the role of class struggle within socialism and the function of race laws within National Socialism.[60] Ideologically, despite their profound differences, the class struggle is to the proletarian state what the racial struggle is to the nationalist state.

58. *Ibid.*, p. 320.
59. *Ibid.*
60. *Ibid.* Klaus Scholder makes much of some of these structural and formal similarities between National Socialism and Marxist socialism. He says, for instance, that "In der Ausführung dieser These argumentierte Hitler ähnlich wie auf der anderen Seite der Marxismus. Während dort der Faschismus zu einem Instrument der kapitalistischen Weltverschwörung wird, erschien bei Hitler der Marxismus als Instrument der jüdischen Weltverschwörung. Nationalisozialistischer Rassenkampf und marxistischer Klassenkampf bekamen bis in die Formulierung hinein den gleichen ideologischen und politischen Stellenwert....Statt der proletarischen Masse gegen ihre kapitalistischen Unterdrücker stand hier die deutsche Masse gegen ihr jüdischen Unterdrücker." *Die Kirchen und das Dritte Reich,* pp. 101-102. While there may be some validity in Scholder's observation, this should not disguise the fact, particularly in the case of Tillich and Hirsch, that they perceived their approach to political ethics to be both formally and materially, methodologically and substantively different. This despite the fact that Tillich was more ready to admit similarities between them than was Hirsch. For a discussion of the similarities and differences between the political theologies of Tillich and of Hirsch see Gunda Schneider-Flume, "Kritische Theologie contra theologisch-politischen Offenbarungsglauben," *Evangelische Theologie* 2,33(March-April 1973), pp. 114-137.

Nation and State

In the third section of Part Two Tillich examines Hirsch's notions of the nation and the state. "At no place in your book," remarks Tillich, "does it seem to me that there is so much constructive work that still needs to be done as here."[61] Tillich argues that at the basis of Hirsch's book and thought there are three identifications which Hirsch assumes but nowhere clearly demonstrates and yet without which his whole conceptual pyramid crumbles. These three presuppositions are the identification of the "holy *horos*" with the origin, of origin (*Ursprung*) with nation (*Volk*), and the nation with the bond of blood (*Blutbund*).

1. Take, for instance, the first of these identifications: that of the "holy *horos*" and the origin. According to Hirsch, "The boundary is powerful in the whole of our human-historical life." The religious socialists also spoke repeatedly of the "abyss" or the sphere of "inexhaustibility"—that part of the structure of our existence which gives meaning to our life and goes beyond a rationalistic form-philosophy. But in contrast to the religious socialists, Hirsch restricts the holy *horos* to the origin.[62] He thereby limits the *horos* to the "wherefrom" of existence and leaves out the dimension of the "whereto."

Surely, says Tillich, the "holy *horos*," to use Hirsch's terminology, must break out of and through the boundary of the origin. "Indeed," he adds, "you recognize the fact that the holy horos is able to consume [*verzehren kann*] the natural-historical, but nowhere do you intimate that it can transcend it, can lead to a new historical reality which is no longer an origin-bound actualization."[63] Hirsch seems to hold that at no time within one's historical existence can an individual escape from the power of his own origin. For Tillich there exists such a possibility; the early Christian community is an example where the "whereto" breaks through the "wherefrom." The early church and the New Testament community represent an estrangement from the origin and the breaking in of a new theonomy.

2. What bothers Tillich about Hirsch's second identification—that of origin with nation—is that Hirsch seems to think of the nation in terms of the European

61. "Die Theologie des Kairos," p. 321.
62. The German reads as follows: "'Am Ganzen unseres menschlich geschichtlichen Lebens ist die Grenze mächtig. Ueberall in ihm offenbart sie sich...ihr Schein des Denkens Licht, ihre Glut des Lebens Blut', sagst Du in Uebereinstimmung mit dem, was wir über den Abgrund, die Unerschöpflichkeit, den sinngebenden Gehalt unserer Existenz gegenüber einer rationalistischen Formphilosophie gesagt haben. Aber warum beschränkst Du dann den Horos, der am Ganzen unseres geschichtlichen Lebens mächtig sein soll, auf den Ursprung?" *Ibid.*, p. 321.
63. For Tillich the divine is not bound to ethnicity or nationality: "Die heilige Grenze als 'des Lebens Blut' glüht in Franziskus und Buddha nicht mit der Macht ihres Ursprungs, sondern in der Macht eines ausdrücklichen Bruches mit ihrem Ursprung. Zwar weisst Du darum, dass der heilige Horos den natürlich-geschichtlichen verzehren kann, aber nirgends wird bei Dir angedeutet, dass er ihn transzendieren kann, dass er zu einer neuen geschichtlichen aber nicht mehr ursprungsgebundenen Verwirklichung führen kann." *Ibid.*, p. 321.

nation-state, a recent phenomenon which has come into existence only since the French Revolution. Tillich once again admits a weakness in his earlier thought:

> Now there can be no doubt that the nation-state in this sense is the unmediated, historically powerful reality of today. And I would concede that Religious Socialism with its interest in the social order of society gave too little attention to the nation state and the powers of the origin concentrated in it (even I in my last book, [*The Socialist Decision*]). I also concede, further, that there can be moments in history in which the destiny [*Schicksal*] of one nation can signify a kairos, a transcending historical hour, to be religiously interpreted, a promise and a demand not only for itself but also for the world. Had your book said only this, I could have spared myself the following critique. But it says much more and something much different. It says, for example, that origin and nation are identical.[64]

To identify nation with origin, says Tillich, one would need to include under the former all the various historical groups such as kindreds, tribes, blood-related groups, races, estates, classes, language groups, and so on, all of them representing powers of the origin. Hirsch does not include all these diverse groups but restricts his notion of nation to a 150-year-old phenomenon. It is because of this, says Tillich, that Hirsch's "metaphysical absolutization" of the nation as the only actualization of the holy *horos* is so problematic.

3. In his third identification—that of nation with the bond of blood—the concept of blood-bond is ill-defined and acquires a type of salvific significance for a certain segment of humanity. For Hirsch it is that which resists the onrush of cosmopolitan "European-American culture."[65] Tillich particularly objects to Hirsch's seeming identification of the "bond-of-blood" with the German nation

---

64. *Ibid.*, pp. 321-322. The German word *"Volk"* as used by the political theologians of the 1920s and by Tillich here as well is difficult to translate accurately into English. To translate it simply as "nation" is to suggest too narrow a geographic-political entity in the sense of the modern nation-state. On the other hand, to translate it merely as "people" is to lose the political dimension of the word. It might best be translated as "national-people." I use a variety of translations—including nation, nationality, a people, peoplehood, folk—depending on the context.

65. In Tillich's words, "Du gibst dieser Identifikation das grösste Gewicht, indem Du behauptest, dass durch die Idee des Blutbundes dem Sturz der 'euramerikanischen Kultur von Klippe zu Klippe' das 'Bis hierher und nicht weiter' entgegengerufen wird. Die Idee des Blutbundes hat also geradezu Heilsbedeutung für einen Teil der Menschheit. Umso wichtiger wäre es, klar herauszuarbeiten, um was es sich dabei handelt. Offenbar meinst Du nicht die Rassengesetzgebung, die ja praktisch nur gegen die Juden gerichtet ist und nicht gegen die übrigen Völker des euramerikanischen Kulturkreises. Blutbund muss also etwas Engeres meinen, entweder die spezifische Blutsbeschaffenheit des sogenannten nordischen Menschen, die aber einerseits nichtdeutsche Völker umfasst, andererseits für grosse Gruppen des deutschen Volkes nicht zutrifft. So bliebe also nur das deutsche Volk selbst und die Forderung, jede Blutsvermischung über seine Grenzen hinaus zu verhindern und Träger schon vorhandener Blutmischungen dieser Art im Sinne der Rassengesetzgebung zu entrechten." *Ibid.*, p. 322.

itself, with the intent of preventing any and every blood mixture beyond its own boundaries, depriving those with such a mixture of certain rights through race laws. However, such steps would tear apart more than a 1000 years of tradition, says Tillich, a tradition that sees the Christian Western world as representing an individual family of people, formed in their origin through Christianity. Has Hirsch, then, as a theologian been called "to superimpose the natural-historical blood community onto the sacramental blood community of Christianity which has been established through the Lord's supper?" Tillich asks. "Would it not have been your task as theologian exactly at the point where you wanted to emphasize so strongly the power of blood origin, to work out the limit of its powers with the help of the symbol of the Lord's supper?"[66] As we have found in our study of Hirsch's thought, Hirsch does not intend to replace the sacramental community of Christianity with the natural-historical blood community, as Tillich here suggests. Rather, Hirsch clearly separates these two communities (one is spiritual and the other is earthly-historical) and has a much stronger conviction than does Tillich that all human beings are bound and destined by natural-historical distinctions and blood ties.

Tillich now proceeds to a concept that is of pivotal importance for Hirsch's theory of the state, and one that Tillich considers to be the only truly original aspect of Hirsch's socio-political thought—namely, the idea of a "hidden sovereign" (*Verborgenen Souverain*). Tillich suspects that Hirsch uses this concept to give substance to his view of the state and to provide a legitimate basis for "revolution"—a right that the old Lutheran teaching denied. Tillich's references to Lutheran theology at this point suggest not only his own disagreement with traditional Lutheran social and political theory, but the widely differing interpretations of Luther that support Tillich's and Hirsch's divergent methodologies. Referring to the development of Lutheran theology during the Weimar period, Tillich asks Hirsch:

> Have you never asked yourself the question...How it is possible that a church which through hundreds of years has subjected itself to every higher authority, including the feudal-dynastic one which was the most ruinous for the nation, and taught an unconditional obedience precisely to these "bad authorities," forgets this teaching at the moment where a state is created in which other than the old classes represent the authority? At the moment when certain groups lose their inherited privileges, Lutheranism, as represented by Young National Lutheran theology, develops a teaching of "conditional obedience." Would not a questioning concerning the theological character of both doctrines have been in order here?[67]

66. *Ibid.*
67. *Ibid.* Tillich's own relationship to Lutheranism—his more mystical interpretation of Luther, on the one hand, and his rejection of the socially conservative elements within Lutheranism in favor

Tillich calls Hirsch's "hidden sovereign" a mystical reality which provides an unlimited right to revolution, free from all objective norms, a right that far exceeds the old Calvinist or even the socialist theory of the state. While Hirsch's category is meant to create a sense of obligation and responsibility on the part of the rulers, it is ill-suited for such a task. The old divine-right-of-kings and sovereignty-of-the-people categories, both in their own way were much better suited to providing such standards for human action. Hirsch's "hidden sovereign" lacks precision; the rulers who are allegedly subordinated to it in fact define it the way they want to. "Would not a realism which sought a genuine anti-autocratic corrective have been more right and honorable precisely at this point, than an enthusiasm which declares that a return to autocracy is 'unlikely'?" asks Tillich.[68] Such an autocracy, adds Tillich, can be prevented only by the addition of aristocratic or democratic correctives.

The religious socialists recognized this fact a long time ago when they argued that a democracy must be seen not as constitutive but as corrective in the creation of a state. Tillich reminds Hirsch of German thinkers such as Hegel, who contrasted the Christian-German concept of freedom with the pre-Christian Asiatic principle of despotism and the democratic ideal of the value of the individual. He suggests that Hirsch's task as a German Christian philosopher of history would have been to draw people's attention to this tradition, rather than making a "declaration of hate against everything democratic without any critical restriction."[69]

As far as Hirsch's defense of totalitarianism is concerned, Tillich agrees theoretically that a totalitarian state must have a worldview or myth as its basis. However, there are some serious logical problems. First, a totalitarian state must be led by charismatic personalities who make decisions on the basis of "creative accountability" (*schöpferischen Verantwortlichkeit*). But how can such personalities appear in the first place? They can appear only, as Hirsch himself admits, through a process of resistance against the previously entrenched political and social structures. Hirsch in fact considers himself to have become strong through his own resistance against the political and spiritual-intellectual powers of the preceding period. "Democracy gave room, certainly too much room, for such opposition," Tillich asserts.[70] Tillich is keenly

of a prophetic interpretation of the "Protestant principle," on the other; as well as his attempt to move beyond Lutheranism in some crucial areas—have already been discussed in an earlier chapter. For a discussion of Tillich's own espousal of Lutheran theology, see James Luther Adams, "Paul Tillich on Luther," *Interpreters of Luther: Essays in Honor of Wilhelm Pauck,* pp. 304-334.

68. "Die Theologie des Kairos," p. 324. Tillich here refers Hirsch to his article, "Der Staat als Erwartung und Forderung," *Religiöse Verwirklichung* (Berlin: Furche, 1930). Also in *GW* IX, pp. 123-138.

69. "Die Theologie des Kairos," p. 324.

70. *Ibid.,* p. 325. In Tillich's biting critique of the spirit of capitalism in his 1926 book *The Religious Situation,* for instance, he establishes the connection between capitalism and democracy and says: "The pillar of democracy is the middle class and particularly that part of the middle class

aware of the shortcomings of Western democracy; nevertheless, he is more willing than Hirsch to defend the Western notion of individual freedom and subjectivity. It was democracy which created space for the development of the very charismatic personalities which now head the totalitarian revolution. Paradoxically, however, totalitarianism itself allows no such room for the development of nonconformist charismatic leadership.

Second, there is no possibility for spiritual-intellectual renewal within the totalitarian context. Tillich agrees with Hirsch that religious leadership is poorly served by bourgeois professors and "pampered literati," adding that "The genuine bearers of the spirit have voluntarily or involuntarily remained at a distance from both forms of existence for the past century. I emphasize in contrast to many liberals that uncertainty, persecution, homelessness, prison, and threat of death have never been able to hurt the genuine spirit and will serve it now as well. But there exists here a boundary."[71] Tillich goes on to say that for spiritual health to exist there must be room for the spirit to say No. Such a possibility does not exist within a totalitarian state.

The Freedom and Independence of the Church

In the fourth section of Part Two Tillich elaborates on the need for the church to have room for deviation and nonconformity (*Ausweichraum*), a prerequisite for both early Christianity and Protestantism. Tillich charges Hirsch with allowing the Catholic church room for such an independent existence within the German nation while denying the same for the Protestant church. It is true, observes Tillich, that if one assumes that a worldview (or myth) is required for the existence of a totalitarian state then one must ask with Hirsch whether "this myth 'is the sustaining, natural, historical life-basis [*Lebensgrund*] and creative space for the evangelical faith and the evangelical spirit for the German people [*deutsche Menschen*]', whether the new picture of the German man and the old picture of the Christian man agree with one another?"[72] Tillich is interested in the methodological principle lying behind this question: "I do not have to examine whether they do. I have to concern myself, as in the whole letter, only with the methodological, with the theological principle. And in this regard I ask: Who is to decide this? A genuine decision can be made only in a situation where a No is possible."[73]

which exercises economic leadership, in whose hands lies the control of capital. Middle class democracy is the political expression of capitalism. Capital creates majorities and with majorities it creates political power," p. 128. Translation by H. Richard Niebuhr.

71. *Ibid.*, p. 325. In the words of Tillich, "Um bedroht und verfolgt zu werden, muss der Geist erst einmal da sein; und um da zu sein, muss er einen Raum haben, in dem er durch Nein-sagen zum Ja-sagen kommen kann. Es ist der erste Schritt alles Geistes, nein zu sagen zum unmittelbar Gegebenen."

72. *Ibid.*, p. 326.

73. *Ibid.* As we have seen, Hirsch also allows for a "No" but he rejects a no in the liberal sense,

If (1) the *state* says No to the above question—that is, whether the two pictures agree with one another—then, in a totalitarian situation, the church will have to surrender its own myth in favor of the myth of the state. The state may disguise its No and the rulers may wipe out or mask aspects of the Christian picture that do not agree with the new picture of the German man. There is, however, the other possibility that (2) the *church* seriously questions the agreement of the two pictures. Would Hirsch in such a case be willing to allow the Protestant church the same room for deviation from the norm as he does the Catholic church? And if so, what becomes of the totalitarian claim of the state since the church also claims the whole person? These are the crucial questions which Protestantism and Christianity must face in the presence of the current totalitarian demands of the German state but which Hirsch "enthusiastically avoids."

Tillich suggests that there is in fact an area of agreement between himself, Barth, and Hirsch, when Hirsch claims that the state has taken over the social and cultural activities of the church, leaving the church in a better position to devote itself to its true task. But he and Barth went further than Hirsch in describing the positive nature of the church's task. "Besides the proclamation of the word and meditation we gave to the church the task of actualizing in itself symbolic-representationally the Christian concept of love in social structures and thus being for the state an impressive pointer to the limits of all coercive dealings and to a reality of a higher order."[74] There could even now be some agreement between them if Hirsch would admit to allowing room for such a Christian stance within a totalitarian state. But no such unity is imaginable as long as Hirsch maintains that the only way to keep the church from becoming a dead church is for all the preachers, workers, and genuinely pious people to give themselves unreservedly, with everything they possess, their work and their talents, to the newly evolving structures and forms of national life.[75] It is this monolithic vision of the church that Tillich finds so objectionable. In a noteworthy passage Tillich voices the importance of allowing for different forms of risk within the church:

where everything is seen in terms of "yes" and "no" in a dialectical way. Hirsch's "Yes" or "No" is the Kierkegaardian existential "either-or." Here Barth, interestingly, agrees with Hirsch when he says: "Hirsch is quite right: 'There is only the Either-Or.'" Barth, "On the Situation, 1933-34," *The German Church Conflict*, p. 33.

74. "Die Theologie des Kairos," p. 326.

75. *Ibid.*, pp. 326-327. The German reads: "Keinerle Einigung ist aber möglich mit folgenden Sätzen von Dir: 'Allein Führung als heisser Wille..., die Verkündiger und die kirchlichen Helfer und Arbeiter und alle lebendigen Frommen mit allem, was sie an Gut und Arbeit und Gaben haben, in die werdenden Formen und Gestaltungen volkhaftstaatlichen Lebens hinüberzureissen, kann unsere Kirche davor bewahren, jetzt eine tote Kirche zu werden....'" p. 327.

Whether the church is alive or dead is dependent upon the power with which she anticipates the kingdom of God, and tries to actualize the kingdom of God in an anticipatory way appropriate to the hour; it is dependent upon nothing else. The judgment concerning which is the hour and what it looks like is risk [*Wagnis*]. It can be a sign of great vitality when different forms of risk are undertaken in the same church and struggle with each other. If you declare that a church is dead when it does not singlemindedly go along with your own form of risk-taking, then you claim that it is more than risk-taking, then you do not place yourself and your risking under the cross but raise it to the rank of a revelation beside the cross.[76]

It becomes clear once again from this passage that at the heart of the differences between Hirsch and Tillich is not only a different concept of the nature of the church but a different conception of the kingdom of God and how it is to be realized. For Tillich the kingdom of God is an eschatological-historical reality which has relevance for the political structuring of society and for which human beings have some responsibility. For Hirsch the kingdom of God is a spiritual reality that is totally independent from human political striving.[77] If it has any relevance it is only through the individual conscience.

Reservation and Obligation

Finally, in the fifth section of Part Two Tillich recalls his own distinction between (1) Religious reservation (*Reservatum religiosum*) and (2) Religious obligation (*Obligatum religiosum*).[78] The attitude of the New Testament church toward the state was primarily one of reservation and, as Hirsch rightly states, was one-sided and conditioned by the times. Because of its situation the church could at that time feel no obligation for the nation, state, culture, and society. But Hirsch unfortunately reverses this and stresses obligation without reservation. He relegates reservation to the individual spiritual realm: "You indeed give to the individual a Reservatum, the personal relation to God; but not to the church, which you deny an independent historical place. Therewith, however, you supercede it [*hebst Du sie auf*], make it powerless over against the world-

76. *Ibid.*, p. 327.

77. Hirsch consistently held this position to the end of his life. In an article entitled "Gottesreich und Menschenreich," which appeared in a *Festgabe aus Pädagogik und Theologie für Helmuth Kittel zum 70. Geburtstag* in 1972, Hirsch says the following: "Die These aber, welche dieser unserm evangelischen Glauben verderbenden Entartung am sichersten entgegenwirkt, ist die, dass das Reich Gottes niemals, in keinen Stadium der Geschichte, ein Menschenreich werden wird, sondern immerdar das durch die Todesgrenze verhüllte Geheimnis bleibt, welches in den dem Evangelium glaubenden Herzen und Gewissen sein heimliches Leben hat." (Dortmund: W. Crüwell, 1972), p. 154.

78. Tillich is referring here to his 1923 article "Grundlinien des Religiösen Sozialismus" *Blätter für Religiösen Sozialismus*, p. 96.

views or myths which carry the totalitarian state."[79]

Protestantism, according to Tillich, could not exist without reservation. "Religious Socialism knew," recalls Tillich, "as it adopted the teaching of Reservatum religiosum, that it dare never annul the religious element in socialism; that the church is something distinct even from the *kairos*; that is, from the promise and the demand that it envisioned in the social and spiritual restructuring of society in the distant foreseeable future. You have appropriated the Obligatum, but at the price of the Reservatum—the accusation [*Vorwurf*] that in essence is the theme of my whole letter."[80]

Tillich alludes to Hirsch's last letter in which Hirsch similarly avoids addressing the above problems. Hirsch maintains that he does not need an attitude of reservation over against present events in Germany because "one's personal relation to God can give one the courage to enter an historical movement with an unbroken Yes."[81] Tillich remarks that he and others are shocked and repelled by Hirsch's whole intellectual direction, especially by sentences like the following: "Where we, out of faith that is obedient to this truth (of the gospel), have the courage with our yes to enter into a human-historical [actuality], there the unfathomable grandeur of truth accompanies us and holds sway over this human-historical in its own way."[82]

Tillich agrees with Hirsch that the Christian must risk involvement in a finite possibility. But this does not give us the right "to assert an unbroken religious and theological yes to this finiteness." As Christians, and particularly as theologians, we dare not fall into an enthusiasm which gives an unqualified yes to something that demands both a yes and a no. Tillich makes a final succinct comparison between himself, the religious socialists, and Hirsch:

It would be wrong for us not to want to make a decision at all because of this, even a religious and theological decision in the sense of risk, to avoid in our theology the judgment that befalls everything human-historical. Neither you nor we have attempted to avoid such [risk]. That is what unites us. You, however, have said yes, while we could say yes only together with a manifold no; not because we considered our cause as worse, it was after all our risk,

79. "Die Theologie des Kairos," p. 327.

80. *Ibid.*, p. 327. What is at stake here, of course, in Tillich's defense of the notion of *Reservatum religiosum*, is one of the central concepts of his whole theology; namely, the category of the "Protestant Principle."

81. *Ibid.* Besides this brief illusion I have no record of this letter by Hirsch to Tillich.

82. The German sentence in its context is as follows: "Ich zitiere den entsprechenden Satz Deines Buches: 'Wo wir aus dem diese Wahrheit (des Evangeliums) gehorchenden Glauben heraus den Mut haben, mit unserem Ja in ein Menschlich-Geschichtliches hinein zu gehen, da geht die unergründliche Hoheit der Wahrheit mit uns und waltet nun nach ihrer Weise an diesem Menschlich-Geschichtlichen.' Zu dem ganzen Gedankengang kann ich nur sagen, dass nicht nur ich, sondern auch andere von ihm erschreckt und zurückgestossen waren." "Die Theologie des Kairos," pp. 327-328.

but because we believed that from the point of the Eternal nothing else could be said about and to a finite reality.[83]

Tillich concludes his long letter with a reference to a personal letter that Hirsch had at one time sent to him, in which he challenged Tillich to write a book that would benefit Germany in its present crisis. Tillich comments that he hopes this public letter will satisfy such a need more adequately than Hirsch's book and many other current writings which are of lesser worth than Hirsch's. He hopes this letter will have an influence on many Germans and help make "believing realists" out of present "enthusiasts." This would be the greatest service he could give to Germany, especially if it could aid in lessening the terrible danger of disappointment that always follows such enthusiasm, a danger that Hirsch unfortunately has helped to intensify rather than mitigate.

A Brief Restatement and Clarification in Tillich's Second Letter

Before turning to the second document in the debate of 1934-35—Hirsch's response to Tillich's devastating attack—we need to consider briefly the third and final document in the controversy: Tillich's "Um was es geht: Antwort an Emanuel Hirsch," which leaves out some of the more personal and irate overtones of the first letter; it appeared in the May 1935 issue of *Theologische Blätter*. This brief restatement of Tillich's fundamental position over against Hirsch is divided into three main parts following a short introductory paragraph.

In the introduction Tillich makes the comment that Hirsch's letter to Stapel combines "defense with attack, the personal with the substantive, individual things with larger points of view." "The attitude of the whole letter," adds Tillich, "above all, the human, gratifying, and conciliatory concluding section makes it possible for me to summarize in more economic form the meaning of my attack on his book, which was not fully grasped by Hirsch."[84] In a footnote Tillich observes that nothing of this reconciling spirit, unfortunately, is evident in the person to whom Hirsch addressed his letter (Stapel) and expresses doubt at the wisdom of choosing Stapel as the addressee.[85]

---

83. *Ibid.*, p. 328.
84. "Um was es geht: Antwort an Emanuel Hirsch," p. 117.
85. Tillich says: "Leider findet sich nichts von dieser Haltung bei dem Adressaten des Briefes. Es würde der Sache und dem Niveau der Auseinandersetzung mit Hirsch widersprechen, wenn ich darauf einginge. Ich begnüge mich damit, mein Bedauern über die Wahl des Adressaten auszudrücken." *Ibid.*, p. 117n. This little footnote of Tillich's against Stapel was included by the editor of *Theologische Blätter* in direct contravention of the publisher's wishes and is the suject of a lengthy defense by Schmidt to J.C. Hinrichs'sche Buchhandlung on May 2, 1935. Schmidt also mentions this same matter in a letter to Tillich dated May 3, 1935.

Historical Indebtedness

Broadly speaking the three parts of the letter deal with Tillich's historical, theological, and political concerns.[86] In Part One he addresses the historical question of intellectual indebtedness. It is, he says, the obligation of those who think academically and not propagandistically, to express proper appreciation for the intellectual stance and achievements of the preceding period of German intellectual history. The first part of his letter, says Tillich, was written primarily with this concern in mind. As far as the question of "plagiarism" is concerned, Tillich clearly modifies his stand in his rejoinder and now maintains that in no way does he perceive the dispute between himself and Hirsch to be over questions such as academic originality. "I have never had the slightest understanding for such squabbling," he adds.[87] Even if Young Lutheran theology had been developed independently of Religious Socialism, Hirsch's interpretation of the German events would still remain just as incomprehensible to him. Hirsch has correctly understood that his position was attacked as "typical" rather than as a "personal" or "individual" one. In fact, Tillich adds, Hirsch's stance "is almost the only one that is worth attacking."[88]

This raises an important question: to what extent is this a personal and partisan political debate between two friends and opponents and to what an extent is it a confrontation between two schools of thought? The intensity of Tillich's letter cannot be understood simply in terms of political differences but must be seen in the light of their long friendship and their ongoing intellectual and personal differences and conflicts, as we have examined them in the first part of this study, as well as the polemics raging between opposing theological and ecclesiastical factions in Germany at the time.

Tillich's main point in this first part of the letter is that no particular historical epoch can ever be put under an unconditional Yes or No. This is especially the case when one acknowledges, as Hirsch does, that the ideas to which one gives an unqualified Yes grew out of the preceding period. This is even more true when opposing sides—like those of Tillich and Hirsch—work with similar categories. "Are we to pass on to future generations of thinking Germans a caricature of German intellectual history or the true dialectical picture of this development?" Tillich asks. "It was that and that alone which concerned me and concerns me now, and not Hirsch and not myself, not originality or plagiarism,"[89] he adds.

Both passion and impartiality must be involved in our historical consciousness. Everyone who deals with intellectual history has the responsibility to

86. Walter Bense calls the three concerns the "apologetic or historical concern," the "systematic or polemical" concern, and the "political or ethical" concern, respectively. See Bense, "Tillich's *Kairos* and Hitler's Seizure of power: The Tillich-Hirsch Exchange of 1934/35," p. 39.

87. "Um was es geht: Antwort an Emanuel Hirsch," p. 118.

88. *Ibid.* pp. 117-118.

89. *Ibid.*, p. 118.

guard against myth-making. For the purpose of historical thinking, "hate towards one period of history and enthusiasm for another are as bad as a spectator-type of indifference."[90] This comment of Tillich's is illuminating in the light of Hirsch's repeated charge that Tillich lacks concrete involvement in historical realities. Tillich once more demonstrates the "boundary" or "dialectical" nature of his historical consciousness.

Theological Heterodoxy
Part Two deals with Tillich's theological concern. Hirsch had expressed astonishment at the fact that Tillich now suddenly sided with Barth over against his old friend, apparently for political rather than theological reasons. In fact, says Tillich, he had sided neither with Barth nor with Hirsch but had tried to provide a third option between the two extremes. The existence and growth of a demonized sacramentalism had demonstrated the urgent need for such a third way, which Tillich describes as follows:

> In the fight against this [sacramentalism] I stand on Barth's side. For in this fight Barth represents the prophetic element which—albeit in secularized form—is also contained in socialism. It is not my intention to exclude the priestly-sacramental element altogether...but indeed it is and was necessary in the whole history and pre-history of Christianity, and it is even more necessary today than previously, to prevent the misuse of the sacramental element for the creation of ideologies and the sanctification of power structures. That is what was at stake in the critique of the central notions that Hirsch employs.[91]

The debate between himself and Hirsch, says Tillich, is like the controversy in the early church concerning the two natures of Christ, or the struggle over the question of grace and nature in the middle ages, or the issue of faith and good works during the Reformation. The *kairos* teaching of the religious socialists was an attempt to find a middle way between two extreme poles. Hirsch has fallen into the heretical error of espousing one of these extremes:

90. *Ibid.* Tillich adds: "Es wäre schön, wenn Hirsch nicht nur von seinen systematischen Lösungsversuchen, sondern auch von seiner Würdigung der vergangenen Periode deutscher Geschichte zugestehen würde, dass die Frage nach ihr offen geblieben ist." In other words, the evaluation of the previous period in German history must remain open.

91. This important German text reads as follows: "Im Kampf dagegen stehe ich auf Barth's Seite. Denn in diesem Kampf vertritt Barth das profetische Element, das—freilich in säkularisierter Form—auch im Sozialismus enthalten ist. Nicht ist es meine Absicht, das priesterlich-sakramentale Element überhaupt auszuscheiden, wie manche sonst zustimmenden Zuschriften befürchten, wohl aber ist es nötig und war es nötig in der ganzen Geschichte und Vorgeschichte des Christentums, und ist es heute nötiger denn je, zu verhindern, dass das sakramentale Element zur Schaffung von Ideologien und Weihung von Machtgebilden missbraucht wird. Darum ging es in der Kritik der zentralen Begriffe, die Hirsch verwendet." *Ibid.*, p. 118.

My question was: Is this heresy, the "Chalcedonian" mixing of the divine and the human, necessary if we want to avoid the Barthian heresy, the "Chalcedonian" tearing apart of both? Is there no "Chalcedonian" solution to the question concerning the "kingdom of God" and the "kingdom of man"? Even if Hirsch's categories arose without dependence on the Kairos-teaching—which is open to further discussion—they would still express exactly that which, in the solution to the problem, needs to be struggled against as the one, always menacing, heresy: the unmediated and unbroken hallowing and consecrating of a human kingdom. Hirsch's teaching of the two kingdoms, of which one refers exclusively to the inwardness of the individual human being, the other just as exclusively to the orders of political and social life, has the consequence of removing these orders from the critique of the anticipation of the coming of the kingdom of God. Also Barth withdraws them from such a critique, but he profanizes them at the same time, and places them under substantive norms which consciously or unconsciously contain an element of prophetic critique. Hirsch gives them an explicit religious consecration and renounces therewith all critique of the demons that are operative in them. These are the problems which concern all present theological work. This is what concerned me in my effort to differentiate the Kairos teaching sharply from the categories of the "two kingdoms" which are often confused with it.[92]

Interestingly, Tillich accuses Hirsch of mixing the divine and the human on the one hand, and separating them too radically through the doctrine of the two kingdoms on the other. What Tillich seems to mean is that by separating the two realms—the internal spiritual kingdom from the external social-political kingdom—Hirsch is in effect collapsing the two realms since he has no adequate

---

92. The original states: "Meine Frage war: Ist dieser Irrweg, das 'chalzedonensische' Vermischen des Göttlichen und Menschlichen notwendig, wenn wir den Bart'schen Irrweg, das 'chalzedonensische' Trennen beider vermeiden wollen? Gibt es keine 'chalzedonensische' Lösung der Frage 'Reich Gottes' und 'menschliches Reich'? Auch wenn die Kategorien Hirsch's ohne Anlehnung an die Kairoslehre entstanden wären—was weiter zur Diskussion stehen mag—, so würden sie gerade das sagen, was in der Lösung des Problems als der eine, immer drohende Irrweg zu bekämpfen ist: Die unmittelbare und ungebrochene Heiligung und Weihung eines menschliches Reiches. Hirsch's Lehre von den zwei Reichen, von denen das eine ausschliesslich bezogen ist auf die Innerlichkeit des einzelnen Menschen, das andere ebenso ausschliesslich auf die Ordnungen des politischen und sozialen Lebens, hat die Folge, dass diese Ordnungen der von der Reich-Gottes-Erwartung kommenden Kritik entzogen sind. Auch Barth entzieht sie der Kritik, aber er profanisiert sie zugleich und stellt sie unter sachliche Normen, die bewusst oder unbewusst ein Element prophetischer Kritik enthalten. Hirsch gibt ihnen ausdrücklich religiöse Weihe und verzichtet damit auf jede Kritik an den in ihnen wirkenden Dämonien. Um diese Probleme geht es in aller gegenwärtigen theologischen Arbeit. Darum ging es mir in meinem Bemühen, die Kairoslehre scharf gegen die oft zum Verwechseln ähnlichen Kategorien der Lehre von den 'zwei Reichen' abzugrenzen." *Ibid.,* p. 119. In this quotation we have the most succinct statement by Tillich of the theological differences between himself, Barth and Hirsch as they affect their political ethics.

basis by which to judge or criticize the social-political order. As we have already seen, however, Hirsch does in fact have a standard that he allegedly uses to critique the temporal orders: it is the criterion of humbly bowing before the Lord of history and being open to correction and scourging (*verzehren*) by the Eternal. Whether this is an adequate standard and whether it can be adequately applied is of course the question.

Political Theology

Part Three focuses on the political question, particularly the relationship between theology and politics. According to Tillich the relation between the two can never be indicated with an "and," especially when a political movement regards itself as a worldview. A distinction must be made between viewing political action from the perspective of a power struggle and expedience, or taking it seriously as a worldview and judging it on the basis of theological categories. The latter is not politics but a "theology of politics [*Theologie der Politik*]," a part of a "theology of culture." Theology cannot escape such a "theology of culture" if it wants to espouse the unconditional nature of the Christian proclamation. A theology which gives up its right to criticize the political as well as any other worldview has truncated itself. The moment politics defines itself in terms of a worldview it must be subjected to a theological critique,[93] even at the price of martyrdom, as Geismar rightly argues in his discussion with Hirsch. It is nonsense, argues Tillich, to denounce, as Hirsch does, the theological critique of a political worldview as being simply an expression of political opposition while at the same time justifying and glorifying the same political worldview theologically.

In conclusion Tillich expresses his hope and optimism that his letter may have contributed to the clarification of the relation between the Christian proclamation and a political worldview, and asserts that his letter and its contents were not meant to be seen as personal vexation. "What I wanted to strike against," says Tillich, "is an intellectual power that expresses itself simultaneously as theology, worldview, ethos, and scholarship, and as such plainly contradicts the prophetic element inherent in Christianity—a conviction that has not been shaken by Hirsch's thesis."[94] He ends by agreeing that the present struggle requires existential involvement, a "personal binding obligation" (*Verbundenheit*) which cannot be avoided even in the context of an existential refusal, and that such involvement is made possible by the evangelical doctrine of justification.[95]

93. "In dem Augenblick, wo Politik sich selbst weltanschaulich begründet, muss diese Begründung verantwortlicher theologischer Kritik unterworfen worden. Auch um den Preis des Märtyrertums, wie Gaismar mit Recht Hirsch gegenüber fordert." *Ibid.*, p. 119.
94. *Ibid.*, p. 120.
95. Tillich's concluding statement reads as follows: "Ich glaube aber, dass der evangelische Rechtfertigungsgedanke die Möglichkeit gibt, dass auch heute, wo niemand, der ernst genommen

A Summary

We have come to the end of our detailed examination of Tillich's first open letter to Hirsch and his final rejoinder. His arguments and accusations can in my opinion be gathered together and summarized in terms of three major charges. First, Tillich charges Hirsch with not giving adequate credit and recognition to the important insights of the preceding period in German intellectual history (the Weimar period) for the development of his own concepts. More specifically, despite the more moderate tone of Tillich's second letter he accuses Hirsch of distorting the meaning of the central concepts of Religious Socialism (categories like the demonic, the boundary, dynamic truth, risk, theonomy, and particularly the *kairos* teaching) and of applying them to National Socialism—an opposite political movement. Implicit in this first accusation, despite his disclaimers in the second letter, is the charge of "plagiarism" and political opportunism, Hirsch having consciously disguised his dependence upon Tillich and the religious socialists.

Second, Tillich attacks Hirsch's basic theological method, saying that he has eliminated the prophetic-eschatological dimension from the above concepts and has used them for a sacramentalization of a finite reality—the German nation-state. This hallowing of a political movement grows out of his non-dialectical espousal of the Lutheran two-kingdom doctrine which radically separates the internal spiritual realm from the external social and political realms. Implicit in this second accusation is the charge of heresy, Hirsch having given ultimacy (an unbroken Yes) to a penultimate reality and of having raised the present events in Germany into a second source of revelation beside that of the biblical proclamation.

Finally, Tillich accuses Hirsch of having an inadequate political theory in which categories like *"horos," "nomos," "logos,"* origin, blood-bond, national-people (*Volk*), hidden sovereign, and obligation without reservation are used by Hirsch to consecrate the present hour without adequate norms by which to be self-critical and politically responsible. Hirsch lacks a profound sociological understanding of the ideological and class nature of the present occurrences in Germany and his defense of totalitarianism against Western notions of freedom and democracy paves the way for an autocratic Machiavellian-type state. Implicit in this final accusation is the charge of uncritical political enthusiasm and naiveté.

werden soll, an dem Einsatz seiner Existenz vorbei kann, persönliche Verbundenheit auch durch existentielle Ablehnung nicht aufgehoben werden muss. Der 'Feind' ist keine wesensnotwendige, sondern eine wesenswidrige, wenn auch 'existentielle' Kategorie." *Ibid.*, p. 120.

9

National Socialism
and Christian Freedom:
Hirsch Responds to Tillich's Charges

At the time of Tillich's open letter to Hirsch, written from Union Theological Seminary, New York, Emanuel Hirsch was a professor of systematic theology at the University of Göttingen, a position which he had occupied since 1936. He had first received his appointment at Göttingen in 1921 and held the chair of church history until 1936. Hirsch's two volumes of Kierkegaard studies appeared in 1933—the year prior to Tillich's letter and the same year that Hirsch gave his lectures which were to make up the book that Tillich attacked.[1] Hirsch's response to Tillich's charges appears as "Ein Brief an Dr. Stapel," written on November 16, 1934 and published in a volume entitled *Christliche Freiheit und politische Bindung: Ein Brief an Dr. Stapel und anderes.* The first 47 pages are devoted to Hirsch's answer to Tillich's accusations and the next 28 pages to Hirsch's response to Eduard Geismar, a Danish philosopher-theologian and significant Kierkegaard scholar with whom Hirsch also had had an ongoing conversation about the German situation and the task of theology. The last 20 pages consist of a series of theses (*Drei Thesenreihen*) in which Hirsch articulates his views on (1) The revelation of God in law and gospel, (2) confession and confessions, and (3) church and state. In this chapter we are concerned primarily with an examination of the first part: Hirsch's response to Tillich.

Hirsch's reply is substantial and deserves careful scrutiny.[2] It consists of a

---

1. Hirsch was convinced that Kierkegaard represented a major turning point in Christian thought and piety. The influence of Kierkegaard on Hirsch's thought, including his interpretation of the political and theological events of 1933 in Germany, should not be underestimated. See Walter Buff, "Emanuel Hirsch," p. 79.

2. North American theologians have tended to dismiss Hirsch's reply as nonsubstantial. An example of such a rather too easy dismissal of Hirsch's response and thought in general is that of David Hopper: "The hope with which Tillich concluded his letter was not, of course, realized. Hirsch rejected all remonstrances and persevered in support of the National Socialist cause. He indirectly answered Tillich's 'open letter' with a small pamphlet entitled *Christian Freedom and Political Obligation.* Part of the pamphet was a letter from Hirsch to Dr. Wilhelm Stapel, a leading figure among the German Christians. In the letter to Stapel, Hirsch replied to some of Tillich's criticisms, chiefly to the charge of plagiarism. Tillich, for his part, found significant misunderstanding in Hirsch's interpretation of the original letter, and, in a brief answer in *Theologische Blätter* (May 1935), he recapitulated the major points. As indicated, however, the original letter and later summary had little or no effect on Hirsch and the German Christians." *Tillich: A Theological*

brief preface in which Hirsch makes some personal remarks about the format of his answer, an introductory section in which he attempts to show the partisan political nature of Tillich's critique, and four major parts. Part one deals with Tillich's "inaccurate" renditions of aspects of Hirsch's thought, particularly statements about foreign countries; Part Two focuses on the charge of "plagiarism" as applied to the concept of the boundary; Part Three continues the discussion of "plagiarism" with regard to the category of the *kairos*; Part Four considers various aspects of Tillich's charge that Hirsch has deified or "sacramentalized" an earthly reality without giving the church room to protest. In the conclusion Hirsch pays tribute to Tillich's personal integrity and briefly sketches their personal and intellectual relationship over the years.

Misrepresentations and Initial Counter-charges

Hirsch begins his short preface with the observation that Tillich has opened a "volley of shots" (*Schützenfeuer*) against him and that editor Karl Ludwig Schmidt has provided him with the appropriate weapon. He feels that his honor is at stake; he cannot address Tillich directly. He says later in the letter: "With Tillich himself I cannot speak any longer. Someone who uses the form of an [open] letter to a friend to accuse his opponent of untruthfulness, ignoble self-interest in the use of alien concepts, theological Machiavellianism...and the betrayal of the eternal for an earthly [reality] without any qualifications, has destroyed the possibility for a direct discussion. Friendship amongst Germans rests on the acknowledgment of mutual honor and the equality of academic disciplines. There remains only one possibility for Hirsch: to defend himself as substantively as possible against an attack on the honor that he as a German teacher and writer deserves and to trouble Stapel and the public as little as possible with the private side of the affair.[3] He refers to Stapel, the addressee, as "a German journalist who is courageous and conscious of his responsibility, with whom I have been linked as possessing the same will-for-Germany against the forces of 1918, and who in his struggles has suffered a heavier and harder affliction of his honor than I have."[4]

Already in the preface, Hirsch introduces what will be one of his central counter-charges against Tillich: namely, that Tillich lacks a responsible commitment to a people and, instead, espouses a free-floating critical individualism:

Portrait, p. 89. An example of Tillich's side being presented without equal attention being given to Hirsch's side of the debate in North America is the recent translation into English of Tillich's "Open Letter to Emanuel Hirsch but not Hirsch's response in *The Thought of Paul Tillich*, edited by James Luther Adams, Wilhelm Pauck, and Roger Lincoln Shinn.

3. Hirsch, "Brief an Herrn Dr. Stapel," *Christliche Freiheit und politische Bindung*, p. 7.
4. *Ibid.*

My controversy with Tillich arises out of various previous stages of struggle, culminating now in a settling of accounts between the nationally-bound historical thinking of the new German spirit [*des Volksgebundenen Geschichtsdenkens neuer deutscher Geistigkeit*] and that of a freely-suspended critical propheticism [*freischwebenden kritischen Prophetie*], which as a kind of guardian angel has traversed Germany on the train of Marxism, which it has tried unsuccessfully to guide along more acceptable and responsible lines.[5]

According to Hirsch, Tillich's criticisms of him grow out of an attitude of cosmopolitan internationalism which has no solid communal roots, a stance which Hirsch finds abhorrent.

In his introduction Hirsch makes two preliminary charges against Tillich: (1) that Tillich uses partisan politics to argue against an old friend who happens to be his political opponent, and (2) that Tillich has written a polemical pamphlet rather than engaging in a careful analysis of his opponent's thought. In the first of these Hirsch charges Tillich with the kind of political opportunism that Tillich had levelled against him. Hirsch describes the partisan-political dimension of the debate in the following terms:

There exists in Tillich an anger, an anger against that German spirit which submits itself to National Socialism, of which I have now become a representative—in my national perspective I have been a basic opponent of his for a long time—through my book "Die gegenwärtige geistige Lage im Spiegel philosophischer und theologischer Besinnung," Göttingen, 1934. He in many ways [*Vielfach*] sees in National Socialism that which has intellectually robbed and plundered Marxism in order to misuse that which it has thus appropriated in the service of its own will. He examines this model [of National Socialism] through me by subjecting to analysis my relation to a Marxism that he represents, one with democratic correctives, one which has been deepened by Christianity and religion, and to some extent also trans-formal. Thus he imposes on me a sincerely held prejudice against political opponents. I have robbed all decisive ideas from him and then corrupted them and twisted them in the direction of a National Socialism.[6]

5. The German reads as follows: "Meine Auseinandersetzung mit Tillich steigt durch einige vorläufige Kampfesschichten empor zu einer Abrechnung des volksgebundenen Geschichtsdenkens neuer deutscher Geistigkeit mit der frei schwebenden kritischen Prophetie, die als eine Art Geleitengel mit auf dem Zug des Marxismus durch Deutschland war und ihn vergebens auf leidlich verantwortliche Bahnen zu lenken suchte." *Ibid.*, p. 5.

6. In the German original, Hirsch's charge against Tillich reads as follows: "Es lebt in Tillich ein Zorn, der Zorn gegen die dem Nationalsozialismus hingegebene deutsche Geistigkeit, deren Repräsentant ich—durch meine nationale Haltung von je ihm sachlich ein Gegner—nun ihm durch mein Buch "Die gegenwärtige geistige Lage im Spiegel philosophischer und theologischer

Such an attack, adds Hirsch, should be made only on the basis of a thorough analysis of the opponent's entire work and education. If it were done honorably and in an unprejudiced way, such a methodological critique would be legitimate. But, instead, Tillich has written a superficial, polemical pamphlet, his second preliminary charge:

> That is, a pamphlet has been written instead of an analysis; a pamphlet, in which neither the genetic nor the systematic unity of the opponent's ideas become visible. Because I as a nationalist am classified, from the perspective of Tillich's political dogma, as a "bourgeois reactionary" (National Socialism, according to him, is purportedly carried by "reactionary" petit-bourgeois and peasant classes), I am on my part till now supposed to have known and thought only what such a type of an individual—according to the dogmatic schema of a Christian-Religious Marxism—could have known or thought. Everything which does not fit this and in any way appears to be a serious and mature, philosophically well-worked through, religious understanding of history, must have been illegitimately appropriated. Political partisans tend to work in such a way when they are dogmatists at the same time.[7]

Here then we have another charge that will continue as a motif throughout Hirsch's letter: namely, that instead of carefully examining the consistency of Hirsch's views from within Hirsch's own theological-political schema, Tillich has examined and judged Hirsch's position through the screen of a doctrinaire socialist-Marxist dogma and view of history.

Besinnung," Göttingen 1934, geworden bin. Er sieht im Nationalsozialismus vielfach den, der den Marxismus geistig beraubt und ausgeplündert hat, um das so Angeeignete nun im Dienst seines eignen Wollens zu missbrauchen. Dies Exempel rechnet er an mir durch, indem er mein Verhältnis zu dem christlich-religiös vertieften und zum Teil auch umgebildeten Marxismus mit demokratischer Korrektur, den er vertreten hat, einer Analyse unterwirft. So wird ein Vorurteil gegen politische Gegner, an das er ehrlich glaubt, an mir exekutiert. Ich habe alle entscheidenden Ideen bei ihm geraubt und dann nationalsozialistisch korrumpiert und umgebogen." *Ibid.*, p. 8.

7. "Das heisst, es wird ein Pamphlet geschrieben statt einer Analyse, ein Pamphlet, in dem weder der genetische noch der systematische Zusammenhang der Ideen des Bekämpften sichtbar wird. Da ich als Nationalist von Tillichs politischem Dogma aus gesehen als 'bürgerlicher Reaktionär' einzuordnen bin (der Nationalsozialismus wird nach ihm angeblich von 'reaktionären' kleinbürgerlichen und bäuerlichen Schichten getragen), so habe ich von mir aus eben nur das bisher gewusst und gedacht zu haben, was ein Individuum solcher Art nach dem dogmatischen Schema des christlich-religiösen Marxismus allein wissen und denken kann, und alles, was dazu nicht passt und irgendwie als Ernst und Reife eines philosophisch durchdrungenen religiösen Geschichtsverständnisses erscheint, das muss unrechtmässig angeeignet sein. So pflegen Parteipolitiker zu arbeiten, wenn sie zugleich Dogmatiker sind." *Ibid.*, pp. 8-9.

Inaccurate Citations and Interpretations

Having made these preliminary remarks, Hirsch proceeds to the four-part letter itself. In Part One Hirsch concentrates on the inaccuracies of some of Tillich's citations, particularly the ones having to do with Hirsch's comments about non-Germans. Without a full translation of Hirsch's text it is difficult to understand the full meaning of Hirsch's technical complaints. Our intention here is not to examine in detail the accuracy or inaccuracy of Tillich's citations but loosely to introduce Hirsch's annoyances in order to get at some of the more fundamental issues. For instance, Hirsch claims that Tillich has taken out of context his remarks about foreign philosophizing as being "subhuman-naturalistic" (*untermenschlich-natürlich*). Here, he says, Tillich gives the word "subhuman" a meaning that was not intended. For Hirsch, the term refers to a naturalistic, scientific, mathematical mode of thought and not to crass materialism.

Further, Hirsch intended to describe foreign philosophizing during the pre-war era, and not foreign philosophizing in general. What Tillich passes over is Hirsch's emphasis on the meta-historical as well as his rigorous criticism of German philosophy itself at this point. Similarly, Tillich has distorted and taken out of context his observations about the cultural imperialism of the French (Welsch). He did not use the phrase "specifically French" (*Welsch*), as Tillich maintains. "In my context it is clear," adds Hirsch, "that I try to distinguish the conscious German and National Socialist idea that an authentic community of nations [*Völkergemeinschaft*] can only grow out of the free unfolding of the *nomos* whose type is appropriate to each nation, from the concept, propagated by Western nations, that the community of nations rests on an international culture. It is an undeniable fact that French imperialism wants to be a cultural imperialism."[8]

In Tillich's criticism of Hirsch's alleged identification of "authoritarian government" with the French, Tillich has once more distorted his meaning, inverted a subjective form into the objective, and left out the qualifying phrase "in the customary sense." Hirsch replies: "It is clear that I, as one who affirms an authoritarian leadership-state [*autoritären Führungsstaats*] in a new sense, cannot simply turn against the authoritarian government of Ludwig XIV or Napoleon and not against all other [authoritarian governments]. Through shortening and taking it out of context, the intent of my assertion—to differentiate the German monarchy, borne by the association of free men, from the absolute sovereignty of the prince that has come to Germany from France—is no longer recognizable."[9] This succinct statement by Hirsch indicates the type of

8. *Ibid.*, p. 11.
9. "Dass ich als Bejaher eines in einem neuen Sinne auktoritären Führungstatts mich nicht schlechtweg gegen jedes auktoritäre Regiment wenden kann, sondern nur gegen das eines Ludwig XIV,

government and political system that Hirsch ideally envisions for Germany—a national German monarchy borne by the association of free men. In effect, Hirsch is here defending a uniquely German version of a constitutional monarchy.

Hirsch points to other citations where Tillich has changed the tone of his statements, all the while surely recognizing what such slight changes of modulation can do to distort another person's thought. Through such devious means Tillich has given an inaccurate picture of Hirsch's intellectual stance. Hirsch has not, for example, taken over from Tillich the belief in the identity of theology and theonomous philosophy. What Hirsch said was "that a conscious Christian philosophy and theology have the same Telos and are differentiated only according to the aim [*Abzweckung*] of their tasks. For me that is something else."[10] Nor has Hirsch suddenly appropriated Tillich's own long-standing view that justification applies to thought as well as sin. "Similarly it is simply untrue that I...have always till now rejected the application of justification to thought and now have taken it over from him. The justification of thought, that is, that my thought and teaching is worth something only in the context of the forgiveness of sin, has been self-evident to me from the time of my student years.... What I have always rejected and still reject is the Tillichian use of this concept for a dissolution of God's act of justification through dialectics."[11] Hirsch's

oder Napoleon, ist klar. Durch die Verkürzung und Herauslösung ist der Sinn meiner Aussage, das germanische Volkskönigtum, dass von dem Bund freier Männer getragen ist, gegen das absolute Fürstentum, dass von Frankreich her nach Deutschland gekommen ist, abzugrenzen, nicht mehr erkennbar." *Ibid.*, pp. 11-12. In his definitive work *The German Idea of Freedom*, Leonard Krieger traces the evolution of the German political tradition as a unique combination of Eastern authoritarianism and Western liberalism. Because of its unique political history, Germany has developed a view of freedom which is distinctive, a synthesis of authoritarianism and autonomy, secular submission and spiritual independence. "The juxtaposition—indeed, even the connection—of one conception of liberty that could be realized only within the authoritarian state and of another that could be realized only in an absolute realm beyond all states is a commonly remarked German phenomenon," observes Krieger. Krieger shows how this connection has developed. *The German Idea of Freedom: History of a Political Tradition* (Chicago: The University of Chicago Press, 1957), p. ix. Hirsch's vision for a uniquely German state must be seen in the light of such a distinctive German political tradition.

10. "Brief an Herrn Dr. Stapel," p. 12. In the German, "Ich habe S.76 gesagt, das eine bewusst christliche Philosophie und die Theologie das gleiche Telos haben und nur nach der Abszweckung ihres Dienstes unterschieden werden. Das ist für nich etwas andres."

11. "Abgelehnt habe ich immer," says Hirsch, "und lehne noch heute ab die Tillichsche Benutzung dieses Gedankens zur Auflösung der Rechtfertigungstat Gottes in Dialektik." "Brief an Herrn Dr. Stapel," p. 12. For Tillich, this insight had come from Martin Kähler: "But there was another element in his thought which was even more important for several of my friends and myself, namely, his application of the principle of the Reformation to the situation of modern man between faith and doubt. He taught us that he who doubts any statement of the Bible and the creed can nevertheless be accepted by God and can combine the certainty of acceptance with the actuality of even radical doubt. This idea made it possible for many of us to become or remain Christian theologians." Martin Kähler, *The So-Called Historical Jesus and the Historic, Biblical Christ*, pp. xi-xii.

critique of Tillich's dialectical method is an underlying motif of his entire letter. Tillich had criticized Hirsch for the pride he took in having undermined (*ausgehöllt*—literally "hollowing out") the state of 1918-1932. Hirsch replies that the term "*ausgehöllt*" appears in Barth's writings but not in his own. He had fought against the state of those years because he did not want it to have a monopoly on shaping the German life and spirit which during the Weimar years was pushed to the abyss through its lack of character and principles. He seriously believed and taught that the state had the responsibility, as executor of the hidden sovereign of the nation, to establish order and further education, to emphasize the sacrifice of individuals for the sake of the whole. He rejects Tillich's implication that he was a pawn in the hands of the capitalists:

> The insinuation that I was somehow at that time a tool of capitalistic forces, I reject. The summons in "Deutschlands Schicksal" (1920) to legitimate state property [*staatlichen Obereigentums*] as protection against the selfishness of property owners who do not recognize themselves as bound to the nation, and in general my whole position with respect to the then so-called social question, was decidedly anti-capitalistic. But one would indeed have had to read me in order to know this, and not simply label me a *priori* as a National Socialist reactionary on the basis of some dogma.[12]

This anti-capitalist theme in Hirsch's writings, dating back to the World War I years, once more illustrates some of the affinities not only between the thinking of Tillich and Hirsch but also between socialism and some of the national movements in Germany during the 1920s.

Concerning Plagiarism: The "Boundary"

In Part Two Hirsch replies to Tillich's charge of plagiarism, especially as it concerns his concept of the "boundary." He repeats his astonishment at the captivating power that the religious-Marxist dogma about the national socialist reactionary obviously has over Tillich. Somehow Tillich just cannot concede that Hirsch is capable of having his own genuinely independent historical view without being a reactionary. Hirsch goes on to show how his notion of the

The question of certainty and scepticism with respect to religious knowledge had been an area of controversy between Tillich and Hirsch for some time. What is really at stake here for Hirsch is not so much that God forgives the doubter but that even believing knowledge requires God's forgiveness because it remains human knowledge.

12. "Brief an Herrn Dr. Stapel," p. 13. Hirsch's long-standing and thoroughgoing critique of rugged individualism and selfish-competitive capitalism is undeniable. As early as 1920 he said: "In dieser unstarren Einordnung der Eigenmacht des Eigentums in die Obmacht des Staates liegt die wahre Uberwindung des Kapitalismus." *Deutschlands Schicksal*, p. 124.

boundary is rooted in his own intellectual heritage. Tillich knows that he (Hirsch) too wrestled with Kant, Fichte, and Hegel.

From the beginning the two crucial questions which preoccupied Hirsch were (1) the notion of the boundary as it relates to a theory of knowledge and the philosophy of religion, and (2) the significant achievements of Kant, Fichte, and Hegel in the philosophy of history. Tillich is well aware that Hirsch published numerous articles and books which were historical—an attempt to go beyond the idealistic conception of God, knowledge, and the philosophy of history. He also knows that Hirsch went through the shattering experience of an encounter with Nietzsche's scepticism and Dilthey's historicism. Hirsch in fact wrote on Nietzsche, whom he regarded with the "antipathetic emotions" of both awe and revulsion. Tillich knows that Hirsch concerned himself for a decade with the thought of Kierkegaard, whom he considers one of the greatest critics and analysts of modern culture, and about whom he has written nearly 1,000 pages. Tillich knows also from personal meetings that despite his (Hirsch's) intense aversion to the irreligious mind of Spengler, he is grateful to him "for helping him understand the crisis of modern culture and for expanding his intellectual view from a Diltheyian analysis of the Western mind to an understanding of the growth and decline of culture."[13]

It is in the light of these struggles with thinkers and issues that Tillich must decide what is original in Hirsch's thought and what is borrowed, what is part of a common German intellectual heritage from which both of them have drawn and what is unique in each of them. Instead, however, Tillich simply "uses the disagreeable schema of economic materialism. Everything that contradicts his picture of the bourgeois ideology of politically-enslaved Lutheranism I have secondhandedly and inauthentically appropriated for the justification of a national socialist mentality...."[14]

In this study we have already shown that Hirsch in fact was not simply an opportunist who plagiarized Tillich's concepts and distorted their meaning, but one who developed his own particular political and theological categories over an extended period of time and applied them, with some change and development to be sure, to political events as they unfolded. These categories were shaped, interpreted, and reinterpreted in light of these political events—as was

---

13. "Brief and Herrn Dr. Stapel," p. 14.

14. "Dann konnte er die Frage stellen, was diesen gemeinsamen Meistern gegenüber an seinem eignen christlich-religiös vertieften und ausgeweiteten Marxismus wirklich Neues und Eigentümliches war, und was er daher, wenn es bei mir wiederkehrte, als sein Eigentum in Anspruch nehmen konnte. Statt dessen hat er hier einfach das—von ihm noch heute verteidigte—widerwärtige Schema des ökonomischen Materialismus angewandt. Alles was seinem Bilde von der bürgerlichen Ideologie des politisch versklavten Luthertums widerspricht, habe ich zur Rechtfertigung nationalso-zialistischer Geistigkeit sekundär und unecht übernommen, und sollten es selbst solche uns beiden schon in der Studienzeit selbstverständlichen Dinge sein wie dass das evangelische Christentum das gegen sich selber kritische Christentum ist." *Ibid.*, pp. 14-15.

true in Tillich's case as well.

Hirsch now moves into a discussion of his notion of the boundary. He defends himself against Tillich's charge that he has used the religious socialist concept of the boundary, applied it to bourgeois society, and then distorted it as meaning the "holy middle." Hirsch first corrects Tillich by saying that the phrase "bourgeois society" does not appear in his own writings. "As a decisive example of a boundary-lacking religiosity I describe instead in ever new ways, not bourgeois religion but the regression into pre-Christian national religion [*vorchristliche Volksreligion*]...."[15] In this important statement, as he had done on a number of previous occasions, Hirsch makes a distinction between a pre-Christian tribal type of religion and a Christianity which takes seriously its national and ethnic roots.

Although he cannot find the phrase "holy middle" in his own work, says Hirsch, he admits that here Tillich has touched on the central nerve of his view of history. It is in his thinking about history that he developed the category which is decisive for his thought—namely, the concept of the "Lord of history." Despite Barth's tendency to caricature him, Hirsch allows that Barth has understood the important place that this notion has in his own work better than Tillich:

> (I want to take this opportunity, because I will certainly not receive such a good one again, to compliment Karl Barth: he has, despite the fact that he likes to caricature this in me, perceived correctly that with my phrase "Lord of History" I say that which he must attack if he wants to attack my central argument; but I can pay Tillich as thinker no such compliment, when he even though Barth's rejection of the religious grounds of history must after all be more disagreeable to him than my "Lord of History"—takes precisely this Barth instead of me as his ally on political grounds.)[16]

It is interesting that Hirsch too views his own thought over against Barth on the one side and Tillich on the other. Both view Barth's theology as one of the three theological alternatives of the period and use him as a foil for clarifying their own similarities and differences with each other. Noteworthy as well is the fact that Hirsch also accuses Tillich of political opportunism. With the concept of

---

15. *Ibid.*, pp. 15-16. Hirsch was critical of any such regression into a pre-Christian identification of religion and nation as found in some supporters of National Socialism. He was critical of and differentiated his own stance from those religious enthusiasts who misused and misinterpreted the events of 1933. *Ibid.*, p. 40; also "Meine Wendjahre (1916-21)," p. 5.

16. "(Ich will bei dieser Gelegenheit, weil ich sie so gut gewiss nicht wieder kriege, Karl Barth mein Kompliment machen: er hat, was er auch an mir zu karikieren liebt, den richtigen Sachverhalt gerochen, dass mit dem Worte 'Herr der Geschichte' das gesagt ist, was er angreifen muss, wenn er zentral angreifen will; ich kann aber Tillich als Denker kein Kompliment machen, wenn er—obwohl ihm Barths Leugnung des religiösen Grundes der Geschichte immerhin widerwärtiger sein muss als mein 'Herr der Geschichte'—eben diesen Barth dann aus politischen Gründen als Bundesgenossen wider mich nimmt.)" *Brief an Herrn Dr. Stapel*, p. 17.

the boundary, says Hirsch, he had attempted to explain in depth and with paradox what for the German awakening (*Aufbruch*) is the connection between a responsibility-laden religious openness (*Erschlossenheit*) and a hard, obliging bondage (*harter Bindung*) to the earthly, national *nomos* of the state with its heavy, earthly, biological presuppositions. Hirsch takes this opportunity to thank Stapel for the *nomos* teaching, a concept which is crucial for his own view of history and which he first appropriated from Stapel and then developed further.

The concept of the boundary, argues Hirsch, functions in a double sense, as (1) the historical reality which in its particularity and the power with which it calls us to service limits and binds reason and freedom, and (2) the infinite divine majesty, the hidden mystery which comes from beyond our historical life and shatters and consumes all historical moments.[17] It was for the purpose of explaining this mystery that Hirsch formulated the view that the historical *horos* and the holy *horos* are paradoxically both separated and related. Is this a concept that bears Hirsch's own stamp or has it been borrowed from Tillich? That is the question!

The term "boundary," says Hirsch, came to him, as it did to everyone who considers it a mark of the unfathomable dialectic between the temporal and the eternal, through years of preoccupation with Kantian-Fichtian philosophy, particularly through his study of Fichte's concept of God. This concerned him in his 1913-14 thesis on Fichte's philosophy of religion, where he talks about Fichte's perception of the boundary of knowledge as the boundary between being and non-being: "'The non-being of knowledge is, however, Being itself [= the Absolute].'"[18] The non-being of knowledge is in actuality the origin of knowledge. His concept of the boundary can only be properly understood, Hirsch says, in relation to this Fichtian sense of knowledge as the root of the whole of human-historical life, and in the light of Fichte's concept of God as it relates to the concrete boundary of knowledge as the unfathomableness of the given historical moment which calls us to dutiful service. While his view of God, knowledge, history, and the boundary was deeply shaped by Fichte's thought, there still always remained a fundamental difference between his own thought and that of Fichte:

---

17. In Hirsch's own words: "Der Begriff der Grenze, der mir dies alles leistet, schwebt in dem ineinander geketteten Doppelsinn von einerseits der geschichtlichen Wirklichkeit, die nach ihrer schlechthin gegebnen Besonderheit und ihrer zu Dienst rufenden Macht die Vernunft und Freiheit grenzt und bindet, und anderseits der unendlichen göttlichen Hoheit und Gewalt, die als das verborgne Geheimnis jenseits des geschichtlichen Lebens das vergängliche geschichtliche Leben erschüttert und verzehrt mit der Macht des Ewigen, indem sie es grenzend bewahrt." *Ibid.*, pp. 17-18.

18. *Ibid.*, p. 18. Hirsch is referring here to his inaugural dissertation, *Die Religionsphilosophie Fichtes zur Zeit des Atheismusstreites in ihrem Zusammenhange mit der Wissenschaftslehre und Ethik* (Göttingen: Vandenhoeck & Ruprecht, 1914).

What distinguishes me from Fichte, and always has distinguished me from him, is this, that he under the illusion of systematic thought did not take seriously in his philosophy of history that which his own assessment demanded: the majesty of God, who alone as the boundary-establishing hiddenness of history fills it with its presence and its life.... In contrast to that two very opposing forces were at work in me: the power of the Lutheran doctrine of creation and the shattering scepticism of Nietzsche and Dilthey. I struggled for a view of history in which the hidden mystery of the living God was understood as a power both giving meaning to and hiding meaning from human-historical life. Thus, in 1920 I gained a view of history expressed in "Deutschlands Schicksal," as the mean between an idealistic and a positivistic, a sceptical and an absolutistic understanding of history.[19]

Hirsch adds that at the time when he wrote his *Deutschlands Schicksal* he had still not adequately understood Luther's teaching on law. It was only through the sense of shame experienced by Germans in 1918, through seeing Marxism increasing its strength throughout Germany, through a struggle with misery and distress, and through his study of Kierkegaard that he began to comprehend Luther's theology. The brokenness and depth of the Lutheran view of history, says Hirsch, can already be felt in his short 1925 essay "Grundlegung einer Christliche Geschichtsphilosophie"[20] The national socialist liberation has, he says, given him a new courage to overcome his paralysis and risk a fresh understanding of the earthly *nomos*. From statements such as these one gains a sense of the degree to which Hirsch's theology was, by his own admission, influenced and shaped by historical events and experiences.[21]

19. Because of the importance of the statement in clarifying Hirsch's relation to Fichte, we once again cite the German original: "Was mich von Fichte scheidet, und von je geschieden hat, ist dies, dass er unter dem Wahn des Systemgedankens mit der durch seinen eignen Ansatz geforderten Majestät Gottes, die allein als eine die Grenze setzende Verborgenheit die Geschichte mit ihrer Gegenwart und ihrem Leben füllt, in seiner Geschichtsphilosophie nicht ernst gemacht hat. Er lässt also den verstehenden Begriff dann doch des Ganzen der Geschichte mächtig werden. Demgegenüber haben in mir zwei sehr entgegengesetzte Potenzen, die Macht des lutherischen Schöpferglaubens und die skeptische Erschütterung durch Nietzsche und Dilthey, zusammengewirkt, und ich habe um eine Geschichtsansicht gerungen, in der das verborgne Geheimnis des lebendigen Gottes zugleich als sinngebende und sinnverschliessende Macht über und am menschlich-geschichtlichen Leben verstanden wurde. So ist mir 1920 die Geschichtsansicht von 'Deutschlands Schicksal,' als Mitte zwischen idealistischer und positivistischer sowie zwischen skeptischer und absoluter Geschichtsansicht entstanden." "Brief an Herrn Dr. Stapel," pp. 18-19. See also *Deutschlands Schicksal,* pp. 9-63.

20. "Brief an Herrn Dr. Stapel," p. 19. See also "Grundlegung einer Christliche Geschichtsphilosophie," *Zeitschrift für systematische Theologie* 3,24(1925), pp. 213-247.

21. Hirsch sees socio-political reality as the living context for the human quest for God. Gunda Schneider-Flume makes much of how the socio-political events of the war years and the Weimar Republic shaped Hirsch's theology and alludes to Hirsch's statement that "...im Verhältnis des Menschen zur politisch-sozialen Wirklichkeit ist der lebendige Sitz der Frage nach Gott." See

Hirsch is quite open about the fact that he and Tillich share some common perceptions about the religious depth of human-historical reality. Where does this similarity come from? Why are there similarities within their concepts of the "boundary?" It is due, says Hirsch, not to plagiarism on his part but because of a common intellectual tradition—German Idealism:

> It is because he, like I, had his point of departure in the Idealistic thinking about history, and [because] like I he had—under the influence of the sceptical and historical crisis of epistemology [*Wahrheitsbewusstsein*] as well as what this crisis revealed about the true depth of human existence—to break this Idealistic thinking exactly at the same point as I: at its false placing of the unconditional [*an seiner falschen Unbedingtsetzung*]. It is, nevertheless, no accident that he has applied this so differently than I have. For he arrived at his position through the thought of the late Schelling, which I have always found repellent. He has, consequently, not had that simple childlike relation to the Lutheran doctrine of creation which has sustained me in every crisis of the intellect no matter how dark it was all around me. Furthermore, he has never had that severity of character [*Herbigkeit*] which allowed me always to find the duty-binding obligation of my historical being within a law of actuality [*die mich immer in einem Gesetz der Wirklichkeit die verpflichtende Bindung meines geschichtliche Daseins finden lies*] prior to any prophetic or other such stance. Therefore, even now the relationship between his and my view of history is circumscribed by the abstract-dialectical relation of the temporal and the eternal, of being shattered and of being pardoned, which oscillates in both of us; and he, because of who he is, has to reject what for me belongs essentially to the boundary, the obligation to the nomos in its specific earthly form. He has not at all seen my concept of the boundary through to its end, when he reclaims it for himself (and Jaspers). Therefore, it will also have no impact on him when I say: It is indeed not meant to be "my" concept of the boundary; it is surely to be the concept of that which is happening to us as Germans at this moment in our history on a most profound level.[22]

In short, according to Hirsch (1) both he and Tillich have their common intellectual roots in German Idealism, (2) their differences are due to the fact that a) Tillich was influenced by the late Schelling (while Hirsch took his point of departure from Fichte), b) Tillich has no serious appreciation for the Lutheran teaching on creation, and c) Hirsch, contrary to Tillich's adoption of a critical-prophetic stance, always saw himself much more existentially obligated to an earthly national *nomos*.

Schneider-Flume, *Die politische Theologie Emanuel Hirschs 1918-1933*, p. 164.
    22. "Brief an Herm Dr. Stapel," p. 20.

Hirsch wonders why Tillich, who is by nature an honorable man, rails against him in such a confused manner. He believes it is because Tillich judges him from the perspective of religious socialist dogma and assumes that Hirsch, as someone who is conscious of his being bound to a nation (*Volksgebundenheit*), does not understand the holy *horos* which consumes (*verzehrt*), does not know anything about the religious boundary of death (*Todesgrenze*). If he had accurately read his works, says Hirsch, Tillich would have discovered that this dogmatic schema does not fit his (Hirsch's) thought and that he too knows things which Tillich considers to be the monopoly of religious Marxism. Instead, Tillich immediately pronounces his indictment: plagiarism.

As far as the concepts of autonomy and theonomy are concerned, here again Hirsch argues that they have their common roots in German Idealism. The idealistic philosophy of history constructs its view on the notion of the dialectic of freedom and being, of the political and the religious. Fichte, whose understanding of history Hirsch examined in his 1914 thesis, pointedly argued that the struggle between reason (*Verstand*) and faith (*Glaube*), autonomy and theonomy, produced the rhythm of historical events and the structuring of an age. Hirsch adds: "I have never seen Tillich here as other than a pupil and disciple of my philosophical teacher Fichte."[23] In fact, says Hirsch, he considers himself to have moved more definitively beyond Idealism than has Tillich.

Concerning Plagiarism: The Kairos

The heart of Tillich's attack is of course Hirsch's alleged misappropriation of Tillich's *kairos* concept. Tillich had suggested that Hirsch deliberately avoided using the Greek term *kairos* in order to disguise his appropriation of this most central of all of Tillich's theological-political categories. In Part Three Hirsch ardently and persuasively defends himself against this accusation and maintains instead that the supposedly *kairos*-related terms that he uses—such as the hour, the moment, national upheaval (*Umbruch*), national awakening (*Aufbruch*)—are not imposed by him on the movement but arise out of and are given their meaning by the events of 1933 themselves. He did not invent these terms nor plagiarize them from Tillich but found them already there. He discovered them as an inherent ingredient of the historical event itself and has tried to understand and interpret them responsibly. Any plagiarism of the philosophy of the *kairos* if there were such, would therefore have been committed by the gods of history.

---

23. *Ibid.*, p. 21. The irony of this lies in the fact that Tillich himself was responsible for initially leading Hirsch to a study of Fichte, the philosopher who to a great degree was responsible for tearing Tillich and Hirsch apart. See the "Nachwort" by Hans-Walter Schütte, entitled "Subjektivität und System," *Hirsch Tillich Briefwechsel 1917-1918.*

Further, the fact that the historical turning point has articulated itself simultaneously as a (1) political and a (2) religious worldview by Germans is in no way Hirsch's own discovery. In Hirsch's words: "My responsibility rests only in the fact that I, claiming rigorous and honest academic accountability, develop a retrospective interpretive affirmation of this self-understanding of the movement."[24] He is, in short, quite willing to accept personal and intellectual responsibility for his book and his use of concepts that may on the surface bear certain similarities to those of Tillich. He reminds Tillich that the conceptual categories he uses in his book have been part of his own thought since he first became a writer. Most of them already appeared in the introduction and first chapter of his *Deutschlands Schicksal*. "I have, to that extent, as Karl Barth has sarcastically pointed out, remained completely incorrigible [*unverbesserlich*] in my historical thinking, and my speech is personally legitimate."[25]

A specific example of a category which is distinctively his own is the concept of national "awakening" (*Aufbruch*). It had its origin in the youth movement, says Hirsch, and entered his vocabulary at the time that a group of German patriots began their struggle against the Young Plan and the spirit of 1918. "For me the German nation ever since then was in the period of national awakening [*Aufbruch*]," he adds, "out of the self-estrangement of the then existent political system, which the *kairos* teaching undertook to deepen and to save religiously and intellectually."[26] In the end, he maintains, it is precisely their opposite perceptions of and reactions to 1918 and the Weimar Republic that lie at the basis of their profound differences in 1933. He and his fellow theological and political compatriots in fact interpreted the events of 1918 and the years following in a way totally different from those, like Tillich, who found themselves in the *kairos* school of thought.

It is in this light, also, that their differing understandings of the demonic must be explained, the category which occupies a special place in the concepts which Tillich claims for himself. Hirsch here admits the influence of Tillich in the evolution of his own thought. Originally Tillich's application of the notion of

24. "Meine Verantwortung liegt allein darin, dass ich mit dem Anspruch strenger wahrhaftiger geistiger Rechenschaft ein ausdeutendes nachverstehendes Ja zu dieser Selbstauffassung der Bewegung entwickle." "Brief an Herrn Dr. Stapel," pp. 22-23.

25. *Ibid.*, p. 23. He is presumably referring here to Barth's statements in his "On the Situation, 1933-34," *The German Church Conflict*, p. 30.

26. The German in its context reads: "Es ist in meinen Begriffsschatz etwa um die Zeit hineingekommen, da die echt deutschen Kämpfer mit dem Volksbegehren gegen den Youngplan die Kampfesansage auf Tod und Leben wider den Geist von 1918 ins Volk riefen. Seitdem war für mich das deutsche Volk im Aufbruche heraus aus der Selbstentfremdung des damaligen politischen Systems, das die Kairoslehre religiös und geistig zu vertiefen und damit zu retten unternahm." "Brief an Herrn Dr. Stapel," pp. 23-24. The Young Plan was a plan adopted and submitted to the allied governments on June 7, 1929 by a committee of financial experts, chaired by Owen Young, for the purpose of solving problems arising out of the reparation demands of the Allies on Germany at the end of World War I.

the demonic to historical life, to the powers that determine the destiny of the whole, seemed strange to him. Hirsch had begun with a Kierkegaardian view of the demonic, which sees it more in terms of a personal fate, a personal ethical-religious stance. Under the terrible experience of the German crisis, however, the demonic received for him a new and wider, more historical meaning. "The lies of the world conscience, the extortion of the reparations and the occurrences within Russia brought me to the acceptance of a widened meaning," says Hirsch.[27] This passage is significant in helping us to understand the movement of Hirsch's thought from a more personal, existential, and ontological understanding of Christianity to one which includes a more historical view.[28]

While Hirsch admits that Tillich's thinking may have influenced him, he insists that his own definition of the demonic remains substantially different from Tillich's. The following lengthy quotation from Hirsch dramatically illustrates the methodological difference between Tillich's dialectical and Hirsch's paradoxical way of interpreting theological concepts:

However, even for Tillich himself there can be no doubt that the content of the words "demonic" and "demon," as widened to include the historical sphere, is defined completely differently by him and me. For him—and one can trace this conceptual motif back to Jacob Boehme—this demonic is the exaltation [*Erhebung*] of the divine itself as that power which is adverse to form, structure, and meaning, which in its negativity contains a remarkably positive significance. For me the historical demonic is simply the perversion [*Verkehrung*] of the divine power which lies within man by rising up [*Empörung*] against bindingness [*Bindung*] and the nomos, thereby becoming a life-destroying force. It is a much simpler, and as far as I am concerned also a more primitive conceptualization. But it is for me the only legitimate linguistic usage because it alone truly corresponds to the demonic in the personal sense.... I understand very well the National Socialist protest against Tillich's concept of the demonic. I share it. Nothing awakened more intense opposition in me than the cleverest [*geistwallste*] of all of the writings of Tillich known to me, the one of 1926 concerning the demonic. A view of life, which in everything is based on law, obligation [*Bindung*], and

27. *Ibid.*, p. 24.

28. It is interesting to note that in Tillich's thought there seems to have been a move toward a more "ontological" view of theological concepts, and a lessening emphasis on the "historical" dimensions after World War II. See Hopper, *Tillich: A Theological Portrait*, pp. 97ff. It would be interesting to examine whether there was here an implicit moving together of Tillich's and Hirsch's theological methods in the post-war period. See also Gordon D. Kaufman, *Relativism, Knowledge and Faith* (Chicago: The University of Chicago Press, 1960), p. 108, n. 3. Kaufman says: "It is regrettable that the tendencies, evident early in Tillich's thinking, to think through the significance of the *historical* foundations of human existence and thought, have given way to absolutistic principles and concepts. Many of Tillich's notions start out as historical conceptions (e.g., Kairos, the Protestant principle) but seem to go over too easily into eternally valid ideas."

discipline, must find Tillich's concept of the demonic as somehow sick. This increases the more one recognizes the depth of his philosophy of religion. There is in him a divine spectator-like stance which violates human existence in a way which does not suit us. From the way Tillich's book is composed it is clear that he himself recognized and felt this. (Here we once again come up against those final differences between his and my intellectual stance. I maintain, and believe he understands me in this, that we are not allowed dialectically to think everything there is to think.)[29]

Hirsch too uses dialectical language but his view of dialectic differs from Tillich's. It is a dialectic which cannot escape the givenness and historical bindingness of corporate existence. What he objects to in Tillich is the latter's alleged escape into dialectical thought in order to avoid a concrete and responsible commitment to a particular historical situation and a national peoplehood. Tillich's view of the "demonic" is simply one more example of this.

Hirsch finds it incomprehensible that Tillich could even dream of him having plagiarized Tillich's categories for propagandistic purposes, since both of them had, despite their many differences, struggled with similar questions over many years. The problem that preoccupied both of them, recalls Hirsch, was the dialectic between truth and history. They both perceived this to be the basic question of the age. Both were, for instance, deeply affected by the realization that the *Notion,* as it initially lay submerged in Fichte's thought and later broke through much more clearly and systematically in Hegel, was historically completely conditioned both in form and in content. This realization was at the basis of Hirsch's concept of justification as well as his view of the *logos.* In fact, says Hirsch, "I had secretly hoped that in my concept of the Logos he [Tillich] would recognize a legitimate attempt to solve the point in question, and I could thus, in virtue of the inseparable connection between the Logos-concept and the spirit of the German national upheaval [*Umbruchs*], draw him over into the new German period and, therewith, win back a dynamic thinker for Germany."[30] Hirsch believed—until 1933 at least—that Tillich had certain affinities with National Socialism and that he might be persuaded to remain in Germany and work along with the movement. This hope is confirmed in a letter from Hirsch to Tillich in 1933, in which he suggests that Tillich's book *The Socialist Decision* is moving in a national socialist direction.[31] But, says Hirsch,

29. "Brief an Herrn Dr. Stapel," pp. 24-25. Hirsch has in mind here Tillich's 1926 essay entitled "Das Dämonische. Ein Beitrag zur Sinndeutung der Geschichte."
30. The German reads: "Ich hatte heimlich gehofft, er würde in meinem Begriff des Logos einen legitimen Einsatz zur Lösung des Fragmals finden, und ich könnte ihn so, vermöge der untrennlichen Verknüpfung dieses Logosbegriffs mit der Geistigkeit des deutschen Umbruchs, hinüberreissen in die neue deutsche Zeit und damit für Deutschland einen lebendigen Denker zurückgewinnen." *Ibid.,* p. 26.
31. An unpublished letter to Tillich, April 14, 1933.

with Tillich's open letter, and particularly with his demolition of Hirsch's *logos-concept*—not because of the concept itself but in opposition to the new German spirit—this hope has shattered.

Hirsch reiterates his view that Tillich's historical as well as theological thinking was never centered on the nation. Hirsch, on the other hand, always saw his thinking as German, and it is this which differentiated his own "talk about the hour, moment, historical turn, decision, calling, risk and so on" from Tillich's concept of the *kairos:*

It becomes immediately apparent in the nationally-bound nature of my historical thinking. All my thought about life and history stresses that I as a German know myself as bound and called by God in an unshaken way within my earthly existence, in the service of that which I call the "hidden sovereign," in the service of a specific historical people [*Volkstum*], in which I have awakened to life and personality; and whoever tries to pull apart my concept of the hidden sovereign the way Tillich tries, has set himself in opposition to all my political and historical concepts. I have never understood how Tillich's Marxist thinking, despite the greater depth that he has, can so bewitch Tillich that he becomes blind to the particular binding and creative center of every earthly-political occurrence, to the nation and state as the historical force to which the trinity of science [*Wissenschaft*], technology [*Technik*], and economics [*Wirtschaft*], which are interconnected in Tillich but also falsely separated, are finally subordinated, because this trinity is not the law of being in the same primary sense as nation and state are.[32]

Hirsch does not want to deny the interwovenness of the various nations and peoples and the depth of cross-cultural human interaction, but maintains that one's primary experience of the "true life-preserving ground" of one's being can be found only in the context of one's own people. Through a people's rediscovery of its national *nomos* the boundary between God and humanity can in some sense be shattered. Hirsch hopes that other nations and peoples will, like Germany, rediscover the uniqueness of their own *nomos*, according to their own situation and type.[33] What Hirsch rejects is a cosmopolitan, international, and

32. "Brief an Herrn Dr. Stapel," pp. 26-27. In 1933 Hirsch had published a lengthy essay on the "Hidden Sovereign," entitled "Vom verborgenen Souverän."

33. Hirsch says: "An der Wiederentdeckung des volkhaften Nomos in seiner verpflichtenden Tiefe, so dass die Grenze gegen Gott darinnen aufbricht, hab ich die deutsche Geschichtswende als das Ende dieses Zeitalters bei uns geschildert und habe nur so, dass überall mit gleicher Ursprünglichkeit die gleiche Wiederentdeckung je besonders nach Lage und Art geschieht, eine Ausweitung unsrer Geschichtswende zur Wende für andere Volkstümer zu erhoffen gewagt. Nicht um die lebendige Verflochtenheit der Volkstümer zu leugnen oder zu zerstören, wie Tillich mir andichtet, wahre ich diese Begrenzung, und erst recht nicht, um die Tiefe des Humanen, in dem das Verstehen von Mensch zu Mensch und Volk zu Volk geschieht, aufzuheben, sondern um dem allen, dass mir zum Menschsein gehört, den wahrhaftigen lebenbewahrenden Grund zu geben." "Brief an

rootless type of theology.[34] The *kairos*-teaching, in the eyes of Hirsch, strives precisely for such a universal interpretation of world history throughout time and space.[35] This is what Hirsch rejects. To be truly human is to take one's place within a particular nation, in responsible obedience to its demands for service, recognizing at the same time the fallibility of one's decision and trusting in the providence of God.

It is this obligation to a historical national people that Hirsch finds lacking in Tillich's thought and life. In one of the most devastating critiques of his whole article Hirsch accuses Tillich of being a "free-floating individual" in the mode of 19th-century individualism and intellectualism:

> Tillich is somehow freed where I am bound. He finds his service to the dynamic historical whole through a "prophetic" stance, as he expresses it; that is, as a free-floating [*frei-schwebender*] individual, who, from a position overlooking the whole teeming life-coherence of the world, defines his place and task through an intuition which is inwardly justified but not rigorously demonstrated. That is the noblest form of individualism and intellectualism of the preceding historical epoch: being bound is known only as a self-binding of the intellect;... I do not deny that in this position there can exist a holy decisiveness. And yet, there is within it just that mentality that you, Doctor Stapel, and I have found in some way to have *transgressed* against the measure and boundary of earth-bound and community-obligated human beings; and over against which we have placed primitive, simple obligation in the sphere of natural-historical powers in the service of the "hidden sovereign," namely, nationality, as that which is genuinely responsible and authentically human. We say no, as German Lutherans, to the individualism of the spiritual [*geistigen*] human being, which is based on detachment, even in this its best and most pious form; and we do not shrink from characterizing it as individualism even when, as in Tillich's case, it has led to a surrender of the self to the Marxist-shaped mass proletarian movement.[36]

Herrn Dr. Stapel," p. 27.

34. Hirsch does not deny the interdependence and interwovenness of nations, nor does he deny the universal dimensions of human nature and existence. But what he does reject is a watered-down international culture which has no sense of national and ethnic identity. He describes it in the following way: "Aber das sieht eben nur der richtig, der den rechten Blickpunkt für Gesetz und Mitte des geschichtlichen Lebens sich nicht verwirren lässt durch ufer-und haltlos werdende welt-geschichtliche Umblicke, die nur, wie bei Tillich geschehen, zu der von Ihnen und mir gehassten alle echte gegliederte Humanität gefährdenden falschen Internationalität des Denkens und Lebens führen. Selbst wenn aber dieser Irrgang vermieden werden könnte, würde für mich eine Totaldeutung der ganzen Weltgeschichte durch alle Räume und Zeiten, worauf die Kairoslehre zustrebt nicht notwendig mit der geisthaften Tiefe des Lebensverständnisses gegeben sein." *Ibid.*, pp. 27-28.

35. *Ibid.*

36. The complex but important German text reads as follows: "Tillich ist irgendwie gelöst, wo

The chaos and confusion of the Weimar period was, according to Hirsch, a direct result of a generation of such "free-floating" (or "freely-suspended") individuals who stressed autonomy and freedom rather than duty, obligation, and being bound to their people. It is out of a disillusionment with this mentality that the Young National Lutheran movement was born. Out of this, also, grew Hirsch's conviction that the divine *horos* calls humankind to an all-encompassing, duty-demanding commitment to a particular nation and people.

According to Hirsch we come to understand ourselves as members of a particular ethnic people because of God's order of creation. Thus, our true freedom and humanity can be found and fulfilled only as we discover and accept our place in that created order:

Every responsible, free decision in a historical situation and in the face of a contemporary power [*Gegenwartsmächtigen*], is genuine for us only on the basis of self-discovery in a self-evident, holy bindingness to a community [*heiliger Gemeinschaftsgebundenheit*]. The law of actuality, which gives and protects the life of us as created humans, exists as a duty-demanding divine order of creation, according to which we are able to be truly free and alive only in the sphere of the earthly interconnectedness of blood and destiny [*im Ring irdischer Bluts- und Schicksalsverbundenheit*], only as those who recognize the duty-demanding Nomos [*verpflichtenden Nomos Anerkennenden*]. God as creator and ruler, as Lord of history, is a harsh law, and yet he is revealed in it through mysterious hiddenness [*Verhüllung*] and darkness [*Verdunkelung*]. We hear ourselves called to responsible decision, not as prophets in Tillich's sense, but as those who, in the paradoxical vitality of conscience that posesses us [*uns habenden*] prior to all thinking and decision-making, recognize a law that is powerful for them.[37]

ich gebunden bin. Er findet seinen Dienst am bewegten geschichtlichen Ganzen in 'prophetischer' Haltung, wie er es ausdrückt, das heisst als ein frei schwebender Einzelner, der in Überschau über den ganzen strömmenden Lebenszusammenhang der Welt sich seine Stellung und Aufgabe bestimmt in einer innerlich gerechtfertigten, aber nicht streng beweisbaren Intuition. Das ist die edelste Gestalt des Individualismus und Intellektualismus der abgelaufnen Geschichtsepoche: die Bindung wird nur als ein Sichselberbinden des Geistes gekannt, der bindende Gott spricht durch den das Telos der Lebensmächte findenden Geist selbst. Ich leugne nicht, dass in dieser Haltung heilige Entschlossenheit liegen kann. Und doch ist eben diejenige Geistigkeit darin, die Sie, Herr Doktor Stapel, und ich irgendwie als Mass und Grenze des erdgebundnen, gemeinschaftsverpflichteten Menschen *überschreitend* empfunden haben, und der wir primitive, schlichte Gebundenheit im Ring der natürlich-geschichtlichen Mächte, im Dienste des 'verborgenen Souveräns,' nämlich des Volkstums, als das wahrhaft Menschliche und wahrhaft Verantwortliche gegenübergestellt haben. Wir verneinen als deutsche Lutheraner den in Lösung gegründeten Individualismus des geistigen Menschen auch in dieser seiner feinsten und frömmsten Gestalt, und wir lassen nicht ab, ihn als Individualismus zu kennzeichnen, auch wenn er wie bei Tillich zu einer Selbsthingabe an die vom Marxismus geformte proletarische Massenbewegung geführt hat." *Ibid.*, pp. 28-29. It is interesting to note that Hirsch pays tribute here to Tillich's form of individualism as being of the finest and most pious type; nevertheless, it is an individualism which he as a Lutheran must reject.

From the beginning, Hirsch, as a person who knew the living Lord of history, always hated wholeheartedly what he considered to be the Judaistic transformation of life into a schema or codex. For him life was a risk with God, open to the divine spirit's disclosure of the demands of the hour and the situation. The person, therefore, who does not have this "self-evident duty-demanding consciousness of himself being bound under the law of natural-historical actuality, which is under the Horos," is like the person who considers himself independent of the "organically-conditioned law of life" and is, with respect to eternal matters, a "dreamer who produces myths at the point where one ought to be honoring the Horos."[38]

In light of all of this, Hirsch concludes, Tillich must surely (1) admit that Hirsch speaks authentically about the "hour" and its call, (2) be pleased that Hirsch has in fact not appropriated Tillich's formulation of the *kairos* for himself (Hirsch says Tillich has not only broadened but also distorted the biblical meaning of *kairos*, as well as the Kierkegaardian sense of the "moment" by giving them an individualistic interpretation which is foreign to Hirsch), and (3) see that the relation between Hirsch and Gogarten is more than simply tactical. Hirsch adds that in his espousal of the new German spirit two sides are always held in tension—sides which fall apart in Tillich: ethos and earthliness, law and historicity, bindingness (*Gebundenheit*) and political risk.[39] Tillich separates these contrary poles and judges Hirsch from one side or the other. Seen from one side alone Hirsch appears to be a sacramentalist. Seen from the other he becomes a moralist.

Concerning the Charge of Heresy

Theologically speaking the most serious charge Tillich levels against Hirsch is that of heresy, a charge that was made repeatedly by the confessing church—of which Tillich was technically never a member—against the German Christians.

---

37. "Alle verantwortliche freie Entscheidung in einer geschichtlichen Lage und gegenüber einem Gegenwartsmächtigen ist uns nur echt auf dem Boden des Sichfindens in selbstverständlicher, heiliger Gemeinschaftsgebundenheit. Das Gesetz der Wirklichkeit, dass uns als geschaffnen Menschen das Leben gibt und bewahrt, ist als eine verpflichtende göttliche Schöpfungsordnung da, gemäss der wir nur im Ring irdischer Bluts- und Schicksalsverbundenheit, nur als die den verpflichtenden Nomos Anerkennenden wahrhaft frei und lebendig zu sein vermögen. Gott als Schöpfer und Walter, als Herr der Geschichte, ist strenges Gesetz, und darinnen in geheimnisvoller Verhüllung und Verdunkelung dennoch offenbar. Nicht als Propheten im Sinne Tillichs, sondern als solche, die in der vor allem Denken und Entscheiden und habenden paradoxen Vitalität des Gewissens ein Gesetz an ihnen mächtig wissen, hören wir uns zu verantwortlicher Entscheidung gerufen." *Ibid.*, pp. 29-30.
38. *Ibid.*, p. 30.
39. *Ibid.*, pp. 30-31.

According to the confessing church the so-called "false doctrine" of the German Christians was—as most clearly expressed in the Barmen Declaration of 1934—that they considered "besides this one Word of God [Jesus Christ], still other events and powers, figures and truths, as God's revelation."[40] In Part Four Hirsch defends himself against this charge.

Tillich's charge of heresy takes place on three levels: (1) According to Tillich, Hirsch has given an absolute value to the German revolutionary upheaval (*Umbruch*), something inadmissible for Christians. Thus, Hirsch functions as a priest consecrating a historical event instead of speaking the critical-prophetic word; (2) Hirsch supports the totalitarian claims of the state without preserving the church's right to protest and deviate from the norm (*Ausweichraum*). Consequently he takes away from the church and the Spirit the possibility of resistance to an anti-Christian development in the political sphere; and (3) Hirsch has made present political events in Germany into a second source of revelation, standing alongside that of the biblical message.[41] What becomes overwhelmingly clear in Hirsch's defense of himself against these charges is the fact that at the heart of their differences is a divergent understanding of Luther and a different attitude toward Lutheranism.

Hirsch begins his defense by turning to Luther's teachings on obedience to parents, lordship and authority, and the Lutheran understanding of loyalty, oaths of loyalty, and obedience. He reminds Tillich of the seriousness with which Lutherans have traditionally regarded the oath of loyalty, adding that he himself had never sworn an oath of loyalty to the Weimar Republic—it had never been demanded of him. To swear an oath of loyalty before God, argues Hirsch, is to commit oneself unconditionally and excludes any mental reservation (*reservatio mentalis.*) Basing his defense of the oath on Romans 13, Hirsch argues that the critique against the oath of allegiance arises out of 19th century liberalism and is

---

40. Article One of the Barmen Declaration states the following: "Jesus Christ, as he is attested for us in Holy Scripture, is the one Word of God which we have to hear and which we have to trust and obey in life and in death. We reject the false doctrine, as though the Church could and would have to acknowledge as a source of its proclamation, apart from and besides this one Word of God, still other events and powers, figures and truths, as God's revelation." Arthur C. Cochrane, *The Church's Confession Under Hitler,* p. 239. The Barmen declaration with its six major articles, while ultimately the product of intensive committee work and the ratification of the 139 delegates of the Barmen Synod in May 24-31, 1934, bears the distinctive marks of Karl Barth's theology, who, it is generally agreed, basically wrote the document and saw it through to its end. Barth's Christocentric crisis theology, which had evolved during the 1920s and had been extremely influential in German theological and ecclesiastical circles during the Weimar period, is evident throughout the declaration. This declaration became the manifesto of the confessing church from 1934 to 1945. Barmen's theology reflects the culmination and triumph of a particular theology—Barth's crisis or Word of God Theology—over at least two other theologies: Tillich's *Kairos* Theology and Hirsch's *Nomos* Theology, theologies which had struggled with each other throughout the Weimar period. See A. James Reimer, "The Theology of Barmen: Its Partisan-Political Dimension," *Toronto School of Theology* 1, 2(Fall, 1985), pp. 155-174.

41. "Brief an Herrn Dr. Stapel," pp. 31-32.

made by theologians who have a broken relation to Lutheran teachings. The liberal oath to a constitution is truly problematic. The conditions of a constitution are artificially produced; and, further, one cannot place one's trust in a paper document the way one can in a living person, a requisite for any oath of loyalty.[42] It is of course logically possible that for the sake of the gospel or because of some unforeseen earthly need, this loyalty and obedience changes into faithful and suffering disobedience, even for the genuine Lutheran Christian.[43]

Faithfulness and obedience demand an all-or-nothing stance. An attitude of critical reservation undermines them. While there is a dialectic present in our earthly and political commitments, it is a dialectic that is God's, not our own. God may choose to shatter our own position and views, but this in no way frees us from making unconditional commitments. Referring to his pledge to earthly authorities, Hirsch makes the following declaration:

> I give and pledge them their earthly place, trusting in the God and being obedient to the God who bids me so to give and to pledge; and this latter trust and obedience carries me and hallows me in my total commitment to earthly bondage [*Bindung*]. If it pleases God to shatter my particular position as false, then out of a sense of crushing shame over such a judgment I have to find my way back to a new trust and obedience under Him and thus struggle for a new and binding position; and the new position will again be a completely genuine actualization of a life in earthly bondage. I cannot want to be a god-like, free-floating spirit with a confident dialectical relation to the law of the earthly community which has laid hold of me. My place within my earthly existence is not a dialectical one at my disposal; it is an immediate and duty-demanding earthly existence and the dialectic in it is not mine but my Creator's and Lord's, who joins life and situation for me.[44]

42. *Ibid.*, p. 34n. Hirsch attaches here a lengthy five-point footnote entitled "Evangelisch-lutherische Lehre vom Treueid [oath of loyalty]."

43. Hirsch describes the theoretical possibility of civil disobedience with the words: "Die abstrakte Möglichkeit, dass um Gottes und des Evangeliums willen, ja nach mir sogar um eines grossen sonst nicht behebbaren irdischen Notstandes willen, die Treue und der Gehorsam sich in die Treue des leidenden Ungehorsams verwandelt, besteht logisch immer, und der echte lutherische Christ würde, wenn solche Stunde kommt, schlicht seinen Mann zu stehen haben." *Ibid.*, p. 33.

44. This highly significant German text reads as follows: "Ich gebe und gelobe sie der irdischen Stelle im Vertrauen auf den Gott, in Gehorsam unter den Gott, der sie mich geben und geloben heisst, und dies letzte Vertrauen und Gehorchen trägt und heiligt mich in meiner ganzen Hingabe hinein in die irdische Bindung. Gefällt es Gott, mir meine bestimmte Haltung als falsch zu zerbrechen, so muss ich aus zernichtender Beschämung über solches Gericht heraus mich wiederum zu Vertrauen und Gehorsam unter ihm hinfinden und darin neu gebundne Haltung erringen, und die neue Haltung wird wiederum ganze echte Verwirklichung des Lebens in irdischer Bindung sein. Ich kann nicht ein göttlich freischwebender Geist sein wollen, der ein dialektisch gesichertes Verhältnis zu dem ihn nehmenden Gesetz der irdischen Gemeinschaft hat. Ich bin nicht auf eine mir verfügbare dialektische Weise in irdischer Existenz, ich bin unmittelbar in verpflichtender irdischer Existenz,

Thus, what ultimately sanctifies one's life and commitment is the integrity of one's personal trust in God, who is the Lord not only of individuals but of history and nations as well. The same God who frees us on an individual level binds us to our earthly obligations and responsibilities in the socio-political sphere. The realms are different but it is the same God who rules in both spheres. This is where "Christian freedom" and "political bondage" come together.[45] The Christian is both free in his immediate spiritual relation to God and bound in his socio-historical existence. The political movement to which one commits oneself, however, is not beyond the pale of critique and judgment. A political authority must trust in God as well and bow before the Lord of history. This is the criterion by which one must judge and evaluate an historical-political movement: "I may be permitted here to make an applicable observation: that in my duty as a German, the established relation between faithfulness and commitment in which I now stand with respect to the movement and the power which is currently renewing Germany, has its solid foundation and its inviolable sanctification in the fact that the leader [*Führer*], the movement and the government humbly submit [*beugen*] themselves and the nation before the Lord of history who demands of all us discipline, honor, sacrifice and risk for the sake of the whole."[46]

Hirsch protests against Tillich's attempt to draw a parallel between his own commitment to the Marxist-formed proletarian movement and that of Hirsch's allegiance to National Socialism. Such a comparison rests on the false assumption that both, because they see earthly movements as combining politics and worldviews, fall under the same religious and Christian judgment. One cannot, as Barth has done against Kittel, name subordination to the swastika and to the Soviet star in the same breath. There is a qualitative difference between the two, both religiously and ethically.[47]

und die Dialektik darinnen ist nicht mein, sondern meines Schöpfers und Herrn, der mir Leben und Lage fügt." *Ibid.*, pp. 34-35. Actually, Tillich and Hirsch have very similar sounding ways of talking about the "holy" and what it means for an earthly event to be "hallowed," as we have seen in an earlier chapter.

45. Hirsch says the following about Christian freedom in the context of earthly bondage: "Wo darum das Vertrauen auf den Gott, der der Herr der Geschichte bleibt, das Bindende ist in der Stunde des Treue Forderns und Treue Gebens, da empfängt die Unmittelbarkeit irdischen Daseins aus der verborgenen Unmittelbarkeit jedes Einzelnen zu Gott beides zugleich, die verpflichtende Ganzheit der Eingliederung und die Freiheit des im Geiste ein einzelner verantwortlicher Mensch Seins." *Ibid.*, p. 35.

46. *Ibid.* For Hirsch, unfaithfulness and betrayal on the part of people to their earthly rulers has the effect of destroying the rulers' faith in God, their own sense of obligation and commitment to God. Hirsch says as much in the following: "Vielleicht kommt das darin zum mächtigsten Ausdruck, dass dies sich durch Gott in Treue an den irdisch Waltenden binden Lassen heisst den irdisch Waltenden durch Treue binden an Gott." *Ibid.*

47. An important quotation in this regard is the following: "Tillichs Vergleich seiner Hingabe an die proletarische Bewegung und meiner an den deutschen Nationalsozialismus beruht auf der Voraussetzung, dass beide, weil sie irdische Bewegungen mit Verknüpfung von Weltanschauung

Tillich has charged him with destroying Christian freedom by uncritically allowing a historical movement the full power to structure all of life in the name of God. Hirsch is, however, fully cognizant of the danger of using the Eternal merely to sanctify an earthly obligation: "If the Eternal is used merely to hallow an earthly obligation [*Bindung*], then the earthly becomes hardened and closed off to any breaking in of the Eternal. Such a deified earthly reality becomes a power which enslaves the faith and love of Christians."[48] Hirsch bases his interpretation of Christian freedom squarely on what he considers to be Luther's view of freedom and bondage, a view which is alien to an age of free-floating freedom and spirituality. For Luther "freedom" applied to the Christian's personal relation to God (forgiveness and justification) and "bondage" to the person's participation in the laws of earthly existence. Citing a passage from his book, *Die gegenwärtige geistige Lage,* Hirsch explicates even more clearly what he means by this double stance of freedom and bondage:

"It is in relation to the earthly embrace of nationality that we correctly learn to see our freedom and bondage. What is it in Luther that shatters the false individualism which is incapable of committing itself totally and unconditionally? It is a genuine Christian individualism that recognizes its freedom and individuality as derived from God. This Christian individualism is the basis for the unbreakable defiance [*Trotz*] of the pious against a wholly tempting world [*eine ganze ihn onfechtende Welt*], against every earthly claim which is not sanctioned by God. Thereby it gives to the commitment of oneself [*Sich heineingeben*] to the earthly and also to nationality the weight of a resolution before God. And thus it secures precisely the unconditionality of service and duty: the free yes to service before God compels one to keep oneself within an earthly relation to God. That is something which earthly nationality [*Volkstum*] with all its raging power could not have made me capable of merely through earthly majesty. Precisely he who is free in God, who knows the contingency of the temporal, can be completely faithful within the earthly."[49]

und Politik seien, unter der gleichen religiösen und christlichen Beurteilung stünden. Und diese Voraussetzung—die Karl Barth z. B. veranlasst hat, gegen Kittel mit noch mehr extremer Anwendung, für die Tillich natürlich nicht verantwortlich ist, das Stehen unter dem Hakenkreuz und das unter dem Sowjetstern in einem Atem zu nennen—ist der Grundfehler in Tillichs analytischer Abwägung meiner und seiner Haltung. Ich würde das nicht sagen, wenn hier nicht Tillich Exponent eines auch sonst jetzt umgehenden theologischen und kirchlichen Vorurteils wäre." *Ibid.*, pp. 35-36. What is noteworthy in this statement is that it is Hirsch who refuses to be compared with Tillich and not the other way around. Tillich is more ready to admit parallels than is Hirsch.

48. "Wenn das Ewige nur gebraucht wird, die irdische Bindung zu heiligen, dann wird das Irdische in sich verhärtet und verschlossen vor dem Hereinbruch des Ewigen. Und ein so vergöttlichtes Irdisches wird zu einer den Glauben und die Liebe des Christen knechtenden Macht." "Brief an Herrn Dr. Stapel," pp. 36-37.

49. *Ibid.*, pp. 37-38. Hirsch is citing here a passage from his *Die gegenwärtige geistige Lage*,

While it is true to say that one's faith and freedom in God hallow one's earthly commitment, it would be wrong, according to Hirsch, to call this a "deification" or "sanctification" of the earthly-historical. Earthly-historical reality must always be recognized as temporal and never confused with the eternal.[50]

It is Tillich, not he himself, who has confused the two realms—the eternal and the temporal. This is because Tillich lacks a proper understanding of the Lutheran teaching of law and gospel. According to this teaching, the gospel applies to one's relation to God and the law applies to one's earthly bondage. For Hirsch the eternal sphere deals with questions of salvation and justification before God; for Tillich the eternal realm somehow structures human activity and the earthly sphere:

My having life and salvation in God, my being a child of the eternal kingdom which will be disclosed finally to me in death and judgment, is not conditioned by the earthly-historical obligation in which the law holds me, or even through my placing myself within it. It is the free gift of God in Christ. Divine love, which is given to me in faith, is not bound to the all-embracing divine rule in law and history. It is the free eternal divine life itself which discloses itself to me and thereby frees me. This is not correctly conceptualized by Tillich (this much I can say even though all his sayings concerning ultimate and eternal things seem to me to have about them a noteworthy uncertainty and therefore an incomprehensibility), because he sees the coming kingdom of God as somehow both promised (to us) and demanded (of us). To me it is that which is purely promised, and thus in the promise, freely given to faith.[51]

This does not mean, for Hirsch, that there is no connection between law and gospel, between the eternal spiritual sphere and the temporal physical sphere. "Is the relationship between that which is believed and the earthly-historical thereby not superceded [*aufgehoben*]?" asks Hirsch. "No. The same God who makes me free in his love places me within earthly-historical life, with its law and its duty. He gives to my faith the historical actuality which stands under the law as his discipline and my way into an undisclosed eternity."[52] The law is the

pp. 163-164.

50. We saw in an earlier chapter how Tillich himself, in his 1921 "Masse und Religion," talks about the mass as holy. Tillich says: *"Die Masse ist heilig; denn sie ist Offenbarung der schöpferischen Unendlichkeit des Unbedingt-Wirklichen* und insofern der Unbedingtkeit des Unbedingten, angeschaut durch die Kategorie der Quantität." "Masse und Religion," *GW* II, p. 72.

51. "Brief an Herrn Dr. Stapel," p. 38.

52. "Hebt sich dann nicht aber das Verhältnis des Glaubenden zum Irdisch-Geschichtlichen auf? Nein. Eben der Gott, der mich in seiner Liebe frei macht, stellt mich in das irdisch-geschichtliche Leben mit seinem Gesetz und seiner Pflicht. Er gibt meinem Glauben die unter dem Gesetz steh-

path through which, not by which, human beings come to the gospel.

Paradoxically, precisely by freeing us from the law as far as personal salvation and justification is concerned, the gospel binds us to the law as far as temporal and earthly reality is concerned: "Thus it is through my faith in the gospel, which makes me free from the law, that I am bound to total service and total commitment [*ganzer Hingabe*] to an earthly life held in custody by the law. The freedom of the conscience from the law in one's relation to God is the unconditional sanctification [*Heiligung*] of service in the fulfillment of the law."[53] For him, Hirsch adds—and this has been expressed both by Stapel and himself in their *nomos* concept—the notion of "law" is not a "bloodless catalogue of commands" but a "governance [*Walten*] and activity [*Wirken*] that preserves life and moves history [*geschichtsbewegtes*]." In one sense law and gospel are strictly separated. The law *qua* law deals with earthly obligations and duties. The gospel *qua* gospel deals with one's personal relation to God. In another sense, however, they are vitally linked. The same God who gives us freedom of conscience in the gospel has created the earthly-historical set of relationships in which he has placed us. Faithfulness and obedience to the law of these relationships demonstrates our freedom in Christ. Thus, to be a Christian means to receive one's personality every moment by divine grace, something which remains incomprehensible and is not at one's own disposal. To be a Christian means to be a free person in the realization and fulfillment of a nationally-bounded (*volkhaft*) humanity, with a trans-human basis and purpose within individual life. Hirsch doubts that Tillich has such a trans-human grounding (*transhumaner Gründung*) in the divine spirit.

Out of this law-gospel duality grows another dualism—that of the two kingdoms—which is central, as we have already seen, to Hirsch's interpretation of the Christian's relation to National Socialism. It is Luther's two-kingdom doctrine—rather than the priestly-sacramental vs. the prophetic-critical schema of Tillich's religious socialism—that provides Hirsch with the schema through which he views the German events of 1933. It is for this reason that he sees his own strong commitment to the German "revolution" in terms of a political realism and not a religious utopianism, as Tillich charged. "A religious utopianism, which acts as if the kingdom of God is now actualizing itself on earth, is one to which I would not give myself either with or without critical reservation," asserts Hirsch.[54] He expresses his "political realism" (in contrast to Tillich's "believing realism") regarding the German Reich in the following remarkable passage:

ende geschichtliche Wirklichkeit als seine Zucht und meinen Weg in die unenthüllte Ewigkeit hinein." *Ibid.*, pp. 38-39.
53. *Ibid.*, p. 39.
54. *Ibid.*

I see in the German political occurrence a hard, sober, and rigorous affair [*angelegenheit*], the building up of a life-regimen for my nation which grasps and shapes the total person out of a sense of accountability and a courage which is kindled by the consciousness of the "boundary." What is to evolve is not the kingdom of God but the kingdom of the Germans, built with an attitude of humble worship of the Lord of history. The joy and gratitude to God for having granted to us the beginning and the possibility, for the will to obedience and accountability against the powers of destruction in the hour of greatest need which has been awakened in our nation, can, to be sure, find extreme forms of expression here and there and in individual cases awaken enthusiastic hopes [*schwärmerische Hoffnungen*].[55]

Here we see how the two-kingdom doctrine works when applied to a concrete political situation and how Hirsch can unequivocally support a totalitarian movement such as National Socialism without, in his view, deifying it as Tillich charges. Furthermore, Hirsch lives under no illusion that there may not be extremists who falsely absolutize it and whose passion turns into false utopianism. Ultimately, however, it is Tillich who is in danger of deifying the state by applying the kingdom of God as a standard for restructuring Germany into a socialist state.

In retrospect it may strike us as surprising that Hirsch at this stage in the evolution of National Socialism still believed that Hitler saw himself as humbly accountable to the Lord of history:

Whoever makes the Führer [Hitler] into a religious utopian and his Third Reich into a kingdom of God because in his actions as a statesman—so completely in contrast to what we have experienced from politicians here and elsewhere—he recognizes himself as accountable to God and because he realizes that no political order can preserve the life of a nation other than one that looks up to God and honors obligation [*Bindung*] under God, that person falsely transfers categories from a religiously-enhanced Marxism and applies them to a movement of a different kind and with different aims.[56]

---

55. *Ibid.*

56. *Ibid.*, p. 40. "Wer aber den Führer deshalb, weil er in seinem Handeln als Staatsmann—so ganz im Gegensatz zu dem, was wir an Politikern bei uns und anderwärts erlebt haben—unter der Verantwortung vor Gott sich weiss, und weil er weiss, dass keine politische Ordnung anders denn als Ordnung eines zu Gott aufblickenden, die Bindung unter Gott ehrenden Volks lebenbewahrend zu sein vermag, zu einen religiösen Utopisten macht und sein drittes Reich zu einem Gottesreich, der überträgt fälschlich die Kategorien des religiös vertieften Marxismus auf eine Bewegung andrer Art und andern Ziels."

His view is more comprehensible once one understands Hirsch's particular critique of the politicians and the political system of the Weimar Republic, which indeed valued the secularization of the state in the name of the separation of church and state. It is not the task of this study to test the accuracy or inaccuracy of Hirsch's appraisal of the religious attitudes of Hitler and other National Socialist leaders. What is clear in the above statement, however, is that (1) Hirsch *believed* Hitler perceived himself as accountable to God in some sense, and (2) Hirsch here disavows any attempts to deify the National Socialist state in a utopian sense.

As far as Tillich's *kairos*-doctrine is concerned, Hirsch evaluates Tillich's philosophy of theonomy more positively than does his friend Stapel. The *kairos*-doctrine, says Hirsch, is an attempt by Tillich to develop a third alternative, half-way between the absurd either-or of the 19th century: *either* viewing history and community totally in terms of self-sufficient human reason and freedom, or seeing history and community as a utopian path to the eternal. Nevertheless, adds Hirsch, he always considered the "critically reflective propheticism" of Tillich's *kairos*-teaching as being neither a commitment to Marxism nor an overcoming of Marxism, but as an illusory solution. What Tillich lacks, according to Hirsch, is a Lutheran understanding of the law-gospel dichotomy and of the two-kingdom doctrine:

> Above all, Tillich lacks that Lutheran understanding of life which expresses and clarifies itself in the knowledge of the dialectic of law and gospel, and the teaching of the two kingdoms which is conditioned by it. In this Lutheran understanding of life lies the possibility of understanding the national political order as hallowed by God; that is, as granted, sustained, and demanded by him, made into a source of creativity and into an undiscussable duty by him, to understand while at the same time to accept it rigorously and clearly as an earthly-temporal matter. In the sense of this understanding of the political I have affirmed the German revolution of 1933 and differentiated myself clearly from the enthusiastic misuse of the event, a fact which Tillich cannot evade.[57]

Again, Hirsch is aware of the danger of extremism in the movement; on numerous occasions he separates himself from those whom he considers overly enthusiastic on the side of nationalism and ethnicity.[58] An important question,

---

57. *Ibid.*

58. In a 1951 autobiographical essay, for instance, Hirsch reflects on this dangerous extremism in the nationalist movement: "Ich habe von da an unter den jungen nationalen evangelischen Theologen und darüber hinaus unter den eine nationale Wiedergeburt ersehnenden geistigen Deutschen manche persönlichen Freunde gehabt und bin stolz darauf gewesen. Aber ich spürte von Anfang an die durch das eherne Schicksal schmerzhaft gezogenen Grenzen dieser Wirkung. Theologie und Kirche gingen unter dem Einfluss der dialektischen Theologie weithin andere, entge-

we might add here, is whether the two-kingdom doctrine, as it evolved in traditional Lutheran theology, was an adequate basis on which to prevent such misuses, or whether it in fact lent itself to being misused.

Hirsch holds that there is a realm dealing with essentials of the common life which must not be subjected to endless debate. An open discussion of all of these matters has taken away human stability, produced a general chaos of meaning, and created a situation in which no young person can be nurtured, no character adequately trained. The spiritual task is to further the common good and not to engender private worldviews. The Christian message is not an alternate worldview but is concerned with inculcating common and shared Christian values. "Faith is something other than a worldview, which is an earthly and a communal affair. When a national-order (*Volksordnung*) is open, within the composite of life and spirituality that sustains it, to the possibility of its natural Nomos and Logos being redemptively wounded (*segnenden Verwundung*) through the gospel, then the Christian has everything he needs gladly to stand within this order and to cooperate in shaping it. Then the boundary of the earthly kingdom is preserved over against the eternal kingdom through its [the boundary] being opened and acknowledged"[59]

Hirsch does not lack all criteria for evaluating a political movement. His criteria, however, are different from those of Tillich. The integrity of a political order must be judged on the basis of its openness to God and the possibility of being "wounded" through the gospel. The problem, however, is how to determine whether a given movement in fact has a sense of humble accountability before the Lord of history and is open to being "wounded"—or corrected—through the gospel. Ultimately, the political decision for Hirsch, as for Tillich, is one of risk.

Is this heavenly freedom then simply something by which we comfort ourselves in our earthly-historical slavery to a political movement? asks Hirsch. No. Hirsch reminds Tillich that he (Hirsch) and his associates joined the national movement which undergirds the German national "revolution" on the basis of conviction and not political opportunism. They gave themselves to the movement before it was in power on the basis of an analysis of the historical

gengesetzte Wege und verschlossen sich, soweit sie das taten, auch um des Gegensatzes zu 'Deutschlands Schicksal' willen allen Einwirkungen meiner theologischen Arbeit. Da wurde es natürlich schwer, wenn nicht unmöglich, radicalen jungen Stürmern und Drängern zur richtigen Einsicht in das Verhältnis des Christlichen und des Humanen zu helfen." "Meine Wandejahre (1916-21)," p. 5.

59. "Der Glaube ist etwas andres als eine Weltanschauung, die eine irdische und eine gemeinsame Angelegenheit ist. Wenn eine Volksordnung in der sie tragenden Lebens- und Geistesverfasstheit geöffnet ist für die Möglichkeit der segnenden Verwundung des natürlichen Nomos und Logos durch des Evangelium, dann ist alles gegeben, dessen ein Christ bedarf, um gerne in ihr stehen und an ihr gestaltend mitarbeiten zu können. Dann ist die Grenze des irdischen Reichs gegen das ewige Reich dadurch gewahrt, dass sie geöffnet und anerkannt ist." "Brief an Herrn Dr. Stapel," p. 42.

crisis in which Germany found itself. Such a decision requires a risk since God has not left human beings any clear recipe for life. While for Tillich concrete personal political freedom is required for personal participation in the structures of society, for Hirsch "the right form of responsible participation is not the critical word, but the constructive and clarifying word of the faithful; and the place where the Christian church fulfills its task of breaking up the hard soil by furrowing German life with the plow of the gospel is not a place of withdrawal [*Ausweichraum*] but the place of work in the middle of the field."[60] The person who reserves for himself his own individual earthly destiny cuts himself off from a genuinely binding national order. Such a person no more belongs to the people who sow and work than does the town dweller who writes a critical and rational article on the work of the farmers.

What does this mean for the German Evangelical church? It means that "If the Evangelical Church is to be a ruling partner in the German Nomos and Logos, then she must be [a part of] the German national order, feel the German distress as her own distress, the German hope as her own hope, and understand her work accountably before the Lord Christ as part of the building up of German life. Such a church will express a constructive, broadening and, where necessary, also a consecrating-wounding [*segnend-verwundend*] voice on behalf of the German spirit and character."[61] There is always the possibility that the movement and personal commitment to it will be wounded, scourged, shattered, or corrected by God.

Concerning a Second Source of Revelation

Hirsch concludes Part Four with a brief defense of himself against the third of Tillich's charges in this section—a charge which is similar to that of Karl Barth and the Barmen group against the German Christians: namely, that they have two sources of revelation—the Bible and Hitler (or the German events of 1933). "Here now the kairos-philosopher and the confession-zealots and persecutors of heretics stand on one front," Hirsch remarks somewhat facetiously. He answers this charge by once again referring to the two kingdoms:

If National Socialism were for me a religious utopia, of which I, myself a Kairos-philosopher, only a clumsier and more naive one, had said that in it the kingdom of God had drawn near or even come completely to pass, then

60. "Ich will kurz antworten: nicht das kritische Wort ist die rechte Gestalt verantwortlicher Mitarbeit, sondern das helfende und klärende Wort des Getreuen, und nicht der Ausweichraum ist die Stelle, an der die christliche Kirche die Verhärtungen aufbrechende Durchfurchung deutschen Lebens mit dem Pflug des Evangeliums vollzieht, sondern der Arbeitsplatz mitten auf dem Acker." *Ibid.*, p. 43.

61. *Ibid.*, pp. 43-44.

Tillich would have obviously been right at this point. But we have indeed already seen that I think in terms of the Lutheran teaching of the two kingdoms. Tillich has here therefore fallen into error, evaluating the assertions of my book, which belong to a different intellectual and theological context, according to what they would have meant in the structure of a religiously-enhanced Marxism. That is the self-deception of a systematic thinker which often underlies the evaluation of unfamiliar [*fremder*] patterns of thought.[62]

Part of the difference between them, Hirsch seems to think, is the fact that he [Hirsch] is an intellectual historian while Tillich is a systematic theologian. Hirsch reveals here a certain mistrust of systematicians, particularly of Tillich when he makes historical judgments: "I am not surprised that now also I am misunderstood by him from the point of a systematic method."[63] He also expresses surprise at Tillich's rigid and orthodox view of revelation, adding that he considers himself to have developed the concept of revelation more fully than Tillich has in his writings.

Here in his response to Tillich and elsewhere Hirsch is adamant in rejecting the confessing church's—and in this case, Tillich's—accusation that he was placing a second revelation beside that of Christ, or that he had other gods beside the one God, Jesus Christ. No, together with Luther, he was proclaiming "Christ alone." He was quite ready to say that in some sense God was revealing his will to Germans through the national awakening that was sweeping across the land. But this had nothing to do with the gospel (justification, salvation, love, mercy, and forgiveness). God's actions in history do not give us personal salvation. Personal salvation and the resurrection to eternal life are granted to us

---

62. *Ibid.*, p. 45: "Wenn der Nationalsozialismus mir eine religiöse Utopie wäre, von der ich, selber ein Kairosphilosoph, nur ein plumper und naiver, gesagt hätte, dass in ihr das Reich Gottes nahe herbeigekommen oder ganz herbeigekommen sei, dann hätte Tillich selbstverständlich hier recht. Aber, wir hapen ja schon gesehen, dass ich in der lutherischen Lehre von den zwei Reichen denke. Tillich ist hier also widerfahren, dass er die einem andern geistigen und theologischen Zusammenhang angehörigen Aussagen meines Buches nach dem beurteilt hat, wass sie in der Struktur des religiös vertieften Marxismus bedeutet hätten. Das ist eine Selbsttäuschung, der systematische Denker in der Beurteilung fremder Gedankengänge des öftern unterliegen."

63. Hirsch adds: "Ich habe so manchen wissenschaftlichen Widerspruch in mir gehabt, wenn ich Tillich irgendwann auf das Gebiet der geisteshistorischen Analyse sich wagen sah. Es wundert mich nicht, dass nun auch ich bei ihm nach systematischer Methode missverstanden worden bin." *Ibid.*, p. 45. Hirsch hints here at a more profound methodological difference between himself and Tillich. Although Hirsch himself had a deep interest in systematic thinking and occupied the chair of systematic theology at the University of Göttingen from 1936-1945, he had a certain suspicion of interpreting the Christian God, the human relation to God, and human ethical responsibilities in history in terms of a comprehensive philosophical system the way it was done in German Idealism as well as by his friend Tillich. Prior to any human system, he felt there was a transcendent God whom one meets in one's individual subjectivity and ethical obedience. Hans-Walter Schütte makes much of this difference in his appropriately titled essay, "Subjektivität und System," *Hirsch Tillich Briefwechsel 1917-1918*, pp. 38-51.

320 Emanuel Hirsch and Paul Tillich

by God in Jesus Christ alone. This is the eternal kingdom, and no earthly reality, nation, political movement, or charismatic leader can be identified with or have the right to infringe upon this kingdom.

Nevertheless, there is a legitimate place also for the earthly kingdom under the sovereignty of God, the Lord of history. This earthly kingdom functions for the purpose of preserving human life through law, coercion, and authority, demanding our ethical obedience, our discipline, and our unconditional commitment. Here in the earthly kingdom we are not free but bound. And this submission and obedience in the earthly realm is a form of obedience to God who has placed us within our particular historical situation.[64]

In his conclusion to the letter Hirsch briefly alludes to one more issue—his view of race and blood—and then ends with a tribute to Tillich and their personal and intellectual relationship over the years. With regard to his notion of race and blood, Hirsch does not go into a substantive explication of his views except to say that Tillich has not understood his concept of blood-bond (*Blutbund*) and that his concept of nation (*Volk*) is broader than what Tillich suggests, consisting of a group of several closely related systems of races. According to Hirsch, "Tillich has overlooked the fact that I, in saying yes to the concern for race and heredity as an unrelinquishable duty in an order which seeks to preserve the nation [*Volksberwahrender Ordnung*], have exactly at this point exercised a piece of responsible academic reflection."[65]

Hirsch closes his letter with some remarkably conciliatory comments about Tillich, saying that he must thank Tillich on two accounts: first, for leading him to the study of Idealistic philosophy in their student years, and second, for being a person with exemplary personal, intellectual, and political integrity even after their 1918 break, one to whom Hirsch and the Young National Lutherans are deeply indebted.

Hirsch makes some further observations which shed light on their relationship: despite their early bond of friendship, there soon developed a divergence in their philosophical views; Tillich was influenced by Schelling and developed a mystical view of the human encounter with God while Hirsch moved in the direction of Fichte and the call to duty and concern with the social question. Because of the importance of these remarks for our whole study, we quote Hirsch's own words at length:

Only one thing remains to be said, without which this letter would be incomplete: to acknowledge to you that I owe Tillich gratitude, and that it has grieved me to be compelled finally to settle the accounts with a friend from my youth, whom I would not like to think out of my life. I thank him on two

64. See A. James Reimer, "The Theology of Barmen: Its Partisan-Political Dimension," *Toronto Journal of Theology* 1,2(Fall 1985), pp. 155-174, pp. 161ff.
65. "Brief an Herrn Dr. Stapel," p. 46.

accounts. First, he is the one who in our student years enticed me into the stream of Idealistic philosophy at a time when I...lacked productive personal initiative. From the Berlin philosophers, who were then authoritative, one learned that the idealists were shoddy [*Stümpler*] and audacious [*Frechlinge*] and that it did not pay to read them; so I limited myself to a serious reading of Kant. That incentive by Tillich was the beginning of a rich intellectual comradeship which extended to the end of the war, and which, despite the ongoing conflict between us—I held to Fichte, he to Schelling; I thought in terms of the call to duty, he in terms of the mystical encounter with God; I was tortured by the social question, he avoided it at the time—was a gift to me (and until now I thought to both of us). And when in 1918 the political rupture occurred between us, which I always perceived to be in some sense a rupture in religious matters as well, I still thought, and that is the second [point of gratitude], that I could learn something from Tillich. Now it was different than it had been earlier. Each one went his own way in his intellectual struggle without really debating with the other, he more rapidly and sensationally [*glänzender*], I with greater heaviness and (for the sake of the political struggle) more intensely [*geballter*]. But throughout all those years he was a singular example to me of a person who in his own way, according to his own law and in line with his own political decision, bore all the miseries of the period of crisis with unheard-of integrity and was intellectually inspiring. One cannot have such an example before oneself without it making one broader and deeper in one's own struggle, even if one opposes and at times is hostile toward every third sentence of every article. I have expressed this second point of gratitude at a particular place in the book, which Tillich attacks, as strongly as the context of the analysis allowed (p. 121).[66]

Hirsch had in fact in his book, which Tillich had attacked so ruthlessly and on the basis of which Tillich had charged Hirsch with plagiarism, admitted that there was a formal similarity between Religious Socialism and Young National Lutheranism: namely, in both cases faith dared to make a political decision, albeit, materially speaking, a different one. He had in that context also clearly identified the concept of the *kairos* as a Religious Socialist (or Theological Marxist) notion, conceptualized as a means of risking a political decision for a future society in the face of the crisis in and decline of Western culture. It was through its struggle with this significant opponent that Young National Lutheranism had been liberated from its own earlier bourgeois underpinnings and had been helped to become a dynamic and coherent movement in its own political decision for National Socialism.[67] In the light of this clearly recognized

66. *Ibid.*, p. 47.
67. In his *Die gegenwärtige geistige Lage*, Hirsch had carefully outlined the important similari-

and articulated indebtedness to Tillich and the religious socialists, while at the same time identifying important differences, one can understand why Hirsch must have been dumbfounded by Tillich's charge of plagiarism.

We must therefore conclude our rather detailed examination of Hirsch's response to Tillich's accursatory open letter by allowing that Hirsch has in fact persuasively defended himself against the charges Tillich levels against him, particularly the charge of plagiarism—an accusation which Tillich himself seems to have modified if not completely withdrawn in his final rejoinder. In the process Hirsch has also raised some substantive countercharges of his own. A careful weighing of these substantive charges on both sides will have to await our final chapter. In the meantime, we might summarize Hirsch's own counter-charges as follows. First, on the more *personal* level, Hirsch claims that Tillich bears a grudge against his friend and has distorted Hirsch's position by inaccurate citations, by taking phrases out of context, by writing a polemical pamphlet rather than a thorough systematic analysis of Hirsch's work. Such a careful reading of Hirsch's writings would have revealed an inner consistency and an intellectual integrity in his thought from early on. Instead, Tillich has personally maligned his friend, charged him with plagiarism, without a proper admission of their common intellectual heritage. Implicit in this first accusation is the charge of partisan politics, in which Tillich disguises their mutual indebtedness to German Idealism, but also the fact that Hirsch's concepts are substantially

ties and differences between Religious Socialism and Young National Lutheranism, and credited the Religious Socialists (implying of course Tillich himself) for making an important contribution to Young National Lutheranism in the development of its own distinctive position: "Die so enstehende Haltung des *religiösen Sozialismus* hatte mit dem, das von ihr am bittersten befehder wurde, dem jungen nationalen Luthertum, formell etwas Verwandtes: der Glaube wagte eine geschichtliche Entscheidung. So ist auch hier der christlichen Theologie ein wesentliches Stück Geschichtsphilosophie zugewachsen. Durch Verwandtschaft und Gegensatz den abstandnehmenden Theologen gegenüber ist hier das Denken auf die Frage der geschichtlichen Dialektik zwischen dem Heiligen und Profanen, dem Geistlichen und dem Weltlichen hingestossen worden.... Die Meinung, in der grossen Krise euramerikanischer Kultur wagend für eine kommende gegen eine untergehende Welt Stellung genommen zu haben, hat den Begriff des *Kairos,* der von Gott gegebnen fordernden geschichtlichen Entscheidungsstunde, erzeugt. Mit alledem hatte diese Geschichtsphilosophie des theologischen Marxismus eine Sendung gerade aum jungen nationalen Luthertum: sie hat es aus der bürgerlichen Enge, die ihm ursprünglich anhaftete, erlösen helfen, hat ihm die andre geschichtliche Entscheidung, die es fällte, in grössre Zusammenhänge stellen helfen. Ohne das innere Ringen mit diesem bedeutenden Gegner—in der Geschichtsphilosophie der theologischen Marxisten war etwas, was im Marxismus sonst fehlte, nämlich Geist—wären die Theologen des jungen nationalen Luthertums kaum lebendig genug geworden, um sich ehrlich an den Nationalsozialismus als die geschichtliche Gestalt der von ihnen geforderten Entscheidung und als den Einsatz eines neuen deutschen Geschichtsalters zu geben" (p. 121). Here we see how carefully and perceptively Hirsch had deliniated his own—and that of Young National Lutheranism—dependence on and independence from Tillichian categories. Particularly noteworthy is Hirsch's observation that the struggle with Religious Socialism helped to free Young National Lutheranism from the narrow middle class values which it had earlier adhered to, and in this way enabled it to develop a more coherent political position of its own.

different from Tillich's own. Tillich is giving vent to a long-standing hostility of Religious Socialists to nationalist-oriented movements such as National Socialism.

Second, on the *theological* level, Tillich lacks a proper understanding of the Lutheran creation teaching (as it relates to the orders of creation such as nationality), the law-gospel dichotomy and the related two-kingdom doctrine. Ironically, therefore, it is Tillich, says Hirsch, who confuses the divine and the human realms by not clearly separating the temporal and the earthly kingdoms. Tillich sees the kingdom of God both as demanded and promised; consequently he assumes that human beings have some part to play in bringing about the kingdom of God on the historical plane. The fallacy of Tillich's critique of Hirsch, according to the latter, is that he judges Hirsch's theology from the perspective of his own religious socialist schema—the priestly-sacramental versus the prophetic-eschatological—a schematization which is foreign to Hirsch's thought. In short, one might say, Hirsch turns Tillich's charge of heresy around by questioning the soundness of Tillich's own theology in the light of Reformation thought.

Third, on the *political* level Tillich lacks a responsible commitment to a particular national community. Instead, he espouses a 19th-century type of liberal, free-floating individualism and intellectualism which takes a critical attitude toward society without itself becoming involved. He does not have a profound sense of duty, destiny, and obligation to his people, but employs the dogmatic and doctrinaire rhetoric of a shallow Marxist-oriented religious socialism in his defense of the proletariat and a rootless international culture. The crisis of the Weimar Republic was a result of just such shallow political thinking, in which individual autonomy rather than an unconditioned commitment to the nation (as an organically-related people) determined German politics. It was out of a disillusionment with this kind of political thinking that Young National Lutheranism was born. Hirsch's own political hopes for Germany rest on the belief that in National Socialism a new authoritative, uniquely German political alternative is emerging (combining individual subjective freedom and external national allegiance) which is quite different from American democracy, British parliamentarianism, French authoritarianism, and Russian "bolshevism."

10
Conclusion: A Critical Evaluation of the Debate and its Implications for the Political Task of Theology

Echoes of the Debate in German Theological Circles

The public debate between Tillich and Hirsch, widely known to have been long-time friends, caused a furor throughout German theological circles and received widespread attention in German periodicals. Karl Ludwig Schmidt, editor of *Theologischer Blätter*, in which Tillich's first open letter to Hirsch appeared in November 1934, sent a copy of that issue to various papers and kept his readers well informed of what he calls the "echo" Tillich's letter received in these other periodicals.[1]

With a few exceptions, all of these echoes, as reported by Schmidt, supported Tillich's critique of Hirsch's position. One of these, that of Karl Ae, in the *Neue Sächsischen Kirchenblatt*, deserves lengthy quotation:

> The response that Tillich gives to Hirsch in his "Open Letter" belongs positively to the most significant and noteworthy statements of the present struggle. In the light of the significance attributed to Theology Professor Hirsch in the present intellectual situation, and in the light of the strong influence that according to all the evidence Hirsch has had and continues to have on the church administration of Ludwig Müller, Hirsch's programatic work needs to be put in question in a particularly clear and critical way....Tillich treats it [Hirsch's position] as a substantive critic, without disputing that something can be learned from it in the particulars. For the sake of discourse

---

1. These echoes included that of Ernst Wolf in *Evangelische Theologie* (November 1934); Karl Ae in *Neue Sächsischen Kirchenblatt* (November 25, 1934); Hermann Mulert in *Christlichen Welt* (December 1, 1934); Hans Schlemmer in *Protestantenblatt* (December 16, 1934); Ernst Bunke in *Deutschen Evangelischen Kirchen-Zeitung für die Gemeinde: Die Reformation* (December 16, 1934); Wilhelm Kolfhaus in *Reformierten Kirchenzeitung* (December 16, 1934); Robert Frick in *Pastoraltheologie* (January 1935); Wilhelm Stapel in *Deutschen Volkstums* (December 2, 1934); and Hans Rückert in *Deutsche Theologie* (April 1935). The above are cited in "Zum offenen Brief Paul Tillichs an Emanuel Hirsch," *Theologische Blätter* 14, 1(January 1935), pp. 25-27; "Nachtrag 'Zum offenen Brief Paul Tillichs an Emanuel Hirsch,'" *Theologische Blätter* 14, 2(February 1935), p. 62; "Zur Auseinandersetzung zwischen Tillich und Hirsch," *Theologische Blätter* 14, 6(June 1935), p. 158.

with the other, Tillich engages the author by taking a stimulating [*spannungs-reichen*] and fruitful middle-position between personal friendship with and objective disavowal of Hirsch. His disavowal and critique is unreserved. To follow it in detail one must read the text itself. It is a masterpiece of Tillichian intellectual-dialectic. At the same time, it is also a Tillichian piece of self-representation and a new portrayal of the nature and limitation of his Kairos teaching. It is also, however, an excellent presentation of the intellectual work of Hirsch....Through it beams of light are cast on our present church situation in general, illuminating its dire inner distress. There are certainly also many theological questions that need to be directed to Tillich. His theological critique of Hirsch here can be supported because it derives from a basic eschatological perspective, a stance defined in terms of the "end" and directed to the "end"; spotlights must today be focussed on various places for the sake of clarity and truth. What concerns us finally and decisively is the truth as given to us in the Biblical revelation; it recognizes to be sure the obligation and the command to take history seriously as standing under the will of God; nevertheless, it also acknowledges the insight that we dare not absolutize (and thereby sacralize) any "moment" of history.[2]

Another echo, as reported by Schmidt, is that of Hans Schlemmer, in the *Protestantenblatt*. Schlemmer makes the point that Tillich's whole article intends to show how Hirsch has taken over Tillich's most important insights from the Religious Socialists and, thus, Hirsch himself [without wanting to] is aligning himself with young Marx. What Schlemmer finds most interesting in Tillich's open letter, however, is the interdependence of theology and philosophy: "...our interest," he says, "in the given context is before all else the extent to which in the whole argument of Tillich theological and philosophical trains-of-thought are intertwined with each other, to the point of 'an identification of theology with a theonomous philosophy,' something affirmed by both opponents; the age of an alleged independence of theology from philosophy is past."[3] This particular response to the debate identifies a point of identity between Hirsch and Tillich—both use philosophy and theology in their interpretation of the present religious and political situation—which, although not explicitly mentioned here, distinguishes them from Barth's theology.

Schmidt does his part, after Tillich's first open letter, to keep his readers informed about the variety of responses, to keep Tillich in New York up to date, and to press other periodicals to take a stand. A series of personal, unpublished letters from Schmidt to Tillich in the years 1934 and 1935 give poignent witness

---

2. This statement by Karl Ae is cited by Karl L. Schmidt in "Zum offenen Brief Paul Tillichs an Emanuel Hirsch," *Theologische Blätter*, p. 26.
3. "Nachtrag 'Zum Offenen Brief Paul Tillichs an Emanuel Hirsch,'" *Theologische Blätter*, p. 62.

to the behind-the-scenes entrigue that characterized the debate, its consequences, and the publishing details surrounding these. In a December 17, 1934 letter, for instance, Schmidt indicates having received numerous letters of support, and complains that some of the larger newspapers like the *Frankfurter Zeitung* have so far remained silent.[4] In a substantial and highly polemical letter dated February 25, 1935 Schmidt tells Tillich that he has requested his publisher (J.C. Hinrichs) to send Hirsch's *Christliche Freiheit und politische Bindung*, containing Hirsch's response to Tillich "Brief an Herrn Dr. Stapel," to Tillich in New York. In this letter Schmidt denounces both Hirsch and Wilhelm Stapel, using unusually strong and vitriolic language. Throughout this letter one gets the overwhelming sense that behind the Tillich-Hirsch controversy there is a much larger and longer antagonism between two theological-political camps, represented by the radically different editorial policies of *Theologische Blätter*, as edited by Karl L. Schmidt, on the one side, and *Deutsches Volkstum*, as edited by Wilhelm Stapel, on the other, each publicly denouncing the other in turn.[5] These letters show that the Tillich-Hirsch debate cannot be separated from the context of this larger Schmidt-Stapel antagonism, which itself represents long-standing partisan hostilities between left-wing and right-wing theological and political camps, each with their own representative periodicals.

This fact has the effect of partly relativizing not only Schmidt's and Stapel's positions, but that of Tillich's and Hirsch's as well. Schmidt tells Tillich in the February 25 letter that, even prior to Hirsch's response (the form of which he finds objectionable because it is not written as an open letter to Tillich but as a letter to Stapel), he reported on the many positive responses to Tillich's letter in order to make his readers aware of how isolated Hirsch was in his views, despite the fact that there were still some theologians who took his side. According to Schmidt, this remarkable phalanx of opponents to Hirsch cannot be disputed.

---

4. Personal letter: Schmidt to Tillich, December 17, 1934. This series of unpublished letters from Schmidt to Tillich are found in the Tillich Archive, Andover Library, Harvard Divinity School.

5. This personal hostility between Schmidt and Stapel, as editors of two periodicals with very different editorial stances, surfaces in letters by Schmidt to Tillich (February 25, 1935), Schmidt to J.C. Hinrichs'sche Buchhandlung (May 2, 1935), and in a lengthy defense by Schmidt against some of Stapel's charges in "Zum offenen Brief Paul Tillichs an Emanuel Hirsch," *Theologische Blätter* (January 1935), pp. 25-27. In the latter, Schmidt says: "Als Herausgeber und Schriftleiter der ThBl muss ich Wert darauf legen, auf dieses erste Echo aufmerksam zu machen, weil Wilhelm Stapel im 2. Dez.-Heft seines '*Deutschen Volkstums*' auf den Gedanken gekommen ist, die ThBl wie auch die 'Christliche Welt' politisch zu denunzieren. Zu Tillichs Brief weiss er nichts anderes zu sagen als dies: 'Tillich benutzt die frühere Jugendfreundschaft, um dem nationalen Theologen (scil. Emanuel Hirsch) per Du Sottisen zu sagen. Ueber die Grenze her. Emigranten-Theologie, Import via Leipzig. Man wird immer ungenierter.' Dass und wie der Herausgeber des 'Deutschen Volkstums' mich als 'alten Spezialgegner aus der Zeit des Kultusministers Grimme' apostrophiert, ist mehr als eine 'Sottise'. Dass ich als evangelischer Pfarrverweser in Lichtensteig—dieses über 700 Jahre alte Toggenburger Städtchen liegt in der *deutschen Schweiz*—'immer noch die 'Theologischen Blätter' in Leipzig leite, wird mir aus einem peinlich durchsichtigen Grunde vorgehalten." Schmidt, "Zum offenen Brief Paul Tillichs an Emanuel Hirsch," pp. 26-27.

He calls the Hirsch-Stapel-Gogarten-H.M. Müller union a political alliance based on a kind of pseudo-theology and vows to fight such views. He thinks Hirsch's response to Tillich is shallow and characterizes the mutual admiration of Hirsch and Stapel for each other as both sad and comical. He depicts Hirsch as avoiding the real issues and being incognizant of what is really happening politically in Germany.

Even Schmidt, however, has his differences with Tillich's theology, a fact which demonstrates the complexity of the issues involved, and indicates the extent to which theologians within the same camp disagreed with each other. In a lengthy letter to Tillich on April 26, 1935 Schmidt thanks Tillich for a good response, both materially and formally, and promises to print it at the head of the May issue, despite what he anticipates will be strong resistance from his publisher Hinrichs, who is beginning to feel the pressure of the new regime on his publication.[6]

Schmidt agrees especially with Tillich's evaluation of both Hirsch and Barth as "sinners" against the Chalcedonian formulation, Barth on one side and Hirsch on the other, confirming his own thesis that Barth is in danger of a docetic Christology and ecclesiology.[7] Schmidt has problems, however, with Tillich's understanding of the Kingdom of God and how it relates to the Church, and goes on to a substantive critical analysis of Tillich's theology at this point. We cannot here go into Schmidt's critique, except to say that he considers the objectification of the Kingdom of God, as represented by the sixteenth-century Enthusiasts, as in some ways foreshadowing the views of the Religious Socialists as well as the German Christians. He stresses that the Kingdom of God and the Church must be seen as two separate realities, which must not be confused even if both are interpreted eschatologically. It is the Church, as an instrument and witness to the Kingdom of God and not the Kingdom of God itself, which must take a stand over against the demonic elements present in the totalitarian state. While he feels Hirsch is a hopeless case, unchangeable in his ways, he as a third person can finally only remain both silent and sceptical about the personal imponderables that exist between Tillich and Hirsch.

This personal evaluation of Tillich's stance by his friend and editor raises some interesting points that we have alluded to on numerous occasions in our study. Despite all the differences between Tillich and Hirsch, there are some deeper affinities between the two, not only personally but also theologically, which Schmidt recognizes here as "imponderables." More specifically, however, he finds that both the German Christians and the Religious Socialists have something in common: they have inherited from the so-called "Enthusiasts" of the sixteenth-century a view of the Kingdom of God as an objective reality. While

---

6. Personal letter: Schmidt to Tillich, April 26, 1935.
7. According to Schmidt, because of this charge Barth is so angry at him that he has for some time now had no contact with Barth. Personal letter: Schmidt to Tillich, April 26, 1935.

this is not an accurate interpretation of Hirsch's view of the Kingdom of God—Hirsch as we have seen again and again clearly separated the Kingdom of God as an inner reality from the kingdom of the world (in this case the German National Socialist state) as an external reality—it bears some truth when applied to Tillich; and does correctly suggest that at the point where both Tillich and Hirsch "politicize" theology they use some similar categories.

A very different view of the Tillich-Hirsch exchange, and the fundamental issues involved, comes from Hans Rückert, in an essay entitled "Echte Probleme und falsche Parolen. Zur Auseinandersetzung zwischen Hirsch und Tillich," in the February-March issue of *Deutsche Theologie*, an article that Schmidt sent to Tillich at Union Theological Seminary.[8] Rückert, who is clearly sympathetic to Hirsch's cause, defends the need for his rather lengthy essay on the grounds that 1) substantive questions are being discussed by Tillich and Hirsch which go far beyond their personal differences, the right answers to which will have great significance for the fate of the German Evangelical Church; and that 2) the Tillich-Hirsch exchange makes plain that a disparity exists between the true theological state of affairs and the momentary church-political situation, a disparity which falsifies, poisons and lames the whole inner life of contemporary German Protestantism. Every theological journal which recognizes its true task, he says, must try to transcend this disparity.

Rückert sees Hirsch's method of answering Tillich's accusations in the form of a letter to Herrn Dr. Stapel, as quite appropriate, a way of getting at the issues more quickly and avoiding the painful personal dimensions of the debate. He is especially critical of Schmidt's role in publicizing the debate and Tillich's central thesis: that Hirsch has stolen some of Tillich's own Religious Socialist categories, and that somehow Hirsch is an example of what National Socialism has done on a much larger scale—intellectually robbed and plundered Marxism of its central concepts. In a revealing passage Rückert says:

> If need be one can overlook these ideas in someone like Tillich who has been hit so hard and become so embittered by circumstances. However, the fact that among the many voices which in German theological and ecclesiastical circles have with satisfaction taken cognizance of the rebuff of Hirsch by Tillich (K.L. Schmidt has faithfully kept record ad maiorem gloriam of them in his periodical) to my knowledge not one has expressed scepticism concerning this charge of spiritual plagiarism—even if it were in the most

---

8. Hans Rückert, "Echte Probleme und falsche Parolen. Zur Auseinandersetzung zwischen Hirsch und Tillich," *Deutsche Theologie: Monatschrift für die Deutsche Evangelische Kirche* 2, 2-3(February/March 1935), pp. 36-45. In the words of Klaus Scholder, Rückert was a young Tübingen church historian in the Karl Holl school of Luther interpretation, who saw the German national revolution as challenging the church with the question "Whether it possessed the inner power to interpret the great turn of German fate as God's working and participate in the shaping of it." *Die Kirchen und das dritte Reich*, p. 545.

charitable form possible toward Tillich—throws a very bad light on the inner attitude toward church-political opponents, something we have in the meantime grown accustomed to accept. Regardless of how one views Hirsch's theological and church-political development, this one thing everyone who can come to his own opinion somewhat free from the influence of partisan-church emotions will have to concede, that it [Hirsch's development] is intrinsically more consistent than much of what we have in the past two years experienced in this regard on both church-political fronts. In the face of the laborious, not to mention agonizing, struggle with Fichte, Luther and Kierkegaard, which has characterized his intellectual development, and the triumphs and failures which are clear for all to see in Hirsch's writings, the charge of borrowing from Religious Socialism, a consciously-disguised borrowing at that, strikes one as simply hilarious. I am amazed at the patience with which Hirsch refutes it in its particulars.[9]

Rückert goes on to discuss Hirsch's response to what he considers to be Tillich's three substantive charges against Hirsch: 1) that Hirsch has done what for Christians is not allowed: absolutized a historical moment—the National Socialist revolution; 2) that Hirsch has supported the totalitarian claims of the state without giving the church and the spirit room for deviation ((*Ausweichsraum*); and 3) that Hirsch has lifted these historical events to a second source of revelation beside the first, the Biblical message. We will not here examine Rückert's defense of Hirsch concerning each of these. On the whole Rückert takes Hirsch's side, although he disagrees on fine points.

He makes much of Hirsch's discussion of the unreserved nature of one's duty to be obedient to parents and rulers, as taught by Luther in the catechisms, and the unqualified character of the oath of loyalty sworn by Christian officials and soldiers. What he says about Hirsch and the oath illumines not only Hirsch's own view of the oath but also graphically portrays the reasoning used by many to support their oath of loyalty to Hitler on the bais of their interpretation of Luther:

I consider the supporting sentence of this annotation as being correct: that the appeal to God in the oath holds within it *no* reservation; that "faithfulness and obedience can also be expressed in the fact that the official"—should at any time some action contrary to the Christian conscience be demanded of him—"willingly take upon himself the refusal to carry out a command and the [consequent] discharge from service or punishment;" that to express a reservation for the purpose of avoiding a potential conflict of conscience or a potential punishment is impossible; and that there are no Christian considerations militating against the oath. After all, all of us who have sworn an oath

9. Rückert, "Echte Probleme und falsche Parolen," p. 38.

of loyalty to Hitler base ourselves on this.[10]

Having expressed his basic agreement with Hirsch, however, Rückert goes on to point out two difficulties he has with Hirsch's line of argument. First, he wishes Hirsch could have distanced himself from the presuppositions of his own situation—as, for example, when Hirsch says he never swore an oath of loyalty to the Weimar constitution because no one ever demanded such an oath of him. What about the many who did swear such an oath to a liberal state? asks Rückert. Second, Rückert finds problematic the grounds upon which Hirsch bases his defense of the unreserved nature of the oath of loyalty. For Hirsch to add a reservation makes the oath ignoble and the person unworthy. "The oath of loyalty is fulfilled...in the trust that the recipient of the promise of loyalty will not bring the one who swears into conflict with his Christian conscience."[11] According to Rückert, "Here Hirsch falls into the same error as does Tillich: he anticipates a bogey [*Popanz*] as opponent or—what is the same—he intends to settle a whole problem with an extreme case [*Grenzfall.*]"[12] Hirsch's way of arguing, says Rückert, does not get to the heart of the problem:

> Whoever unreservedly gives the oath of loyalty invoking the name of God with the proviso [*mit weiter nichts als*] that he trusts that the recipient of the promise of loyalty will not lead the one who swears into conflict with his Christian conscience, swears frivolously and is unworthy to give the oath; for he places his trust in the goodwill of human beings. Only he who faces the serious fact that the God upon whom he calls moves history toward its goal through human fallibilities [*durch menschlichen Irrtümer*]; and that the conscience of the person who receives loyalty as well as the one who pledges loyalty have fallible human consciences, which despite the purest of subjective intentions on both sides may come into conflict with each other; only such a person is worthy to give the oath without reservation.[13]

10. *Ibid.*, p. 39. Rückert is referring here to a lengthy footnote by Hirsch on the "Evangelische-Lutherische Lehre vom Treueid," "Brief an Herrn Dr. Stapel," pp. 32-34.

11. *Ibid.*, p. 40.

12. *Ibid.*

13. *Ibid.* Rückert finds Hirsch's other formulation of the same issue more acceptable: "'Ich gebe und gelobe' Treue und Gehorsam 'der irdischen Stelle im Vertauen auf den Gott, in Gehorsam unter den Gott, der sie mich geben und geloben heisst, und dies letzte Vertrauen und Gehorchen trägt und heiligt mich in meiner ganzen Hingabe hinein in die irdische Bindung. Gefällt es Gott, mir meine bestimmte Haltung als falsch zu zerbrechen, so muss ich aus zernichtender Beschämung über solches Gericht heraus mich wiederum zu Vertrauen und Gehorsam unter ihm hinfinden und darin neu gebundene Haltung erringen, und die neue Haltung wird wiederum echte Verwirklichung des Lebens in irdischer Bindung sein.'" *Ibid.*, pp. 40-41. This extremely important statement by Hirsch is a pithy summary of his whole ethic-of-conscience which lies at the basis of his political decision-making, reflecting the influence of Kierkegaard, in which ultimately ethical decisions are based not on rational criteria but on an existentialist leap of faith in a given situation. See Robert Ericksen,

Rückert enthusiastically supports Hirsch's use of Luther's two-kingdom doctrine against Tillich, and elaborates on Hirsch's critical statement concerning theologians who "are still inclined, like formerly St. Augustine was, to equate nation and state with the kingdom of the world, and the constituted and administered [*geordnete*] church with the kingdom of God...."[14] Although both Hirsch and Rückert have primarily Tillich in mind here, Rückert sees the same danger present in the revitalization that is occurring under National Socialism—the danger that some in the movement may identify the empirical church too much with the eschatological church, and thus inadvertently succumb to the liberal spirit:

> If the church misunderstands itself as the earthly order that is defined by law, in which a "kingdom of God as both promised (to us) *and* demanded (of us)" is actualizing itself, then a liberalism which believes—even if in a completely different way—in the immanent realization of God's kingdom, can think of it [the church] as an ally and in turn it [liberalism] can be seen as an ally; and a confusion can occur which is tantamount to the inner dissolution of the church. That precisely Tillich is now considered to be a welcome champion of the Evangelical church in so many circles where two years earlier three exes [*Kreuze*] were still put behind his name, is a sign that this is conceivable.[15]

In Rückert then we have a contemporary on the side of Hirsch who sees the basic issues very differently than does Schmidt. He is highly critical of the Tillich-Schmidt alliance and, if anything, feels that Hirsch is not strident enough in his criticisms of Tillich. In the June 1935 issue of *Theologische Blätter* Schmidt draws attention to Rückert's critical essay, particularly to the personal remarks about Schmidt, and the characterization of Tillich as an "embittered man." He mentions that he has had the Rückert article sent to Tillich in New York and is leaving it up to Tillich whether he wants to respond to Rückert's charge: that Hirsch has dealt with the "genuine problems" and Tillich only with the "false problems."[16] Tillich appears not to have taken up the challenge.

The nature and extent of the responses by German thinkers in well-known theological and church periodicals to the Tillich-Hirsch exchange, as we have briefly looked at them in the preceding pages, demonstrate some significant aspects of the debate and its context. They show how far the Tillich-Hirsch controversy goes beyond private differences and touches on fundamental and highly sensitive issues within the German theological and church-political

    14. "Echte Probleme und falsche Parolen," p. 43.
    15. *Ibid.*, p. 43.
    16. Hirsch, "Zur Auseinandersetzung zwischen Tillich und Hirsch," p. 158.

community at large. They illustrate as well the passionate intensity and antagonism with which various opposing theological-political fronts regarded each
other, as exemplified by the Schmidt-Stapel denunciations of one another.
Tillich and Hirsch, while clearly both dependent thinkers, still embodied and
represented in their positions larger theological, ecclesiastical and political
fronts in Germany. We catch a glimpse, finally, into the complexity of the
various fronts; how variant the positions are even amongst allies within the same
camp. Schmidt, for instance, while a great defender and publicizer of Tillich's
critique of Hirsch, nevertheless finds fault with Tillich's understanding of the
kingdom of God and its relation to the church. Rückert, on the other side,
staunchly defends Hirsch against Tillich but thinks Hirsch has not distanced
himself adequately from his own situation and has some difficulty with Hirsch's
explication of the oath of loyalty.

A Critical Evaluation of the Charges

We have come to the end of our study of the life and thought of Emanuel Hirsch
and Paul Tillich, their relationship with each other culminating in their
1934-1935 debate, and the "echoes" to that controversy in German theological
circles. It remains now for us to take another look at the accuracy of the charges
they levelled against each other, as we have summarized them at the end of
Chapters 8 and 9, and slightly rephrased them here for further analysis. In our
study of Hirsch's thought as it evolved from 1914 to 1933 we have emphasized,
in contrast to Gunda Schneider-Flume and in agreement with Jens Holger
Schjørring, the *continuity* of Hirsch's theological and political development as
an argument against Tillich's first charge in his open letter of 1934: that Hirsch
opportunistically plagiarized Tillich's Religious Socialist categories and filled
them with National Socialist content.[17] It is true that the historical events of
1933 did profoundly influence and shape Hirsch's theological perceptions and
formulations as had the events of 1914 and 1918 earlier. It is true, as well, that
the National Socialist revolution—which represented the kind of strong
leadership-oriented movement of national rebirth that Hirsch had longed for and
struggled for throughout the 1920s—and the theological foment associated with
it in the summer of 1933 provided Hirsch with some new concepts and terminology, particularly that of *horos* and *nomos*. Admittedly, also, Hirsch's
concept of *horos* (holy *horos* and historical *horos*), which he used to explicate

17. One of Schneider-Flume's theses is that Hirsch's political and theological thought underwent a fundamental shift between the years of the Weimar Republic, which he opposed, and the
triumph of National Socialism, which he wholeheartedly endorses. Schneider-Flume argues that this
shift was a sudden change from a decision-oriented ethics-of-conscience (*Gewissensethik*) in the
1920s to an ethics-of-realism (*Wirklichkeitsethik*) in the 1930s. Gunda Schneider-Flume, *Die politische Theologie Emanuel Hirschs 1918-1933*, see esp. pp. 128ff.

the relation of the eternal to the human-historical, bore some resemblance to Tillich's notion of the *kairos*. Nevertheless, the charge that Hirsch plagiarized these categories from the Religious Socialists—and disguised this plagiarism at that—simply does not bear up under close scrutiny, under the careful study of· Hirsch's independent and consistent theological development from 1914 onward. Hirsch was much too independent and consistent a thinker—as Barth, his passionate opponent and colleague already in the early 1920s rightly acknowledged—for him deceptively to borrow from another man's thought.[18] If Hirsch was such an independent thinker, and if he in fact brought different theological and political presuppositions and commitments to his categories of *horos* and *nomos* than does Tillich to his *kairos*, why then does Tillich make this serious charge?

The most obvious reason appears to be a personal one: Tillich's reputation was at stake. His friendship with Hirsch over the years was well known and he wanted to make publicly clear his differences with Hirsch on all things political. His outburst suggests a keen sensitivity to the potential charge that his own Religious Socialist theology and Hirsch's particular form of political theology had substantial elements in common. Tillich's own theological-political thought as he developed it throughout the 1920s and early 1930s was on trial. Tillich does in fact admit that his *kairos* doctrine was not stringent enough, and suggests that a stronger notion of revelation must go along with the concept of *kairos* (a kairos-revelation correlation) if the latter is to be protected from misuse.

Despite their theological and political differences, we have found that there were some strong affinities between these two thinkers. This is why Tillich and Hirsch were drawn to each other in the first place. There is a resemblance in their critique of previous Lutheran theology, in their ambivalent attitude toward the Enlightenment, in their lament for a more coherent society built on common values, and in their conviction that the divine and the human, theology and politics need somehow to be bridged.

Both Tillich and Hirsch were critical of theological orthodoxy (Lutheran scholasticism or confessionalism), on the one hand, and nineteenth-century liberal Protestantism with its bourgeois individualism, on the other. Each was concerned to take cultural and political life more seriously in their theology than

18. Barth, *The German Church Conflict*, p. 30. In the words of Barth, "We can and must praise it [*Die gegenwärtige geistige Lage*] too for the fact that its author, in contrast to many of his fellow-believers, has, with what he declared today, remained in line with what he has always meant, intended and maintained. If anyone is genuine and has the right to speak in this affair, it is Emanuel Hirsch." In a similar vein Barth writes in a personal letter to Hirsch in 1953, after many years of silence following their controversy in the 1930s, that of the German theologians known to him, Hirsch was the only one of those who supported Adolf Hitler and his cause who had the inner consistency and the moral right to take this step. Personal letter: Barth to Hirsch, September 12, 1953. Karl Barth Archive, Basel, made available to me by Walter Buff, Hannover.

the previous era of Lutheran theology had done. Each was intent on developing a "political theology" (Tillich aligning his theology with the political left and Hirsch with the political right) in which the political imperative would become a determinative factor; although to my knowledge they never used the term "political theology" to describe their theology.

The categories which they used to draw out the political consequences of their theology, while based on different theological presuppositions and filled with opposite political content, functioned similarly in their thought. Hirsch built on the two-kingdom theology of Luther to legitimate the "nation [*das Volk*]" and Tillich relied on the prophetic-eschatological motif of the Jewish tradition and the "Protestant Principle" of the Reformation to defend the "proletariat." While commitment to *Volk* and *Proletariat* obviously reflected diverse orientations—one is particularist the other internationalist—both represented *politicial* readings of theology. Analysts like West German historians Klaus Scholder and Gunda Schneider-Flume, and East German thinker Detlef Döring have pointed out these similarities between a political theology of the left and the right. This danger—namely, that because a political theology of the left and a political theology of the right use similar categories and are thus potentially interchangeable—may have in part driven Karl Barth in the 1920s to forsake his early Religious Socialism in favor of a theological orthodoxy which is never nonpolitical (or apolitical) but in some sense always stands prior to politics. Barth proceeded to spend the rest of his life writing a Church Dogmatics, intent on developing stringent doctrinal criteria for social and political ethics.

A second charge of Tillich's is that in Hirsch's unqualified support for National Socialism, premised on his use of the two-kingdom doctrine of Luther, Hirsch is heretical; that is, he has given an unbroken "Yes" to and in effect deified a penultimate historical reality. The accuracy of Hirsch's interpretation of Luther's two-kingdom doctrine is beyond the scope of this study. Further, the extent to which, if any, Hirsch's interpretation of the two kingdoms underwent a change to fit the situation toward the end of the Weimar years, as Gunda Schneider-Flume argues, would require a more detailed examination of Hirsch's early and later explication of Luther's two kingdoms than this study can undertake.[19]

It is true that from 1918 to 1932 Hirsch found himself outside of and in opposition to the political mainstream of the Weimar Republic. His stance changed from one of "critical opposition" in the 1920s to wholehearted support when the National Socialists came into power in 1933. This political shift did not, however, represent a fundamental shift in Hirsch's theological views but was in

19. Schneider-Flume maintains that with Hirsch's growing disillusionment with German politics in the Weimar period his interpretation of the two-kingdom doctrine also underwent a change, the split between the two realms becoming ever more sharp and his intellectual secession from the existing state ever more pronounced. Schneider-Flume, *Die politische Theologie Emanuel Hirschs 1918-1933*, p. 122.

continuity with his "conservative" understanding of the God-ordained nature and task of government and authority (*Obrigkeit*) from the beginning. The basis upon which he distanced himself from the political assumptions of the Weimar Republic—to which he never swore an oath of allegiance—and his unequivocal support of Hitler and National Socialism in 1933 (although for some strange reason he joined the Party only in 1937 when most well-known Protestant theologians had become thoroughly disillusioned with the movement) was consistent throughout.

It was based on what he perceived to be the legitimate task of earthly political authority. It was premised on the strict separation of 1) the visible, external political-legal sphere, governed by the norm of justice, the demand for obedience, and its particular God-given task of punishing evil and protecting the good through the appropriate use of force, from 2) the invisible, internal, spiritual sphere of conscience—the individual's hidden relation to God, governed by the norm of noncoercive love and the reality of spiritual freedom.

He believed the political perceptions at the foundation of the Weimar Republic together with the "theological-Marxist" options of the period, such as Religious Socialism, were not consistent with the unique Reformation-Germanic-Christian understanding of the relation of the human-historical to the Christian as formulated most profoundly by Luther. His support for National Socialism—although he was fully aware of the fluidity of the situation and the dangerous and abortive possibilities of the revolution—was not an opportunistic one but was conditioned on his firm conviction that the leaders of the revolution rightly understood their God-ordained earthly human-historical task and considered themselves accountable to the Lord of history. The success of the revolution, he thought, would depend to a great extent on how unreservedly the evangelical church would participate and co-operate in the educational task of the new era.

Tillich's charge of idolatry or the absolutization of a finite earthly reality, is a serious one. To what an extent did Hirsch unconditionally sanctify National Socialism or German nationality in general? This question must be addressed on two levels. First, did Hirsch consciously and deliberately, in his understanding of *Volk* and theological support of the events of 1933, deify National Socialism and the German nation? Second, if the answer to the first question is no, then one still needs to ask whether he did *de facto* deify National Socialism as a political movement and the German nation as an earthly, human-historical, finite reality without intending to do so?

The answer to the first question must certainly be *No*. Hirsch did not intentionally give divine or absolute status to National Socialism and the German nation. It is true that he did in some sense understand the National Socialist revolution as a "holy movement"—that is, as expressive of and an embodiment of God's holy will for the German nation—but then so does Tillich in his interpretation of the proletarian movement of the early 1920s. In fact, ironically, it is Hirsch who in 1920s with some justification accused Tillich of deifying an earthly-historical reality (the proletariat) as a "holy movement," linking it in a preparatory way to the realization of the kingdom of God on earth. Hirsch repeatedly stresses that the kingdom of God and the kingdom of the world must be distinquished to avoid idolatry. His whole Lutheran understanding of the two kingdoms is an attempt to guard against the kind of idolatry and deification that Tillich accuses him of. Hirsch says quite clearly that the kingdom of Hitler and the National Socialists (the Third Reich) is not the kingdom of God but the kingdom of the world, the kingdom of Germany.

Hirsch reminds overly-enthusiastic German nationalists of the dangers of deifying the nation, of the fact that the nation (*das Volk*) is the highest earthly corporate community but remains all the same a temporal, finite reality that will pass away. To regard the nation as in any way eternal, says Hirsch, manifests a lack of serious theological reflection. He warns German Christians against slipping back into a pre-Christian national religion. His whole understanding and defense of war is linked to the notion that in war the destiny and will of a nation are tested. In war God judges nations. One of his strong criticisms of the German Christians, and the reason why he withdrew his formal membership, is precisely that certain fanatic segments of the movement confused the two kingdoms and slipped into a pre-Christian pagan identification of religion and nation. On this level, therefore, Tillich's charge of deification is unjustified.

On the deeper level—the *de facto* absolutization of the German nation and the National Socialist state—however, Tillich's charge carries more weight. In the strict sense, the term "deification" is inaccurate to describe Hirsch's stance toward National Socialism and the German nation (*Volk*). Hirsch clearly does not deify National Socialism, the National Socialist revolution, or the German nation—he does not give them divine, eternal absolute status. *The fundamental problem with Hirsch's socio-political ethics appears, however, to be the lack of adequate theological criteria by which one's allegiance to one's earthly own— one's own family, tribe, nationality and state—can be adjudicated. There seem to be few if any publicly available and discussible theological norms by which the Christian can evaluate, judge and criticize the activities of political movements such as National Socialism and one's nation; and upon which the extent and locus of one's allegiance and resistance can be determined. One simply finds oneself thrown by God into a particular earthly situation and obedience to God demands unquestioning earthly faithfulness to one's own in this ambiguous situation.*

Already in the years 1911-16, Hirsch says, he learned the riddle-like character of God's will for one in historical situations. There are no clear ethical-religious guidelines for historical action. One cannot know before hand whether one is making the right decision in ambiguous situations. One discovers God's will only in retrospect, through taking risks, once the dice have fallen, and even then only partially. It is here where the doctrine of Justification, being pardoned for wrong choices, is particularly applicable.[20] One should, however, not press this point about no criteria too far. Hirsch *does* have some general conditions which a government has to meet in order to deserve full support. It is upon some general notions of good and bad government that Hirsch bases his own decision against Weimar and for National Socialism. Political regimes need to be evaluated by whether their leaders in their individual consciences see themselves as accountable before the Lord of history; whether the national *nomos* is respected as a boundary that dare not be crossed; whether the state demands discipline, honor, sacrifice of individuals for the sake of the whole; and whether the nation-state recognizes its temporal nature and limits itself to the structuring of earthly historical and political life.[21] Hirsch thought that National Socialism and its leaders (not including some of its fanatical extremists) met there conditions in a way that the Weimar government had not.

Despite these general criteria for good government there is some truth to Schneider-Flume's rather too strongly put charge that Hirsch flees into irrationalism, into the inward conscience where no external rational norms apply.[22] Hirsch is quite ready to defend reason and freedom but only as servants of an ultimate allegiance to nation and state. At the start of his 1933 lectures [*Die gegenwärtige geistige Lage*] he maintains that what is called for is "clear and assisting thought." Hirsch rejects what he considers to be a nineteenth-century Tillichian type of free-floating freedom and autonomous reason that has no ethical "bindingness" to one's own (primarily nation and state). He repeatedly argues against a false individualism and a false spirituality which flees from history. Nevertheless, he himself strongly individualizes and spiritualizes all theological norms by relegating them to the realm of individual conscience.

In the final analysis, therefore, Hirsch's sense of obligation to fatherland, nationality and the state remains beyond and outside of the realm of rational critique, public discussion and open questioning. Nationality is simply an historical given which cannot be challenged, a boundary that cannot be crossed.

20. "Mein Weg in die Wissenschaft," p. 3.
21. "Brief an Herm Dr. Stapel," pp. 35ff.
22. One of the main charges that Schneider-Flume levels against Hirsch is that his ethics-of-conscience is in essence a flight from historical reality into the inward conscience. Outside of the conscience there are no norms—the only norms are those that the conscience recognizes as the expression of the eternal good but these are not open to external discussion or evaluation. The conscience is in effect absolutized as the only normative instance and is combined with a holy duty to perform one's historical task. Reason is replaced with intuitive decision-making. Schneider-Flume, *Die politische Theologie Emanuel Hirschs 1918-1933*, pp. 77, 84, 88ff. In some sense, of course, Hirsch's "Political Theology" was precisely an attempt to correct and avoid that flight from historical reality into pure spirituality and false individualism that characterized some earlier forms of Lutheran thought and Dialectical theology, in order to emphasize the historical-social context of one's search for God.

It calls forth unconditional commitment (*Hingabe*)—a daring decision (*Wagnis*) in the face of uncertainty, trusting in the Lord of History that it is the right decision. To make one's allegiance to a finite, earthly reality immune to criticism and debate is in effect—despite all the claims to the contrary—a form of absolutization. Here Tillich's charge is surely justified. It is this lack of theological criteria by which one can ultimately guide political decision-making and determine the marks of God's action within history that is the problem. This intuitionism implicit in Hirsch's thought is not, however, a sudden opportunistic shift in his thinking in the early 1930s in the face of a political movement more to his taste, but is present in his theology from the beginning. More exactly, it is implicit in his particular understanding and appropriation of Luther's two kingdom doctrine, and his fateful view of nationality with its God-ordained status.

Hirsch maintains that the holy boundary of nationality cannot be crossed. One's nationality—not synonymous with but certainly including biological, material, racial as well as spiritual qualities—is the highest earthly communal bond, created by God, to which one must submit oneself and be obligated if one is to find meaning within human existence. Hirsch is tragically aware of the origin, givenness, and inescapability of one's own historical situation. By giving such a high status to nationality, however, and, further, by tying it so closely to the legal, political and coercive arm of the state, he makes nationality into an "untouchable" entity. He does not shrink from drawing certain objectionable conclusions from this, declaring, for instance, that Jews and Germans are racially distinct and ought to be kept separate from each other. While spiritually united in Christ, historically they are alien to each other and Jews ought to be given "guest status" in Germany. In contrast to many, he speaks warmly of individual Jews; encourages Christians to continue their personal fellowship with individual Jews without thereby withholding their support for the restructuring of German society; and makes a point of rejecting terms of inferiority when talking about the Jew as a people.[23] Nevertheless, he must together with many others be held accountable for not speaking out clearly against Jewish atrocities, and in his ideology of the nation for sharing in the creation of a theological atmosphere conducive to the antisemitic spirit of the times.

Hirsch did stress that the nation is itself subject to change, evolution and upheaval. Nationality stands under the judgment of God—a judgment borne out

23. In Hirsch's words, "Die Kategorie, unter die der Jude zu stellen ist, ist nicht die Minderwertigen, Unwerthaften, in der Substanz Verdorbenen, sondern einfach die Kategorie des Fremden, das für uns nicht passt, und mit dem wir uns nicht vermischen können, ohne Schaden zu leiden....Darüber hinaus haben Christen, ohen deshalb ihr Ja zur Neuordnung verdunkein zu dürfen, etwa früher von ihnen geknüpfte und gepflegte menschliche und persönliche Gemeinschaft mit einzelnen Menschen jüdischen Blutes festzuhalten, nicht nur um der persönlichen Treue willen, sondern auch um der menschlichen Ehre willen." "Theologisches Gutachten in der Nichtarierfrage," *Deutsche Theologie*, p. 184.

in the birth, growth, power, decline and defeat of nations, most dramatically manifest during times of war and crisis. Further, he declared that the health of a nation is finally dependent upon its leaders' and citizens' openness to and sense of accountability to the Lord of history. In all of this, however, those who lead and those who are led must courageously risk a total and unswerving obedience to the nation-state: a reality which is not divine but is divinely willed as the holy boundary which dare not be crossed. This unswerving allegiance takes the form of a decision, the rightness or wrongness cannot be determined ahead of time but is rooted in the inwardness of the individual conscience, and becomes clear only in retrospect. The daring decision may turn out to have been a wrong one but this God will reveal in God's own good time, at which time the individual will need to correct his course and once again make an unconditional decision for nation and state.

By separating the external socio-political sphere (kingdom of the world) from the inward-spiritual sphere of conscience (kingdom of God) so sharply, by applying two different sets of norms for each, Hirsch is removing the political sphere from the normativeness of the kingdom of God, as Tillich correctly perceives. Tillich rightly points out that by relegating the norms of the kingdom of God (gospel, love, freedom, equality, unity) to the inward, personal sphere of conscience and the norms of the kingdom of the world (justice, law, order, coercion, obedience, differentiation) to the external, political sphere, Hirsch is unable to bring to bear the radical critique of the political realm that Christian theology requires. Tillich's critique of Hirsch's stance toward National Socialism may be more than anything a criticism of Luther's two-kingdom doctrine. In short, Hirsch's uncritical support of National Socialism may in fact be a logical consequences of the conservative social ethic implicit in Luther's two-kingdom doctrine, a doctrine which Tillich clearly rejects precisely for this reason.

We turn now to an evaluation of Hirsch's charges against Tillich. In attempting to identify the soft spots in Tillich's theology, especially as it pertains to politics, in the light of Hirsch's critique, it needs to be remembered that Tillich sooner than most Protestant theologians in Germany took an unequivocal stand against the demonic aspects of German nationalism in the early 1930s, including its concomitant anti-semitism. His early recognition and incisive denunciation of totalitarianism, suppression of individual and social freedoms, racism and anti-semitism are exemplary. For these reasons, among others, Tillich was among the first, together with his Jewish friends and colleagues, to be censured, to be suspended and dismissed from his job at the University of Frankfurt, and driven into unwanted exile in a foreign country. Tillich's early socialist thought has often not been given the serious attention it deserves, especially in North America where his later less radical and less politically-oriented work seems to have caught the imagination of the general public. It is precisely this early political thought, however, which must be more carefully scrutinized in order to gain a clearer understanding of this great theological, social and political thinker. It is in this early political period, during the War and Weimar years, that we find the clue to his later abhorrence of totalitarian authoritarianism even to the point of leaving behind an already well-established professional career and a beloved homeland.

This well-known side to Tillich needs, however, to be balanced with another side: his alter-ego: the side represented by his friend Emanuel Hirsch; the side that was both repulsive to him and attracted him to the end. To better understand this side, we look at the way Hirsch saw Tillich. This picture of Tillich cannot simply be dismissed. Hirsch's charges need to be taken seriously, not only to gain an understanding of Hirsch and many others who supported National Socialism and the German Christians, but also to gain a better insight into Tillich himself. Hirsch, after all, knew Tillich both personally and intellectually perhaps better than anyone else. They had known each other, read each other's writings, and discussed each other's ideas for some 27 years prior to the 1934-1935 debate.

At the end of chapter 9 we summarized Hirsch's counter-charges against Tillich under the categories of personal, theological and political. 1) *Personal charges.* On the *personal* level Hirsch defends himself persuasively against the charge of plagiarism and with some justification blames Tillich for not working through his work carefully and systematically enough, for failing to point out the inner consistency of his thought, and for not emphasizing their common intellectual heritage. Much more important, however, are the political and theological charges. It is to these we now turn. The *political* charges are a) that Tillich reflects a nineteenth-century type of free-floating (or freely-suspended) individualism and intellectualism which takes a critical stance toward socio-historical realities without itself becoming actively engaged; and the related charge b) that Tillich does not have a sense of duty and obligation to his own national-community (*das Volk*) but espouses a dogmatic, doctrinaire and shallow Marxist-oriented religious socialism in defense of the proletariat and a rootless, international culture. The *theological* accusations simply put are a) that Tillich does not adequately ground his thought in Luther's theology, particularly Luther's two-kingdom doctrine; and b) that as a result it is Tillich, not he (Hirsch), who, by confusing the two kingdoms and collapsing them into one earthly kingdom, sanctifies the earthly-historical sphere.

2) *Political charges.* The first of the political criticisms of Tillich—that he represents a freely-suspended nineteenth-century individualism—can be evaluated from a number of vantage points. Tillich is a complex and many-sided personality and this charge, as the others that Hirsch makes, must be addressed from a number of different perspectives. In one sense it is simply false to accuse

Tillich of espousing a free-floating individualism. Tillich, as we have seen, is all too aware of the dialectical nature of the Enlightenment tradition—both its positive and its negative aspects. He affirms the Enlightenment view of autonomy as a positive emancipatory impulse, but is highly critical of the demonic distortion of Enlightenment assumptions into a self-sufficient liberal form of autonomy, as well as the positivistic reduction of reason to technical or instrumental reason which is empty of all religious substance and communal ties. His whole book *Die religiöse Lage der Gegenwart* (a book whose title and contents ironically bear some remarkable resemblances to Hirsch's 1933-1934 book *Die gegenwärtige geistige Lage*), for instance, is devoted to unmasking precisely the shallowness of self-sufficient, rationalistic, and individualistic bourgeois culture (referred to by Tillich as the "spirit of capitalism") that Hirsch also so passionately disavows. His *The Socialist Decision*, as we have seen, is a masterful exposition of the negative consequences of the bourgeois principle— the dissolving of all human bonds and the rationalizing, autonomizing and indi- vidualizing of all human existence. In it he defends a future form of socialism— and here Tillich's own originality comes through in a way which is still relevant for today—that will recover religious substance and a sense of rootedness and belongingness (the bonds of origin). On this more theoretical and abstract level, therefore, Hirsch's argument against Tillich appears to be off the mark. In fact, they share similar ambivalences about the Enlightenment and the triumph of a rationalist culture which destroys the cohesion of society, a romanticism on the part of Tillich that has been persuasively demonstrated by the East German Detlef Döring.

What then is Hirsch's charge all about? Does it hold some validity on the more practical level? Does Tillich remain practically disengaged politically and uncommited? It has been frequently pointed out by Tillich scholars that the "Kairos Circle" was in fact a circle of intellectuals who were more preoccupied with critizing society and shaping the theoretical direction of socialism than with actual partisan politics. Tillich himself admits his own aversion to partisan- political involvement on the practical level. But then so was Hirsch suspicious of party politics. Surely, it is not on this level that Hirsch's accusations must be considered. What Hirsch is challenging is Tillich's basic methodology and its practical consequences, including his particular form of socialist decision. In the mind of Hirsch, it is Tillich's dialectical method of theologizing that prevents him from making unequivocal and binding commitments to a particular duty, woman, people, nation, God. Everything remains broken and dialectical! What is one to make of this charge?

There can be no doubt that Tillich's philosophical-theological method remains dialectical from beginning to end. But what exactly is the nature of his dialectical method? On one level, I would suggest, Hirsch's judgment is a valid one. Since the very essence of Tillich's method entails a "Yes" and a "No" to all aspects of human life and thought, Tillich is driven always to sit on a boundary between two equally unacceptable, or attractive extremes, never quite able to make up his mind for the one or the other, always trying to combine both in a higher abstract unity. In fact, the terms "boundary," "frontier," "emigre" become determinative motifs in his theology. Tillich is not unaware of the danger inherent in this stance (and one can assume of the validity of Hirsch's judgment) but is unwilling to give it up.

In his autobiographical sketch *On the Boundary* he refers to this danger. Written just a year after his debate with Hirsch, Tillich in this book describes his whole life up to that point in terms of existence on the boundary between two contraries: two temperaments, city and country, two social classes, reality and imagination, theory and practice, heteronomy and autonomy, theology and philosophy, church and society, religion and culture, Lutheranism and socialism, Idealism and Marxism, native and alien land. He begins the book with the following admission:

> When I was asked to give an account of the way my ideas have developed from my life, I thought that the concept of the boundary might be the fitting symbol for the whole of my personal and intellectual development. At almost every point, I have had to stand between alternative possibilities of existence, to be completely at home in neither and to take no definitive stand against either. Since thinking presupposes receptiveness to new possibilities, this position is fruitful for thought; but it is difficult and dangerous in life, which again and again demands decisions and thus the exclusion of alternatives. This disposition and its tension have determined both my destiny and my work.[24]

Although he does not mention Hirsch by name, Tillich here implicitly admits to a kernel of truth in Hirsch's criticism of his dialectical mode of thinking. Tillich draws an interesting distinction between "thought" and "life" suggesting that in contrast to pure thought, life "again and again demands decisions and thus the exclusion of alternatives." Tillich's whole book betrays the fact that it was his life and not simply his thought that stood on the boundary between alternatives.

The fact remains, however, that Tillich did not simply sit on the fence between two alternatives either in thought or in life. Tillich did not in real life defend a spectator-like stance. He did decide for Religious Socialism and against National Socialism, and was willing to suffer the consequences. These decisions were, however, always made with the recognition of the tragic, broken, and fragmentary nature of every position, and with the recognition that the other side held some truth within it. His theoretical and practical call to decision-making grows out of his understanding of the dialectical method itself.

24. *On the Boundary*, p. 13.

What Tillich rejects is a commitment which does not take into account the finite nature of all decisions and the negative elements in every cause. This is what distinguishes "dialectical thinking" from "paradoxical thinking." Dialectical thinking is always in danger of absolutizing itself and deteriorating into paradoxical thinking in which the "Yes" and the "No" are torn apart and become fixed in relation to each other. This is what, rightly or wrongly, Tillich accuses the so-called "Dialectical Theologians" Karl Barth and Friedrich Gogarten of doing. Of this kind of "Dialectical Theology," Tillich says: "It remains conscious of an abstract No to the time, [but] it does not become concretely critical of the time."[25]

Tillich describes Hirsch as undialectically and unparadoxically absolutizing ethical-personalistic piety (Frömigkeit) on the one side, and the Dialectical Theologians as absolutizing their own so-called dialectical position on the other side.[26] While he considers his own dialectical method as having more in common with Barth and Gogarten than with Hirsch, he argues that Barth's theology is not authentically dialectical but remains paradoxical and supernaturalistic. It tears apart and fixes the Yes and the No. It sees revelatory truth not in dynamic terms but fixes and thus absolutizes God's revelation in particular historical moments, especially in the historical Christ.[27] In Tillich's view a theology is truly dialectical when the Yes and No are kept inseparably together and become a dynamic mode of historical understanding and concrete historical action. Dialectical theology in effect assumes a positive Yes (historical commitment) as a presupposition for the critical historical No. This is in a sense the reverse of Barth's method which assumes a critical historical No as a prelude to an historical affirmative Yes. Tillich eloquently describes his method in his 1923 debate with Barth and Gogarten:

> The dialectician must realize that he as dialectician has a position among others which does not cease to be a position through any dialectical self-annulment [*Selbstaufhebung*]; and he must prepare, just as he is ready to place his stance under the No in spite of his conviction of its truth, to grant the other positions the same Yes that he grants himself, despite the No which he applies against them. He must bind himself together with them under the unity of No and Yes. This is no relativism; the conviction of the superiority

25. Tillich, "Kairos II: Ideen zur Geisteslage der Gegenwart," *GW* VI, p. 32. This essay was initially published by Tillich as part of a work edited by him under the title *Zur Geisteslage und Geisteswendung* (Darmstadt: Reichl, 1926), pp. 1-21.

26. Tillich, "Kritisches und Positives Paradox: Eine Auseinandersetzung mit Karl Barth und Friedrich Gogarten," *GW* VII, p. 220. This essay initially appeared in *Theologische Blätter* 2 (1923), pp. 263-269.

27. Tillich, "Was ist Falsch in der 'Dialektischen' Theologie?" *GW* VII, pp. 247-262. This essay first appeared as "What is Wrong with the 'Dialectical Theology?'" *The Journal of Religion* 15, 2 (1935), pp. 127-145.

of the dialectical position *under* the Yes and No does not need to be given up because of this but it is the bringing-into-consciousness of the ineradicable [*unaufhebaren*] stance which too is hidden in the proclamation of the crisis; it is the recognition of the Yes that is the presupposition of the No; it is the moving back [*Rückgang*] from critical to positive paradox.[28]

In this short statement we have perhaps the most concise clarification of how Tillich views his own dialectical method. His dialectical method is ultimately not a "sitting on the fence," not a situating of oneself abstractly on the boundary between two alternatives, but the genuine affirmation of a position without the absolutization of that stance—that is, always recognizing the broken and fragmentary nature of one's own choices.

The consequences of this method are evident in his *The Socialist Decision*. Here, he remains critical of much contemporary socialist doctrine and party politics because it has rejected all sacramental substance (all rootedness in the myth of origin). Nevertheless, he is unequivocal in his own socialist decision and call to Germany to make a socialist decision. Having stated his own decision for socialism, however, he is quick to place his Yes under a No—a No to all demonic forms of socialism. His commitment to socialism is thus not ambiguous but dialectical. He negates certain aspects of socialism from within his commitment to it, and thus hopes to contribute to the positive direction of socialism. This contribution is not only theoretical but practical and political as well. His head-on conflict with the Brownshirts and National Socialist enthusiasts and officials in the early 1930s demonstrates this practical-political outworking of his thought.

It is precisely this dialectical form of historical and political commitment—taking a stand but with certain critical reservations—that Hirsch finds objectionable. There are certain situations in life—one's inescapable bond with one's own nationality and the responsibilities that come with this, for instance—that cannot be described in dialectical terms the way Tillich does. This brings us to Hirsch's second and related political charge. Hirsch's observation that Tillich is a doctrinaire Marxist-oriented Socialist is, as we have seen, unfounded and need not be elaborated upon. While it is true that Tillich defended the early Marx and wanted to reconcile this genuine Marx with Christianty, challenging socialism to recover its lost religious substance, he does this to expose the error of doctrinaire socialism dominating much of German socialist politics.

The more substantive part of the charge, however—namely, that Tillich does not see himself as obligated and unreservedly bound to the nation but defends a rootless international culture (that of the proletariat)—requires a more elaborate answer. This takes us into an examination of Tillich's view of the nation and the myth of origin. We have discovered in our study that Tillich does in his writings

---

28. Tillich, "Kritisches und Positives Paradox," p. 218.

in the 1920s and early 1930s place a remarkably strongly emphasis on the importance of these so-called powers of the origin. In our extensive analysis of Tillich's *The Socialist Decision* we have tried to explicate his critical understanding of the nation, for instance, as it relates to the socialist commitment. What Tillich espouses is both the *universality* and the *particularity* of genuine socialism. He rejects the notion of a rootless, international, proletarian culture, identifying it as the demonic absolutization of pure form that comes with an autonomous reason which is devoid of all religious substance. The proletariat must recover, he says, a lost sense of rootedness within a national-people (*Volk*). Hirsch understood this about Tillich and, consequently, wrote him in 1933 urging him to stay in Germany and contribute to the National Socialist movement, suggesting that that was where he truly belonged.

Underneath their differences there is, one might say, a different understanding of the relation between the particular and the universal. For Hirsch there is no possibility within history of breaking out of one's historical particularity. Universality is an important inward spiritual reality identified with the Kingdom of God but historically unrealizable. For Tillich universality is a historical goal. National particularity is important but ultimately only a means to an international end: the universal and just human community, most adequately expressed in the prophetic vision of the kingdom of God. The way to this universal human community is through the national good. One's struggle for this universal community of love and justice must remain superior to one's fidelity to one particular nation; the universal must stand as a judgment over and critique of all particular national identities thereby relativizing the particular without dissolving it.

Although blood, soil, nation and ethnicity are all important for Tillich, he refuses to bind himself uncritically and unreservedly to these the way Hirsch does, first, because he believes it is *possible* to break out of one's particularity, and, second, because he believes it is *necessary* to do so. The "ought" and "whence" of human existence are finally on the side of a universal international order of justice. It is precisely this dialectical understanding of the nation—affirming the myth of origin embodied in one's nationality while at the same time denouncing the demonic oppression of "strangers" in the land in the light of the prophetic vision of universal justice—that distinguishes Tillich's methodologically from that of Hirsch. Tillich, unlike Hirsch, consciously shapes his "political theology" along the lines of Jewish-prophetic theology. The Jewish prophetic tradition, according to Tillich was critical of all religious nationalism, including its own, and aspired to a universal humanity. The symbol for this is Abraham as the emigre; the one whom God called out from his own country to an unknown land.[29] This is why the motif of the *emigre* becomes such an

---

29. Tillich says in this regard: "The God who demands obedience of him is the God of an alien country, a God not bound to the local soil, as are pagan deities, but the God of history, who means to

important symbol, both for Tillich's life and his thought. He always had, as he says, an instinctive appreciation for the German landscape, language, tradition and historical destiny; nevertheless, he always lived on the boundary between alien and native land, never quite feeling at home in either.

Hirsch understands Tillich's theology quite well at this point but disagrees with him. Precisely because he believes in the temporality of all historical existence, he objects to what he considers Tillich's historical absolutization of the universal, and his consequent dialectical relation to all historical particulars, symbolized by the emigre motif. Hirsch has a much more tragic sense of the giveness of life, of the inescapable and fateful role of race, blood, ethnicity and nationality in determining human existence than does Tillich. It is this limiting or restraining factor of all human-historical life that he calls the boundary. Tillich refuses to accept this deterministic captivity to the birth, life and death cycle represented by the powers of origin. It is Tillich's firm conviction that human beings can break through and transcend the boundaries of ethnos and work toward a universal humanity within history that most profoundly separates him from Hirsch. Hirsch does not believe that the ethnic boundaries and national antagonism can be overcome and translated into an international community of love as long as the sun shines, other than in a spiritual sense.

For Hirsch, the human relation to one's particular national ethnos (or *nomos*) can best be described in terms of Luther's concept of "earthly bondage." One finds one's universality in one's union with all of humanity of whatever national culture, not in the arena of earthly justice and power but in the realm of "spiritual freedom." Tillich, in contrast, hopes and believes that human beings will be able to shape earthly, social structures in relative correspondence to the moral and ethical claims of the Kingdom of God. The universality of the prophetic promise has for Tillich, to the chagrin of Hirsch, earthly, historical and political relevance. The earthly, historical, international order stands in some kind of continuity with the kingdom of God.[30]

3) *Theological charges.* This brings us to the theological charges made by Hirsch against Tillich: that Tillich is unfaithful to Luther's theology (particularly his two-kingdom doctrine), and as a result collapses the eternal kingdom into the temporal one, thereby absolutizing earthly-historical existence. We have tried to show throughout this study how a constellation of personal, political and theological factors contributed to their 1934-1935 public fight. Their divergent political choices in 1933 are rooted in differences of personal temper-

---

bless all the races of the earth. This God, the God of the prophet and of Jesus, utterly demolishes all religious nationalism—the nationalism of the Jews, which he opposes constantly, and that of the pagans, which is repudiated in the command to Abraham." *On the Boundary*, pp. 91-92.

30. In Tillich's view, "The increasing realization of a united mankind represents and anticipates, so to speak, the truth implicit in a belief in the Kingdom of God to which all nations and all races belong. Denying the unity of mankind as aim includes, therefore, denying the Christian doctrine that the Kingdom of God is 'at hand.'" *On the Boundary*, p. 96.

ment, psychology, family upbringing and so on. There is a capriciousness to the way people decided for and against Hitler in 1933 that defies logical and rational analysis. Nevertheless, we have argued in our study that there are theological differences between Tillich and Hirsch which help to explain their opposite political allegiance. Whether their split was primarily a theological one with practical-political consequences is open to dispute. It seems rather that their personal idiosyncrasies, their philosophical-theological orientations and method-ologies, and their political perceptions and decisions informed and reinforced each other.

Hirsch, for instance, who had a particular view of the true Germany as a rela-tively monolithic and unitary evangelical-*volkisch* tradition, did not simply take over Luther's two-kingdom doctrine and apply it in an unmediated fashion to the German situation. He interpreted the doctrine in the light of his particular experience of German social and political reality. Others with a different perception of the German and European situation interpreted and applied the same doctrine quite differently. Tillich, who rejected a unitary concept of German nationality, opposed any attempt to recover a monolithic German myth of origin, and recognized secularization as a not altogether negative fact. He sees the Lutheran tradition as having been historically too closely allied with the ruling classes against the legitimate claims of the secularized working classes and dissociates himself from the two-kingdom doctrine altogether.

Hirsch is quite right, therefore, when he claims that Tillich does not have an appreciation for Luther's two-kingdom doctrine. Tillich rejects it deliberately. He objects to the confusion of his *kairos*-doctrine with the two-kingdom doctrine. Unlike Hirsch, who was greatly concerned with remaining faithful to Luther's thought, Tillich is quite ready to take liberties with it. James Luther Adams points out that Tillich was no Luther scholar (as Hirsch was), and, although he perceived his theology to be essentially grounded in Luther's theology, he adapted Luther freely to suit his own existential and systematic concerns. His relationship to Luther was not one of "filial obedience" and at points he was openly critical of Luther's theology.[31]

One such point was Luther's two-kingdom doctrine. We have found in our study that one of Tillich's main criticisms of Hirsch was his dualism—his sepa-ration of the two kingdoms, relegating the kingdom of God to the inner spiritual sphere (gospel, love, and so on) and the human kingdom to the outer social-political sphere (law, justice), thus in effect insulating the external social order from the theological norms of the kingdom of God. Tillich's criticism here goes back to Luther himself, who, he thought, put too great an emphasis on "the role of force and the obligation of obedience to political authority," as Adams describes it.[32] Tillich goes beyond Luther in his desire to relate gospel and law,

---

31. James Luther Adams, "Paul Tillich on Luther," *Interpreters of Luther: Essays in Honor of Wilhelm Pauck,* p. 305.

love and justice, the kingdom of God and the kingdom of the world to each other. In place of Luther's two-kingdom doctrine Tillich appropriates what he considers to be another more central Protestant doctrine: the "Protestant Principle"—the protest against all forms of heteronomy, ideology and idolatry.

Hirsch considers this to be a "confusion of the two kingdoms" and objects to it in the second part of his theological charge. He maintains that Tillich, by relating the two kingdoms in this way, by considering the kingdom of God as in some sense continuous and structurally relevent to the historical political sphere, is in fact collapsing the two kingdoms into one—a historical one—and thus is himself guilty of absolutizing the historical sphere. Hirsch is thinking here especially of Tillich's early 1920s view of the proletariat as holy, as bearer of the kingdom of God. Implicit here is the insinuation that Tillich has weakened the transcendence of God by too readily identifying God's presence with a particular historical moment and socio-political movement.

The irony in this is that Hirsch too in 1933 claimed that National Socialism was like a "holy storm" sweeping across Germany; and that Tillich makes the same charge of Hirsch that the latter had made against him in the early 1920s. The charge seems more convincing when it comes from the mouths of Barthians and neo-Orthodox theologians of the period. What can be said in defense of Tillich here, however, is that, although he rejects what he considers to be Hirsch's non-dialectical view of God and transcendence, he himself never intentionally collapses the transcendent into the immanent, the infinite into the finite, the unconditioned into the conditioned. His whole apology for a Jewish-prophetic-eschatology in the face of what he describes as the supernaturalism of Barth and the demonic-sacramentalism of Hirsch and the young national Lutherans is to guard against a deification of the present. The kingdom of God always remains that which is to come, never to be fully realized historically but always relevant to historical socio-political life. The kingdom of God remains above and yet enters history. In Tillich's theology transcendence is never so transcendent that it is irrelevant to history, nor so immanent that it cannot judge history. It is an immanent transcendence and a transcendent immanence.[33]

Tillich cannot be accused of deifying, or absolutizing finite historical reality. Nevertheless, John Stumme has rightly detected an ambiguity in Tillich's notion of transcendence as it pertains to the kingdom of God.[34] Tillich vacillates

32. *Ibid.*, p. 330.
33. John R. Stumme, *Socialism in Theological Perspective: A Study of Paul Tillich 1918-1933*, pp. 234ff.
34. Stumme maintains that "Escatology for Tillich, it will be recalled, had its origin with the prophets who raised 'time over space' and envisioned a '"new heaven and a new earth,"' that is, a new structure of being 'that cannot be grasped ontologically.' Tillich decided for the priority of time over space and did to a degree 'break' his ontological thinking through consideration of the forward direction of history. In the final analysis, however, it is not sufficiently opened up for Tillich consis-

between an ontological-vertical view of transcendence (more in line with Hirsch's theology) and a historical-horizontal notion. He wants to combine the priestly-sacramental and the prophetic-eschatological approaches to reality. It is this vacillation in Tillich's view of transcendence that makes him vulnerable to charges on the left as well as charges from the right. In the end, it is not at all clear whether such an ideal balance can be maintained. Tillich himself seemed in his later years to move more and more toward an ontological view of reality and transcendence. For Hirsch, however, Tillich's God, whether ontologically or eschatologically conceived, was not transcendent enough, and too much part of his own philosophical system. According to Hirsch, Tillich's concepts did not entail a personal, binding faith to the God of Evangelical Lutheran Christianity, a God who was Lord of history and demanded ethical obedience both in personal-private life as well as in public-national-political life.

Implications for the Political Task of Theology

One of the obvious lessons to be learned from the Tillich-Hirsch debate is that all Christian theology must seek to reject political resignation and quietism as well as any simple sanctification of "changes in prevailing ideological and polit-ical convictions."[35] There are, however, a number of critical questions raised for all modern theology by this controversy. How can theology take its political task seriously without losing its distinctive theological character; that is without theology becoming simply an ideological ally for a political movement of the left, right, or centre? What are the criteria by which the Christian church can take the socio-political imperative of its kerygma seriously, making political decisions and entering political alliances with integrity, without reducing theology to politics? In short, what is the *theological* starting point for a polit-ical theology, for a theology which sees all of theology as having an intrinsic social, economic and political component? What are the *theological norms* by which political choices can be positively guided, on the one hand, and *all* polit-ical movements critically judged, on the other?[36]

Klaus Scholder devotes considerable space in his *Kirchen und das Dritte Reich* to appraising the political theologies of the 1920s and 1930s in Germany.

tently to carry through an historical-eschatological approach to reality. Eschatology is subordinated to ontology, and time is made into something spatial. A concept of the new in accord with his onto-logical assumption of the eternal present replaces the universal hope of a 'new heaven and a new earth' of a future non-ontological new being." *Ibid.*, p. 238.

35. See Article Three of the Barmen Declaration. Arthur C. Cochrane, *The Church's Confession Under Hitler* (Pittsburgh: The Pickwick Press, 1976), pp. 240-241.

36. See A. James Reimer, "Theological Stringency and Political Engagement: The Paul Tillich-Emanuel Hirsch Controversy over National Socialism," *Studies in Religion/Sciences Religieuses* 16, 3 (1987), pp. 331-345.

He maintains that with the political theology of these years a new modern type of theology was born which makes political ethics the key to theological understanding. In his words, "Certainly every theology is political. In the modern political theology, however, political ethics becomes the key question of theological understanding and church behaviour. That is its general mark and point of recognition."[37] Political ethics becomes the standard for good theology and not the other way around: "Political theology is bound to no confession. Where political ethics becomes the key to theological understanding and church activity, there the political theme defines theology and not theology the political theme."[38] Scholder is highly critical of this kind of politically-determined theology: "Where political decision becomes the criterion of theology—and that happens in every political theology—politics and theology become blind, helpless and corrupt. That is a realization that one arrives at forcefully out of the history of political theology in the twentieth century."[39]

Whether one agrees with Scholder's general assessment of twentieth-century political theology or not, his analysis of the political theology of the 1920s and 1930s needs to be taken seriously and in part confirms our own analysis of the similarities between Tillich and Hirsch. Scholder includes under the umbrella of political theology not only the theology of Emanuel Hirsch, Wilhelm Stapel and Paul Althaus but also Marxist-oriented theology such as Paul Tillich's Religious Socialism. He considers this political theology of the left formally and structurally similar to that of nationally-oriented political theology of the right, as represented by young national Lutheranism. Both are political theologies: that is, for both political allegiance becomes a hermeneutical key for theological understanding. Both struggled against individualism, and for community, solidarity, commitment and sacrifice. The way the category of "nation (*Volk*)" functioned for the political theology of the right (the religious nationalists), so the category of "proletariat" functioned for the political theology of the left (the Religious Socialists), even though the content of each—that is, the specific solutions they offered to the crisis within German society—differed radically.

In Scholder's view it was precisely because they were formally so similar that Religious Socialists were ineffective in their struggle against the National Socialists. They argued against the national-movement largely on political-ideological grounds and won comparatively few followers because they used similar arguments on the other side, without being able to take hold of the populace, incapable of illuminating the churchly-theological significance of the conflict.[40] Religious Socialists tried unsuccessfully to pit one political theology

37. Scholder, *Die Kirchen und das Dritte Reich*, p. 130. See also my review essay of Scholder's book: A. James Reimer, "German Theology and National Socialism," *The Eumenist* 19, 1(November-December, 1980), pp. 1-8.

38. *Die Kirchen und das Dritte Reich*, p. 539.

39. *Ibid.*, p. 133.

40. *Ibid.*, p. 181.

over against another, to replace a national-oriented theology with a Marxist-oriented one.[41] In fact, Scholder finds historical evidence to show that the NSDAP first took hold in churches where Religious Socialists had politicized congregations earlier. Ironically, Religious Socialists in this way prepared the way for National Socialism in certain parts of Germany (such as Thuringia and Baden).[42]

In Scholder's historical analysis there are three major options that were available to the church in the 1920s and 1930s: 1) political theologies of the left or right, 2) theologies which falsely claimed to be neutral (in which case one could be accused of practical opportunism or pietistic flight from the world), or 3) a critique of political theology and National Socialism on theological grounds.[43] Scholder thinks this latter alternative found expression in Barthian theology. While he is critical of Barth at a number of points—his negative critique of all culture weakened the supports for the Weimar Republic, for example—he believes that it is Barth who accurately perceived theology to be in some sense distinct from and prior to politics. Barth did not advocate a neutral theology—he was fully aware that all theology is political, whether one is conscious of it or not—but he rightly recognized that one's political stance must be derived from and based on theological arguments. So, for Barth, the question in the 1930s was not so much whether one's politics was of the right or the left (Barth personally aligned himself politically with the left) but whether one argued on adequate theological grounds, whatever political position one espoused.[44]

Gunda Schneider-Flume argues likewise that the Religious Socialism of Paul Tillich, the political theology of Emanuel Hirsch (as well as the more recent revolutionary theology of Richard Shaull) are structurally similar.[45] While all three come to very different political conclusions, they all work with similar theological-political categories. Each stresses the political starting point of theology and develops categories to describe divine presence in the sociopolitical structuring of reality. Tillich describes this divine-historical connection with the category of "theonomy," Hirsch with the concept of the "boundary," and Shaull stresses "the dynamic activity of God." Each describes the specific point of divine entrance into historical-political reality: for Tillich it is the "*kairos,*" for Hirsch it is the "turning point [*Wende*]," and for Shaull it is "revolutionary change."[46]

41. *Ibid.,* p. 546.
42. *Ibid.,* p. 248.
43. *Ibid.,* p. 216.
44. *Ibid.,* p. 547.
45. Gunda   Schneider-Flume,   "Kritische   Theologie   contra   theologisch-politischen Offenbarungsglauben: Eine vergleichende Strukturanalyse der politischen Theologie Paul Tillichs, Emanuel Hirschs und Richard Shaulls," pp. 114-137.
46. *Ibid.,* pp. 123-124.

In each case, says Schneider-Flume, the norms are not absolutes that stand over against reality but ones that arise out of a perception of the political situation itself. Of the three, however, Tillich is the only one who achieves a certain distance from the political situation, and develops a critical stance toward socio-political reality. Tillich's concepts of "dynamic truth" and "believing realism" give his socio-political analysis incomparably more depth than either Hirsch's or Shaull's. Unfortunately, Tillich's strength is also his weakness: his ambivalent attitude toward utopia and the realization of the kingdom of God in history gives his theological-political theory critical power but weakens his concrete engagement in the struggle for political change. All the same, the strength of his theory outweighs its weakness; ultimately it makes impossible any belief in "absolute political truth." For this reason he could never on the basis of his political theory have decided for National Socialism, as some have suggested, even though his *kairos*-doctrine lacked sufficient stringency. Although the *kairos* moment was the point at which Unconditioned truth entered history, this divine truth could itself never be equated with the *kairos* itself.[47]

Despite Schneider-Flume's defense of Tillich here, it needs to be recalled that in his *Masse und Geist* in the early 1920s Tillich came close to identifying the proletariat as *the* holy movement through which the Unconditioned was entering human history. The problem with Tillich's category of the *kairos* during these early years was that it remained largely a formal notion without adequate theological criteria by which to determine when a *kairos* moment was actually occuring, and by which to prevent its being distorted for wrong political ends. The Tillich-Hirsch controversy hinged to a large degree on the interchangeability of theological categories and political content; and, consequently, the problem of norms by which to determine when and through whom God was acting in history.

Schneider-Flume and particularly Klaus Scholder, in my opinion, give inadequate attention to the theological presuppositions behind modern political theology, including that of Hirsch and Tillich. They too quickly lump all political theologians, whether of the left or right, together as formally similar (making politics rather than theology the starting point of their ethical reflection). Although both Tillich and Hirsch would emphasize the cultural and political task of theology—in contrast to what they considered to be Barth's supernaturalism—neither would perceive their theology as having a political starting point with theology being simply an addendum to politics. Particularly Hirsch would object to this caricature of this thought, on grounds of his strong advocacy of the separation of the two kingdoms. We have in our study spent considerable time elucidating the theological differences between Tillich and Hirsch and have proposed that theological-philosophical presuppositions were in fact determinative in their divergent political decisions in 1933.

47. *Ibid.*, p. 125.

What is one then to make of Robert Erickson's recent provocative thesis, in his illuminating study of "Nazi theologians" Gerhard Kittel, Paul Althaus, and Emanuel Hirsch, that "In the end arbitrary factors of background and environment may explain the political stance of these individuals more effectively than do their intellectual positions"?[48] He goes on to say that because "political judgments are ultimately existential, the differences between Barth, Tillich and Bonhoeffer on the one hand and Kittel, Althaus and Hirsch on the other cannot be explained on the basis of superior or inferior intelligence or insight. Stated another way, we cannot rely upon intelligence or rationalism to protect us from political error."[49] In order more fully to understand Ericksen's important hypothesis, and how our own study either corroborates or differs from his thesis, his argument needs more detailed scrutiny.

According to Ericksen, the western world but particularly Germany was hit by a genuine crisis at the beginning of the twentieth century, a crisis that was especially acute for theologians and academics, whose comforts of respectability and prestige were being threatened. The "crisis of modernity" had to do with the disintegration of social cohesiveness resulting from the Enlightenment; the erosion of traditional moral values and family ties as a consequence of the *industrial revolution*; the undermining of established class privileges and shared values in favour of an egaliatrian, autonomous society through the *democratic revolution*; and the shaking of previous pillars of certainty (such as rationalism, empiricism and positivism) following the *intellectual revolution*.[50] Modern German theology was largely an attempt to find certainty in the face of the post-Enlightenment "crisis of faith" through the myths of science, reason and religion. With the coming of the twentieth-century, and particularly with the First World War these myths themselves were broken. During the years of the Weimar Republic this crisis was experienced in microcosm and all the major theologians—whether of the left, centre or right—were affected by this new more radical crisis.

By and large these theologians "responded to the crisis of liberal theology by denying the efficacy of reason," evident in the theology of theologians who opposed Hitler: the neo-orthodoxy of Karl Barth, the existentialism of Rudolf Bultmann, and the more liberal theology of Paul Tillich.[51] Although Tillich was less willing to deny the importance of reason than Barth, for instance, in crucial areas where reason and faith conflict he sided with the latter. This rejection of rationalist theology also, however, characterized many who supported Hitler and National Socialism, particularly Kittel, Althaus and Hirsch. The important link between all of these diverse theologians was the impact of existentialism,

48. Ericksen, *Theologians Under Hitler*, pp. 25-26.

49. *Ibid.*, p. 26.

50. *Ibid.*, p. 4. See also A. James Reimer, "Book Review: *Theologians Under Hitler* by Robert P. Ericksen," *Grail: An Ecumenical Journal* 3, 3(September 1987), pp. 103-107.

51. Ericksen, *Theologians Under Hitler*, pp. 14ff.

particularly the influence of Kierkegaardian thought. In the final analysis what mattered was a "leap of faith." Herein lies the difficulty of adjudicating political choices. In the words of Ericksen, "In terms of value judgments, the problem with existentialism is that it is morally neutral. A leap of faith towards Hitler is no less valid than a leap of faith away from him."[52] Take for instance Bonhoeffer's decision to participate in the assassination plot against Hitler. On what grounds did he make his political choice against Hitler? In Ericksen's opinion Bonhoeffer's Christocentric ethics depended on "the same irrational assumption recognized by Kierkegaard as the crux of faith" that others who supported Hitler too acknowledged.[53]

In short, what Ericksen persuasively shows is that there were no theological assumptions that made one "Hitler-proof." To think dialectically, to have a Christocentric theology, to accept a two-kingdom theology, or to emphasize the law-gospel distinction—assumptions sometimes cited to explain the differences between those who supported Hitler and those who resisted him—in the end do not explain those differences. Theologians and pastors on both political fronts frequently had similar theological emphases. "In the end arbitrary factors of background and environment may explain the politcal stance of these individuals more effectively than do their intellectual positions."[54] Barth's Swiss background helped to determine his anti-German nationalism. Tillich's association with Religious Socialism in the 1920s made him immune to National Socialism. Bonhoeffer's international connections particularly with England made him cosmopolitan. Hirsch, Althaus and Kittel, on the other hand, were raised in patriotic, conservative environments. According to Ericksen, "Freud's suggestion that subconscious factors motivate human behaviour must be recalled in this context. The irrational leap of faith basic to every political stance may find its source in background and environment."[55]

Ericksen's conclusions are persuasive and certainly contain a large element of truth to them—namely, that ultimately, political decisions for or against Hitler were not rooted in rational theological presuppositions but were irrational "leaps of faith" determined more by arbitrary factors such as personal upbringing, family background and social environment, personality and psychological compensation than anything else. Nevertheless, we have tried to show in our study of Hirsch and Tillich that their intellectual and theological development and differences did play an important role in determining their different choices in 1933. Ericksen himself is not entirely consistent in defending his own thesis, for in his analysis of each of the three theologians under consideration—Kittel, Althaus, and Hirsch—he amply demonstrates how each

52. *Ibid.*, p. 24.
53. *Ibid.*, p. 25.
54. *Ibid.*, pp. 25-26.
55. *Ibid.*, p. 26.

of them grounded their rejection of the Enlightenment and support of National Socialism on astute rational thinking. In fact, in the end, Ericksen is not satisfied to remain with his earlier hypothesis that all decision-making is ultimately an irrational choice but maintains that rational criteria—"the values of the liberal, democratic traditions, humanitarianism and justice"—may still be the best guardians against political error.[56] Further, Ericksen implies how it was in fact the dominant influence of Kierkegaardian existentialism on most of the theologians under consideration, including not only those who supported Hitler but also many of those who rejected him, that relativized theological and dogmatic normativity in political decision-making, and may have been their downfall. Ericksen fails to deal adequately with the theological-dogmatic differences between theologians on the various sides that, in my opinion, help to explain different political choices.

Our study points to the dogmatic inadequacy of both Hirsch's and Tillich's theology and political theory. As we have seen, both were convinced that the Enlightenment had radically emptied Christian doctrines of their traditional meaning, and sought new ways of bridging the divine and the human realms. In the process they understandably rejected Protestant orthodoxy in favor of a more existentially-understood theology closely alligned with distinctive political options for German society. For Tillich this took the form of a Religious Socialist *kairos* theology, and for Hirsch it took the form of a nationally-oriented *nomos* theology. Both of them were serious theologians whose political ethic was grounded in prior theological understandings. In neither case, however, we have argued, was their political allegiance sufficently determined by stringent theological norms which both transcended the given political situation and had a direct bearing on that situation. For Tillich the *kairos* doctrine (and later the category of revelation which he correlated with the notion of *kairos*) remained largely a formal category without sufficient Christological and ecclesiological content. For Hirsch, revealed theology (in particular his Christology) pertained to the spiritual realm and had little to do with social and political choices. Our study suggests but does not demonstrate (this must remain the goal of another study) that Barth's more classical dogmatic theology was not an escape into supernaturalism, as charged by Tillich and Hirsch, but was precisely an attempt to develop normative theological-dogmatic criteria relevant for historical and political action.

---

56. *Ibid.*, p. 191.

Bibliography

The Works of Emanuel Hirsch

"Arier und Nichtarier in der deutschen evangelischen Kirche," *Kirche und Volkstum in Niedersachsen* 1, 2 (1933), pp. 1-4.

Betrachtungen zu Wort und Geschichte Jesu. Berlin, 1969.

Bibliographie Emanuel Hirsch 1888-1972. Edited by Hans-Walter Schütte. Berlin und Schleswig-Holstein: Verlag Die Spur, 1972. A comprehensive bibliography of primary sources and writings by Emanuel Hirsch. Cited as *Bibliographie Emanuel Hirsch.*

"Brief an Herrn Dr. Stapel," *Christliche Freiheit und Politische Bindung: Ein Brief an Dr. Stapel und anderes.* Hamburg: Hanseatische Verlagsanstalt, 1935, pp. 7-47. Cited as "Brief an Herrn Dr. Stapel."

Christentum und Geschichte in Fichtes Philosophie. Tübingen: Mohr, 1920.

Das Alte Testament und die Predigt des Evangeliums. Tübingen: Mohr, 1936.

"Das Ewige und das Zeitliche," *Glaube und Volk* 1, 5 (May 15, 1932), pp. 65-71.

Das kirchliche Wollen der Deutschen Christen. Berlin-Steglitz: Evangelischer Pressverband für Deutschland, 1933. A collection of eight short essays written during the spring and summer of 1933. Cited as *Das kirchliche Wollen.*

"Das kirchlichen Wollen der Deutschen Christen. Zur Beurteilung des Angriffs von Karl Barth (Theologische Existenz heute, München 1933)," *Das kirchlichen Wollen,* pp. 5-17. Dated July 15-16, 1933.

Das vierte Evangelium in seiner ursprünglichen Gestalt verdeutscht und erklärt. Tübingen: Mohr, 1936.

"Demokratie und Christentum," *Der Geisteskampf der Gegenwart* 54, 3 (1918), pp. 57-60.

"Der Pazifismus," Sonderdruck aus den *Wingolfs-Blätter*. Mühlhausen: Paul Fischer, 1918, pp. 1-16.

Der Prozess: eine Individual-typologische Vorehekomödie verfasst von Paul Tillich, Gelegenheitsdichter und Zufallskomödiant, meistens Doktor der Philosophie unter respektive Gegenwirkung der "Prinzesskafécommission 'Gemischtes Bis'" sowie des philosophischen Ehesachverständiger "Mane Hirsch." An unpublished manuscript in typewritten form, Tillich Archive, Marburg, Germany.

Der Sinn des Gebets. Fragen und Antworten. Göttingen: Vandenhoeck & Ruprecht, 1921 and 1928.

Der Wille des Herrn. Gütersloh: Bertelsmann, 1925.
"Deutsche Zukunft," *Wingolfs-Blätter* 47 (1917-1918), pp. 1-8.

Deutsches Volkstum und evangelischer Glaube. Hamburg: Hanseatische Verlagsanstalt, 1934.

Deutschlands Schicksal: Staat, Volk und Menschheit im Lichte einer ethischen Geschichtsansicht. Göttingen: Vandenhoeck & Ruprecht, 1920, 1922, 1925. Cited as *Deutschlands Schicksal.*

Die Auferstehungsgeschichten und der christliche Glaube. Tübingen: Mohr, 1940.

Die gegenwärtige geistige Lage im Spiegel philosophischer und theologischer Besinnung: Akademische Vorlesungen zum Verständnis des deutschen Jahrs 1933. Göttingen: Vandenhoeck & Ruprecht, 1934. Referred to as *Die gegenwärtige geistige Lage.*

Die idealistische Philosophie und das Christentum. Gesammelte Aufsätze, Studien des apologetischen Seminars. Gütersloh: Bertelsmann, 1926.

"Die Lage der Theologie," *Deutsche Theologie* 3, 2/3 (February/March, 1936), pp. 36-66.

"Die Liebe zum Vaterlande," *Pädagogisches Magazin,* Heft 975 (Langensalza, 1924).

Die Reich-Gottes-Begriffe des neueren europäischen Denkens. Ein Versuch zur Geschichte der Staats- und Gesellschaftsphilosophie. Göttingen: Vandenhoeck & Ruprecht, 1921. Cited as *Die Reich-Gottes-Begriffe.*

Die Religionsphilosophie Fichtes zur Zeit des Atheismusstreites in ihrem Zusammenhange mit der Wissenschaftslehre und Ethik. Göttingen: Vandenhoeck & Ruprecht, 1914.

Die Theologie des Andreas Osiander und ihre geschichtlichen Voraussetzungen. Göttingen: Vandenhoeck & Ruprecht, 1919.

"Die wirkliche Lage unsere Kirche," *Das kirchliche Wollen,* pp. 20-23. This article first appeared in *Monatschrift für Pastoraltheologie* 4, 5 (May/June, 1933), pp. 182-185.

"Ein Christliches Volk," *Der Geisteskampf der Gegenwart* 54, 7 (1918), pp. 163-166.

Emanuel Hirsch Paul Tillich Briefwechsel 1917-1918. Edited with a postscript by Hans-Walter Schütte. Berlin und Schleswig-Holstein, Verlag Die Spur, 1973. Reprinted in Paul Tillich, *Briefwechsel und Streitschriften.* Ergänzungs- und Nachlassbände zu den Gesammelten Werken VI. Frankfurt/M: Evangelisches Verlagswerk, 1983, pp. 98-136.

Erklärung, Monatsschrift für Pastoraltheologie 22, 3 (1927), pp. 62-63.

Fichtes Religionsphilosophie im Rahmen der philosophischen Gesamtentwicklung Fichtes. Göttingen: Vandenhoeck & Ruprecht, 1914.

Fichtes, Schleiermachers und Hegels Verhältnis zur Reformation. Göttingen: Vandenhoeck & Ruprecht, 1930.

"Freiheit der Kirche, Reinheit des Evangeliums. Ein Wort zur kirchlichen Lage," *Das kirchlichen Wollen,* pp. 27-28. First published in *Evangelisches Deutschland* 10, 28 (July 9, 1933), pp. 245ff.

"Friedrich Schleiermacher, Dogmatische Predigten der Reifezeit, Ausgewählt und Erläutert," *Friedrich Schleiermacher, Kleine Schriften und Predigten,* ed. by Hayo Gerdes and Emanuel Hirsch, Vol. 3. Berlin, 1969.

Frühgeschichte des Evangeliums. Erstes Buch: Das Werden des Markusevangeliums. Tübingen: Mohr, 1941. *Zweites Buch: Die Vorlagen des Lukas und das Sondergut des Matthäus.* Tübingen: Mohr, 1941.

Geschichte der neuern evangelischen Theologie im Zusammenhang mit den allgemeinen Bewegungen des europäischen Denkens. Gütersloh: Bertelsmann; Band 1, 1949; Band 2, 1951; Band 3, 1951; Band 4, 1952; Band 5, 1954. Cited as *Geschichte der neuern evangelischen Theologie.*

"Gottesreich und Menschenreich," *Mutuum Colloquium: Festgabe aus Pädagogik und Theologie für Helmuth Kittel zum 70. Geburtstag,* ed. by Peter C. Both, et al. Dortmund: W. Crüwell, 1972.

"Grundlegung einer Christliche Geschichtsphilosophie," *Zeitschrift für systematische Theologie* 3, 24 (1925), pp. 213-247.

Jesus Christus der Herr. Theologische Vorlesungen. Göttingen: Vandenhoeck & Ruprecht, 1926.

"Kurzer Unterricht in der christlichen Religion," *Das kirchlichen Wollen,* pp. 17-20.

Leitfaden zur Christlichen Lehre. Tübingen: Mohr, 1938.

Letters to Hans Grimm, June 19, 1948 and June 3, 1958. Unpublished. In Hans Grimm Archive, Lippoldsberg/Weser, Germany. Made available by Walter Buff, Hannover, Germany.

Letters to Karl Barth, August 9, 1921 and September 12, 1953. Unpublished. In Karl Barth Archive, Basel. Made available by Walter Buff, Hannover, Germany.

Letter to Nikolaus Christiansen, September 16, 1934. Made available by Walter Buff, Hannover, Germany.

Letters to Paul Tillich. Unpublished. Most of these are located in the Tillich Archive, Andover Library, Harvard Divinity School, Cambridge, Massachusetts. Referred to in the text as "Personal letter, Hirsch to Tillich, date."

Letter to Walter Buff, August 3, 1970. Unpublished. Provided by Walter Buff, Hannover, Germany.

"Luthers Gedanken über Staat und Krieg," *Wingolfs-Blätter* 46, 7 (January, 1917), pp. 175-179.

Luthers Gottesanschauung. Göttingen: Vandenhoeck & Ruprecht, 1918.

"Meine Theologischen Anfänge," *Freies Christentum* 3, 10 (1951), pp. 2-4.

"Mein Weg in die Wissenschaft (1911-1916)," *Freies Christentum* 3, 11 (1951), pp. 3-5.

"Meine Wendejahre (1916-1921)," *Freies Christentum* 3, 12 (1951), pp. 3-6.

"Nachruf auf Oxford," *Deutsches Volkstum* (October, 1937), pp. 738-740.

"Nachwort," *Das kirchlichen Wollen*, pp. 31-32. Dated July 15, 1933.

"Nation, Staat und Christentum, 30 Thesen," *Mitteilungen zur Förderung einer deutschen christlichen Studentenbewegung* 6 (1923), pp. 82-84.

"Nationalsozialismus und Kirche: Um die Berufung des evangelischen Reichsbischofs," *Das kirchlichen Wollen*, pp. 23-25. First published in *Völkischer Beobachter* 26, 148/149 (May 28/29, 1933).

"Oxford 1937 und Herr Oldham," *Deutsches Volkstum: Monatschrift für das Geistesleben*, (March, 1937), pp. 196-203.

"Paul Tillich: *Religionsphilosophie*" in *Theologische Literaturzeitung* 51, 5 (March, 1926), pp. 97-103.

"Rauschgeist und Glaubensgeist," *Der Geisteskampf der Gegenwart* 55, 2 (1919), pp. 40-42.

"Rede auf der Kundgebung deutscher Wissenschaft. Veranstaltet vom sächsischen Gau des nationalsozialistischen Lehrerbundes zu Leipzig am 11. November 1933. Nach dem durchgesehenen Stenogramm. Die Rede wird auch in der Gesamtveröffentlichung jener Kundgebung gedruckt."

Schöpfung und Sünde in der natürlich-geschichtlichen Wirklichkeit des einzelnen Menschen. Versuch einer Grundlegung christlicher Lebensweisung. Beiträge zur systematischen Theologie. Tübingen: Mohr, 1931. Referred to as *Schöpfung und Sünde.*

Staat und Kirche im 19. und 20. Jahrhundert. Göttingen: Vandenhoeck & Ruprecht, 1929.

Studien zum vierten Evangelium. Text, Literarkritik, Entstehungsgeschichte, Beiträge zur historischen Theologie. Tübingen: Mohr, 1936.

"Theologisches Gutachten in der Nichtarierfrage," *Deutsche Theologie* 1 (May, 1934), pp. 182-199.

"Unsere Frage an Gott," *Evangelische Wahrheit* 5, 22 (1914), pp. 370-372.

"Volk, Staat, Kirche," *Das kirchichen Wollen,* pp. 25-27. This article first appeared in *Evangelisches Deutschland* 10, 23 (June 4, 1933), pp. 204ff.

"Volksernährung und Biergenus," *Wingolfs-Blätter* (1916).

"Vom verborgenen Souverän," *Glaube und Volk* 2, 1 (1933), pp. 4-13.

"Was die Liebe tut," *Der Geisteskampf der Gegenwart* 55, 10 (1919), pp. 192-193.

"Weltanschauung, Glaube und Heimat," *Zweifel und Glaube.* Frankfurt a.M.: Verlag Moritz Diesterweg, 1937, pp. 52-64; originally published in *Deutsches Volkstum* (January, 1936), pp. 17-35.

"Zum halleschen Universitätskonflikt," *Die Wartburg* 31, 2 (1932), pp. 46-47. Issued jointly by Hirsch and Hermann Dörries.

"Zum Problem der Ethik," *Zwischen den Zeiten* 3 (1923), pp. 52-57.

"Zur Geschichte des Streits um den Reichsbischof," *Das kirchlichen Wollen,* pp. 29-31. First published in *Der Reichsbote,* Tageszeitung für das evangelische Deutschland, 130, 7 (June, 1933).

"Zur Grundlegung der Ethik. Eine Auseinandersetzung mit Albert Schweitzer," *Die Tat* 16, 4 (1924), pp. 249-260.

"Author's Introduction," *The Protestant Era.* Translated by James Luther Adams. Chicago: The University of Chicago Press, 1966. First published in 1948.

"Autobiographical Reflections," *The Theology of Paul Tillich,* ed. by Charles W. Kegley and Robert W. Bretall. New York: Macmillan, 1964.

"Bericht über die Monate November und Dezember 1915." Handwritten manuscript of 1915, first published in *GW* XIII, pp. 77-79.

"Christentum und Emigration," *GW* XIII, pp. 187-191. Originally published in *The Presbyterian Tribune* 52, 3 (1936), pp. 13, 16.

"Christentum, Sozialismus und Nationalismus," *Wingolfs-Blätter* 53 (1924), pp. 78-80. Also in *GW* XIII, pp. 161-166.

"Christentum und Idealismus. Zum Verständnis der Diskussionslage," *Theologische Blätter* 6 (1927), pp. 29-40. Also in *GW* XII, pp. 219-238.

"Christentum und Sozialismus (I)," *Das neue Deutschland* 8 (December, 1919), pp. 106-110. Also in *GW* II, pp. 21-28.

"Christentum und Sozialismus (II)," *Freideutsche Jugend* 6 (1920), pp. 167-170. Also in *GW* II, pp. 29-33.

"Christentum und Sozialismus. Bericht an das Konsistorium der Mark Brandenburg," *GW* XIII, pp. 154-160. Translated by James Luther Adams as "Answer to an Inquiry of the Protestant Consistory of Brandenburg," *Metanoia* 3, 3 (September, 1971), pp. 10-12, 9, 16.

"Christologie und Geschichtsdeutung," *Religiöse Verwirklichung.* Berlin: Furche, 1930. Also in *GW* VI, pp. 83-96.

"Das Christentum und die Moderne," *Schule und Wissenschaft* 2 (1928), pp. 121-131, 170-177. Also in *GW* XIII, pp. 113-130.

"Das Christentum und die moderne Gesellschaft," *The Student World* 21 (Geneva, 1928), pp. 282-290. Also in *GW* X, pp. 100-107.

Das Dämonische. Ein Beitrag zur Sinndeutung der Geschichte. Tübingen: Mohr, 1926. Also in *GW* VI, pp. 42-71.

"Das Problem der Macht. Versuch einer philosophischen Grundlegung," *Neue Blätter für den Sozialismus* 2 (1931), pp. 157-170. Also in *GW* II, pp. 193-208.

Das System der Wissenschaften nach Gegenständen und Methoden. Ein Entwurf. Göttingen: Vandenhoeck & Ruprecht, 1923. Also in *GW* I, pp. 109-293.

"Das Wohnen, der Raum und die Zeit," *Die Form* 8 (1933), pp. 11-12. Also in *GW* IX, pp. 328-332.

Der Begriff des Ubernatürlichen, sein dialektischer Charakter und das Prinzip der Identität, dargestellt an der supranaturalistischen Theologie vor Schleiermacher. Part One: Königsberg/Neumark: Madrasch, 1915. Part Two: Unpublished manuscript: Theol. Habilitationsschrift, Halle-Wittenberg. Cited in *Register und Bibliographie, GW* XIV, p. 139.

Der Sozialismus als Kirchenfrage. Leitsätze von Paul Tillich und Carl Richard Wegener. Berlin: Gracht, 1919. Also in *GW* II, pp. 13-20.

"Der Sozialismus und die Geistige Lage der Gegenwart," *Neue Blätter für den Sozialismus* 3 (1932), pp. 14-16.

"Der Staat als Erwartung und Forderung," *Religiöse Verwirklichung.* Berlin: Furche, 1930. Also in *GW* IX, pp. 123-138.

"Die Bedeutung des Antisemitismus," *GW* XIII, pp. 216-220. First published as "German Americans Take Stand For Democracy Against Nazis," in *Deutsches Volksecho-German People's Echo* 2, 48 (1938), pp. 1-2.

Die religionsgeschichtliche Konstruktion in Schellings positiver Philosophie. Ihre Voraussetzungen und Prinzipien. Breslau: Fleischmann, 1910. Translated as *The Construction of the History of Religion in Schelling's Positive Philosophy*, trans. and with an Introduction and Notes by Victor Nuovo. Lewisburg: Bucknell University Press, 1974. Cited as *Schelling's Positive Philosophy*.

Die religiöse Lage der Gegenwart. Berlin: Ullstein, 1926. Also in *GW* X, pp. 9-93. Translated into the English by H. Richard Niebuhr as *The Religious Situation.* New York: Holt, 1932. The edition used in this study is The World Publishing Company (New York) edition, 1967.

"Die religiöse Lage im heutigen Deutschland," *GW* XIII, pp. 226-238. First published as "The Religious Situation in Germany Today," in *Religion in Life* 3, 2 (1934), pp. 163-173.

Die Sozialistische Entscheidung. Potsdam: Protte, 1933. Also in *GW* II, pp. 219-365. Translated as *The Socialist Decision* by Franklin Sherman with an Introduction by John R. Stumme. New York: Harper & Row, Publishers, 1977.

"Die technische Stadt als Symbol," *Dresdner Neueste Nachrichten* 115 (1928), p. 5. Also in *GW* IX, pp. 307-311.

"Die Theologie des Kairos und die Gegenwärtige Geistige Lage: Offener Brief an Emanuel Hirsch," *Theologische Blätter* 11, 13 (November, 1934), pp. 305-328. Also in *Briefwechsel und Streitschriften.* Ergänzungs- und Nachlassbände zu *GW* VI, pp. 142-176. Now translated into English as "Open Letter to Emanuel Hirsch" by Victor Nuovo and Robert P. Scharlemann in *The Thought of Paul Tillich,* edited by James Luther Adams, Wilhelm Pauck, Roger Lincoln Shinn. San Francisco: Harper & Row, Publishers, pp. 353-387.

"Eine geschichtliche Diagnose: Eindrücke von einer Europareise," *GW* XIII, pp. 238-248. First published as "A Historical Diagnosis: Impressions of an European Trip," *Radical Religion* 2, 1 (1936/1937), pp. 11-17.

"Emanuel Hirsch: Der Sinn des Gebets," *Theologische Blätter* 1 (1922), pp. 137-138.

"Emanuel Hirsch: Die Reich-Gottes-Begriffe des neuren Europäischen Denkens. Ein Versuch zur Geschichte der Staats- und Gesellschafts-Philosophie," *Theologische Blätter* 1 (1922), pp. 42-43.

"Foreward," Martin Kähler, *The So-Called Historical Jesus and the Historic Biblical Christ.* Translated, edited, and with an introduction by Carl E. Broaten. Philadelphia: Fortress Press, 1964.

"Geist und Wanderung," *GW* XIII, pp. 191-200. Originally published as "Mind and Migration," in *Social Research* 4, 3 (1937), pp. 295-305.

Gesammelte Werke, Vols. I-XIII, edited by Ranate Albrecht. Stuttgart: Evangelisches Verlagswerk, 1959-1972. Also, *Register, Bibliographie und Textgeschichte zu den Gesammelten Werken von Paul Tillich*, Vol. XIV, edited by Ranate Albrecht. Stuttgart: Evangelisches Verlagswerk, 1975. These will be cited simply in the form *GW*, Vol., page. In addition there are six supplemental volumes, or *Ergänzungs- und Nachlassbände*. In August 1986, marking the 100th anniversary of Tillich's birth, the publication of a new edition of Tillich's *Main Works Hauptwerke* in six volumes was announced, to be published by De Gruyter—Evangelisches Verlagswerk GmbH (Berlin and New York). Although some of these volumes have now appeared our study is based on the older edition.

"Gläubiger Realismus," *Theologenrundbrief für den Bund deutscher Jugendvereine* 2 (November, 1927), pp. 3-13. Also as "Gläubiger Realismus I," *GW* IV, pp. 77-87.

"Grundlinien des Religiösen Sozialismus: Ein systematischer Entrourf," *Blätter für Religiösen Sozialismus* 4, 8-10 (1923), pp. 1-24. Also in *GW* II, pp. 91-119.

"Kirche und humanistische Gesellschaft," *Neuwerk* 13 (1931), pp. 4-18. Also in *GW* IX, pp. 47-61.

"Kairos I," *Die Tat* 14 (1922), pp. 330-350. Also in *GW* VI, pp. 9-28.

"Kairos II. Ideen zur Geisteslage der Gegenwart," *Kairos. Zur Geisteslage und Geisteswendung*. Darmstadt: Reichl, 1926, pp. 1-21. Also in *GW* VI, pp. 29-41.

"Kairos und Logos," *Kairos. Zur Geisteslage und Geisteswendung*. Darmstadt: Reichl, 1926. Also in *GW* IV, pp. 43-76.

"Kirche und Humanistische Gesellschaft," *Neuwerk* 13 (1931). Also in *GW* IX, pp. 47-61.

Kirche und Kultur. Tübingen: Mohr, 1924. Also in *GW* IX, pp. 32-46.

"Kritisches und Positives Paradox: Eine Auseinandersetzung mit Karl Barth und Friedrich Gogarten," *Theologische Blätter* 2 (1923), pp. 263-269. Also in *GW* VII, pp. 216-225.

Letters to Emanuel Hirsch. Unpublished. In Tillich Archive, Andover Library, Harvard Divinity School, Cambridge, Massachusetts. Cited in the form "Personal Letter, Tillich to Hirsch, date."

"Logos und Mythos der Technik," *Logos* 16 (1927), pp. 356-365. Also in *GW* IX, pp. 297-306.

Love, Power and Justice. New York: Oxford University Press, 1954.

Masse und Geist. Studien zur Philosophie der Masse. Berlin, Frankfort/M: Verlag der Arbeitsgemeinschaft, 1922. Also in *GW* II, pp. 35-90. Referred to as *Masse und Geist.*

"Masse und Persönlichkeit," *Die Verhandlungen des 27. und 28. Evangelisch-Sozialen Kongresses,* ed. by W. Schneemelcher. Göttingen: Vandenhoeck & Ruprecht, 1920. Also in *GW* II, pp. 36-56.

"Masse und Religion," *Blätter für Religiösen Sozialismus* 2 (1921), pp. 1-3, 5-7, 9-12. Also in *GW* II, pp. 70-90.

Mystik und Schuldbewusstsein in Schellings philosophischer Entwicklung. Gütersloh: Bertelsmann, 1912. Also in *GW* I, pp. 13-108. Translated as *Mysticism and Guilt-Consciousness in Schelling's Philosophical Development* with Introduction and Notes by Victor Nuovo. Lewisburg: Bucknell University Press, 1974.

On the Boundary: An Autobiographical Sketch. New York: Charles Scribner's Sons, 1936.

Perspectives on 19th and 20th Century Protestant Theology, ed. and with an Introduction by Carl E. Braaten. New York: Harper & Row, 1967.

"Philosophie und Schicksal," *Kant-Studien* 34 (1929), pp. 300-311. Also in *GW* IV, pp. 23-35.

Protestantisches Prinzip und Proletarische Situation. Bonn: Cohen, 1931. Also in *GW* VII, pp. 84-104. Translated by James Luther Adams as "The Protestant Principle and the Proletarian Situation," *The Protestant Era.* Chicago: The University of Chicago Press, 1966. First published in 1948.

"Protestantismus und politische Romantik," *Neue Blätter für den Sozialismus* 3 (1932), pp. 413-422. Also in *GW* II, pp. 209-218.

"Religionsphilosophie," *Lehrbuch der Philosophie*. Berlin: Ullstein, 1925, pp. 765-835. Also in *GW* I, pp. 297-364.

Religiöse Verwirklichung. Berlin: Furche, 1930.

"Religiöser Sozialismus," *Neue Blätter für den Sozialismus* 1 (1930), pp. 396-403. Also in *GW* II, pp. 151-158.

"Sozialismus," *Neue Blätter für den Sozialismus* 1 (1930), pp. 1-12. Also in *GW* II, pp. 139-150.

"Sozialismus: II. Religiöser Sozialismus," *Die Religion in Geschichte und Gegenwart*, ed. by Hermann Gunkel und Leopold Zscharnack. Tübingen: Mohr, 1931, pp. 637-648. Also in *GW* II, pp. 159-174.

Systematic Theology, Vol. I-III. Chicago: The University of Chicago Press, 1951, 1957, 1963.

The Protestant Era. A collection of Tillich's German writings trans. by James Luther Adams. Chicago: The University of Chicago Press, 1966. First published in 1948.

"Über die Idee eine Theologie der Kultur," *Religionsphilosophie der Kultur*. Berlin: Reuther & Reichard, 1919. Also in *GW* IX, pp. 13-31.

"Uber Gläubigen Realismus," *Theologische Blätter* 7 (1928), pp. 109-118. Also as "Gläubiger Realismus II," *GW* IV, pp. 88-106.

"Um was es geht: Antwort an Emanuel Hirsch," *Theologische Blätter* 5, 14 (May, 1935), pp. 117-120. Also in *Briefwechsel und Streitschriften, Ergänzung- und Nachlassbände zu GW* VI, pp. 214-218.

"What is Wrong With the 'Dialectic' Theology?" *The Journal of Religion* 15, 2 (1935), pp. 127-145. Translated into German in *Die Christliche Welt* 50 (1936), pp. 353-364. Also in *GW* VII, pp. 247-262.

"Zehn Thesen," *Die Kirche und das Dritte Reich. Fragen und Forderungen deutscher Theologen*, ed. by Leopold Klotz. Gotha: Klotz, 1932, pp. 126-128. Also in *GW* XIII, pp. 177-179.

Other Sources

Adams, James Luther. "Paul Tillich on Luther," *Interpreters of Luther: Essays in Honor of Wilhelm Pauck,* ed. by Jaroslav Pelikan. Philadelphia: Fortress Press, 1968, pp. 304-334.

_____. *Paul Tillich's Philosophy of Culture, Science & Religion.* New York: Harper & Row, 1970.

_____. Wilhelm Pauck and Roger Lincoln Shinn, ed. *The Thought of Paul Tillich.* San Franciso: Harper & Row Publishers, 1985.

Barth, Karl. *The German Church Conflict,* ed. by A.M. Allchin, et al., trans. by T.H.L. Parker. London: Lutterworth Press, 1965.

Bense, Walter F. "Tillich's *Kairos* and Hitler's Seizure of Power: The Tillich-Hirsch Exchange of 1934/35," *Tillich Studies: 1975,* ed. by John J. Carey. Tallahassee: North American Paul Tillich Society, pp. 39-50.

_____. Private letter to A.J. Reimer, July 1, 1976.

Buff, Walter. Unpublished manuscript "Abschied Von Emanuel Hirsch." Made available to me by Walter Buff.

_____. "Emanuel Hirsch," *Die Spur: Beiträge, Mitteilungen, Kommentare.* Berlin: Bund Evangelischer Lehrer, 1968, pp. 76-81.

_____. Extensive correspondence with A. James Reimer, Waterloo, Ontario. Letters in Reimer's private collection. These letters (as other correspondence) are cited in the form "Personal letter, Buff to Reimer, date."

_____. Letter to Emanuel Hirsch (August 2, 1970). In Buff's private collection.

Busch, Eberhard. *Karl Barth: His Life from Letters and Autobiographical Texts,* trans. by John Bowden. Philadelphia: Fortress Press, 1976.

Carr, E.H. *International Relations Between the Two World Wars 1919-1939.* London: Macmillan & Co., 1965. First published as International Relations Since the Peace Treaties in 1937.

Cochrane, Arthur C. *The Church's Confession under Hitler.* Pittsburgh: The Pickwick Press, 1976. First published in 1962.

Documents from the Berlin Document Center, Berlin, Germany. Mission of the United States of America. Wasserkaefersteig 1, 1000 Berlin 37 West Germany.

Döring, Detlef. *Christentum und Faschismus: Die Faschismusdeutung der religiösen Sozialisten.* Stuttgart: Verlag W. Kohlhammer, 1982. Cited as *Christentum und Faschismus.*

Ericksen, Robert P. *Theologians Under Hitler: Gerhard Kittel, Paul Althaus and Emanuel Hirsch.* New Haven: Yale University Press, 1985. Referred to as *Theologians Under Hitler.*

_____. "The Barmen Synod and its Declaration: A Historical Synopsis," *The Church Confronts the Nazis: Barmen Then and Now,* Herbert C. Locke, ed. New York and Toronto: The Edwin Mellen Press, 1984.

Graf, Friedrich W. "Bürgerliche Seelenreligion? Zum politische Engagement des Kulturprotestantismus" *Mittwoch* 2, 76 (April, 1986).

Halperin, William S. *Germany Tried Democracy: A Political History of the Reich from 1918 to 1933.* New York: W.W. Norton & Co., 1965. First published by Thomas Y. Crowell Co., 1946.

Helmreich, Ernst. *The German Churches Under Hitler: Background, Struggle, and Epilogue.* Detroit: Wayne State University Press, 1979. Cited as *The German Churches Under Hitler.*

Hopper, David. *Tillich: A Theological Portrait.* Philadelphia: J.B. Lippincott Co., 1968.

Jay, Martin. *The Dialectical Imagination: A History of the Frankfurt School, and the Institute of Social Research, 1923-1950.* Boston and Toronto: Little, Brown and Company, 1973.

Kähler, Martin. *The So-called Historical Jesus and the Historic, Biblical Christ,* trans. and ed. by Carl E. Braaten. Philadelphia: Fortress Press, 1964.

Kaufman, Gordon D. *Relativism, Knowledge and Faith.* Chicago: The University of Chicago Press, 1960.

Krieger, Leonard. *The German Idea of Freedom: History of a Political Tradition.* Chicago: The University of Chicago Press, 1957.

Locke, Herbert C., ed. *The Church Confronts the Nazis: Barmen Then and Now.* New York and Toronto: The Edwin Mellen Press, 1984.

Marquardt, Friedrich-Wilhelm. "Socialism in the Theology of Karl Barth," *Karl Barth and Radical Politics,* ed. and trans. by George Hunsinger. Philadelphia: The Westminster Press, 1976, pp. 47-76.

Niebuhr, H. Richard. "Translator's Preface," *The Religious Situation* by Paul Tillich. Cleveland: The World Publishing Co., 1967, pp. 9-24. First translated by Niebuhr in 1932.

Pauck, Marion and Wilhelm. *Paul Tillich: His Life and Thought,* Vol. I and II. New York: Harper & Row, 1976. Cited as *Tillich: Life.*

Reimer, A. James. "Book Review: *Theologians Under Hitler* by Robert P. Ericksen," *Grail: An Ecumenical Journal* 3, 3 (September, 1987), pp. 103-107.

_____. "German Theology and National Socialism," *The Ecumenist* 19, 1 (November-December, 1980), pp. 1-8.

_____. "Nation and the Myth of Origin in Paul Tillich's Radical Social Thought," *Consensus: A Canadian Lutheran Journal of Theology* 14, 2 (1988), pp. 35-48.

_____. "Paul Tillich's Theology of Culture—An Ambivalence Toward Nineteenth-Century 'Culture Protestantism'," *Religion et Culture,* ed. Michael Despland, Jean-Claude Petit, and Jean Richard. Quebec: Les Presses de L'Université Laval Les Editions Du Cerf, 1987.

_____. "The Theology of Barmen: Its Partisan-Political Dimension," *Toronto School of Theology* 1, 2 (Fall, 1985), pp. 155-174.

_____. "Theological Method and Political Ethics: The Paul Tillich-Emanuel Hirsch Debate," *Journal of the American Academy of Religion,* XLVII/1 Supplement (March, 1979), pp. 177-192.

_____. "Theological stringency and political engagement: The Paul Tillich-Emanuel Hirsch controversy over National Socialism," *Studies in Religion/Sciences Religieuses* 16, 3 (1987), pp. 331-345.

Rückert, Hans. "Echte Probleme und falsche Parolen. Zur Auseinandersetzung zwischen Hirsch und Tillich," *Deutsche Theologie* 2, 2-3 (February-March, 1935), pp. 36-45.

Rupp, George. *Culture-Protestantism: German Liberal Theology at the Turn of the Century.* Missoula: Scholars Press, 1977.

Schjørring, Jens Holger. *Theologische Gewissensethik und Politische Wirklichkeit: Das Beispiel Eduard Geismars und Emanuel Hirschs.* Göttingen: Vandenhoeck & Ruprecht, 1979. Cited as *Theologische Gewissensethik.*

Schmidt, Karl Ludwig. Letters to Paul Tillich and J.C. Hinrichs'sche Buchhandlung. Unpublished. In Tillich Archive, Andover Library, Harvard Divinity School, Cambridge, Massachusetts.

_____, ed. "Nachtrag 'Zum offenen Brief Paul Tillichs an Emanuel Hirsch,'" *Theologische Blätter* 14, 2 (February, 1935), p. 62.

_____, ed. "Zum offenen Brief Paul Tillichs an Emanuel Hirsch," *Theologische Blätter* 14, 1 (January, 1935), pp. 25-27.

_____, ed. "Zur Auseinandersetzung zwischen Tillich und Hirsch," *Theologische Blätter* 14, 6 (June, 1935), p. 158.

Schneider-Flume, Gunda. *Die politische Theologie Emanuel Hirschs 1918-1933.* Frankfurt/M: Verlag Peter Lang GmbH, 1971.

_____. "Kritische Theologie contra theologisch-politischen Offenbarungsglauben: Eine vergleichende Strukturanalyse der politischen Theologie Paul Tillichs, Emanuel Hirschs und Richard Shaulls," *Evangelische Theologie* 33, 2 (March-April, 1973), pp. 114-137.

Scholder, Klaus. *Die Kirchen und Das Dritte Reich:* Band I: *Vorgeschichte und Zeit der Illusionen 1918-1934.* Frankfurt/M: Verlag Ullstein GmbH, 1977. Cited as *Die Kirchen und Das Dritte Reich.* This volume has now been translated into the English by John Bowden as *The Churches and the Third Reich: Volume One: 1918-1934.* Philadelphia: Fortress Press, 1988. My study relies on the original German. Also, my study does not take into account Klaus Scholder's second volume, *Die Kirchen und das Dritte Reich. Band 2: Das Jahr der Ernüchterung 1934: Barmen und Rom.* Frankfurt/M-Berlin: Verlag Ullstein GmbH., 1988.

Schütte, Hans-Walter. "Subjektivität und System," *Emanuel Hirsch Paul Tillich Briefwechsel 1917-1918.* Berlin und Schleswig-Holstein: Verlag Die Spur, 1973. Cited as *Hirsch Tillich Briefwechsel.*

_____, ed. *Bibliographie Emanuel Hirsch 1888-1972.* Berlin und Schleswig-Holstein: Verlag Die Spur, 1972.

_____, ed. *Emanuel Hirsch Paul Tillich Briefwechsel 1917-1918.* Berlin und Schleswig-Holstein: Verlag Die Spur, 1973.

Stone, Ronald H. *Paul Tillich's Radical Social Thought.* New York: University of America Press, 1986.

Stumme, John R. "Introduction," *The Socialist Decision* by Paul Tillich, trans. by Franklin Sherman. New York: Harper & Row, 1977, pp. ix-xxvi.

_____. *Socialism in Theological Perspective: A Study of Paul Tillich 1918-1933.* Missoula: Scholars Press, 1978.

Tillich, Hannah. *From Time to Time.* New York: Stein and Day Publishers, 1974.

Yoder, John Howard. *The Original Revolution.* Scottdale: Herald Press, 1972.

_____. *The Politics of Jesus.* Grand Rapids: Wm. B. Eerdmans, 1972.

Zabel, James A. *Nazism and the Pastors.* Missoula: Scholars Press, 1976.

Index

TORONTO STUDIES IN THEOLOGY

41. William C. Marceau, **Optimism in the Works of St. Francis De Sales**

42. A.J. Reimer, **The Emanuel Hirch and Paul Tillich Debate: A Study in the Political Ramifications of Theology**

43. George Grant, et al., *Two Theological Languages* **by George Grant and Other Essays in Honor of His Work,** Wayne Whiller and Frank Dlinn(ed.)

44. William C. Marceau, **Stoicism and St. Francis de Sales**

45. Lise van der Molen, **A Complete Bibliography of the Writings of Eugene Rosenstock-Huessy**

46. Franklin H. Littell (ed.), **The Growth of Interreligious Dialogue, 1939 - 1989: Enlarging the Circle**